Money Management for Lawyers and Clients

Money Management for Lawyers and Clients

Essential Concepts and Applications

Robert W. Hamilton

Minerva House Drysdale Regents
Chair in Law
University of Texas Law School

ASPEN LAW & BUSINESS
Aspen Publishers, Inc.

Library of Congress Catalog Card No. 93-77456

ISBN 0-7355-0632-9

Published by Aspen Law & Business
Formerly published by Little, Brown & Company

Summary of Contents

v

PART III

INVESTMENTS FOR INDIVIDUALS   285

PART IV

TAXATION   461

Table of Contents

PART I

BASIC CONCEPTS OF DEBT AND INTEREST 1

vii

Table of Contents

PART II

APPLICATIONS   97

Chapter 11.   Life Insurance   239

Chapter 12. The Laid Off White Collar Employee   275

PART III

INVESTMENTS FOR INDIVIDUALS   285

Chapter 13. Investment Strategy: Of Risk and Return   287

PART IV

TAXATION 461

List of Tables and Forms

List of Tables and Forms

Preface

The major purpose of this book is to provide background and guidance for individuals in the present and future ordering of their own personal financial affairs. It is written specifically for the benefit of law students and young lawyers, though, of course, what is desirable for a law student, and later a lawyer, is usually also desirable for most individuals. Thus, this book is equally about individual and consumer financial matters in general.

One usually learns to manage his or her own personal financial affairs by experience. Some persons entering law school have a head start on others: They may be somewhat older than the average college graduate and have gained experience through employment and assuming family responsibilities before going to law school, or even while in school. Former military personnel, who often decide to go to law school after a career of ten or more years in the military, are a good example. Some may have tried their hand at operating their own businesses; others may have worked in offices that regularly deal with financial matters; a few may have been fortunate enough to have inherited money that they have invested and as a result learned something about handling personal finances in the process. Some entering law students may be quite sophisticated and knowledgeable. One sometimes encounters in a beginning law school class certified public accountants with years of experience, former employees of investment companies or stock brokerage firms, life insurance actuaries, economics or business school professors, and the like. But these students are rare. Much more common is the recent college graduate whose experience with handling money is limited to knowing how to apply for a student loan, to fill out a blank check and later, perhaps, to suffer the cost, pain, and embarrassment of "bouncing" a check. Often the first real lesson in financial management that one learns is to balance the check book before writing those last few checks.

This book is designed primarily for the person who is closer to the recent college graduate than the experienced older student. It assumes that the reader has little or no prior experience or knowledge. It concentrates on practical fundamentals: how a real estate mortgage or "whole life" insurance policy really works, for example. Throughout there is an emphasis on vocabulary. Words such as "amortize," "discount," and "balloon note" may strike fear in the heart of the uninitiated: Such terms are defined and discussed in this book, and the underlying concepts are not difficult. A glossary is also provided.

Perhaps one further word about focus is appropriate. This book primarily discusses the relatively affluent individual whose income places him or her on the top half of the economic ladder. Looked at another way, this book is principally designed for the family that from time to time has spare funds to invest, a family whose entire income is not consumed in basic survival and subsistence. Most lawyers fit this profile; indeed, the starting salaries for associates at large or medium-sized firms in most American cities place the recipients easily in the top half of family incomes in the United States from the day they start work. Of course, not all lawyers automatically step from law school directly onto the top half of the economic ladder. Many as a matter of principle accept employment in legal aid or other programs that provide only subsistence or limited remuneration. Others may "hang out their shingle" and attempt to make it in solo practice, where incomes, particularly in the early years, may be scant.

Even individuals or families with very modest incomes will find much of this book useful. Such persons purchase or lease automobiles, they may have one or more credit cards, they may purchase a residence. In difficult times they may borrow emergency funds either from banks or credit unions or from sources that cater to the less affluent: small loan companies and pawn shops, for example. They may be laid off and face the grim reality that salary checks will not be coming in for a while.

More sophisticated persons may find some of the discussion in this book to be elementary: On the other hand, it is unlikely that anyone will find nothing useful or helpful in this book.

This book had its genesis in a project that was published in 1989 by Little, Brown and Company under the title "Fundamentals of Modern Business." When Little, Brown decided to create a series called "Essentials for Law Students," it seemed sensible to revise the portions of the Fundamentals book that dealt with consumer and individual matters and place this discussion in a separate volume. The balance of the Fundamentals book dealing with business, accounting, and corporate matters is to be a separate volume in the "Essentials for Law Students" series. In the process of making this division, a considerable amount of revision and editing was undertaken. This volume, in short, is much more than a simple restatement of portions of the Fundamentals book. It is a new book, and the information in it is current as of March 1, 1993.

Robert W. Hamilton

April 1993

Acknowledgments

I wish to express my appreciation for the assistance provided by my secretary, Judy Dodson, in the preparation and editing of the manuscript for this book. The editorial assistance of Patty Bergin of Little, Brown and Company is also deeply appreciated. Finally, I express my appreciation to Carol McGeehan, Richard Heuser, Nick Niemeyer, and Ilene Breitbarth of Little, Brown and Company, and my wife, Dagmar S. Hamilton, for resolving the difficult question of the best title for this book at a restaurant in San Francisco.

I gratefully acknowledge the permissions granted to reproduce excerpts from the following materials.

The Wall Street Journal. Reprinted by permission of *The Wall Street Journal* © 1992, 1993 Dow Jones & Company, Inc. All rights reserved worldwide.

R. Hamilton, *Fundamentals of Modern Business*. Copyright © 1989 by Robert W. Hamilton. Reprinted by permission of Little, Brown and Company.

Andrew and Winston, Defining Suitability, Kentucky Law Journal, vol. 81, pages 105, 111, 112 (1982-1983). Reprinted with permission.

Money Management for Lawyers and Clients

PART I

BASIC CONCEPTS OF DEBT AND INTEREST

1

Debt and Interest
in General

§1.1 INTRODUCTION

Debt is what makes the modern American economy go around. For individual consumers, the purchase of houses, of automobiles, of washing machines, and of other so-called big ticket items would be very difficult if not impossible without the widespread availability of easy credit. In the 1990s, it is a rare individual or family that does not carry a significant amount of debt. Both small and large businesses also rely heavily on debt in their operations, though the reasons are usually different. Individuals borrow primarily in order to satisfy immediate desires or needs and pay for them from future income or earnings. Businesses that rely on debt to finance their operations usually do so in order to improve their profitability. From a business standpoint, there are substantial tax incentives and economic forces (including sheer necessity for more capital than owners can sometimes provide) that encourage every business in the modern economy to utilize borrowed money on a large scale. Debt, in short, is not only a practical necessity for individuals and businesses; it encourages consumption and economic activity, fuels economic growth in the modern economy, and helps to maximize enjoyment and earnings.

On the other hand, debt is dangerous. When an individual borrows money, he or she usually assumes fixed commitments that may run many years into the future. Economic conditions may change, and debt incurred in an earlier era may become a crushing burden. In short, debt increases risk. An individual or family that does not understand and control debt may find credit cut off, the home and automobile lost to creditors, debt collection agencies telephoning repeatedly, and, ultimately, bankruptcy under Chapter 7 or 13 of the federal Bankruptcy Code. Businesses that incur excessive debt may suffer a similar fate, though the terminal point may be reorganization under Chapter 11 of the Bankruptcy Code.

In order to understand financial transactions in a variety of different settings, basic knowledge about debt, interest rates, the calculation of interest, and the effect of time on the value of payments to be made in the future is essential. This chapter deals with debt and interest; the following chapter deals with the effect of time on the value of future payments. If these concepts are not understood one cannot fully understand all aspects of personal finance.

This chapter includes a number of tables. It is not really important that the reader become conversant with how these tables are used to solve problems of increasing complexity. It is important, however, that the reader understand what the tables represent and how they are constructed. They also permit easy calculations of solutions to relatively simple problems that defy intuitive analysis.

The development of inexpensive, hand-held financial calculators has revolutionized the computation of various financial calculations. Paper and pencil or slide rules have been eliminated; one now needs only to punch in critical numbers at critical places and the answer can be read out on the calculator display. The examples set forth in this and the following chapter were figured with such a calculator. The development of this calculating miracle does not in the slightest render unnecessary the knowledge of the basic concepts discussed in this chapter. One has to know what one is trying to calculate and why. Further, use of these devices is itself complex; entering of numbers in the wrong sequence or the wrong place may result in numbers appearing in the display that bear no relationship to the problem that is being worked on. One has to know enough about the problem and the range in which the solution must fall to be able to recognize a ridiculous result if it appears.

§1.2 DEBTS AND THE RIGHTS OF CREDITORS

When one person (the creditor) lends money to another (the debtor), the first question that arises is what evidence of that debt the creditor should demand. Many consumer finance transactions are on "open account." A gasoline credit card is a good example: When one fills up, one "pays" by the use of the credit card; the cost of the gasoline is electronically communicated to a central accounting office and added to the buyer's account; at the end of the month, the company selling the gasoline sends a bill for purchases made during the month.

Small noncommercial loans are frequently evidenced simply by a canceled check, or acknowledged by a handshake, or a simple "thank you." A slightly greater level of formality occurs when the debtor executes an IOU—a written acknowledgment by the debtor that a debt exists. The initials "I.O.U." simply stand for "I owe you." An IOU may simplify the evidentiary requirements otherwise imposed on a creditor seeking to enforce a debt but it is not, by itself, a promise to repay the debt. Of course, a debt exists any time there is a loan, even if it is not evidenced by any writing or formality, and the creditor may enforce the repayment obligation upon proving that a loan was in fact made and not repaid.

Many individuals eventually default on consumer loans they have received for one reason or another. Rather surprisingly, it is relatively uncommon for a creditor to bring a lawsuit against such a defaulting debtor, obtain a judgment, and then use legal processes to collect upon that judgment. How one goes about collecting upon a judgment is discussed in section 6.2. The reason the traditional judicial process studied in law school is not routinely resorted to is that it is costly and inefficient. Even when a creditor gets a judgment, it is usually not easy to levy upon assets in order to obtain satisfaction. The more common "collection" practice is to cut off future credit, report the default to credit agencies, and then assign the account to a collection agency. Debts that cannot be collected in this way are usually written off as part of the cost of doing business. See Chapter 6. Many jurisdictions have small claims courts where judicial assistance for debt collection may be obtained inexpensively and usually without hiring a lawyer. These courts have limited jurisdiction; the maximum claim that a small claims court may consider has traditionally been $500 or $1,000, but some states have higher ceilings: New York and Connecticut, for example, have $2,000 ceilings while the ceiling in Pennsylvania and California is $5,000. A grocer who sold groceries on credit and was not paid, or a noncommercial creditor holding an IOU, might resort to these courts for assistance (even though the plaintiff, if successful, still must collect upon the judgment). These courts may also hear small business-related disputes, for example, between the photographer and the ad agency or the architect and the builder. However, larger retailers and commercial lenders rarely use these small claims courts.

In the modern world, debts may be freely sold, assigned, or traded without the prior consent of the debtor. A person purchasing or otherwise acquiring a debt is known as an assignee and may enforce the creditor's claim against the debtor (subject to whatever defenses arising out of the same transaction that the original debtor may have against the original creditor). The debtor may also agree in the original transaction to waive defenses he or she may have in a suit brought by an assignee, and such a waiver will be given effect in some circumstances. In the modern world of consumer finance, many open account claims of consumers are assigned to financial institutions; the consumer may not be aware that the assignment has been made. Many thousands of such debts may be "packaged" together into artificial securities and sold publicly. See sections 16.19 and 16.20.

Banks, small loan companies, and other moneylending agencies routinely require a potential debtor to sign a promissory note before extending credit. A promissory note has different legal consequences than an open account or an IOU. A promissory note states that the debtor "promises to pay to the order of" the creditor the amount of the debt, together with interest. Unlike an IOU, a promissory note itself embodies a promise to make a payment at some future time. One advantage of a promissory note is that the holder can sell or assign the underlying obligation simply by transferring the promissory note to a third person.

Form 1-1 is a modern commercial promissory note. A promissory note may be made payable to the order of a specific person or to "bearer." A bearer note is payable to whoever has physical possession of the piece of paper; the debt is transferred simply by physical transfer of the paper. A promissory note payable to the order of a person is usually transferred by indorsement. The payee of the note writes on the back of the note "Pay to the order of Y," signs his or her name, and delivers the note to Y. Y can then enforce the note as though he or she were the payee or may indorse the note to Z by following the same process.

A promissory note is said to be in negotiable form if it meets minimal statutory requirements: It must: 1) be signed by the maker; 2) contain only an unconditional promise to pay a certain sum in money; 3) be payable on demand or at a definite time; and 4) be payable to order or bearer. Most notes used in commercial transactions are in negotiable form. The advantage of a note in this form is that if the person acquiring the note is a holder in due course (that is, a person who acquires the note for value and without knowledge of possible defenses), that person is able to enforce the promise of payment set forth in the note free of certain defenses that the debtor might have had if suit had been brought directly by the creditor on the underlying transaction. The negotiation of a promissory note to a holder in due course results in a debt becoming an article of commerce largely freed from the underlying transaction that gave rise to it: The debt ceases to be a personal obligation between the creditor and debtor.

To illustrate: Assume that a seller of an expensive personal computer originally received cash for a portion of the purchase price and lent the buyer the balance, taking a negotiable promissory note executed by the buyer. The buyer, however, has stopped making payments on the ground that the computer did not perform as warranted. Obviously, if the seller

Form 1-1. Negotiable Promissory Note

Michigan National Bank

PROMISSORY NOTE
(Time or Term Loan)

Note No. _____

Amount $ _____

_____ , Michigan

Due Date _____

Dated: _____

FOR VALUE RECEIVED the undersigned, jointly and severally (the "Borrower"), promise to pay to the order of _____

_____ , a
(Full Proper Bank Name)

(the "Bank"), at Bank's office set forth below or at such other place as Bank may designate in writing, the principal sum of _____

_____ Dollars

($ _____), together with interest as hereinafter provided, all in lawful money of the United States of America.

The unpaid principal balance of this promissory note ("Note") shall bear interest computed upon the basis of a year of 360 days for the actual number of days elapsed in a month, at a rate of interest (the "Effective Interest Rate") which is equal to:
(COMPLETE ONE:)

(1) _____ percent (_____ %) per annum.

(2) _____ percent (_____ %) per annum in excess of that rate of interest established by

_____ as its _____ rate (the "Index"), as such Index may vary
(the "Designee Bank")

from time to time. Borrower understands and agrees that the Effective Interest Rate payable to Bank under this Note shall be determined by reference to the Index, and not by reference to the actual rate of interest charged by the Designee Bank to any particular borrower(s). If the Index shall be increased or decreased the Effective Interest Rate under this Note shall be increased or decreased by the same amount, effective the day of each increase or decrease in the Index. If at any time the Designee Bank shall abandon the use and quotation of the rate of interest used as the Index for this Note, the Index shall be Bank's own Prime Rate of interest. Principal and interest shall be paid to Bank as follows:
(COMPLETE ONE:)

(1) On _____ , 19 _____ . (Single Payment)

(2) Consecutive payments of $ _____ ☐ plus interest ☐ including interest (if neither of the foregoing boxes is checked, the payment stated above shall be "plus interest") accrued to the date of such payment, commencing on the _____

of _____ , 19 _____ , and continuing on the _____ day of each _____ thereafter, until the Due Date, upon which date the entire unpaid principal balance of this Note and all accrued and unpaid interest shall be due and payable to Bank in full.

Borrower expressly assumes all risks of loss or delay in the delivery of any payments made by mail, and no course of conduct or dealing shall affect Borrower's assumption of these risks. If Bank shall determine that the Effective Interest Rate under this Note is, or may be, usurious or otherwise limited by law, the unpaid balance of this Note, with accrued interest at the highest rate then permitted shall, at the option of the Bank, become immediately due and payable.

☐ This Note may be prepaid, in full or in part, at any time, without any prepayment fee. All partial prepayments shall be applied against the last accruing installment or amount due under this Note and no partial prepayments shall affect the obligation of Borrower to continue making all payments specified in this Note until the entire unpaid principal and all accrued interest shall have been paid in full.

☐ Upon prepayment of this Note, Borrower agrees to pay Bank that prepayment fee stated in the Prepayment Addendum attached to this Note.

Upon the occurrence of any of the following events of default, Bank, at its option and without notice to Borrower, may declare the entire unpaid principal balance of this Note and all accrued interest, together with all other indebtedness of Borrower to Bank, to be immediately due and payable: (a) Borrower's failure to pay any installment of principal or of interest when due; (b) any breach by Borrower of any warranty, representation, covenant, term, or condition stated in any loan agreement, security agreement, mortgage or other agreement executed in connection with this Note; (c) the death, dissolution or termination of existence of Borrower; (d) if Borrower is generally not paying debts as such debts become due; (e) the commencement of any proceedings under any bankruptcy or insolvency laws by or against Borrower; (f) if any other indebtedness of Borrower to the Bank or to any other creditor shall become due and remain unpaid after acceleration of the maturity or after the maturity stated; (g) if any writ of attachment, garnishment, execution, tax lien, or similar process shall be issued against any property of Borrower; or (h) Borrower's business shall be sold to, or merged with, any other business, individual, or entity.

Upon the occurrence of any event of default, the unpaid principal balance of this Note shall bear interest at a rate which is two percent (2%) greater than the Effective Interest Rate otherwise applicable. If any payment under this Note is not paid within ten (10) days after the date due, then, at the option of the Bank, a late charge of not more than four cents ($0.04) for each dollar of the installment past due may be charged by Bank. In addition to any other security interests granted, Borrower grants Bank a security interest in all of Borrower's bank deposits, instruments, negotiable documents, and chattel paper which at any time are in the possession or control of Bank, and after the occurrence of any event of default Bank may apply its own indebtedness or liability to Borrower or to any guarantor in payment of any indebtedness due under this Note.

Acceptance by Bank of any payment in an amount less than the amount then due shall be deemed an acceptance on account only, and Borrower's failure to pay the entire amount due shall be and continue to be an event of default. Borrower and all guarantors hereof do hereby jointly and severally waive presentment for payment, demand, notice of nonpayment, notice of protest or protest of this Note, and Bank diligence in collection or bringing suit, and hereby consent to any and all extensions of time, renewals, waivers, or modifications as may be granted by Bank with respect to payment or any other provisions of this Note, and to the release of any collateral or any part thereof with or without substitution. The liability of the Borrower under this Note shall be absolute and unconditional, without regard to the liability of any other party. Borrower agrees to pay all of Bank's costs incurred in the collection of this Note, including reasonable attorney fees. This Note shall be deemed to have been executed in, and all rights and obligations hereunder shall be governed by, the laws of the State of Michigan.

This Note is secured by (CHECK WHERE APPLICABLE):
☐ Security Agreement dated _____ , 19 _____   ☐ Loan Agreement dated _____ , 19 _____
☐ Real Estate Mortgage dated _____ , 19 _____   ☐ Guaranty dated _____ , 19 _____
☐ Other _____

Reference is hereby made to the document(s) and agreement(s) described above for additional terms and conditions relating to this Note.

Borrower Address: _____

BORROWER

_____

Bank Address: _____

SPECIMEN

_____

Tax I.D. or Social Security No.

10016 (12/88)

© 1987 MICHIGAN NATIONAL CORPORATION

WHITE - BANK ORIGINAL   YELLOW - BANK PROCESSING COPY   PINK - CUSTOMER COPY

7

directly seeks to enforce the buyer's promise to pay the balance of the purchase price, the defense of breach of warranty will be raised. It may not be completely ethical, but if the seller can negotiate the promissory note to a holder in due course, for example, a bank, the buyer will not be able to assert the defense of breach of warranty against the holder in due course. In other words, in the hands of a holder in due course, the promissory note is enforceable in and of itself without regard to the underlying commercial transaction that gave rise to it. If the buyer is forced to pay the holder in due course in full, he or she may then turn around and sue the seller for breach of warranty, so that at least theoretically, the wrongdoer — the seller whose product did not conform with his or her warranties — ends up ultimately being held responsible. In the process, however, the innocent purchaser of the promissory note is permitted to enforce it in accordance with its terms, and the defense of the maker can only be asserted against the other party to the original transaction in a separate law suit.

It is, of course, possible in the preceding hypothetical that the holder in due course will be unable to get satisfaction from the buyer. The seller, who indorsed the note to the holder in due course, is then liable to take back the note from the holder in due course and return any consideration paid since an indorser warrants that the instrument will be honored when it is presented. Other persons in the chain of transfer may also be liable on their warranties inherent in their indorsements of the note. They in turn may have rights against prior indorsers, until ultimately the loss falls on the first indorser — the seller. In other words, if the buyer refuses to pay and the holder in due course is compelled to go back against the seller/indorser or earlier transferees on their warranties, the same result is reached — the wrongdoer ends up holding the bag.

The cutting off of defenses described in the previous paragraphs does not apply to certain "real" defenses, such as forgery or duress. Also, if the person acquiring the note is not a holder in due course or if the transfer is cast as an "assignment" of a note rather than as a "negotiation," no defenses are shut off (unless the maker agrees to waive them), and the holder of the note stands in precisely the same shoes as the original lender. The difference between assignment, ("I hereby assign the attached note to Z") and negotiation ("pay to the order of Z") may seem to be mere semantics; however, different legal consequences often flow from different words. The detailed rules about the negotiation of promissory notes and other types of commercial paper, who qualifies as a holder in due course, and the rights of such a holder, all appear in Articles 3 and 4 of the Uniform Commercial Code and are covered in detail in advanced law school courses in commercial law.

Almost all commercial loan-type transactions are evidenced by promissory notes. Most of them are in negotiable form. Forms for negotiable promissory notes appear in all form books, and printed promissory notes in negotiable form with blanks to be filled in can be obtained from a legal stationer. Form 1-1 is an example of such a preprinted form.

§1.3 SECURED AND UNSECURED LOANS

Creditors often are not satisfied with the protections and rights available to a simple creditor, or even to a holder in due course of negotiable commercial paper. Such a creditor is unsecured: His or her right to collect on the claim (or the right of a holder in due course to enforce the note in accordance with its terms) depends on the debtor being good for the amount due when a judgment is obtained. The time when collection is sought is more critical than the time the transaction occurred: An unsecured debtor may have numerous assets and a good credit record when the debt is created, but unexpected illness, business reverses, or unwise transactions may make the debt uncollectible when enforcement is sought. A holder in due course is no better off than the original creditor in this regard since even if the holder gets a judgment on the promissory note, he or she still has to collect on the judgment. Not even a holder in due course can squeeze blood from a turnip.

Creditors increase the likelihood of repayment by requiring, at the time of the transaction, that the debtor grant an interest in some or all of his or her property to secure the repayment of the loan. In the case of sales of goods, the document granting this interest is called a "security agreement." Form 1-2 is an example of such an agreement. This property may be referred to as the "collateral" for the loan. Larger transactions or larger loans typically involve such requirements, as do many small consumer loan transactions. If the transaction involves the sale of goods on credit, the seller will normally take a security interest in the actual goods sold; in other types of transactions, the security interest may involve various kinds of tangible or intangible property or rights, including real estate, insurance policies, an automobile, or anything else that may be reduced to cash if the borrower defaults. State laws may restrict the types or kinds of property that individual consumers may pledge as security for loans. Typically the property or assets remain in the control of the debtor until a default on the loan occurs, when the creditor may take judicial steps or self-help to seize the property or rights in which he or she has an interest in order to satisfy the debt. Historically, these creditor-owned interests in debtors' property were called liens or chattel mortgages; under the Uniform Commercial Code, they are called security interests or purchase money security interests, though references to liens still regularly appear in cases involving personal property. Basically, a lien or security interest is an intangible property interest that allows the creditor, if the loan is not

Form 1-2. Security Agreement (General)

SECURITY AGREEMENT
(General)

I.   The parties to this agreement are as follows:

Debtor:_____

Secured Party:_____

II.   The Debtor for valuable consideration, receipt whereof is hereby acknowledged, hereby transfers to the Secured Party a security interest in the following property and any and all additions and accessions thereto:

SPECIMEN

III.   The Collateral has been acquired and is used by the Debtor (or will be acquired and will be used) primarily for the purpose checked below:

☐ Equipment used in business.   ☐ Consumer goods (personal, family or household goods).

If checked here ☐, the Collateral will be acquired with proceeds of loans from the Secured Party which may disburse the proceeds thereof directly to the Seller.

IV.   The Collateral will be kept at_____
                                         (No. and Street)

_____   _____   _____
         (City or Town)   (County)   (State)

and the record owner of said premises is_____

Debtor agrees to promptly notify Secured Party of any change in the location of the Collateral and that Debtor will not remove the Collateral from said State without the written consent of the Secured Party.

V.   The aforesaid security interest shall secure the obligations evidenced by notes described as follows:

Date_____Amount_____

and shall secure the payment of any and all indebtednesses and liabilities whatsoever of the Debtor to the Secured Party, whether now existing or hereafter arising, together with all costs and expenses of Secured Party in respect of or connected with any of the indebtedness or Collateral.

VI.   Debtor at its expense will keep and maintain in force such insurance in such amounts covering loss or damage to the Collateral, including extended coverage, as is usually and customarily carried by owners of like property or as may be requested by Secured Party, including loss payable clauses if demanded.

VII.   Debtor hereby warrants and covenants that except for the security interest granted hereby Debtor is, or to the extent that this agreement states that the Collateral is to be acquired after the date hereof, will be, the owner of the Collateral free from any adverse lien, security interest or encumbrance and that Debtor will defend the Collateral against all claims and demands of all persons at any time claiming the same or any interest therein.

VIII.   If any or all of the Collateral has been or is to be attached to real estate, Debtor on demand of Secured Party shall furnish the Secured Party with a disclaimer or disclaimers signed by all persons having an interest in the real estate (including landowners, mortgage holders, and lessees) disclaiming any interest in the Collateral prior to the interest of the Secured Party.

IX.   Debtor will pay on demand all costs and expenses of filing and recording, including the costs of any searches deemed necessary by Secured Party, to establish and determine the validity and the priority of the security interest of the Secured Party and also all other claims and charges which in the opinion of Secured Party might prejudice, imperil or otherwise affect the Collateral or its security interest therein. At its option, Secured Party may discharge taxes, liens or security interests or other encumbrances at any time levied or placed on the Collateral, may pay for insurance on the Collateral and may pay for the maintenance and preservation of the Collateral. Debtor agrees to reimburse Secured Party on demand for any payment made, or any expense incurred by Secured Party pursuant to the foregoing authorization.

X.   Debtor will keep the Collateral free from any adverse lien, security interest or encumbrance and in good order and repair and will not waste or destroy the Collateral or any part thereof. Debtor will not use the Collateral in violation of any statute or ordinance. Secured Party may examine and inspect the Collateral at any time, wherever located.

XI.   In the event the Debtor fails to pay when due any installment of interest or principal of any indebtedness secured by this Security Agreement, or in the event the Debtor violates any term of this Security Agreement, or in the event the Secured Party in good faith deems itself insecure either as to the payment of the obligations secured by this agreement, as to the Debtor's ability to perform this Security Agreement, or as to the sufficiency of the collateral securing the indebtedness, then the Debtor shall be in default of this Security Agreement and the Secured Party may proceed in accordance with law. In furtherance of and not in limitation of the foregoing, in the event of default, the Secured Party shall have the right to take immediate possession of the Collateral, and for that purpose may pursue the same wherever it may be found and may enter any of the Debtor's premises, with or without force or process of law, wherever said Collateral may be, or be supposed to be, and search for the same, and if found, may take possession of and remove and sell the Collateral or any part thereof at public or private sale. Unless the Collateral is perishable or threatens to decline speedily in value or is of a type customarily sold on a recognized market, the Secured Party will give the Debtor reasonable notice of the time and place of any public sale or of the time after which any other intended disposition is to be made. The requirement of reasonable notice shall be met if such notice is mailed, postage prepaid, to the Debtor at the address given herein or if none to any address in the Secured Party's files, at least five days before the time of sale or other disposition. Expenses of retaking, holding, preparing for sale, selling or the like shall include Secured Party's reasonable attorney's fees and legal expenses. Out of the money arising from such sale, Secured Party may retain all costs and charges for pursuing, searching for, retaking, removing, keeping, storing, advertising and selling such Collateral, together with the amount due and unpaid upon any notes held by it, accounting to the Debtor for any surplus.

XII.   No default shall be waived by Secured Party except in writing and no waiver of any default shall operate as a waiver of any other default or of the same default on a future occasion. All rights of Secured Party hereunder shall be cumulative and shall inure to the benefit of itself, its successors and assigns; and all obligations of Debtor shall bind legal representatives and successors. If there is more than one Debtor, all undertakings, warranties and covenants made by the Debtor and all rights, powers and authorities given to or conferred on the Secured Party shall be made or given jointly and severally.

Dated:_____, 19_____   Signed: _____

_____   _____
            Address   Debtor

repaid, to seize the property subject to the lien to satisfy the unpaid loan; usually the property may be seized without judicial process and is thereafter sold and the proceeds applied against the unpaid loan.

Notice of a security interest in the debtor's property is "perfected," that is, made valid against the world, usually by filing a public notice. For security interests in goods, a "financing statement" must be filed in the office of the Secretary of State. UCC Form 1, set forth as Form 1-3, is the standard form financing statement used in most states. (There are some important exceptions to the filing requirement for perfection; where an exception is applicable the security interest is perfected either by other means, such as taking possession of the collateral, or automatically.) A

Form 1-3. Financing Statement

STATE OF MICHIGAN
UNIFORM COMMERCIAL CODE FINANCING STATEMENT
(Approved by the Secretary of State and Michigan Association of Registers of Deeds)

INSTRUCTIONS:
1. TYPE OR PRINT All information required on this Form.
2. If filing is made with the Secretary of State, send the **WHITE** copies to the Secretary of State, Lansing, Michigan. If filing is made with the Register of Deeds, send the **YELLOW** copies to the Local Register of Deeds. Retain the **PINK** copies for files of secured party and debtor.
3. Enclose filing fee.
4. IF ADDITIONAL SPACE IS NEEDED for any items on this Form, continue the items on separate sheets of paper (5'' x 8''). One copy of these additional sheets should accompany the WHITE Forms, and one copy should accompany the YELLOW Forms. USE PAPER CLIPS to attach these sheets to the Forms (DO NOT USE STAPLES, GLUE, TAPE, ETC.) and indicate in Item 1 the number of additional sheets attached.
5. At the time of filing, the filing officer will return acknowledgement. At a later time, the secured party may date and sign the termination legend and use acknowledgement copy as a termination statement.
6. Both the WHITE and YELLOW Filing Officer copies must have original signatures. Only the debtor must sign the financing statement, and the signature of the secured party is not necessary, except that the secured party alone may sign the financing statement in the following 4 instances: Please specify action in Item 7 below.
   (1) Where the collateral which is subject to the security interest in another state is brought into Michigan or the location of the debtor is changed to Michigan.
   (2) "For proceeds if the security interest in the original collateral was perfected."
   (3) The previous filing has lapsed.
   (4) For collateral acquired after a change of debtor name etc., and a filing is required under MCLA 440.9402 (2) and (7); MSA 19.9402 (2) and (7).

1. No. of additional sheets			For Filing Officer (Date, Time, Number, and Filing Office)
	Liber	Page	
2. Debtor(s) (Last Name First) and address(es)	3. Secured Party(ies) and address(es)		
4. Name and address(es) of assignee(s) (if any)	CHECK ☒ if applicable		
	5. ☐ Products of collateral are also covered.		
	6. ☐ Collateral was brought into this state subject to a security interest in another jurisdiction.		

7. This financing statement covers the following types (or items) of property:

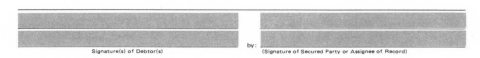

Signature(s) of Debtor(s)	by: (Signature of Secured Party or Assignee of Record)

failure to perfect means that subsequent creditors may obtain competing security interests senior to the unfiled interest and that a bankruptcy trustee may be able to avoid the unfiled security interest, reducing the creditor to unsecured status.

The process by which a secured creditor realizes upon the security is usually described as foreclosure, though in the case of consumer goods it may involve repossession. As indicated above, typically, the seized property, no matter how recovered, is sold and the proceeds applied to the payment of the debt. If the proceeds of the sale of seized property are not sufficient to discharge the loan (as is usually the case), the creditor continues to have an unsecured claim against the debtor for the balance, usually called a "deficiency" or "deficiency judgment." In the rare event that the proceeds exceed the loan balance, unpaid interest, and allowable fees or charges (often including attorney's fees), the debtor is entitled to the balance.

Everyone has heard of automobiles or washing machines of luckless debtors being repossessed by hard-hearted creditors, or the equipment and land of farmers being put up for sale at auction at the direction of one or more banks or other creditors. While such events do obviously happen with some regularity when debtors are individuals, most enforcement efforts involve something less than foreclosure. For one thing, creditors often take as collateral property of dubious value but of personal value to the debtor as a device to encourage payment. Secondhand furniture probably will not bring very much upon resale, but the threat of foreclosure could mean the potential loss of a family's cherished items and only furniture, and payment of the secured loan may be made to ensure that the furniture is not lost. Many secured creditors threaten and cajole: They may make telephone calls threatening to foreclose or seize the property, or even post it for foreclosure and sale at some definite time and place. Foreclosure, however, is not itself free of cost and in most industries, at least, is a last resort. Automobile repossession in many areas is an exception to these statements because of the relative mobility and ease of marketability of the collateral. Most automobile repossessions occur without advance warning to the debtor and may involve entering a locked vehicle and crossing the ignition to secure possession of the collateral.

If the debtor goes bankrupt, a secured creditor is in a more favorable position than an unsecured creditor when the distribution of assets to creditors is made. This is an additional reason for a creditor to take security for a loan, though as a practical matter in most consumer bankruptcies, there are no assets to be distributed to creditors. See Chapter 6.

Much of the law relating to obtaining and perfecting security interests appears in Article Nine of the Uniform Commercial Code and is covered in detail in advanced commercial law courses in law school. However, legal problems relating to security interests also involve bankruptcy, collection practices, and the like. These problems are sufficiently complicated that there is often at least one additional advanced course in law school curricula to deal with them.

§1.4 SIMPLE INTEREST AND COMPOUND INTEREST

At the most basic level, everyone understands the concept of interest on a debt: Interest is the amount paid by a borrower for the use of the lender's money. Interest is the cost of a loan to a borrower; it is the return from owning capital to the lender. The amount of interest owed by a borrower is apparently a function of three variables: (1) the number of dollars borrowed; (2) the period for which they are borrowed; and (3) the rate of interest being charged.

Rather surprisingly, interest is a concept of some complexity. For one thing, it often masquerades under different names, particularly in consumer transactions: for example, "finance charge," "service charge," "points," and "transaction fee." Further, in order to determine how much interest actually is to be earned on a specific loan, one must know not only the stated interest rate, the period the loan is to be outstanding, and the amount borrowed, but also the periods when interest is to be computed, and, if the loan is to continue for more than one interest period, whether the interest is to be calculated as simple interest or compound interest.

The virtually universal practice is to quote interest rates on an annual basis. There is no uniformity, however, as to the manner in which the actual computation is to be made. Interest quoted at the rate of 6 percent per year may actually mean interest calculated at 0.5 percent per month due at the end of each month or it may mean interest at the rate of 1.5 percent per quarter due at the end of every three-month period, or 3 percent semiannually due at the end of six months, or 6 percent due at the end of a year. Usually, these different calculations lead to different results that become increasingly significant the larger the sums involved. The times when payments are to be made on a loan may or may not coincide with the times when interest is calculated.

The computation of interest over several periods also involves an assumption as to whether the earned interest is in effect withdrawn every period so that each period's interest is computed on a stable principal, or whether the earned interest from the previous period is left with the borrower and treated as principal thereafter, itself to earn interest in the future period. The former is called "simple" interest and the latter "compound" interest.

A good example of compound interest involves the deposit of money with your friendly Savings and Loan Association. In this transaction, you are, of course, the lender and the Association is the borrower who pays you interest at a specified rate. Let us assume that you deposit $10,000 with an Association that advertises that it pays 8 percent per year, compounded quarterly. (In 1992, when this is written, interest rates offered by Savings and Loans are way below 8 percent per year; however, rates in that range were offered less than five years ago and it is quite possible that they will be offered again. As a result, this book continues to use rates that were realistic several years ago and may become realistic again in the future.)

The phrase "8 percent per year, compounded quarterly" carries a lot of freight. The word "quarterly" means, first of all, that while the Association quotes its interest rate as 8 percent per year, it actually calculates interest at the rate of 2 percent for each accounting period of three months and adds that amount of interest to your account at the end of that period. Thus, if you left your $10,000 with the Association for three months, you would be credited with $200 (2 percent of $10,000), which you could withdraw without reducing your account below $10,000.

Let us assume that you do not do this; rather you do not do anything except let the Association use your money for another three months. If the Association computed its obligation on a simple interest basis, you would simply earn another $200 during the second three months. If the Association computed its obligation on a compound interest basis (as most savings and loans institutions do and as your Association expressly promised to do when it advertised that its 8 percent rate was "compounded" quarterly), it would consider that you had $10,200 on loan to the Association throughout the second quarter, and interest would be calculated on this amount at the end of six months so that you would earn $204 during this period rather than simply $200. This is compound interest. The additional $4 reflects interest on the last period's interest. Over several accounting periods, the difference between compound and simple interest becomes increasingly significant. If you left your compound interest investment with the Association for a full year, you would have an account worth $10,824.32; at the end of two years, it would be worth $11,716.59. If only simple interest were paid, the investment would be worth $10,800 after one year and $11,600 after two years. At the end of ten years your investment will be $22,080.40 at compound interest; if only simple interest were paid, the account would be worth $18,000.

The compounding of interest thus significantly increases the growth rate of capital. If the interest rate is 6 percent (compounded quarterly), the investment doubles in 11.75 years; at 8 percent, in about nine years; at 10 percent, in about seven years. There is a rough way to estimate approximately how long it will take for a savings account to double in value at a specified interest rate. The "rule of 72" states that a savings account will double in value in the number of years that equals 72 divided by the interest rate (ignoring the decimal). Thus, an 8 percent savings account doubles in nine years (72 ÷ 8 = 9).

If the Association had calculated the interest it owed you on a simple interest basis, in effect it would be ignoring the interest earned in previous periods in calculating the current period's interest; or to put it another way, it would assume that you had withdrawn the interest earned at the end of each accounting period even though you had not in fact done so. Presented in this way, it seems clear that compound interest more accurately reflects the reality of loan transactions over several accounting periods than does simple interest. The continued existence of simple interest computations here and there in the economy probably reflects a lack of sophistication by some lenders, the somewhat greater complexity of compound interest calculations as compared to simple interest calculations, and possibly an illogical remnant of the historical antipathy to the payment of interest at all.

One can readily imagine, for example, an unsophisticated creditor making a two-year, 6 percent loan and concluding that he should receive the original principal of the loan plus an aggregate of 12 percent in interest at the end of two years. The creditor may not realize that he is in fact charging less than 6 percent per year; or in other words that he is worse off setting up the transaction this way than if he made a one-year loan at 6 percent for that year and then "rolled over" the entire loan — principal and interest — at the end of that year into a second one-year loan at 6 percent for the second year.

The apparent complexity of compound interest transactions may have been a problem when all calculations were made with paper and pencil, and some lenders may have concluded that the additional interest was just not worth the apparent number of repetitive calculations or the use of a mathematical formula. This calculation problem, however, has been entirely eliminated by the development of compound interest tables, and recently, with the development of inexpensive and convenient electronic calculating devices and computers described briefly in section 1.1.

One of the peculiarities of compound interest calculations is that whenever interest is compounded more frequently than the quoted annual rate, the actual interest rate earned for the year is more favorable to the lender than the quoted rate. In the above example, the quoted rate is 8 percent, but the actual rate of return for the first year is 8.243 percent. The quoted rate is sometimes also called the "nominal" rate, while the actual rate earned is usually called the "effective" rate of interest, the "yield," or the "annual effective yield." In consumer transactions subject to the federal Truth In Lending Act, both the amount of the financing charges and the "annual percentage rate" (or "APR" as it is often abbreviated) must be set forth. Regulation Z, issued by the Federal Reserve Board, contains detailed rules as to how these should be calculated for a variety of transactions. If compound interest is calculated on an annual period, of course, the effective rate at the end of one year is identical to the quoted nominal rate.

Table 1-1
Future Value after n Periods of $1 Invested Today

No. of periods	2%	3%	4%	5%	6%	7%	8%
1	1.0200	1.0300	1.0400	1.0500	1.0600	1.0700	1.0800
2	1.0404	1.0609	1.0816	1.1025	1.1236	1.1449	1.1664
3	1.0612	1.0927	1.1249	1.1576	1.1910	1.2250	1.2597
4	1.0824	1.1255	1.1699	1.2155	1.2625	1.3108	1.3605
5	1.1041	1.1593	1.2167	1.2763	1.3382	1.4026	1.4693
6	1.1262	1.1941	1.2653	1.3401	1.4185	1.5007	1.5869
7	1.1487	1.2299	1.3159	1.4071	1.5036	1.6058	1.7138
8	1.1717	1.2668	1.3686	1.4775	1.5938	1.7182	1.8509
9	1.1951	1.3048	1.4233	1.5513	1.6895	1.8365	1.9990
10	1.2190	1.3439	1.4802	1.6289	1.7908	1.9672	2.1589
11	1.2434	1.3842	1.5395	1.7103	1.8983	2.1049	2.3316
12	1.2682	1.4258	1.6010	1.7959	2.0122	2.2522	2.5182
13	1.2936	1.4685	1.6651	1.8856	2.1329	2.4098	2.7196
14	1.3195	1.5126	1.7317	1.9799	2.2609	2.5785	2.9372
15	1.3459	1.5580	1.8009	2.0789	2.3966	2.7590	3.1722
16	1.3728	1.6047	1.8730	2.1829	2.5404	2.9522	3.4259
17	1.4002	1.6528	1.9479	2.2920	2.6928	3.1588	3.7000
18	1.4282	1.7024	2.0258	2.4066	2.8543	3.3799	3.9960
19	1.4568	1.7535	2.1068	2.5270	3.0256	3.6165	4.3157
20	1.4859	1.8061	2.1911	2.6533	3.2071	3.8697	4.6610
21	1.5157	1.8603	2.2788	2.7860	3.3996	4.1406	5.0338
22	1.5460	1.9161	2.3699	2.9253	3.6035	4.4304	5.4365
23	1.5769	1.9736	2.4647	3.0715	3.8197	4.7405	5.8715
24	1.6084	2.0328	2.5633	3.2251	4.0489	5.0724	6.3412
25	1.6406	2.0938	2.6658	3.3864	4.2919	5.4274	6.8485

16

Table 1-1 (*continued*)
Future Value after n Periods of $1 Invested Today

No. of periods	2%	3%	4%	5%	6%	7%	8%
26	1.6734	2.1566	2.7725	3.5557	4.4594	5.8074	7.3964
27	1.7069	2.2213	2.8834	3.7335	4.8223	6.2139	7.9881
28	1.7410	2.2879	2.9987	3.9201	5.1117	6.6488	8.6271
29	1.7758	2.3566	3.1187	4.1161	5.4184	7.1143	9.3173
30	1.8114	2.4273	3.2434	4.3219	5.7435	7.6123	10.0627
31	1.8476	2.5001	3.3731	4.5380	6.0881	8.1451	10.8677
32	1.8845	2.5751	3.5081	4.7649	6.4534	8.7153	11.7371
33	1.9222	2.6523	3.6484	5.0032	6.8406	9.3253	12.6760
34	1.9607	2.7319	3.7943	5.2533	7.2510	9.9781	13.6901
35	1.9999	2.8139	3.9461	5.5160	7.6861	10.6766	14.7853
36	2.0399	2.8983	4.1039	5.7918	8.1473	11.4239	15.9682
37	2.0807	2.9852	4.2681	6.0814	8.6361	12.2236	17.2456
38	2.1223	3.0748	4.4388	6.3855	9.1543	13.0793	18.6253
39	2.1647	3.1670	4.6164	6.7048	9.7035	13.9948	20.1153
40	2.2080	3.2620	4.8010	7.0400	10.2857	14.9745	21.7245
41	2.2522	3.3599	4.9931	7.3920	10.9029	16.0227	23.4625
42	2.2972	3.4607	5.1928	7.7616	11.5570	17.1443	25.3395
43	2.3432	3.5645	5.4005	8.1497	12.2505	18.3444	27.3666
44	2.3901	3.6715	5.6165	8.5572	12.9855	19.6285	29.5560
45	2.4379	3.7816	5.8412	8.9850	13.7646	21.0025	31.9204
46	2.4866	3.8950	6.0748	9.4343	14.5905	22.4726	34.4741
47	2.5363	4.0119	6.3178	9.9060	15.4659	24.0457	37.2320
48	2.5871	4.1323	6.5705	10.4013	16.3939	25.7289	40.2106
49	2.6388	4.2562	6.8333	10.9213	17.3775	27.5299	43.4274
50	2.6916	4.3839	7.1067	11.4674	18.4202	29.4570	46.9016

Chapter 16 contains a more complete description of cash-equivalent investments, including deposits in banks, credit unions, and savings and loan associations, and the purchase of "certificates of deposit" from such institutions.

§1.5 THE CALCULATION OF COMPOUND INTEREST

The examples so far make one important point about compound interest problems: The calculations appear to be complex since they involve repetitive transactions rather than simple arithmetic manipulation or multiplication. Indeed, if one were to compute the interest at the end of each period, add it to the previous balance, and then compute the interest for the next period, the calculation in many instances would be laborious if not interminable. There is, however, a formula for computing compound interest that has frightened generations of non-mathematicians. That formula is:

$$FV = P \times (i + 1)^t$$

where i is the interest rate, t the number of time periods, P the principal and FV the future value after t periods.

Obviously there must be a way to make the calculations even quicker than by using this formula. For many years financial institution employees used a set of tables that gave compound interest computations (and other calculations described below) for one dollar by interest rates and by periods. These tables were called, not surprisingly, compound interest tables.

Table 1-1 is an example of a compound interest table. It shows the future value of $1 at various interest rates for 50 time periods. This table is very easy to use. Assume you deposit $1,000 in a bank that pays 8 percent per year compounded quarterly. If you leave the money there for ten years, how much will be in the account after ten years? Since the interest is compounded quarterly, the question involves a calculation over 40 periods at 2 percent per period. Looking in the "40" row and "2%" column, we see that $1 will grow to $2.2080 after 40 periods. Hence, $1,000 will have grown to $2,208.

Another example closer to home might be useful: Assume you plan to start law school in five years and will need $10,000 for the first year's tuition. If a bank will guarantee a 6 percent rate compounded semiannually, how much must you deposit today to have $10,000 in five years? This requires a calculation over 10 periods at 3 percent. Using the "10" row and "3%" column, we find that $1 deposited today will have grown to $1.3439 in five years. Hence you must deposit

$$\frac{\$10,000}{1.3439} = \$7,441.03$$

It should be cautioned that these hypotheticals are not entirely realistic. First, no account is taken of the income tax that would be due on the periodic interest earned. Second, most banks today will not guarantee a fixed interest rate over time (though other financial devices exist that may permit "locking in" a fixed rate).

Within the last few years handheld calculators have become available with compound interest and other calculations built into their memories. One has only to enter any three of the four possible variables: the interest rate per period, the number of periods, the original principal amount and the future value. The calculator supplies the missing variable in a matter of seconds. The calculations in this and the preceding section, and the other calculations in this chapter were all made with the use of such a calculator, which originally cost about $30.

2 Present Values of Future Payments

§2.1 INTRODUCTION

One of the most fundamental financial concepts involved in both consumer and business financial transactions is that money to be paid in the future is not worth as much as money to be paid today. Relatively simple formulas permit a direct comparison of the value of amounts to be paid at different times. This chapter discusses this concept, which underlies practically all of modern financial theory and much of current business practice. The process by which amounts payable at different times are made comparable is usually referred to as "discounting" future payments to current values or to net present values. The word discounting in this context simply means reducing. Another phrase that describes this process is determining the "time value" of money.

§2.2 THE BASIC CONCEPT

What is the right to receive $1,000 a year from now worth today? Assuming that there is no risk that the payer will default, is it not clear that the right is worth something less than $1,000? For if one had $1,000 today, one could invest it for a year in a riskless investment and thereby earn one year's interest in addition to the original $1,000. Thus, $1,000 payable a year from now has to be worth somewhat less than $1,000 in hand today. How much less? One way that such a question can be answered is to approach it from the point of view of a hypothetical investor: If that investor can make 12 percent per year on his or her money in a riskless investment, how much should he or she pay today for the right to receive that $1,000 in a year? So phrased, the issue becomes an algebraic calculation:

$$X + .12X = \$1,000$$
$$1.12X \quad = \$1,000$$
$$X \quad\quad = \$1,000/1.12 = \$892.86$$

To such an investor, the right to receive $1,000 a year from now is worth precisely $892.86. But, it may be rejoined, why choose a 12 percent return? Why not, say, an 8 percent return, in which case the calculation becomes

$$X + .08X = \$1,000$$

and the value of the right to receive the $1,000 in 12 months becomes $925.93? The difference between these two amounts is significant. Of course, there is no one single rate of return that is correct in an absolute sense. But that element of uncertainty as to what the correct value is should not hide certain basic truths revealed by these simple examples: (1) Since interest rates are positive, a dollar in the future is always worth less than a dollar today; and (2) the higher the interest that can be earned on a riskless investment, the lower is the current value of a right to receive a future payment. In other words, there is an inverse relationship between interest rates and current values of future payments. This leads to yet a third basic truth: (3) The riskier an investment that is to yield returns in future years, the lower the current value of the right to receive those future returns.

The present value of a future sum is the same thing as the future value of a present sum invested at the same interest rate. It is looking at the same transaction from different ends. For example, assume that one plans to buy a $1,000 stereo a year from now; how much do you have to put aside today in an account earning 12 percent per year to have $1,000 in one year? The answer, of course, is the now familiar amount, $892.96; determining that the present value of $1,000 payable one year from now is $892.96 is simply looking at the same transaction from a different perspective. Compare the example relating to funding the tuition for the first year of law school in Chapter 1.

When speaking of the earning power of a present amount over time, one usually speaks of the interest rate. When going the other way and computing the present value of a future payment, one usually speaks of the discount rate. However, it is the same rate, since the present value of a future sum and the future value of a present sum involve precisely the same calculation, examined from opposite perspectives.

§2.3 PRESENT VALUE CALCULATIONS OVER MULTIPLE PERIODS

Following the same line, what is $1,000 payable two years in the future worth today? If we again assume a 12 percent interest rate, it turns out that a $797.19 investment today grows to $892.86 after one year and to precisely $1,000 after two years. Thus, the present value of $1,000 payable two years from today is $797.19 at 12 percent interest. This involves a compound interest calculation, since the comparison is with a $797.19 investment today that is left untouched until the end of the two-year period. (The concept of compound interest is discussed in sections 1.4 and 1.5 of the previous chapter, and this discussion should be reread if you are not certain how compound interest differs from simple interest.) A formula to determine present values of future payments over multiple periods, derived from the formula for compound interest, is:

$$PV = \frac{FV}{(1 + i)^n}$$

where PV = present value; FV = future value; i is the interest rate; and n the number of periods. The simple calculations of one-year present values set forth in section 2.2 are obviously special applications of this formula.

Despite the apparent mathematical certainty of the formula, it is important to recognize that the precise calculation of the present value of a future sum over a specified period depends not only on the applicable interest or discount rate but also on the number of subperiods within the period over which interest is compounded. In other words, in order to get mathematical precision, one must know both the applicable discount rate and whether interest is compounded quarterly, annually, or over some other set of subperiods during the two-year period in question. In the foregoing calculations, it is assumed that interest is compounded only annually so that the number of periods is two. In most calculations like this, involving relatively short time periods, the number of subperiods used does not change the results significantly. For example, if one calculates a 12 percent discount rate compounded quarterly over the two-year period, interest is compounded eight times at 3 percent per quarter, and the present value of $1,000 payable two years from now is $789.41 as compared with the $791.19 obtained above on the assumption that interest is compounded only annually. Do you see why increasing the number of subperiods reduces the present value of a future payment?

§2.4 EXAMPLES OF PRESENT VALUE CALCULATIONS

Table 2-1 indicates what $1,000 payable at various times in the future is worth today at 12 percent and at 6 percent. Several fundamental relationships described in this table should be emphasized:

First, as one should intuitively expect, the longer the period before the payment is to be received, the smaller the value.

Second, the present value of the right to receive even large sums of money in the far distant future is not worth very much, if anything. For example, how much should you pay for the right to receive $100,000 in a lump sum 100 years from now? Not very much: According to the table below, you should pay no more than one dollar at a 12 percent discount rate and $294 at a 6 percent rate. Since practically no one living today will be living when this payment is due, even these numbers are suspect. Indeed the entries in the table for all payments to be made in the distant future—25 years or more—are so theoretical and subject to so many contingencies that little credence can be given to them.

Third, in making these present value computations, the discount rate that is chosen has a tremendous effect on the outcome of the calculation. One can manipulate answers obtained by superficially minor changes in that number. Section 2.8 of this chapter speculates briefly on how this rate should be selected in real-world calculations.

Table 2-1
Present Value of a Future Payment of $1,000

Number of years until payment	Present value of $1,000 at 12%	Present value of $1,000 at 6%
1	$892.90	$943.40
2	797.20	890.00
3	711.80	839.60
4	635.50	792.10
5	567.40	747.30
10	322.00	558.40
25	58.80	233.00
50	3.50	54.30
100	0.01	2.94

Table 2-2 on page 26 shows the present values of one dollar payable at various time periods in the future at most plausible interest rates. It will be noted that the numbers in Table 2-2 are all decimals less than one while in Table 1-1 all the entries are one or larger. That is because each entry in Table 2-2 is the reciprocal of each entry in Table 1-1:

$$\text{Entry in Table 2-2} = \frac{1}{\text{Entry in Table 1-1}}$$

The mathematically inclined may easily satisfy themselves that this reciprocal relationship indeed exists. The formula actually used to generate the entries in Table 2-2 is set forth on page 23.

A simple illustration of the use of Table 2-2 is the hypothetical set forth in section 1.4 of a person planning to set aside a sum of money today to provide $10,000 for tuition for the first year of law school five years from now. The problem further stipulates an interest rate of 6 percent compounded semiannually. One simply has to look up the discount factor for 3 percent over ten periods in Table 2-2, which yields 0.7441, and multiply by $10,000 to get $7,441.00, the same answer obtained by a division by a decimal in Chapter 1.

The decimal numbers in Table 2-2 are sometimes called discount factors because they can be added together to determine the present values of future payments. Most people find it easier to add and multiply decimals than to divide by decimals.

§2.5 A PRELIMINARY LOOK AT ANNUITIES

An annuity is a stream of constant payments to be made at fixed intervals. Commercial annuities are the subject of Chapter 10. This section provides a preliminary examination of the underlying concept.

Assume that we want to know the present value of the right to receive $1,000 each year, beginning next year and continuing for five years. The appropriate discount factor is 12 percent compounded annually. The value of this stream of payments is exactly $3,604.80. This result can be determined in several ways from the tables set forth in this book. First, one could simply add up the present values of each of the first five payments in Table 2-1, which appears at the beginning of section 2.4. The sum is $3,604.80. A second way to calculate the present value of the same annuity is to add up the first five discount factors in Table 2-2 under the 12 percent column (.8929 + .7972 + .7118 + .6355 + .5674 = 3.6048) and multiply the sum by $1,000. Of course this process works only if the payments are identical in amount and evenly spaced.

An even simpler method exists. Table 2-3 is a table of the present

Table 2-2
Present Value of $1 Payable after n Periods in the Future

No. of periods	2%	3%	4%	5%	6%	7%	8%
1	.9804	.9709	.9615	.9524	.9434	.9346	.9259
2	.9612	.9426	.9246	.9070	.8900	.8734	.8573
3	.9423	.9151	.8890	.8638	.8396	.8163	.7938
4	.9238	.8885	.8548	.8227	.7921	.7629	.7350
5	.9057	.8626	.8219	.7835	.7473	.7130	.6806
6	.8880	.8375	.7903	.7462	.7050	.6663	.6302
7	.8706	.8131	.7599	.7107	.6651	.6227	.5835
8	.8535	.7894	.7307	.6768	.6274	.5820	.5403
9	.8368	.7664	.7026	.6446	.5919	.5439	.5002
10	.8203	.7441	.6756	.6139	.5584	.5083	.4632
11	.8043	.7224	.6496	.5847	.5268	.4751	.4289
12	.7885	.7014	.6246	.5568	.4970	.4440	.3971
13	.7730	.6810	.6006	.5303	.4688	.4150	.3677
14	.7579	.6611	.5775	.5051	.4423	.3878	.3405
15	.7430	.6419	.5553	.4810	.4173	.3624	.3152
16	.7284	.6232	.5339	.4581	.3936	.3387	.2919
17	.7142	.6050	.5134	.4363	.3714	.3166	.2703
18	.7002	.5874	.4936	.4155	.3503	.2959	.2502
19	.6864	.5703	.4746	.3957	.3305	.2765	.2317
20	.6730	.5537	.4564	.3769	.3118	.2584	.2145
21	.6598	.5375	.4388	.3589	.2942	.2415	.1987
22	.6468	.5219	.4220	.3418	.2775	.2257	.1839
23	.6342	.5067	.4057	.3256	.2618	.2109	.1703
24	.6217	.4919	.3901	.3101	.2470	.1971	.1577
25	.6095	.4776	.3751	.2953	.2330	.1842	.1460

Table 2-2 (continued)
Present Value of $1 Payable after n Periods in the Future

No. of periods	2%	3%	4%	5%	6%	7%	8%
26	.5976	.4637	.3607	.2812	.2198	.1722	.1352
27	.5859	.4502	.3468	.2678	.2074	.1609	.1252
28	.5744	.4371	.3335	.2551	.1956	.1504	.1159
29	.5631	.4243	.3207	.2429	.1846	.1406	.1073
30	.5521	.4120	.3083	.2314	.1741	.1314	.0994
31	.5412	.4000	.2965	.2204	.1643	.1228	.0920
32	.5306	.3883	.2851	.2099	.1550	.1147	.0852
33	.5202	.3770	.2741	.1999	.1462	.1072	.0789
34	.5100	.3660	.2636	.1904	.1379	.1002	.0730
35	.5000	.3554	.2534	.1813	.1301	.0937	.0676
36	.4902	.3450	.2437	.1727	.1227	.0875	.0626
37	.4806	.3350	.2343	.1644	.1158	.0818	.0580
38	.4712	.3252	.2253	.1566	.1092	.0765	.0537
39	.4619	.3158	.2166	.1491	.1031	.0715	.0497
40	.4529	.3066	.2083	.1420	.0972	.0668	.0460
41	.4440	.2976	.2003	.1353	.0917	.0624	.0426
42	.4353	.2890	.1926	.1288	.0865	.0583	.0395
43	.4268	.2805	.1852	.1227	.0816	.0545	.0365
44	.4184	.2724	.1780	.1169	.0770	.0509	.0338
45	.4102	.2644	.1712	.1113	.0727	.0476	.0313
46	.4022	.2567	.1646	.1060	.0685	.0445	.0290
47	.3943	.2493	.1583	.1009	.0647	.0416	.0269
48	.3865	.2420	.1522	.0961	.0610	.0389	.0249
49	.3790	.2350	.1463	.0916	.0575	.0363	.0230
50	.3715	.2281	.1407	.0872	.0543	.0339	.0213

Table 2-2 (continued)
Present Value of $1 Payable after n Periods in the Future

No. of periods	9%	10%	11%	12%	13%	14%	15%
1	.9174	.9091	.9009	.8929	.8850	.8772	.8696
2	.8417	.8264	.8116	.7972	.7831	.7695	.7561
3	.7722	.7513	.7312	.7118	.6931	.6750	.6575
4	.7084	.6830	.6587	.6355	.6133	.5921	.5718
5	.6499	.6209	.5935	.5674	.5428	.5194	.4972
6	.5963	.5645	.5346	.5066	.4803	.4556	.4323
7	.5470	.5132	.4817	.4523	.4251	.3996	.3759
8	.5019	.4665	.4339	.4039	.3762	.3506	.3269
9	.4604	.4241	.3909	.3606	.3329	.3075	.2843
10	.4224	.3855	.3522	.3220	.2946	.2697	.2472
11	.3875	.3505	.3173	.2875	.2607	.2366	.2149
12	.3555	.3186	.2858	.2567	.2307	.2076	.1869
13	.3262	.2897	.2575	.2292	.2042	.1821	.1625
14	.2992	.2633	.2320	.2046	.1807	.1597	.1413
15	.2745	.2394	.2090	.1827	.1599	.1401	.1229
16	.2519	.2176	.1883	.1631	.1415	.1229	.1069
17	.2311	.1978	.1696	.1456	.1252	.1078	.0929
18	.2120	.1799	.1528	.1300	.1108	.0946	.0808
19	.1945	.1635	.1377	.1161	.0981	.0829	.0703
20	.1784	.1486	.1240	.1037	.0868	.0728	.0611
21	.1637	.1351	.1117	.0926	.0768	.0638	.0531
22	.1502	.1228	.1007	.0826	.0680	.0560	.0462
23	.1378	.1117	.0907	.0738	.0601	.0491	.0402
24	.1264	.1015	.0817	.0659	.0532	.0431	.0349
25	.1160	.0923	.0736	.0588	.0471	.0378	.0304

Table 2-2 (continued)
Present Value of $1 Payable after n Periods in the Future

No. of periods	9%	10%	11%	12%	13%	14%	15%
26	.1064	.0839	.0663	.0525	.0417	.0331	.0264
27	.0976	.0763	.0597	.0469	.0369	.0291	.0230
28	.0895	.0693	.0538	.0419	.0326	.0255	.0200
29	.0822	.0630	.0485	.0374	.0289	.0224	.0714
30	.0754	.0573	.0437	.0334	.0256	.0196	.0151
31	.0691	.0521	.0394	.0298	.0226	.0172	.0131
32	.0634	.0474	.0355	.0266	.0200	.0151	.0114
33	.0582	.0431	.0319	.0238	.0177	.0132	.0099
34	.0534	.0391	.0288	.0212	.0157	.0116	.0086
35	.0490	.0356	.0259	.0189	.0139	.0102	.0075
36	.0449	.0323	.0234	.0169	.0123	.0089	.0065
37	.0412	.0294	.0210	.0151	.0109	.0078	.0057
38	.0378	.0267	.0190	.0135	.0096	.0069	.0049
39	.0347	.0243	.0171	.0120	.0085	.0060	.0043
40	.0318	.0221	.0154	.0107	.0075	.0053	.0037
41	.0292	.0201	.0139	.0096	.0067	.0046	.0032
42	.0268	.0183	.0125	.0086	.0059	.0041	.0028
43	.0246	.0166	.0112	.0076	.0052	.0036	.0025
44	.0226	.0151	.0101	.0068	.0046	.0031	.0021
45	.0207	.0137	.0091	.0061	.0041	.0027	.0019
46	.0190	.0125	.0082	.0054	.0036	.0024	.0016
47	.0174	.0113	.0074	.0049	.0032	.0021	.0014
48	.0160	.0103	.0067	.0043	.0028	.0019	.0012
49	.0147	.0094	.0060	.0039	.0025	.0016	.0011
50	.0134	.0085	.0054	.0035	.0022	.0014	.0009

Table 2-3
Present Value of an Annuity of $1 Payable at the End of Each Period for n Periods

No. of periods	2%	3%	4%	5%	6%	7%	8%
1	.9804	.9709	.9615	.9524	.9434	.9346	.9259
2	1.9416	1.9135	1.8861	1.8594	1.8334	1.8080	1.7833
3	2.8839	2.8286	2.7751	2.7232	2.6730	2.6243	2.5771
4	3.8077	3.7171	3.6299	3.5460	3.4651	3.3872	3.3121
5	4.7135	4.5797	4.4518	4.3295	4.2124	4.1002	3.9927
6	5.6014	5.4172	5.2421	5.0757	4.9173	4.7665	4.6229
7	6.4720	6.2303	6.0021	5.7864	5.5824	5.3893	5.2064
8	7.3255	7.0197	6.7327	6.4632	6.2098	5.9713	5.7466
9	8.1622	7.7861	7.4353	7.1078	6.8017	6.5152	6.2469
10	8.9826	8.5302	8.1109	7.7217	7.3601	7.0236	6.7101
11	9.7868	9.2526	8.7605	8.3064	7.8869	7.4987	7.1390
12	10.5753	9.9540	9.3851	8.8633	8.3838	7.9427	7.5361
13	11.3484	10.6350	9.9856	9.3936	8.8527	8.3577	7.9038
14	12.1062	11.2961	10.5631	9.8986	9.2950	8.7455	8.2442
15	12.8493	11.9379	11.1184	10.3797	9.7122	9.1079	8.5595
16	13.5777	12.5611	11.6523	10.8378	10.1059	9.4466	8.8514
17	14.2919	13.1661	12.1657	11.2741	10.4773	9.7632	9.1216
18	14.9920	13.7535	12.6593	11.6896	10.8276	10.0591	9.3719
19	15.6785	14.3238	13.1339	12.0853	11.1581	10.3356	9.6036
20	16.3514	14.8775	13.5903	12.4622	11.4699	10.5940	9.8181
21	17.0112	15.4150	14.0292	12.8212	11.7641	10.8355	10.0168
22	17.6580	15.9369	14.4511	13.1630	12.0416	11.0612	10.2007
23	18.2922	16.4436	14.8568	13.4886	12.3034	11.2722	10.3711
24	18.9139	16.9355	15.2470	13.7986	12.5504	11.4693	10.5288
25	19.5235	17.4131	15.6221	14.0939	12.7834	11.6536	10.6748

Table 2-3 (continued)
Present Value of an Annuity of $1 Payable at the End of Each Period for n Periods

No. of periods	2%	3%	4%	5%	6%	7%	8%
26	20.1210	17.8768	15.9828	14.3752	13.0032	11.8258	10.8100
27	20.7069	18.3270	16.3296	14.6430	13.2105	11.9867	10.9352
28	21.2813	18.7641	16.6631	14.8981	13.4062	12.1371	11.0511
29	21.8444	19.1885	16.9837	15.1411	13.5907	12.2777	11.1584
30	22.3965	19.6004	17.2920	15.3725	13.7648	12.4090	11.2578
31	22.9377	20.0004	17.5885	15.5928	13.9291	12.5318	11.3498
32	23.4683	20.3888	17.8736	15.8027	14.0840	12.6466	11.4350
33	23.9886	20.7658	18.1476	16.0025	14.2302	12.7538	11.5139
34	24.4986	21.1318	18.4112	16.1929	14.3681	12.8540	11.5869
35	24.9986	21.4872	18.6646	16.3742	14.4982	12.9477	11.6546
36	25.4888	21.8323	18.9083	16.5469	14.6210	13.0352	11.7172
37	25.9695	22.1672	19.1426	16.7113	14.7368	13.1170	11.7752
38	26.4406	22.4925	19.3679	16.8679	14.8460	13.1935	11.8289
39	26.9026	22.8082	19.5845	17.0170	14.9491	13.2649	11.8786
40	27.3555	23.1148	19.7928	17.1591	15.0463	13.3317	11.9246
41	27.7995	23.4124	19.9931	17.2944	15.1380	13.3941	11.9672
42	28.2348	23.7014	20.1856	17.4232	15.2245	13.4524	12.0067
43	28.6616	23.9819	20.3708	17.5459	15.3062	13.5070	12.0432
44	29.0800	24.2543	20.5488	17.6628	15.3832	13.5579	12.0771
45	29.4902	24.5187	20.7200	17.7741	15.4558	13.6055	12.1084
46	29.8923	24.7754	20.8847	17.8801	15.5244	13.6500	12.1374
47	30.2866	25.0247	21.0429	17.9810	15.5890	13.6916	12.1643
48	30.6731	25.2667	21.1951	18.0772	15.6500	13.7305	12.1891
49	31.0521	25.5017	21.3415	18.1687	15.7076	13.7668	12.2122
50	31.4236	25.7298	21.4822	18.2559	15.7619	13.8007	12.2335

Table 2-3 (*continued*)

Present Value of an Annuity of $1 Payable at the End of Each Period for n Periods

No. of periods	9%	10%	11%	12%	13%	14%	15%
1	.9174	.9091	.9009	.8929	.8850	.87723	.8696
2	1.7591	1.7355	1.7125	1.6901	1.6681	1.6467	1.6257
3	2.5313	2.4869	2.4437	2.4018	2.3612	2.3216	2.2832
4	3.2397	3.1699	3.1024	3.0373	2.9745	2.9137	2.8550
5	3.8897	3.7908	3.6959	3.6048	3.5172	3.4331	3.3522
6	4.4859	4.3553	4.2305	4.1114	3.9975	3.8887	3.7845
7	5.0330	4.8684	4.7122	4.5638	4.4226	4.2883	4.1604
8	5.5348	5.3349	5.1461	4.9676	4.7988	4.6389	4.4873
9	5.9952	5.7590	5.5370	5.3282	5.1317	4.9464	4.7716
10	6.4177	6.1446	5.8892	5.6502	5.4262	5.2161	5.0188
11	6.8052	6.4951	6.2065	5.9377	5.6869	5.4527	5.2337
12	7.1607	6.8137	6.4924	6.1944	5.9176	5.6603	5.4206
13	7.4869	7.1034	6.7499	6.4235	6.1218	5.8424	5.5831
14	7.7862	7.3667	6.9819	6.6282	6.3025	6.0021	5.7245
15	8.0607	7.6061	7.1909	6.8109	6.4624	6.1422	5.8474
16	8.3126	7.8237	7.3792	6.9740	6.6039	6.2651	5.9542
17	8.5436	8.0216	7.5488	7.1196	6.7291	6.3729	6.0472
18	8.7556	8.2014	7.7016	7.2497	6.8399	6.4674	6.1280
19	8.9501	8.3649	7.8393	7.3658	6.9380	6.5504	6.1982
20	9.1285	8.5136	7.9633	7.4694	7.0248	6.6231	6.2593
21	9.2922	8.6487	8.0751	7.5620	7.1016	6.6870	6.3125
22	9.4424	8.7715	8.1757	7.6446	7.1695	6.7429	6.3587
23	9.5802	8.8832	8.2664	7.7184	7.2297	6.7921	6.3988
24	9.7066	8.9847	8.3481	7.7843	7.2829	6.8351	6.4338
25	9.8226	9.0770	8.4217	7.8431	7.3300	6.8729	6.4641

Table 2-3 (continued)
Present Value of an Annuity of $1 Payable at the End of Each Period for n Periods

No. of periods	9%	10%	11%	12%	13%	14%	15%
26	9.9290	9.1609	8.4881	7.8957	7.3717	6.9061	6.4906
27	10.0266	9.2372	8.5478	7.9426	7.4086	6.9352	6.5135
28	10.1161	9.3066	8.6016	7.9844	7.4412	6.9607	6.5335
29	10.1983	9.3696	8.6501	8.0218	7.4701	6.9830	6.5509
30	10.2737	9.4269	8.6938	8.0552	7.4957	7.0027	6.5660
31	10.3428	9.4790	8.7331	8.0850	7.5183	7.0199	6.5791
32	10.4062	9.5264	8.7686	8.1116	7.5383	7.0350	6.5905
33	10.4644	9.5694	8.8005	8.1354	7.5560	7.0482	6.6005
34	10.5178	9.6086	8.8293	8.1566	7.5717	7.0599	6.6091
35	10.5668	9.6442	8.8552	8.1755	7.5856	7.0700	6.6166
36	10.6118	9.6765	8.8786	8.1924	7.5979	7.0790	6.6231
37	10.6530	9.7059	8.8996	8.2075	7.6087	7.0868	6.6288
38	10.6908	9.7327	8.9186	8.2210	7.6183	7.0937	6.6338
39	10.7255	9.7570	8.9357	8.2330	7.6268	7.0997	6.6380
40	10.7574	9.7791	8.9511	8.2438	7.6344	7.1050	6.6418
41	10.7866	9.7991	8.9649	8.2534	7.6410	7.1097	6.6450
42	10.8134	9.8174	8.9774	8.2619	7.6469	7.1138	6.6478
43	10.8380	9.8340	8.9886	8.2696	7.6522	7.1173	6.6503
44	10.8605	9.8491	8.9988	8.2764	7.6568	7.1205	6.6524
45	10.8812	9.8628	9.0079	8.2825	7.6609	7.1232	6.6543
46	10.9002	9.8753	9.0161	8.2880	7.6645	7.1256	6.6559
47	10.9176	9.8866	9.0235	8.2928	7.6677	7.1277	6.6573
48	10.9336	9.8969	9.0302	8.2972	7.6705	7.1296	6.6585
49	10.9482	9.9063	9.0362	8.3010	7.6730	7.1312	6.6596
50	10.9617	9.9148	9.0417	8.3045	7.6752	7.1327	6.6605

values of annuities (payable at the end of each period). To get the present value of the 12 percent, 5-year annuity one simply looks up the "five year" row and "12 percent" column to find the number 3.6048. Obviously, Table 2-3 may be obtained from Table 2-2 by a process of systematic summing of amounts.

These various methods of calculation all show that the present value of the right to receive an aggregate amount of $5,000 in increments of $1,000 per year over the next five years is $3,604.80. It seems odd that the right to receive $100,000 in a lump sum 100 years from now, also discounted at 12 percent, is worth only one dollar, while the right to receive only $1,000 per year over the next five years is worth thousands of times as much. Yet that is the magic of the time value of money.

For those mathematically inclined, a nice complex formula to derive the present value of a stream of constant payments in the future is:

$$PV = \frac{P(1 - (1 + i)^{-N})}{i}$$

where P = the recurring payment; and PV, i, and n all have the same meanings as in the previous section.

Handheld calculators have also been programmed to compute present and future values of annuities directly. For the current generation, that may be even easier, but one should understand the underlying theory.

§2.6 THE VALUE OF A PERPETUAL ANNUITY

Let us take a leap of fancy and assume that an annuity will continue forever —$1,000 per year forever. That must be worth an infinite amount, mustn't it, because the number of payments are infinite?

For simplicity, let us assume that the appropriate discount rate is 12 percent, so that we know that the first five years of the annuity is worth $3,604.80. If you turn back to the table at the beginning of section 2.3, it appears that the "infinity" answer must be wrong because the present value of future payments drops off dramatically. Similarly, if one looks at Table 2-3 under the 12 percent column, the value of a 5-year annuity is $3,604.80; a 10-year annuity, $5,650.20; a 15-year annuity, $6,810.90; a 20-year annuity, $7,469.40; a 25-year annuity, $7,843.10; a 30-year annuity, $8,055.20. The present value of the five $1,000 payments from 25 years to 30 years is only $212.00. The present value of a 45-year annuity is $8,285.00; of a 50-year annuity, $8,3045.00. From the 45th to the 50th year, the five years of payments increase the present value by only $22. Clearly the value of a perpetual annuity is not infinite.

The present value of a perpetual stream of fixed payments is precisely equal to the reciprocal of the discount rate:

$$\frac{1}{\text{discount rate}}$$

In the above hypothetical,

$$\frac{1}{.12} = 8.3333;$$

the present value of the right to receive $1,000 per year forever (at a 12 percent discount rate) is $8,333.33. This should become intuitively obvious when you realize that $8,333.33 invested at 12 percent yields $1,000 per year ($8,333.33 × .12 = $999.99), year after year, forever. Since the present value of a 50-year annuity on those terms is $8,304.50, it follows that the present value of the right to receive every payment, from the 51st on to infinity, is only $28.80. When one values a long-term annuity, a simple way to approximate its value is to assume that it is infinite and multiply by the reciprocal of the discount factor.

§2.7 VALUING VARIABLE FUTURE PAYMENTS

Skill in discounting future payments to present value is useful in a variety of contexts. An individual may be offered a variety of different payment alternatives for a major purchase. A homeowner planning to sell her home may be faced with selecting the most attractive of several offers that involve payments at different times and in different amounts, or choosing between two or more strategies that involve payments of various amounts at various times under various assumptions. In order to avoid the common mistake of comparing oranges and apples, that is, of comparing dollars payable at different times without taking into account the time value of money, it is necessary to reduce all future payments to current values. In doing this one must select one or more interest rates: If all the payments are to be made by the same entity under apparently constant circumstances, it is customary to use a single interest rate for all calculations. Consider the following example: A homeowner is planning to sell his present home and purchase a larger one. He is considering three offers that involve the following terms:

a) Offer A, $90,000 cash on settlement;
b) Offer B, $10,000 cash on settlement, thereafter $1,000 per month for 120 months;
c) Offer C, $25,000 down, $1,200 per month for 72 months.

The total payment to be received under Offer A is $90,000, payable immediately. Under Offer B, the total payments to be received are $130,000 ($10,000 plus 120 times $1,000). The contract presented by this hopeful purchaser ignores the interest component entirely and states, as the purchase price, the full $130,000. Under Offer C, the total payments are $111,400 ($25,000 plus 72 times $1,200). However, because of the time value of money, this comparison of gross amounts to be received is misleading. Calculation shows that at a 9 percent interest rate, and ignoring income taxes, the present value of $1,000 per month for 120 months is $78,941.69, and the present value of $1,200 per month for 72 months is $66,572.22. Thus, the present values of the three offers are:

Offer A: $90,000
Offer B: $88,941.69
Offer C: $91,572.22

Even though Offer B yields the largest gross amount, it has the smallest present value. This occurs because the immediate down payment in Offer B is rather small and periodic payments continue over ten years rather than six years, as in the case of Offer C. On the other hand, since the present values of the three offers are very close, most persons would probably recommend that the all-cash offer be accepted on the theory that there is some advantage in being disentangled from a property immediately. However, it certainly is not intuitively obvious that this is the most sensible solution.

In this hypothetical, different conclusions may be reached if a different discount rate is chosen. For example, if one computes the present value of the three payment options using a discount rate of 6 percent rather than 9 percent, the results are as follows:

Offer A: $90,000
Offer B: $95,366
Offer C: $94,990

Suddenly, the payments to be spread out over a period of time have become more attractive. Reflection shows that this is a result of the fact that the present value of future payments is higher at lower discount rates, so that at the lower discount rate the future payments become relatively more valuable compared with the cash payments on closing. As noted before, there is an inverse relationship between value and discount rates: The higher the rate, the less a future payment is worth.

§2.8 WHAT DISCOUNT RATE TO USE IN CALCULATING PRESENT VALUES

In light of the foregoing discussion, certainly, a reasonable question at this point is why the interest rate of 12 percent was used in most of the above calculations. Why, in the last example comparing three different payment schedules, were the rates compared unexpectedly changed to 9 percent and 6 percent? Where do rates in the real world come from anyway?

Unfortunately, there is no simple answer to the question of which discount rate to use in all circumstances in the real world. It depends on what the question is, the current level of market interest rates, and the investment alternatives available to the parties. As described above, the differences in results reached vary significantly depending on the rate chosen, though the differences between choosing a 6 percent or a 6.5 percent rate is nowhere near as substantial as the difference between choosing between 6 percent and 12 percent, as Table 2-1 illustrates. However, that does not give much guidance as to whether a 6 percent or a 12 percent rate should actually be used.

Most real-life problems in determining present values come down to a choice between one of the three following rates:

1. The market interest rate for essentially risk-free investments, the yield on short-term debt securities issued by the federal government, for example.
2. The highest interest rate that a person could obtain for a deposit within his or her means at a local financial institution.
3. The lowest interest rate that a person would be charged in order to borrow funds of the same magnitude as the transaction involves.

In instances in which a person of doubtful wealth has the obligation to make a future payment, an appropriate upward adjustment may be made to the discount rate to reflect the possibility that obligor may be unable or unwilling to make the payment. In other words, the risk has increased, and therefore a higher discount rate is appropriate. Of course, the higher the discount rate is, the lower the present value of that payment will be. In most instances, however, the calculations are made using one of the three basic rates set forth above without express adjustment in the discount rate for the risk of nonpayment. Rather, that risk is taken into account in a subjective way in deciding whether or not to enter the transaction at all, even if the calculation shows the value of the transaction to be attractive.

3

Modern Payment Mechanisms

§3.1 INTRODUCTION

This chapter introduces readers to modern payment mechanisms. The nature of these mechanisms has changed dramatically in the last 20 years with the development of modern electronic systems of recordkeeping; it is likely that further changes will continue to occur in the future.

Historically, the simplest and most common type of payment mechanism was currency, pieces of paper or coins that were "legal tender for all debts public and private." For small transactions, currency is still the simplest and most convenient payment mechanism. Today, when I go down to the corner store for a gallon of milk, the storekeeper gives me the milk and I give him the price in cash. In the nineteenth and early twentieth centuries, many persons mistrusted banks and kept their accumulated wealth under the mattress or in the sock drawer. Even relatively large transactions were then routinely settled by cash payments.

Today, currency is rarely used for the settlement of legitimate large transactions. It is awkward and frequently dangerous to carry around large amounts of cash. And, because currency is the preferred method of settlement of illegal transactions in drugs, guns, and other contraband, the federal government has imposed reporting requirements on persons paying or receiving cash in excess of $5,000. Compliance with these requirements may call unwanted attention to legitimate transactions if currency were used to settle such transactions.

Barter is another payment mechanism that was doubtless relatively common in rural economies and survives in limited forms today. The plumber puts in a new bathroom and is "paid" in the form of a butchered side of beef which is ready to be placed in the plumber's freezer. Such private arrangements doubtless occur from time to time today. There also exist "clubs" or membership organizations that essentially serve as clearing organizations for barter transactions. The plumber who is a member of such an organization puts in a bathroom for another member of the organization and receives a "chit" that enables him to acquire a designated amount of services or products from any other member of the organization. Barter is probably economically insignificant today, though the full extent of it is unknown; it is attractive in part because it may facilitate income tax evasion. See section 19.23. For example, it is unlikely in the above example that either the farmer or the plumber will include, as they unquestionably are required to do, the value of the bathroom or the beef as income in their state and federal income tax returns. The barter organizations deny they are designed to facilitate tax evasion and make clear to their members the income tax obligations arising from barter transactions cleared through their organizations. How much cheating actually goes on is unknown.

§3.2 PERSONAL CHECKS

Unquestionably most personal obligations today are paid through the medium of personal checking accounts. Most such accounts are with banks. If money is defined as something creditors or sellers will accept in payment of obligations, checks drawn on bank deposits are clearly a type of money. Of course, before writing checks, one has to open an account, deposit some money in it, execute a form contract, and sign a signature card that permits the bank to verify that in case of a dispute it was in fact the depositor who signed a disputed check.

When one deposits money in a checking account, the depositor is making a loan to the bank; the depositor is a creditor, and the bank becomes a debtor. A personal check is simply a written order to the bank to transfer specific funds owed to the depositor to a third person. When a depositor pays a debt by a personal check, the creditor receives the check and presents it to its bank. The creditor immediately receives a deposit slip showing that its account has been increased by the amount of the check. The check then makes its way back through the banking system to the bank of the original depositor, a process that may take a few days. Thus there exists a period of time when the amount of the check appears as a deposit in the creditor's account and yet has not been subtracted from the debtor's account. This period is called the "float."

The depositor's bank may refuse to pay ("dishonor" is the technical word usually used) a check for a variety of reasons: The depositor may not have sufficient funds to cover the check; the depositor may have entered a "stop payment order" directing the bank not to pay the check; or the account may have been closed in the meantime. The creditor depositing the check will learn that one of these events occurred only when its bank notifies it that the check has been dishonored by returning it to the creditor.

The creditor does not affirmatively learn that a check has cleared. Silence in this respect is good news. A creditor who deposits a check drawn on another bank may be prevented from drawing upon those funds for a brief period after the deposit. This period is set by the federal Expedited Funds Availability Act (EFAA), a statute that was designed to (and did) cause the banking system to speed up the process of clearing checks. However, even after funds are made available, the creditor cannot safely use the funds until the check is presented to the debtor's bank and is cleared, since the creditor's bank will deduct the amount of the check from the creditor's account if the check is thereafter dishonored. In other words, the EFAA relates to when funds must be made available by the creditor's bank, not when the transaction is final. The funds availability rules of EFAA are subject to "safeguard" exceptions: For example, funds need not be made available until the check has actually cleared in cases of checks in excess of $5,000, redeposited checks, checks drawn on repeatedly overdrawn accounts, and checks the bank has reasonable cause to believe are uncollectible. Notice may have to be given before a safeguard exception may be invoked.

The processes by which checks are presented through the Federal Reserve System and dishonored checks are returned to the depositor are described in detail in Professor John F. Dolan's book on the Uniform Commercial Code in the Essentials for Law Students series. The discussion below describes only those features of the system that directly impact on individuals using regular checking accounts.

It is estimated that the banking system clears about 52 billion checks per year. It is obviously not possible for banks to verify the signature on each check presented for payment. Instead, check clearing is done almost entirely electronically. The key is the strangelooking numbers appearing at the bottom of the check: They are machine readable magnetic numbers, and the process is called magnetic ink character recognition (MICR). (The fraction that appears in the upper right-hand corner of the check is not MICR and is used only if the MICR system fails; the numerator identifies the branch and bank of the writer of the check; the denominator the proper federal reserve destination for the check, that is, the component of the federal reserve system within which that bank and branch are located.) Form 3-1 is familiar to practically all readers: It is a simple check with the MICR notation and fraction that is supplied by a bank to a depositor.

The only human involvement with the routine check is the entry of the amount of the check by a bank clerk in MICR format on the check itself so that the amount thereafter may be machine-read; everything else happens electronically. What is important to appreciate is that no one compares the signature on a check with a signature on a signature card unless there is a complaint that a check has been forged. If blank checks are lost or stolen, one must keep a careful watch to make sure that someone is not filling them in and placing them in the collection system.

For the same reason, one cannot send "instructions" to the bank by notations on the check itself. A postdated check will clear routinely when it is deposited; no one at the bank reads the date. Similarly, a restrictive indorsement on the back of the check will be ignored since no bank employee reads it.

When one fills in a check, care should be taken that blanks are not left that enable an unscrupulous person to alter the amount—from "$9.50" to "$1009.50," for example. The careless filling out of a check that permits this type of alteration may be the responsibility of the depositor, not the bank.

The banking system is national in character; checks may be presented for payment anywhere in the United States. The clearing process occurs at different levels. About 20 percent of all checks are "on us" checks that are presented for payment to the bank on which the check is drawn. Funds availability for "on us" checks is the first business day after the day the check is deposited. Checks presented to other banks in the same community ("local checks") usually clear through a local clearinghouse. Funds availability for local checks is the second business day following the day of deposit. Each Federal Reserve Bank maintains its own regional clearinghouse for the multistate area it serves, and the Federal Reserve Banks operate a national clearinghouse among themselves to handle checks that are presented to banks in districts of other Federal Reserve Banks. Funds availability in the case of non-local checks is the fifth business day following the day of deposit of the check.

A clearinghouse is a very simple concept: All checks drawn on and presented by a single bank are netted together each day, and the bank in effect pays only the net amount. This "payment" is actually made by a charge to or deposit in a special account (called a clearing account) maintained for that bank with the clearinghouse, which is usually physically located in the Federal Reserve Bank.

When checks in very large amounts are presented to a bank other

Form 3-1. Check with MICR Symbols

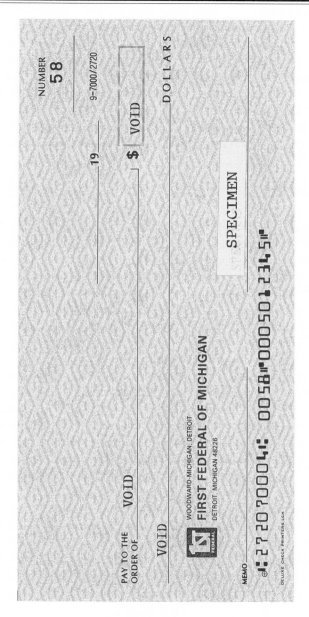

Reprinted with the permission of First Federal of Michigan.

than the bank on which they are drawn, the federal reserve clearing system may be avoided, and a direct presentment system used. The checks are sent via private messenger service by the presenting bank to the bank on which they are drawn (the receiving bank). The amount is deposited in an account maintained by the presenting bank with the receiving bank, and the amount is immediately transferred by wire transfer to the presenting bank. Large banks maintain such accounts in banks in other large cities throughout the country.

The legal principles applicable to checks and the presentment system appear in articles 3 and 4 of the Uniform Commercial Code.

§3.3 CHECKING AND SAVINGS ACCOUNTS

Until the 1970s, checking accounts were the exclusive province of commercial banks. So-called savings institutions — credit unions and savings and loan associations, for example — were depositories for savings but did not make those funds available through checks. Similarly, commercial banks maintained basically two different kinds of accounts: checking accounts and savings accounts. Funds deposited in savings accounts could be accessed only by passbook entry and not by check. This sharp distinction between two related functions has now largely disappeared. Savings institutions provide checks to draw on funds on deposit with them, as do brokerage firms, credit card companies, and other financial institutions.

Commercial banks have largely eliminated the distinction between savings and checking accounts. Interest may be paid on checking account balances, and checks may be used to access funds in traditional savings accounts. A single bank may offer as many as 10 or 12 different accounts blending to some degree savings and checking privileges to appeal to persons with varying needs. Many banks have developed fancy names for these accounts that may promise more than they deliver.

The suitability of these accounts as investment vehicles is discussed in section 16.3. Certificates of deposit are discussed in section 16.4.

The blurring or elimination of the distinction between checking and savings accounts, and the creation of multiple varieties of accounts has increased the need for sensitivity about service charges, fees, and handling charges imposed by banks. For example, a bank might advertise a savings account with checking privileges paying a relatively high rate of interest but not disclose that a service charge of $2.00 per check is imposed if more than four checks are written each month and that a $5.00 fee is charged if the amount deposited in the account drops below $1,000 during any month. The $5.00 fee will more than wipe out the month's earnings on the less than $1,000 in the account. The same bank may also offer another account that does not earn interest but provides unlimited checkwriting privileges without a service charge if the balance in the account remains above $500 and a $0.25 service charge on checks if the account is below that amount. While both of these accounts have their attractive features, certainly the first should not be used as a general checking account for household accounts, and the second should not be used as a depository for excess funds not currently needed for living expenses.

In 1992, interest rates on checking accounts were so low that they must be viewed as unattractive investments. See section 16.3. Only funds that must be available for immediate use should be kept in such accounts. Indeed, interest rates on these accounts are so low that the return is less than the inflation rate, and bank charges for such unnecessary things as overdrafts or use of automated teller machines may wipe out any interest earned on these accounts.

The traditional practice by commercial banks is to return to the depositor each month all checks that have cleared through the account. Increasingly, banks provide only a monthly statement describing checks that have cleared but do not return the checks themselves. The checks are destroyed after photocopies are made in the event of future disputes. Nonbanking institutions that offer checkwriting privileges usually follow this practice, which is sometimes called "truncated checking accounts." Institutions that do not return checks may provide depositors with check blanks that have carbonless paper attached so that the depositor has a record of precisely what was written on each check.

§3.4 OVERDRAFT PROTECTION

It is relatively easy for anyone to "bounce" a check by writing it for an amount greater than the funds on deposit when the check is presented. Many persons maintain checking accounts with balances close to zero in order to avoid the loss of interest income; others maintain balances close to zero simply because they have no choice. A check that exceeds the funds on deposit is called an "overdraft." An overdraft may occur because the depositor did not keep accurate records of checks previously written or because a deposit made recently has not been made available by the bank as permitted by Federal Reserve System regulation.

There is some additional cost to the system when an overdraft is dishonored and returned to the creditor. The depository bank, on which most of the cost rests, usually imposes a fairly hefty charge for a bounced check, for example, $25 or $30. Obviously, it is not only embarrassing but a costly matter to lose track of one's balance and write a half dozen or so small checks to cover household expenses, all of which bounce. Furthermore, since overdraft charges snowball, the dishonored check charge may well result in additional checks bouncing.

A recipient of a dishonored check may also seek to impose a fee on the writer of the bad check to cover its handling costs.

The usual practice of a creditor which receives back a dishonored check for insufficient funds is to redeposit the check on the hope that the check will clear when presented a second time.

Many banks offer overdraft protection. The bank agrees that it will honor a check even though there are insufficient funds in the account, in effect making a loan to the depositor of the amount necessary to clear the check, and imposing a service charge that is usually the same as the charge for dishonoring a check. Overdraft protection is desirable because it avoids the embarrassment and inconvenience of having a creditor learn that a check was written upon insufficient funds.

Overdraft protection may be provided free of charge as a service to desirable customers; the name of a bank officer who knows the depositor may be placed on the depositor's record and whose approval is necessary before the bank will clear the check. More likely today, the overdraft will be viewed as a loan and interest charged at the highest unsecured interest rate then in effect at the bank — on credit cards that may be one and one-half percent per month. See Chapter 7. Typically, interest continues to accrue until the loan itself is paid off by the customer; the deposit of funds in the overdrawn account sufficient to "cover" the overdraft does not stop the running of interest.

If the depositor maintains other inactive accounts at the bank — for example, a savings account or a home equity loan account — an arrangement may be made by which a bank may automatically use funds in these accounts to cover the overdraft. If charged to a home equity loan account, the interest cost is much lower than on an unsecured account. A fee of perhaps $5 may be charged whenever this crossover occurs.

Some banks permit overdrafts written by one person to be charged to another person's account; this arrangement may be appropriate for a parent who wishes to guarantee his or her child's account.

Overdraft protection is obviously a desirable feature of any active checking account and often may be obtained simply by asking for it.

In many states, it is a criminal offense to write checks when one knows there are not sufficient funds to cover the check. In these states, the prosecutor's office may find itself a bad check collection agency as it exercises prosecutorial discretion with respect to complaints filed by merchants.

§3.5 CASHIER'S CHECKS AND OTHER GUARANTEED PAYMENT DEVICES

Many creditors are willing to take the risk that a check will be dishonored. A seller of goods on credit has already extended credit; the risk is not increased by the receipt of a check drawn on the debtor's account. On the other hand, a seller of goods may be reluctant to release them to the purchaser simply on the faith of a personal check. In other words, if it is a cash transaction not involving the extension of credit, a personal check is not the same as currency. Several devices exist that avoid this extension of credit through the use of the payment system.

A cashier's check is a check issued by the bank itself to a designated third party. Form 3-2 on page 48 is an example of such a check. When the check is issued, the amount is deducted from the depositor's account so that the dishonor risk is avoided. A typical cashier's check is a two-party instrument: the bank and the payee. The name of the depositor purchasing the cashier's check usually appears on the face of the cashier's check as the "remitter."

A certified check is a check made out by the depositor who presents it for certification to the bank. The bank signifies its "acceptance" of the check by a stamp placed on the check itself. When a bank certifies a check, the amount is immediately deducted from the remitter's account. Form 3-3 on page 49 is an example of a certified check.

Both cashier's and certified checks eliminate the risk of dishonor. Furthermore, deposit insurance provided by the Federal Deposit Insurance Corporation provides protection against the risk of bank failure. Finally, stop payment orders are not permitted with respect to such instruments, so that the creditor essentially is assured of payment. Hence these checks are virtually the same as cash.

The major disadvantage with these instruments is a matter of convenience, since the depositor must go down to his or her bank to obtain a cashier's check or the bank certification. It also results in the amount of the check being deducted from the depositor's account a few days earlier than it normally would be if a personal check were used.

Some banks offer check-guaranty programs so that local retailers may accept personal checks without concern of risk of dishonor. These plans may require the retailer to make a telephone call to a designated bank office, or increasingly, to require the purchaser to present a plastic card similar to a credit card along with the personal check. These guaranty programs are contractual between the bank and participating retailers, and typically apply only to checks below some designated amount.

A new type of check guaranty program, based on modern computer technology, was first introduced in 1990 and is now offered by several companies. One such company is a subsidiary of a national credit reporting agency (see section 4.2). Under its program, it guarantees the payment of individual checks written to member retail stores in exchange for a small fee for each check guaranteed. A cashier accepting a personal check is required to enter the account number and amount of the check into the cash register, which electronically sends the information to the guaranteeing agency; the guaranteeing agency processes the account number and

Form 3-2. Cashier's Check

Printed with the permission of Manufacturers National Bank of Detroit.

Form 3-3. Certified Check

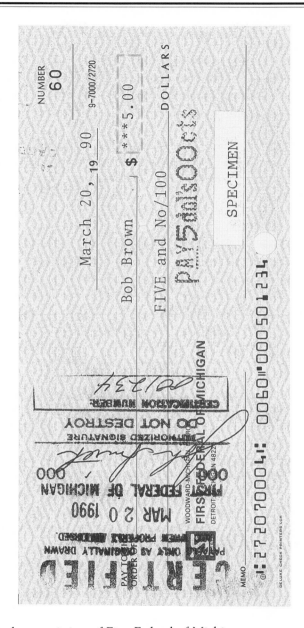

Printed with the permission of First Federal of Michigan.

amount through a computer and in a few seconds signals the cashier whether or not payment of the check is guaranteed. The interesting aspect of this program is that the guaranteeing agency does not have legal access either to bank balances or to credit reports on the check writer. Rather, a person enters the guaranteeing agency's computer when he or she first purchases something by check at a business that is a member of the guarantee program. The first check is not reviewed. If a check written on an account bounces, all other checks on the same account are automatically rejected until the dishonored check is made good. However, the system also may reject checks based on other patterns that do not necessarily imply that the check will be dishonored: for example, checks aggregating a large amount being written within a specified time or many checks being written within a short period of time (a pattern that may indicate that someone has stolen or found another's checkbook and is passing as many bad checks as possible). If a check is not guaranteed during business hours, the retailer may ask the check writer for additional information, such as a driver license number or credit card numbers, and then telephone the guaranteeing agency with this information, which may then guarantee the check. Obviously, it is a nuisance and potentially embarrassing to be pulled from the cash register line and asked for additional information when presenting a check for a small purchase. Presumably, when the database increases in size over a period of time, such incidents involving persons with good credit and sufficient funds in the bank to cover the questioned check will diminish.

Other payment systems exist. Some persons do not have checking accounts at all because of their personal financial circumstances and exigencies. These persons may make payment to creditors through postal or bank money orders. Form 3-4 is a bank personal money order while form 3-5 is a postal money order. The debtor takes currency to the issuer of the money order and receives a form that may be made payable to the debtor himself or to a creditor of the debtor. Traveler's checks (see section 3.7) work on somewhat the same principle. These alternative payment systems are rarely used by persons who maintain checking accounts. Funds availability for cashier's checks, certified checks, and Postal Service money orders under the EFAA is one business day after the day of deposit.

Private money order firms also exist, many with offices in the poorest sections of town. There is an insolvency risk in these forms of payment in the event the company writing the money order ceases doing business after the money order is purchased but before it is "cashed."

§3.6 PRIVATE CHECK CASHING FIRMS

Private check cashing firms flourish in many cities, particularly in the poorer sections. These firms cash salary, government, and welfare checks

Form 3-4. Money Order

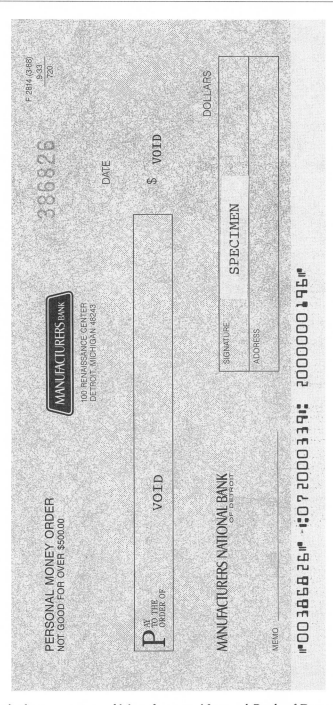

Printed with the permission of Manufacturers National Bank of Detroit.

Form 3-5. Postal Money Order

for a fee for persons who do not have a bank account. A typical charge might be $13 to cash a $500 check, though fees vary widely.

Some persons with a bank account may use private check cashing services because of their convenient location and their immediate need for cash. Private check cashing firms avoid the problem created by the funds availability rules. See section 3.2.

The number of check cashing outlets has been estimated to have increased from 3,000 in 1988 to 5,000 in 1993. This is doubtless due to the tightening of minimum deposit requirements by traditional banks and the closing of bank branches, particularly in the less affluent parts of American cities. In addition to cashing checks, many also sell postage stamps, money orders, lottery tickets, and simplify the process of wiring funds through Western Union or other types of electronic funds transfers. Some dispense food stamps under contract with the state. A few give cash-advance loans on individual income tax refunds.

A number of states regulate check cashing firms by imposing a maximum amount that can be charged for cashing checks. Nevertheless, there have been numerous complaints about gouging, and proposals have been made to subject these firms to regulations in states where they are not now regulated, and nationally, by federal law. Other legislative proposals include a requirement that regular banks be required to cash checks even if the payee does not maintain an account at the bank.

While the charge for cashing checks is only a few dollars, this is an expensive service — running into the hundreds of dollars per year — if used each week or each month.

§3.7 TRAVELER'S CHECKS

Another traditional and widely advertised payment mechanism involves traveler's checks issued by several banks and other organizations — the best known of which is the American Express Co. — primarily for the use of travelers or vacationers in places where they do not have normal banking connections. Form 3-6 is a typical traveler's check. At first blush, these traveler's checks appear to be bargains: For the nominal charge of one dollar for each hundred dollars of checks (payable in advance), the traveler is promised the convenience of worldwide acceptance as payment and free replacement of lost checks. The purchaser of traveler's checks signs each check twice — once when they are purchased and a second time when they are actually used. In this way it is difficult for a thief or finder of checks to negotiate them. But if they are stolen, the risk is on the organization issuing the checks and not the traveler. How can a bank possibly make money charging only one dollar per hundred dollars of checks, assuming the risk of loss, let alone meeting the cost of expensive

Form 3-6. Traveler's Check

Printed with the permision of Barclays Bank Plc.

radio and TV advertising commonly used to promote the use of traveler's checks? Furthermore, many organizations that issue traveler's checks waive the one dollar per hundred fee for card holders or depositors using certain kinds of accounts, and issue traveler's checks free. This seems to be an example of something for nothing.

The answer lies in the fact that the purchaser must pay the face value of the checks immediately but they are not "cashed in" until some time later. However, unlike money orders and cashiers or certified checks, traveler's checks are often not cashed immediately. Rather, they are carried around for days or weeks during the purchaser's travels. In the meantime, the bank invests the funds used to purchase the traveler's checks and earns interest without paying any interest at all to the purchaser. Further, since people are constantly buying new traveler's checks, the available funds for investment remain reasonably stable, subject, of course, to seasonal variations. The amount available for investment by the issuers of traveler's checks may be a very large sum — running into the hundreds of millions or billions of dollars for the larger companies — and is usually called "the float." The interest on the float is what makes traveler's checks profitable for the issuer.

One major issuer of traveler's checks has an advertisement in which the announcer suggests that on returning from vacation, "keep your last traveler's check in case of an emergency." Might there be an ulterior motive behind this helpful and friendly suggestion?

Developments in electronic banking (discussed in the following sections) have cut into the traveler's check business and may spell the ultimate demise of this familiar device. As electronic interlocking of credit cards has evolved on an international scale, it may be easier, safer, and more convenient to carry a piece of plastic rather than bulky traveler's checks. With a Visa or Mastercard today one can obtain a "cash advance" in local currency in most foreign countries simply by going to a local bank. ATM machines may provide cash at the local machine as well. Why carry traveler's checks?

Two related developments also are tipping the scale against traditional traveler's checks. Increasingly, foreign stores, hotels, and restaurants are charging "encashment fees" when they accept traveler's checks. These fees may range from 2 to 10 percent of the face value of the check and reflect the preference of foreign establishments to deal with plastic and electronic communication rather than paper. Second, obtaining foreign currency electronically may result in a more favorable exchange rate than one can obtain by presenting a traveler's check payable in dollars to a foreign restaurant or hotel. ATM transactions are aggregated, and a "wholesale" exchange rate applied. Of course, to the extent a cash advance involves a loan by the credit card issuer to the user, interest is charged. When a person buys traveler's checks, he or she loses interest on the money paid for the checks themselves, but that loss may be smaller than the interest charged on a cash advance.

A traveler getting $500 of foreign currency today usually gets the equivalent of as much as $20 or $25 more by using an ATM machine outside a foreign bank than by cashing traveler's checks at the counter inside. Likewise, visitors to an American Express office in a major European city will do better by using their card to get money from a machine than by going inside and cashing traveler's checks or a personal check at the counter.

§3.8 ELECTRONIC BANKING

The last decade has seen major changes in banking practices as a result of the revolution in electronic communication and recordkeeping. Most banks have opened automated teller machines (ATMs) that accept deposits and provide cash up to designated amounts through the use of a plastic card and personal identification number (PIN). The latter is a number selected by the depositor that is designed to prevent a person who steals or finds a lost bank card from emptying the depositor's account. The PIN must be entered manually by the user to effectuate the transaction.

Depending on the ATM involved, these cash transactions may involve either the short-term extension of credit by the bank or a direct charge to the customer's account. Co-operative arrangements exist among many banks so that one bank's customers may make deposits or draw cash from another bank's ATM machines. Thus, electronic banking is gradually becoming national or international in scope. Deposits made in "nonproprietary" ATMs (an ATM owned by the bank in which the deposit is to be made is known as a "proprietary" ATM) are subject to the same funds availability rules under the EFAA as non-local checks, that is, five business days after the day of deposit. The convenience of ATMs cannot be doubted, even though they may create security problems for their users and provide an attractive target for thieves with access to heavy equipment.

Many banks also have programs that permit depositors to arrange for automatic payment of recurring bills, such as utility bills, insurance premiums, and the like. Many employers have adopted programs that permit salary payments to be automatically deposited in the employee's checking accounts. These transactions are arranged electronically through automated clearing houses (usually called ACHs). It is likely that significant changes will continue to occur in payment systems in these areas in the future.

§3.9 CREDIT AND DEBIT CARDS

The proliferation of Visa and Mastercard credit cards used as payment media is perhaps the most visible product of the electronic revolution.

When one buys goods or services using one of these cards, one naturally thinks that one is making payment when one in fact uses a credit card. As described in Chapter 7, however, one is usually creating a consumer loan from the bank by the use of such a card. Along with the proliferation of credit cards there has been the widespread use of point-of-sale (POS) telephone systems that enable the retailer to determine whether the use of the card is authorized by the issuer of the card.

Some plastic cards are debit cards rather than credit cards. As described in Chapter 7, a debit card involves an immediate deduction of the amount of the purchase from the account of the user rather than the extension of credit. Most ATM cards are debit cards. Banks have tried to encourage the use of debit cards rather than credit cards, but they remain relatively unpopular with many users.

So-called "smart cards" are cards that permit credit and personal information to be placed on the card itself so that the call to the credit card center is eliminated when a smart card is used for a purchase. Perhaps these cards are the wave of the future.

Legal principles relating to consumer electronic funds transfers can be found in a variety of federal and state statutes, particularly, the Truth in Lending Act, Regulation Z of the Federal Reserve System, and the Electronic Fund Transfers Act.

A major problem with modern credit cards is the loss or theft of cards. The maximum that a cardholder is liable for if there is an unauthorized use of the card is $50. There is no charge if the loss of the card is reported promptly. A new credit card with a new number may be issued almost immediately when a card is reported lost by telephone.

As every cardholder knows, it is possible to use a credit card by telephone. Hence an eavesdropper (or a person who acquires your card number from other sources) may be able to place charges on your account without having physical possession of your card. It is important, when reporting that a charge appearing on your bill was not authorized, to use the phrase "unauthorized use" to distinguish it from a mere "billing error." Billing errors must be reported within 60 days, but there is no time limit on reporting unauthorized uses. This is an important principle because a person obtaining a credit card number may be able to divert monthly statements away from the card holder's address. When this occurs the cardholder is likely to learn of the unauthorized use only when the credit limit has been exceeded and the use of the card by the cardholder is unexpectedly rejected.

§3.10 WIRE TRANSFERS

Today, payments made in connection with substantial transactions are usually made by wholesale wire transfers. The previous section discussed consumer electronic transfers; this section discusses an immense payment network that involves trillions of dollars per year and an average transaction of about two million dollars each. One popular article on this topic described wire transfers as the "uncharted frontiers of finance . . . where money consists of magnetized specks of iron oxide in computer memories and great fortunes move from continent to continent as weightless photons through the electromagnetic ether."

There are two wire transfer systems in existence: "Fedwire" operated by the Federal Reserve System and the Clearinghouse Interbank Payment Systems ("CHIPS") operated by the New York Clearinghouse Association. Fedwire requires the use of depository institutions that maintain accounts with the Federal Reserve System; daily Fedwire transfer transactions exceed 165,000 and the total dollar volume per year is in the $100 trillion dollar range. CHIPS is largely used in international transactions in which settlement is to occur in dollars in New York City.

Wire transfer is a "paperless" transfer. Transfers of funds are made by instant electronic communication between banks with funds being deposited directly into the account of the recipient. The arrangement is much faster than traditional check clearing procedures. Today it is routine to provide that a transaction involving, say, the sale of certain oil and gas properties for $70,000,000 in cash, be closed by the wire transfer of this amount from sets of accounts used by the buyer to sets of accounts used by the seller.

Of course, these transactions do involve the use of paper in most respects. There is a contract between the parties and a written direction to the bank to wire funds from account A to account B in another bank. The only paperless aspect of the transaction is the actual movement of funds by electronic communication through members of the Federal Reserve System.

Legal principles with respect to wholesale wire transfers are set forth in article 4A of the Uniform Commercial Code, an article that was approved in 1989 and has been adopted by a number of states.

4

Credit Reporting: Why You May Not Qualify for a Loan or a Lease

§4.1   INTRODUCTION

Today credit decisions by most lenders (including banks, mortgage companies, and issuers of VISA, Mastercard, and other credit cards) are based not on an independent investigation of the applicant or on financial information supplied by that applicant. Rather those decisions are likely to be based on a "credit report" assembled by a national organization from information supplied routinely by millions of stores, banks, and other creditors. If the information in a credit report is erroneous — perhaps because information about someone else was included in the credit report — an applicant for credit may be turned down summarily. Furthermore, unless the applicant does something to correct that error, it is very likely that subsequent applications for credit will also be denied by other credit-granting organizations on the basis of the same erroneous information.

The modern credit reporting industry is a product of the electronic age. As late as the 1970s, credit reporting was done on a local basis. Potential lenders relied on information supplied by the applicant (usually verified by direct inquiry with references supplied by the applicant) and possibly an examination of public records of bankruptcies, judgments and foreclosures. Some credit information on individuals was maintained by local credit bureaus in large cities, which entered information manually in their records. A decision to refuse to grant credit in this earlier era could usually be discussed with a responsible officer of the lending organization that declined to grant credit or with a representative of the local credit bureau itself. That era has largely ended. A denial of credit today usually is the product of negative information supplied by a national credit reporting company and the consumer usually must look exclusively to that credit reporting company, not the organization denying credit, for an explanation.

The credit reporting industry is regulated by the Fair Credit Reporting Act of 1971, a federal statute that grants consumers the right to inspect their credit files. Prior to the enactment of this statute, there was no right of consumer access to credit information. Under this statute, anyone who is turned down for credit may obtain a copy of their credit report free; consumers who are "just curious" usually must pay a small fee to inspect their report.

§4.2 THE MODERN CREDIT REPORTING INDUSTRY

There are three major credit reporting companies today: TRW Credit Data, Equifax Credit Information Services, Inc., and Trans Union Corporation. Each of these organizations maintains files on approximately 150 million persons. Data is supplied by banks, department stores, and other lenders about loans, bill payments, and credit cards. Data is also routinely culled from public records, particularly money judgments, liens, foreclosures, alimony and child support obligations, lists of delinquent taxpayers, and related credit matters. Hundreds of local credit bureaus are linked electronically with each of these three national organizations, supplying information to them and providing credit reports to customers of the local bureau. Indicative of the magnitude of the information collecting activities of these credit reporting organizations is the fact that each of them makes about two billion updates on individuals' activities each month.

What is recorded in the national system is credit paying history. No record is maintained of salaries, assets owned, criminal convictions, or other nonfinancial information a potential creditor might desire or find useful. If the creditor desires that kind of information, it must obtain it directly from the credit applicant, or, possibly, from a local credit bureau.

Information — particularly negative information — is generally retained in credit reports for seven years. A bankruptcy filing is retained for ten years. Thus, an individual who defaults on a real estate mortgage and permits the property to be foreclosed will have destroyed, or at least seriously damaged, his or her credit standing for seven years. See Chapter 6.

The three major credit reporting firms supply about 1.5 million reports per day, most of which are communicated electronically directly to computer terminals of credit-granting organizations and others: banks, local credit bureaus, stores, insurance companies, employers, automobile dealers, and landlords. These reports enable United States consumers to purchase about 5,000 homes, 40,000 cars, and 300,000 appliances each day.

Unfortunately, access to credit reports is relatively easy to obtain by persons without a direct right of access to the information, since there are no controls over what happens to the information after it has been received by an organization that is legitimately entitled to it. For example, a "headhunter," seeking to lure employees away from their employers, may obtain credit reports of people who are being considered for employment by a competitor. Indeed, the comment has been made that access to this information is relatively easy for everyone to obtain except for the individual who is the subject of the credit report.

In the past, the three major credit reporting firms sold names, addresses, and some limited financial data to "direct mailers," the providers of "junk mail" that seems to fill most mailboxes. This practice has been widely criticized and has been discontinued by at least one of the three major firms. Similarly, banks that voluntarily offer to send out credit cards to "pre-approved applicants" without delay are relying on national credit reports; pre-approval in that context means persons with good credit histories.

§4.3 HOW TO GET INTO THE CREDIT REPORTING SYSTEM

A young person, just starting out, usually applies for one or more credit cards as much for their convenience as for the extension of credit that they normally entail. However, in a typical catch-22 situation, the first application for a credit card may be denied because the applicant has no credit history and thus is ineligible for credit.

Because of the practices of the credit reporting industry, it does not help to show that the applicant has a good job, a bank account, and that he or she has carefully lived within his or her income for several months or years. Conservative, sound financial practice may dictate that one should pay cash for everything, but that does not create a credit history that enables one to borrow money when the need arises. Rather paradoxically, what is needed is the grant of credit and the repayment of loans before one can get a loan.

In order to obtain the initial grant of credit so that one can enter the reporting system, it may be necessary for a friend or family member with a good reporting history to guarantee or act as surety for the new applicant.

A gasoline credit card is usually somewhat easier to obtain than a bank credit card; many young people begin with such a card.

Students who have received student loans and are making payments on them will usually have entered the credit reporting system through payments on that loan. They should be able to obtain additional credit.

If none of these avenues are open, a person may establish a credit record through the use of a "secured" credit card. See section 7.12.

§4.4 ERRORS IN CREDIT REPORTS

There are numerous horror stories about mistakes in modern credit reports. A study in 1989 showed that nine million consumers checked their credit files, and that about three million of them found information they believed to be erroneous. Of course, this does not necessarily mean that one of every three credit reports contains erroneous information, since there is an element of self selection within the nine million who checked their files; presumably many of them had some reason to believe that erroneous negative information was included in them.

Anecdotal horror stories are numerous. The following is taken from a Wall Street Journal article on the credit reporting firms in September, 1991:

> Joseph Pazos of West New York, N.J., a typical example, says he checked his credit report in 1987 after he was turned down for a credit card. He found the report was littered with negative information about his father, Jose Pazos, who lives at the same address. The younger Mr. Pazos obtained letters from more than a dozen of his father's old creditors, stating that their dealings were with Jose, not Joseph. He even changed his mailing address to a post-office box in another town.
>
> But four years later, he says his father's data is still cluttering his reports. Meanwhile, he has been turned down for two more credit cards and a student loan. The loan fell through just before he was going to start bachelors-degree night courses, and he had to postpone them for a year.

The confusion of persons with similar or identical names is apparently a recurring problem within the credit reporting industry. Part of the problem obviously is that individuals often use variants of their name on credit applications; married women may continue to use their maiden name for some, but not all purposes, and so forth. However, unique social security numbers are routinely required on credit applications so that the credit reporting organizations at least have the capability of avoiding much of this confusion.

More serious was the mistake made in collecting information about the citizens of Norwich, Vermont. A part-time employee of TRW was sent to the Norwich town office to look up the names of delinquent taxpayers. However, she was given a list of tax receipts rather than tax delinquencies, and she carefully copied down, and duly reported as delinquent, the 1,400 residents of Norwich who had paid their taxes. When the town clerk of Norwich learned that many residents were suddenly having credit problems she called TRW. She left six messages over the course of a week asking for a review of what had happened. A week later, the mistake was discovered and eventually corrected. Ultimately, TRW agreed to pay $250 to each Vermont resident who could prove that credit applications were denied or delayed in 1991 by more than 48 hours as a result of errors in a TRW report and up to $1,000 to any person who can prove that he or she actually suffered damages due to those errors.

Credit reports often do not reflect payments that have actually been made on credit cards or other loans; such a mistake can be readily corrected by following the standard dispute resolution mechanism described in the following section.

Given the magnitude of the national credit reporting system, it is easy to overstate the significance of anecdotal stories like the above. The credit reporting companies insist that the great bulk of the information in their files is accurate. The author of this book checked his credit report in connection with writing this chapter and discovered no errors.

§4.5 HOW TO LOCATE AND CORRECT ERRORS IN A CREDIT REPORT

The first indication that a person's credit report may contain an error that has a negative impact on one's credit rating is usually the denial of a credit application. However, it is not necessary to wait for this to happen; one can obtain a copy of one's credit report simply by requesting one in writing and perhaps paying a small fee. Consumer organizations recommend that a person obtain a copy of his or her credit report at least once a year. It is sensible to order a credit report from each of the three major credit reporting companies, since transactions may be reported differently by each company.

If one is planning to enter into a major transaction several months in the future — for example, applying for a mortgage to purchase a new house — it may be sensible to obtain a copy of credit reports several months in advance of the application to make sure there are no unexpected problems, and if there are, they can be resolved in advance of the transaction. Again, reports from all three companies should be obtained since one does not know from which company a report will be obtained by potential lenders.

If one has discovered an error in a credit report and filed a dispute resolution form, it is prudent to order a new credit report after being notified that a correction has been made, to ensure that the correction has in fact been made in a satisfactory way.

A credit report is not an easy thing to understand. If an error is found on a credit report, the dispute resolution form accompanying the credit report should be filled out and returned, along with copies of supporting documents. If the error is discovered because credit was denied, a copy of the form and accompanying documents should also be sent to the bank or organization that actually denied the credit application.

The credit reporting company reverifies disputed or inaccurate information; if it is not reverified, it is deleted from the credit report. If the information is deleted, the other major credit reporting companies should be notified by the consumer since it is likely that the same erroneous information was reported to them. If the credit reporting company refuses to remove the negative information, the information, of course, remains in the file. However, the consumer may request the credit reporting company to note that the item is disputed and include a brief statement explaining the transaction, which the company will include in future credit reports.

If one does not receive satisfaction from the credit reporting company, complaint may be made to the consumer protection division of the state's attorney general office or to the Federal Trade Commission (which administers the Fair Credit Reporting Act). As a last resort, one might resort to litigation against the credit reporting company; in many states punitive damages and attorneys' fees may be recovered in addition to actual damages if the credit reporting company fails to remove erroneous information without justification.

§4.6 HOW TO REACH CREDIT REPORTING COMPANIES

The names and addresses of the three major credit reporting companies (as of 1992) are as follows:

> Equifax Information Service Center. Attention: Consumer Dept., P.O. Box 740241, Atlanta, Georgia 30375-0241. Telephone: 1-800-685-1111
> Trans Union National Consumer Disclosure Center, 25249 Country Club Boulevard, P.O. Box 7000, North Olmstead, Ohio 44070
> TRW Consumer Assistance, P.O. Box 2350, Chatsworth, California 91313-2350. 1-214-235-1200

§4.7 LOAN AND CREDIT CARD APPLICATIONS

When one applies for a loan or a credit card, one has to fill out a loan application form that is submitted to the lender or the credit card issuer. The information requested may serve several different purposes.

One important purpose is to assure that the applicant is properly identified to the credit reporting company by the lender or credit card issuer. This may be accomplished by asking for the applicant's social security number and residential address. Prior residential addresses may also be requested for the same reason.

Applications for credit also often request some additional information that may not appear in a credit report but which may be relevant to the decision to grant credit. For example, the application may ask whether the applicant owns or rents his home; presumably a homeowner is more financially secure (and therefore a better credit risk) than a renter. Information may be requested about the person's employer and the number of years the applicant has been employed by that employer. Presumably a long-term employee is a better credit risk than one who has been employed for a shorter period.

Questions may also be asked about income, asset holdings, and monthly payments. In this regard loan application forms vary widely, depending in part on the size of the contemplated loan transaction. Many forms only ask one or two general questions (for example, "Please identify the range in which your annual income falls."). Some forms may also inquire about a spouse's employment history and income. Some forms may require additional detail about one's finances, including estimates of monthly expenses, outstanding balances on other loans, and other credit cards. The numbers of three outstanding credit cards may be requested. Some questions may appear on loan application forms simply because they appeared on forms developed before the emergence of the national credit reporting firms and have never been deleted. Some loan applications may inquire about other denials of credit or mortgage foreclosures or the like. Much of this information also appears on the applicant's credit report. Presumably, if the credit report shows that a question was answered falsely on the application form, the loan may be denied on that ground alone.

§4.8 HOW TO ESTIMATE A PERSON'S LOAN-REPAYING ABILITY

There are two plausible ways to ascertain the ability to repay a loan. The first method examines the applicant's assets and liabilities. If the assets exceed the liabilities, a creditor may be able to seize the excess assets if there is a default. This is sometimes called the "net worth" or "balance sheet approach," since a balance sheet shows one's assets and liabilities at an instant in time, and the difference is one's net worth at that instant. The granting of credit on the basis of a net worth statement is sometimes called the "pounce" approach since the creditor is proceeding on the theory that if required payments are not made, the creditor will pounce on assets to repay its loan.

The second method uses a cash flow analysis concentrating not on one's net worth at an instant in time but on one's anticipated inflows and outflows of cash over the period of the loan. Inflows presumably arise from receipt of salaries and other income; outflows from repayment obligations, living expenses, transportation costs, insurance premiums, and the like. This analysis is known as a "cash flow" or "equity solvency" approach and is generally viewed as a more realistic measure of a debtor's ability to repay a specified loan. The ability to repay a loan is obviously enhanced if one has a substantial positive anticipated cash flow — that is, if anticipated cash inflows exceed anticipated cash outflows.

Questions asked on loan application forms may be directed at either or both of these two analyses. Indeed, in many applications, some questions appear to be directed at a balance sheet test while others are directed at a cash flow analysis.

The two approaches toward repayment ability discussed in this section appear and reappear throughout business law and practice. They are discussed further, for example, in Chapter 6 in connection with a discussion of the federal bankruptcy law.

5

Techniques for Saving on a Fixed Income

§5.1 INTRODUCTION

Many individuals just starting out find it extremely difficult to save. Needs are usually so great and immediate that a systematic savings plan seems impossible, and if some money is left over, an impetuous decision to "reward myself for being so good" exhausts what little has been set aside. Indeed, saving always seems to be something that can be started tomorrow.

Saving is an essential attribute of effective financial management, but certainly one of the most difficult to achieve for persons living on fixed, limited incomes. This short chapter is largely hortatory in nature, giving general suggestions as to how a savings program might be initiated. It also discusses general questions, such as the problems that may arise when one unexpectedly receives a windfall or faces financial decisions during some kind of personal crisis.

§5.2 GENERATIONAL ATTITUDES TOWARD SAVING

A young adult in the early 1990s is likely to have a different attitude toward saving than her parents. The attitudes of the current young adult are much closer to those of her grandparents who remember the great depression and became adults during the 1940s and 1950s. Today's young adults are not sure they will have a job in the future; they are not sure that they will be able to educate their children, buy a house, or provide for their elderly parents or their own old age. Borrowing money is a risky thing to do in light of such uncertainty, and saving and saving programs are currently very much in vogue. These attitudes are remarkably similar to those of the older generation who experienced the pessimism of the 1930s.

The different attitude of persons who grew up during the 1960s and 1970s may be traced to the fact that these were decades of optimism, of rising incomes (and of rising prices and inflation), of rising residential real estate values. Persons reaching adulthood during these decades tended to view saving as old fashioned: Why concentrate on saving dollars today when they would doubtless be worth less tomorrow? Why be concerned about putting a few dollars away each month "for a rainy day" when the value of one's house was appreciating at a rate of 10 percent per year, and one just received a "cost of living" raise of 7 percent last year? Spending and enjoying was the way to go, not hoarding funds for something that was unlikely ever to occur.

Three events during the 1980s largely signaled the current attitude about saving and the future. These events were: first, the stock market collapse in October, 1987; second, the collapse in residential real estate values in many areas of the country in the middle and late 1980s; and third, the lingering recession of the late 1980s and early 1990s when the job market for white collar professionals dried up and significant numbers of middle managers in the 40 to 60 year age bracket were laid off. Even the legal profession, which had proved to be recession-proof since World War II and in which law firms had grown by a factor of tenfold in a couple of decades, suffered these maladies for the first time. Suddenly, the secure life of legal practice was no longer secure; the number of summer clerkships declined precipitously; and some firms actually began downsizing by firing associates and expelling partners. These events were surprising and dismaying because they demonstrated the ephemeral nature of the assumptions underlying the go-go years that ended sometime in the 1980s. For the first time since the 1930s, the feeling was widespread that economic conditions were continuing to get worse rather than better and that the generation coming into adulthood was not going to be as well off as their parents.

§5.3 THE GOALS OF A SAVING PLAN

Many persons consciously adopt a strategy to save money with specific goals in mind. One may decide to save toward a down payment on a house to have more space for a growing family. One may decide to save in order to pay down educational loans or credit card debts incurred during more optimistic (or less self-controlled) periods. One may decide to save in order to provide education for children, to augment one's retirement income, to provide care for elderly parents, to purchase a new car, or simply to have a reserve fund for contingencies.

For most persons starting a savings program, it is usually easiest to save if one has a specific goal. If a person has a specific goal, he or she is less apt to "make an exception just this time" and ignore the savings program. On the other hand, once habits of saving become sufficiently ingrained, a person can usually continue to save money even though a specific goal has been attained and no other additional goal has been set. There has been lot of discussion about "baby boomers," those persons between the ages of approximately 27 to 46 (in 1992) who are struggling with economic stagnation at an age when their parents were enjoying a steady improvement in their standard of living. Persons in this age group often married later in life than the earlier generation, and therefore started a family and assumed financial burdens also later in life. The three major financial goals of the baby boom generation are: 1) to care for elderly parents; 2) to save to educate children; and 3) to plan for their own retirement. All this must be done in a shorter time period than the previous generation.

Section 5.6 discusses saving for children's college educations. A later section of this book discusses saving for retirement (section 10.18). This topic is discussed in a later chapter largely because it may involve the use of annuities and insurance products that are the subject of subsequent chapters.

§5.4 THE SECRETS OF SYSTEMATIC SAVING

Unquestionably, the first requirement of any saving program is to get control of one's cash flow. Significant portions of one's take-home income can easily be dribbled away on small expenses that could readily be avoided. For most people, this means establishing a household budget for recurring items. But a budget is not essential; one can do much the same thing by meticulously recording every expenditure for a week or month and then reviewing where the money went and deciding what expenditures could be avoided in the future. Reading one's checkbook can also be illuminating: Do you really need an expensive health club membership? Is a $200 birthday present a little larger than necessary, when after all it is the thought that counts? Did I really need that extra blouse and two pairs of shoes that I bought last month?

A second secret of any savings plan is to resist the temptation to make impulse purchases. Leave the plastic credit cards at home and pay cash.

That stings a bit more when one has the impulse to buy something in a store window. Avoid the use of automatic teller machines to supplement one's "walking around" money except for true emergencies. Impulsive withdrawals of small amounts "to tide matters over" are also budget busters.

Of course, the convenience of credit cards probably dictate their continued, limited use. Cards should be used only for purchases that have been carefully planned. They are also useful on a trip as recordkeeping devices of expenses for which your employer will reimburse you. However, they can be devastating to a budget when a person on vacation decides to buy personal items or gifts. If one continues to use credit cards, they should carry minimal costs. See section 7.10.

Third, savers should think small. The way to save is to control small expenditures as well as large. A small, steady stream of savings mounts up. Assume one's goal is a $10,000 nest egg for the purchase of a home. Given the budget exigencies of a particular family, it is clear that saving more than $100 per month will be difficult. One should not be put off by the fact that $100 seems like a trivial amount when compared to the lofty goal of $10,000. Of course, each month's saving will earn interest thereafter, so that the nest egg will grow at a compound rate. See section 1.4. If we assume that the local bank is paying only 4 percent a year (compounded monthly) on small savings accounts, it will take a little over seven years to accumulate $10,000. If one can increase the payment to $125 per month, it will take less than six years to reach the desired goal. And, it is likely that interest rates will go up at some point over the next few years, so the goal will be reached even more quickly. If one assumes an interest rate of 6 percent, rather than 4 percent, and payments of $125 per month, it will take about five and one-half years to accumulate $10,000. These examples illustrate that even large amounts can be saved if one has patience. (These examples do not take into account the income tax that is due on the interest paid on the account.)

Finally, take the savings off the top before the regular monthly budget kicks in. A variety of devices exist to make saving easier, even painless.

The best arrangement is for the amount of the saving to be deducted by the employer before the take-home pay is calculated. What one never gets cannot be spent. Furthermore, one's life-style tends to accommodate itself to one's take-home pay. Many employers have plans by which they will deposit a portion of each paycheck directly into a savings account in a bank or credit union, or into a money market fund. Other off-the-top saving devices exist. An employee may elect to purchase a specified amount of Series EE United States Savings Bonds each month. See section 16.9. One might also ask the employer to over-withhold federal income taxes so that one has a refund coming at the end of the year. (This, however, loses the interest accumulation on monthly payments during the year, since no interest is paid by the Internal Revenue Service on over-withholding.)

A variety of tax deferred savings arrangements exist. See Chapter 10. Some involve deferral of tax on both the amount contributed and the income earned from the account. Many employees may obtain tax benefits from contributions to an Individual Retirement Account. These arrangements are desirable from a long-term standpoint — for example, saving for college education of small children or for retirement — but are usually not desirable for shorter term saving plans, since penalties and income tax liabilities may be imposed if these funds are withdrawn before age fifty-nine and one-half. These penalties and tax liabilities wipe out much of the savings otherwise provided by these plans.

All of these arrangements work on the principle that if you don't have it, you won't spend it. Where this is not the case, one should arrange to have the deposit in a savings account or mutual fund be the first check written or withdrawal made each month rather than the last.

Many banks have plans by which they will withdraw a specified amount from your checking account at the beginning of each month and deposit it into a savings vehicle. American Express offers a plan through which a cardholder may choose an amount — between $50 and $5,000 each month that American Express adds to each monthly bill; the cardholder is not obligated to pay this amount, but if he or she does the payment goes into an interestbearing savings account. These plans are not as good as having an employer do it directly, but they serve much the same purpose.

A number of other psychological savings devices exist. For example, assume that you are paying off a car loan at the rate of $200 per month. You finally pay it off. Why not keep making the same $200 payments but this time to your savings account rather than to a lender? Another device is to factor a reward into a savings program. Many consumers identify specific things that they are saving for, but then set up a savings program that yields a little something extra. For example, one may budget to save, say, $1,000 per year; why not set aside $100 per month beginning in January for this goal and then enjoy the "free" $200 at the end of the year?

In the last analysis, however, if one is spending one's entire take-home income and not saving anything, or worse, one is gradually sinking further into debt, changes in expenditure patterns and life-style are essential before meaningful saving can begin.

§5.5 HOW TO INCREASE THE RATE OF SAVING

Assume that you have $10,000 saved, and you wish to see that amount grow as quickly as possible without taking undue risks. If one invests this amount in a virtually riskless money market mutual fund (see section 16.8), the yield may be, say, 3.7 percent. If no funds are withdrawn, this amount will grow to about $10,376 after one year, $10,767 after two years, and $11,172 after three years. If you can add $100 per month to this money market fund, it will grow to about $11,597 after one year, $13,254 after two years, and $14,973 after three years. That is a significant improvement if one can afford the $100 per month.

Another method of improving yield is to shift the funds to a somewhat more risky class of investment. Stock or bond mutual funds (see section 15.4) might yield 7 percent at the same time the money market fund is yielding 3.7 percent. If one shifts the $10,000 to such a fund with a 4 percent "load" (discussed in section 15.5), the $10,000 will grow to $10,294 after one year, $11,038 after two years, and $11,836 after three years. If one adds $100 per month to the mutual fund, the yield will be $11,533 after one year, $13,606 after two years, and $15,829 after three years. The addition of $100 per month to this fund leads to dollar cost averaging of securities prices; you buy more shares in a month when prices are lower and fewer shares in a month when prices are higher. Of course, the yield of 7 percent is not guaranteed, and indeed is a lot less secure than the 3.7 percent yield on the money market fund. But as discussed in Chapter 13, a higher yield carries with it higher risk.

§5.6 SAVING FOR COLLEGE COSTS

Parents of small children look forward with concern and dread to the costs of their children's college education. Growth of tuition costs have far exceeded the rate of inflation since the 1970s, particularly for private colleges and universities. During the late 1980s and early 1990s, the costs of attending public universities and junior colleges increased substantially as states faced large budget shortfalls. In 1992, the annual cost of attending a state school was nearly $6,000 per year and the annual cost of a private school was about $20,000 per year. While the gap between the cost of a private and a public education has narrowed, certainly education at public institutions remains much less expensive than at the more prestigious private institutions of higher education.

Many middle class parents today desire to send children to private schools, beginning with nursery school and extending all the way through high school. When tuition bills start in pre-school at an annual cost of $3,000 to $4,000 per year, and rise to as much $5,000 to $12,000 per year in high school, there is not much room to save for college. Indeed, even two-income upper middle class families find such tuition costs difficult to meet. Many institutions permit tuition to be paid in 12 equal installments rather than in a single lump sum. It is recommended that pre-college tuition be met from income sources because costs usually escalate upwards when the child begins college. If possible, one should not borrow against retirement funds or cash surrender values of life insurance policies to meet pre-college expenses.

Of course, scholarship assistance may be available, and the child may be able to borrow against future income while in college, as well as earning something during summers. However, most higher two-income families find that they are not eligible for scholarship assistance, at least if their family is small. There are, however, very attractive loan programs offered by the federal government that permit many children of less affluent families to attend college. These loan programs are described briefly in section 7.18.

The obvious way to provide for a college education many years in the future is to begin saving at the birth of the child. The simplest plan is to set aside money each month in a traditional savings program. Because of the historic inflation in the cost of higher education (a phenomenon that may not continue in the future), it is usually recommended that funds be invested in diversified equity securities, usually mutual funds, to take advantage of the historic growth in value of such investments. A similar strategy involves the purchase of a "laddered portfolio" of bonds that mature in approximately annual intervals during the period a child is likely to be in college. See section 16.13. The laddered portfolio mixes together shorter and longer term bonds and may result in a higher yield than a straight investment in an equity mutual fund.

Brokerage firms and banks offer a variety of savings plans that are specifically tailored to cover future educational costs. Governmental entities have also offered plans that may be attractive to some parents. While these plans may offer advantages, they also have limitations.

One type of tailored investment involves certificates of deposit pegged to indices of college costs. These were widely advertised and offered during the 1980s when yields on certificates of deposit were in the 8 or 9 percent range. Some private financial institutions advertised "college sure" or "tuition guaranteed" certificates of deposit. One advertisement stated that a new parent may invest $1,000 or more in a college sure CD and the growth in income will assure that the CD will keep pace with college costs no matter how fast they climb.

Closer examination revealed that while the growth in income was pegged to a college cost index, the promised growth was not guaranteed. For one thing, a CD of this type had no special tax protection, and the income each year was taxable to the parents. For another, the variable interest rate of the CD was pegged to an index that measured the average increases of tuition, fees, and living expenses at 500 colleges. A child who elected to attend a more expensive than average institution might find that he or she had a lot of uncovered costs. There was also no assurance that the investments of the bank offering this CD would cover the promised interest rate. The bank did maintain a large asset buffer to protect against college costs outstripping bank investment income. In addition, the CDs were insured by the Federal Deposit Insurance Corporation so that presumably the Federal Government would become responsible if the bank defaulted. Nevertheless, the bank would be in serious trouble if, say, college costs increased at a rate of 25 percent per year while investment income stalled out at 5 percent per year.

Further, even though the income from the CD was pegged to increases in college costs, the coverage was not 100 percent. Interest was paid once a year when the index was calculated, but the actual amount of interest paid depended to some extent on the amount invested. Investors with more than $10,000 invested earn 1 percent less than the index; those with less than $10,000 invested earn 1.5 percent less than the index. Thus, in order to cover this gap, parents were urged to invest more up front to make up the difference when the child entered college. Illustrations were provided: Someone wishing to have $8,000 available for tuition in ten years should invest $9,200 if one assumed a 10 percent average college inflation rate (and therefore an 8.5 percent return on the investment). Withdrawal penalties were also imposed unless the withdrawal occurred in the last year of the CD; in addition, interest may be withdrawn in any year without penalty during a narrow "window" following the calculation of the interest rate.

The terms set forth in the preceding paragraph permit a straight comparison of this CD and an investment in treasury bonds. For example, over the period 1988 through 1991 the CollegeSure CD paid significantly less than a 10 year Treasury note:

	1988	1989	1990	1991
Treasury note	8.85	8.49	8.55	7.86
CollegeSure	6.33	7.11	6.39	5.89

Of course, as interest rates fell in 1992, this tailored CD became much less attractive; however, during the same period, the index of college costs also stabilized. In any event, a tailored CD does not appear to be the way to go even if they are still offered in the current period of low interest rates.

An alternative approach to financing college costs is to invest in zero coupon bonds, or zeroes, as they are usually called. These investments are discussed in section 16.16. Because zeroes lock in a fixed interest rate, they appear at first blush to be an ideal vehicle for saving for college tuition. Their major disadvantage is that the imputed income is taxed to the holder; this disadvantage may be partially avoided by placing the zeroes in a custodial account for the minor child. The tax may also be avoided by investing in tax-exempt zeroes issued by states or municipalities, though the yield is lower.

Yet another alternative approach involves residents of Michigan and Florida. These two states have created tuition prepayment plans to protect families from the cost of financing college educations. Essentially the state sells investment contracts to new parents for a lump sum and invests the proceeds, promising to cover tuition when the child enters college. In Michigan, a lump sum payment of $6,756 by the parents of a newborn would cover four years of tuition beginning 18 years later at a Michigan public university. Such a deal appeared too good to be true, and apparently it was. In 1991, Michigan suspended its program (after writing some 55,000 contracts) when it became apparent that the income of the fund was not coming close to funding its future obligations. At the present time, the average four-year tuition cost at Michigan public universities is over $9,000 and over $11,000 at the premier schools, the University of Michigan and Michigan State University. The future status of contract holders remains to be seen.

The Florida program was created on a more realistic financial basis, in part because tuition at state schools is lower in that state. The contract for a newborn cost $3,796, but that was more than the cost of four years of education at a public Florida university.

If a systematic plan of saving is adopted, it may be sensible to make annual gifts to the child to take maximum advantage of the splitting of income for tax purposes. A common strategy is to give $10,000 per year per child to avoid gift taxation. In order to avoid the kiddie income tax (see section 19.17), the income must be under $600 per year. The next $600 of investment or unearned income is taxed at the child's 15 percent rate. If the child is under 14, all investment income above $1,200 is taxed at the parent's top rate of 28 or 31 percent. One way to avoid this higher rate is to invest the child's income in tax-exempt bonds. See section 16.18. Another possibility is the purchase of growth stocks that pay a small dividend. The growth in value escapes tax until the child is an adult, when the stock is sold. One possible disadvantage of this approach is that the child becomes entitled absolutely to the money when he or she reaches the age of 18. The child may decide to spend the money on something else rather than education.

Many financial advisers play on parental despair to sell life insurance or annuities as a type of so-called "college investments." The chief selling point is usually the tax deferral feature of these investments. See sections 10.6 and 11.21. But most of these investments carry high costs and may limit the investor to a low rate of return. For example, life insurance may be recommended for this purpose, since savings are tax deferred. Meanwhile the child is protected should the parents get hit by a truck. But there are fees and commissions that greatly reduce the attractiveness of insurance as a savings vehicle — in effect, much of the money is paying for the college education of the agent's children, not the insured's. Illustrations may compare a tax deferred life insurance policy with a taxable investment, assuming a market rate of return but without taking into account commissions or fees. The comparison also may not take into account income taxes that may be payable when insurance money is withdrawn.

In some cases, United States Government series EE bonds may be attractive, in part because of the forgiveness of income tax for lower income families when proceeds are used for educational purposes. See section 16.9. Under the 1992 tax laws, this tax break is phased out, beginning when a couple's income reaches $62,900 and disappearing completely at $94,350.

§5.7 NONRECURRING WINDFALLS

What happens when one inherits money, a lot of money? Or what happens when one draws a winning lottery ticket? People usually view windfalls as fortunate, a pathway to financial happiness. Rather surprisingly, such events may have very negative personal repercussions: They may create a large amount of strife, unpleasantness, and unhappy recollections of matters long past.

One basic point is that a windfall, by definition, is not likely to recur again. To spend it helter-skelter, without any particular plan in mind, leads to eventual exhaustion with little to show for it and often a sense a regret of a once in a lifetime opportunity that was not used to advantage.

A windfall may put a distance between the recipient and his or her friends. There may be a feeling that friends are now friends more because of the money than because they get along together and enjoy each other's company. New friends are apt to be viewed particularly skeptically. Relations with members of the opposite sex may be colored by the fear that the partner is a "gold digger." Indeed, money may become an obsession, and there may be a concern that it must be handled responsibly by the recipient, that no one else may be trusted. A spouse may suddenly be viewed with mistrust if he or she proposes spending even modest amounts of the windfall on things the family clearly needs. A very common syndrome of the newly wealthy is to simultaneously want to spend everything and not to spend anything. To escape this syndrome, it may help to make a single purchase and then consider what to do next. And, of course, there is always the fear of the smooth talking stranger who is working on the assumption that "there is a fool born every minute," and you are today's victim.

Much can be done to prepare persons to handle money responsibly, when an inheritance is clearly in the cards. For example, it may help to warn such persons not to be too trusting and to be cautious about persons who offer to manage the money for you.

Some rules of thumb for the recipient of an unexpected windfall:

1) Move slowly: If a deal looks too good to pass up, there is probably something wrong with it and it should be avoided.
2) Put off major life decisions, like opening your own business, for at least a year. Invest funds gradually, and keep control over your own accounts; in particular, avoid "wrap accounts" that entail money management for a large fee.
3) Finally, diversify by spreading money among several different investments, and do not put all the new-found eggs into a single basket.

§5.8 FINANCIAL DECISIONS IN PERIODS OF STRESS

As a corollary to the previous section, it is usually a mistake to make major financial decisions when an important personal event has either just occurred or is about to occur. For example, it is generally desirable to defer important financial decisions when any of the following has recently occurred:

1) You have bought a house.
2) You have just had a child.
3) You have just changed or lost a job.
4) There has been a death in the immediate family.
5) You have just inherited money.

Many brokers, agents, and scam artists scan the papers for persons in these positions and seek to sell them insurance, recommend that they make invest funds in some scheme, or assist them in handling their funds. Generally, it is a good idea to put important financial decisions off until one can reflect on them.

6

Debt Collection and Bankruptcy

§6.1 INTRODUCTION

This chapter discusses the individual who is a troubled debtor — unable to manage his or her financial affairs. It includes a discussion of modern collection practices, the various legal remedies available to the debtor, and the ultimate debtor's remedy of bankruptcy.

Of course, individuals may have serious financial problems for a large variety of reasons. The nonprofit Consumer Credit Counseling Service (CCCS) lists over 60 causes of financial problems, including loss of job, illness that prevents the individual from working, alcoholism or drug abuse, gambling losses, misuse of credit cards, poor shopping habits, the purchase of an automobile that is beyond the means of the individual to maintain, student loan problems, separation, divorce, widowhood, child support obligations, job changes, inability to sell a house when expected, and on and on. No matter what the cause, the result is that the individual finds himself or herself so far in debt that there seems to be no possible way out. Furthermore, the individual may be faced with eviction from his or her apartment or foreclosure of the mortgage on the residence. The specter of bankruptcy, and even homelessness, looms in the background.

Most individuals facing serious credit problems have incomes somewhat below the national median family income (about $35,000 per year in 1991). The composite client of CCCS in Maine in 1991 was 35 years old with an average gross annual income of $24,120 and an average unsecured debt of $17,335 owed to 12 creditors. These numbers are typical of the entire country except for the average amount owed on a national basis, which was higher—about $19,688. About 33 percent of the unsecured debt was owed to banks (much of it presumably credit card debt), 18 percent to retailers, 14 percent to issuers of major credit cards, 11 percent to finance companies, 5 percent to credit unions, 4 percent to collection agencies, and 4 percent to doctors, hospitals, and other medical providers. The average client was married (55 percent), supported two dependents, had a monthly income of $2,010, and spent $497 on housing, and $1,420 on living expenses. Fifty-three percent were female.

The average figures described in the previous paragraph should not hide the fact that many persons with much higher incomes also are troubled debtors. Many persons simply adopt lifestyles that exceed their earning capacity. Others have never learned the most rudimentary principles of living within one's income, or have adopted risky wealth-increasing strategies that have failed.

Perhaps the two most basic lessons of this chapter are: (1) it is not a crime to be unable to pay one's debts; and (2) a lot of people successfully avoid paying their debts even though they have the assets to do so if they wish. The federal bankruptcy law provides a fresh start for most individual debtors and enables one to preserve a portion of one's assets and continue living without hounding and threats by unpaid creditors. On the other hand, consumer bankruptcy is a last resort, and several devices short of bankruptcy exist to rescue the individual who has gotten in over his or her head.

This chapter concentrates on the rights of unsecured creditors and the rights and duties of the debtor: It does not generally deal with the rights of secured creditors with respect to the collateral securing their debts or the rights of creditors to proceed against sureties and others who may have guaranteed the payment of debts to certain creditors. It also does not discuss issues that tangentially involve the troubled debtor, such as bounced checks discussed in section 3.4.

Detailed analyses of the topics touched on in this chapter appear primarily in third-year law school courses and seminars devoted to bankruptcy, debt collection, and creditors' and debtors' rights. This chapter does not go into much detail on these topics; rather it simply introduces the reader to the modern treatment of the insolvent or financially troubled debtor.

§6.2 "I JUST LOST A LAWSUIT. WHAT HAPPENS NEXT?"

Much of law school is devoted to teaching how one goes about getting a judgment and how one gets it affirmed on appeal. Not very much is taught about how one translates a final judgment into money in the bank. Indeed, most students are probably unaware that most judgments against consumers are judgments entered by default. The debt is admittedly due and unpaid; the debtor cannot or will not voluntarily pay the amount due.

First of all, the fact that a plaintiff has been awarded a dollar judgment against a defendant does not mean that money flies automatically out of the defendant's bank account and into the plaintiff's account. Indeed, after a final judgment has been entered (and all appeals exhausted), not very much at all happens. The plaintiff simply has a court determination that the plaintiff should recover a specified amount from the defendant. There is no promise by the judgment defendant to cooperate by voluntarily making the required payment. A judgment defendant that does not want to pay the amount of the judgment can simply sit tight. The next move is up to the plaintiff.

Each state provides procedures for collecting upon a judgment. While the procedures available vary from state to state, the basic remedy is to obtain a writ of execution and have the sheriff seize nonexempt property and sell it at public sale. The proceeds of the sale are paid to the judgment creditor to satisfy its claim, and any excess is paid to the judgment debtor. Every state provides that certain types of property are exempt from execution, which means that they cannot be levied upon to satisfy a judgment. The property that is exempt varies widely from state to state. It may be enumerated by item (for example, one automobile or horse or certain household furniture) or may be enumerated as an amount (for example, $5,000 of personal property). Most states have a variety of exemptions, some by category and some by dollar amounts within other categories. In some states, a person's residence (or homestead) may be exempt from execution either in whole or up to a specified value. A uniform federal exemption effective only in federal bankruptcy proceedings is applicable in about a dozen states.

In addition, a judgment creditor may garnish amounts owed to the judgment debtor. A writ of garnishment is served on a person who owes the judgment debtor money and commands that person to pay the amount due to the judgment creditor rather than the judgment debtor. Wages and bank accounts are the most commonly garnished property. States usually limit the kinds of accounts that may be garnished; many, for example, limit or prohibit the garnishment of wages due to the judgment debtor. Federal law also prohibits wage garnishments in excess of 25 percent of disposable earnings of any employee in any work week.

Many states provide, as an alternative method of enforcement, that the entry of a judgment, or the abstracting and recording of judgments in the county records, impresses a lien on real (and in some cases personal) property located within the state or within that specific county. The principal advantage of the lien is that the judgment debtor is thereafter unable to dispose of the property without "clearing up" (that is, paying off) the judgment lien. The creditor does not have to persuade the sheriff to go out and seize property but can simply sit back and wait patiently for the lien to produce the needed payment.

The execution process is relatively costly. Property must be located, care must be taken that the sheriff seizes and sells the right property, and the sheriff may require a bond or indemnification in the event the property he is directed to seize turns out not to be owned by the judgment debtor or to be exempt from execution. Even though the judgment creditor may take the deposition of the judgment debtor and seek information about the ownership and location of property, the judgment debtor is under no obligation to cooperate. Under these circumstances, it is not uncommon for a judgment debtor to offer to make a partial payment in full settlement of the judgment, and for the judgment creditor to accept this offer rather than seeking to obtain the full amount of the judgment by legal process.

§6.3 DEBT COLLECTION AGENCIES

Given the cost of obtaining a judgment and the problematic nature of finding any valuable assets that may be levied upon after a judgment is obtained, most unsecured creditors may threaten to, but do not actually, bring suit. Creditors may simply write off as uncollectible substantial amounts of claims, and they view this as a part of the cost of doing business.

When debts are not paid when due, the creditor usually writes dunning letters that are increasingly threatening in tone. If these letters do not produce the desired result, the creditor may adopt a quite different tone, suggesting that the debtor may be having financial difficulties and some arrangement for paying the debt should be discussed. If this approach also does not produce results, the failure to make timely payment may be reported to the credit reporting companies and the debt assigned to a collection agency.

The practices of collection agencies vary widely. Historically, collection agencies used "tough guy" or "strong-arm" approaches to persuade the debtor to pay. An agency might employ "operatives" — typically beefy former security guards or policemen — to serve notices in person. Repeated telephone calls might be made to the debtor at work or late in the evening involving thinly veiled threats to enlist the aid of a person's employer to garnish wages or to seize assets. Many of these tactics are now outlawed by the federal Fair Debt Collection Practices Act of 1977 and by similar state laws. In addition, state courts have been sympathetic toward law suits brought by individuals against collection agencies using or threatening abusive tactics.

Some collection agencies continue to rely on relatively strong-arm tactics. During the recession in the late 1980s and early 1990s, the number of debtors unable to pay their bills increased and, as a result, so did the business of collection agencies. Sometimes new employees were added without adequate training. During this period, the number of illegal and harassing practices grew to such a level that further legislation was being discussed. Administrative proceedings were also successfully brought against organizations such as American Family Publishers and the American Express Company on the theory that they hired collection firms and knowingly approved or assisted these firms in using deceptive and harassing debt collection practices. Of course, not all collection agencies use these tactics; some adopt a much more low-key approach. Rather than threatening, they offer to help. They may listen sympathetically to the individual's plight and suggest that the individual seek assistance in reorganizing his or her financial affairs. Some prefer to call themselves "accounts receivable managers" rather than collection agencies.

At one time, collection agencies purchased delinquent accounts at a percentage of the face amount. The agency kept whatever was collected. Today the customary practice is to make collection efforts for a fee based on the age of the accounts and the amount collected.

§6.4 THE COLLECTION OF UNPAID FEDERAL INCOME TAXES

Most individual taxpayers regularly pay their federal income taxes through the "pay as you go" collection system described in section 19.19. Many persons, however, have significant amounts of income that are not subject to withholding. These persons are required to make quarterly declarations of estimated tax, but they may nevertheless be tempted to use available cash for purposes other than the payment of income taxes and may reach a position that they are unable to pay their tax obligations when they become due. Other persons may fail to report income entirely or may treat items improperly on their tax returns only to be audited or notified that additional amounts of tax are due. Other persons may fail to report income entirely or may treat items improperly on their tax returns only to be audited or notified that additional amounts of tax are due. A person in a difficult financial position who is faced with a demand that additional tax be paid should not ignore the tax claim. The Internal Revenue Service has powerful collection procedures to assure that defaulting taxpayers do not escape their obligations. The Internal Revenue Service may simply seize bank accounts, wages, or property (subject to fairly narrow exemptions); property that is seized may be sold for a fraction of market value, and the defaulting taxpayer's bill is reduced only by what the Internal Revenue Service actually receives on the resale.

The collection process is so unpleasant that professional tax advisers recommend that every effort be made to satisfy the tax obligation before other obligations. The sale of investments to raise immediate cash, if possible at all, may give rise to a subsequent tax obligation since the gain is itself subject to tax; it is more sensible to borrow the money in a tax deductible form, such as a home equity loan if that is practical. If a taxpayer cannot borrow money and has no assets to sell, he or she should try to work out an arrangement with the IRS. A persuasive showing of a good faith intention to pay the tax obligation may lead to an agreement that permits the obligation to be paid over a period of time, thereby avoiding compulsory collection procedures. A taxpayer may also make an "offer in compromise," in which the taxpayer agrees to settle for a fraction of the total amount claimed by the IRS; however, such an offer will be considered only if the amount offered exceeds the total value of equity in the taxpayer's assets. Only about 9,000 such offers were received by the IRS in 1991. If the tax obligation is eligible to be discharged in bankruptcy, the threat by a taxpayer to file a bankruptcy petition may persuade the IRS to discuss an offer in compromise seriously.

§6.5 CREDIT EDUCATION AND COUNSELING

The National Foundation for Consumer Credit is a nonprofit umbrella organization for some 700 consumer credit counseling services (CCCSs) scattered around the country. It sets guidelines and policies for the local organizations that provide extensive educational programs for individuals as well as assistance to specific individuals in budgeting, financial management, and repayment of debts. CCCSs maintain speakers bureaus to provide speakers to schools, clubs, work sites, church groups, and the like on a wide variety of financial topics. Typical topics include "Consumer and Personal Credit," "Women and Credit," "Getting a Home Loan," "Teach Your Kids the Value of Money," and "Your Credit Rating."

The central function of CCCSs is to provide confidential and professional financial and debt counseling to individual debtors and, where possible, to aid and rehabilitate financially distressed families and individuals. While many individuals voluntary request the assistance of CCCSs, referrals are also made by creditors, employers, social service agencies, and collection agencies.

Individual counseling includes a complete review of the individual's income, expenses, and debts. A small fee is charged for this service. In many instances, all that is required is counseling or the creation of a more realistic budget for the troubled individual or family; in others, a debt management plan is created with the consent of creditors and administered by the CCCS.

A debt management plan is usually one step short of bankruptcy. If the review of the individual's financial position shows that there is no possibility of satisfying all creditors, the CCCS will contact the individual's creditors and seek to work out a modified payment schedule with the consent and approval of those creditors. Such a plan is usually attractive to creditors since it promises that they will receive something, while bankruptcy normally means that they will receive nothing. Creditors, for example, may accept a partial forgiveness of the debt and a plan that involves repayment of the balance over a period of time. If a creditor declines to accept a plan, it reserves its various collection rights, thereby assuring that the debtor probably will be forced into bankruptcy.

The typical debt management plan involves the deposit by the debtor of a monthly payment into a trust account administered by the CCCS. This payment may be due on the 22nd of each month. After the debtor's check clears, the CCCS mails out checks to each participating creditor on the 26th of the month. Participating creditors are requested to make a 15 percent tax deductible donation to the CCCS for this service, and the debtor is also expected to pay a small fee.

The problems faced by many debtors have been resolved through this voluntary settlement device. An advantage of this device is that the CCCS contacts creditors and credit reporting agencies and may eliminate harassing calls and preserve the debtor's credit rating, an important step in the rehabilitation of a troubled debtor. Some for-profit credit counselors may offer similar debt restructuring programs.

§6.6 DEBT CONSOLIDATION

Private debt consolidation is sometimes recommended for consumers who have lost control of their budgets and find themselves lacking immediate funds to pay a number of different creditors. Instead of paying dozens of debts individually — credit cards, auto loans, medical bills, etc. — the debtor on his or her own takes out a single loan to repay all of these immediately due obligations. One monthly payment is all that is required, and as that consolidation loan is paid off over time, the debtor gradually returns to financial solvency.

In many instances a debt consolidation loan may save consumers from bankruptcy. However it is important to recognize that a debt consolidation loan will be successful only if the debtor's monthly take-home cash flow is able to stretch to meet the payments on the consolidation loan, to continue to provide for basic needs of food, clothing, and shelter, and to cover unexpected problems that may arise. If it is not, debt reduction must be negotiated.

Banks, credit unions, and finance companies all offer debt consolidation loans, and many advertise them heavily. These loans may be secured or unsecured, but the interest costs of an unsecured personal loan to consolidate debts may make such a transaction unattractive. A popular form of debt consolidation loan today is a home equity loan — a second mortgage on the debtor's residence. See section 7.13. The terms of such a loan are likely to be more favorable than other types of loans, and the interest may be tax deductible. However, if the debt consolidation loan is a lien on the debtor's residence, a failure to make payments may lead to foreclosure and the loss of a place to live.

One needs to be cautious when debt consolidating. Even where the interest rate on a debt consolidation loan is lower than current borrowing costs, the debtor must realize that when the length of the loan is stretched out to reduce the size of the monthly payment, the total loan costs are increased. In the long run, more cash flow will be tied up the longer the consolidation loan is outstanding. Further, it makes little sense to pay off noninterestbearing debt — such as most doctors' bills — with interest-incurring indebtedness. That simply increases the interest cost. Noninterestbearing debt should generally not be included in the consolidation but should be paid off directly in one or more payments.

Private debt consolidation generally leads to a loss of flexibility in purchasing, in paying, and possibly in negotiating with creditors. In many instances, the services of a CCCS may be preferable to a do-it-yourself consolidation.

§6.7 STATE LAW: ASSIGNMENTS FOR BENEFIT OF CREDITORS

A debtor who is in a hopeless position financially may take advantage of a long established state procedure and make an assignment of property for the benefit of creditors. Such an assignment is to a third person for the benefit of the creditors and is theoretically a voluntary act on the part of the debtor. The theory is that the debtor has recognized the hopelessness of his or her financial situation and has decided to turn the available property over to a trustee for the benefit of creditors to be administered and divided up on an equitable basis. Of course, the reality is usually more complex: Debtors are usually reluctant to throw in the towel and make a voluntary assignment for creditors. Usually such an assignment is made after considerable pressure from major creditors who argue that the only alternative is a more expensive proceeding in the federal bankruptcy courts. The major creditors may also insist that a specific person be named as the assignee to administer the debtor's property.

Many states have statutes that regulate, in whole or in part, assignments for the benefit of creditors. These statutes generally follow the common law principles developed with respect to such assignments. They may require recording of the assignment, the filing of schedules of assets and liabilities with a court, and the giving of notice to all creditors.

An assignee for the benefit of creditors is viewed as a trustee and is subject to the standard trustee's fiduciary duties. His or her duty is to liquidate the assets of the estate and distribute the proceeds to creditors as expeditiously as possible. The assignee has limited power to set aside recent transactions with specific creditors: The assignee may have power to set aside fraudulent conveyances (discussed in section 6.10) and some unperfected liens, but does not have a general power to set aside transactions that may have the effect of giving preferential treatment to some creditors over others. The power to set aside preferences, as they are called, does exist in federal bankruptcy court: If a debtor has made one or more voidable preferences, that may make impractical the assignment for benefit of creditors route. Also, a relatively new uniform statute intended for state adoption dealing with fraudulent transfers (also discussed in section 6.10) does give the assignee for benefit of creditors power to attack certain preferences.

An assignment for the benefit of creditors usually occurs only when the debtor's assets are insufficient to pay off the creditors in full, and all of the debtor's nonexempt property is included within the assignment. The receipt by a creditor of a partial payment from the assignee does not discharge the debtor from residual liability on the unpaid balance. As a result, assignments are much more likely to be used by corporate than by individual debtors, who prefer the federal bankruptcy route, since a discharge from this residual liability may be available.

An assignment for the benefit of creditors does not need the consent of specific creditors. However, a partial or qualified assignment may be set aside as a fraudulent conveyance. And, creditors who object to an assignment for the benefit of creditors may be able to commence an involuntary bankruptcy proceeding in the federal courts since the execution of an assignment for the benefit of creditors is a basis for ordering relief against the debtor in a creditor-commenced bankruptcy proceeding. An assignment for the benefit of creditors prevents unsecured creditors from attaching or seizing the assigned property to secure the payment of their debts.

§6.8 STATE LAW: COMPOSITIONS AND EXTENSIONS

A "composition" is an agreement between a debtor and two or more creditors by which the creditors agree to accept a partial satisfaction of their claims and forgive the balance. The typical debt management plan administered by the CCCS is a type of composition. An extension agreement is an agreement between creditors and a debtor that gives the debtor additional time to discharge the debts but does not forgive them.

A creditor who is not a party to a composition or extension agreement is not affected by it. Such a creditor may continue to seek to enforce its claims against the debtor and its property by legal or extra-legal means. As a practical matter, a creditor who does so is likely to force the debtor into federal bankruptcy.

A composition differs from an assignment for the benefit of creditors primarily because it is a contractual understanding between the debtor and specific creditors settling their claims. An *assignment*, on the other hand, is a liquidation arrangement not dependent on the assent of creditors and not involving any release of the unpaid portions of any claims. A composition and an assignment for the benefit of creditors nevertheless may occur simultaneously, as when a debtor agrees to make an assignment for the benefit of creditors, and each creditor agrees to forgive the excess by which its claims exceed the amount available for that creditor from the assignment.

§6.9 BANKRUPTCY AND INSOLVENCY

The words "insolvent" and "bankrupt" are often thrown around loosely. From a legal standpoint the word insolvent is much the more precise term even though it has two quite different possible meanings. The most common meaning of "insolvent" is simply that the debtor is unable to meet its obligations as they come due. This is usually referred to as "equity insolvency" or "insolvency in the equity sense." The second meaning is that used in section 101(26) of the Federal Bankruptcy Code: A debtor is "insolvent" if "the sum of such entity's debts is greater than all of such entity's property, at a fair valuation" exclusive of exempt property and certain other items. This is usually referred to as "balance sheet insolvency" or "insolvency in the bankruptcy sense," phrases that are somewhat misleading because the Federal Bankruptcy Code also uses the concept of equity insolvency in a number of different sections. Balance sheet insolvency requires acceptance of some kind of accounting principles, though the phrase "at a fair valuation" obviously assumes that realistic asset values may be substituted for book values.

In real life, the difference between equity and balance sheet insolvency can be very great. Equity insolvency focuses on the liquidity of or cash flow of the person, while balance sheet insolvency focuses on the liquidation of his or her assets. A person may well be insolvent in the bankruptcy sense but solvent in the equity sense: A debtor may have sufficient cash flow to enable it to deal with the bills as they roll in, month after month indefinitely, even though his or her aggregate liabilities greatly exceed assets. Many persons starting their first job with large educational debts are insolvent in the bankruptcy sense. Or, a debtor could have a large slug of indebtedness that does not come due for another three years or so. Similarly, a debtor may lack sufficient liquidity to meet his or her obligations as they are coming due today and thus be insolvent in an equity sense, but at the same time have illiquid assets and resources with a value far in excess of all of its liabilities, so that the person is not insolvent in the bankruptcy sense.

The word bankrupt has several varied and loose meanings. In the most technical sense, "bankrupt" means that a person is the subject of a federal bankruptcy proceeding. At one time it also meant that the person had committed one or more acts of bankruptcy (a concept that was eliminated from the Federal Bankruptcy Code in 1978 but continues to be referred to in the literature). It may mean a commercial trader who is insolvent (either in the equity or balance sheet sense). It also may be used as a synonym for "insolvent." Generally, the word should be limited to its technical meaning — a person who is subject to a federal bankruptcy proceeding — to avoid confusion and uncertainty.

§6.10 FRAUDULENT CONVEYANCES

The state law doctrine of fraudulent conveyances (or fraud on creditors) is designed to protect creditors from transactions entered into by debtors that have the purpose or effect of hindering or defeating the creditor's ability to collect on the indebtedness. The doctrine has its roots in the statute of 13 Elizabeth enacted in 1570 and is part of the received English common law inheritance in all states. The Commissioners on Uniform State Laws adopted a Uniform Fraudulent Conveyance Act (UFCA) in 1919 that has been adopted by some 25 states. In addition, a complete revision and modernization of this Act was approved in 1984 under the name Uniform Fraudulent Transfers Act (UFTA). The description below is based on the assumption that in the future states will continue to substitute the UFTA for the old UFCA, and that additional states that did not adopt the UFCA will codify their rules relating to fraudulent conveyances by adopting the UFTA.

One class of fraudulent conveyance covered by the statute involves transfers made with an actual intent to defraud or under such circumstances in which such an intent may be reasonably inferred. Section 4 of the UFTA defines these conveyances in the following terms:

> (a) A transfer made or obligation incurred by a debtor is fraudulent as to a creditor, whether the creditor's claim arose within a reasonable time before or after the transfer was made or the obligation was incurred, if the debtor made the transfer or incurred the obligation:
> (1) With actual intent to hinder, delay, or defraud any creditor of the debtor; or
> (2) without receiving a reasonably equivalent value in exchange for the transfer or obligation, and the debtor:
> (A) was engaged or was about to engage in a business or a transaction for which the remaining assets of the debtor were unreasonably small in relation to the business or transaction; or
> (B) intended to incur, or believed that the debtor would incur, debts beyond the debtor's ability to pay as they became due.

This is an "actual intent" section. Actual intent may be difficult to prove, but section 4(b) makes proof easier by in effect creating a series of presumptions. Section 4(b) states that, when determining whether actual intent to defraud exists, consideration may be given to 11 different factors — for example, that the debtor absconded (factor 6) or removed or concealed assets (factor 7). These factors are usually referred to as "badges of fraud."

A second category of fraudulent conveyance involves transfers when the debtor is insolvent. Such transfers are actionable without regard to actual intent. The operative language of section 5 of the UFTA is as follows:

> (a) A transfer made or obligation incurred by a debtor is fraudulent as to a creditor whose claim arose before the transfer was made or the obligation was incurred if the debtor made the transfer or incurred the obligation without receiving a reasonably equivalent value in exchange for the transfer or obligation and the debtor was insolvent at that time or the debtor became insolvent as a result of the transfer of obligation.

(b) A transfer made by a debtor is fraudulent as to a creditor whose claim arose before the transfer was made if the transfer was made to an insider for an antecedent debt, the debtor was insolvent at that time, and the insider had reasonable cause to believe that the debtor was insolvent.

This section protects existing creditors from asset-depleting transactions when the debtor is insolvent.

The UFTA contains a carefully drafted set of definitions that flesh out many of the general terms used in sections 4 and 5. It defines *insolvent* as the situation in which "the sum of the debtor's debts is greater than all of the debtor's assets at a fair valuation," but adds that a debtor "who is generally not able to pay the debtor's debts as they become due is presumed to be insolvent." It also defines terms such as reasonably equivalent value, insider and transfer.

Generally, a conveyance that falls within one of the categories of fraudulent conveyance is voidable at the suit of a creditor, an assignee for the benefit of creditors, or a bankruptcy trustee. Alternatively, the creditor may ignore the transfer and simply proceed against the property by attachment or other private remedy. Protection, however, is given to a transferee who takes the property in good faith and for a reasonably equivalent value. A good faith transferee is also protected to the extent of the value of any improvements he may have made in good faith to the property.

§6.11 AN OVERVIEW OF THE FEDERAL BANKRUPTCY CODE

The Federal Bankruptcy Code was enacted pursuant to the constitutional provision authorizing Congress to enact "uniform bankruptcy laws." The current code was enacted in 1978, replacing an earlier statute enacted in 1898. Substantial amendments to the administrative provisions of the 1978 Act were made in 1984. The 1978 Act made numerous changes in the bankruptcy code, so the pre-1978 literature cannot be safely relied upon.

Major features of federal bankruptcy law that distinguish it from state law are: (1) a broad power to avoid prefiling transfers of property — particularly preferences — to ensure equality of treatment among creditors of the same class; (2) the existence of an automatic stay against collection efforts by creditors immediately upon filing a bankruptcy petition; and (3) the grant to a bankrupt of a discharge from prefiling debts in most circumstances. The underlying theory of a discharge is that an "honest" debtor should be given a fresh start.

The major chapters of the Bankruptcy Code dealing with individual bankruptcies are Chapters 7 and 13. A few individuals also may petition for reorganization under Chapter 11, but that is uncommon.

Chapter 7 governs traditional or "straight" bankruptcy proceedings for both individuals and businesses. The nonexempt assets of the bankrupt are liquidated under the supervision of a trustee and distributed to creditors in accordance with relative priorities. A Chapter 7 proceeding may lead to a discharge of an individual debtor from most obligations. In a Chapter 7 proceeding, the discharged debtor is not left penniless since substantial amounts of property may be exempt from creditors' claims under state law and therefore not subject to the bankruptcy proceeding. Court decisions hold, for example, that certain retirement and pension rights are exempt from seizure and liquidation in a Chapter 7 proceeding.

Chapter 13 deals with reorganizations by individuals with a regular income with unsecured debts of less than $100,000 (and secured debts of less than $350,000) — many consumer bankruptcies, in short. A Chapter 13 reorganization requires court confirmation but not creditor approval. Chapter 13 involves the anticipated payment in full of all debts over a period of time. If this is not practical — and many Chapter 13 plans turn out to be unworkable in practice — the proceeding may be converted to a Chapter 7 liquidation and possible discharge from unpaid obligations.

Bankruptcy proceedings are generally administered by federal district judges. Judicial districts also have bankruptcy judges to assist the district judges: Bankruptcy judges are not Article III judges. In addition, Chapter 7 cases involve a trustee to administer the estate of the bankrupt. A trustee is a private individual (named either by the district judge or by the creditors, depending on the type of case) who is charged with representing the interests of creditors generally in the property of the bankrupt that is available for distribution to the creditors.

Most bankruptcy proceedings are initiated by a voluntary filing by the debtor. Any person with debts may make a voluntary filing; it is not a requirement for filing that the debtor be "insolvent" in either the balance sheet or equity senses. Chapter 7 proceedings may also be instituted by creditors seeking the involuntary institution of bankruptcy procedures against a debtor. Generally three creditors with unsecured claims totaling at least $5,000 must join in the petition for involuntary bankruptcy, though debtors with less than twelve creditors may be placed into involuntary bankruptcy by a single creditor with an unsecured claim exceeding $5,000. An involuntary petition must allege either that the debtor is not paying debts as they mature (i.e., is insolvent in the equity sense) or that the debtor has made an assignment for the benefit of creditors within the preceding 120 days.

The filing of an involuntary bankruptcy proceeding almost always severely disrupts the debtor's activities and adversely affects its credit standing since such filings are quickly picked up by the credit reporting agencies. Severe sanctions may be imposed on a creditor who files such a petition in bad faith.

§6.12 UNEXPECTED CONSEQUENCES OF A BANKRUPTCY

A complete description of bankruptcy proceedings is well beyond the scope of this book. There are certain consequences of a bankruptcy proceeding, however, that should be part of the general knowledge of every lawyer.

From the standpoint of creditors, the filing of a bankruptcy proceeding by a debtor has several unpleasant consequences. First, the automatic stay requires the immediate cessation of collection efforts. This includes attempts to foreclose on liens or security interests in specific property as well as attempts to collect upon unsecured claims. After the petition is filed, the rights of the creditor are to be determined in the bankruptcy proceeding and that may entail delays of two years or more in payment. Except for this delay, liens or security interests in property are respected in bankruptcy. Second, the bankruptcy trustee has the power to disaffirm executory contracts, so that persons with contract rights against the debtor may find that the contract is no longer enforceable, and they have an unsecured claim arising under the contract that must be established in the bankruptcy proceeding. Alternatively, the bankruptcy trustee may elect to enforce the contract against the other party for the benefit of the estate. Third, if a creditor has been successful in obtaining payment of an antecedent debt shortly before the bankruptcy proceeding is commenced, that payment may be a voidable preference and the creditor may be compelled to return the payment to the trustee for the benefit of the bankruptcy estate. Preferences may be set aside if made within 90 days before the filing of the bankruptcy petition, or, within one year of the filing if the preference is to an insider, for example, a relative of an individual debtor.

For the individual debtor considering whether or not to file a voluntary bankruptcy petition, the major goal is usually the bankruptcy discharge, which provides for the fresh start that is the justification for federal bankruptcy. A secondary motivation may be the automatic stay, which ends collection efforts subject to court review.

Debtors sometimes do not appreciate that not all debtors are entitled to a bankruptcy discharge, and even where such a discharge is granted, it does not cover all classes or types of claims. There is, thus, a two-step inquiry in determining whether a debt is discharged in bankruptcy. First, it must be determined if the debtor is entitled to a discharge at all. Second, if so, it must be determined if the specific debt is covered by the discharge.

1. *Debtors that are not entitled to a discharge.* A debtor is not entitled to a discharge at all if it is determined that he or she engaged in acts of dishonesty or refused to cooperate with the bankruptcy proceeding in specified ways. These grounds include the making of a fraudulent conveyance within a year of filing the bankruptcy petition, failing to keep or preserve financial records, refusing to testify after immunity is granted following the invocation of the privilege against self-incrimination, failing to explain satisfactorily the loss of assets in connection with the bankruptcy proceeding, or making a false claim against the estate. If a debtor is not eligible for a discharge, he or she remains liable on all prefiling debts. As a result, it is customary to investigate carefully the availability of a discharge before the decision is made to file a voluntary bankruptcy petition.

2. *Debts not covered by a discharge.* Even when granted, a bankruptcy discharge does not cover several classes of claims: (1) most federal tax claims; (2) debts for money, property, or services obtained through fraud, false representations, or false financial statements relied upon by the specific creditor; (3) debts that are not scheduled in the bankruptcy proceeding; (4) child support and alimony; (5) tort liabilities arising from "willful and malicious" conduct; (6) fines, penalties or forfeitures payable to governmental entities; (7) educational loans; and (8) claims arising from driving while intoxicated. The exclusions of these items from the bankruptcy discharge are based upon policy and social considerations relating to inappropriate conduct by a debtor. Some of these limitations on the bankruptcy discharge are applicable automatically based on the nature of the debt. Others, particularly item (2) above, must be expressly pleaded by a specific creditor who must then be prepared to establish at a hearing that the conduct of the bankrupt with respect to his or her claim makes the bankruptcy discharge inapplicable to that creditor's claim.

§6.13 CREDIT AND CREDIT CARDS AFTER A BANKRUPTCY DISCHARGE

As indicated earlier, an individual who has gone through Chapter 7 bankruptcy emerges with a destroyed credit record. The fact that a bankruptcy petition has been filed is picked up almost immediately by the credit reporting firms and remains in the credit records for ten years. As a result, any routine credit check after the filing will reveal the fact of bankruptcy and probably the denial of credit. Even regular telephone service and utilities may be a problem as these suppliers may insist on a cash deposit to cover monthly charges. This section discusses devices that may ameliorate some of the post-bankruptcy problems.

In a typical personal bankruptcy, the debtor is in default on payments on all existing credit cards. As a result each of the issuers will be listed as creditors in the bankruptcy filing and will receive notice of the filing. As a result, all of the debtor's outstanding credit cards will be deactivated promptly by the issuers who become aware of the filing, and new applications for credit cards will be rejected as a result of the credit check.

A credit card is a virtual necessity today for most middle-class living. It is virtually impossible to check into a hotel or rent a car at an airport without a valid credit card. If a potential bankrupt is well advised, he or she will make sure that at least one credit card is current when the bankruptcy filing occurs. Since that credit card issuer will not be listed as a creditor in the bankruptcy filing, it probably will not be aware of the filing. And, if that card is kept religiously current, it may not become aware of the filing for an extended period.

A person who has been discharged under Chapter 7 is ineligible for another bankruptcy discharge for seven years. Rather perversely, this provision tends to improve the potential credit standing of the newly discharged bankrupt who emerges from Chapter 7 with virtually no debt and a vastly improved net worth and no right to a new discharge for several years. Recognizing this, some department stores (for example, Sears), automobile dealers, and commercial insurance companies are willing to extend credit if the bankrupt has a steady income.

A bankrupt's credit record may also be improved by the use of a so-called secured credit card, with a record of conscientious and timely payments. See section 7.12.

Individuals who successfully complete the Chapter 13 reorganization plan have an easier time reestablishing credit since they have repaid in full their prebankruptcy creditors under the plan. When all is said and done, however, the newly discharged bankrupt may be expected to have difficulty obtaining credit, particularly for substantial transactions. A classic case is the bankrupt who applies for a large mortgage to acquire a vacation home; the prior bankruptcy filing just about ensures that such an application for credit will be rejected.

PART II

APPLICATIONS

7

Modern Consumer Credit Transactions

§7.1 INTRODUCTION

This chapter describes the most popular forms of general credit available to individuals. It deals with the individual as borrower.

Unsecured loans to individuals are generally viewed as high risk loans, and most such loans carry high interest rates though affluent individuals may be able to borrow money on terms that approximate those available to small commercial borrowers. An important exception to this pattern are educational loans provided by many universities and colleges as part of their educational obligation; these loans (discussed in section 7.18) may be government-subsidized and embody favorable terms: They may be interest-free until the borrower graduates and thereafter interest may be charged at below-market rates for consumer loans. Educational loans obtained through an institution of higher learning are much more attractive and less costly than loans obtainable through commercial sources.

Secured loans generally involve lower interest rates than unsecured loans. Subsequent chapters deal with the two most important consumer loan transactions: purchases of real estate and purchases of new automobiles. Loans for these purposes are secured by liens on the property being acquired, and this security largely explains why they, too, carry relatively low rates of interest. Loans for these two purposes are sufficiently unique to justify special treatment.

The modern home equity loan is another important type of secured loan that is available to homeowners at attractive rates.

The federal Truth in Lending Act (formally known as the Consumer Credit Protection Act, Title 1) is designed to assure that every customer who has need for consumer credit is given meaningful information with respect to the cost of that credit. This legislation is applicable to banks, savings and loan associations, department stores, credit card issuers, credit unions, automobile dealers, consumer finance companies, residential mortgage brokers, craftsmen (for example, plumbers or electricians), doctors, dentists, other professionals, hospitals, and any other individual or organization that extends or arranges credit for which a finance charge is or may be payable or which is repayable in more than four installments. In most cases, the financing cost must be expressed in the dollar amount of the finance charge and as an annual percentage rate computed on the unpaid amount of the amount financed. The ubiquitous abbreviation "APR," which appears in advertisements and financing statements, refers to the annual percentage rate calculated in accordance with regulation Z, the regulation that implements the Truth in Lending Act. Other relevant information also may have to be disclosed. Regulation Z contains detailed rules as to how the annual percentage rate is to be calculated on a variety of different transactions. This legislation does not set forth maximum charges that may be imposed on consumers in credit transactions.

§7.2 CONSUMER FINANCE COMPANIES

Everyone has seen advertisements for "easy" loans, "household" loans, and "small" loans offered by consumer finance companies. Companies involved in this loan business are usually regulated by state law, but the essence of their business is lending money at very high rates of interest. These rates may be advertised on a monthly basis; a rate of 3 percent per month is 36 percent per year. Small loan companies operate under special exceptions to usury statutes (discussed in section 7.14); rates of 50 percent per year or more are not uncommon.

In 1992, one small loan company offered a "tax refund" loan based on one's anticipated tax refund. The finance charge was a flat $29, which was advertised to be 6 percent on the average $500 refund. The ads, however, did not point out that since the loan might be outstanding for only two or three weeks (until the borrower obtained his or her tax refund), the annualized interest rate was closer to 200 percent than to 6 percent. While this was an ingenious idea, and doubtless popular with many marginal taxpayers who were looking forward every day to receipt of their tax refunds, it also reveals something about the cost of borrowing from small loan companies.

Pawnshops are also a common feature of many cities. Pawnshops make short-term small loans to individuals on the security of valuable personal possessions: watches, fur coats, musical instruments, guns, and what have you. They usually do not lend more than 50 percent of their estimate of the value of the collateral being provided. They may charge even higher effective rates of interest than finance companies. Rates of 100 percent or more per year are not uncommon. The default rate on pawn-secured loans is high and the resale of items left as security is an important aspect of pawnshop operation. The cost of loans from these sources is so great that they should be utilized only as a last resort.

§7.3 SMALL LOANS FROM BANKS AND CREDIT UNIONS

An individual with a good credit record and a history of employment may be able to establish a relationship with a bank or credit union that permits him or her to borrow from that bank or credit union on terms that are considerably more favorable than from consumer finance companies. Interest rates may be based on the prime rate (discussed below in section 7.16); if the prime rate is, say, 8 percent, the interest rate charged to an individual may be 10 or 12 percent per year — two to four points above the prime rate. If the borrower can provide security in the form of marketable securities or retirement funds in an account with the bank, the interest rate on an unsecured loan may be even lower.

The cost of unsecured loans from these sources is so much more favorable than from small loan companies that, where practicable, they should always be sought. Loans may be made to permit the borrower to make a tax payment, to contribute to an individual retirement account, to purchase appliances, to cover uninsured medical expenses, to finance a vacation, to pay off higher interest rate loans, or for a variety of other purposes. The lender is not so much interested in what the loan is to be used for as the assurance of repayment.

As a practical matter, credit card loans (see section 7.10) and home equity loans (see section 7.13) have supplanted many personal unsecured signature loans from banks and credit unions.

§7.4 EXACT OR ORDINARY INTEREST

Banks and other financial institutions distinguish between ordinary interest and exact interest in connection with loans. These terms relate to the manner of calculating interest for periods of less than one year. When calculating interest, it is customary to exclude the day the loan is made and include the day in which it is repaid. When calculations were made by paper and pencil, and many loans were for days, weeks, months, or fractions of years, it greatly simplified matters to consider a year to consist of 360 days based on 12 months of 30 days each. Interest computed on the basis of these simplifying assumptions is called "ordinary interest" and is still used by many banks and in the computation of interest on some types of securities, particularly corporate, agency, and municipal bonds. "Exact interest," in contrast, is more realistic: It treats the year as consisting of 365 or 366 days, as the case may be, and ignores months. With the development of modern calculating devices, the computation of exact interest, like the calculation of compound interest, has been greatly simplified, though it is obviously more complicated to count the specific number of days in each month than it is to assume that each month has 30 days. While the difference involved is usually relatively small, one suspects that many financial institutions continue to use ordinary interest because it imparts a small upward bias in the amount of interest charged borrowers.

§7.5 MARGIN LOANS

An individual who owns marketable securities may borrow up to 50 percent of the value of those securities from the broker holding the securities. Margin loans do not have to be used for the purchase of securities (though that is the most common use). Some brokerage firms encourage customers to use margin loans for personal purposes, for example, to consolidate credit card obligations or to pay for big ticket items. The interest rate on margin loans is somewhat below the rates charged by banks and credit unions on consumer loans generally. On the other hand, individuals with securities accounts are unlikely to have extensive credit card obligations and may have sufficient resources to purchase consumer items they decide to buy with cash. There also may be a feeling that it is undesirable to mix personal transactions with a stock brokerage account; in any event, it is uncommon to use margin loans for personal purposes.

The Federal Reserve System regulates the use of borrowed funds to purchase additional marketable securities. This regulation only affects loans that are themselves secured by marketable securities. Hence, if one pledges marketable securities to a bank to secure a loan, the bank will require the borrower to sign a statement certifying that the proceeds will not be used to purchase additional marketable securities.

§7.6 OTHER CONSUMER LOANS TO PURCHASE GOODS

Retailers of big ticket goods and appliances may finance their purchase, thereby in effect lending purchasers the bulk of the purchase price. Retailers that finance their purchasers' transactions fall into two broad categories: stores selling (or "renting to own") goods, appliances, and furniture to low income individuals that require weekly or monthly payments (where the risk of default is extremely high and the prices for the goods greatly inflated) and traditional stores catering to individuals with higher income levels and good credit standing.

Sellers in the first category are concentrated in the lower income areas of cities; their prices are so high (and often the quality of the goods being sold or rented so low) that they are unlikely to be patronized by persons who have access to conventional credit sources.

This section discusses loans by stores of the second type. Many loans by these stores appear to involve favorable interest rates and other terms. "No payments until April" and low advertised finance charges are typical appeals in advertising by such stores.

Of course, the favorable loan terms may be in part because the loans are secured by the goods being sold. Because used goods often depreciate very markedly when they leave the store, however, this is often not the most likely explanation. Since the loans are arranged through the seller, there is also the possibility that, like the stores selling to low income individuals, the prices offered are somewhat higher than they would be if the store did not extend credit but sold only through straight cash transactions. In effect, the higher prices are compensation for the favorable credit terms. And the "no payments until April" offer usually means that interest and finance charges run during the period that no payments are required to be made, so that that aspect of the transaction is not as attractive as first appears.

As a general rule, it is usually preferable to arrange for a straight cash purchase of the appliance and then to arrange for the financing independently through one's own credit source. At least, this should clarify what is the real price of the goods or appliance and what is the cost of the credit.

Many department stores and other high-end merchants that at one time provided "charge accounts" and extended credit for large ticket purchases are increasingly relying on bank credit cards rather than extending credit on their own. The substitution of bank credit for loans to customers permit significant savings for stores: They may close down their credit and finance departments entirely and do not have to worry about the collectability of delinquent accounts. However, many stores retain their private credit programs; financing charges in these programs are typically in the 21 to 22 percent range, higher than the 17 or 18 percent imposed on carryover charges on ordinary VISA and Mastercard cards. These "store cards," as they are usually called, have different economics than the bank card. There is neither an annual fee nor a transaction fee. See section 7.10. Also, the balances carried over on stores cards—perhaps $200 or $300 on the average—is significantly lower than the balances carried over on bank cards. Finally, the rate of default is higher, because stores usually issue cards to persons who cannot qualify for bank credit cards. Despite these differences, there have been complaints about the high interest rates on stores cards, and calls for their reduction.

§7.7 ADD-ON INTEREST

Interest on some consumer loans (either cash loans or loans to finance a purchase of a major appliance) is computed on an "add-on" basis that permits a mild deception about the effective interest rate. Add-on interest can best be described by an example. A $1,000 two-year loan is stated to be available at 8 percent "on an add-on basis." When the actual computation is made, interest of $160 (.08 × $1,000 × 2) is added to the principal amount, and the total ($1,160) is divided by 24 to determine the monthly payment ($48.33). The actual rate of interest on this transaction is 14.67 percent and not 8 percent. Do you see why the effective rate is considerably greater than 8 percent? (Hint: If interest of $160 per month is being added to the loan each month while it is outstanding, what is the average balance outstanding on the loan?) Under federal disclosure regulations the actual as well as the add-on rate must be disclosed. Whether or not this actually helps the average consumer is debatable.

Consumer loans also often involve a variety of small (or not-so-small) charges for credit checks, credit life insurance, or a variety of other financing or handling charges. Often the services or benefits provided by these charges cost considerably less than the amount charged, so that some uncertain portion of these charges also may legitimately be viewed as a charge for the use of money (i.e., interest).

§7.8 REFINANCING TERM LOANS: THE RULE OF 78's

Refinancing or paying off a long-term loan that requires monthly payments by the borrower in advance of its maturity entails a calculation of the unpaid balance of the loan at the time the loan is paid off. This in turn requires a calculation of how much of the earlier payments constituted principal and how much constituted interest. That is easy, one might say, since one should simply calculate the interest due at the time each payment was made and the excess should be applied to reduce the principal. When the next payment is made, the interest should be calculated on the principal as reduced by previous payments. This is usually called the "*simple interest*" method and is undoubtedly the fairest way to determine the unpaid balance, since the borrower is being charged interest at the stated rate only on the unpaid balance.

Another method widely used in many states is the "rule of 78's" or "sum of digits" method of calculating interest. This method of calculating is much more favorable to the creditor than the simple interest method. The rule of 78's gets its name from the sum of the digits applicable to a 12-month loan. Using a 12-month loan as an example, the rule of 78's first assigns the numbers one through twelve to the months the loan is outstanding and then adds the numbers together. The total is 78. If the borrower pays off or refinances the mortgage after one payment, he or she is assumed to have paid 12 seventy-eighths of the total interest owed; after two payments, 23 seventy-eighths of the interest has been paid off, and so forth. On a two-year loan, the digits one through twenty-four are added together to form the denominator. This method allocates a significantly higher portion of the total payments to interest in the early months than the simple interest method, and therefore increases the amount of principal that remains due.

The rule of 78's maximizes the inflation of interest about a third of the way through a loan. When a large, long-term loan is involved, the inflation can amount to thousands of dollars. For example, on a $30,000 15-year loan to purchase a mobile home at 16 percent interest (terms not uncommon during the early 1980s), a borrower who refinances the loan after the end of five years would discover that he has paid an additional $4,595 in interest by the use of the rule of 78's than would be due by the simple interest calculation.

Before deciding to refinance or prepay an outstanding loan, one should determine whether the rule of 78's will be applied to the transaction, and if so, one should take into account the cost involved before deciding whether refinancing or prepayment is desirable. This may be done most simply by requesting the lender to estimate in writing the amount necessary to pay off the loan and whether the rule of 78's is applicable to the loan. It is possible that the original loan documents will indicate that the rule of 78's is to be applied in calculating prepayments, but the rule may be applied even if the documents are silent, so inquiry is therefore necessary.

The rule of 78's is widely viewed as unfair to consumers and its use is barred in about 16 states. When negotiating a loan in a state in which its use is permitted, it is sometimes possible to insist that a simple interest calculation be incorporated in a new loan.

The rule of 78's apparently developed in the 1930s as a matter of convenient calculation of interest on proposed prepayments. At the time, most loans were relatively short-term, and the differences between the rule of 78's and simple interest were small. That is not true today, however, when five-year automobile loans are practically standard.

One of the quirky aspects of the rule of 78's is that because the formula applies so much of the interest to the early periods of the loan, the effective interest rate applied on later payments drops steadily. It may make little sense, for example, to refinance the mobile home loan described above after ten years, because the payments thereafter represent primarily principal, and the effective interest rate on the balance of the loan might well be lower than the interest rate on a loan obtained to refinance that obligation.

§7.9 HOW TO READ FINE PRINT IN LOAN AGREEMENTS

The language of loan agreements is often so opaque as to defy even sophisticated analysis. When an important provision — such as a prepayment privilege — cannot be readily understood, it is necessary to ask the lender to give an illustration of how the provision is to be applied.

A good illustration is a form used in a Small Business Administration loan program. The program is known as the 503 loan program for small businesses financed through the Federal Financing Bank, an arm of the United States Treasury. This program was active during the early 1980s, years of high interest rates. With interest rates on outstanding loans as high as 15.7 percent, the prepayment privilege was obviously of considerable practical importance. When attorneys for borrowers were asked to review the loan documents, they were faced with the following prepayment provision:

The debenture may be prepaid at such price as will result in a yield from the date of prepayment to maturity, equal to the U.S. Treasury new issued yield for a security with a maturity and payment schedule comparable to the remaining maturity and payment schedule of the debenture, computed as of the close of business two business days prior to the date of prepayment, plus accrued interest on the amount prepaid to the date of payment.

Many attorneys failed to appreciate the draconian implications of this opaque language. The substance of this provision requires the borrower to pay the equivalent of the principal balance and all the interest he or she would have had to pay had the loan been paid over the contractual period. If interest rates have dropped significantly since the loan was taken out (the usual situation in which prepayment is advantageous), the resulting prepayment penalty might be astonishing: A 25-year, $336,000 loan for which refinancing was sought after 10 years carried a penalty of $123,123; another entrepreneur discovered that a refinancing of a $177,000 loan carried a $45,000 penalty.

A more recent SBA program for essentially the same class of borrowers, the 504 program, has a much more traditional prepayment arrangement: Any loan may be prepaid during the first year upon the payment of one year's interest; the penalty decreases thereafter on an annual basis and completely disappears if the remaining life of the loan is less than one-half of the original term of the loan. If the luckless borrowers described in the previous paragraph had participated in the 504 program rather than the 503 program, the prepayment penalties would have been about $4,800 and $7,400, respectively.

Rather curiously, legislation designed to change the prepayment penalties under the 503 program was enacted by Congress but was vetoed by President Reagan; a similar repeal proposal was opposed by the Bush Administration on the ground that it would create a revenue loss that must be made up by cuts in other small business programs.

§7.10 TRADITIONAL BANK CREDIT CARDS

Everyone is familiar with bank credit cards that charge interest at the rate of 1.5 percent per month (or a lower rate for larger transactions). Indeed, these credit cards have become the principal source of credit for most individuals. One can use these cards to buy things now and pay later; one can also use them to buy traveler's checks, to borrow money, to get cash advances from automated machines, or to cover overdrafts in a checking account. All of these transactions essentially constitute loans on which the annual interest rate may well exceed 18 percent per year. Credit cards, in other words, are a source of easy credit, not of cheap credit. In terms of interest costs, they are intermediate between personal bank and credit union loans, on the one hand, and small loan finance charges, on the other.

The issuer of a credit card imposes a more or less arbitrary maximum amount of loans that may be outstanding on a credit card at any one time. This maximum frequently may be increased upon the request of the user of the card. A person with several credit cards may easily borrow tens of thousands of dollars in the aggregate by using those cards to the maximum.

The effective interest rate involved in the use of credit cards depends on specific transactions and on the manner of calculating the monthly finance charge. The traditional card involves a finance charge or fee of 1.5 percent per month on the "average daily balance." The amount outstanding each day is added up, and the result is divided by the number of days in the month to get an average daily balance. The finance charge is calculated on this figure. Traditional credit cards also provide, however, for no finance charge if there is prompt payment of the entire balance within the following billing period (or within the first 25 days of that billing period). To the extent the balance is in fact paid off in full to avoid the imposition of finance charges, these cards provide what are in effect short-term interest-free loans. Credit cards are good for consumers who take advantage of these interest-free loans. Plans with this feature may still be profitable to the issuer because: (1) Many users of the card do not pay off the balance each month and thus incur the finance charge; (2) banks also may charge card holders an annual membership fee ($50 per year is a common charge); and (3) retailers and other merchants are also charged a fee of about 2.15 percent on each transaction.

Credit cards increasingly may offer other "free" benefits. They may offer frequent flier miles (a mile per dollar of purchases) to obtain free airplane tickets or free upgrades, extended warranties on goods purchased through the card, car rental insurance waivers, 24-hour customer service, discounts on purchases of new vehicles, and emergency card replacement for lost cards. These "free" benefits may represent competition for the consumer and may explain why interest rates on credit card loans have generally not declined as rapidly as interest rates. In addition, more and more cards are eliminating the days of grace to pay outstanding balances without the imposition of a financing charge, and more and more cards are imposing an annual fee.

For persons who can obtain bank credit cards (and that may not always be easy for young individuals just starting out), the best type of card to use is a traditional card that charges no annual membership fee and no finance charge if the unpaid balance is paid in full during the first 25 days of the next billing period. No-fee cards are widely available, but some issuers of no-fee cards have eliminated the once standard 25-day grace period to avoid the finance charge by paying off the balance in full; these banks assess charges immediately upon any purchase with the card.

Some banks in smaller communities may offer bank credit cards on a national basis, seeking to acquire users by charging lower interest rates than banks in larger cities. Thus, one may be able to reduce borrowing costs even when it is contemplated to make only the minimum required payment each month.

Credit card rates and charges, in sum, vary widely in terms of interest rates, membership fees, and the granting of days of grace for payment to avoid the financing charge. Benefits and credit limits also may vary widely. As in many other areas, comparison shopping is sensible for persons with good credit ratings before selecting a specific bank credit card.

Some card issuers have advertised plans that waive minimum payments for several months; since finance charges continue to accumulate during this grace period, these plans are more of a boon to the issuer than to the carduser.

In addition to the finance charge, some credit card issuers also charge "late fees" if payments are not received by the closing date of the account. A "late fee" of, say, $10.00 may significantly increase the effective interest rate on credit card debt. A few states have enacted statutes prohibiting the imposition of such charges, and the issue whether this legislation is preempted by the federal regulation of consumer credit is being actively litigated as this is written.

Because of the high interest rate inherent in credit card finance charges, an individual's general strategy should be to pay off these obligations as promptly as possible. Of course, in many situations the cardholder in fact is unable to pay off the full balance each month. Indeed, many people pay only the minimum required amount to avoid a default and use the card as a type of unsecured loan. Some people have obtained a dozen or so credit cards and carry substantial balances over each month on a number of cards. This is an extremely expensive form of borrowing; if one cannot pay off the balance in full, it is sensible to obtain a bank loan to pay off the credit card balances since the interest cost on a personal loan from the bank should be about half the cost of financing the same loan through credit cards. Unfortunately, people who use credit cards as a financing device may not qualify for such loans.

Credit counseling services report that excessive use of credit cards and the carrying over of monthly balances on several cards is common among financially distressed individuals, and in fact is often a major cause of that financial distress. See section 6.5.

§7.11 MORE ON CALCULATIONS OF FINANCE CHARGES

During the late 1980s and early 1990s, interest rates declined to the lowest levels in three decades. However, finance charges for credit cards seemed to remain stuck at 1.5 percent per month. This resulted in adverse publicity about "gouging" by credit card issuers, whose cost of lendable funds had declined precipitously. The rate on which finance charges were calculated thereafter gradually began to come down. However, some card issuers at the same time quietly changed the method by which finance charges were calculated in order to increase credit card fees.

As indicated above, most card issuers assess finance charges on the basis of the average daily balance over a one month period. A number of card issuers, however, have changed to different systems of calculating finance charges that have one thing in common: They yield higher finance charges than the simple average daily balance over the one month system. Many card issuers bill on an odd day of the month so that customers who write checks at the end of the month may be charged a finance charge. Other companies have instituted a two-cycle average daily balance computation. With the two-cycle method, the balance used to calculate finance charges is the sum of the average daily balances for two monthly cycles — the current billing period and the one before. As a result, a person who spends $1,150 in the first month and $200 in the second month, and pays the balance off at the end of the first month finds that the paid-off balance continues to be used in the calculation of finance charges for the following month.

Some issuers in effect have eliminated the one month free interest privilege by imposing finance charges on new purchases from the date they are reported without regard to whether the balance is paid off during the following billing period. Others may impose finance charges from the reporting date on cash advances but continue the days of grace approach for other transactions. Other methods of calculating finance charges are sometimes used. While these differences in the method of calculating finance charges probably do not seem to be large to the average card user and are more an irritant than anything else, the differences from the standpoint of the issuer of thousands of cards may be quite substantial.

Federal regulations require issuers to disclose the type of method used for the calculation of finance charges. Examples are rarely provided, however.

§7.12 BANK DEBIT CARDS AND SECURED CREDIT CARDS

A number of banks now offer "secured" credit cards. Bankrupts and persons who do not qualify for regular credit cards may deposit, say, $500 and be issued a piece of plastic that permits them to "charge" up to that amount. This, of course, is not credit at all. In effect, the bank is lending the customer his or her own money. Secured credit cards are designed for bad credit risks. No interest may be paid on the deposit, and an issuance fee and service charges may be imposed. For example, interest rates may be as high as 22 percent, nonwaivable annual fees of $20 to $75 may be imposed as well as an initial application fee of $65. Many banks permit the substitution of a certificate of deposit paying perhaps 5 percent instead of an noninterestbearing deposit. The justification for these high rates and charges is that the issuer must incur additional costs in monitoring the use of these cards to avoid the inadvertent extension of credit. As a result, the cost of servicing these cards is relatively high and justifies the loading on of expenses despite the absence of any extension of credit. It is, of course, also true that persons who are unable to obtain a regular credit card may be seriously inconvenienced in their day-to-day affairs, and may be willing to pay these expenses in order to have the convenience of a piece of modern plastic.

Another type of card that is superficially quite similar to both a secured credit card and a traditional bank credit card is the so-called "bank debit card." These cards, like the secured credit card, usually do not involve the extension of credit at all. Rather, cards are issued only to persons with demand deposit or immediately available funds on deposit with the issuer. The cardholder's account is immediately and automatically charged with the amount of each purchase as soon as the merchant reports it. These cards may involve short-term extension of credit by the issuer until the account is charged, but essentially there is no credit component with respect to the use of the card. There is no financing charge and, typically, no annual fee for the issuance of the card. The merchant accepting a debit card normally is not aware that a debit card rather than a credit card is being used. Banks have sometimes encouraged the use of debit cards, apparently without a great degree of success, since most customers appear to prefer the traditional credit card even if the cost is somewhat higher.

§7.13 HOME EQUITY LOANS

In 1986, Congress enacted major amendments to the federal income tax statutes. (See generally Chapter 19.) One change eliminated the deductibility of interest on most consumer loans. This change affected various classes of taxpayers quite differently. By and large, it did not affect the middle- or lower-middle-income borrower who did not itemize personal deductions on his or her personal income tax return: That type of borrower generally used only the "standard deduction" (see section 19.13) and did not itemize personal deductions at all. However, it did adversely affect persons who itemized deductions; generally, these are people who owned residential property. The mortgage interest and real estate tax payments due each year in connection with the ownership of a residence remained tax deductible and usually made itemization of personal deductions advantageous. Before the 1986 Act, these taxpayers also were able to deduct the interest paid on loans for a vacation, a new car, a boat, or credit card debt. Indeed the deductibility of the interest on these consumer loans probably increased somewhat the willingness of taxpayers to borrow money for these purposes.

Since most taxpayers affected by the elimination of the deduction for consumer interest were homeowners, the obvious solution for a taxpayer who wished to buy, say, a new automobile on credit and deduct the interest payments after the effective date of the 1986 Act, was to take out a loan using his or her residence as security — a second mortgage — and use the proceeds to buy the automobile. Such a second mortgage was called a home equity loan, and Congress ringed the deductibility of interest on such loans with limitations to avoid revenue loss.

A "home equity loan" is a loan secured by a mortgage on a residence. The proceeds of that loan need not be reinvested in the residence itself but may be used for other purposes. To deduct the interest on a home equity loan used for purposes other than improving the real estate — to buy an automobile, for example — the taxpayer may borrow only an amount equal to the cash invested in the residence (purchase price plus cost of improvements) and cannot deduct interest to the extent the loan is secured by general appreciation in value of the residence. However, this restriction is eliminated for loans for medical or educational purposes. In 1991, the maximum home equity loan for which the interest deduction was allowed was capped at $100,000.

As described in Chapter 9, placing or refinancing a mortgage on a home has traditionally been a rather costly proposition, since it is viewed as a conveyance of real estate and is subject to all the traditional and costly conveyancing requirements for real estate. Home equity loans minimize these costs, particularly if the holder of the first mortgage also is providing the home equity loan. Home equity loans typically involve the creation of a line of credit secured by a lien on the value of the home. The line of credit is arranged in advance up to a specified maximum that is a fraction of the estimated value of the residence reduced by any outstanding first mortgage on the property. Since these are loans secured by a mortgage on real estate, the interest rate charged is significantly lower than that on the other types of consumer loans discussed above (except for margin loans secured by marketable securities). The interest is itself tax deductible if the taxpayer itemizes deductions. See section 19.13. The home equity loan, in short, is generally the best consumer loan around from a cost standpoint for people who own their own residences but who have limited additional resources.

With increased experience, the practices and uses of home equity loans have evolved. There are now two types of home equity loans offered that qualify for favorable income tax treatment:

a) Closed end home equity loans are loans of a fixed sum secured by a second mortgage on the residence at a fixed rate for a fixed term, for example, 15 years at 9.9 percent per year. Traditional real estate closing costs and points may also be charged on such a transaction.

b) Open end second mortgages are revolving credit lines secured by a second mortgage on the residence. One may access this credit line by writing checks drawn on the home equity account. Banks may also issue plastic cards that enable a person to access this credit line much as though it were an ordinary credit card account. Outstanding home equity loans of this type are charged a floating interest rate that is about 2 percent over the prime rate. See section 7.16. Closing costs may be waived entirely or may be imposed when the line of credit is created but at considerably lower rates than applicable to a closed end mortgage. Most home equity loans are of this second variety.

Statistics indicate that the most common use of home equity loans is, in fact, to pay for home improvements. The second most common use is for debt consolidation: 24 percent of closed end loans and 30 percent of home equity credit line loans were used for this purpose in 1990. Undoubtedly, many persons use this new line of credit cautiously for desirable purposes. Nevertheless, there is clearly a substantial use of home equity loans as a substitute for traditional consumer debt. Home equity loans are available at lower rates than credit card or automobile loans and may readily be substituted for them.

Of course, a borrower accustomed to using unsecured credit devices and writing personal checks may not realize that transactions using a home equity loan check or home equity loan credit card actually involve placing or increasing a second mortgage on the borrower's residence. Nonpayment (or even the failure to make prompt payments) may cause the borrower to lose his or her home, or at least, create significant discomfort and insecurity. (See the discussion of foreclosure of second mortgages in section 9.22.) Taking expensive vacation trips with the proceeds of home equity loans may be a recipe for disaster for a family, since the cost of those vacations becomes a lien on the family's residence, which otherwise might be exempt from seizure for nonpayment of unsecured loans.

Home equity loans have had the effect of increasing the long-term debt of American homeowners at the same time that residential values are declining in many areas. Some banks may be holding a first mortgage and a home equity loan on a residence, when the sum of the two exceeds the fair market value of the residence. Further, a home equity loan involves a homeowner in a second payment each month to keep his or her residence. A large home equity loan coupled with the unexpected loss of a job may lead to disaster. Some homeowners may view an unused home equity line of credit as a substitute for temporary cash reserves for medical expenses or for loss of jobs. While this line of credit does provide instant cash, it also creates or increases a second lien on the borrower's residence. Unless the need is truly temporary, the use of the home equity credit line may compound the financial problems faced by the homeowner. For these reasons, concern has been expressed that many families may overuse this inexpensive line of credit without full understanding of the consequences.

One study by a credit counseling service estimated that fully 75 percent of all people who use home equity loans for debt consolidation purposes find themselves twice as indebted within two years. Homeowners simply may not have enough discipline to restrain long held buying habits.

Some unexpected problems also may crop up with home equity loans. For example, usually the husband and wife have equal access to the home equity credit line. When one party plans to separate and seek a divorce, he or she may empty the credit line before announcing the intention to separate and move out, leaving the other party with a major debt to repay. Second, large home equity loans have to be repaid when a house is sold, thereby reducing the free cash that may be used to purchase a more expensive residence. Third, as interest rates drop a homeowner may wish to refinance the first mortgage (see section 9.35); a large home equity second mortgage may complicate this transaction since it will have to be refinanced or folded into the new mortgage when the old one is refinanced.

Despite potential problems of these types, the home equity loan is clearly an attractive credit source for individuals who may take advantage of it — that is, those who own their own homes and who have capital invested in the house in excess of the outstanding mortgages.

§7.14 USURY STATUTES

Most states have usury statutes that purport to limit the maximum legal interest rate to 12 or 14 percent. Because of unusually high interest rates during a period in the early 1980s, many of these statutes were amended to raise the maximum rate significantly or to apply a floating maximum rate that is dependent on some external market rate of interest. As a result, the potential importance of these statutes has diminished with the decline in interest rates.

The maximum interest rate permitted by the usury statutes is significantly lower than the effective interest rates being charged on many consumer loans. In a handful of states the usury statute has created problems for credit card or consumer loans, but in most they have been held inapplicable for two reasons. First, in most states the usury rate is created by statute and may be changed by statute. Small loan companies and pawnshops, for example, operate under special statutes that expressly authorize the charging of high interest rates. It is somewhat ironic that the persons for whom the usury rate was designed — lower- and middle-class citizens — are often able to borrow money only from businesses operating under one of these special statutes that permit interest rates significantly above the statutory usury rate. However, that is often the market reality. Second, the courts in most states have developed a distinction between a "cash sale" and a "credit sale" that permits retailers to avoid usury problems. The cash sale/credit sale distinction allows the seller to establish a higher price for credit sales than for cash sales of the identical goods without the difference being considered interest for purposes of the usury statute. This so-called time-price differential has an element of fiction about it but is widely accepted.

The usury statutes of many states are also expressly made inapplicable to all corporate borrowers or to transactions over a certain size. Other states permit a higher maximum legal interest rate for corporate transactions than for individual transactions. The theory of these provisions is that borrowers in such transactions are inherently commercial entities that can take care of themselves. These exceptions provide a device to avoid the usury statute. A person buying a piece of real estate may do so in his or her own name or may form a wholly owned corporation to do so at only a modestly greater cost. If the proposed interest rate on a loan to finance the purchase of that real estate exceeds the maximum legal rate permitted by the usury statute, the transaction may be cast in corporate form rather than as an individual transaction in order to avoid the usury "problem."

A fair amount of controversy exists about usury statutes. They are clearly well-meaning consumer legislation: That they have the counterproductive effect of making credit unavailable at above-usury levels, but still lower than small loan levels, has been widely suggested. Certainly, if the usury statutes were made broadly applicable to all types of loans, and all loopholes or evasions were eliminated, many persons might be entirely unable to obtain credit legitimately; such persons may be driven to loan sharks or worse to obtain essential loans.

§7.15 THE BEWILDERING VARIETY OF CONSUMER INTEREST RATES

How are consumer interest rates established in the real world? The prior sections reveal a wide variety of interest rates applicable to various types of consumer loans. While consumer interest rates are part of a larger market for consumer and commercial loans, they have some unique characteristics, which are discussed below.

Two major variables determine the level of interest rates generally: One is the general price level in the market for lendable funds, and the other is the risk of nonpayment in the particular type of transaction. In some kinds of loans, other variables become important, such as whether interest income is subject to income taxation at the federal or state levels, or whether proceeds of transactions may be subject to the risk of currency exchange rate fluctuations, but these variables generally have no application to the market for consumer loans. The following two sections discuss these two variables in general terms.

§7.16 THE MARKET FOR LENDABLE FUNDS

There is in the modern American economy a clearly defined market for commercially loanable funds to individuals and enterprises: Interest is the factor that balances the supply and demand for money in this market. Here the commercial banks are the sellers of money, and the individuals and commercial enterprises that borrow funds are the buyers. Consumer loans are thus part of a retail market for money, which can be distinguished from the market where commercial banks obtain funds—a wholesale market. The weathervane interest rate in the retail market is called the "prime rate." That is the rate usually (and not always accurately) defined as the rate large commercial banks charge large borrowers that involves essentially no risk of default. Loans that carry greater risk will be made at higher rates to compensate the lenders for taking that additional risk.

Banks announce publicly the prime rate that they are using in making loans. Competition requires large commercial banks throughout the nation to maintain a largely uniform prime rate; however, the rate often changes, and there may be periods of transition in which some banks quote the old rate while others quote the new. If the demand for funds appears to be increasing, one or more banks may announce a quarter-point or even a half-point increase in the prime rate. If other banks believe the higher rate is supportable by the market for funds, they, too, announce an increase, and the movement becomes nationwide. If other banks do not go along, the innovative banks will probably rescind the increase in order to ensure that their large borrowers do not go elsewhere for funds. A similar pattern appears when the demand for loanable funds appears to be slack and a decline in the prime rate is being considered. At least one major commercial bank uses a formula based on several money market factors to establish a tentative prime rate, but competition may force this bank to adjust its rate.

The federal government plays a major role in the establishment of the prime rate and, thus, the general level of retail interest rates. Acting through the Federal Reserve System, it uses interest rates and the supply of money in commercial banks as devices to fight inflation and unemployment and to encourage a high level of economic activity. (The fact that these may be partially conflicting goals need not detain us.) This control is exercised by the Federal Reserve System through several devices, the most important of which are: (1) open market transactions in federal securities; (2) changes in bank reserve requirements; (3) federal debt management transactions; and (4) the discount rate. These controls work efficiently on state-chartered as well as federally chartered institutions.

A detailed discussion of how reserve requirements, open market transactions, and debt management transactions by the Federal Reserve System indirectly influences the supply of money and the prime rate is beyond the scope of this book. These devices all operate indirectly and somewhat silently by increasing or decreasing the supply of funds banks have available to lend to customers. The fourth, the discount rate, is more visible since it is an interest rate charged by the Federal Reserve System on loans to commercial banks. The discount rate is set by the Federal Reserve System partly on political and partly on economic considerations: Changes in this rate receive as much publicity as changes in the prime rate. The relationship between the discount rate and the prime rate can be most simply visualized as the former being the wholesale rate and the latter being the retail rate for money. This, of course, is from the bank's perspective. The spread between the discount and prime rate is usually about two percentage points. If the Fed raises the discount rate, the prime rate also rises, and if the Fed reduces the discount rate (as it has done dramatically several times during the early 1990s) the prime rate almost always drops also.

The prime rate not only measures the market level of the demand for money but also the rates banks are willing to pay on certificates of deposit and savings accounts — part of the retail supply of lendable funds.

§7.17 RISK CATEGORIES AND CONSUMER INTEREST RATES

One unique aspect of most consumer interest rates is that they appear to be relatively insensitive to changes in the prime rate. Rates for credit card loans and loans by small loan companies or pawnshops are quite "sticky" and stable despite significant changes in the prime rate and discount rate. This has been dramatically demonstrated during the early 1990s as the recession caused the Federal Reserve System repeatedly to reduce the discount rate and increase the supply of lendable funds, thereby causing the prime rate to decline from 9.5 percent to 6 percent — about a one-third decline in the cost of money.

Some consumer interest rates are quite sensitive to changes in rates. Rates for unsecured signature bank loans, margin loans, automobile loans, and home equity loans have declined steadily along with other retail interest rates. For example, an individual with a good credit rating may have sought an unsecured signature loan from a commercial bank for $5,000 five years ago. (A *signature loan* is simply an unsecured loan made solely on the borrower's signature.) At that time the borrower was charged 11 percent interest. Today, the same borrower in the same financial condition is quoted an interest rate of 8 percent for the identical loan. "After all," the friendly banker happily explains, "two years ago the prime rate was 9 percent; today it is 6 percent." This individual is in effect being charged two points over the prime rate.

Illustrative of the "sticky" consumer loan rate is the 1.5 percent per month charge made on credit cards. That rate has remained remarkably stable as the prime rate declined, triggering accusations that banks were "gouging" by refusing to reduce their charges. The usual explanations for the slowness of consumer interest rates to reflect market rate changes are: (1) Risk factors are high in such loans; and (2) credit cards are more than a simple credit device; they also make available costly services to the cardholder.

Loans made by a small loan company are unquestionably more risky than loans made by banks and credit unions. Credit card loans are clearly more risky than home equity loans. These differences in risk help to explain the relative costs of these various types of credit but do not explain why the general level of rates for consumer loans fails to be sensitive to the market level of interest rates for at least the credit component of such transactions.

One point is of central importance to individuals, however. There is a fair degree of self-selection as to which risk category an individual planning to borrow money decides to place himself or herself. An individual may seek a loan from a local bank or credit union or may go down to his friendly credit union or pawnshop. That individual may or may not qualify for a low interest rate signature loan at his local bank, but he should certainly try that source before placing himself in the high risk small loan company market. It is equally irrational for a person with a secure income, who might readily qualify for a home equity loan, to use a credit card as a loan source. Or, put another way, if that individual is unable to pay off the balances on his credit card each month, it would be sensible to borrow the money to do so by activating his home equity loan line of credit. If there is any doubt about the ability of that individual to repay the loan in due course, neither loan should be taken out.

§7.18 EDUCATION LOANS

In 1992, the annual cost of attending a state school was nearly $6,000 per year and the annual cost of a private school was about $20,000 per year. It is the unusual family that can educate two or three children at these costs without extensive borrowing. Some banks offer education loans through second party sponsors, such as Nellie Mae, Inc., and Education Resources Institute. Many companies permit loans from profit sharing or section 401(k) plans for educational costs at favorable terms. Most educational loans, however, are made through government programs.

Among the very best bargains available to consumers today are federally guaranteed educational loans for college and graduate students. For most students, the principal loan source is the "guaranteed student loan," also called a "Stafford loan." In 1993, a student may borrow up to $23,000 over four years and a graduate student may borrow up to $65,000. Interest rates on these loans is the three-month Treasury bill rate plus 3.1 percent, with a 9 percent cap. In 1993, the interest rate is 6.94 percent plus a 5 percent origination fee. If a family's income is below a certain maximum criterion, the interest on this loan is paid by the United States while the borrower is in school; starting six months after graduation, students repay the loans over a five- or ten-year period. If the family income exceeds the maximum criterion, the same amounts may be borrowed, but interest begins to run at the time the loans are made.

For the poorer student, Pell grants are outright financial contributions ranging from $400 to $2,300 per year.

Finally, the PLUS (Parent Loans for Undergraduate Students) parent loan program permits parents to borrow up to the entire annual cost of the student's education (less financial aid) from a bank. Eligibility is based on creditworthiness, not financial need; there is no arbitrary maximum loan limit. The interest rate on a PLUS loan is based on the one-year Treasury bill interest rate plus 3.1 percent, with a 10 percent maximum rate. In 1993, the interest rate is 7.36 percent with a 5 percent origination fee. Payments of interest and principal begin 60 days after the loan is made, though individual banks may permit interest to be deferred during the period the child is in school and to be added to the principal of the loan.

In establishing the expected family contribution that parents are expected to make under federal student loan criteria, the equity in the family home is not taken into account.

It is essential to file the required financial aid form and family financial statement on a timely basis and to apply for Pell grants even if it is reasonably clear that the student is not eligible for that program. The right to participate in these various attractive loan and grant programs is dependent on timely and complete applications; loans are made available only after it has been determined that the student is not eligible for a Pell grant.

8

Automobile Financing and Leasing

§8.1 INTRODUCTION

A few years ago the purchase of an automobile was, for most buyers, a rather straightforward major credit transaction. Some buyers could pay cash for the entire cost of the automobile, but for most individuals an automobile could only be bought on credit, a purchase larger than any other consumer credit transaction except a home. The purchaser selected an automobile and negotiated the price with a salesman who then presented the transaction to his superior for final approval. A cash down payment of about 25 percent was required (or more commonly, the buyer traded in his or her used car as part or all of the down payment). The balance was then financed through the dealer (actually through a captive financing agency owned by the automobile manufacturer) or through a bank, credit union, or other financing agency selected by the purchaser. Automobile loans were for three or four years at competitive consumer interest rates. The lender took a security interest in the car, planning to repossess it if payments were not made regularly. After three or four years, the buyer owned the automobile outright, though it was not uncommon for the purchaser to decide to trade-in the car on yet a newer vehicle before the loan was fully paid off. For many consumers, "car payments" were therefore a permanent part of the budget. From the standpoint of the lender, the principal financial concerns were to ensure that the car was insured against loss and that the resale value ("blue book" value) always exceeded the amount due on the loan.

A major development in the retail automobile industry is the growth of long-term leasing as an alternative to the purchase of new automobiles. For no money down (usually) and monthly payments that are less than the monthly payment due on a 75 percent automobile loan, the lessee may drive away in a brand new, expensive automobile. It seems almost too good to be true.

In 1990, 20 percent of all of General Motors Acceptance Corporation's retail finance transactions involved a lease rather than purchase transaction. In 1989, the corresponding figure was 7 percent. Captive finance companies — GMAC, for example — now finance over 80 percent of all leases written by dealerships. Whether or not leasing is too good to be true, its increasing popularity cannot be questioned.

Both purchases and leases of automobiles are subject to the Truth in Lending Act so that the finance charge and the annual percentage rate of interest on the extension of credit must be disclosed. See section 7.1.

§8.2 THE COMPLEXITIES OF A PURCHASE

Automobile purchases usually involve three important variables: the price of the new vehicle, the value placed on the trade-in, and the cost of financing the difference. Failure to pay attention to any one of these variables may lead to paying too much for what the buyer is getting. Most salesmen are paid on a commission basis, and they quickly become expert in manipulating one or more of these variables. Furthermore, the turnover of salesmen at most automobile agencies is relatively high and the amount of training small. As a result, questionable sales techniques used by automobile salesmen may be passed on by word of mouth and may occur without the knowledge of the dealer. The vocabulary of automobile salesmen indicates the major tactics that the purchaser should be on guard against:

1) *Selling the payments* — focusing discussion on the monthly payments, thereby diverting the shopper's attention from the total price.
2) *Slam dunk* — negotiating an unreasonably high price from an unsophisticated and unsuspecting buyer.
3) *Heavy turnover* — a system of pressuring customers to buy by placing them in a small, windowless salesroom where a succession of salesmen try to wear down the buyer's sales resistance.
4) *Low balling* — the quotation of an unrealistically low price to a comparison shopper; the shopper finds only higher prices elsewhere, but when he or she returns, the salesman reports that the sales manager will not approve the quoted price and negotiates a higher price.

5) *Hull-Dobbs* — obtaining a large cash deposit or the keys of the prospective trade-in and holding them hostage until the buyer agrees to purchase a vehicle on the seller's terms.

6) *Stealing the trade-in* — quoting a low price on the new car but buying the trade-in at an even lower price; the profit on the trade-in more than covers the loss on the sale of the newer vehicle.

7) *The puppy dog* — letting the customer take the newer vehicle home under the belief that only minor details of the deal need to be worked out; when the customer returns happy with the new purchase, the financing costs of the transaction are jacked up as a "detail."

As the "sticker price" of new automobiles has grown, there has been a liberalization of credit terms. It is now routine to offer a four-year loan on a brand new automobile; five-year loans are also offered. These longer term loans create problems: The depreciation of the automobile may exceed the rate of pay-down on the loan, so that the loan is not fully secured. Further, many purchasers desire to trade in an automobile in less than four years; the lower pay-down rate may significantly reduce the value of the used car traditionally used to cover all or most of the down payment on the new car.

Some dealers have broken away from the traditional salesman-on-a-commission method of selling cars. Some have adopted a fixed price, no haggling philosophy; the price on the vehicle is not subject to negotiation. Others hire salesmen on a fixed salary basis or provide that commissions are paid out only over several years. A few dealers are experimenting with a policy of auctioning off traded-in vehicles and the customer receives the difference in cash if the trade-in sells for more than the allowance given by the dealer.

Perhaps one final word should be added: Unfortunately, some automobile salesmen are male chauvinists who view women as incompetent on the aspects of automobile purchases: "Honey, your husband (or boyfriend) will tell you this is a great deal." Not only are such comments personally distasteful but women purchasing a car on their own may sometimes be viewed as easy marks and should generally look at the offered terms extremely carefully.

§8.3 THE BASIC LEASE TRANSACTION

A long-term lease can best be illustrated by an example. In 1989, a potential purchaser can purchase a brand new Range Rover for $37,000. For many persons that is a rather startling figure. To purchase the Range Rover, the buyer would face a down payment of $9,250 (25 percent of the purchase price) and monthly payments of $731.42 on a four-year loan. The salesman, however, can offer an alternative: an irrevocable lease for four years with no money down and payments of "only" $595 per month. There is no option to return the car before the end of the lease term. At the end of four years, the lessee may return the Rover or purchase it for $22,800, the anticipated blue book value of the Range Rover at that time. (Some lease transactions do not have this purchase option; at the end of the lease, the Range Rover must be returned to the dealer.) At first blush, everyone should lease rather than buy, since there is no down payment and the monthly payments are more than $100 per month less. Of course, in the case of the lease, the lessee must pay an additional $22,800 in four years or give up the car; in the case of the credit sale, the buyer owns the Range Rover outright at the end of the four-year term. Nevertheless, for a person with limited financial resources and a taste for new expensive cars, leasing is an attractive, though costly, alternative.

This transaction can readily be analyzed in traditional present value fashion. Each monthly payment of $595 has two components: Part of each payment compensates the leasing company for the loss of the use of the $37,000 purchase price for the Range Rover, and part of it covers the depreciation in the value of the car over the four years of the lease. Presumably, the $22,800 option figure is an accurate estimate of the probable blue book value of the Rover in four years. If so, it is a matter of indifference to the lessor whether or not the option is exercised; if it is not, the Rover will be sold at its blue book value. Hence, from the standpoint of the lessor, it is putting out $37,000 and receiving $595 per month for 48 months plus a single payment of $22,800 at the end of the 48 months. This is a return of about 12 percent per year.

Lease transactions are structured so that they are as riskless as possible. A number of possible problems are anticipated. For example, it is quite possible that the Range Rover might be driven many more miles than contemplated, thus reducing its resale value, or it may be driven over rough terrain, abused, dented, or otherwise damaged with the same consequence. To avoid this risk, lease agreements provide that if the lessee returns the Range Rover at the end of the four-year term, he may owe an additional payment when the car is returned, depending on how much the automobile has been driven and its condition. Obviously, such an obligation is an area of potentially serious disagreement if the option is not exercised and the car is returned. Further, there is the risk that the car might be "totaled" before the 48-month lease period expires. Given the economics of the "no down payment" lease transaction, it is almost certain that the unrecouped investment of the leasing company in the Rover will exceed its insurable valuable for most of the lease period, thus creating a "gap" in protection. To protect its interest, leasing companies require lessees to also purchase "gap insurance" to protect the leasing company from loss in the event the car is "totaled." Such insurance costs several hundred dollars, depending on the value of the car being leased, and reduces somewhat the attractiveness of leasing an expensive vehicle.

The analysis from the standpoint of the lessee is also interesting. For a payment of $595 per month, he or she gets the use for four years of an automobile originally worth $37,000. Assuming that the lessee does not plan to exercise the option, this is analogous to a straight loan of $37,000 for five years at an interest rate of about 19 percent per year — about the cost of a credit card loan. However, this is deceptive since the actual value of what is being leased declines steadily in value over the term of the lease.

The monthly payment in the lease transaction is so relatively low compared to the outright purchase alternative because there is no amortization of the loan during this period. The entire $595 monthly payment represents "interest" in this calculation. From the standpoint of the lessor, however, this payment is viewed as consisting of two components: Part of the payment constitutes interest on the purchase price of the Range Rover, and part of it covers the depreciation in the value of the car during the term of the lease.

If the lessee enters into the lease planning to exercise the option to purchase the car for $22,800 in four years, he or she is considerably better off by buying the car at the outset and financing the purchase in a conventional manner even though a down payment has to be made, and the payments on the automobile loan are higher than the rental payments under the lease. If the lessee planned to acquire a new car at the end of four years regardless of whether she bought or leased, however, leasing may be more attractive than buying. In part, this is because the lessee has the use of the down payment that would be required in a purchase transaction. In part, also, it is due to the fact that the buyer, if she buys the car outright, incurs the loss of the value of the car when she resells it after four years.

A lease agreement for a new automobile is negotiable in somewhat the same way that a purchase of a new car is negotiable within a limited range. More and more lease agreements require an up-front payment of several hundred dollars, which may be described as "capitalized cost reduction," or a commitment fee. These are thinly disguised payments of advance interest at the commencement of the lease that permit lower advertised monthly payments. Such payments reduce the attractiveness of the lease transaction and may sometimes be negotiated around. Such advance payments should be particularly avoided, if possible, if one expects to return the vehicle at the end of the lease term.

The monthly lease payment is a function of three major variables: interest rates, the purchase price used by the leasing company to calculate payments, and the predicted value of the car at the end of the leasing period. The higher this latter value is, the lower are the monthly lease payments. A sophisticated lessee may sometimes negotiate the last two variables in order to reduce the amount of the monthly payments. The terms under which further payments may be due upon the expiration of the lease also may sometimes be negotiated in part in advance.

§8.4 COMPARISON OF LEASING AND PURCHASING

The advantages of leasing are illustrated by Table 8-1, which compares the purchase and lease of a 1992 Mercedes 300SE ($55,000 list price) and a 1992 Honda Accord LX (price $15,000). The loan payments are calculated after a down payment of $5,500 on the Mercedes and $1,600 on the Honda.

Table 8-1
Automobile Purchase and Lease Transactions Compared

Term	Lease Payment	Loan Payment
The Mercedes		
2 years	$1,275.59	$2,307.09
3 years	$1,034.11	$1,620.57
4 years	$907.84	$1,076.25
5 years	$827.66	$1,076.25
The Honda		
2 years	$357.73	$671.15
3 years	$307.57	$471.44
4 years	$276.92	$372.18
5 years	$254.50	$313.09

Examining these transactions and given the uncertainties as to what will happen over the next five years, one may well ask why should anyone today pay down $5,500 in cash and then pay $1,076 each month for 60 months when the same car can be driven for five years with no down payment and a monthly payment of $827.66?

§8.5 OTHER ADVANTAGES OF LEASING TRANSACTIONS

One of the major advantages of leasing, from the standpoint of the dealer, is that it encourages consumer loyalty. More than 80 percent of leasing customers return to the same dealership for another vehicle as compared to about 34 percent for outright sale transactions. In addition, the lower monthly payment distracts attention from the sticker price of new vehicles, now averaging about $16,000 per vehicle, sold by dealers and avoids rebates and incentives that have cut into profits of dealers and manufacturers.

The major problem with the leasing alternative, from the standpoint of the dealer, remains the accurate assessment of trade in value when the car is originally sold and the lease terms established. The major source of losses by lessors on automobile leases has been the result of overestimates of the value of the car at the expiration of the lease term.

Nevertheless, the automobile lease appears to offer major advantages to both the dealer and to the purchaser who has a taste for expensive automobiles. It therefore appears to be a permanent addition to the economic scene.

9
Residential Real Estate

PART I.   THE PURCHASE OF REAL ESTATE

§9.1   INTRODUCTION

This chapter focuses on residential real estate transactions, including negotiating the contract to purchase, financing the purchase, title assurance,
and conveyancing.

The purchase of a home is the largest single commercial transaction
ever made by most persons. In almost every instance, the purchase requires
borrowing most of the purchase price; this loan is universally secured by a
mortgage on the property being acquired. Payments on this debt are usually
the largest single component of the average homeowner's monthly budget.

Part I of this chapter focuses on the transaction itself: the purchase
of real estate. It discusses the financial limitations faced by most families
when deciding to purchase a residence. It also generally discusses the roles,
perspectives, and objectives of modern facilitators of traditional real estate
transactions: brokers, title assurers, lending institutions, and others. The
basic pattern of residential real estate conveyancing — a two-step transaction consisting of the execution of a contract of sale followed at a later
time by a formal closing of the transaction — is typical of most important
commercial transactions. An understanding of this basic structure is therefore necessary for every person who hopes to participate in substantial
commercial transactions.

Part II discusses modern financing instruments used in real estate
transactions. A person planning to purchase residential real estate faces a
bewildering array of alternative mortgage instruments: The two basic types
are conventional real estate mortgages and adjustable rate mortgages. However, most real estate lenders offer a variety of options of each type, at
varying interest rates, varying "points" charged at closing, varying time
periods for repayment, and in some instances, alternative amortization
schedules.

Part II also discusses the consequences of a default on a mortgage. In the 1990s, consumer bankruptcy has risen to an all time high. Many of these bankruptcy proceedings involve real estate mortgages and possible foreclosure on them, causing the loss of the family's residence.

Part III discusses innovative financing techniques that developed during the 1970s and 1980s (a period of high mortgage interest rates and inflation of real estate values). In this economic scene, purchasers naturally desire to assume outstanding low interest rate mortgages; this in turn leads to the practice of conveying real estate subject to outstanding encumbrances, and reliance on due-on-sale clauses by lenders to compel purchasers to refinance the purchase. It also leads to seller-financed transactions.

Part IV discusses financing techniques during the 1990s, when economic conditions have changed dramatically since the 1980s. The inflation in real estate values of the 1970s and 1980s appears to have been replaced by stable or declining prices, interest rates have declined by approximately 50 percent from their peak in the previous decade, and higher standards for qualification for real estate loans have been imposed on lending institutions. Since 1986, many areas of the country have even seen substantial declines in real estate values. For the first time, large numbers of persons who purchased real estate at relatively high prices, with the firm belief that prices were sure to go even higher, have had to deal with the unexpected problem of mortgages and real estate liens that are larger than the current value of the underlying real estate that is the security for the loan. Defaults and foreclosures have soared, and many financing institutions have collapsed, in part because of "bad" real estate loans. Further, concerns about job security in this period have made many potential purchasers of real estate reluctant to make long-term financial commitments. Seller-financed transactions, therefore, reappear during this period for quite different reasons than during the 1970s and 1980s. These problems are the final topic discussed in this chapter.

§9.2 CONTRACTS FOR DEED AND OTHER DEVICES FOR TRANSFERRING TITLE TO REAL ESTATE

This chapter concentrates on the traditional residential real estate transaction in which title passes immediately to the purchaser (subject to a mortgage to a commercial lender) at the closing of the transaction. The conveyance is typically by warranty deed. (If you do not know what a warranty deed is, see section 9.16.)

In many states there exists an alternative method of conveyancing—an installment sales contract, or "contract for deed," as it is often called. In this type of transaction, the buyer enters into a contract agreeing to make specified payments over a period of years in return for which he or she is entitled to immediate possession and use of the property. However, title to the property is conveyed to the purchaser only after the last required payment is made. Often used for low income and speculative resort properties, the contract for deed transaction has its own problems and peculiarities, which are often considered in real property or conveyancing courses. They are not discussed further here.

In a few areas of the United States, conveyancing transactions may take the form of long term ground leases rather than outright conveyances of title to real estate. Ground lease conveyancing is also common in England. Also sometimes considered in real property or conveyancing courses, these types of conveyances are also not discussed further here.

§9.3 SOURCES OF FUNDS FOR ACQUIRING RESIDENTIAL REAL ESTATE

Relatively few persons or families buying a home or personal residence today have the necessary capital to purchase their home with cash. As used in this chapter, "home" or "personal residence" includes cooperative apartments and condominiums as well as traditional urban, suburban, or rural residential real estate. A home is the largest single purchase ever made by most persons; a purchaser typically has difficulty scraping up the minimum down payment required by a lender, let alone paying the entire purchase price in cash. As a result, most of the purchase price of a residence is almost always borrowed.

Unlike commercial real estate, residential real estate does not have a cash flow from which payments on loans may be made in the future. Rather, the payments typically must come from the future earnings of the owners of the real estate. As a result, eligibility for a residential real estate loan is largely based on the earning capacity of the purchasers. Rules of thumb to determine how large a mortgage a specific income will support are discussed in section 9.6. In the event of default, attempts to collect a judgment from financially troubled families are not likely to be successful or cost-justifiable since, if the mortgage is in default, the family has probably already exhausted its financial resources. As a result, relatively large down payments are usually required for residential property, because the lender is necessarily relying primarily on the resale value of the property being purchased as security for its loan and desires to have a cushion between the amount of the loan and the value of the property securing it.

§9.4 THE DOWN PAYMENT

The minimum down payment actually required for a loan to purchase residential property varies with the type of lender and the economic conditions at the time of the transaction, but the amount required is relatively standardized. The percentage of the purchase price required to be paid at the closing depends in part on the source of the loan. There are two traditional sources for residential real estate financing: (1) conventional loans made by savings and loan associations, commercial banks, and other types of organizations, and (2) government guaranteed loans (usually guaranteed by the Veterans' Administration (VA) or the Federal Housing Administration (FHA)).

The terms of conventional loans are largely dictated by market forces, but the down payment required is traditionally 20 percent of the purchase price: In some circumstances lenders may accept a somewhat smaller down payment, perhaps 15 percent or even less. If private mortgage insurance is available, lenders accept an even lower down payment — sometimes as low as 5 or 10 percent — but the purchaser then has to pay a monthly insurance premium for the duration of the mortgage. Private mortgage insurance is written by a handful of insurance companies and obligates the insurance company to pay the loan in the event the borrower defaults. Mortgage insurance is available only for families with relatively high and secure income.

In concrete terms, in 1992, the median house price in the United States was $103,600. The purchase of this house required a down payment of about $23,000. The median family income in 1992 was about $36,900, more than enough to qualify for a loan of about $80,000 at the then average mortgage rate of 8.46 percent under the rules of thumb discussed in section 9.6. Doubtless, for most families at or close to the median, raising a down payment of this magnitude is extremely difficult. Sources include gifts from relatives, savings, inheritances, the proceeds of sale of prior residences, and, in some cases, loans from other sources. (It should be added that if a portion of the down payment is borrowed through a commercial second mortgage or from a short-term commercial lender on an unsecured basis, the risk of default by the purchaser is greatly increased, since the purchaser now has two loans to deal with. A second mortgage may disqualify the purchaser from a maximum 80 percent first mortgage.)

Some lenders have programs designed to assist the first-time homebuyer. One such program called "Parent Power," for example, provides 100 percent financing (i.e., no down payment is required and the mortgage covers the entire cost of the property) if a relative (a parent, grandparent, aunt, or uncle) puts up collateral valued at more than 30 percent of the purchase price of the home. If the purchaser defaults, the relative is liable only for the 30 percent. The collateral may be made available by depositing marketable securities with the lender or by placing a home equity loan on the relative's residence. There is a one-time application fee of $300 for a "Parent Power" loan, and an annual fee equal to 2 percent of the guaranteed amount is added to the monthly payments of the borrower. These arrangements are relatively new; inquiry should be made to banks and other financial institutions to determine whether they offer similar programs.

A large down payment may also be avoided if the borrower and the purchase qualify for a VA or FHA loan. The terms of VA and FHA loans are largely circumscribed by federal regulation: They typically are available only for smaller or less expensive properties and the down payment required is 10 percent or less. Eligibility may be restricted to specific classes of persons, and in the past many persons qualified for 100 percent loans under these programs. In other words, there was no down payment required at all. Because of the governmental guarantee of payment, the lender does not have the same concern about having a cushion as it does with mortgages that are not guaranteed.

In addition to the down payment, the purchaser must be prepared to meet a variety of additional costs, called closing costs, which may easily add several thousand dollars to the amount of cash that is required "up front." These costs may include points, an interest-related concept that is discussed in section 9.13.

A person buying a residence may have liquid funds (available from a modest inheritance, for example) in excess of the required 20 percent of the purchase price. If such a purchaser is concerned whether her income can comfortably support the monthly payments required by the mortgage, she may reduce the size of the mortgage by increasing the down payment, thereby reducing future monthly payments and the total interest cost of the loan needed to finance the purchase of the residence. This strategy may appear attractive during periods of concern about job security and future income, but to the extent such concerns are justified, it is usually more sensible to retain the flexibility of having liquid resources than to have a lower down payment. In other words, a person who has concern about future job security should probably opt for a lower down payment rather than a larger one. Indeed, it may be more sensible for such a person to defer the real estate purchase entirely until economic conditions improve or the potential purchaser's personal situation has been clarified.

Even in the rare case in which a person has the capital necessary to purchase a residence outright and has no concern about the stability of her future income, she often prefers for personal reasons to borrow a substantial part of the purchase price. For one thing, it is important for every individual to retain readily available funds for emergencies, and capital invested in a home certainly cannot be obtained quickly. In a word, capital invested in a residence traditionally is illiquid. The development of home equity loans (see section 7.13) during the last decade has changed this attitude to some extent since a home equity loan may be accessed (up to the maximum amount authorized by the lender) as readily as a line of credit under a credit card. The availability of home equity loans may make persons more willing to use available liquid capital to increase the size of down payments than they have been in the past.

In addition, a person with substantial capital is usually interested in diversifying his or her investments; diversification is simply another word for the common sense principle of not putting all one's financial eggs in one basket. See Chapter 13. Putting a large amount of capital into a residence usually decreases diversification, though in the case of extremely wealthy individuals, this decrease may not be viewed as serious. Finally, the purchaser may prefer to borrow most of the purchase price of the residence to leave his or her capital free for speculation or commercial investment. A loan secured by residential real estate may be on more attractive terms than the purchaser could obtain if he or she were to invest capital in a residence and then borrow funds for outside investments through normal commercial channels. Since interest rates on mortgages are relatively high in contrast with most riskless short-term investments (see Chapter 16), however, persons would be better off (contingency and diversification concerns aside) investing the capital in the mortgage rather than in conservative, cash equivalent investments.

Of course, the purchase of a residence is also an investment. Most persons and families own several homes at one time or another during their lifetimes, usually selling one home in order to provide the down payment (and usually part of the purchase price) for the next one. In the past, there has been a general inflation of residential real estate values in many areas, so that people usually profited from buying a residence, living in it a few years, and then selling it in order to buy a new one. In some cases, individuals may have profited so substantially from this speculation in residential real estate that the sales price for the old residence will buy the new one without significant additional financing. The federal income tax law encourages this practice since it permits a person who sells his or her principal residence and invests the proceeds in a new principal residence within two years to "roll over" the proceeds without paying tax on the gain on the sale of the old residence to the extent that the cost of the new residence equals or exceeds the sales price of the old. In addition, gain of up to $125,000 on residential real estate is exempt on a one-time basis by a person over 55 years old. Much of this exempt gain may arise from earlier "rollovers" in which no gain was recognized.

In many areas of the United States, the pattern of steadily increasing residential real estate values appears to have ended and residential real estate prices have stabilized or even begun to decline. Thus, for many persons, the possibility of "trading up" by taking advantage of automatic appreciation of real estate values for down payments has ended, at least in the early 1990s.

§9.5 HOW MUCH IS A RESIDENCE WORTH?

A person thinking about the purchase or sale of residential real estate has to resolve the question of how much the residence is worth. If a purchaser, what is the maximum amount she is willing to pay for the residence, or if a seller, what is the minimum amount she is willing to accept for the residence?

Of course, the owner of residential real estate is familiar with the property — its advantages, its idiosyncrasies, and its defects — and usually has some idea as to its value. When the property is put up for sale, the owner must set an asking price on that property. That price, however, is not a reliable indication of what the owner is willing to accept, because owners often put inflated and unrealistic asking prices on their properties. Since it is quite common for some negotiation over price to occur in connection with residential real estate, a slightly inflated price may be justified in the owner's mind as providing some room to negotiate while keeping the price within an acceptable range. Not all sellers use this tactic, however. Some simply set what they view to be a realistic or acceptable price and refuse to negotiate at all. As a result, an asking price is not a reliable indication of value or even of what the seller thinks the value is.

A second source of information is the appraised value of the residence for local real estate taxation purposes. Most taxing authorities maintain appraisal offices that are skilled at estimating values of properties within their jurisdictions. Their valuations usually may be obtained simply by a telephone call. The usefulness of this information is limited, however. For one thing, tax appraisals are often not current; they may be redetermined once every few years (or even less frequently) with some kind of automatic adjustment made in the intervening years. More seriously, however, many jurisdictions do not appraise properties for tax purposes at 100 percent of market value. Assessments may be generally set at two-thirds, one-half, or some smaller fraction of estimated value. In the absence of specific knowledge about the practices followed by the local assessment office, these tax valuations should not be viewed as reliable indicators of value.

The most reliable method of estimating value is to employ an independent appraiser who is skilled in the techniques of appraising market values and is familiar with properties in the community. There is no central list of qualified appraisers; indeed, most real estate brokers feel they are qualified to estimate the market value of specific homes. Federal law requires appraisers of property with a value of more than $100,000 to be certified if the appraisal is to be submitted as part of a loan application to a federally insured institution. There is not, however, any generally accepted certifying organization. Nevertheless, appraisals of real estate are usually uncomplicated, and a ball park figure usually suffices for the purpose of setting an asking price on a piece of property.

How does an experienced appraiser estimate the value of residential property? The most widely used method estimates the market value of the residence based upon recent sales of similar nearby properties — comparables, as they are usually called. This comparison is obviously best suited to appraising homes that are substantially similar to other homes in the immediate neighborhood and is less reliable for residences that are unique. Examination of sale prices of other homes will create a range of prices and terms. The appraiser must then adjust these figures, either up or down, to take into account the specific residence's features and deficiencies. It is at this point that the appraiser's judgment and skill are most important.

Another method of appraisal involves an estimate of the replacement cost of the residence. Appraisers estimating the replacement cost of a residence usually rely on appraisal handbooks that give current construction costs for various materials; this approach often involves long and complicated calculations. Replacement cost may be relied upon as the principal method of valuation if the property is unique and there are no comparable properties for which independent sales data are available. Replacement cost also is widely used for fire and casualty insurance purposes.

Finally, the appraiser may consider the sales history of the property in question. If the present owner purchased the property in the recent past, the price he or she paid may be indicative of its current value. This information, however, may not always be easy to obtain. Further, it is always possible that the present owner obtained the property at a bargain price, or made substantial repairs or improvements, or that recent market trends show that the historical price is no longer an accurate estimate of current value. As a result, most appraisers place less weight on historical data than on recent sales of similar properties in the community.

If a property has been on the market for several months or years at a specified price but has not sold in an active real estate market, that is a quite reliable indication that the market value of the residence is less than the asking price.

In making a formal appraisal, a skilled appraiser may estimate value on more than one basis and then compare values obtained by using different approaches. In some cases, the appraiser may average the values obtained by these different methods, but a more accepted practice is to select a value that appears to be representative and ignore other approaches that lead to divergent values.

§9.6 HOW MUCH CAN I AFFORD TO PAY?

The two variables that determine how expensive a house a specific person or family can afford are: (1) the amount of the down payment the person or family can, or is willing, to make; and (2) the size of the loan that a lender will make based on its expected income. Where a family has two or more wage earners, the combined incomes are ordinarily considered for loan eligibility purposes unless circumstances indicate that one wage earner is likely thereafter to drop out of the labor force. Lenders have rules of thumb that provide a variety of different guides for the benefit (or sorrow) of potential home purchasers. It must also be recognized that these are only guides, and that lenders are often flexible in granting loans in close cases, depending on the demand for real estate loans. Often a lender will decline to make a specific loan on a specific property at the requested interest rate but will offer to make the loan at a somewhat higher rate to compensate for the perceived increased riskiness of the loan. Regrettably, there are many documented instances of different standards being applied based on the location of the specific property in question or on the ethnicity of the applicants. A white family with several minor "problems" in their credit report might be given a mortgage, while a black family with similar income and similar minor credit report problems might be rejected. While these patterns appear to becoming less common, there is still a broad, gray area in the granting of mortgage loans, and an applicant rejected by one mortgage lender may be accepted by another.

Assuming a 20 percent down payment and a conventional loan at 10 percent interest, a widely followed rule is that the purchase price should not exceed two and one-half times the family's gross income. (How the monthly mortgage payments on a conventional loan of a specified size are determined is the subject of sections 9.18 and 9.19.) A somewhat different rule is that the monthly mortgage payments for principal and interest should not exceed 25 percent of the family's take-home pay. Under these rules of thumb, a family with a median income of $36,900 in 1992 has sufficient income to purchase a house selling for about $103,600, the median price of a residence in that year.

Another commonly used "rule" is that aggregate monthly housing costs should not exceed 40 percent of take-home pay, though many families have demonstrated that one can survive a much higher percentage — over 50 percent — if there are no unexpected emergencies. In comparing these various rules it should be noted (a) that aggregate monthly housing costs are significantly greater than the payments of principal and interest on a mortgage (the major additional items are taxes, insurance, and repairs), and (b) that take-home pay is significantly smaller than gross earnings. Of particular importance in these calculations is appreciation of the difference between PI and PITI payments discussed in section 9.19.

These rules of thumb were developed during a period when all mortgages involved level payments for the life of the mortgage. They proceed on the assumption that the purchaser's income will also remain level for the period of the mortgage. As discussed in section 9.25, many modern mortgages are adjustable rate, and the monthly payments are tied to interest rates so that they may increase or decrease during the life of the mortgage. Nevertheless, rules of thumb based on level rate mortgages are routinely applied to adjustable-rate mortgages. A person who can show a steady growth in earning power may be able to persuade a lender to make a larger loan than the rules of thumb might indicate by arguing that his or her income growth is likely to continue. Correspondingly, a lender may be reluctant to make a loan to persons employed in businesses in which lay-offs are occurring or are threatened, or to use both a husband's and wife's income in the calculation of mortgage eligibility when it is likely that one of them will drop out of the labor force in the near future.

Of course, the larger the down payment a family can make, the lower the anticipated mortgage payment, and other things being equal, the more expensive the residence that can be acquired.

§9.7 THE STRUCTURE OF A REAL ESTATE PURCHASE

The purchase of real estate is usually a two-step process that resembles most substantial commercial transactions. The first step is the execution of a contract of sale, setting forth the terms of the transaction. There then follows a period, often lasting a month or more, during which each party prepares to perform his or her obligations under the contract. Usually the most important responsibility of the purchaser during this period is arranging the necessary financing; another important matter (which may be the responsibility of either the purchaser or the seller, depending on the conventions followed by local realtors) is establishing that the seller has marketable title satisfactory to the purchaser. Marketable title is a title that a reasonable attorney in the community should accept. The second step is the closing, at which the formal steps required to complete the transaction take place. Of course, upon the execution of the contract the parties are legally bound to complete the transaction; the closing occurs when legal title to the property is conveyed to the purchaser.

The two-step transaction described above is the pattern for virtually all significant commercial transactions, whether it involves the sale of a business, the purchase of an automobile, or the purchase or sale of securities. This same pattern occurs when the purchaser has an "option" and is not committed to complete the purchase; after the formal exercise of the option, a closing is scheduled at the mutual convenience of the parties.

§9.8 THE ROLE OF REAL ESTATE BROKERS

Most purchases and sales of residential real estate involve real estate brokers. Often, neither the purchaser nor the seller of residential real estate are skilled at such large financial transactions. In addition, they often lack the services of a lawyer. Real estate brokers routinely guide such persons through the intricacies of buying and selling properties. In contrast, purchasers and sellers of commercial real estate typically have considerably greater sophistication, are accustomed to dealing with lawyers, and may deal directly with each other, thereby limiting the role of the brokers.

The first question that an owner of real estate who wishes to sell must face is whether to list the property with a broker or seek a purchaser directly. A broker is, of course, a professional in selling real estate; the major disadvantage of using a broker is the cost of his or her commission, which typically runs 5 or 6 percent of the aggregate selling price, and in the case of unusual or difficult properties may run higher. This commission, it is important to emphasize, is payable independently of the amount of effort exerted by the broker and is computed on the aggregate selling price, not on the amount of cash that changes hands: On a $120,000 property for which the purchaser is to pay $20,000 in cash and assume an existing $100,000 mortgage, the commission is, nevertheless, $6,000 or $7,200, exactly the same as if the purchaser were paying all cash for the property. It is usually not possible to negotiate with a broker over the amount of the commission, at least with respect to the average residential property, since the broker usually states firmly that the demanded commission is standard in the community and refuses to consider any change in the commission rate.

Many owners of residential property, at least initially, seek to sell their properties on their own to avoid the cost of the broker's commission. They may advertise in local newspapers and place signs on the property. This is often unsuccessful because the seller may be unfamiliar with the real estate market and set an unrealistic price on the property, even without a commission. Also, most brokers refuse to show unlisted properties to potential purchasers, and many potential purchasers immediately contact a real estate broker rather than trying first to find a suitable unlisted property. Many properties initially offered "for sale by owner" (a phrase that implies that no brokerage commission is involved) are later listed with a broker.

Properties listed for sale with a real estate broker are referred to as "listings." Most brokers refuse to accept listings unless they are given an "exclusive" for at least a limited period of time. The wording of exclusive clauses varies, but usually the seller's broker is entitled to a commission if (a) the property is sold to anyone during the period of the exclusive, or (b) is sold at any time to a person who was shown the property by the broker during the period of the exclusive. Real estate brokers in most communities have a "multiple listing service," that is, a centralized system that gives participating brokers access to all (or most) current listings that have been placed with all other participating brokers. In most communities, brokers also have systems by which participating brokers can obtain access to keys for the property so that it may be shown in the absence of the owner and the broker for the seller.

A potential purchaser usually consults a broker to help him or her locate a suitable property. This broker could be, by chance, the same broker that has the original listing, but usually it is not. If different brokers are involved in a successful transaction, they will share the commission on some predetermined basis that may vary over time, depending on the market for real estate in the community. The division may be 50/50, or two-thirds/one-third, or on some other basis. The brokers' commissions are typically paid solely by the seller out of the proceeds of the sale: The purchaser may not be aware that the very helpful broker showing him or her around, seemingly out of graciousness, is viewed as a subagent of the seller, owing a fiduciary to the seller but not to the buyer. This may come as a shock to the potential buyer, who may actually and erroneously rely fully on the broker, disclosing price strategies and plans. It should be obvious, however, that the broker, who shows a potential buyer around, is motivated at least partially by the fact that he or she will receive a portion of a substantial commission payable by the seller upon the purchase of a residence shown by the broker. In many cities, firms of avowedly "buyer's brokers" who represent only the buyer and expressly do not represent the seller have appeared since 1980, and if they prove to give value, it is possible that a gradual change may take place in traditional real estate brokerage relationships. Some traditional brokers, however, have resisted sharing commissions with "buyer's brokers."

One study showed that less than one-third of potential buyers realize that the broker they are dealing with, and relying on, owe fiduciary duties to the seller. Depending on the circumstances, of course, the buyer's broker might also assume fiduciary duties to the buyer, placing himself or herself in a potentially conflicting situation.

Everyone familiar with the real estate industry has heard stories of brokers who earned full commissions on the basis of practically no effort. The broker accepts the listing one morning; that afternoon, the telephone rings, and it is a person dying to purchase the just-listed property. If the sale goes through, the broker will have earned perhaps a $7,200 commission for two telephone calls. One must balance stories about such windfalls with stories about the broker who conducts an open house every weekend for six months, advertises the property in the newspaper, and takes unusual steps to try to sell a specific property. Also, a broker assisting a purchaser may show a potential purchaser 50 different houses and then fail to earn even a partial commission when the purchasers stumble upon the perfect house on their own. The hard luck stories are probably more common than the windfalls: One does not hear of real estate brokers retiring rich after a few years of sales efforts.

§9.9 NEGOTIATION OF THE CONTRACT OF SALE

After locating a suitable property, the potential purchaser makes a bid, or offer, on the property. This usually takes the form of a proposed contract of sale, which is usually prepared by the purchaser's broker (on a standard form contract that is typically more favorable to the broker than to either the purchaser or the seller), setting forth the terms on which the purchaser hopes to purchase the property. This contract covers the basic terms of the sale — the price, the terms of financing hoped to be obtained, the time when possession is to be transferred, what personal property is included in the sale, and so forth. Many unsophisticated purchasers may not appreciate the potential binding effect that this document has on their rights in connection with the proposed purchase, for if the seller simply accepts the proposed contract, the purchaser is bound in accordance with its terms. Because this initial document is so important, a lawyer should examine it on behalf of the purchaser before it is submitted, but brokers usually do not suggest this, and the purchaser may not be sophisticated enough to insist on it. In any event, it is quite common for real estate brokers to draft contract language for offers to be made by potential purchasers.

After the proposed contract of sale is completed with the assistance of the purchaser's broker, it is signed by the potential purchasers, delivered by the purchaser's broker to the seller's broker, and then presented by the seller's broker to the seller. A nominal down payment, or "earnest money" payment, in the form of a check is attached to the document. A typical down payment on a $120,000 transaction might be as low as $1,000 or $2,000. It is not uncommon for contracts to provide that if the offer is accepted, the buyer will increase the earnest money to at least cover the brokers' commission (in the above example that would be $6,000, assuming a 5 percent commission). The earnest money is usually held "in escrow" until the transaction closes and is not turned over to the seller. Escrows are discussed in section 9.11.

Brokers usually prefer to act as intermediaries between the potential purchaser and seller throughout the negotiation rather than to allow them to negotiate directly. (The brokers' expressed concern is that a direct confrontation may lead to a breakdown in the negotiations. There may also be concern that, if there is direct negotiation, the purchaser and seller will get along too well and may try to work out a private deal that does not include the brokers' commission.) The seller may make a counteroffer by changing the terms of the contract of sale, perhaps by increasing the price or by requiring the buyer to increase the size of the down payment upon acceptance, and the revised form of contract is returned to the purchaser's broker, who then presents this counteroffer to the purchaser. In the process, the brokers tend to act as facilitators of the sale, urging the seller to come down and the purchaser to go up, rather than as true agents or representatives of one party or the other.

If the purchaser is represented by an attorney, the attorney prepares a formal contract of sale that is usually not based on the standardized contract used by real estate brokers. A contract prepared by the purchaser's attorney doubtless represents the purchaser's interests more effectively than does the standard brokers' contract.

§9.10 WARRANTIES AND CONDITIONS

A person who is planning to purchase a used home should not assume that appliances work, that the roof is free of leaks, that there is no termite infestation, and so forth. These matters are usually the subject of warranty or condition. A warranty is simply a promise by the present owner that certain things are true; warranties generally must be expressly set forth in the contract of sale if they are to be enforced. More commonly, the owner does not want to make warranties since he or she wants to be entirely free of responsibility for the old residence when the sale closes. Then the purchaser must rely on personal investigation or the investigation of experts he or she hires. To assure that the purchaser can back out if it turns out, for example, that an expensive new roof is needed, the contract must set forth, as a condition to closing, that the purchaser has received a certificate from a qualified roofer that the roof is sound and free of leaks. A condition differs basically from a warranty: A warranty is in effect a promise by the seller to fix matters if they are not as represented, while a condition in effect states, "you may back out if your expert determines that something is wrong, but you are relying on him, and not on me, to fix matters." The purchaser, of course, must arrange for the roofer to come out and make an examination of the roof at the purchaser's expense.

In some instances, a seller may be so anxious to complete the sale that he will say things that he knows to be untrue; if the statements are factual and material, the buyer may have grounds to rescind or seek damages because of fraud, even though the statements were not made in writing.

In some areas of the country the problem of termite or pest infestation is so serious that standard forms assume that a certificate from a qualified exterminator will routinely be provided as a cost of settlement.

Buyers of new homes often are encouraged to purchase home warranty insurance to guard against shoddy construction. This insurance has grown in popularity during the extended weak market in construction which has placed pressures on developers to cut corners. As many as 90 percent of new homeowners purchase such policies, which cost several hundred dollars and provide insurance against defects for as long as ten years.

The fine print of home warranty insurance should be examined carefully because the policies often do not extend as far as homeowners may orally be led to believe. Also, policies usually require all disputes to be resolved through arbitration. However, this insurance may provide valuable peace of mind protection to the purchaser.

§9.11 THE CLOSING

The second step of the process is the closing, which occurs when the title has been examined and the necessary financing arranged. Subsequent sections of this chapter outline some aspects of these intermediate steps. The contract of sale generally contains a time period during which the closing is to occur, but, in practice, the time is usually set by the availability of the financing commitment and the convenience of the parties.

The closing may also be referred to as the "settlement" of the transaction. Many aspects of the settlement process for real estate transactions are governed by the federal Real Estate Settlement Procedures Act (RESPA), enacted in 1974. RESPA also governs many aspects of mortgage loans, insurance and tax escrows, and the like. RESPA was enacted to make significant reforms in the settlement process and to curb abusive practices in connection with the sale and financing of residential real estate.

The closing usually occurs at the offices of an attorney, or the title company, or the lender. When a closing takes place in the office of a title company or lender, an officer or employee of the title company or lender usually acts as the closing officer. In an attorney's office, the attorney is the closing officer. It is at this point that the formal deeds, promissory notes, mortgages, etc. are executed, the cash to be paid by the purchaser, and the loan to be made by the new lender are paid in, and all the necessary documents to effect a transfer of title to real estate are executed. All checks are usually made payable to the closing officer or to the company he or she represents. All the documents are executed and left along with the checks in escrow with the closing officer. "Escrow" is a fancy word that describes the status of documents (and money) that have been delivered to a disinterested third person (here the closing officer) with instructions to deliver documents and disburse funds to specified persons only upon the occurrence of specified conditions or events. Escrow is a convenient device for any type of closing transaction that requires a series of steps to be taken in a specific sequence, yet virtually instantaneously.

Pursuant to the escrow instructions, the closing officer first makes sure that all checks have cleared and the funds deposited in a special trust account. He or she then records in the local land records in the proper sequence the release of the old mortgage, the new deed, and the new mortgage executed by the buyers. Funds are then disbursed to the various parties in accordance with the agreed upon settlement sheet, and the recorded documents are delivered to the persons entitled to them: The promissory note originally executed by the sellers is marked "paid" and delivered to them. This disbursement of funds and delivery of documents takes place a few days after the closing. The seller receives the portion of the purchase price to which he or she is entitled, the brokers receive their shares of the commission, the old mortgagee receives the entire unpaid balance of its loan, and the purchaser receives the deed, and, shortly thereafter, the payment or coupon book reflecting his or her obligation to make payments on the new mortgage.

Possession of the property is often also transferred at the closing by the delivery of keys, but this is a matter of agreement between the parties, and possession may be transferred either before or after the closing.

§9.12 ALLOCATION OF CLOSING COSTS

Before the closing, the closing officer prepares a proposed "settlement sheet" showing charges allocable to the purchaser, charges allocable to the seller, and the disposition of all cash held in or to be received by the closing escrow. Federal law requires copies of this preliminary settlement sheet to be distributed to the purchaser and seller for their preliminary review. Even with this advance disclosure, settlement sheets tend to be rather complicated, and many purchasers or sellers probably "trust in God" and do not fully analyze or understand these important documents. The Department of Housing and Urban Development has prepared a helpful pamphlet entitled "Settlement Costs and You."

An examination of a proposed settlement sheet shows that a number of charges are imposed on the purchaser and a number imposed on the seller. Some of the charges relate to the costs of preparing and filing the basic documents in the public land records; others relate to items required by the lender, such as an appraisal, a credit report, loan origination fees, points, and other vague charges; still others relate to the costs of obtaining title assurance and a survey. These charges add up to substantial amounts, several thousands of dollars at a minimum, even in a routine transaction. Form 9-1 is the standard HUD-approved settlement statement.

Points, and other charges that relate to the financing of the purchase (as contrasted with the purchase itself) are discussed in section 9.13 below.

Federal regulation also requires that the purchaser receive a statement detailing his or her obligations to escrow amounts to pay insurance and real estate taxes on the property. See section 9.19 below.

At first glance, the allocation of certain charges to the purchaser and others to the seller seem quite arbitrary. If one asks the closing officer how these responsibilities are split, he or she will probably respond, "custom of the community" or "contract provisions." In fact, a careful reading of the

Figure 9-1. Standard HUD-approved Settlement Statement

HUD-1 REV. 9/76 | FORM APPROVED OMB NO. 2502 C 0265 (EXP. 12/31/86)

A.

B. TYPE OF LOAN

1. ☐ FHA 2. ☐ FMHA 3. ☐ CONV. UNINS.
4. ☐ VA 5. ☐ CONV. INS.
6. FILE NUMBER: 7. LOAN NUMBER:

SETTLEMENT STATEMENT
U.S. DEPARTMENT OF HOUSING AND URBAN DEVELOPMENT

8. MORTGAGE INSURANCE CASE NUMBER:

C. NOTE: This form is furnished to give you a statement of actual settlement costs. Amounts paid to and by the settlement agent are shown. Items marked "(p.o.c.)" were paid outside the closing; they are shown here for informational purposes and are not included in totals.

D. NAME OF BORROWER | E. NAME OF SELLER: | F. NAME OF LENDER:

G. PROPERTY LOCATION: | H. SETTLEMENT AGENT: | PLACE OF SETTLEMENT

I. SETTLEMENT DATE:

J. SUMMARY OF BORROWER'S TRANSACTION		K. SUMMARY OF SELLER'S TRANSACTION	
100. GROSS AMOUNT DUE FROM BORROWER:		**400. GROSS AMOUNT DUE TO SELLER:**	
101. Contract sales price		401. Contract sales price	
102. Personal property		402. Personal property	
103. Settlement charges to borrower (line 1400)		403.	
104.		404.	
105.		405.	
Adjustments for items paid by seller in advance		*Adjustments for items paid by seller in advance*	
106. City/town taxes to		406. City/town taxes to	
107. County taxes to		407. County taxes to	
108. Assessments to		408. Assessments to	
109.		409.	
110.		410.	
111.		411.	
112.		412.	
120. GROSS AMOUNT DUE FROM BORROWER		**420. GROSS AMOUNT DUE TO SELLER**	
200. AMOUNTS PAID BY OR IN BEHALF OF BORROWER:		**500. REDUCTIONS IN AMOUNT DUE TO SELLER:**	
201. Deposit or earnest money		501. Excess deposit (see instructions)	
202. Principal amount of new loan(s)		502. Settlement charges to seller (line 1400)	
203. Existing loan(s) taken subject to		503. Existing loan(s) taken subject to	
204.		504. Payoff of first mortgage loan	
205.		505. Payoff of second mortgage loan	
206.		506.	
207.		507.	
208.		508.	
209.		509.	
Adjustments for items unpaid by seller:		*Adjustments for items unpaid by seller:*	
210. City/town taxes to		510. City/town taxes to	
211. County taxes to		511. County taxes to	
212. Assessments to		512. Assessments to	
213.		513.	
214.		514.	
215.		515.	
216.		516.	
217.		517.	
218.		518.	
219.		519.	
220. TOTAL PAID BY/FOR BORROWER		**520. TOTAL REDUCTION AMOUNT DUE SELLER**	
300. CASH AT SETTLEMENT FROM/TO BORROWER		**600. CASH AT SETTLEMENT TO/FROM SELLER**	
301. Gross amount due from borrower (line 120)		601. Gross amount due to seller (line 420)	
302. Less amounts paid by/for borrower (line 220)	( )	602. Less reductions in amt. due to seller (line 520)	( )
303. CASH (☐ FROM) (☐ TO) BORROWER		603. CASH (☐ TO) (☐ FROM) SELLER	

Page 1

Figure 9-1. (*continued*) Standard HUD-approved Settlement Statement

HUD-1 REV. 5/76   Page 2

L. SETTLEMENT CHARGES		PAID FROM BORROWER'S FUNDS AT SETTLEMENT	PAID FROM SELLER'S FUNDS AT SETTLEMENT
700. TOTAL SALES/BROKER'S COMMISSION based on price $ @ % =			
Division of Commission (line 700) as follows:			
701. $ to			
702. $ to			
703. Commission paid at Settlement			
704.			
800. ITEMS PAYABLE IN CONNECTION WITH LOAN			
801. Loan Origination Fee %			
802. Loan Discount %			
803. Appraisal Fee to			
804. Credit Report to			
805. Lender's Inspection Fee			
806. Mortgage Insurance Application Fee to			
807. Assumption Fee			
808.			
809.			
810.			
811.			
900. ITEMS REQUIRED BY LENDER TO BE PAID IN ADVANCE			
901. Interest from to @ $ /day			
902. Mortgage Insurance Premium for months to			
903. Hazard Insurance Premium for years to			
904. years to			
905.			
1000. RESERVES DEPOSITED WITH LENDER			
1001. Hazard insurance months @ $ per month			
1002. Mortgage insurance months @ $ per month			
1003. City property taxes months @ $ per month			
1004. County property taxes months @ $ per month			
1005. Annual assessments months @ $ per month			
1006. months @ $ per month			
1007. months @ $ per month			
1008. months @ $ per month			
1100. TITLE CHARGES			
1101. Settlement or closing fee to			
1102. Abstract or title search to			
1103. Title examination to			
1104. Title insurance binder to			
1105. Document preparation to			
1106. Notary fees to			
1107. Attorney's fees to			
(includes above items numbers:			
1108. Title insurance to			
(includes above items numbers:			
1109. Lender's coverage $			
1110. Owner's coverage $			
1111.			
1112.			
1113.			
1200. GOVERNMENT RECORDING AND TRANSFER CHARGES			
1201. Recording fees: Deed $; Mortgage $; Releases $			
1202. City/county tax/stamps: Deed $; Mortgage $			
1203. State tax/stamps: Deed $; Mortgage $			
1204.			
1205.			
1300. ADDITIONAL SETTLEMENT CHARGES			
1301. Survey to			
1302. Pest inspection to			
1303.			
1304.			
1305.			
1400. TOTAL SETTLEMENT CHARGES (*enter on lines 103, Section J and 502, Section K*)			

We, the undersigned, identified as Borrower in section D hereof and Seller in section E hereof, hereby acknowledge receipt of this completed Uniform Settlement Statement (pages 1 & 2) on   19

Borrower: Seller:

_____   _____

_____   _____

This form provided by

Figure 9-1. (*continued*) Standard HUD-approved Settlement Statement

ADDENDUM TO HUD-I
SETTLEMENT STATEMENT

G.F. No. _____

I have carefully reviewed the HUD-I Settlement Statement and to the best of my knowledge and
belief, it is a true and accurate statement of all receipts and disbursements made on my account or
by me in this transaction. I further certify that I have received a copy of the HUD-I Settlement
Statement.

_____   _____

_____   _____

Borrowers   Sellers

The HUD-I Settlement Statement which I have prepared is a true and accurate account of this
transaction. I have caused or will cause the funds to be disbursed in accordance with this
statement.

_____   _____

Settlement Agent   Date

WARNING: It is a crime to knowingly make false statements to the United States on this or any
other similar form. Penalties upon conviction can include a fine and imprisonment. For details
see: Title 18 U. S. Code Section 1001 and Section 1010.

printed boilerplate in the form real estate contract shows that it does
contain language that allocates most or all of these costs to one party or
the other. The line between custom and contract in this connection is
rather blurred because of the widespread use of standard form contracts in
most communities. At least theoretically there is no reason why the potential purchaser in the original contract of sale cannot include provisions
shifting some or most of these costs to the seller, or vice versa. This is not
the norm, however, in part because this must be done at the time the
original contract is prepared, and as indicated above, this is usually prepared by a broker rather than a lawyer. Even lawyers, however, may be
reluctant to change the customary allocation of costs, since the amounts
are relatively small in light of the purchase price of the house, and an
attempt to shift the responsibility for these costs may make the contract
unacceptable to the seller.

It is customary to allocate real estate taxes (and insurance, if a new
policy is not to be written) between purchaser and seller in the year in

which the sale occurs on the basis of the fraction of the year each owned the property.

It is important to recognize that practices with respect to the allocation of significant costs vary widely from community to community. For example, on the basic matter of title insurance premiums, it is the custom in some communities for this to be a charge to the seller (on the theory that he or she has to provide acceptable proof of title). In others, it is customary for this to be charged to the purchaser (on the theory that this is in part a cost of obtaining a loan).

§9.13 "POINTS"

A later section in this chapter (section 9.29) discusses the substantial increases in interest rates that occurred in the 1970s and early 1980s. One important consequence of this development was the institutionalization of the practice of lenders of charging points in connection with the making of long-term loans for residential real estate. This practice is discussed here because points appear on the settlement sheet as a cost of closing.

A point (or a discount point as it is sometimes called) is simply a charge equal to 1 percent of the loan amount; a lender who charges 3 points on a $100,000 loan in effect imposes an additional $3,000 fee at closing. Originally, points were charged to the borrower as a device to keep real estate loans from exceeding nominal state usury ceilings or to keep quoted interest rates more in line with other competitive rates. So, if a purchaser of real estate "borrows" $100,000 at 11 percent for 30 years but then is immediately required to pay 3 points (or $3,000) back to the lender at closing, he or she is really borrowing only $97,000, but is paying back $100,000 on the regular amortization schedule for that amount. The effect of charging three points on this loan is to increase the effective interest rate on the $97,000 actually borrowed from the 11 percent quoted figure to 11.38 percent without calling attention to it.

The economic effect of charging points against the borrower is so obvious that the federal government in its guaranteed loan programs generally prohibits the evasion of maximum ceiling rates on interest by charging the borrower points. However, both the Veteran's Administration and the Department of Housing and Urban Development generally permit points to be charged against the seller on the theory that this does not increase the borrowing cost to the purchaser. However, it seems evident that the probable effect of charging the seller points is to cause sellers to increase the price of the property by the amount that they expect they will have to pay to allow the borrower to get the federally guaranteed loan. As a result, points that are charged against the seller probably are, in fact, paid by the purchaser over the lifetime of the loan through larger payments.

The practice of charging points in loan closings is practically universal today in residential real estate transactions. Many additional fees that may not be described as points but, say, as a "loan acceptance fee" or "loan origination fee," are economically equivalent to points if they are received by the lender and do not reflect the actual cost of providing services. For reasons discussed below, purchasers and sellers of residential real estate sometimes agree between themselves in advance to share, in some predetermined ratio, the cost of the points that almost certainly will be charged at closing.

§9.14 TITLE ASSURANCE

Title assurance procedures and techniques are an important part of many law school courses on real property and conveyancing. The purpose of this section is to give a brief introduction to the subject.

Virtually all states provide that documents relating to interests in land are binding on third persons only if publicly filed and recorded in the land records of the county or other local governmental unit. The public records are usually filed in the order in which they are received, and the filing office usually maintains grantor-grantee and grantee-grantor indexes. Unfortunately, it is practically impossible to find out the current status of the title to a piece of real estate using these records. Instead, in these states a private industry, the members of which may be referred to as title companies, abstract companies, or title plants, maintain private summaries of the same records organized on a much more useful tract index basis. To obtain a current and accurate picture of the title of a tract without incurring excessive search costs, one usually uses the services of one of these private companies, which update their title records daily on a tract basis to reflect every document filed every day in the public land records.

In some areas public records may be maintained on a tract index basis. Also, some areas have adopted the Torrens system, which is a form of direct title registration. The discussion below does not deal with these systems of title assurance.

In most urban areas today, title assurance is provided by title insurance, though in some areas, lawyers' opinions of title based on studies of title abstracts may still be used. Title insurance is normally written by specialized companies that maintain tract indexes: Companies involved in writing life or casualty insurance usually are not involved in title insurance.

Title insurance is an unusual type of insurance in some respects. Historically, it has always been a profitable backwater of the insurance market. It is little studied and virtually unregulated at the federal and state level; ratings agencies do not assess the financial strength of title insurers; the leading companies have little cachet or investor interest, and consumers do not usually shop around for title insurance. In F.T.C. v. Ticor Title Ins. Co., a case which was decided by the Supreme Court of the United States in 1992, involving a price fixing complaint under the antitrust laws, the title insurance business was described as follows:

> Title insurance is the business of insuring the record title of real property for persons with an interest in the estate, including owners, occupiers, and lenders. A title insurance policy insures against certain losses or damages sustained by reason of a defect in title not shown on the policy or title report to which it refers. Before issuing a title insurance policy, the insurance company or one of its agents performs a title search and examination. The search produces a chronological list of the public documents in the chain of title to the real property. The examination is a critical analysis or interpretation of the condition of title revealed by the documents disclosed through this search.
>
> The title search and examination are major components of the insurance company's services. There are certain variances from State to State and from policy to policy, but a brief summary of the functions performed by the title companies can be given. The insurance companies exclude from coverage defects uncovered during the search; that is, the insurers conduct searches in order to inform the insured and to reduce their own liability by identifying and excluding known risks. The insured is protected from some losses resulting from title defects not discoverable from a search of the public records, such as forgery, missing heirs, previous marriages, impersonation, or confusion in names. They are protected also against errors or mistakes in the search and examination. Negligence need not be proved in order to recover. Title insurance also includes the obligation to defend in the event that an insured is issued by reason of some defect within the scope of the policy's guarantee.

Six title insurers handle three-fourths of all the nation's properties. Major companies are Chicago Title and Trust, First American Title Insurance, Commonwealth Title Insurance, Lawyers Title Insurance of Richmond, Stewart Title Guaranty, and the Old Republic group. Concern has been expressed about the long-term solvency of some of these major issuers of title insurance. Virtually everyone in title insurance agrees that the rate of claims has risen sharply to about 12 to 15 cents of every dollar taken in through premiums as of 1992. In contrast, in the mid-1970s the loss ratio was about 3 cents on every dollar of premiums. Generally, insurers may not have placed enough money in reserves to pay the higher claims; at least 10 percent of premiums should be set aside at current claims levels. In 1992, the reserves at First American Insurance Company were 3 percent; Lawyers Title Insurance Company had a reserve ratio of 7 percent; Stewart Title and Guaranty, 6.8 percent; Old Republic International's group, of which Title Insurance Company of Minnesota is the main subsidiary, had a reserve ratio of 11.1 percent.

Increases in claims since the 1970s are the result of several factors. Some builders have walked away from partially finished construction, leaving mechanics and materialmen's liens. Also, title companies have made a much greater use of freelance title researchers; as a result the number of mistakes in title searches has increased. Third, discovery of hazardous waste under homes and factories, which makes it difficult to transfer title to property, has led to an increased number of claims. Insurers argue that while property with hazardous wastes may be unmarketable, title is still technically good. But, in any event, they have to defend against such claims.

Title insurance policies are unusual in several respects. For one thing, title insurance is not an annual or recurring policy: There is only a single premium, and a title insurance policy, once written, theoretically remains outstanding forever to protect the insured from claims asserted by others. It is more similar to an indemnification agreement in this respect than to an insurance policy. For another, as noted by the United States Supreme Court, title insurance companies generally do not take risks that they know about. If the title search shows that a risk exists, the company will exclude that risk from the coverage of the policy. If a title search reveals a trivial potential defect (such defects are colloquially referred to as "flyspecks"), the company is nevertheless likely to include an express exception not providing protection against that defect. Also, it is to the interest of both the purchaser and the lender to try to persuade a title company to eliminate as many exceptions of this nature as possible. It is sometimes possible to do this by arguing that the excepted defect was cured by the statute of limitations or that an exception, for example, for an unconveyed dower interest arising from a marriage that took place in 1912 is unlikely to be a real defect today simply because of the passage of time. A third unusual aspect of title insurance is that the premium is based solely on the purchase price of the property and is not dependent on what problems there are in the title. As indicated above, a major problem in the title is excepted from the coverage if it is known, though presumably a title company may decline to issue a policy at all if it concludes that the potential seller does not in fact have title to the property.

Title insurance does protect against some things even if the title company expressly excepts every risk that it is aware of: forged deeds, misfiled deeds, and the like. As a practical matter, however, the risk involved in the average title insurance is not very great, though occasionally one hears of cases in which the title company is compelled to acquire land or cover losses incurred by insureds.

Before issuing a title policy, a title company sets forth the results of its title search for the benefit of the parties. This may take the form of a "binder," "commitment to insure," or "title report." This is an important document that every purchaser should examine carefully since his or her title is subject to the exceptions set forth in that document. If a substantial defect appears, the purchaser may reject the title, that is, refuse to complete the transaction on the ground the title is not marketable. What should be done, however, if the report shows a "defect" that is unlikely to affect the purchaser's use and enjoyment of the residence, but the title company refuses to remove it? There is a risk in simply ignoring the problem and completing the purchase of the property, which may not be self-evident. The risk is that presumably the same defect will reappear when the purchaser tries to resell the property in the future, and the new purchaser (or his or her lawyer) may take a less charitable attitude toward the problem and reject the title. In other words, the concern is as much whether the purchaser will be able to resell the property subject to the defect as whether the defect is one that may hinder the purchaser's use and enjoyment of the property. Where a defect such as this appears, the purchaser may be able to negotiate a reduction in the agreed purchase price if he or she agrees to purchase subject to the defect.

Title companies offer a "mortgagee policy" and an "owner's policy." The first protects the lender up to the extent of the unpaid balance of the mortgage and is the only policy required by the lender as a condition to making the loan. The second protects the purchaser both with respect to his or her equity in the property and, more importantly, against subrogation claims that might be brought by the title company against the owner on the mortgage note or on his or her warranties of title in the mortgage if a claim is made on the mortgagee policy. "Subrogation" means stepping into the shoes of another: The title company pays off the mortgage, takes an assignment of the mortgage note, and then sues the owner for the unpaid balance of the full amount of the mortgage note as subrogee of the mortgagee's interest. The cost of the owner's policy is not great (when purchased in connection with the mortgagee policy), and a purchaser should always be advised to acquire the owner's policy as well as the mortgagee policy.

§9.15 WARRANTIES OF TITLE

The subject of title insurance naturally leads to a discussion of warranties of title. There are three basic types of deeds: general warranty deeds, special warranty deeds, and quitclaim deeds. (In some areas of the country general or special warranty deeds may be known by different names.) The first, as its name implies, includes a general warranty by the seller that his or her title is valid as against the world. The second warrants title as against any act of the seller but does not warrant good title against the world, and the third simply conveys whatever title the seller possesses without any warranty of any kind. These title warranties may serve as a basis for litigation by the grantee or a subsequent purchaser against the grantor if there is a title defect. (This is an additional reason to insist that purchasers acquire the owner's title policy, since that policy insures against such warranty claims made by a subsequent purchaser as well.)

The type of warranty deed that must be tendered at the closing of a routine real estate transaction is also part of the custom of the community. In most areas, general warranty deeds are the custom, though in some areas the custom is to convey by special warranty deed. If a seller refuses to give the customary type of deed used in the community, that is a powerful warning that there is some title defect somewhere. In particular, if a seller is willing only to give a quitclaim deed in a community in which warranty deeds are the custom, that is almost a guarantee that there is something fundamentally wrong with the title to the property, and the purchaser is probably buying a lawsuit.

§9.16 THE SURVEY

Lenders often require a reasonably current survey of the property as a condition for making a loan. The cost, which is usually not great, is usually allocated to the purchaser. Even where a current survey is not required by the lender, lawyers recommend that the purchaser obtain a new survey for his or her own protection. If it should turn out that the fence at the back of the lot was put up after the last survey and is six inches on the neighbor's land, the purchaser typically has no recourse. Title warranties and title policies are expressly or impliedly subject to whatever state of facts an accurate survey would show; as a result, the cost of a survey should be viewed as a relatively inexpensive "peace of mind" insurance in most cases.

§9.17 MORTGAGOR LIFE INSURANCE

Many mortgage companies offer a type of life insurance to purchasers of real estate that, at first glance, appears to provide additional peace of mind. For a relatively small additional monthly payment, this policy guarantees that upon the unexpected death of the borrower, the insurance policy will provide an amount sufficient to pay off the mortgage in full. As described more fully in Chapter 11, this is a declining balance term life insurance policy, and its cost should be evaluated along with other term life insurance policies offered by commercial companies generally. An investigation will usually reveal that the cost of this insurance is high given the amount of protection that is afforded by the policy, though an offsetting feature is that adding the payment to the monthly mortgage payment makes the carrying of this insurance relatively painless.

PART II.   FINANCING THE PURCHASE

§9.18 THE CONVENTIONAL REAL ESTATE MORTGAGE

This section discusses the classic level-payment real estate loan, widely used for both commercial and residential real estate financing. This type of mortgage is sometimes called a conventional mortgage. Subsequent sections discuss the principal alternative offered to residential homebuyers today — the adjustable rate mortgage and its numerous variants. See sections 9.25 to 9.27.

A traditional real estate mortgage is for a long term — 25 or 30 years — at a fixed interest rate established at or close to the market rate of interest at the time the loan is made. Monthly payments are required, and interest is computed on the unpaid balance each month. The loan is amortized over its life by these monthly payments, which are fixed in advance and remain constant throughout the life of the mortgage. The words "amortize" and "amortization" are fancy terms that simply mean the loan is set up so that a portion of each monthly payment is applied to principal as well as interest: In the classic mortgage of this type the monthly payment is computed so that the final level payment — the 360th payment on a 30-year mortgage — reduces the loan balance to zero.

The first payment on a traditional mortgage represents virtually all interest with a few dollars or cents being applied to principal; the second payment consists of a tiny bit less interest (since the first payment reduced the principal slightly) and therefore a tiny bit more is available to be applied to reduce principal. This process continues over the life of the mortgage, with each payment representing a somewhat larger amount of principal and smaller amount of interest than the previous one.

To illustrate: On a $75,000 9 percent loan for 30 years, the level monthly payment is $603.47 over the 30 years. The first payment reduces principal by $40.97 (the remaining $562.50 is interest); the second payment reduces principal by $41.27 (the remaining $562.19 is interest); and so on. The twelfth payment reduces principal by $44.48; after this payment the principal has been reduced to $74,487.60. The payment made on the fifth anniversary of the mortgage (the 60th payment), reduces principal by $63.66, and the mortgage then has been reduced to $71,910.10. Obviously, only a small amount of the unpaid balance is amortized in the early years of the mortgage. After 10 years, the principal has been reduced to $67,072.31; after 15 years, it has been reduced to $59,497.86; after 20 years to $47,638.70; after 25 years to $29,071.04. During the last five years, most of each payment is principal and upon making the 360th payment, the principal is reduced to zero.

It may seem difficult to set up the amount of the monthly payment so that everything comes out exactly even 25 or 30 years later. But these things need be worked out only once mathematically for each plausible interest rate (for example, by each one-fourth of a percent) and for each plausible time period — for example, 10 years, 15 years, etc., up to 30 years) in order to create a set of tables providing the monthly payment per $1.00 of loan for specified interest rates over specified periods. The monthly payment required for a specific transaction can then be computed simply by multiplying the figure shown in the table by the size of the contemplated mortgage. Other tables permit a person to determine precisely what part of each payment on any loan represents principal and what part represents interest. These calculations are also well within the capacity of modern handheld financial calculators, which have largely replaced tables and pencil-and-paper in such calculations.

The fixed-interest, level-payment loan described here is so common and so widely used that it is sometimes referred to as a "conventional" loan. (The term "conventional" is also sometimes used in a different context to describe residential real estate loans made by a savings and loan association or other lender in contrast to loans guaranteed under federal programs such as FHA or VA.)

In discussing the parties to a mortgage, the lender is referred to as the "mortgagee" and the owner/debtor is referred to as the "mortgagor."

§9.19 INSURANCE AND TAXES

This section deals with a major post-closing charge that is usually added by lenders to the monthly payment on residential real estate mortgages. The discussion in the rest of this chapter assumes that you understand the concepts underlying the traditional long-term level-payment mortgage described in section 9.17 of this chapter.

Lenders who make residential real estate loans tend to rely more on the value of the property as security than on the personal promise to pay the note made by the purchaser. (See section 9.3) In order to preserve their principal security (the residence), lenders must assure themselves that real estate taxes are paid when they are due and casualty insurance (for example, fire or storm) is kept up. Together or separately, taxes and insurance are rather big ticket items for many families, and to ensure that funds are available when needed, lenders usually require the purchaser to pay, each month, an additional amount equal to one-twelfth of the estimated cost of insurance and taxes. These amounts are held in escrow by the lender and disbursed more or less on a timely basis directly to the insurer and the taxing authorities to pay the insurance premium and the tax bill.

The internal treatment of these escrow funds varies from area to area. In some areas the lenders collect the escrow amounts but do not pay interest on them. Since a lender may have hundreds or thousands of mortgages outstanding, the amount of interest-free money may be quite substantial and provides a significant additional return to the lender who, of course, is free to invest these funds profitably until they are needed. Where interest is not paid on escrow funds, knowledgeable purchasers feel there is a rip-off by lenders. Where negotiation with a lender is possible (and often it is not), attorneys should seek to eliminate the tax and insurance escrows completely or to work out an arrangement by which escrow payments earn interest. It should be noted, however, that there are two sides to this issue. The handling of these escrowed funds and the paying of taxes and insurance involve some cost to the mortgagee (though this cost is probably far less than the earnings on these funds), and in a sense is a convenience to the mortgagor. The issue of whether interest should be paid on escrowed funds has been the subject of litigation in several states. In some communities, escrow payments are treated as reducing the principal of the mortgage, and payments of taxes or insurance premiums as increasing the mortgage. In effect, this pays interest on escrow funds at the rate of the mortgage. While such treatment affects the mathematical accuracy of the amortization schedule, that is relatively unimportant, since the overall effect is small.

Complaints about overcharging for, and refusing to pay interest on, tax and insurance escrows by lenders were so widespread that Congress, in 1974, enacted the Real Estate Settlement Procedures Act (RESPA) that prohibited lending institutions from holding excessive sums in escrow accounts. Section 10 of RESPA allowed lenders to require monthly escrow payments equal to one-twelfth of the next year's anticipated bills, plus an additional one-twelfth of one month's escrow payment as a cushion. Abuses, however, appear to have continued, and in 1990 Congress enacted section 942 of the Cranston-Gonzales National Affordable Housing Act to require servicers of federally related mortgage loans to issue: (1) an initial escrow statement to the borrower at the time of closing or within 45 days of opening the account; (2) an annual escrow statement analyzing the account; and (3) a notice of any shortage in the escrow account. Regulations issued by HUD detail the information required to be included in the annual escrow statement.

Excessive escrow payments were apparently exacerbated by the increasingly common practice of selling packages of mortgages into the secondary market. Escrow amounts were sometimes determined by distant companies based on regional averages rather than the actual amounts due for taxes and insurance on specific properties. RESPA was also amended in 1991 to require lenders to advise potential purchasers whether the lender plans to service the loan itself or to assign that function to others. An actual assignment of these functions must also be communicated to holders of outstanding mortgages when they occur.

The monthly payment needed to amortize the borrowed amount is sometimes referred to as the "PI" (principal and interest) payment. The full payment, including tax and insurance escrows, is referred to as the "PITI" payment. When monthly mortgage costs are discussed with purchasers, usually only the PI amount is quoted because there is no current information about the TI portion of the payment. Some naive purchasers have relied on a PI quotation of the monthly cost of a mortgage of a specified amount and later discovered to their dismay that PITI is considerably larger than PI.

§9.20 REAL ESTATE LOANS ARE SECURED BY LIENS

A loan made to enable the borrower to purchase real estate is represented by a promissory note, which is usually on a standard printed form. The obligation to pay is routinely secured by a lien on the real estate that is the subject of the transaction. The lien is actually created in a separate document, either a mortgage or deed of trust, which is also executed at the closing. The terms of these documents are so standardized that printed forms are usually used with a few blanks filled in. (Typed-in clauses referring to special terms such as prepayment privileges are also sometimes added.) These standardized forms are typically prepared by the lender, who usually resists making changes in them. A "deed of trust" differs from a "mortgage" in only minor respects: The type of instrument used in a particular state or community depends more on tradition or convention than on the differences between the two forms of instruments. Hereafter, the word mortgage will be used to refer to both types of instruments.

The lien created by a mortgage covers the entire property that is the subject of the transaction. It covers improvements existing on the land, as well as new improvements as they are constructed, and the land itself. Liens have both a geographic and a temporal aspect. Temporal rights, such as the rights of a lessee to possess the property under a ten-year lease, are subject to the lien of the mortgagee, though usually in the event of a default the mortgagee does not want to try to dispossess tenants. In some cities rent control laws may limit the power of owners to dispossess tenants even when they wish to do so.

§9.21 IS ANYBODY LIABLE ON THE REAL ESTATE LOAN?

The promissory note secured by a real estate mortgage is, of course, a promise by the person signing it to pay the amount set forth in the note. In practically all residential real estate transactions, the owners are required to sign the note individually so that they have personal liability (as well as the threatened loss of the property) if a default occurs. In commercial real estate, however, it is not unknown for the lender to agree to look solely to the property as the source of payment and not require the developer to assume personal liability. This may be done by having some third person (a "straw party") or a corporation without substantial assets be the owner of the property and sign the note. The same result may be reached by a provision in the note limiting the power of the holder to recover from the maker in the event of default. This is often referred to as a "non recourse" loan. In the case of such a loan, the owner then is faced with the loss of the property, including whatever equity he has in the property, if there is a default, but is not personally liable for the debt. In rare instances, similar practices may be used in residential real estate transactions.

Individual liability on real estate notes may be discharged through the bankruptcy process if the individual is insolvent. A personal discharge does not, of itself, release the lien on the property so that a bankruptcy discharge does not prevent foreclosure. (See section 9.37.)

§9.22 WHAT HAPPENS IF THERE IS DEFAULT?

What happens if the owner of a residence defaults on his or her obligation to make monthly payments? Not all defaults lead immediately to foreclosure on the property or suits brought to recover missed payments. Loan instruments often provide for grace periods in which missed payments may be made up, often upon the payment of an additional charge. Also, legal action is expensive and taken only as a matter of last resort. It is not uncommon for lenders to threaten foreclosure and even post property for sale under the procedures set forth in the mortgage, without completing the threatened action. In many instances, the financially troubled owner, threatened with the loss of his or her residence, may seek to avoid foreclosure by trying to work out an arrangement with the mortgagee that will enable the owner to keep the residence. He or she may agree to seek credit counseling or to make at least current payments of interest until his or her financial condition improves. Mortgagees are often willing to cooperate with financially distressed owners in part because a partially performing mortgage is better than a totally nonperforming one. Mortgagees are particularly likely to cooperate in this regard if the mortgagor's financial problems are temporary and not his or her "fault"—for example, an illness or temporary loss of a job.

An uncorrected default on a mortgage leads to a foreclosure and ultimately the public sale of the property by auction after public announcement. The procedures to be followed are set forth in the mortgage itself; usually no judicial order is required before the sale may be made by the trustee or the sheriff. The proceeds of the sale, after deduction of expenses, are applied to the mortgage in default. If there is a second mortgage on the property—a home equity loan, for example—two rules of priority apply: (1) A foreclosure of a junior mortgage does not affect a senior mortgage, and the purchaser at the foreclosure sale takes the property subject to the senior mortgage; and (2) foreclosure of a senior mortgage automatically wipes out the liens of all junior mortgages. Thus, if Bank A holds the original, first mortgage, and Bank B has made a home equity loan, and the mortgagor stops making payments to both banks, if Bank B forecloses, it will become the owner of the property subject to Bank A's first mortgage. If Bank A forecloses while Bank B remains inactive, Bank B's lien will be wiped out in Bank A's foreclosure action.

The most common pattern at a foreclosure sale is that the foreclosing lender purchases the property for the amount of the outstanding indebtedness. The reasons for this can best be appreciated by a concrete example. Assume that Smith has defaulted on both a first mortgage in the amount of $150,000 and a second mortgage (a home equity loan held by a different lender) with a current unpaid balance of $50,000. The value of Smith's house has declined significantly as a result of the collapse of real estate prices in the community with the result that the fair market value of the house is $125,000.

On these assumptions, Bank B, the holder of the home equity loan, has essentially an unsecured and almost certainly uncollectible loan. Smith is personally liable to repay the $50,000 but is probably judgment proof. Why should Bank B go through an expensive foreclosure procedure in order to acquire a property worth $125,000 subject to a senior $150,000 lien? In a word, it won't.

What about a foreclosure by Bank A? Bank A presumably could buy the property if it bids $125,000 or higher; presumably no third person will bid more than its present market value. At first blush, it does not appear to make much difference whether Bank A bids $125,000, or $150,000, or something in between. In any event it will get property worth $125,000 and will probably never recover anything from Smith. What Bank A bids, however, does affect Bank A's rights against Smith. If Bank A bids in the property at its current market value of $125,000, it will have to take (or "book") an immediate loss of $25,000; however, Bank A will have a continuing claim against Smith, since the sale did not produce sufficient funds to discharge Smith's debt. The sale, in other words, has produced a "deficiency." On the other hand, if Bank A bids in the property at $150,000, until recently it did not have to book an immediate loss but it gave up its probably worthless deficiency claim against Smith. In the modern era, however, lenders are required to write down properties to their current market values promptly after foreclosing on them. There is now little chance for a bank to overstate its financial condition by bidding in properties at or above their market value.

A lender in the position of Bank A that has purchased property at foreclosure may seek to resell it to a third party or may hold it off the market in the hope that prices improve. When it does decide to resell the property, it may offer the purchaser favorable financing terms: After all, it already has $150,000 invested in the property so that it may grant a new purchaser a mortgage of up to that amount without investing an additional dollar in the property. Any payments are better than holding the property vacant in its inventory and off the market.

If we assume that the value of Smith's property is between $150,000 and $200,000, both Bank A and Bank B have positive security on their loans. In this situation, Bank A, if it is the foreclosing lender, will bid the amount of its lien, $150,000, and no more. If it gets the property at that price, it will be getting a bargain (since Bank B's lien disappears on the foreclosure of the first lien). If it bids any more, the excess proceeds will belong to Bank B. Since Bank A's economic interest in the property is only $150,000, it has no incentive to bid more than that. Bank B, on the other hand, has an incentive to bid at least up to the fair market value of the property and possibly up to the amount of its claim against Smith. If it does so when Bank A is foreclosing, it will have to pay Bank A $150,000 in cash; if it acts first and forecloses, it will take subject to Bank A's mortgage and will have to make up any overdue payments and thereafter keep that mortgage current in order to prevent Bank A from foreclosing.

If we assume that the value of Smith's property is somewhat in excess of $200,000, Smith has a positive equity in the property. He should, at least theoretically, bid on the property to preserve his equity (i.e., the difference between the mortgages and the fair market value of the property). Of course, if Smith could not meet the monthly payments on the two loans, he probably also will not be able to raise $200,000 to pay off the loans in cash at the foreclosure sale. As a result, whatever equity he has in the property is, as a practical matter, probably gone. An opportunistic third person should theoretically bid $200,001: He or she will then outbid Bank B (which has no incentive to bid above $200,000) and get Smith's equity for $1. It would be an unusual opportunistic third person, however, who could come up with $200,000 in cash, or who would be willing to invest $200,000 in a problematic venture in order to secure the equity ownership of an interest that may be worth only a small amount in excess of $200,000. Where Smith's equity is larger, however, it is quite possible that an opportunistic third person or Smith himself may be able to raise the necessary funds through a short-term loan, which may thereafter be paid off when the foreclosure purchaser refinances or resells the property. One thing is clear: If the owner has a substantial equity in the foreclosed property, he or she must scramble. If he or she does not, someone else will obtain a bargain at his or her expense — either one of the lending institutions or an opportunistic third person, since each will naturally bid the smallest amount necessary to purchase the property.

As a practical matter, lenders usually foreclose on residential property rather than ignore the property and sue Smith directly on the promissory note he signed. However, such a direct suit for a money judgment might be attractive if the lender believes that the owner has elected to default on the mortgage voluntarily while having ample resources to continue making payments on the mortgage.

This analysis is somewhat unrealistic because it is usually impossible to estimate with any degree of exactness the fair market value of property on which an owner has defaulted. It is therefore not uncommon for mistakes to be made, for junior lienholders to bid to obtain the property because they are uncertain whether the value of the property exceeds the senior liens. Some things can be said with confidence, however. It is theoretically possible to obtain real bargains on foreclosure. However, in the normal course of things in the real world, the secured debts usually significantly exceed the most optimistic estimate of market value. Thus, there is no positive equity, and the only bidders are the representatives of the lenders.

§9.23 MODERN TRENDS IN RESIDENTIAL REAL ESTATE PRICING AND FINANCING

Prior to about 1970, the financing of residential real estate purchases was fairly straightforward. Conventional financing required a down payment of 20 percent and a 25- or 30-year mortgage at the going rate of approximately 5 to 7 percent a year. All mortgages were of the conventional level-payment type described in section 9.18. Special financing — FHA or VA — permitted selected purchasers even more favorable terms as to minimum down payment and interest rates, though the level-payment schedules were rigorously followed in connection with such loans as well. In effect, the federal government was subsidizing the selected purchaser by capping the interest rate and making the down payment requirement easier to meet.

It is a little hard to recreate today the attitudes of the post-World War II and pre-1970 era towards real estate ownership. The 1950s and early 1960s were periods of unprecedented optimism in the United States. It was the era of the tract home with a choice of brick, stone, or redwood facades; of cars with tail fins; of hope and enthusiasm. The notion that every middle-class family could own its own home seemed to be an accepted fact since residential real estate was relatively inexpensive in most areas during this period, and most middle-class American families could find financing that enabled them to purchase housing.

For example, in the 1960s an average upper-middle-class house cost approximately $30,000. A more modest house in a standardized subdivision might sell for half of that, and the median price for homes was even lower. A family purchasing the $15,000 house might need a $3,000 down payment (though veterans could obtain such a house with no down payment) plus a $12,000 mortgage at 6 percent over 25 years. The monthly payment PI on such a mortgage is only $71.95 per month, and on a PITI basis the payment might be $100 or $110 per month. The purchase of the much larger $30,000 house might require a $7,500 down payment plus a $22,500 mortgage at 6 percent per year for 30 years. The monthly payment on such a mortgage was only $134.90 per month, PI, and about $200 to $225 per month, PITI. Thus, the payment for housing out of a family budget was relatively modest and well within the means of most of the middle class. Of course, the purchasers of the more expensive house would have to scrape together the down payment plus closing costs either from savings, family gifts, inheritances, or loans from family or other sources. Many families had small nest eggs based on World War II military service, and the special VA or FHA governmental programs often provided for reduced or even zero down payments for those who did not.

Beginning in the 1970s, the price of residential real estate began to increase dramatically in many areas. In part, this was due to inflationary pressures in the economy generally, to increases in construction costs, and to the widespread demand for family-owned housing. In 1986, the median price, nationwide, for a used home was about $80,000, a fivefold increase in 20 years. This increase was accompanied by a sudden and unprecedented (at least since World War II) increase in the level of interest rates during the 1970s and early 1980s. In the 1960s, long-term fixed payment mortgages were available in the range of 6 to 8 percent; by the late 1970s and early 1980s mortgages carrying interest rates of 13 or 14 percent per year were the norm, and in some periods and areas, mortgages carrying rates as high as 16 or 17 percent per year were written. Even as late as 1988, after several years of prosperity during the "Reagan era," general growth in the economy, and substantial declines in interest rates, interest rates for residential real estate were above 10 percent per year.

The dual factors of rising real estate values and rising interest rates greatly increased the cost of purchasing housing, both in terms of the down payment required and the family's income necessary to qualify for the mortgage. Many persons resisted the notion of committing themselves to 30 years of payments at 14 or 15 percent per year, particularly since many of them remembered the era of 6 percent interest rates paid by their parents.

One major consequence of the increase in housing costs was doubtless the increase in the number of wives in the work force; the two-income family became an economic necessity in the 1980s in order to purchase housing that a generation ago could readily be purchased on a single income.

In an effort to keep the residential market moving and to shore up the appreciation in real estate values, the housing and real estate finance industries developed new techniques and novel financing devices. To some extent the rules of thumb were bent to economic necessity. For example, 10 percent down payments became common, particularly on more expensive properties, and lenders increasingly accepted borrowers who devoted a relatively large fraction of their disposable income to housing. However, lower down payments increase the amount of the loan and the size of the monthly payment. Much more promising were changes in the traditional structures of mortgage repayment schedules that tended to defer much of the ultimate cost of the purchase to the future. During periods of inflation (such as occurred in the 1970s), this seemed to make obvious sense from the standpoint of the borrower since these loans would be repaid with depreciated dollars in the future. Also, the market saw more and more transactions involving assumptions of existing low interest rate mortgages and the increased use of second mortgages and other creative financing techniques. These developments form the subject of the following sections.

In retrospect, one should perhaps have been able to foresee in the 1980s that trends could not continue indefinitely and that a correction in real estate prices would occur. When such a correction did occur in the late 1980s, however, many persons were shocked and uncomprehending. Inflation of real estate prices was so common in so many areas that many people simply did not believe that prices could go down as well as up, and that a decision to pay too much, or to accept repayment terms that were onerous, would not be rescued by an increase in take-home pay or the value of the residence. It is ironic that some of the devices adopted during the 1970s to permit individuals to acquire expensive real estate increased the magnitude of the correction and the number of mortgage foreclosures and consumer bankruptcies in the 1980s and 1990s. Other important factors also contributed to the magnitude of the correction that did occur: the Tax Reform Act of 1986 (which had its primary impact on commercial real estate development and real estate tax shelters), the overbuilding of multi-family and office buildings based on overly optimistic estimates of future growth, the collapse of oil prices, which particularly devastated the southwest, the scandals of the savings and loan industry, and the lingering recession, which occurred during the same period.

As this is written in 1992, the real estate industry has not recovered in many areas of the country. In the early 1990s, after a long recession and generally weak economy (during which time the Federal Reserve System repeatedly reduced the discount rate in order to try to stimulate the economy), mortgage rates have declined to between 8 and 9 percent. In 1992, the average interest rate on fixed payment mortgages was 8.46 percent. Yet real estate prices have not improved in many areas and continue to decline in some.

§9.24 THE FIXED-PAYMENT MORTGAGE IN CONTEXT

The basic premises underlying the traditional fixed-payment mortgage appear to be: (1) The person making payments on the mortgage has a level income over the term of the mortgage; (2) interest rates and real estate values are going to remain relatively stable over the term of the mortgage; and (3) there is no systemic inflation in the economy. These premises obviously were not true in the recent past. Interest rates have varied dramatically in the last 20 years; inflation has been a constant factor since World War II and has continued at a reduced rate during the recessionary period of the early 1990s. And, real estate values have proved to be subject to significant deflation as well as inflation.

There is, of course, no inherent reason why the interest rate on a mortgage or its amortization schedule need be fixed for the entire life of the mortgage. One might, for example, establish a fixed amortization schedule for the loan based on the initial interest rate, but then increase or decrease the monthly payment to take into account changes in the effective interest rate on new mortgages. Or, one might provide for an amortization schedule that permitted the loan to be amortized slowly in the early years of the mortgage and more rapidly in later years.

These variations on the traditional fixed-rate mortgage seem abstractly realistic in light of normal expectations about what people do under conditions of varying interest rates and continuing inflation:

(1) In periods of inflation, one should expect family incomes to increase gradually over time. Hence, an accelerating amortization schedule appears to be quite consistent with general trends in family income.
(2) Level-payment loans taken out during a period of high interest rates will probably be refinanced when interest rates drop significantly (see section 9.35).
(3) Level-payment loans taken out during a period of low interest rates will be assumed rather than paid off when properties are bought and sold during periods of high interest rates (see section 9.30). Widespread assumptions of low rate mortgages during periods of high interest rates warp the financing of many real estate transactions and may cause serious economic injury to the lending industry.

It would seem sensible, therefore, to structure both amortization schedules and interest rates not on a fixed or static level over the term of the mortgage, but on a basis that varies with time and with current interest rates. Thus was born the nontraditional mortgages discussed in the following sections.

§9.25 ADJUSTABLE-RATE AND OTHER NONTRADITIONAL TYPES OF MORTGAGES

Adjustable-rate and other nontraditional mortgages are sometimes called "alternative mortgages" since they are alternatives to the conventional fixed-rate mortgage described in section 9.18. They were developed during the 1970s and 1980s when real estate markets were faced with high interest rates and rapid inflation in real estate values. The principal alternative mortgages are described in the following paragraphs. As this section amply demonstrates, these mortgages are part of the modern wonderland of acronyms.

Several important caveats should be noted about alternative mortgages at the outset: (1) Nomenclature is not always uniform and some of the instruments described below may have different names in some areas; (2) there are a great many variants and hybrids of alternative mortgages, perhaps as many as 500 in all, though most of them differ in only minor respects, such as the type of index used to calculate adjustments in interest rates or differences in maximum changes in any one year; and (3) some of the variants described below may not be offered by lending institutions in some areas. Indeed, some of the nontraditional mortgages discussed below were devised on the assumption that real estate values would continue to increase indefinitely and have fallen into disuse when real estate values unexpectedly declined in many areas.

The conventional, level-payment long-term mortgage described in section 9.18 is referred to below as the fixed-rate conventional mortgage or FRCM.

1. **Graduated Payment Mortgage (GPM).** A "graduated" payment mortgage has a fixed interest rate and a fixed time for repayment like an FRCM. However, rather than having level payments over the life of the mortgage to amortize the principal, the monthly payments for a GPM start out at a lower level than those called for by the FRCM but rise usually in three or four steps in later years. A GPM might have, for example, scheduled increases in payments at the end of the third, fifth, and seventh years of the mortgage. Obviously, payments in later years must be higher than the payment schedule of an equivalent FRCM in order to make up for the lower amortization payments in earlier years. The graduation rate,

the term of graduation, and the interest rate are all fixed throughout the life of the loan.

The theory behind a graduated payment mortgage is that the purchaser's income is likely to be lowest in the first years after the purchase of the residence and is likely to increase thereafter with inflation and with promotions, enabling the purchaser to make larger payments in later years. In effect, a GPM attempts to match mortgage payments with the borrower's anticipated future income stream. The aggregate amount of interest that must be paid over the life of a GPM is larger than the cost of a fixed-payment conventional mortgage since the loan is paid off at a slower rate in the early years.

A GPM carries a significant capacity for deception of or misjudgment by a marginal purchaser of residential real estate and appears to have disappeared in the 1990s. Even though the purchaser is warned that mortgage payments will increase in later years, household budgets are usually calculated on current receipts and current expenses. The sudden significant increase in monthly mortgage payments when the increased amortization schedules kick in may come as a cruel blow to the household budget if hoped for increases in salary or take-home pay have not materialized, if additional expenses caused by illness or increase in the size of the family have been incurred, or if, most disastrous of all, the individual family members have been laid off rather than receiving the promotions and salary increases they expected. Indeed, GPMs were generally marketed by heavily emphasizing the low payments in the initial years, often showing them as a percentage of the loan amount, with only a footnote in fine print warning the reader that the mortgage was a GPM and later payments would be much higher. The rates shown in these ads are sometimes called "teaser rates."

2. **Deferred Interest Mortgage (DIM).** The DIM is a type of GPM with a fixed interest payment and a fixed date of maturity; however, initial payments for the first few years are fixed at such a low level that they do not cover the original monthly interest cost of the loan. The result is "negative" amortization. During the early years, the unpaid portion of the interest is added to the principal of the mortgage each month so that the amount of the loan *increases* rather than *decreases* after each payment. After perhaps the second step in the graduated payments — the fifth year — the payments are large enough to cover the full interest cost and begin the amortization of the principal. Later payments must be fixed at a higher rate than a regular GPM in order to cover the unpaid interest of the earlier years.

3. **Pledged Account Mortgage (PAM).** A pledged account mortgage is simply a DIM or GPM in which a fund is created at the closing that is used to finance the lower initial payments. A not uncommon arrangement

requires the purchaser to pay points at the closing (see section 9.13), and the points form the fund to finance the lower initial payments. In some instances the seller of the property may be persuaded to place a portion of the sales price into the fund for this purpose; presumably, the price of the residence is inflated by the amount of this payment. The seller is willing to do this in order to permit the sale of the property; it is a kind of creative financing (see section 9.33). This arrangement is sometimes called a "buy-down option" and may be acceptable to the seller in order to dispose of hard-to-sell real estate.

4. **Adjustable-Rate Mortgage (ARM).** The interest rate on an ARM (sometimes called a variable-rate mortgage or "VRM") is not fixed at the market interest rate when the loan is created but is tied to some index that reflects changes in market rates of interest. Thus, future monthly payments are not precisely known when the loan is originated. Adjustable-rate mortgages have proved to be widely popular during the 1980s and 1990s and are offered by virtually all lenders today. Indeed, one of the more difficult questions faced by purchasers of real estate during periods of reduced interest rates is whether to "lock in" the current interest rate by taking a FRCM or to gamble that rates may go even lower in the future by taking an ARM. These and other issues relating to the choice between FRCMs and ARMs are discussed in sections 9.26 and 9.27.

If there are significant increases in interest rates, it is possible that an ARM may lead to very large increases in monthly payments over a relatively brief period. Many borrowers initially objected to the open-endedness of these mortgages. To increase their attractiveness, many ARMs carry initial interest rates about two percentage points below the market rate on FRCMs. They limit the maximum change in interest rate that can occur in the ARM over the life of the mortgage (for example, to not more than a 5 percent increase) and provide caps on the maximum change in monthly payment that may occur because of an annual rate adjustment. If the indexed change is greater than the cap, the excess is added to the principal of the loan much like in a DIM.

Of course, as the 1990s have vividly demonstrated, interest rates may go down as readily as they go up. The holders of many ARMs have, therefore, seen their payments decline dramatically: Of course, this decline does not help the holder of a GPM.

5. **Graduated Payment Adjustable Rate Mortgage (GPARM).** Two of the above features, a graduated payment and an adjustable rate, may be combined into a single real estate mortgage. Payments go up over time to amortize the principal and the payments are simultaneously adjusted to reflect changes in interest rates. The acronym of such a mortgage often includes a slash: GP/ARM. GP/ARMs were widely used to finance speculative commercial real estate transactions in the 1980s.

6. **Rollover Mortgage (ROM).** The ROM (currently used extensively

in Canada but not in the United States) is a long-term loan for which the interest rate and monthly payments are usually renegotiated every five years. The rate adjustment is based on an index or formula that reflects current market conditions, with a maximum increase of five percentage points over the life of the mortgage.

7. **Price Level Adjusted Mortgage (PLAM).** In a PLAM the interest rate and the term of the mortgage are fixed, but the outstanding balance is adjusted periodically in accordance with changes in some agreed-upon index of real estate values. In other words, the payments may increase as the value of the underlying property increases. A PLAM permits the lender to share along with the owner in the anticipated appreciation in the value of the underlying real estate. It presumably also would permit the lender to share in declines in real estate value as they occur, an event apparently not seriously contemplated by the persons who devised this type of alternative mortgage.

8. **Reverse Annuity Mortgage (RAM).** A RAM is, in effect, an annuity purchased by an increasing loan against the accumulated equity in a residence. It is designed for the elderly and the retired who have a large equity in their home because of inflation and need to use the equity to support themselves. Basically, it enables the owners of an appreciated residence to continue to live in the family home, receiving a monthly payment that reduces their equity in the house. The loan becomes due either on a specific date or when a specified event occurs, such as the sale of the property or the death of the borrower. If the loan becomes due on a specified date, and the owners are still alive, the residence will probably have to be sold, with considerable discomfort to the owners.

RAMs appear to be attractive to elderly homeowners who live in homes that have appreciated in value. They remained unavailable in most areas of the United States until the late 1980s. In 1989, the Federal Housing Administration announced a pilot program to provide loan guarantees for RAMs. In 1991, the pilot plan was extended to 25,000 loans, still a small quantity given the estimated demand from millions of Americans over 65 who own their own homes.

The FHA program limited available maximum loans to a range of $67,500 to $124,875, depending on the region of the United States in which the home was located. Guidelines for non-guaranteed mortgages are being prepared so that these loans may be placed in the secondary markets for mortgage loans. When these programs are in place, the availability of RAMs is expected to improve rapidly.

It is probably not necessary to remember all of these modern variants to the traditional fixed-rate conventional mortgage. If one is faced with a mortgage with an unfamiliar name, ask what it is. All of the variations are spin-offs from the conventional fixed-rate mortgage: There is nothing mysterious or incomprehensible about them.

§9.26 MORE ON ADJUSTABLE-RATE MORTGAGES

Adjustable-rate mortgages have proved to be the most profitable and durable type of nonconventional loans. In the 1990s, the initial interest rate on ARMs is between one and two percentage points lower than an interest rate of a FRCM. This differential reflects both a conscious sales decision to increase the attractiveness of these mortgages and the fact that interest rates are at a low level when compared to the recent past. The assumption is that in the future rates are more likely to increase than to decrease further. From the standpoint of the lender, an ARM is less risky than a FRCM in this scenario, since the ARM is self-adjusting.

A variety of different indexes are used to determine the amount of adjustment in the interest rates of ARMs: (1) indexes based on six-month, one-year, three-year, or five-year treasury securities; (2) indexes based on actual mortgage rates, such as the national average mortgage contract rate on the purchase of previously occupied homes calculated by the Federal Home Loan Bank Board; (3) the average cost of funds to federally insured savings and loan associations in the area, the state, or nationally; or (4) LIBOR (the London Interbank Offered Rate, an interbank lending rate used by London banks on dollar-denominated deposits). ARMs on the East Coast are usually tied to interest rates on six-month or one-year Treasury bills, or on three- or five-year Treasury notes. These rates may be determined as of a specific day — for example, 45 days before the adjustment day, or on a weekly average. Cost-of-funds indexes are widely used on the West Coast. All of these indexes are readily available and widely used.

As a practical matter, most ARMs provide for adjustments yearly or semiannually based on changes in the applicable market interest rate. A few may provide for adjustments on a different schedule. Usually, these adjustments are also reflected by changes in the amount of the monthly payment on an annual or semiannual basis.

§9.27 WHICH IS BETTER, A FIXED-RATE OR AN ADJUSTABLE-RATE MORTGAGE?

The choice between a FRCM and an ARM appears to be strongly influenced by perceptions about future trends in interest rates. In August 1989, when interest rates were relatively high and the trend was downward, 50 percent of all new mortgages written were adjustable-rate. Two years later, in August 1991, a period of relatively low rates, only 10 percent of new mortgages were adjustable-rate. This is not surprising: If people perceive that interest rates are low they will "lock in" the low rates with a FRCM; if rates are viewed as high and the trend is downward, they will select an

ARM so that they may take advantage of the anticipated lower rates without having the expense of refinancing the mortgage.

In general terms, fixed rates have the advantage of certainty and security. With a FRCM one knows what one's financial obligations will be for the duration of the mortgage. Variable rates, on the other hand, are a gamble on future interest rates and involve a greater amount of uncertainty as to one's future obligations.

Statistics show that in the recent past persons who selected adjustable-rate mortgages have done somewhat better than those who selected fixed-rate mortgages. Of course, this is based on what has happened in the past and there is no assurance that the same will be true in the future.

Table 9-2 shows the monthly payments due and total interest paid by persons taking out fixed- and variable-rate mortgages for $100,000 during a period of high interest rates and during a period of lower rates:

Table 9-2
Comparison of FRCMs and ARMs under Various Assumptions

	Monthly payment	Total interest through 8/91
1. When rates were high (July 1984):		
14.67% 30 year fixed rate	$1,236	$102,930
Same, refinanced in Aug., 86 at 10.2%	$1,238 $ 897	$ 77,372
ARM 12.41% first year	$1,060 Highest $ 784 Lowest	$ 70,314
2. When rates were low (March 1987):		
9.08% 30 year fixed	$ 810	$ 39,464
ARM 6.41% first year	$ 626 Lowest $ 922 Highest	$ 38,767

It is interesting that the adjustable-rate mortgage performed somewhat better than the fixed-rate mortgage under different interest rates during different periods.

The decision as to which type of loan to take is complicated by the fact that lenders now offer a variety of mortgages of each type at various interest rates that are dependent on the number of "points" being charged at closing. For example, zero-point loans carry higher interest rates and, if they are adjustable, higher caps on lifetime rate increases than loans that carry a three or four point obligation. It is difficult to make concrete suggestions as to which alternative is the most attractive. Generally, if one expects to resell or refinance the property in a few years, one should select the zero point alternative and pay a somewhat higher annual interest rate. If one has excess funds at the time of closing but is concerned about the impact of high mortgage payments on the monthly budget, one should select the high points alternative that carries the lowest PI monthly payment.

§9.28 HOW LONG SHOULD A RESIDENTIAL REAL ESTATE MORTGAGE RUN?

A person with a good salary and good cash flow purchasing a residence will have a choice as to the length of the mortgage. For most people, trying to purchase the most expensive house they can afford, the choice is easy: One should choose the longest mortgage available — 30 years, for example — in order to make the monthly payment as small as possible. One will have to make more payments, but each payment will be smaller and month-to-month living will be somewhat easier.

The choice is not so easy for a person who can afford higher payments. Consider a $100,000 mortgage and a person who can easily afford $1,000 in PI payments; a 15-year mortgage may be available at 8.5 percent that involves a $985 monthly payment as compared to a 30-year mortgage at 8.9 percent carrying a $797 monthly payment. Which should the potential homeowner select? The owner saves $188 in payments per month by selecting the 30-year mortgage. However, after 15 years the shorter mortgage will have been paid off while $79,000 will still be owed on the 30-year mortgage. Looked at another way, if one simply adds up the total payments on the two mortgages (without taking into account the time value of money) the 15-year mortgage involves aggregate payments of $177,000, while the 30-year mortgage costs a total of $287,000. The 15-year mortgage seems clearly the most sensible choice, and, indeed, increasing numbers of purchasers facing this choice are opting for the shorter, higher payment mortgage.

There are other variables, however. Over the first 15 years, the payments on the 30-year mortgage are $188 per month less than the 15-year mortgage; this is a "saving" of $33,840 which may be invested over the 15-year period. Furthermore, the payments on the 30-year mortgage are mostly interest, which is deductible for federal income tax purposes; a considerably smaller amount of each payment is deductible on the 15-year mortgage. If one invests these two savings — the $188 per month saved on the payment and the tax reduction caused by the increased interest deductions — the 30-year mortgage looks much more attractive. If one assumes a 10 percent return (approximately the annual historical return provided by the Dow Jones Industrial Average), the nest egg created by these two savings will grow to $98,000 at the end of 15 years, $19,000 more than the amount of the loan balance on the 30-year mortgage at the end of 15 years.

Of course, there are major assumptions underlying this analysis, particularly the assumptions that the borrower has the will power to invest the $188 saving every month and that he will be able to average a 10 percent return over the 15 year period, a return higher than the interest rate on the mortgage. Indeed, there is probably sufficient doubt about these assumptions that one might well simply select the shorter mortgage, if one has a viable choice.

PART III.   FINANCING STRATEGIES OF THE 1980s

§9.29 THE BACKGROUND OF CREATIVE FINANCING

As interest rates and property values increased during the 1970s and 1980s, a number of innovative financing devices developed that enabled persons to acquire residential properties, which they could never have afforded under traditional standards. These practices are generally referred to as "creative financing" of residential real estate transactions; the word "creative" in this context implies a higher degree of speculation and risk than "standard" financing. Thus, the term "creative" is not necessarily a word of praise but rather implies skirting close to a line of unacceptability because of excessive risk.

Creative financing was a natural response to high interest rates and substantial appreciation in real estate values. High interest rates and high prices made potential purchasers unable to qualify for the financing of a desired purchase. Such conditions occurred during much of the 1970s and 1980s but do not exist as this is written in 1992.

As a consequence of the difficult conditions of the 1970s and 1980s, sellers often faced a shortage, or even a total absence of, qualified buyers. A critically important factor that explains almost all creative financing transactions of residential real estate is that owners of appreciated property who desire to sell are often as distressed as the purchasers themselves. And that was certainly the case in many instances during the period under discussion. It was wonderful to own a house that cost $35,000 a decade before and was now appraised at $200,000, but who could afford to buy it when interest rates were hovering at 14 percent? Sellers who had hoped to get all-cash offers (as was routinely the case ten or so years earlier when prices and interest rates were lower and most mortgages were refinanced upon the sale of the property) found that their property remained on the market for extended periods of time. Further, when they did receive offers, they stipulated that the seller was not to receive the entire purchase price immediately. Usually, a traditional counteroffer proposing a small reduction in the asking price by the seller in this situation was fruitless: The problem was much more basic than a few thousand dollars. The buyer was willing to pay the asking price but could not obtain financing for any purchase within a reasonable range of the asking price.

Creative financing was also encouraged by the fact that the seller was acutely aware that the current market price reflected a substantial profit component. For example, a house that cost $35,000 a decade ago now was now on the market for $200,000; the mortgage had been paid down to $18,000, and the owner's original $7,000 equity would grow to about $180,000 if someone paid the asking price. (Such profits were not uncommon during the early years of the real estate boom in the late 1970s.) However, after watching a few unsuccessful attempts by purchasers to finance the $200,000 asking price, many sellers concluded that it was sensible to put a portion of the potential profit at risk for a period of time in order to help the purchaser finance the transaction.

Another fundamental factor in the development of creative financing was increasing recognition that because of the rise in interest rates, older fixed-rate mortgages at low interest rates were attractive assets if they could be transferred to a potential purchaser of the house. If interest rates were at 11 percent, the opportunity to "borrow" a portion of the purchase price by taking over an outstanding mortgage at 6 percent was obviously attractive, since the payments on an 11 percent loan could easily be hundreds of dollars per month higher than those on a 6 percent loan of the same amount. Furthermore, an assumption of a loan cost the seller relatively little: The real losers were the lending institutions that had older 6 percent loans outstanding. Lenders would naturally prefer that they be paid off when the property was transferred so that they could make a new loan with the proceeds at the effective market rate of 11 percent. Thus, before considering the nature of creative financing for residential real estate, the next three sections consider the rules governing assumptions of mortgages.

In any event, once the seller recognizes that a straightforward, all-cash sale is not likely to occur, the stage for creative financing is set.

§9.30 ASSUMPTIONS AND REFINANCINGS OF MORTGAGES

This section assumes that there are no contractual restrictions on assumptions of loans. This is an artificial assumption since most fixed-payment conventional mortgages do contain such restrictions; the effect of these contractual provisions is discussed in the following section.

When a person or family decides to buy a residence on which there is already a mortgage, there are theoretically several ways of handling the transaction, and it is helpful to consider the factors affecting the choice of which method is to be followed.

The first alternative is for the new purchaser simply to obtain outside financing for the entire purchase price (over and above the down payment) from independent sources. To use the example from the previous section, the purchaser applies for a new first mortgage at 11 percent; a portion of this loan is, in effect, applied to paying off the old 6 percent mortgage on the property. This is called a refinancing and is the pattern usually followed when interest rates are stable.

An alternative transaction is an assumption. In this transaction the buyer simply pays the owner the difference between the mortgage and the sales price and agrees to make the monthly payments on the mortgage being assumed. Suppose, for example, that there is a $70,000 mortgage on a house that the owner has advertised for sale at $100,000. The purchaser has available $30,000 in cash. If the transaction is refinanced, the purchaser places a new mortgage for, say, $75,000. The proceeds of that mortgage, and $25,000 of the purchaser's outside capital, are used to pay off the $70,000 mortgage and give the seller his $30,000 of equity. In an assumption, the buyer simply pays the owner his equity of $30,000 and also agrees to make the payments required on the $70,000 mortgage.

In the absence of an interest rate differential, both the purchaser and the seller — but particularly the seller — usually prefer that the existing mortgage be refinanced. The seller, who signed the original note for the existing mortgage, usually wants the purchaser to refinance since the seller has a contingent liability on the original mortgage. In an assumption, the purchaser agrees to make the required payments on the assumed mortgage. If the purchaser defaults on this promise, the lender may go after the seller as the person who originally signed the note and who therefore remains personally liable on it. Purchasers also prefer to refinance in the absence of an interest rate differential because an assumption transaction may be more difficult to work out and (as explained below) often requires simultaneous payments on two mortgages. If we are talking about a $100,000 purchase price, and there is an outstanding first mortgage with an unpaid balance of $60,000, somehow the purchaser must come up with $40,000 to make up the difference. If the purchaser were to refinance the mortgage, he or she could presumably get an 80 percent mortgage and thus would have to come up with only $20,000 in cash. If the purchaser wishes to assume the existing mortgage but has only $20,000 in cash, he or she will have to take out a second mortgage for $20,000 and will inevitably end up making two monthly payments rather than one for a period of several years. Payments on two mortgages totaling $80,000 are significantly higher than the payment on a first mortgage for $80,000 because: (1) The interest rate on a second mortgage is higher due to greater risk; (2) the purchaser is amortizing the principal of two mortgages simultaneously; and (3) second mortgages usually mature within a shorter period, requiring larger principal payments to amortize the unpaid balance.

If the purchaser is to take over the seller's mortgage, there are two alternative forms that the transaction may take. The most common is for the purchaser to "assume and agree to pay" the mortgage. The other is for the purchaser to take "subject to" the mortgage. If the purchaser takes subject to the mortgage, the purchaser thereafter makes the payments on the seller's mortgage but is not personally liable on it. The purchaser has not promised either the lender or the seller that he will make the monthly payments or pay the amount of the loan. Such a purchaser, theoretically at least, is free to walk away and abandon the property at any time; the incentive to remain and make the payments arises from the fact that he or she will lose whatever cash payment and mortgage reductions made before the mortgage is foreclosed. The seller, of course, remains personally liable on the loan, a disagreeable fact that the seller may regret if economic conditions change dramatically and the purchaser in fact exercises his privilege and "walks."

Alternatively, if the seller requires the purchaser to assume and agree to pay the mortgage, the purchaser makes a promise to the seller that he will make all the payments the seller is obligated to make, and if the purchaser fails to do so, he becomes personally liable to the seller. The original lender may also have the right to sue on the purchaser's promise to assume the mortgage on a theory of third-party beneficiary though as a practical matter this question does not come up very often. The seller who originally signed the note, of course, remains personally liable on the loan, but the seller has some protection if the purchaser walks because the purchaser is liable on the mortgage and can be sued by the seller if he or she is compelled to pay it. On the other hand, this right to sue may not be very valuable if, as is often the case, the purchaser walked because he or she was unable to keep up the payments.

Considering the exposure of the seller in both subject to and assumption transactions, it might seem plausible for the seller to request the lender to accept the new purchaser in his or her place and release the seller from his or her obligation on the mortgage. This type of transaction is technically a novation since it constitutes the substitution of one debtor for another with the consent of the creditor. Most commercial lenders simply refuse to even consider accepting a novation or releasing the original borrower from that obligation. This position is understandable because there is no benefit to the lender in releasing anyone, and, in any event, the lender usually prefers that the loan be refinanced so that it can collect the prepayment penalty and current market interest rates. Certainly the lender will not consider releasing the original borrower if the purchaser of the property does not appear to be as creditworthy as that borrower.

If the seller does not approach the lender for a novation, the lender is usually unaware that the property has been sold and that some new person is making payments on the mortgage. One might think that it would learn of the transaction because it suddenly starts receiving checks from a different payee; most lenders, however, are large bureaucratic organizations that are concerned about receiving a payment but pay no attention to its source. A lender is more likely to learn of the transaction when it receives an inquiry from the purchaser, who explains, during the course of the conversation, that he or she is now making the payments on the outstanding mortgage.

§9.31 PREPAYMENT PENALTIES

Another factor sometimes affecting the decision whether or not to refinance an existing mortgage is the differences in closing costs. Many lending institutions impose prepayment penalties for an early retirement of the mortgage. This penalty, usually fixed at 1 or 2 percent of the unpaid balance, is nominally a charge for the cost to the lender of accepting prepayment of the loan and redeploying the funds into another mortgage; in fact, prepayment penalties are simply another way of modestly increasing the profitability of the lending business since, in periods of stable interest rates, most mortgages are refinanced when properties are sold and relatively few of them continue in existence for the full term of 25 or 30 years. Prepayment penalties, of course, tend to encourage assumptions, other things being equal.

Adjustable-rate mortgages generally permit prepayment in whole or in part at any time without penalty.

Where a loan is to be refinanced, the lender who made the original loan may be willing to refinance the transaction charging no prepayment penalty, lower closing costs, and possibly make some small reduction in interest rates over what would be charged if a new loan were made by a third party.

§9.32 RESTRICTIONS ON MORTGAGE ASSUMPTIONS

The increase in interest rates, which occurred in the late 1970s, greatly changed the dynamics of refinancing and assumptions. Lenders, who were often indifferent to the identity of the person making the payments when interest rates were stable, became much more sensitive about trafficking in mortgages that carried less than market interest rates and began to insist whenever they could that outstanding mortgages should be refinanced when the property was sold. A refinancing, of course, would be at current market rates and may yield a prepayment penalty. During this period, many banks and savings and loan associations were losing money hand-over-fist from their real estate operations. In order to attract funds in an increasingly competitive capital market, they were forced to pay investors market rates of interest, which were sometimes as high as 14 or 15 percent, while at the same time they were receiving 1960s' level interest rates of 6 percent or so on their old fixed-rate mortgages. Compulsory refinancing of these older mortgages became a matter of survival rather than profitability to many lending organizations.

Whether or not the lender's approval of an assumption or subject to transaction is required depends at least initially on the terms of the mortgage. Many older form mortgages conditioned an assumption of the mortgage on the consent of the lender, a provision that apparently had been included to ensure protection of the security in some vague way. Some mortgage forms contained specific and express clauses automatically accelerating the entire unpaid portion of the loan on any sale of the property (a so-called "due-on-sale" clause). Lenders quickly began to use these clauses to try to persuade the purchaser and seller to refinance or, at least, to agree to raise the interest rate on the mortgage being assumed toward current market levels. In other words, these clauses were often not used as a total veto of any assumption or a mandatory refinancing, but rather were used as a lever to increase the effective interest on the mortgage. The screams of anger by both purchaser and seller as they saw the asset consisting of the below-market interest rate loan apparently disappear could be clearly heard throughout the country, and such clauses rapidly became a political issue in many states. Several states prohibited such clauses either by legislation or by judicial decision, but they are permitted by federal law in connection with federally insured mortgages. The Supreme Court has held that state legislation prohibiting such clauses was preempted by the federal rule under the supremacy clause.

Of course, it is one thing to include a due-on-sale or consent-to-assignment clause in a mortgage: It is quite another to locate the transactions when both parties realize the importance of not calling the attention of the lending agency to an assignment. At one time, some lending agencies were scrutinizing recent filings in the land records in an effort to locate unapproved assumptions. Further, even when a transaction in violation of such a clause was discovered, the lender often found it difficult to compel the unwilling parties to recognize the rights of the lender. Litigation is costly, and courts and juries are seldom sympathetic with the lender's claim that even though they are receiving each payment when it is due, they are entitled to negotiate considerably higher payments because the parties did not obtain the consent of the lender as required by the boilerplate language of the mortgage.

The issues discussed in this section arise almost exclusively in connection with fixed-interest rate mortgages. They are unlikely to be a problem with adjustable-rate mortgages.

§9.33 TECHNIQUES OF CREATIVE FINANCING

The purpose of creative financing, basically, is to enable the purchaser, with the cooperation and assistance of the seller, to buy a residence that the purchaser could not afford using the traditional technique of conventional mortgage financing. With the decline in mortgage interest rates since the early 1980s, these techniques are used much less frequently than they were in the 1970s and 1980s, though they are well understood in the real estate financial community and are used in specific situations at the present time. See section 9.37.

Perhaps the simplest form of creative financing involves situations in which there is no first mortgage, or the unpaid balance of the outstanding first mortgage is so small that the seller can use the down payment to pay it off. Under these circumstances, the seller may herself make a first mortgage loan, typically at an interest rate or on terms that are more favorable to the purchaser than terms that would be available from commercial real estate loan sources. A first mortgage loan on commercial terms is salable in the market for real estate mortgages, but typically the specially negotiated terms of a creatively financed mortgage makes the loan unattractive as a commercial investment, or, at the very least, salable only at a significant discount. Hence, this technique is usually practical only when the seller is willing to hold the mortgage for a substantial period of time.

Whether or not the seller comes out ahead by accepting and holding a first mortgage depends on a host of unknowable and unpredictable factors: the terms of the new first mortgage, future changes in interest rates while the seller owns the mortgage, the strength of the market for outstanding first liens on real estate in the community, and, if the purchaser decides to resell the property, what terms can be worked out for the resale. One suspects that, in most situations, the seller ends up losing if he or she agrees to take a privately negotiated first mortgage, though the loss may be mitigated if market rates of interest thereafter decline.

Another example of creative financing is the seller who agrees to take a balloon note for a portion of the purchase price that represents unrealized profit. A balloon note is basically a very simple idea: It is a note that requires periodic payments, but the unpaid balance comes due long before the payments fully amortize the borrowed amount. In the real estate context, a balloon note might come due in 5 or 10 years, but the periodic monthly payments are computed based on a 25- or 30-year amortization schedule. Such a note might be described as a 5-year balloon with payments based on a 25-year 10 percent amortization schedule. This means that monthly payments are computed on the 25-year 10 percent table, but the loan itself comes due in 5 years. When it comes due, there is, of course, a huge final payment due—the balloon—since the monthly payments have mostly gone to the payment of interest, and the principal has been reduced only slightly. Because most borrowers do not have the funds to pay the balloon in cash when it comes due, the property is usually then sold or the loan is refinanced. Refinancing may involve a second balloon note, which in turn may lead to a third. If interest rates have risen or fallen when the balloon comes due, the new mortgage covering the balloon is written at the then-current market rate. A balloon note, in other words, is not unlike an ARM in ultimate economic effect. An owner of appreciated property may be willing to accept a low-payment balloon note reflecting most of the potential profit; why not take a chance as long as the balloon note will require refinancing or sale in five years? If worst comes to worst and the buyer is unable to pay off the balloon and refinancing is impractical, the seller gets the property back, but his or her disappointment is assuaged by any down payment and principal reduction payments made by the purchaser, which the seller retains. Most balloon notes are probably carried by sellers of property, though some financial institutions also accept short-term balloon notes.

Somewhat similar is a short-term first mortgage for the bulk of the purchase price, which serves as a stopgap for the seller and reflects the willingness of the purchaser to live dangerously. When the purchaser is unable to come up with acceptable traditional financing, the seller may offer to carry a first lien on the property on an interest-only basis for a short time, perhaps two years. This mortgage may be for 80 percent or more of the agreed sales price with the seller paying cash for the balance. It is understood that the purchaser will either find acceptable permanent financing in the interim or resell the property. The purchaser is living dangerously, since he is gambling on being able to either resell the property on favorable terms or work out acceptable financing in two years when it is not possible today. If neither alternative is feasible, a default on the short-term loan is inevitable, and the purchaser loses all the cash invested in the property. The seller, of course, gets the property back, but his or her disappointment is again assuaged by the down payment made by the purchaser, which the seller retains.

A much more common type of creative financing is for the purchaser to assume (or take subject to) a below-market-rate first mortgage and for the seller to agree to accept a second mortgage for a short term. Assume, for example, that the parties have agreed upon a price of $100,000 for a residence on which there is a first mortgage that has a current balance of

$40,000, payable at the rate of $350 per month, PI, at 9 percent interest. This mortgage was placed on the property eight years earlier to secure a $43,500 loan taken out by the present seller. Current market interest rates are 15 percent per year. The purchaser has $20,000 for the down payment but cannot afford to pay $1,011 per month PI on a conventional $80,000 mortgage. If the first mortgage can be assumed or transferred, the seller may offer to take back a $40,000 second mortgage, also at 9 percent, over 10 years. The payments on this second mortgage are $507 per month, which when added to the $350 first mortgage payment, total $857 per month, a monthly payment that is feasible. A number of variations may occur at this point. The seller may agree to accept interest-only payments for the second mortgage, in effect making it a long-term balloon note, or seek a shorter term for repayment, or a higher interest rate, offset by smaller payments in earlier years. These variations are unpredictable because the terms are entirely the subject of negotiation between two private persons who may reach whatever terms they find mutually acceptable.

If the first mortgage is not assumable, and the purchaser must obtain a 15 percent, current-market-rate mortgage, the seller may agree to buy down the purchaser's monthly payments of $1,011 by agreeing to pay points or to contribute a portion of the purchase price to an escrow held by the lender. Presumably, either the points or the contribution are in effect added to the sales price of the residence. These techniques are sometimes called equity sharing. This arrangement was described above as a pledged account mortgage, or a PAM.

Lease-purchase option arrangements may also be used as creative financing devices. A purchaser faced with unacceptable market interest rates may lease a residence for a period of one or two years with an option to buy. The parties agree that the option to buy at a price set forth in the lease will be exercised; indeed, the purchaser may contractually commit to exercising the option. Even though the formal arrangement is landlord/tenant, the parties view it as purchaser/seller. The purchaser may be required to pay a substantial sum for this option, a payment that is lost if he does not complete the purchase. The lease payments in part, as well as the option payment in full, may be credited by the purchaser against the purchase price when the option is exercised. The amount of the lease payments before the option is exercised is usually affected by the size of the outstanding mortgage being carried by the seller as well by the fact that interest and taxes are deductible for federal income tax purposes by the seller during the term of the lease, while the payments of "rent" are not deductible by the purchaser.

Creative residential financing also may involve obtaining multiple mortgages on the property in order to finance its acquisition. A not entirely hypothetical case may illustrate this technique. In 1973, a law school teacher had accepted the position of a senior government bureaucrat in Washington, D.C., a notoriously expensive area for residential real estate at the time. He had six or seven children and a government salary of $47,000. He obviously needed a large and expensive house. In 1974, he bought a $175,000 house in a Washington suburb, substantially on the following basis: (1) a down payment of $20,000 and an $80,000 first mortgage by a savings and loan association for 30 years at the then current market rate of 9.5 percent, with a monthly payment PI of $672; (2) a second mortgage for $25,000 repayable over ten years, interest (11 percent) only for five years, with the principal to be paid in equal installments over the following five years. The lender was an unregulated commercial lending corporation. For five years the payment was $229 per month; thereafter the payments would jump to $543 per month; (3) a third mortgage for $50,000. This third mortgage was held by the seller. Its terms were interest at the rate of 12 percent per year, plus an amortization schedule that required the purchaser to reduce principal at the rate of $100 per month for five years, followed by a single balloon payment of $44,000. For five years the monthly payment on this mortgage was $600 per month ($500 per month interest plus $100 principal).

When the monthly payments were added up, the bureaucrat's housing costs were $1,500 per month, PI, or $1,900 per month, PITI. Approximately 42 percent of his salary was spent on housing. He actually had a modest amount of outside income so that his housing costs were about 35 percent of his actual income. Since virtually all of his monthly payments in the first few years constituted interest that was deductible on his federal income tax return, Uncle Sam assisted him significantly. But what would happen at the end of five years when $44,000 cash must be raised to pay off the third mortgage? The answer is simple: There is no way the bureaucrat could afford to live in the house after the fifth year unless he could refinance it. At the time he decided to buy the house, he knew he must resell or refinance it at the end of five years, if not before. If inflation in real estate values continued in the Washington, D.C. area, the appreciation in the value of the house should permit him to meet his obligations without difficulty, and if he resold the house at that time, he might pay off all the obligations and have a profit besides which, presumably, would be invested in another, and potentially even larger, house. If prices continued to increase, he probably could refinance on more satisfactory terms in light of hoped for governmental salary increases. What actually happened was entirely favorable to the law teacher: Real estate values in the area continued to increase substantially, and after three years he resigned his government position, sold the house promptly for $205,000, and went back into teaching outside of the Washington, D.C. area. His down payment for his next house had increased from $20,000 to about $35,000 as a result of living in Washington. Not too bad, in retrospect.

§9.34 WRAPAROUND MORTGAGES

A "wraparound mortgage" is an assumption-related device, which was originally designed for use in financing commercial real estate but turned out to be ideal for the quiet assumptions of mortgages on residential real estate as well. A wraparound mortgage sounds mysterious but is really not. It is described most easily by an example.

Assume that a residence is for sale for $120,000. There is presently a $70,000, 8 percent mortgage on the property, which has 28 years to run. Current mortgage rates are 12 to 13 percent for a new first mortgage. The purchaser has $25,000 in cash, which is enough for the required 20 percent down payment. If the property were refinanced with the purchaser paying the $25,000 down and taking a $96,000 mortgage for 30 years at 13 percent, the monthly payment would be $1,061.95, PI. That is more than the purchaser feels she can afford to pay on a monthly basis for housing. The purchaser therefore proposes that she assume the first mortgage and the seller carry a second mortgage of $26,000 for ten years at 5 percent. The monthly payments on the first mortgage are $513.64 PI; the payment on the second mortgage is $275.77, for a total expected monthly PI payment of about $790, which the purchaser feels that she can handle. Seller responds by offering the purchaser a single wraparound mortgage of $96,000 at 9.5 percent over 30 years, with the seller continuing to be responsible for and making the payments on the $70,000 first mortgage. The payment on the wraparound is $807, roughly what the purchaser feels she is able to pay. The wraparound mortgage is a junior lien since the first mortgage remains unaffected with payments continued to be made by the seller. Everyone but the lender benefits from this arrangement. The purchaser has bought the desired residence for a down payment and monthly payment that she believes she can afford. The seller receives the $24,000 down payment in cash as well as the right to receive $807 per month, out of which $513 per month must be used to make the payments on the "wrapped-around" first mortgage. After making this payment, the seller keeps $287 per month. This is a 13 percent return on the $26,000 actually borrowed by the purchaser from the seller.

The reason a wraparound is financially attractive to the seller is that the purchaser is in effect paying the seller 9.5 percent interest on the $70,000 mortgage that is actually costing the seller 8 percent. The extra 1.5 percent on this amount results in the dramatic increase in the effective interest rate on the portion of the purchase price being financed by the seller. The difference between the 9.5 percent wraparound rate and the 8 percent rate of the first mortgage is usually referred to as the "spread."

Two further comments are appropriate. First, in a wraparound, the seller remains involved with the property and is not out cleanly. Second, the wraparound mortgage cannot be readily sold in the open market, since it is a second mortgage at less than current market rates of interest for such mortgages.

The wraparound concept violates due on sale clauses but may not violate prohibitions against assignment of the mortgage, since the transaction does not technically involve an assignment of the first mortgage.

PART IV.   FINANCING STRATEGIES OF THE 1990s

§9.35 REFINANCING THE HIGH INTEREST RATE MORTGAGE

The previous sections discussed residential financing techniques that developed during periods of high interest rates and escalating real estate values. The 1990s have seen dramatic declines in interest rates and, in many areas at least, static or declining real estate values. In some areas hard hit by overbuilding and substantial unemployment, real estate values have declined substantially. Further, lending agencies, stung by the collapse of the savings and loan industry, have tightened loan requirements and required more careful evaluation of loan applications. These developments have led to new problems and new strategies by homeowners and would-be homeowners.

Consider the plight of a real estate owner who purchased property in the early 1980s and at that time decided to take out a fixed-rate conventional mortgage at 13 percent. By 1992, interest rates had declined to 8.75 percent for a 30-year fixed loan, 8.34 percent for a 15-year fixed loan, and 6.27 percent for the first year of an adjustable-rate mortgage. If the owner can place a new first mortgage on the property, using the proceeds to pay off the existing mortgage, monthly payments will be reduced by more than $250 per month over the next 20 years. In other words, this is an owner who should consider "refinancing" his mortgage.

The rule of thumb is that one should consider refinancing when current interest rates are 2 percent or more below the rate of the mortgage. However, there are other factors that should be considered.

Prepayment penalties and closing costs for the new mortgage, of course, must be considered. Refinancing usually involves closing costs similar to the sale of real estate (except for the broker's commission). The out-of-pocket costs of refinancing, including discount points and miscellaneous fees (which may easily amount to several thousand dollars), should be compared with the monthly reduction in the mortgage payment (PI only) to determine how many months it will take to recoup the costs. If the loan is refinanced through the same lender, however, some closing costs may be avoided. There is also a "hassle factor," which may deter refinancing since the paperwork may be substantial.

Refinancing is attractive only when the owner plans to remain in the house for a period of several years (so that the costs of refinancing can be recouped from the lower mortgage payments). A somewhat more sophisticated rule of thumb is that refinancing should be undertaken only if: (1) the up-front costs can be recouped in three years through the savings on monthly payments; and (2) the homeowner expects that the mortgage will remain in effect for at least five years.

It is sometimes naively believed that lenders are always happy to have their loans prepaid early; that is not true when current market interest rates are below the interest rate on the loan. The small print in some high interest rate mortgages may contain extremely onerous restrictions on prepayment, varying from flat prohibitions against prepayment to provisions limiting the percentage of the outstanding loan that may be prepaid in any one year and providing that such prepayments shall be applied to the last payments due on the loan. Such clauses, if valid, may effectively prevent refinancing altogether, and their validity has been litigated on theories of unreasonable restraints on alienation and violation of state law. In some instances, restrictions on prepayment may appear in the fine print of the promissory note itself rather than in the mortgage.

Individuals with adjustable-rate mortgages may also wish to refinance in order to lock in a lower rate (though one might inadvertently lock in a higher rate if interest rates continue to decline).

In areas in which the value of residential real estate has declined, one must also make sure that the current real estate value will support the refinanced mortgage. Lenders generally will not lend more than 80 percent of the current value of a residence; if the current mortgage is larger than that amount (and that may well be the case in some depressed areas of the country), the mortgage cannot be refinanced unless the owner is willing to bring cash to the table to pay down the current mortgage to a level that permits refinancing. If there is an outstanding home equity loan, that must be treated as part of the mortgage to determine whether refinancing is feasible.

Over the long haul, refinancing at even a one percentage point saving is attractive. If an individual took out a $150,000 30-year mortgage at 10.5 percent, refinancing at 9.5 percent one year later would save $25,700 in interest over the life of the loan.

§9.36 VOLUNTARY INCREASES IN MONTHLY PAYMENTS

During the 1990s, many homeowners have adopted the strategy of voluntarily increasing the amount they pay each month, thereby in effect prepaying the mortgage. In part this may be due to a pessimistic view of future earning power; in part it may be due to the realization that alternative riskless investments of excess funds in the 1990s have yields considerably lower than the interest rate on the mortgage. See sections 16.3, 16.4, 16.7, and 16.8. Why invest funds in investments that yield 3 or 4 percent a year when one can use the same funds to make partial prepayments on a personal obligation that carries a 10.5 percent interest rate? For example, in the case of the $150,000 mortgage described in the last paragraph of the previous section, a strategy of reducing principal by an extra $100 per month would save thousands of dollars of interest, as well as shortening the repayment period by eight and one-half years. Of course, those savings are many years in the future and must be discounted to present values, but a low discount factor would be used in this calculation. See Chapter 2. As with many other financial questions, there are books and software programs available to assist. the homeowner in deciding whether to refinance (as suggested in the preceding section) or to systematically reduce principal by a voluntary monthly payment.

§9.37 RESIDENTIAL MORTGAGES AND BANKRUPTCY

The 1990s have seen a rise in consumer bankruptcies, many of which involve individuals who own residential real estate that is subject to one or more mortgages. In a number of cases, the current market value of the real estate is substantially less than the face amounts of the mortgages on the property. An earlier chapter discusses the broad outlines of federal bankruptcy law; this section describes several unique problems relating to the interaction between residential mortgages and the insolvent owner.

The personal obligation incurred by a purchaser of real estate when he or she signs a promissory note that is secured by a mortgage on the real estate is dischargeable in bankruptcy. That discharge, however, does not affect the lien of the mortgage, and the mortgagee may foreclose on the property even if the debt is discharged. In an effort to preserve the personal residence, some insolvent debtors have filed for bankruptcy under Chapter 7 to obtain a bankruptcy discharge, and then shortly thereafter filed under Chapter 13 to establish a plan of repayment of outstanding obligations to prevent the mortgagee from foreclosing on the mortgage lien. This combination of different chapters of the bankruptcy code is sometimes called a "Chapter 20" bankruptcy proceeding.

In 1990 and 1991, several bankruptcy courts permitted real estate owners who were in bankruptcy under Chapter 7 and facing deficiencies on their defaulted real estate mortgages to retain the real estate by ordering the mortgage debt to be lowered to the fair market value of the property. It was unclear whether the monthly payments would thereafter be reduced to amortize the reduced principal over the original mortgage term or would continue at their former level (thereby paying off the mortgage in a shorter time). Lenders objected vigorously to this "cram down" because it deprived them of any interest in possible appreciation of the real estate. Lenders would prefer to foreclose and take their chances on later disposing of the property when prices improve rather than being compelled to reduce the loan immediately to the current fair market value of the property. In 1992, the Supreme Court held that lenders could not be compelled to accept such cram downs under Chapter 7, based on technical language in that chapter of the Bankruptcy Act. Hence, a bankrupt who obtains a discharge from personal liability on a mortgage loses his residence unless that liability is paid in full.

In some states, a personal residence is exempt from involuntary seizure by creditors and, as a result, from administration in bankruptcy. However, a mortgage is a voluntary lien and may be foreclosed upon by the holder of the mortgage consistently with state exemption statutes.

§9.38 RESIDENTIAL MORTGAGES AND THE FEDERAL INCOME TAX

Chapter 19 describes briefly the federal income tax treatment of individuals. This section describes several unique problems relating to the interaction between residential mortgages and the traps created by the forgiveness of indebtedness concept under the federal income tax. These issues arise only in the case of financially troubled homeowners who sell their residences at a loss.

The sale of a residence is generally a transaction that gives rise to taxable gain or loss. There are two major exceptions: (1) If a taxpayer purchases another residence at a higher price, the tax on the gain is deferred; and (2) a one-time exclusion exists for up to $125,000 of gain for persons over the age of 55. Neither of these exceptions applies when a residence is sold at a loss. Many people are shocked to learn that the sale of a residence at a significant loss may give rise to taxable income.

Assume that a person purchased a residence for $150,000 and placed a $120,000 mortgage on the property. Real estate values in the area have collapsed and the property is now worth only $100,000. The owner is now clearly insolvent and in default on his payments on the mortgage and other debts. The holder of the mortgage agrees to release the lien of the mortgage and forgive the obligation of the owner upon the sale of the residence to a third party for $100,000. All the proceeds of the sale are to be paid to the holder of the mortgage, but the homeowner's responsibility for the deficiency is forgiven. The tax treatment of this transaction from the standpoint of the defaulting owner is little short of disastrous: The owner has a $50,000 economic loss that is not deductible because it arises out of a personal, and not a business, obligation. He also has $20,000 of ordinary income that is subject to tax, arising from the forgiveness of the balance of the mortgage obligation. The tax due on this additional amount of income may be as much as $6,200. That is forgiveness of indebtedness income.

Essentially the same tax result occurs if the holder of the mortgage forecloses on the mortgage, buys it in at $100,000, and then releases the debtor from the potential deficiency.

If the owner files for bankruptcy after his indebtedness is forgiven, he will discover that the tax bill of $6,200 is not dischargeable. In this situation, it would be much more sensible for the owner to declare bankruptcy before entering into any transactions that involve a release of a portion of his obligation since any deficiency is dischargeable without income tax consequences in bankruptcy.

As indicated, one can defer gain on the sale of a residence to the extent the proceeds of the sale are invested in a new residence within two years. This provision, however, does not apply if the owner moves to a less expensive house. Again, the tax law may give rise to unexpected and unpleasant consequences. Assume, for example, that a homeowner bought a house for $100,000 in 1978. In 1987, it had appreciated to $300,000, and the owner refinanced the mortgage, placing a $250,000 mortgage on the property. In addition to paying off the old mortgage, this amount was used for educational purposes and stock market investments, most of which turned out badly. By early 1992, the value of the property has declined to $220,000, and the owner is having difficulty meeting the $2,700 per month payments on the $250,000 mortgage. The owner decides to sell the present house and purchase a $175,000 condominium. First, after finding a buyer at $220,000 the owner must "bring to the table" $30,000 in cash to pay off the balance of the current mortgage. Second, the owner may defer recognition of gain only on the difference between the basis of the old house ($100,000) and the cost of the new one ($175,000). Thus, the owner has a taxable gain on the difference between the sales price of the old residence ($220,000) and its basis ($100,000) and the non-deferred portion of the gain ($75,000). As a result, taxable income of $45,000 arises from the transaction. Finally, the owner must come up with the down payment on the condominium. All this without receiving any cash from the sale of the old house!

§9.39 "TAKE BACK" MORTGAGES

Tight money and a sluggish economy make residences hard to sell. This is particularly true of second homes or vacation homes that are a luxury rather than a necessity. In the 1990s, owners increasingly are finding it necessary to offer an incentive to prospective buyers in the form of seller-provided financing. Such loans have come to be called "take back" mortgages, but they are identical to some forms of creative financing in the 1990s. The difference is that they are now an incentive to unload slow-moving properties rather than to assist the eager buyer in financing a purchaser that is beyond his means as judged by commercial standards.

A take back may be entirely "home made," avoiding closing costs and providing a better interest rate than the purchaser could find on the commercial market. After all, the seller is facing returns of 3 or 4 percent on riskless investments; a take back secured by the vacation home paying 5 or 6 percent looks like a pretty good investment. Take backs often are five to fifteen year loans, with a balloon payment of the principal at the end. Monthly payments may be based on a 15- or 30-year amortization schedule.

Further, if the seller religiously reinvests the payments made by a buyer on a 6 percent loan in current riskless investments paying 3 percent, the aggregate return approaches that of a commercial mortgage.

There are obvious pitfalls in this approach. If the seller thereafter needs funds, she may find it difficult to resell the take back into the commercial mortgage market except at a significant discount. Further, the risk of default and expensive foreclosure proceedings must be taken into account. The credit, financial, and housing history of the buyer should be investigated. A substantial down payment should be required to reduce the risk that the buyer will "walk." Finally, the risk is greatly increased if the seller is asked to take back a second mortgage rather than a first lien. If the buyer defaults on the first mortgage, the seller is in serious risk of getting nothing from the second mortgage.

Owner-provided financing clearly has not returned to the levels of the 1980s. But they are used in the 1990s because that may be the only way to make a deal.

10 Annuities and Retirement

§10.1 INTRODUCTION

A stream of payments payable at specified intervals in the future is called an annuity. Annuities significantly affect the lives of most persons in the United States at some time, even though many persons may have never seen the word and may not know what it means. Rather, annuities are better known as pensions, social security, retirement benefits, or in-service benefits. Modern private annuities form an essential part of retirement plans for employed and self-employed persons, often supplementing social security and related public benefit programs. Almost all of these modern annuities arise directly from the employment relationship and constitute a type of deferred compensation for personal services. They may be referred to in employment manuals or brochures as the employer's "retirement plan" or as "fringe benefits" of employment.

This chapter introduces the real-world modern annuity in a logical, but indirect, way, dealing first with simple and somewhat artificial examples, and then progressing to present-day retirement annuities.

§10.2 COMMERCIAL ANNUITIES IN GENERAL

Many annuities are actually purchased in the marketplace, usually from life insurance companies. In 1991, it was estimated that 15 million annuity contracts issued by life insurance companies were outstanding. If payments are of fixed amounts for a fixed period, the determination of the present values of such payments is a straightforward application of the time value of money, that is, the principle of discounting future payments to present values, applying an appropriate discount rate to each payment to determine the present value of each payment, and then adding up those present values. This subject was introduced in sections 2.5 and 2.6, and an actual example is given in section 10.3.

Most commercial annuities are designed not to make payments for a fixed period but rather to continue for the lifetime of one or more persons. The pricing of such annuities requires an estimate of the probable lifespans involved, which in turn involves reliance on mortality or life expectancy tables, a topic discussed in sections 10.18 and 11.6. Indeed, if the word annuity conjures up any image at all to the average person, it is probably to an elderly person receiving a payment each month for the balance of his or her life. A person receiving an annuity is sometimes referred to as an annuitant. Mortality and life expectancy tables are discussed briefly in sections 10.18 and 11.6. To an increasing extent, modern retirement programs utilize commercial annuities, usually by the purchase of a lifetime annuity shortly before the retirement of the employee or sometimes by the purchase of a guaranteed investment contract from an insurance company for the benefit of each covered employee.

An annuity for the life of a person is in a sense the converse of life insurance on the life of that person: The annuity pays during the lifetime of the person and ends upon his or her death, while life insurance becomes due and payable on death and provides for the period following the death of the person.

In the discussion of commercial annuities below, the person creating the annuity is referred to as the creator or the contributor. The person receiving the annuity is referred to as the annuitant; the annuitant and the contributor can, of course, be the same person. The person or entity agreeing to make the payments is referred to as the "seller" or "writer" of the annuity. Often the seller of an annuity is a life insurance company that is also in the business of selling annuities.

§10.3 SINGLE-PREMIUM IMMEDIATE ANNUITIES

It is easiest to begin with a specific example of the simplest kind of annuity that does not involve any mortality calculation. A rather well-to-do 55-year-old widower is considering the purchase of an annuity. For $100,000 cash paid to a large life insurance company, the company will agree to pay him, or his estate, $1,200 per month each year for ten years. The $100,000 represents more than 50 percent of his current liquid resources: It may have resulted from a lifetime of incremental saving, from life insurance proceeds on the life of his deceased spouse, or from a variety of other sources. The theory behind the ten-year provision is that in ten years he will begin receiving retirement income from other sources: social security payments and a lifetime annuity from an employee pension plan. The ten-year annuity is thus a stopgap. There is no gambling on the death of the annuitant in this example; payments are guaranteed for ten years, whether or not the widower is alive. If he dies within the ten years, the payments will continue to be made to his estate or to whom he directs in his will for the balance of the ten-year term. At the end of ten years, the obligation of the writer of the annuity ends.

An annuity of the type described in the previous paragraph that has payments beginning immediately is called an "immediate annuity." Most immediate annuities today are written so that payments will continue for the life of the annuitant rather than, as in our initial example, for a specified period of years. Most immediate annuities, in other words, are complicated by an assessment of a life expectancy.

It should be obvious in our example that each monthly payment received by the widower consists partly of return of his principal and partly of interest earned on the balance of the money. Without taking into account the time value of money, it appears that he is investing $100,000 and receiving back a total of $144,000 ($1,200 per month times 120 months). However, the discussion in Chapter 2 should make clear the fallacy of that simplistic approach. The reason that this is attractive from the standpoint of the writer of the annuity is that each month it is earning interest on that portion of the $100,000 that it has not yet repaid to the annuitant. In other words, each payment except for the last has an interest component as well as a return of principal component. A computation (difficult with pencil and paper but easy with a preprogrammed handheld calculator) reveals that the annuitant is actually receiving a 7.75 percent return on his $100,000 investment over ten years. In other words, the sum of the present values of the 120 payments of $1,200 each, computed at 7.75 percent, is almost $100,000. Mathematically, at 7.75 percent, the first monthly payment of $1,200 (the first annuity payment) constitutes $645.83 of interest on the $100,000 and $554.17 return of principal. The second payment consists of $642.25 of interest (one month's interest on $99,445.83 ($100,000 minus $554.17)) and $557.75 return of principal; the third payment consists of $638.65 of interest (one month's interest on $98,887.88 (99,445.83 minus $557.75)) and $561.35 of principal. And so on, for each of the remaining payments until the last $1,200 payment, which consists almost entirely of principal and finally exhausts the original $100,000 of principal. In each month the remaining principal is calculated by subtracting the amount of principal repaid the previous month. If these figures look vaguely familiar, compare the analysis of the conventional level-premium mortgage in section 9.17. From the mortgagee's perspective, one can analogize the amortization of a loan to an "annuity" being received from the mortgagor.

If the current market rate for riskless investments is 9 percent at the time of the proposed purchase (an assumption that is not realistic in 1992 when this is being written but quite realistic only five years earlier), this annuity at first glance does not appear to be a very attractive deal. The annuitant would apparently be better off simply investing the money in a federally insured bank account at the higher market interest rate of 9 percent, and withdrawing each month the accumulated interest and a portion of principal necessary to yield his $1,200 each month. In the discussion below, this will be referred as a "do-it-yourself annuity." The economic difference between the life insurance company's product and the do-it-yourself variety of annuity in this example can be made graphic by considering the composition of the first few payments. If the same amount were invested at 9 percent, the first month's interest would have been $750, and only $450 would have had to be drawn from principal to make the $1,200 payment. The life insurance company only gave the annuitant credit for interest of $645.83 and repaid him $554.17 from his principal. At 9 percent, the interest for the second month would be $746.63 and the amount of principal that would have to be drawn out would be $453.38. Corresponding figures for the life insurance company annuity are $642.25 of principal and $557.75 of interest. In each month thereafter the performance of the do-it-yourself annuity appears to be superior, reflecting the fact that the dollars are invested at a 9 percent annual rate rather than at a 7.75 percent annual rate. At the end of the ten-year pay-out period, the bank account would still have $12,918 in it while the commercial annuity would have been exhausted.

Why might a person be interested in buying an immediate annuity at apparently disadvantageous terms rather than simply investing the money directly in a higher yielding investment? There are several possible advantages. For one thing, there is a certain amount of convenience in simply receiving a check each month rather than withdrawing $1,200 from an investment account each month. There is also the matter of self-discipline. Does the annuitant have the mental resolve to follow the routine each month without taking out "a little extra, just this time"? Third, an elderly person with an investment account may be defrauded by a smooth talking swindler; investment of funds in an annuity provides protection to the annuitant against unwise dissipation of assets. These personal factors may not appear to be of great importance in this simple example, but in individual cases they may well justify the decision to purchase an immediate annuity rather than to simply turn over a large sum of money to an annuitant who must rely on that sum over a long period of time to provide his or her livelihood.

A much more substantial advantage of the life insurance company annuity from the standpoint of the widower is that the return of 7.5 percent is guaranteed by the writer of the annuity for the next ten years; even if an investment account is returning 9 percent per year when it is opened, there is normally no assurance that the 9 percent market rate will remain available for that period. A graphic illustration of this point occurred during the period 1988 to 1992. Many retirees with comfortable nest eggs were, in fact, creating "do it yourself" annuities in part by investing their nest eggs in high yielding, but federally guaranteed, certificates of deposit ("CDs") issued by savings and loan associations. They were withdrawing the interest each quarter for living expenses, usually supplemented by a modest reduction in principal. Others were living entirely on the interest generated by the CDs. A four-year "jumbo" certificate of deposit might well have yielded 9 percent compounded interest when it was taken out in 1987. However, when that certificate matured in 1991, it could be renewed ("rolled over" is the phrase often used) only at 6 percent per year. Those retirees were faced with a difficult choice: They could make major reductions in their lifestyle to reflect the one-third decline in their incomes, or they could increase the rate they invaded principal, thereby increasing their risk and anxiety that their nest egg would not last as long as they did. Many of these retirees would doubtless have done better (if they had had the benefit of foresight in predicting the decline in interest rates) — and would have had more peace of mind — if they had purchased an annuity rather than "doing it yourself."

The writer of an immediate annuity (such as in the example under discussion) obviously suffers if interest rates drop as they did during the early 1990s, and it earns 5 percent on invested funds while being required to pay an annuitant 7.75 percent. In effect, the writer of an immediate annuity takes the risk of market fluctuations in interest rates. It is able to do this profitably because it can diversify against this risk since it enters into many different arrangements and many different investments of varying maturities and varying yields at different times. It would be difficult for most annuitants on their own to spread the risk being assumed by an insurance company when it writes a fixed annuity at a specified interest rate.

Of course, there are two sides to changes in investment rates. If interest rates go up, the writer of an immediate annuity gets fat from investing the annuitant's funds at 15 percent, say, while continuing to make fixed payments at a rate of 7.75 percent.

An immediate annuity obviously can provide a considerable amount of convenience and security at the cost of some loss of yield. One way of looking at this transaction is that for a premium of one and one-fourth percent, the insurance company is assuming the administrative costs of handling the transaction as well as the risk that interest rates may decline during the next ten years.

If the immediate annuity is to continue for the life of the widower, the writer is also taking an actuarial risk that the widower might outlive his life expectancy, so that payments will continue longer than expected. The insurance company writing the annuity normally charges an additional premium of 1 percent or so — or quietly reduces the promised payments by a small amount — to assume this additional risk.

An argument may be made against the immediate annuity based on the possibility that the annuitant may become ill and need a significant portion of his principal back immediately rather than in bits of $1,200 per month. This, of course, is not a problem with the do-it-yourself annuity. Also, it is not a problem with most immediate annuities since they generally allow cancellation upon the payment of a surrender fee and a refund of most of the remaining unpaid principal. While cancellation may be relatively expensive, it at least permits most financial emergencies to be met.

A retiree considering the purchase of an immediate annuity is likely to compare the monthly payment under the annuity with the earnings he or she should receive if the purchase price were invested in a riskless investment such as a certificate of deposit. This is not an accurate comparison, of course, since a portion of each annuity payment represents a return of a portion of principal while the earnings on the CD do not. However, from the standpoint of the retiree, the entire annuity payment can be used for living expenses, and the goal of such a person is, typically, to live as comfortably as possible rather than to maximize the amount to be distributed on the retiree's death.

Another psychological benefit of the immediate annuity is that the older the retiree who takes the death benefit option, the higher the annuity payment.

It should also be mentioned that other legal devices exist that may be a substitute for an immediate annuity. For example, a retiree might consider creating an inter vivos trust for his own benefit, which would invest and disburse the retiree's savings. The relatively small amount that is usually involved, however, and the attendant fees and expenses of creating an express trust probably would make this alternative unattractive in most cases. There is, furthermore, the question of who would serve as trustee and make the decisions with respect to investments and distributions to the beneficiary of the trust.

The tax treatment of an immediate annuity is discussed in section 10.6.

§10.4 THE RISK OF DEFAULT

A countervailing factor, which must be taken into account when purchasing a commercial fixed annuity, is the possibility of insolvency of the writer of the annuity. The do-it-yourself annuity may be invested in certificates of deposit or savings accounts that are insured against loss by the federal government, but the right of an annuitant to receive payments from the writer of a commercial annuity is not secured in any way and is dependent on the continued solvency of the writer. Most commercial annuities are written by life insurance companies. This default risk may seem to be theoretical because life insurance companies seem to be large, solvent institutions with lots of money. Appearances, however, can be deceiving.

In the early 1980s, one major company writing single-premium annuities became insolvent after it had promised annuity payments at higher interest rates than it could maintain. A major brokerage firm that had an interest in this company and actively sold its products to its customers stepped in, however, and ultimately protected the investors against loss. Those customers were fortunate. In the late 1980s, three large general insurance companies failed because of disastrous junk bond or real estate investments, and unfortunately no solvent entity was willing to bail them out. The parent corporation of another major insurer also failed, although the insurance subsidiary appeared unaffected. The collapse of a general insurance company, of course, affects many persons in addition to annuitants; it may affect owners of life insurance policies, property and casualty insurance policyholders, private pension plans created by employers for the benefit of their employees, and all persons who have dealt with the failed company. For many individuals such a collapse is a calamity because, at worst, insurance protection and invested funds threaten to disappear entirely, and, at best, badly needed funds may be unavailable to their owners for extended periods.

Insurance companies are generally regulated and insured (in a limited fashion) under state rather than federal law. It was doubtful that the available state insurance funds were adequate to cover the potential losses of insureds and annuitants arising from these failures, let alone possible additional failures. The insolvency risk when one deposits funds with an insurance company is a real one, and it is important to make an assessment of the solvency of an insurance company before investing significant funds. Unfortunately, that is not always easy to do. Insurers are allowed to carry most of their investments at cost rather than present market values, an accounting system that masks potential losses in real estate investments, for example. Proposals are currently being considered to require insurers to report current market values for major portions of their balance sheets but have not been implemented as this is written.

Further, organizations such as A.M. Best Co., which rate the solvency of insurance companies, may use data that is more than 12 months old and may rely on reported book value rather than market value when assessing the insolvency risk. Some companies that rate insurers also charge a fee for supplying anything more than nominal information.

In December 1992, the National Association of Insurance Commissioners (NAIC) approved a model act that would require the development of risk based capital standards for life/health insurers. These standards would provide an index to assess the probability that a specific company might fail. The proposal prohibits the use of this information in the selling of annuities or insurance but makes the index number for each insurer available to the general public.

The insolvency of these well-known insurance companies has sent a shiver through retirees and doubtless has caused many persons to decide to keep their nest eggs rather than using them to purchase an annuity.

§10.5 SINGLE-PREMIUM DEFERRED ANNUITIES

The example set forth in section 10.3 is not typical of most modern single-premium annuity transactions since the annuity commences immediately following the payment. Much more representative is a single-premium annuity that does not begin to involve payments to the contributor/annuitant for a period of years.

Assume that a contributor makes a single, lump sum payment of $100,000 when he is 35 years old for an annuity commencing at age 65. In effect, this person is seeking to fund or supplement his or her retirement by making a long-term investment. Originally, most annuities of this type provided a fixed dollar return beginning at the age of 65. In other words, both the interest rate being paid on the $100,000 contribution over the 30 years before the first payment comes due and the interest rate that determines the amount of the annuity to be paid each month thereafter are, in effect, set forth in the original contract. Typically, a series of elections is provided so that before the annuitant reaches the age at which the first payment is due to be made, he or she could select a payment option: Options might include a single lump sum payment, payments for the balance of the contributor's life, or for the lives of the contributor and his or her spouse, or for the contributor's life with a guaranteed period of payments in the event he or she dies shortly after retirement.

The growth that naturally occurs over the 30-year period between the time the annuity is purchased and the time the first payment is due is called the "buildup." Mathematically, the buildup over 30 years on $100,000 is very substantial. If the insurance company agrees to pay 4 percent per year, the amount available at age 65 would be $331,349.80; at 6 percent, it is $602,257.22; and at 8 percent, $1,093,572.96. Thus, if the contributor can afford to put aside a substantial sum at a relatively young age, there is quite a pot at the end of the rainbow.

Thirty years is, of course, a long time. A similar investment over ten years shows results that are not as spectacular but are still substantial. A $100,000 investment made at age 55, with payments to begin in ten years, grows to $149,083.27 at 4 percent; to $181,939.67 at 6 percent; and to $221,964.02, at 8 percent.

§10.6 THE CONCEPT OF TAX DEFERRAL

In section 10.3, a commercial annuity was compared with a do-it-yourself annuity providing essentially the same benefits. The do-it-yourself possibility, while viable for a single-premium annuity with payments to commence immediately, is not attractive when compared with a deferred annuity such as the one described in section 10.5. The reason for this is the difference in the income tax treatment of an annuity, on the one hand, and a savings account, on the other.

If our hypothetical 35-year-old in section 10.5 were to try to create a do-it-yourself annuity, he would presumably create a savings account and deposit $100,000 in it, planning to allow it to accumulate for 30 years. However, he would have to pay income taxes each year on the interest earned on that account, whether or not any amount was withdrawn from the account. Assuming that the creator was in the 31 percent bracket, the interest income each year would have to be reduced by 31 percent in evaluating the benefits of a do-it-yourself annuity. As a practical matter, if the contributor created a do-it-yourself annuity, it is likely that he would not actually reduce the account by the 31 percent tax but would simply pay the taxes out of other earnings or other assets, allowing the account to grow unchecked or unconstrained. But it should be obvious that from a total net worth standpoint these tax payments must be viewed as part of the cost of the do-it-yourself alternative since the interest on the commercial annuity is not taxed as it is earned.

In the case of the commercial annuity, no income tax is due from the annuitant on the interest on the savings until that person actually begins to receive the annuity payments at age 65. In other words, a deferred annuity offers tax deferral whereas the savings account does not. Because of the 31 percent tax rate differential, an 8 percent do-it-yourself deferred annuity accumulates at about the same rate as a 5.5 percent commercial deferred annuity. This advantage, however, is not permanent. The tax deferral under the annuity continues only during the period of the buildup. Once payments on the annuity commence, a significant portion of each payment becomes subject to income tax. On the other hand, the person creating the do-it-yourself annuity has been paying taxes all along, and a much smaller proportion of each subsequent payment will be subject to tax.

The underlying concept of tax deferral (which applies to many different kinds of transactions) does not mean that the 30 years of buildup escapes tax forever. It is merely postponed until the time the annuitant receives his or her first payment under the annuity after reaching the age of 65. At that time, taxation of the buildup begins. Each payment under the annuity is viewed as having two different components: Part of the payment is a refund of a portion of the $100,000 contribution made by the contributor, and part of the payment represents a distribution from the buildup. The first portion of each payment is viewed as a tax-free return of capital, and the second portion is taxed as ordinary income. The ratio is called the "exclusion ratio," and the Internal Revenue Code and the regulations issued thereunder contain precise rules for calculating it. That ratio, however, is calculated only once at the time of the first payment and is thereafter applied to each payment. Assuming that the exclusion ratio is properly computed; all the contemplated payments are made as scheduled; the annuity is for the lifetime of the contributor; and he or she lives to his or her life expectancy, then the contributor ultimately pays income taxes on every dollar of the buildup. Of course, in most cases the taxation of the buildup will not be precise because one or more of these assumptions will not be true.

A single-premium annuity with payments to commence immediately is taxed in precisely the same way as a deferred annuity. Thus, even though the creator of the do-it-yourself annuity does not defer taxes during the buildup, an exclusion ratio is created to reflect the interest component earned after the annuity begins paying out.

Investors in commercial annuities gain tax deferral, not tax avoidance. Ultimately, the buildup is subject to tax; the only difference between it and the taxation of a do-it-yourself savings account is that the income is taxed immediately in the case of the savings account. Why is tax deferral so advantageous if — come the millennium — the contributor's tax position is unchanged? Basically, it comes down again to the time value of money. Where tax deferral is available, the contributor has the use of the funds otherwise needed to pay taxes in order to earn additional income for an extended period. A dollar today is always worth more than a dollar in the future. A dollar not paid in tax today is worth more than the same dollar paid in tax in 30 years. For this reason alone, tax deferral is always advantageous. Furthermore, since the tax deferral in an annuity usually extends over several years, the buildup occurs at an accelerated rate, because subsequent earnings on prior years' tax deferrals are also tax deferred. Tax deferral offers other possible advantages as well. For example, tax rates may be lower by the time the tax payments must begin than they were during the buildup. Because of the significant reductions in rates that occurred in 1986, however, this is unlikely to be an important factor in the immediate future. Tax rates are now more likely to go up than to go down, particularly for high-income taxpayers. Another possible advantage is that after retirement, persons may be in a lower tax bracket then they were when employed (though again this seems less likely to be important given the current rate structure described in Chapter 19), and thus the deferral may again result in the application of lower tax rates. These differences were obviously more important in earlier years than they are today, but in some individual cases advantages remain. The tax rates applicable to income in 1992 are discussed in section 19.5. The favored tax deferral treatment of annuities is usually rationalized on the ground that Congress desires to encourage private savings and private arrangements to provide retirement income.

Any premature distribution (or loan) from an annuity is deemed to be from the buildup and is subject to ordinary income tax. In addition, if withdrawals occur before the investor reaches the age of fifty-nine and one-half, they are subject to a 10 percent penalty tax, a penalty that may be avoided if the investor takes a lifetime annuity. The purpose of this penalty is to encourage the use of the benefits of tax deferral for long-term retirement needs. There is no similar penalty applicable to mutual funds or other fixed income investments.

A successful tax-oriented device often leads to a legislative response in order to protect the federal revenue base. And so it has with annuities. In recognition of the tax avoidance motive that was becoming increasingly predominant in this type of investment, Congress during the 1980s tightened up the annuity rules significantly. Today, any borrowing from an annuity is viewed as being a taxable distribution from the buildup rather than a loan out of the original contribution; other changes in the tax treatment of annuity payments have also been made to reduce further the attractiveness of deferred annuities from a tax standpoint.

In 1992, the Bush tax plan proposed the total elimination of the tax deferred feature of annuities. This proposal was promptly dropped following a hail of criticism. Apparently the annuity is to remain as a tax deferral device.

§10.7 VARIABLE INTEREST RATE ANNUITIES

The fixed-rate annuities described in the previous sections lost much of their attractiveness during the period of high interest rates in the late 1970s and early 1980s. Even with the advantage of tax deferral, an investment yielding perhaps 4 percent per year is unattractive when compared with riskless market investments yielding 12 or 14 percent per year, as was the case in the early 1980s. A person who has invested in a low-rate fixed annuity will naturally seek to suspend or terminate the annuity, even at a sacrifice if necessary, in order to invest the remaining proceeds at the higher market interest rate. Secondly, the relatively high level of inflation during this period made fixed-rate annuities extremely unattractive: The contributor was making a payment with 1965 dollars, say, in order to receive an annuity of a fixed amount in deflated dollars starting in 1995. These two problems are related since higher inflation levels tend to cause higher interest rates; together they make any long-term, fixed-payment investment relatively unattractive.

There is no inherent reason why the company writing an annuity must create an interest rate gamble. The gamble arises from the decision to pay interest at a fixed rate established in advance. Why not let the company put all payments for future annuities into an investment fund and have the amount of the ultimate annuity depend on what the company actually earns from investing this fund? This proposal eliminates much of the gamble on interest rates that inevitably occurs whenever a long-term investment is made at a fixed interest rate. On the other hand, this arrangement makes retirement planning less precise because the amount of the ultimate annuity to be paid becomes expressly dependent on the investment success of the fund. Commercial annuities of this type are called variable annuities.

The earliest versions of variable annuities date back to the 1950s. These early variable annuities eliminated the completely fixed return feature but assumed that the premium would be invested in traditional fixed income investments. The "variable" feature resulted only from changes in interest earned from such fixed investments over the years. The policies that were developed permitted the writer to designate the interest rate to be paid on funds each year (subject, however, to a minimum rate, which constituted a floor below which rates could not go). Rather confusingly, annuities of this type have come to be known as "fixed annuities" in order to distinguish them from the truly variable annuity discussed in the next section. They are referred to here, however, as "variable interest rate" annuities.

Once the notion that the payout of an annuity was not fixed in advance and could depend on investment results during the buildup, it was a logical step to increase flexibility by allowing contributors to borrow back a portion of their initial contribution whenever they wanted. Now that the amount of the ultimate annuity is not fixed but is dependent on investment results, such borrowing is essentially a matter of indifference to the issuer of the annuity. If the loan is never repaid, the annuity is simply reduced appropriately. If the loan is repaid, it reduces principal for the period it is outstanding, which reduces the amount of the buildup but does not affect the long-term obligation of the company. For exactly the same reason, variable annuity plans usually permit contributors to make additional discretionary payments from time to time. With such flexibility, the annuity ultimately resulting is variable indeed.

A variety of companies continue to offer single-premium, variable interest rate annuities, sold largely on the basis of their favorable tax-deferral characteristics and relatively high initial rates of interest (in the 8 to 10 percent range in late 1988). These rates expressly are not guaranteed in later years and, in fact, appear to be "teaser rates" designed primarily to attract business. Interest rates on these annuities in later years have been significantly lowered even while higher initial rates continue to be advertised for new annuities. In late 1988, one company continued to advertise an initial rate of 9.5 percent for new annuities while paying only 7 percent on money invested in annuities between 1979 and 1984.

For example, in 1992 the following annuities were offered by companies rated "A+" by A.M. Best & Co.:

Table 10-1
Variable Interest Rate Annuities

Issuer	Initial rate	Number of years guaranteed	Years until penalty free surrender
Acacia	6.40	5	5
Sun Life	6.00	5	5
Life of Southwest	6.00	3	1
Federal Home Life	5.75	1	1
Jackson Life	5.25	1	1

Commercial variable interest rate annuities traditionally are offered by insurance companies (sold through insurance agents) and securities brokerage firms (sold by brokers as alternatives to the traditional securities investments described in Chapters 14 through 17. Increasingly, these annuities are now being offered through banks and thrift institutions as alternatives to passbook savings accounts, certificates of deposit, or other traditional investment alternatives. The principal advantage of these bank-related annuities appears to be convenience since most customers apparently visit bank offices more often than they visit brokerage firms or the offices of insurance agents.

Even though sold in bank lobbies, these bank-offered variable interest rate annuities are in fact issued by insurance companies. Commercial annuities written at the offices of Security Pacific Bank, for example, are actually written by Colonial Penn Life Insurance Company. These annuities are not guaranteed by the bank itself and are not protected by federal deposit insurance. Like all commercial annuities, bank-offered annuities should be evaluated on the basis of the surrender charges applicable upon premature withdrawal, on the period the advertised interest rates are guaranteed, and on the risk of possible insolvency of the writer.

Further, it should be recognized that, unlike other bank-offered time investments, an income tax penalty may be applicable on withdrawals before age fifty-nine and one-half.

§10.8 VARIABLE EQUITY ANNUITIES

Once the variable annuity concept is recognized, it is a relatively small additional step to relax the requirement that investments be in long-term interest-yielding investments: Any kind of equity or debt investment might be appropriate for the investment fund. Further, it is also only a relatively small additional step for the company to create several different funds with different investment goals and permit the contributor to designate in which fund or funds he or she would like the funds to be placed, and to permit changes in the investment mix from time to time.

At this point, it is useful to step back and look at what the annuity has become. The power to make decisions as to the investments to be made during the buildup period and the power to withdraw contributions makes the plan not terribly different from an income-producing brokerage account or bank deposit. Yet tax deferral is still available. During the 1970s, the Internal Revenue Service resisted the argument that such an account should be subject to deferred taxation as an annuity, but eventually the IRS lost that argument. As a result, the earnings are still tax deferred (since the transaction is cast in the form of an annuity), and human ingenuity has created a tax deferred investment vehicle that competes with mutual funds, brokerage accounts, and other savings plans. Needless to say, this type of investment quickly became very attractive in the early

1980s because of this feature. Of course, there are administrative costs associated with all annuities. These costs for variable annuities are presumably higher than the costs associated with a fixed annuity. It has been estimated that the yearly administrative costs associated with the management of a variable annuity are about 2 percent of the contributions and buildup.

Variable interest rate and equity annuities are often sold today as tax deferred mutual fund investments (which in some ways they resemble). See Chapter 15 for a description of mutual funds. There are, however, major differences: Variable annuity fees are higher, the alternative investments that are available are fewer, and one is locked in, as a practical matter, for a much longer period. Advertisements for variable annuities regularly compare the growth of a tax deferred annuity with the growth of a taxable certificate of deposit or other fixed-income investments. This comparison is potentially misleading because no account is taken of the deferred tax obligation on the buildup. The comparison, in other words, is stacked against the taxable investment. "What they're really selling you is a compounded interest table," one financial planner has stated.

Heavy surrender charges of up to 7 percent may be applicable to variable annuities if early withdrawal occurs; these charges typically decline over time and disappear entirely after the annuity contract has been in existence for a specified period — typically, after seven years. A common pattern is 6 percent the first year, 5 percent the second year, and so forth. Because of initial charges and early withdrawal fees, a variable annuity should remain undisturbed for an extended period so that the tax deferred compounding can offset these fees. A ten-year holding period for a variable annuity is a good rule of thumb. Some variable annuities soften surrender charges by permitting a 10 percent withdrawal each year without penalty; variable annuities also generally permit the transfer of funds into a lifetime annuity without penalty.

Variable annuity contracts also provide death benefits in the event of death during the buildup period. The named beneficiary is entitled to receive the value of the total investment. Annuity writers may charge a small premium for this death benefit.

Since a variable annuity is an interest in a fund, there is probably no default risk in the purchase of such an investment. However, if the investor elects to take a lifetime annuity, the interest in the fund disappears and the continued payment of that annuity depends on the solvency of the insurance company.

Despite these disadvantages, variable annuities are attractive to many persons. More than 100 billion dollars of such contracts were outstanding at the end of 1991. Comparative information about the performance of specific variable annuities is publicly available from Lipper Analytical Systems, Inc.

§10.9 ASSIGNMENT OF ANNUITY CONTRACT OBLIGATIONS

Annuity contracts may be assigned by the issuing company to assuming companies under the practice generally known as *assumption reinsurance*. The same practice occurs in connection with life insurance policies. See section 11.18. There is a risk, therefore, that vested annuity contracts may be assigned to weaker companies in which the risk of default is materially increased. A person owning such an annuity contract should be particularly vigilant and object to any assignment that appears to increase the default risk on the annuity.

§10.10 MULTIPLE-PREMIUM ANNUITIES

Consider the situation of a 35-year-old person who lacks the resources to make the $100,000 investment described in an earlier section, but who strongly feels that some provision should be made for retirement in 30 years. Commercial insurance companies have long offered annuity plans that are designed precisely to meet the needs of such a person. They involve monthly payment plans under which the contributor gradually builds up a nest egg; the payments accumulate and are converted into an annuity shortly before retirement.

Perhaps the person under discussion feels he or she can contribute $5,000 per year toward ultimate retirement. Traditionally, a fixed-interest rate was involved, so that the amount accumulated after the 30 years of payments could be calculated mathematically. For simplicity, let us assume that each payment is made at the end of the year, that the person plans to retire at the end of the thirtieth year, that interest is compounded annually, and that the insurance company guarantees a 7 percent annual return. The value in 30 years of the stream of $5,000 payments is then equal to the future value of $5,000 over 30 years plus the future value of $5,000 over 29 years plus the future value of $5,000 over 28 years, and so forth. This calculation is made much simpler by the development of tables for the future value of annuities (which in effect is what is involved). Table 10-2 is such a table. To determine the amount that will be available in this example for the purchase of an annuity in 30 years, one need merely look in the 30 row and 7 percent column of Table 10-2. The number (94.4608) is simply multiplied by $5,000 to determine that the amount available for the retirement annuity will build up to $472,304 in 30 years. At today's prices that amount should yield a reasonably comfortable retirement, particularly if it is supplemented by social security and possibly other retirement benefits.

Three important points should be made about the accumulation as-

Table 10-2
Future Value of a Stream of $1 Payments Made at the End of Each Period after n Periods

No. of periods	2%	3%	4%	5%	6%	7%	8%
1	1.0000	1.0000	1.0000	1.0000	1.0000	1.0000	1.0000
2	2.0200	2.0300	2.0400	2.0500	2.0600	2.0700	2.0800
3	3.0604	3.0909	3.1216	3.1525	3.1836	3.2149	3.2464
4	4.1216	4.1836	4.2465	4.3101	4.3746	4.4399	4.5061
5	5.2040	5.3091	5.4163	5.5256	5.6371	5.7507	5.8666
6	6.3081	6.4684	6.6330	6.8019	6.9753	7.1533	7.3359
7	7.4343	7.6625	7.8983	8.1420	8.3938	8.6540	8.9228
8	8.5830	8.8923	9.2142	9.5491	9.8975	10.2598	10.6366
9	9.7546	10.1591	10.5828	11.0266	11.4913	11.9780	12.4876
10	10.9497	11.4639	12.0061	12.5779	13.1808	13.8164	14.4866
11	12.1687	12.8078	13.4864	14.2068	14.9716	15.7836	16.6455
12	13.4121	14.1920	15.0258	15.9171	16.8699	17.8885	18.9771
13	14.6803	15.6178	16.6268	17.7130	18.8821	20.1406	21.4953
14	15.9739	17.0863	18.2919	19.5986	21.0151	22.5505	24.2149
15	17.2934	18.5989	20.0236	21.5786	23.2760	25.1290	27.1521
16	18.6393	20.1569	21.8245	23.6575	25.6725	27.8881	30.3243
17	20.0121	21.7616	23.6975	25.8404	28.2129	30.8402	33.7502
18	21.4123	23.4144	25.6454	28.1324	30.9057	33.9990	37.4502
19	22.8406	25.1169	27.6712	30.5390	33.7600	37.3790	41.4463
20	24.2974	26.8704	29.7781	33.0660	36.7856	40.9955	45.7620
21	25.7833	28.6765	31.9692	35.7193	39.9927	44.8652	50.4229
22	27.2990	30.5368	34.2480	38.5052	43.3923	49.0057	55.4568
23	28.8450	32.4529	36.6179	41.4305	46.9958	53.4361	60.8933
24	30.4219	34.4265	39.0826	44.5020	50.8156	58.1767	66.7648
25	32.0303	36.4593	41.6459	47.7271	54.8645	63.2490	73.1059

Table 10-2 (continued)
Future Value of a Stream of $1 Payments Made at the End of Each Period after n Periods

No. of periods	2%	3%	4%	5%	6%	7%	8%
26	33.6709	38.5530	44.3117	51.1135	59.1564	68.6765	79.9544
27	35.3443	40.7096	47.0842	54.6691	63.7058	74.4838	87.3508
28	37.0512	42.9309	49.9676	58.4026	68.5281	80.6977	95.3388
29	38.7922	45.2189	52.9663	62.3227	73.6398	87.3465	103.9659
30	40.5681	47.5754	56.0849	66.4388	79.0582	94.4608	113.2832
31	42.3794	50.0027	59.3283	70.7608	84.8017	102.0730	123.3459
32	44.2270	52.5028	62.7015	75.2988	90.8898	110.2182	134.2135
33	46.1116	55.0778	66.2095	80.0638	97.3432	118.9334	145.9506
34	48.0338	57.7302	69.8579	85.0670	104.1838	128.2588	158.6267
35	49.9945	60.4621	73.6522	90.3203	111.4348	138.2369	172.3168
36	51.9944	63.2759	77.5983	95.8363	119.1209	148.9135	187.1021
37	54.0343	66.1742	81.7022	101.6281	127.2681	160.3374	203.0703
38	56.1149	69.1594	85.9703	107.7095	135.9042	172.5610	220.3159
39	58.2372	72.2342	90.4091	114.0950	145.0585	185.6403	238.9412
40	60.4020	75.4013	95.0255	120.7998	154.7620	199.6351	259.0565
41	62.6100	78.6633	99.8265	127.8398	165.0477	214.6096	280.7810
42	64.8622	82.0232	104.8196	135.2318	175.9505	230.6322	304.2435
43	67.1595	85.4839	110.0124	142.9933	187.5076	247.7765	329.5830
44	69.5027	89.0484	115.4129	151.1430	199.7580	266.1209	356.9496
45	71.8927	92.7199	121.0294	159.7002	212.7435	285.7493	386.5056
46	74.3306	96.5015	126.8706	168.6852	226.5081	306.7518	418.4261
47	76.8172	100.3965	132.9454	178.1194	241.0986	329.2244	452.9002
48	79.3535	104.4084	139.2632	188.0254	256.5645	353.2701	490.1322
49	81.9406	108.5406	145.8337	198.4267	272.9584	378.9990	530.3427
50	84.5794	112.7969	152.6671	209.3480	290.3359	406.5289	573.7702

208

Table 10-2 (continued)

Future Value of a Stream of $1 Payments Made at the End of Each Period after n Periods

No. of periods	9%	10%	11%	12%	13%	14%	15%
1	1.0000	1.0000	1.0000	1.0000	1.0000	1.0000	1.0000
2	2.0900	2.1000	2.1100	2.1200	2.1300	2.1400	2.1500
3	3.2781	3.3100	3.3421	3.3744	3.4069	3.4396	3.4725
4	4.5731	4.6410	4.7097	4.7793	4.8498	4.9211	4.9934
5	5.9847	6.1051	6.2278	6.3528	6.4803	6.6101	6.7424
6	7.5233	7.7156	7.9129	8.1152	8.3227	8.5355	8.7537
7	9.2004	9.4872	9.7833	10.0890	10.4047	10.7305	11.0668
8	11.0285	11.4359	11.8594	12.2997	12.7573	13.2328	13.7268
9	13.0210	13.5795	14.1640	14.7757	15.4157	16.0853	16.7858
10	15.1929	15.9374	16.7220	17.5487	18.4197	19.3373	20.3037
11	17.5603	18.5312	19.5614	20.6546	21.8143	23.0445	24.3493
12	20.1407	21.3834	22.7132	24.1331	25.6502	27.2707	29.0017
13	22.9534	24.5227	26.2116	28.0291	29.9847	32.0887	34.3519
14	26.0192	27.9750	30.0949	32.3926	34.8827	37.5811	40.5047
15	29.3609	31.7725	34.4054	37.2797	40.4175	43.8424	47.5804
16	33.0034	35.9497	39.1899	42.7533	46.6717	50.9804	55.7175
17	36.9737	40.5447	44.5008	48.8837	53.7391	59.1176	65.0751
18	41.3013	45.5992	50.3959	55.7497	61.7251	68.3941	75.8364
19	46.0185	51.1591	56.9395	63.4397	70.7494	78.9692	88.2118
20	51.1601	57.2750	64.2028	72.0524	80.9468	91.0249	102.4436
21	56.7645	64.0025	72.2651	81.6987	92.4699	104.7684	118.8101
22	62.8733	71.4027	81.2143	92.5026	105.4910	120.4360	137.6316
23	69.5319	79.5430	91.1479	104.6029	120.2048	138.2970	159.2764
24	76.7898	88.4973	102.1742	118.1552	136.8315	158.6586	184.1678
25	84.7009	98.3471	114.4133	133.3339	155.6196	181.8708	212.7930

Table 10-2 (continued)
Future Value of a Stream of $1 Payments Made at the End of Each Period after n Periods

No. of periods	9%	10%	11%	12%	13%	14%	15%
26	93.3240	109.1818	127.9988	150.3339	176.8501	208.3327	245.7120
27	102.7231	121.0999	143.0786	169.3740	200.8406	238.4993	283.5688
28	112.9682	134.2099	159.8173	190.6989	227.9499	272.8892	327.1041
29	124.1354	148.6309	178.3972	214.5828	258.5834	312.0937	377.1697
30	136.3075	164.4940	199.0209	241.3327	293.1992	356.7868	434.7451
31	149.5752	181.9434	221.9132	271.2926	332.3151	407.7370	500.9569
32	164.0370	201.1378	247.3236	304.8477	376.5161	465.8202	577.1005
33	179.8003	222.2515	275.5292	342.4294	426.4632	532.0350	664.6655
34	196.9823	245.4767	306.8374	384.5210	482.9034	607.5199	765.3654
35	215.7108	271.0244	341.5896	431.6635	546.6808	693.5727	881.1702
36	236.1247	299.1268	380.1644	484.4631	618.7493	791.6729	1014.3457
37	258.3759	330.0395	422.9825	543.5987	700.1867	903.5071	1167.4975
38	282.6298	364.0434	470.5106	609.8305	792.2110	1030.0981	1343.6222
39	309.0665	401.4478	523.2667	684.0102	896.1984	1176.3378	1546.1655
40	337.8824	442.5926	581.8261	767.0914	1013.7042	1342.0251	1779.0903
41	369.2919	487.8518	646.8269	860.1424	1146.4858	1530.9086	2046.9539
42	403.5281	537.6370	718.9779	964.3595	1296.5289	1746.2358	2354.9969
43	440.8457	592.4007	799.0655	1081.0826	1466.0777	1991.7088	2709.2465
44	481.5218	652.6408	887.9627	1211.8125	1657.6678	2271.5481	3116.6334
45	525.8587	718.9048	986.6386	1358.2300	1874.1646	2590.5648	3585.1285
46	574.1860	791.7953	1096.1688	1522.2176	2118.8060	2954.2439	4123.8977
47	626.8628	871.9749	1217.7474	1705.8838	2395.2508	3368.8380	4743.4824
48	684.2804	960.1723	1352.6996	1911.5898	2707.6334	3841.4753	5456.0047
49	746.8656	1057.1896	1502.4965	2141.9806	3060.6258	4380.2819	6275.4055
50	815.0836	1163.9085	1668.7712	2400.0182	3459.5071	4994.5213	7217.7163

pects of this kind of transaction. First, any kind of regular contribution made over a long period of time builds up to a large amount in absolute terms over 30 years. Whether or not this is considered advantageous, however, depends on what assumptions one makes about inflation over 30 years. If inflation remains low, a comfortable retirement may be expected; under the worst inflation scenarios, $472,304 may be only the cost of a haircut in the year 2020. Second, the interest rate that is used in the accumulation phase has an immense impact on the amount of the ultimate annuity. Third, if the build-up phase involves monthly payments and monthly compounding of interest (rather than annual payments and compounding, as in the previous hypothetical), the amount of the buildup is significantly increased. Do you see why?

This kind of annuity seems to be precisely the type envisioned by the Internal Revenue Code when it granted the advantages of tax deferral described in section 10.6. The earnings from the investment of the $5,000 payments accumulate without taxation until the annuity becomes due; at that point an exclusion ratio is calculated, and a portion of each payment is subject to taxation, and a portion is excluded as a return of capital. In calculating this ratio the capital invested is the total amount contributed without adjustment for the time value of money — 30 payments of $5,000 each equals $150,000.

For the reasons set forth earlier, the fixed interest rate is not an essential aspect of the multiple-premium annuity. The multiple-payment annuity can readily be a variable annuity dependent on the investment results obtained through actual experience in the manner described in sections 10.7 and 10.8.

This example involves a tax deferred annuity, but the tax advantages of this plan are not as attractive as the tax benefits available through the device of qualified retirement plans, discussed in section 10.11.

§10.11 EMPLOYEE RETIREMENT PLANS: BEFORE-TAX AND AFTER-TAX DOLLARS

The preceding section considered an example in which a person agreed to make annual payments of $5,000 per year to fund a retirement annuity. It was implicitly assumed that the payments would be made voluntarily each year, presumably by a check drawn on the contributor's available funds. Such a plan has some of the disadvantages of a do-it-yourself annuity in that payments require a degree of mental discipline and willpower on the part of the contributor. It also suffers, however, from a more fundamental problem.

Let us assume — as will usually be the case — that the contributor plans to make the payments out of his or her current earnings from employment. This plan is financed with after-tax dollars. This means simply that the contributor must pay income tax on the dollars he or she earns and then must make the contribution to fund the annuity out of the dollars that remain. In other words, if the employee is in the 31 percent bracket, each dollar earned only leads to a $0.69 contribution to the retirement plan.

If the contributor's employer has created a pension or profit-sharing plan that meets the requirements of the federal Employee Retirement Income Security Act (ERISA) and the Internal Revenue Code, contributions may be made by the employer directly for the employee's retirement program without the contributions being included in the employee's tax return and without affecting the deductibility of the contributions from the standpoint of the employer. A plan that meets the requirements of these federal statutes is referred to as a qualified plan. Such a plan provides for a much greater degree of tax deferral than the plan financed with after-tax dollars since no tax is imposed on either the employer's contribution or on the buildup from such contributions, until the employee retires (or in some circumstances, leaves the employer's employment). At the same time, the employer continues to deduct currently on its federal income tax return the gross amount of salary paid to the employee plus the amounts contributed by the employer for his or her benefit to the qualified plan. Payments made to a qualified retirement plan are said to be made with "before tax" dollars.

A qualified plan requires that the employer in some way physically set aside the funds to be used for retirement purposes. Usually the employer makes contributions directly to a trust or other entity, which invests the funds for the benefit of employees, and, upon their retirement, the fund may either pay annuity benefits directly or may purchase a commercial retirement annuity for the employee. Some employers may take advantage of a simplified plan that does not require the creation of a separate trust but provides direct payments for employees' commercial retirement annuities.

In some qualified plans, the employee, as well as the employer, is required to make a contribution; in others, the employer funds the entire plan. The former is called, logically enough, a contributory plan, the latter, a noncontributory plan. If the plan is a contributory plan, the portion contributed by the employee is usually with after-tax dollars and the portion contributed by the employer is with before-tax dollars. Employees in some limited occupational groups may make contributions to retirement plans with before-tax dollars — in other words, they may take a tax deduction for their contribution to the plan.

Federal law imposes a number of very specific requirements on qualified retirement plans. These requirements include vesting (which deals with the question whether the retirement benefits will be paid if the employee quits before retirement), and nondiscrimination (which ensures that lower paid as well as higher paid employees are covered by the plan). It is not necessary to describe these technical requirements: The important point is to recognize the significant degree of additional tax deferral that results from the creation of a qualified retirement plan.

In a qualified plan, everyone appears to gain at the expense of Uncle Sam. The obvious justification for these significant tax benefits is that they provide employers with an incentive to make adequate provision for the retirement of their employees, supplementing the social security system. And, indeed, qualified retirement plans are an important source of retirement income for most working people today.

Qualified retirement plans are divided into defined benefit and defined contribution plans. In a defined benefit plan, the size of the employer's contribution is determined on an actuarial basis to provide employees with designated benefits: An example might be a defined retirement benefit equal to 2 percent of the employee's average salary over the last three years of his or her employment multiplied by the number of years of employment. Thus, an employee with 30 years of service would receive a retirement benefit equal to 60 percent of his or her average three-year pre-retirement salary. The military retirement plan is a well-known defined benefit plan. Defined benefit plans involve annual contributions by employers to fund the anticipated future benefits. In addition to the actuarial determination, the amount of the annual contribution must also be based on an assumption or estimate about the future yield on funds previously contributed and funds to be contributed in the future.

A defined contribution plan, on the other hand, does not establish the amount to be paid by the employer on the basis of the benefits ultimately to be conferred on employees. Rather the contribution is established by reference to extrinsic information during each period, such as the employer's profits, or the actual salary paid to the employee during the period in question. For example, a defined contribution plan might provide an annual contribution by the employer equal to 7 percent of the employee's salary each year. The employee receives 100 percent of his or her salary. The employer contributes an additional 7 percent of this amount to the qualified plan and claims as a deduction for tax purposes 107 percent of the employee's salary. The 7 percent each year builds up in a fund until retirement. The amount in that fund upon retirement cannot be ascertained until retirement: Whatever the amount is, it will then be used to provide retirement benefits for the employee; the plan may purchase a commercial annuity for the life of the retired employee or pay the employee directly an actuarially determined pension based on the amount available upon retirement. The amount of that annuity is determined solely by the amount in that employee's fund.

Qualified plans may also be subdivided into pension plans, profit-sharing plans, and stock bonus plans. Qualified profit-sharing and stock bonus plans involve contributions based on a percentage of profits earned by the employer during the period. A qualified pension plan may be either a defined benefit plan or a defined contribution plan. In the case of all these retirement plans, federal law limits the maximum contributions that may be made in order to cap the maximum tax benefits. Plans may provide for investment of contributed funds at the sole discretion of the trustees of the plan or may permit each individual employee to have a limited choice as to how funds contributed on his or her behalf are to be invested. In general terms, plans increasingly are defined contribution rather than defined benefit plans, and increasingly beneficiaries are given some choice as to the investments to be made with funds contributed on their behalf.

The tax sheltering of the contributions to a qualified plan is in addition to the tax deferral of buildup that occurs within the fund or trust to which the contributions are made. Thus, the employee not only excludes the employer contributions from his or her taxable income but also excludes investment earnings from prior years' contributions. This also involves tax deferral because the retirement benefits, when actually received, are taxable.

§10.12 SOURCES OF RETIREMENT INCOME

The qualified employee retirement plans described in the previous section are extremely popular with both employers and employees. Most major employers have created such plans, and many smaller employers offer some type of plan as well. For many employees, their interest in their employer's retirement plan is their largest single asset, eclipsing the equity in their home and all other savings.

In 1992, about 55 percent of all full-time workers in America's work force were covered by pension or deferred compensation plans. About 24 percent of employees of small firms were covered. There were about 100,000 plans that gave beneficiaries choice as to investment strategy; these plans covered approximately 19 million people and held assets of approximately $335 billion.

In the average retirement in the 1990s, social security accounted for about 25 percent of post-retirement annual income while employer-provided retirement plans made up between 30 and 40 percent of that income. The balance was from savings, private annuities, investments, and other sources. It is anticipated that the percentage of income that social security provides will slowly decline in the future.

The amount of retirement income provided to an employee by a private retirement plan is a function not only of the terms of the plan itself, but also by the number of years the person remains in the employ of that employer. Generally speaking, an individual who changes jobs a number of times during his or her employment career will have a lower retirement income from this source than an individual who remains a member of a single company retirement plan during his or her productive working lifetime. In part this is a function of losses in contributions because the employee quit a job before retirement benefits had vested; in part because plans are usually structured to favor the long-term employee.

The long-term trend in the provision of pension or deferred compensation benefits appears to be slightly downward. In a survey conducted in 1992 (a recession year in which pessimistic economic forecasts were common) only 16 percent of benefits managers expected employers to increase benefits offered to retirees, while 36 percent expected benefits to decline.

As experience with private retirement plans has increased, so have unexpected losses of benefits from a variety of different causes. Some plans have invested unwisely and imprudently. Defined contribution plans are not protected by federal insurance. Trustees of such plans have investment authority but may lack the sophistication to invest cautiously given the fact that they are dealing with their employees' retirement funds. This risk appears to be greatest in smaller plans in which the employer's officers may manage the funds but lack sophistication about basic principles of diversification and conservatism in investment policy. In the 1970s and 1980s, for example, many plan administrators were persuaded to invest heavily in real estate or oil and gas limited partnerships, ventures whose performances have generally varied from poor to disastrous. Unwise investments may also occur in plans in which beneficiaries have some choice as to investment strategy since decisions about specific investments within each broad category continue to be made by trustees.

Different problems have arisen in defined benefit plans. The subsequent obligations of these plans to provide retirement benefits are actuarially determined based on assumed future yields. During the 1980s, a number of companies made contributions on the basis of assumed yields of 10 or 12 percent per year. In the early 1990s, however, interest rates declined significantly and the prices of investments remained generally stable or declined. The result was that many pension funds were not yielding anything close to the projections. In the case of General Motors, for example, the corporation assumed a yield of 11 percent on a pension fund with assets of $42 billion in 1992, but the actual yield was well below that figure. In late 1992, General Motors announced a $1.1 billion charge against corporate earnings because of the underfunding of pension plan obligations caused by this decline in yield. During the 1980s, the opposite problem arose on a number of occasions. As a result of successful investments and increases in stock prices and interest rates, many of these plans find themselves "overfunded," that is, the assets in the trust are greater than needed to meet the plan's obligations. During the 1980s, many employers successfully retrieved these excess funds by terminating the plan, purchasing so-called "guaranteed investment contracts" (GICs) from an insurance company to cover its obligations under the pension plan, and then pocketed what remained. This strategy imposed a new risk on the employees — an insolvency risk that the insurance company writing the GICs may become insolvent. Unfortunately, a major insurance company (First Executive Corporation) writing GICs in discontinued plans was one of the three insurance companies that became insolvent during the late 1980s and defaulted on its obligations. Some employers recognized a moral obligation to its employees in this situation and have quietly assumed the responsibility to provide retirement benefits to its employees while others have not.

Defined benefit plans are insured by the federal Pension Benefits Guaranty Corporation. As a practical matter, this eliminates the risk that the employer will be unable to meet its obligations as they become due. Corporations in reorganization under Chapter 11 of the Bankruptcy Code, however, have defaulted on their pension obligations to employees in an effort to escape these onerous obligations with the expectation that even though the business emerges from reorganization, the responsibility for the continued financing of the plan would remain with the Pension Benefits Guaranty Corporation. These attempts, while not successful, have led to litigation and certainly to increases in insecurity among the employees covered by the plan in question.

Many defined contribution plans give each employee some option as to how his or her retirement funds are to be invested. The choices are usually in broad categories: money market funds, bond funds, stock funds, guaranteed investment contracts with insurers, and so forth. The general nature of these classes of investments is discussed in Chapters 13 through 17 of this book. Undoubtedly many employees lack the sophistication to make sensible choices about investments in funds that are not to become available to them for 20 or 30 years. As this type of plan has continued to increase in popularity, the lack of sophistication or education on the part of many middle and lower level employees is an increasingly serious problem. For example, among the options offered by most plans are investments in GICs written by insurance companies. The funds set aside for employees electing this option were simply turned over to the insurance company. In most instances, the default risk inherent in these plans was not disclosed to the employees. As the default risk came into perspective, many employers began recommending to employees that they consider interests in bond funds and other alternatives (see Chapter 15) rather than the easily understood, but somewhat risky, GIC.

Some $150 to $200 billion in retirement funds were invested in insurers' GICs as of 1992, many of which were acquired by trustees of non-directed plans in which the employees have no investment choice. Employers increasingly are spreading the risk inherent in these outstanding GICs by purchasing contracts from several different employers; others are placing new funds into Treasury bills or mutual funds that invest in treasuries or high quality corporate bonds rather than simply turning the funds over to the writer of the GICs. A number of insurers have also created separate funds in which retirement funds may be invested directly in securities, presumably free of the credit risk of default by the insurance company writing the GICs. The status of these pools of assets in the event of insurer insolvency, however, has not been determined. These funded GICs are called "synthetic GICs" within the insurance industry.

If a person's employment is terminated after the vesting of retirement benefits, benefits typically are paid from the plan only after the person retires, often many years later. Increasingly, however, plans provide that a person with vested retirement benefits may roll over vested amounts into an individual retirement account or into another pension plan. Such treatment is usually permitted in defined contribution plans.

§10.13 KEOGH PLANS

For many years, the significant tax benefits provided by qualified employee retirement plans could not be obtained by self-employed individuals, who, like the 35-year-old providing a do-it-yourself retirement plan, could only fund retirement plans with after-tax dollars. Today, this discrimination against the self-employed has been eliminated by amendments to the tax laws.

Self-employed persons may create devices called Keogh plans (also known as H.R. 10 plans) that basically allows them to set up a retirement trust or retirement account and make contributions to it that may be deducted from the self-employed person's individual income tax return. Tax penalties are imposed for premature withdrawals. Keogh plans are defined contribution plans. For many years the maximum allowable deductible contribution to a Keogh plan was significantly lower than the amount an employer could provide its employees under a qualified retirement plan, but this discrimination against the self-employed has been largely eliminated.

Where a self-employed person can incorporate his or her own business, he or she can also obtain retirement benefits as an "employee" of the corporation. There is generally no reason why the same person cannot be both the sole shareholder and an employee of a corporation. Limitations, however, have been placed on retirement benefits of owner-employees in personal service businesses.

§10.14 INDIVIDUAL RETIREMENT ACCOUNTS (IRAs)

There is yet another class of workers who cannot take advantage of either qualified retirement plans or Keogh plans. These are persons who are employed, but the employer has not elected to create a qualified retirement plan. Individual retirement accounts (IRAs) were originally designed to permit these persons to obtain some parity in tax treatment. They permitted employees to create special retirement accounts with banks and other financial institutions into which they could make periodic contributions and then deduct the payments from their federal income tax returns. Like Keogh plans, maximum deductions and contributions are specified and a tax penalty is imposed if funds are withdrawn prematurely. In 1981, the IRA concept was broadened to permit any employee (including those covered by employer-sponsored retirement plans) to create an IRA and make a contribution of up to $2,000 ($2,250 for an employee and a non working spouse) each year. As a result of this change, IRAs quickly became tax-deferred savings accounts primarily utilized by the relatively affluent rather than by the persons for whom they were originally designed.

In 1986, Congress largely closed off this tax-deferred savings loophole for the well-to-do by limiting IRA deductions to persons not covered by other plans and to those below specified income levels. Individuals who are not covered by any pension plan may make tax-deductible contributions of up to $2,000 per year to an IRA without regard to income. For other persons, tax-deductible contributions may be made only if their gross incomes are less than $35,000 for individuals or $50,000 for married couples. Other individuals may make nondeductible contributions of up to $2,000 per year to an IRA. The advantage of doing this is that the income is tax-deferred until retirement or until the amounts are withdrawn. Therefore, for most moderately wealthy individuals, the IRA is now a tax-deferred savings account that should be compared directly with other tax deferred or tax-exempt investments: annuities, tax-free municipal bonds, or even United States savings bonds. However, based on 1992 interest rates, nondeductible IRA contributions appear justified only where the individual plans to make relatively risky investments in an effort to obtain a return significantly higher than that available from tax-exempt municipals.

Nondeductible IRAs, furthermore, have certain disadvantages. Withdrawals before the age of fifty-nine and one-half are subject to a 10 percent penalty. Further, a person with both deductible (i.e., pre-1986) and nondeductible IRAs must pay taxes proportionately on all the IRAs they hold whenever they make a distribution from any of them. The bookkeeping complexities thereby created deter many persons from utilizing nondeductible IRAs.

§10.15 SECTION 401(k) PLANS

Section 401(k) of the Internal Revenue Code permits employers to create tax-deferred plans for employees in addition to the main pension plan described in section 10.11. Some smaller employers treat their 401(k) plan as their main pension program.

A 401(k) plan permits employees to defer paying taxes on part of their salary — up to a maximum of $8,728 each year in 1992 — by making a contribution to a special account created by the employer. Many employers set a ceiling on contributions, perhaps 6 percent of annual salary and voluntarily contribute to these plans by matching employee contributions either on a 50 percent or full matching basis. The employee may deduct his or her contribution each year; no tax is due on the employer's contribution, if any, or on the earnings from the fund until withdrawals are made, typically upon retirement. The funds may be invested in one or more investment options created by the employer, for example, the employer's stock, a stock mutual fund, a balanced fund of stocks and bonds, a money market fund, or a guaranteed investment contract. About 65 percent of all 401(k) plans invest in guaranteed investment contracts, but that percentage appears to be declining as concern increases about the credit risk of such contracts. Like IRAs and Keogh plans, there is a tax penalty for premature withdrawals of funds before retirement or age fifty-nine and one-half.

Section 401(k) plans are currently the fastest growing type of retirement plan. Over $50 billion per year is flowing into these plans in the early 1990s, contributed by more than 15 million workers. By the end of the decade, it is estimated that 401(k) assets should reach $1 trillion, with many individual account balances well into six figures. In 1988, the average account balance was about $10,000; in 1993, it was $30,000, and many workers with incomes of $20,000 or $30,000 per year have 401(k) account balances over $100,000. Many new companies today simply offer section 401(k) plans as their sole retirement plan. Employees who already have section 401(k) plans usually desire to continue to make contributions to these plans after they change jobs, a fact not lost on employers generally considering the adoption of such plans.

An advantage of 401(k) plans is that they are in addition to IRAs, Keogh plans, and regular employee retirement plans. There is, however, a maximum of $30,000 applicable to the aggregate discretionary annual contributions to IRAs, Keogh plans, and 401(k) plans.

Many employers qualify their section 401(k) plans under section 404(c) of ERISA to limit their fiduciary obligations under the plan. To qualify under section 404(c), the plan must offer at least three different diversified investment options, permit changes in investments within specified time periods, and provide information with respect to the options that are offered. Neither GICs nor employer stock investments are considered to be diversified but may be offered in section 404(c) plans so long as three diversified options are offered. For example, a qualified section 404(c) plan may include a fund that replicates the movements of the Standard & Poor's 500-stock index, an index fund that follows the broader stock market, a bond fund that replicates bond market movements, a balanced fund split between the S&P 500 index fund and the bond fund, a basic income fund that invests in GICs, and investments in the employer's stock. See Chapter 15 for a further discussion of diversified investments.

Employees of state and local governments and agencies are permitted to create analogous plans under section 403(b) of the Internal Revenue Code. Self-employed individuals or employees of small business enterprises may take advantage of "simplified employee pension plans (usually called SEPs or SEP-IRAs) that permit deduction of up to 15 percent of salary or self-employed income (up to $30,000) each year.

§10.16 PRIVATE ANNUITIES

Brief mention should also be made of a device that has some limited usefulness in certain family-related or tax-oriented transactions. A private annuity is created by the transfer of property to a person in exchange for a promise by that person to make fixed periodic payments for the life of the transferor. The rights must be unsecured and the transferor cannot be in the business of writing annuities. In other words, it is an annuity based on the credit of a private individual not in the business of writing annuities. Such private annuities may offer tax benefits by deferring the recognition of gain on the transaction. See section 19.23.

§10.17 LUMP SUM DISTRIBUTIONS

When an individual leaves employment that provides qualified retirement benefits for any reason, he or she may become entitled to a lump sum payment of all vested retirement benefits. The potential distribution may be very large: An employee who has worked for ten or fifteen years may be entitled to a payment in the high five or low six figures. Usually, this is the largest potential payment the employee has ever been entitled to, and the temptation to withdraw this money is obviously very strong, particularly if the employee has been laid off or has voluntarily decided to leave the work force for an extended period.

Despite the temptation, however, the general rule is that one should take the money only as a very last resort, particularly if the employee is less than 55 years old.

An example should make clear the reason for this rule. Assume that a 45-year-old employee has been laid off, and he has $100,000 vested retirement funds in a non-contributory plan. If this amount is taken as a lump sum, the entire amount is subject to federal income tax in the year of withdrawal. Such a payment would put the employee in the 31 percent bracket, so that the tax cost is as much as $31,000. The distribution may also be subject to state income tax. Furthermore, the employee would become subject to a 10 percent penalty for premature withdrawal of retirement funds. As a result, the amount the employee will actually receive is $59,000 ($100,000 − $31,000 − $10,000 = $59,000). This is expensive money: If the withdrawal is not made, the employee will continue to have $100,000 in retirement benefits that continue to grow on a tax-deferred basis even if the employer makes no further contributions on behalf of the employee.

If the employee is older than 55 or agrees to accept an immediate annuity of at least five years (or until the employee reaches the age of fifty-nine and one-half), the 10 percent penalty is not imposed.

There is another "glitch" as well. The employer may be required to withhold 20 percent of the lump sum distribution on account of federal income taxes. See point (4) below. Thus, the check the employee actually receives in the foregoing illustration will be only $80,000; the employee gets the benefit of this withheld amount only when he or she files a federal income tax return many months later.

The lump sum distribution may be avoided by at least four different strategies:

1) The employer's plan may provide the option of simply leaving retirement funds in the plan until retirement. At a later date the amount may be transferred without tax consequences into an IRA or another retirement plan.

2) Transfer the funds directly into an IRA or another qualified plan in a plan-to-plan transfer that does not entail the receipt of funds by the employee.

3) Accept an immediate annuity that continues for at least five years or until the employee reaches the age of fifty-nine and one-half, whichever is earlier.

4) Take the funds and place them into an IRA within 60 days. In this event, the employer must withhold 20 percent of the distribution so that the employee receives only $80,000, but the employee must transfer into the IRA within 60 days $100,000 if the transaction is not to have tax consequences. Where the employee comes up with the additional $20,000 may be a serious problem.

If the employee transfers only $80,000 into the IRA, he is viewed as having received a $20,000 taxable distribution. When his tax return is filed months later, he will have the benefit of a tax payment of $20,000, but will have lost a significant fraction of his retirement.

§10.18 PLANNING FOR RETIREMENT

Retirement planning works from three basic income sources: Social Security, company retirement plans, and individual investments. A comfortable retirement is generally thought to consist of an income equal to 80 percent of pre-retirement income, but the actual amount needed for a comfortable retirement (depending on debts, one's health and health insurance, one's life style, and continuing educational obligations) may actually vary from 50 percent to 100 percent of pre-retirement income.

As indicated above, in the average retirement in the early 1990s, social security accounted for about 25 percent of the retiree's annual income; company pensions made up between 30 and 40 percent. The balance must be covered from lifetime savings, IRA plans, 401(k) plans, variable annuities, and the like. In the future, it is estimated that social security will drop to less than 20 percent of total retirement income, with a concomitant increase needed in personal savings.

In a sense it is never too early to begin planning for retirement since the above figures demonstrate that some portion of retirement income must come from sources other than social security and mandatory employee retirement plans provided by employers. However, for most persons, retirement planning does not seriously begin until about age 40 or so. In many instances, retirement planning does not seriously begin until educational responsibilities to children have been fulfilled.

To assure $30,000 per year in additional income after tax, over and above social security and a company pension, one would need a portfolio valued in 1992 at about $430,000 invested in stock mutual funds. See section 15.4. A portfolio of this size can easily be created if a savings program is begun at an early enough age and continued religiously. For example, if one invests $2,000 a year beginning at age 30 in an Individual Retirement Account that is invested in growth stocks that return 10 percent per year, the IRA will have a value of $542,000 at age 65; if the IRA is opened at age 40, it will have grown only to $197,000 at age 65.

In calculating retirement needs, one should assume that one will live for 20 or 25 years after retiring. Account must be taken of even modest inflation, which seems irrelevant over the short run but has major effect over longer periods. If inflation runs at 5 percent a year, one dollar will be worth 61 cents in 10 years and 38 cents in 20 years. A common fallacy in retirement planning is to determine cash flow requirements for the year of retirement and assume that the same amount should be available every year thereafter.

When the date of actual retirement nears, a person should seek professional advice about retirement options in pension plans. Most retirees have the option to take benefits in a lump sum with a variety of ameliorating tax treatments, depending on the date of birth, or to take a variety of lifetime annuity options. These annuity options are described generally in the following sections.

A major problem for retirees is health care. Until relatively recently, many former employers provided health care to retirees either as a fully paid for benefit or on a costsharing basis by which the former employer paid the bulk of the cost. In recent years, as the cost of medical care has skyrocketed, large corporations have increasingly amended their health care benefits to require retirees to pay an additional part of their health care costs; many small corporations have totally discontinued health services for retirees (if they ever provided such services). In 1992, the accounting rules for most large employers were changed to require that the potential cost of future retiree health care be reflected as an immediate liability on the books of the former employer; this change in the accounting rule has accelerated the movement away from providing free or low cost medical protection for retirees. A retiree who loses, or who does not have, employer provided health care should consider acquiring a comprehensive long-term medical policy from private insurers even though the cost is substantial. In addition to employer-provided medical care, retirees may also rely on Medicare to cover some medical bills after they reach the age of 65. However, Medicare provides only partial protection — for example, under Medicare, a person must still pay $163 daily after the first 60 days of a hospital stay, and $326 daily if the hospital stay exceeds 150 days. Because of these gaps in coverage, many persons covered by Medicare also purchase Medicare supplement policies (medigap) for an additional premium. The selection of such policies has been materially simplified since Congress in 1989 forced states to develop models for medigap policies; these standardized policies greatly simplify the problem of choosing the most appropriate policy for a specific individual.

A few employers have created voluntary employee benefits associations (VEBAs). A VEBA is like a section 401(k) plan but the plan proceeds must be used specifically for health costs or medical insurance premiums.

§10.19 ANNUITY RETIREMENT OPTIONS—DEFINED CONTRIBUTION PLANS

Most deferred contribution retirement plans provide that upon retirement the employee may elect among a variety of annuities that are payable for the life or lives of one or more persons. Such annuities involve actuarial calculations of life expectancies as well as estimates of the time value of money. Actuaries determine rates, returns, and the like on the basis of recorded data, particularly records of mortality that show numbers of persons of various ages and occupations who die each year. See section 11.6. These records form the basis for the widely used tables of life expectancies of persons of various ages, which in turn form the backbone of both the life insurance industry and the annuity industry. The Internal Revenue Service also has published a table of life expectancies to be used for the calculation of the tax consequences of transactions involving annuities and lifetime interests. Portions of these tables appear as Tables 10-3, 10-4, 10-5, and 10-6 later in this chapter.

Let us assume that a faithful employee has reached the age of retirement after participating for many years in one or more plans that provide tax deferred benefits arising upon retirement. Specifically, the employer has contributed to a noncontributory qualified pension plan on behalf of the employee for 25 years. The plan is a defined contribution plan; the most recent statement from the plan shows that the tax deferred savings credited to the employee's account is $200,000. Now 67, the employee has decided to retire, as he is entitled to do. He must now choose what to do with the $200,000 "nest egg." The plan provides that a retiring employee has the following alternatives upon retirement:

(a) Take the total accumulation in cash;
(b) Elect a single life annuity payable for his life;
(c) Elect a life annuity for the life of the employee with payments for ten years guaranteed; that is, if he dies within ten years, payments will continue to be made to his beneficiary;
(d) Elect a life annuity for the combined lives of the employee and his spouse; that is, the payments are to continue while either the employee or his spouse are alive;
(e) Elect a life annuity for the combined lives of the employee and his spouse with a guaranteed ten-year period; or
(f) Elect a life annuity for the combined lives of the employee and his spouse with a further election that if the employee dies first,
  (i) the annuity drops to two-thirds the level at which it was paid while both are alive; or
  (ii) the annuity drops to half the level at which it was paid while both are alive.

In the case of each of the various lifetime annuity options, the plan assumes that the amount credited to the account of the retiring employee on the date of retirement is used to purchase a commercial annuity. The complete selection from the list of elections must be made before the actual date of retirement, and the selection, once made and payments commenced, is usually irrevocable.

At first glance, these choices may seem confusing and complicated, but they really are not. They are familiar to persons who give financial advice to employees contemplating retirement. Choice (a) is obvious and the simplest, though often not the most advantageous; since the plan was noncontributory, the employee has made no contributions into the plan and the entire amount of $200,000 will be taxable to him. When the federal income tax rate structure was strongly progressive, this lumping of income into a single year tended to increase the tax cost of electing an all-cash option, but with the present 31 percent maximum rate, the tax cost has been significantly reduced. In addition, the employee may qualify for an income averaging election upon taking a lump sum payment that also reduces the tax cost.

A more serious problem with the lump sum option is that if the employee elects this option, he then faces the problem of providing for himself and his spouse; there is always some risk that on a do-it-yourself retirement plan the money may run out while one or both of the beneficiaries are still alive.

Choice (b) requires knowledge of two factors: the life expectancy of a 67-year-old man and the interest rate used by the commercial insurance company in calculating the amount of a lifetime annuity for a single person of a specified age. Table 10-3 is the old Internal Revenue Service table showing the expected return on an ordinary life annuity. It will be noted that Table 10-3, like most nongovernmental mortality tables, expressly takes the sex of an annuitant as well as age into account. Since females live longer on the average than males, a contribution of a fixed amount made for the benefit of a female annuitant leads to a smaller monthly payment under this table than if the same payment were made for the benefit of a male. In 1986, the IRS adopted a revised "unisex" table (Table 10-4) that governs present annuity calculations.

In the present example, one may determine the life expectancy of a 67-year-old person under the current IRS expected return schedule. Tables actually used by a writer of an annuity may vary from the IRS table. From Table 10-4 one sees that in effect the retiring employee's life expectancy is an additional 18.4 years. Basically, the plan is purchasing a single-premium annuity commencing immediately and continuing for the life of the employee, but in determining how much is to be paid, the writer of the annuity assumes that the annuitant will precisely live out his life expectancy. This type of annuity is therefore basically the same as the ten-year annuity described in section 10.3. If we assume that an interest rate of 6 percent is used (a reasonable assumption), a $200,000 payment for 18.4 years yields a monthly payment of $1,495.54 per month. It is important to recognize that the payments in this amount continue for the balance

Table 10-3
Pre-1986 Internal Revenue Code Table:
Ordinary Life Annuities — One Life — Expected Return Multiples

Ages			Ages			Ages		
Male	Female	Multiples	Male	Female	Multiples	Male	Female	Multiples
6	11	65.0	41	46	33.0	76	81	9.1
7	12	64.1	42	47	32.1	77	82	8.7
8	13	63.2	43	48	31.2	78	83	8.3
9	14	62.3	44	49	30.4	79	84	7.8
10	15	61.4	45	50	29.6	80	85	7.5
11	16	60.4	46	51	28.7	81	86	7.1
12	17	59.5	47	52	27.9	82	87	6.7
13	18	58.6	48	53	27.1	83	88	6.3
14	19	57.7	49	54	26.3	84	89	6.0
15	20	56.7	50	55	25.5	85	90	5.7
16	21	55.8	51	56	24.7	86	91	5.4
17	22	54.9	52	57	24.0	87	92	5.1
18	23	53.9	53	58	23.2	88	93	4.8
19	24	53.0	54	59	22.4	89	94	4.5
20	25	52.1	55	60	21.7	90	95	4.2
21	26	51.1	56	61	21.0	91	96	4.0
22	27	50.2	57	62	20.3	92	97	3.7
23	28	49.3	58	63	19.6	93	98	3.5
24	29	48.3	59	64	18.9	94	99	3.3
25	30	47.4	60	65	18.2	95	100	3.1
26	31	46.5	61	66	17.5	96	101	2.9
27	32	45.6	62	67	16.9	97	102	2.7
28	33	44.6	63	68	16.2	98	103	2.5
29	34	43.7	64	69	15.6	99	104	2.3
30	35	42.8	65	70	15.0	100	105	2.1
31	36	41.9	66	71	14.4	101	106	1.9
32	37	41.0	67	72	13.8	102	107	1.7
33	38	40.0	68	73	13.2	103	108	1.5
34	39	39.1	69	74	12.6	104	109	1.3
35	40	38.2	70	75	12.1	105	110	1.2
						106	111	1.0
36	41	37.3	71	76	11.6	107	112	.8
37	42	36.5	72	77	11.0	108	113	.7
38	43	35.6	73	78	10.5	109	114	.6
39	44	34.7	74	79	10.1	110	115	.5
40	45	33.8	75	80	9.6	111	116	0

Table 10-4
1986 Internal Revenue Code Table
Ordinary Life Annuities — One Life — Expected Return Multiples

Age	Multiple	Age	Multiple	Age	Multiple
5	76.6	42	40.6	79	10.0
6	75.6	43	39.6	80	9.5
7	74.7	44	38.7	81	8.9
8	73.7	45	37.7	82	8.4
9	72.7	46	36.8	83	7.9
10	71.7	47	35.9	84	7.4
11	70.7	48	34.9	85	6.9
12	69.7	49	34.0	86	6.5
13	68.8	50	33.1	87	6.1
14	67.8	51	32.2	88	5.7
15	66.8	52	31.3	89	5.3
16	65.8	53	30.4	90	5.0
17	64.8	54	29.5	91	4.7
18	63.9	55	28.6	92	4.4
19	62.9	56	27.7	93	4.1
20	61.9	57	26.8	94	3.9
21	60.9	58	25.9	95	3.7
22	59.9	59	25.0	96	3.4
23	59.0	60	24.2	97	3.2
24	58.0	61	23.3	98	3.0
25	57.0	62	22.5	99	2.8
26	56.0	63	21.6	100	2.7
27	55.1	64	20.8	101	2.5
28	54.1	65	20.0	102	2.3
29	53.1	66	19.2	103	2.1
30	52.2	67	18.4	104	1.9
31	51.2	68	17.6	105	1.8
32	50.2	69	16.8	106	1.6
33	49.3	70	16.0	107	1.4
34	48.3	71	15.3	108	1.3
35	47.3	72	14.6	109	1.1
36	46.4	73	13.9	110	1.0
37	45.4	74	13.2	111	.9
38	44.4	75	12.5	112	.8
39	43.5	76	11.9	113	.7
40	42.5	77	11.2	114	.6
41	41.5	78	10.6	115	.5

of the employee's life, no matter how long or how short that life in fact turns out to be. A particularly long-lived annuitant causes a loss to the insurance company, while one who dies tomorrow gives the company a windfall. From the standpoint of the insurance company that writes the annuity, however, the use of reasonably accurate mortality tables eliminates virtually all of the underlying risk, since if many annuities are written, in the long run the longer-lived lifetime annuitants are, on the average, balanced and canceled out by the shorter-lived.

Federal law requires the written consent of the spouse of an employee making a retirement election of an annuity solely for the life of the employee.

Choice (c) is like choice (b) except that payments are guaranteed for ten years. This also involves an actuarial computation. A moment's thought should reveal that the $200,000 payment will purchase a smaller monthly payment under option (c) than under option (b). The reason is that the premature death of the annuitant under option (c) does not benefit the writer of the annuity as it does under option (b); as a result, the total obligation of the writer of the annuity is increased. In the above example, the monthly payment under choice (c) will be approximately $1,400 per month, the $95 difference from the annuity payable under option (c) compensating the writer of the annuity for the possibility that the annuity must continue for a full ten years even if the annuitant dies before then.

Choice (d) is obviously somewhat more complicated since payments are to continue while either the annuitant or his spouse are alive. Tables 10-5 and 10-6 are portions of the "ordinary joint life and last survivor annuity" tables published by the Internal Revenue Service. Table 10-5 is the old table taking the sex of the joint lives into account, while Table 10-6 is the unisex table in current use. In order to ascertain the amount of the monthly payment if this choice is elected, one must know the age of the spouse as well as of the principal annuitant. If we apply the current table and assume an age of 60 for the wife and 67 for the husband, the expected duration of the annuity is 27.0 years (from Table 10-6). This table is read by selecting one annuitant's age from the horizontal axis and the other annuitant's age from the vertical axis. At 27.0 years of expected return, the monthly payment (at 6 percent) is $1,246.73. Obviously, the difference between this amount and the $1,495.54 that would be payable for the life of the husband alone (option (b) is likely to affect significantly the lifestyle of the retirees. The reduction is large because of the younger age of the wife. Under the pre-1986 tables, younger wives had an even greater impact on their husbands' annuities.

Choice (e) is a compromise between preserving current lifestyles in the immediate post-retirement period and not leaving the surviving spouse, most likely a younger wife, in dire straits following the death of her husband. The amount of the monthly payments under these plans may be

Table 10-5

Per 1986 Internal Revenue Code:

Ordinary Joint Life and Last Survivor Annuities — Two Lives — Expected Return Multiples

Ages														
Male	Female	61	62	63	64	65	66	67	68	69	70	71	72	73
Male	Female	66	67	68	69	70	71	72	73	74	75	76	77	78
35	40	39.4	39.3	39.2	39.1	39.0	38.9	38.9	38.8	38.8	38.7	38.7	38.6	38.6
36	41	38.5	38.4	38.3	38.2	38.2	38.1	38.0	38.0	37.9	37.9	37.8	37.8	37.7
37	42	37.7	37.6	37.5	37.4	37.3	37.3	37.2	37.1	37.1	37.0	36.9	36.9	36.9
38	43	36.9	36.8	36.7	36.6	36.5	36.4	36.4	36.3	36.2	36.2	36.1	36.0	36.0
39	44	36.2	36.0	35.9	35.8	35.7	35.6	35.5	35.5	35.4	35.3	35.3	35.2	35.2
40	45	35.4	35.3	35.1	35.0	34.9	34.8	34.7	34.6	34.6	34.5	34.4	34.4	34.3
41	46	34.6	34.5	34.4	34.2	34.1	34.0	33.9	33.8	33.8	33.7	33.6	33.5	33.5
42	47	33.9	33.7	33.6	33.5	33.4	33.2	33.1	33.0	33.0	32.9	32.8	32.7	32.7
43	48	33.2	33.0	32.9	32.7	32.6	32.5	32.4	32.3	32.2	32.1	32.0	31.9	31.9
44	49	32.5	32.3	32.1	32.0	31.8	31.7	31.6	31.5	31.4	31.3	31.2	31.1	31.1
45	50	31.8	31.6	31.4	31.3	31.1	31.0	30.8	30.7	30.6	30.5	30.4	30.4	30.3
46	51	31.1	30.9	30.7	30.5	30.4	30.2	30.1	30.0	29.9	29.8	29.7	29.6	29.5
47	52	30.4	30.2	30.0	29.8	29.7	29.5	29.4	29.3	29.1	29.0	28.9	28.8	28.7
48	53	29.8	29.5	29.3	29.2	29.0	28.8	28.7	28.5	28.4	28.3	28.2	28.1	28.0
49	54	29.1	28.9	28.7	28.5	28.3	28.1	28.0	27.8	27.7	27.6	27.5	27.4	27.3
50	55	28.5	28.3	28.1	27.8	27.6	27.5	27.3	27.1	27.0	26.9	26.7	26.6	26.5

Table 10-5 (continued)
Per 1986 Internal Revenue Code:
Ordinary Joint Life and Last Survivor Annuities — Two Lives — Expected Return Multiples

Ages Male	Female	61 / 66	62 / 67	63 / 68	64 / 69	65 / 70	66 / 71	67 / 72	68 / 73	69 / 74	70 / 75	71 / 76	72 / 77	73 / 78
51	56	27.9	27.7	27.4	27.2	27.0	26.8	26.6	26.5	26.3	26.2	26.0	25.9	25.8
52	57	27.3	27.1	26.8	26.6	26.4	26.2	26.0	25.8	25.7	25.5	25.4	25.2	25.1
53	58	26.8	26.5	26.2	26.0	25.8	25.6	25.4	25.2	25.0	24.8	24.7	24.6	24.4
54	59	26.2	25.9	25.7	25.4	25.2	25.0	24.7	24.6	24.4	24.2	24.0	23.9	23.8
55	60	25.7	25.4	25.1	24.9	24.6	24.4	24.1	23.9	23.8	23.6	23.4	23.3	23.1
56	61	25.2	24.9	24.6	24.3	24.1	23.8	23.6	23.4	23.2	23.0	22.8	22.6	22.5
57	62	24.7	24.4	24.1	23.8	23.5	23.3	23.0	22.8	22.6	22.4	22.2	22.0	21.9
58	63	24.3	23.9	23.6	23.3	23.0	22.7	22.5	22.2	22.0	21.8	21.6	21.4	21.3
59	64	23.8	23.5	23.1	22.8	22.5	22.2	21.9	21.7	21.5	21.2	21.0	20.9	20.7
60	65	23.4	23.0	22.7	22.3	22.0	21.7	21.4	21.2	20.9	20.7	20.5	20.3	20.1
61	66	23.0	22.6	22.2	21.9	21.6	21.3	21.0	20.7	20.4	20.2	20.0	19.8	19.6
62	67	22.6	22.2	21.8	21.5	21.1	20.8	20.5	20.2	19.9	19.7	19.5	19.2	19.0
63	68	22.2	21.8	21.4	21.1	20.7	20.4	20.1	19.8	19.5	19.2	19.0	18.7	18.5
64	69	21.9	21.5	21.1	20.7	20.3	20.0	19.6	19.3	19.0	18.7	18.5	18.2	18.0
65	70	21.6	21.1	20.7	20.3	19.9	19.6	19.2	18.9	18.6	18.3	18.0	17.8	17.5
66	71	21.3	20.8	20.4	20.0	19.6	19.2	18.8	18.5	18.2	17.9	17.6	17.3	17.1
67	72	21.0	20.5	20.1	19.6	19.2	18.8	18.5	18.1	17.8	17.5	17.2	16.9	16.7
68	73	20.7	20.2	19.8	19.3	18.9	18.5	18.1	17.8	17.4	17.1	16.8	16.5	16.2
69	74	20.4	19.9	19.5	19.0	18.6	18.2	17.8	17.4	17.1	16.7	16.4	16.1	15.8
70	75	20.2	19.7	19.2	18.7	18.3	17.9	17.5	17.1	16.7	16.4	16.1	15.8	15.5
71	76	20.0	19.5	19.0	18.5	18.0	17.6	17.2	16.8	16.4	16.1	15.7	15.4	15.1
72	77	19.8	19.2	18.7	18.2	17.8	17.3	16.9	16.5	16.1	15.8	15.4	15.1	14.8
73	78	19.6	19.0	18.5	18.0	17.5	17.1	16.7	16.2	15.8	15.5	15.1	14.8	14.4

Table 10-6
1986 Internal Revenue Code Table
Ordinary Joint Life and Last Survivor Annuities
Two Lives — Expected Return Multiples

Ages	55	56	57	58	59	60	61	62	63	64
55	34.4	33.9	33.5	33.1	32.7	32.3	32.0	31.7	31.4	31.1
56	33.9	33.4	33.0	32.5	32.1	31.7	31.4	31.0	30.7	30.4
57	33.5	33.0	32.5	32.0	31.6	31.2	30.8	30.4	30.1	29.8
58	33.1	32.5	32.0	31.5	31.1	30.6	30.2	29.9	29.5	29.2
59	32.7	32.1	31.6	31.1	30.6	30.1	29.7	29.3	28.9	28.6
60	32.3	31.7	31.2	30.6	30.1	29.7	29.2	28.8	28.4	28.0
61	32.0	31.4	30.8	30.2	29.7	29.2	28.7	28.3	27.8	27.4
62	31.7	31.0	30.4	29.9	29.3	28.8	28.3	27.8	27.3	26.9
63	31.4	30.7	30.1	29.5	28.9	28.4	27.8	27.3	26.9	26.4
64	31.1	30.4	29.8	29.2	28.6	28.0	27.4	26.9	26.4	25.9
65	30.9	30.2	29.5	28.9	28.2	27.6	27.1	26.5	26.0	25.5
66	30.6	29.9	29.2	28.6	27.9	27.3	26.7	26.1	25.6	25.1
67	30.4	29.7	29.0	28.3	27.6	27.0	26.4	25.8	25.2	24.7
68	30.2	29.5	28.8	28.1	27.4	26.7	26.1	25.5	24.9	24.3
69	30.1	29.3	28.6	27.8	27.1	26.5	25.8	25.2	24.6	24.0
70	29.9	29.1	28.4	27.6	26.9	26.2	25.6	24.9	24.3	23.7
71	29.7	29.0	28.2	27.5	26.7	26.0	25.3	24.7	24.0	23.4
72	29.6	28.8	28.1	27.3	26.5	25.8	25.1	24.4	23.8	23.1
73	29.5	28.7	27.9	27.1	26.4	25.6	24.9	24.2	23.5	22.9
74	29.4	28.6	27.8	27.0	26.2	25.5	24.7	24.0	23.3	22.7
75	29.3	28.5	27.7	26.9	26.1	25.3	24.6	23.8	23.1	22.4
76	29.2	28.4	27.6	26.8	26.0	25.2	24.4	23.7	23.0	22.3
77	29.1	28.3	27.5	26.7	25.9	25.1	24.3	23.6	22.8	22.1
78	29.1	28.2	27.4	26.6	25.8	25.0	24.2	23.4	22.7	21.9
79	29.0	28.2	27.3	26.5	25.7	24.9	24.1	23.3	22.6	21.8
80	29.0	28.1	27.3	26.4	25.6	24.8	24.0	23.2	22.4	21.7
81	28.9	28.1	27.2	26.4	25.5	24.7	23.9	23.1	22.3	21.6
82	28.9	28.0	27.2	26.3	25.5	24.6	23.8	23.0	22.3	21.5
83	28.8	28.0	27.1	26.3	25.4	24.6	23.8	23.0	22.2	21.4
84	28.8	27.9	27.1	26.2	25.4	24.5	23.7	22.9	22.1	21.3
85	28.8	27.9	27.0	26.2	25.3	24.5	23.7	22.8	22.0	21.3

Table 10-6 (*continued*)
1986 Internal Revenue Code Table
Ordinary Joint Life and Last Survivor Annuities
Two Lives — Expected Return Multiples

Ages	55	56	57	58	59	60	61	62	63	64
86	28.7	27.9	27.0	26.1	25.3	24.5	23.6	22.8	22.0	21.2
87	28.7	27.8	27.0	26.1	25.3	24.4	23.6	22.8	21.9	21.1
88	28.7	27.8	27.0	26.1	25.2	24.4	23.5	22.7	21.9	21.1
89	28.7	27.8	26.9	26.1	25.2	24.4	23.5	22.7	21.9	21.1
90	28.7	27.8	26.9	26.1	25.2	24.3	23.5	22.7	21.8	21.0
91	28.7	27.8	26.9	26.0	25.2	24.3	23.5	22.6	21.8	21.0
92	28.6	27.8	26.9	26.0	25.2	24.3	23.5	22.6	21.8	21.0
93	28.6	27.8	26.9	26.0	25.1	24.3	23.4	22.6	21.8	20.9
94	28.6	27.7	26.9	26.0	25.1	24.3	23.4	22.6	21.7	20.9
95	28.6	27.7	26.9	26.0	25.1	24.3	23.4	22.6	21.7	20.9
96	26.6	27.7	26.9	26.0	25.1	24.2	23.4	22.6	21.7	20.9
97	28.6	27.7	26.8	26.0	25.1	24.2	23.4	22.5	21.7	20.9
98	28.6	27.7	26.8	26.0	25.1	24.2	23.4	22.5	21.7	20.9
99	28.6	27.7	26.8	26.0	25.1	24.2	23.4	22.5	21.7	20.9
100	28.6	27.7	26.8	26.0	25.1	24.2	23.4	22.5	21.7	20.8
101	28.6	27.7	26.8	25.9	25.1	24.2	23.4	22.5	21.7	20.8
102	28.6	27.7	26.8	25.9	25.1	24.2	23.3	22.5	21.7	20.8
103	28.6	27.7	26.8	25.9	25.1	24.2	23.3	22.5	21.7	20.8
104	28.6	27.7	26.8	25.9	25.1	24.2	23.3	22.5	21.6	20.8
105	28.6	27.7	26.8	25.9	25.1	24.2	23.3	22.5	21.6	20.8
106	28.6	27.7	26.8	25.9	25.1	24.2	23.3	22.5	21.6	20.8
107	28.6	27.7	26.8	25.9	25.1	24.2	23.3	22.5	21.6	20.8
108	28.6	27.7	26.8	25.9	25.1	24.2	23.3	22.5	21.6	20.8
109	28.6	27.7	26.8	25.9	25.1	24.2	23.3	22.5	21.6	20.8
110	28.6	27.7	26.8	25.9	25.1	24.2	23.3	22.5	21.6	20.8
111	28.6	27.7	26.8	25.9	25.0	24.2	23.3	22.5	21.6	20.8
112	28.6	27.7	26.8	25.9	25.0	24.2	23.3	22.5	21.6	20.8
113	28.6	27.7	26.8	25.9	25.0	24.2	23.3	22.5	21.6	20.8
114	28.6	27.7	26.8	25.9	25.0	24.2	23.3	22.5	21.6	20.8
115	28.6	27.7	26.8	25.9	25.0	24.2	23.3	22.5	21.6	20.8

readily determined on an actuarial basis, though the calculations are more complex than those set forth above.

The selection of any of these options must take into account the peculiar needs of the retiree and his or her spouse, their ages, their general health, other available assets and insurance, and so forth. These factors are discussed generally in the following section.

Retirement plans that offer a variety of lifetime annuity arrangements sometimes describe the effect of the various arrangements as a percentage of a standard benefit. A plan widely used by institutions of higher education to provide retirement benefits for faculty and administrators, for example, estimates the benefit that would be payable on the basis of a life annuity with ten-year guaranteed payments as 100 percent. If the annuitant is 65 at the age of retirement, the election of a lifetime annuity with a 20-year guaranteed payment pays 93 percent of the base annuity. A single life annuity without guaranteed payments pays 104 percent of the base annuity. An annuity for the life of both a 67-year-old husband and his 60-year-old wife, and the survivor of them, with a guaranteed ten-year payment, pays 85 percent of the base amount. These percentages are sometimes more meaningful in the eyes of a person selecting irrevocably among these bewildering choices than dollar figures based on a hypothetical example.

§10.20 ANNUITY RETIREMENT OPTIONS—DEFINED BENEFIT PLAN

In a defined benefit plan, the retirement options are not based on the value of a fund on the date of retirement but on other factors, usually years of employment with the employer and the employee's salary during a period ending at or shortly before retirement. A typical program may provide that a person retiring at age 65 receives a pension equal to 1.5 percent of final pay for each year of service. Thus, an employee earning $100,000 at retirement with 30 years of service receives an annual pension of $45,000.

Defined benefit plans also may provide a menu of alternative annuities for the retiree. For example, a defined benefit plan may provide a retiree with the following options:

Single-life annuity—$4,000 per month for life

Joint and survivor annuities:

50 percent survivor's benefit—$3,520 per month for life; $1,760 for spouse's life if retiree dies first

75 percent survivor's benefit—$3,320 per month for life; $2,490 for spouse's life if retiree dies first

100 percent survivor's benefit — $3,120 for retiree and spouse until the death of the survivor

Single life annuity with ten years certain — $3,640 for life of retiree with payment to continue for ten years even if retiree dies.

These all may have about the same actuarial value, based on average risks and life expectancies. The actual selection must depend on a consideration of factors of health, financial condition, and so forth. For example, if a person is married and in ill health, the 100 percent survivor option may be most attractive. Likewise, if a person or spouse expects a significant inheritance, or if he or she has separate pension income or is already the beneficiary of a substantial life insurance policy, the higher single-life payout may be most attractive. An unmarried employee with close family relatives should consider taking the ten-years-certain annuity on the theory that this provides something for collateral relatives if the annuitant dies shortly after retiring.

Federal law requires the written consent of the spouse of an employee making a retirement election of an annuity solely for the life of the employee.

In some defined benefit plans, a retiree adopting a single-life annuity may cause the spouse to lose all retiree medical benefits when the retiree dies. Of course, the availability of Medicare may reduce (though not eliminate) this disadvantage.

§10.21 MULTIPLE PENSIONS

Many persons at retirement have benefits under more than a single pension plan. They may have worked for more than one employer or may have elected to invest retirement funds with more than a single carrier. Both husband and wife may have worked and each may be participants in separate retirement plans. Some may have cash value life insurance policies, which may be converted into an annuity.

It is usually not desirable to select the same annuity option under each plan; considerable flexibility may be obtained by electing different options, for example, the husband elects a joint and survivor annuity under his retirement plan and the wife elects an annuity for her single life under her plan. In making such decisions, the availability of social security and Medicare benefits should be considered, as should the possible availability of life insurance proceeds to help support the surviving spouse where the other has elected an annuity for his or her single life but is covered by an outstanding life insurance policy.

§10.22 PENSION MAX

"Pension max" is a strategy by which a retiree attempts to maximize retirement benefits through a combination of life insurance with a pension election. The strategy calls for a married retiree to take the highest single-life annuity option and then use part of the pension payment to purchase a life insurance policy to provide income for the spouse if the retiree dies first. Actuaries who evaluate this strategy nearly always dismiss it as inferior to coverage under the pension plan itself.

An example of the pension max strategy based on an illustration used to sell this strategy may be useful. A teacher retires at 55. He can choose $28,000 a year for the rest of his life or $21,000 per year until both he and his spouse die. Under the pension max strategy the teacher elects the single life benefit and buys a life insurance policy with a face value equal to 10 times the annual benefit under the joint-and-survivor option—$210,000—to provide the same protection for his wife. An ordinary life policy paid up in seven to ten years (see section 11.20 if you do not understand what this policy covers) costs about $6,500 a year. The $7,000 increase in the pension covers the cost of this premium and still leaves the retiree with $500 more than he would have had if he elected the lower paying joint and survivor option. After ten years the life insurance policy is self-sustaining so that further payments need not be made, and the retiree would have the extra $7,000 in benefits to spend each year.

One problem is that the pension plan in this example uses a more modest assumption about interest rates than does the typical insurance policy. A pension plan calculates the survivor benefit by assuming that the money one foregoes by not taking the single annuity benefit will earn 5 to 8 percent until the death of the annuitant and payments for the spouse begin. In contrast, the pension max illustration may assume that premium dollars will grow at the rate of 9 or 10 percent a year so that the policy will be self-sustaining after the prescribed period of ten years. But the self-sustaining point is speculative: If interest rates go down, the growth in the value of the policy fails to meet the projections in the policy illustration. At that point, there are three options: Pay higher premiums, get less insurance, or drop the policy.

Also, tax consequences are usually not taken into account in the policy illustrations for pension max; they assume that all funds are available for payment of premiums, whereas, in fact, some or all of the pension will be subject to tax.

Pension max may have additional disadvantages. Some retirement programs index for inflation, whereas pension max never does; it assumes that all payments are level. Other retirement plans may provide subsidized survivors' benefits or charge less than actuarial cost for survivor's benefits.

Pension max cannot match the benefits of these policies. Pension max also assumes that the retiree will remain in good health; if he becomes ill, money set aside for premiums to protect the other spouse may have to be used to pay for medical expenses or care maintenance.

The pension max strategy works best if the insurance policy is purchased before retirement. Also, one may sometimes be able to take advantage of the unisex life expectancy tables currently in use in many plans. A couple, both employed, approaching retirement might have the wife adopt the pension max strategy on the theory that she is likely to outlive the average expectancy used to calculate her annuity, while providing insurance proceeds for her husband on the reduced chance that she will die first. Nevertheless, the pension max strategy appears to be more a device to sell life insurance than to provide additional funds to a retiree.

§10.23 EARLY RETIREMENT

Many employers offer "early" retirement to workers in an effort to avoid involuntary layoffs. Such offers may be made to all or selected workers who are 50 years old or older; in rare cases offers may be made to men and women in their 40s. Typically, there is a small "window" of time during which offers of early retirement must be accepted; if the offer is not accepted there may be an implicit threat that involuntary layoffs will follow with financial terms much less attractive than those being offered for early retirement.

Offers of early retirement are usually much less attractive when they are carefully analyzed than when they are presented. Except for offers to very top level management (or to persons who have substantial outside assets), a person accepting early retirement usually finds he or she cannot live comfortably on the benefits promised. Hence a person considering early retirement should plan on finding continued employment in some other area, something that may not be easy for a person in his or her early 50s to do.

The benefits provided for early retirement usually work off of and augment the employer's regular retirement program. A typical defined benefit retirement program may provide that a person retiring at age 65 receives a pension equal to 1.5 percent of final pay for each year of service. Thus an employee earning $100,000 at retirement with 30 years of service receives an annual pension of $45,000 (30 × 1.5 × $100,000). However, if the employee retires before the age of 65 — at 55, say — benefits under this program are reduced, first, because they are calculated on 20 years of service rather than on 30 years, and, second, the employer must pay the pension for an additional ten years. This second factor alone may result in a pension reduction of as much as 50 percent from the age 65 pension if a person retires at 55. Since no one is likely to accept early retirement under such terms, an employer usually offers one or more "sweeteners" for persons who agree to retire early during the "window." The sweetener may consist of a lump sum severance pay plus the addition of an arbitrary number of years of age and of service when calculating the retiring employee's pension. For example, in 1992, Digital Equipment Corporation offered a "sweetener" consisting of a severance payment equal to 26 weeks pay plus the addition of five years to the retiring employee's age and five years to his or her service record for purposes of calculating the person's pension.

While these "sweeteners" sound attractive, an employee is almost always considerably better off working until retirement. For example, an employee who is earning $100,000 at age 55, who accepts early retirement with 25 years of service, will have a pension of only $18,750 if he retires without sweeteners; if five years are added to his age and to his years of service as sweeteners, the early retirement pension grows to $33,750. However, if the employee continued to work for another ten years and received annual salary increases of 7 percent per year, the pension would be $105,000 upon retirement at age 65.

While early retirement has its disadvantages, it is certainly preferable to being laid off at a later date with only nominal benefits. The attractiveness of early retirement plans therefore are directly proportional to the probability of being terminated at a later date.

Early retirement also negatively affects other benefits. Social security benefits are reduced with early retirement if benefits are begun at age 62. Contributions to Keogh or IRA plans normally end with early retirement; even if benefits are deferred until age 65, they are much smaller than if contributions continued to be made.

Sometimes an early retirement offer is so "sweetened" that a person close to retirement finds himself or herself in virtually the same position by retiring as by continuing to work. An example: In 1991, Jane, age 62, has a salary of $72,000. After federal income taxes of $22,320, social security and Medicare taxes of $4,355, and commuting and work related expenses of $5,040 per year, Jane nets $40,285. She is unlikely to receive any significant increases in salary between 1991 and 1994, when she plans to retire at age 65. An early retirement offer is made: a $30,000 cash bonus ($10,000 for each of the three years until retirement) plus full pension benefits of $21,000 (equal to 30 percent of her average earnings of $70,000 for the last three years). After retirement, she will also get IRA benefits of $10,000 per year, social security benefits of $9,400, and distributions from her 401(k) plan of $2,000 per year. If she retires early, she will have to pay $14,787 in federal income taxes and $4,800 in medical insurance premiums that her employer now pays. On these figures — not untypical of persons in their early 60s considering early retirement — the difference between working and retiring is only $7,472 per year, and if Jane works 1,960 hours per year, she is in effect working for $3.82 per hour. It is not surprising that many persons in this category accept early retirement.

A person who accepts early retirement at age 60 can expect to live another 25 or 30 years. During this period, retirement income may be relatively constant while inflation is open-ended. It is particularly important for such a person to take into account the probability that inflation will cause a significant erosion in purchasing power during the period of retirement. While this is a concern for all retirees, it is particularly serious for the person accepting early retirement who does not plan to find alternative employment.

11

Life Insurance

§11.1 INTRODUCTION

Everyone is generally familiar with the institution of life insurance. In 1987, there were approximately 182,000,000 policyholders in the United States; thus, about three out of every five persons living in the United

States have some kind of life insurance. This insurance is purchased individually, primarily through agents. In addition, there were 326,000 mas-
ter group life insurance policies, covering 85,000,000 participants. Group
insurance is usually provided through employers or membership organizations. The average American household owning insurance at all had approximately $102,000 worth of life insurance in force in 1987. About 5
percent of disposable income is spent on life insurance and insurance
products.

Life insurance is an immense industry: In 1987, annual premium
payments on life insurance policies exceeded $213 billion, and the assets
of life insurance companies exceeded $1.0 trillion, much of which repre-
sented reserves to cover future obligations under insurance policies already
in existence. The management, investment, and reinvestment of this huge
pool of capital alone makes this industry an important force in the American economy. The amount of ordinary life insurance in force has increased
steadily since the 1930s and in 1987 exceeded $7.4 trillion. Life insurance
companies also write annuities and may be involved in other kinds of
insurance as well. About 15 million persons own annuity contracts written
by insurance companies. The discussion in this chapter, however, is limited
exclusively to life insurance.

It is probable that a very large percentage of all purchasers of life
insurance are not aware of exactly what they have purchased and do not
know whether they have purchased what they need.

Until the 1970s, the life insurance industry sold a limited number of
products. These traditional products are generally known as "term" insurance and "whole life" insurance, though there are a number of variations
of these basic types of insurance. Together they are often described as
ordinary life insurance. These traditional products were designed basically
to provide protection against the unexpected death of wage earners and
their spouses and, in the case of whole life policies, to encourage savings
in low yielding investments in the guise of providing lifetime life insurance
protection.

The twin factors of high inflation and high interest rates in the period
since the late 1960s has shaken up the life insurance industry. The traditional policies became less attractive, and new types of life insurance have
been developed: flexible premium life insurance (often called universal life
insurance or variable rate life insurance), adjustable life insurance, second
to die insurance, blended life insurance, vanishing premium insurance,
and more importantly, variable life insurance (often called single premium
insurance), a type of policy that contains significant tax shelter benefits.
Tax legislation during the 1980s generally attempted to eliminate or minimize tax shelter and tax deferral devices, and the variable life insurance
product was no exception. While much of the recent growth in the
purchase of life insurance products has been fueled by these new, tax-

oriented policies, their appeal has been dulled in the 1990s by reduced tax advantages and declining rates of return on investments generally.

The first sections of this chapter describe the fundamental relationships and actuarial principles underlying every life insurance contract. The following sections discuss the standard and traditional life insurance products as well as the newer products sold by the life insurance industry today. Consideration is also given to the factors that enter into the decision of the type and amount of insurance a person should own.

§11.2 THE PERSONS INVOLVED IN LIFE INSURANCE POLICIES

In addition to the life insurance company that writes the policy, every life insurance policy involves three actors: the insured, the beneficiary, and the owner of the policy. The insured is the person whose demise triggers the obligation of the insurance company to pay the face value of the policy, and the beneficiary is the person to whom the face value is paid. Often the beneficiary of the policy will be the insured's spouse or children, but it may also be the insured's estate or persons unrelated to the insured. The owner of the policy is the person who has the power to exercise a number of options with respect to the policy: to name or change the designation of the beneficiary, to borrow against the policy or pledge it as security for a loan (if it has a cash surrender value), and to surrender the policy or decide to let it lapse for nonpayment. Usually the owner of the policy is the person who pays the premiums. The owner and the insured may be the same person, but they need not be, and indeed it is often advantageous from a tax standpoint for them to be different persons. Under the federal estate tax law, if the insured has retained the incidents of ownership (for example, the right to change beneficiaries or to pledge the policy as security for a loan) at the time of death, the policy is includable in his or her estate. This is true even if the beneficiary of the policy is a spouse, other family member, or another individual.

§11.3 MUTUAL LIFE INSURANCE COMPANIES AND STOCK COMPANIES

Basically there are two types of life insurance companies writing policies today: mutual companies and stock companies. About 40 percent of all life insurance is written today by mutual companies. A mutual company does not have shareholders; its board of directors is elected by its policyholders, and excess earnings of the company are paid to its policyholders in the form of annual dividends. In a broad sense, the "owners" of a mutual life insurance company are the policyholders. One should not put too much weight on this "ownership," however. Policyholders are widely scattered and unorganized and as a result have virtually no voice in how a mutual company is actually managed. Also, most policyholders are indifferent to management issues so long as their individual policies are not adversely affected. Management of a mutual company can therefore run the company with almost complete freedom from oversight by the owners, the only discipline being provided by the need to offer relatively competitive products with those offered by other insurance companies.

The second type of insurance company is a stock company. It is in form a traditional corporation with shareholders who purchase stock in the company and who are entitled to elect the company's board of directors. Dividends in a stock company are paid to the shareholders, not to the policyholders as in a mutual company. In a stock company, policyholders are more analogous to customers of the corporation than to owners.

When dealing with any insurance company, the possibility that the company may become insolvent in the future should be considered. The potential insolvency risk of insurance companies, and the difficulties of assessing this risk, are discussed in section 10.4

§11.4 PARTICIPATING AND NONPARTICIPATING POLICIES

Policies that are entitled to share in dividends are called participating policies and are usually written by mutual companies. In effect, each year when the premium notice is sent, the amount of the dividend is set forth and the owner of the policy may elect to have the dividend credited against the amount of next year's premium. In mutual companies, dividends may be paid on all types of life insurance outstanding or only on specified classes or types of policies. Policies written by stock companies are usually nonparticipating, that is, they are not entitled to receive dividends. The amount of the annual premium is fixed and is not subject to reduction by a dividend. In making comparisons between various life insurance policies and the costs of similar policies issued by different companies, it is necessary to take into account whether the proposed policy is participating or nonparticipating. While the amount of a dividend on a participating policy is apt to be rather small in contrast with the amount of a premium, it tends to be stable and reasonably predictable, and a complete assessment of the relative costs of two otherwise equivalent policies should take the dividend into account.

Of course, dividends on participating policies do not have to be used to reduce premiums. They may be used to purchase additional "paid up" insurance (see section 11.16), or they may be left with the company to draw interest.

Even though a mutual company pays dividends to policyholders while stock companies pay dividends to shareholders, one should not assume that mutual companies offer cheaper products. Both types of companies compete vigorously with each other for the same insurance dollar. It is not uncommon for a stock company to offer a cheaper policy even after the mutual company dividend is taken into account.

§11.5 THE TRADITIONAL GOALS OF LIFE INSURANCE: FAMILY PROTECTION AND LIQUIDITY

Death may strike a person at any age. The most serious family crises are likely to arise from the unexpected death of a person who is the sole or principal income producer for young and dependent children and a spouse who lacks salable job skills. Life insurance obviously provides essential benefits in this type of situation, and, as a result, it is not surprising that traditionally most life insurance was sold to "breadwinners," in the classic sense. Today, it is not uncommon for both spouses to work even when the children are relatively young, but life insurance may still provide essential protection since the loss of one income may have devastating consequences. Even when one spouse remains home to care for young children, it is increasingly recognized that his or her services are also essential to the family unit, and life insurance protection should be purchased for both spouses.

Even where the death of the insured does not create an immediate financial crisis for a family with young children, life insurance is often a desirable component of contingency financial planning because it provides a large degree of immediate liquidity upon the death of the insured. Many persons have assets that may have substantial value if they can be disposed of in an orderly way but relatively little value if they must be sold immediately at "fire sale" or "distress" prices. Good examples of such assets include real estate such as the family home, a wholly owned business, or shares of stock in a family corporation. Also, a person's heirs may desire to retain certain assets for their own use after the death of the insured, such as the family home, a cabin in the mountains, or an art collection. Whether or not this is practical may depend on whether the estate has other liquid assets sufficient to cover taxes, expenses, cash bequests, and outstanding indebtedness. If the estate does not, something more must be sold to enable the estate to be administered and closed in a timely fashion, and what is most salable is often precisely what the heirs desire to keep for their own use. Life insurance provides liquidity in the form of ready cash that may be of inestimable value in simplifying the immediate post-death affairs of the deceased person's estate and his or her heirs.

Life insurance that is payable to the estate of the decedent is, of course, available for the payment of estate obligations, while life insurance that is payable to an individual usually is not. However, the proceeds of an insurance policy are includable in the estate of the decedent for federal estate tax purposes if the policy is payable to the estate of the decedent, no matter who owns the policy. The use of life insurance to improve the liquidity of the estate may therefore increase the taxes imposed on the estate.

The rules about when life insurance must be included in the taxable estate of the decedent for federal estate tax purposes described above are not as important for most persons today as they were a few years ago because changes in federal tax laws during the 1980s greatly reduced the impact of this tax so that now it affects only the most wealthy individuals. Today there is a $600,000 exclusion applicable to all estates, whereas the exemption was only $60,000 as late as the mid-1970s. Obviously, as a practical matter, the average estate today, with a $600,000 exemption, does not need to be concerned about federal estate taxes. The federal estate tax law also grants an unlimited deduction for transfers to the spouse of the decedent. Of course, if the spouse dies shortly after the decedent, the estate tax saving that may be obtained in the estate of the decedent by taking advantage of this so-called marital deduction largely disappears because the estate of the spouse who dies second will not have the advantage of a marital deduction, and most of the property transferred from the decedent to the spouse will be subject to estate tax upon the death of the spouse. Nevertheless, with proper planning, an aggregate of $1,200,000 (the $600,000 exclusion for the decedent plus the $600,000 exclusion for the spouse of the decedent) may pass tax-free upon the death of both spouses.

§11.6 GAMBLING AND LIFE INSURANCE

Some people doubtless view life insurance (and perhaps other types of insurance as well) as a form of ghoulish gambling on the life of a person. In this view, the person buying life insurance on her life is betting that she will not live beyond her life expectancy, while the insurance company is betting that she will live to a ripe old age. It is important to recognize, however, that from the standpoint of the life insurance company, life insurance is not gambling at all.

Consider, for example, the situation in which a new insured, Jane Doe, aged 30 with three small children, pays her first premium but is hit and killed by a truck ten minutes later while leaving the insurance agent's office. The face amount of the policy is certainly due in this situation even though the insurance was in effect for only the briefest of periods. Even if the policy had not been formally issued, Jane Doe was almost certainly insured at the time of her death because insurance companies universally give their agents authority to bind the insurance companies on prospective insurance policies while the companies assess the risk and decide whether to issue a permanent policy. (A binder, in other words, is a kind of temporary insurance policy.)

The unexpected demise of Jane Doe does not mean that the insurance company writing the policy lost a gamble. Insurance companies diversify the risk by writing many policies on many different people in many different situations. The whole foundation of life insurance is the existence of reliable mortality tables for members of the population as a whole. The earliest such tables date from the late 1600s, and data have been collected on a regular basis ever since. The translation of this information into tables, which permit the determination of theoretical premiums to be charged an average person for a life insurance policy in a specified amount on his or her life, is generally the subject of actuarial science. The principal variable is, of course, age, but other more controversial variables that do reliably assist actuaries in predicting mortality rates, such as sex and race, may be used because mortality tables are available for these subgroups of the population. So long as the population of insureds drawn from a specific risk group covered by a specific company resembles the population of that risk group as a whole, and the premiums are established on an actuarial basis to cover not only the risk but also the insurance company's costs and expenses, the element of gambling is largely eliminated. Indeed, from this perspective, the premature death of our unfortunate Jane Doe is not an unexpected event at all. The mortality tables build in the fact that on average a certain number of 30-year-old women of Jane Doe's race will die in motor vehicle accidents each year. From the perspective of the actuary, this tragedy is a predictable statistic.

Table 11-1 sets forth published data on the expectation of life at various ages in the United States both by race and by sex. Table 11-2 describes the historical changes in life expectancies since 1970. Considerably more elaborate tables are, of course, used by insurance companies to develop premiums applicable to specific applicants, but the general relevance of these tables for purposes of life insurance should be obvious. As long as the individuals being insured by a life insurance company reflect the mortality experience of the population from which they are drawn, premiums may be safely calculated on the basis of available statistics on average mortality tables or life expectancies.

Tables 11-1 and 11-2 deserve some examination since they provide

Table 11-1
Expectation of Life by Race, Sex, and Age: 1989

Age in 1989 (years)	Expectation of Life in Years				
		White		Black	
	Total	Male	Female	Male	Female
At birth	75.3	72.7	79.2	64.8	73.5
1	75.0	72.3	78.8	65.2	73.8
2	74.1	71.4	77.8	64.2	72.9
3	73.1	70.4	76.9	63.3	71.9
4	72.1	69.5	75.9	62.3	71.0
5	71.1	68.5	74.9	61.4	70.0
6	70.2	67.5	73.9	60.4	69.0
7	69.2	66.5	73.0	59.4	68.0
8	68.2	65.5	72.0	58.5	67.1
9	67.2	64.5	71.0	57.5	66.1
10	66.2	63.6	70.0	56.5	65.1
11	65.2	62.6	69.0	55.5	64.1
12	64.3	61.6	68.0	54.5	63.1
13	63.3	60.6	67.0	53.5	62.1
14	62.3	59.6	66.0	52.6	61.2
15	61.3	58.6	65.1	51.6	60.2
16	60.4	57.7	64.1	50.7	59.2
17	59.4	56.8	63.1	49.8	58.2
18	58.5	55.8	62.1	48.8	57.3
19	57.5	54.9	61.2	47.9	56.3
20	56.6	54.0	60.2	47.1	55.3
21	55.6	53.0	59.2	46.2	54.4
22	54.7	52.1	58.3	45.3	53.4
23	53.8	51.2	57.3	44.4	52.4
24	52.8	50.3	56.3	43.6	51.5
25	51.9	49.4	55.3	42.7	50.6
26	50.9	48.4	54.4	41.9	49.6
27	50.0	47.5	53.4	41.0	48.7
28	49.1	46.6	52.4	40.2	47.7
29	48.1	45.7	51.5	39.3	46.8
30	47.2	44.7	50.5	38.5	45.9
31	46.2	43.8	49.5	37.6	44.9
32	45.3	42.9	48.6	36.8	44.0
33	44.4	42.0	47.6	36.0	43.1
34	43.5	41.0	46.6	35.1	42.2
35	42.5	40.1	45.7	34.3	41.3
36	41.6	39.2	44.7	33.5	40.4
37	40.7	38.3	43.7	32.7	39.5
38	39.8	37.4	42.8	32.0	38.6
39	38.8	36.5	41.8	31.2	37.7

Table 11-1 (continued)

| Age in 1989 (years) | Expectation of Life in Years | | | | |
| | | White | | Black | |
	Total	Male	Female	Male	Female
40	37.9	35.6	40.9	30.4	36.8
41	37.0	34.7	39.9	29.7	35.9
42	36.1	33.8	39.0	28.9	35.0
43	35.2	32.9	38.0	28.1	34.1
44	34.3	32.0	37.1	27.4	33.3
45	33.4	31.1	36.1	26.6	32.4
46	32.5	30.2	35.2	25.9	31.5
47	31.6	29.3	34.3	25.1	30.7
48	30.7	28.4	33.4	24.4	29.8
49	29.8	27.5	32.4	23.7	29.0
50	28.9	26.7	31.5	23.0	28.2
51	28.1	25.8	30.6	22.3	27.3
52	27.2	25.0	29.7	21.6	26.5
53	26.4	24.2	28.8	20.9	25.7
54	25.6	23.3	28.0	20.3	24.9
55	24.7	22.5	27.1	19.6	24.1
56	23.9	21.7	26.2	18.9	23.4
57	23.1	21.0	25.4	18.3	22.6
58	22.3	20.2	24.6	17.7	21.8
59	21.6	19.4	23.7	17.1	21.1
60	20.8	18.7	22.9	16.4	20.4
61	20.1	18.0	22.1	15.9	19.7
62	19.3	17.3	21.3	15.3	19.0
63	18.6	16.6	20.5	14.7	18.3
64	17.9	15.9	19.7	14.1	17.7
65	17.2	15.2	19.0	13.6	17.0
70	13.9	12.1	15.3	11.0	13.9
75	10.9	9.4	11.9	8.8	11.0
80	8.3	7.1	8.9	6.9	8.5
85 and over	6.2	5.3	6.5	5.6	6.7

Source: U.S. National Center for Health Statistics, *Vital Statistics of the United States*, annual; and unpublished data.

Table 11-2
Expectation of Life at Birth, 1970 to 1990, and Projections, 1995 to 2010
In years. Excludes deaths of nonresidents of the United States.

Year	Total			White			Black and Other			Black		
	Total	Male	Female	Total	Male	Female	Total	Male	Female	Total	Male	Female
1970	70.8	67.1	74.7	71.7	68.0	75.6	65.3	61.3	69.4	64.1	60.0	68.3
1975	72.6	68.8	76.6	73.4	69.5	77.3	68.0	63.7	72.4	66.8	62.4	71.3
1976	72.9	69.1	76.8	73.6	69.9	77.5	68.4	64.2	72.7	67.2	62.9	71.6
1977	73.3	69.5	77.2	74.0	70.2	77.9	68.9	64.7	73.2	67.7	63.4	72.0
1978	73.5	69.6	77.3	74.1	70.4	78.0	69.3	65.0	73.5	68.1	63.7	72.4
1979	73.9	70.0	77.8	74.6	70.8	78.4	69.8	65.4	74.1	68.5	64.0	72.9
1980	73.7	70.0	77.4	74.4	70.7	78.1	69.5	65.3	73.6	68.1	63.8	72.5
1981	74.2	70.4	77.8	74.8	71.1	78.4	70.3	66.1	74.4	68.9	64.5	73.2
1982	74.5	70.9	78.1	75.1	71.5	78.7	71.0	66.8	75.0	69.4	65.1	73.7
1983	74.6	71.0	78.1	75.2	71.7	78.7	71.1	67.2	74.9	69.6	65.4	73.6
1984	74.7	71.2	78.2	75.3	71.8	78.7	71.3	67.4	75.0	69.7	65.6	73.7
1985	74.7	71.2	78.2	75.3	71.9	78.7	71.2	67.2	75.0	69.5	65.3	73.5
1986	74.8	71.3	78.3	75.4	72.0	78.8	71.2	67.2	75.1	69.4	65.2	73.5
1987	75.0	71.5	78.4	75.6	72.2	78.9	71.3	67.3	75.2	69.4	65.2	73.6
1988	74.9	71.5	78.3	75.6	72.3	78.9	71.2	67.1	75.1	69.2	64.9	73.4
1989	75.3	71.8	78.6	76.0	72.7	79.2	71.2	67.1	75.2	69.2	64.8	73.5
1990, prel.	75.4	72.0	78.8	76.0	72.6	79.3	72.4	68.4	76.3	70.3	66.0	74.5
Projections:[1] 1995	76.3	72.8	79.7	76.8	73.4	80.2	(NA)	(NA)	(NA)	72.4	68.8	76.0
2000	77.0	73.5	80.4	77.5	74.0	80.9	(NA)	(NA)	(NA)	73.5	69.9	77.1
2005	77.6	74.2	81.0	78.1	74.6	81.5	(NA)	(NA)	(NA)	74.6	71.0	78.1
2010	77.9	74.4	81.3	78.3	74.9	81.7	(NA)	(NA)	(NA)	75.0	71.4	78.5

NA Not available. [1]Based on middle mortality assumptions; for details, see source. Source: U.S. Bureau of the Census, *Current Population Reports*, series P-25, No. 1018.

Source: Except as noted, U.S. National Center for Health Statistics, *Vital Statistics of the United States*, annual; *Monthly Vital Statistics Report*; and unpublished data.

interesting information that the reader may not be aware of; for example, what is your life expectancy at your present age? Why do life expectancies tend to increase steadily? Obviously improvements in medical care, the development of antibiotics, and the like largely explain this trend. The life expectancy of a white male born in 1900 was less than 50 years while it was over 72 years for a white male born in 1986. Average figures, however, have a tendency to mislead. Much of the increase in life expectancy since 1900 has been caused by decreases in infant and child mortality rather than by improving the life expectancy of a person who reaches adulthood.

Is it proper or appropriate (or constitutional?) for life insurance companies to use sex-based and race-based tables? The accumulated statistics that support these distinctions provide valid predictors, but they have come under increasing criticism. The reason for this is political more than economic because a longer life expectancy may sometimes be favorable and sometimes not. In 1989, a 65-year-old white male had a life expectancy of 15.2 years while a white female of the same age had an expectancy of 19 years. If we assume that both the male and the female retire at the same time and have precisely $100,000 to invest in a lifetime retirement annuity which is based on their respective life expectancies, the male would receive monthly payments that are significantly higher than the female: At 7 percent per year, the monthly annuity would be $893.20 for the male and $794.19 for the female. On the other hand, if the transaction contemplates the purchase of life insurance, on the same assumptions the female would be charged a significantly lower premium for the same amount of insurance since she will, on average, be paying premiums for several more years and the insurance company will have the use of her money for a longer period.

§11.7 TERM INSURANCE

"Term insurance" is a traditional type of life insurance that provides basic life insurance protection. It provides solely death protection for a fixed period of time such as one, five, or ten years. The face amount of the policy is paid only if the insured dies within the time or term stated in the policy. Term insurance is pure insurance, based on actuarial data on the probability of death occurring within the fixed period of the policy. As the insured gets older, the probability of his or her death during the current time period obviously increases; thus the cost of term insurance increases with the age of the person involved. This is graphically illustrated by the following 1991 price quotations for $100,000 of term insurance for non-smoking males set forth in Table 11-3.

Table 11-3
Term Life Insurance Premiums by Age

Age	Annual Premium
30	$155
40	$173
50	$251
60	$710
70	$2,156

At about age 65, the cost of pure term insurance becomes prohibitive. However, for a 35-year-old breadwinner with a nonworking spouse and two or three young children to support — perhaps the prototypical individual needing life insurance — term insurance provides a very large degree of temporary protection at a relatively modest cost.

Even though term insurance is based on actuarial principles, there may be wide variations in price quotations, based on different assessments of risk, different premium structures, different commission rates payable to agents, and so forth. In addition, a variety of options may be offered in connection with a term policy: double payment in the event of accidental death, for example, or an option to convert term insurance at a later date into other types of insurance without a new medical examination.

Term insurance policies usually require a medical examination, though some companies may write small term policies for younger persons solely on the basis of written health-related questions. Persons in certain risky occupations or having risky avocations may not be able to obtain term insurance at all or may be able to obtain it only by paying an additional premium. Term insurance policies are usually renewable for additional terms (at higher premiums) without another medical examination or questionnaire. Many policies provide for level premiums for periods of up to five years, with the level premium during this period being approximately equal to the average of annual premiums over the period for a person of the age in question. Term insurance is also often sold at bargain prices in connection with, or as a sweetener for, other types of life insurance.

Term insurance may be either face amount insurance (in which event the face amount is constant and the premium increases periodically) or declining balance (in which event the premium remains constant but the face amount of insurance coverage declines as the person gets older). A very common kind of declining balance insurance is mortgage insurance, sold in connection with a mortgage on a home, or credit insurance, required by many lenders when they make small consumer loans. The theory is that for a small additional monthly fixed sum, life insurance equal to the unpaid balance of the loan is maintained to make sure the loan is repaid in the event the borrower dies before the indebtedness is paid. The charges for this type of insurance are often significantly higher than the cost of a straight term policy; many consumer loan organizations maintain relationships with insurers and try to have those insurers write all of this lucrative type of insurance.

Declining balance term insurance is also sold through magazine or newspaper advertisements that promise small amounts of insurance and claim that premiums will not increase before a person reaches some specified age. These policies are usually extremely expensive for the coverage provided. A giveaway that declining balance term is being advertised is usually that the amount of the insurance is either not set forth or is described as "up to" some specified amount.

§11.8 GROUP LIFE INSURANCE

"Group life insurance" is a type of term insurance usually provided by employers for their employees and also is offered by a wide variety of different kinds of membership organizations, fraternal organizations, trade associations, social clubs, investment clubs, and so forth — to their members through the organization.

Under current tax rules, an employer may provide up to $50,000 of group life insurance on a nondiscriminatory basis to its employees on a tax-free basis (that is, the premiums are deductible by the employer, but the value of the insurance is not includable in the income of covered employees for tax purposes). This modest tax benefit is very popular.

The individual's premium for group life insurance is usually lower than the premium for the equivalent amount of term insurance that could be purchased individually for the same person. There are several reasons for this. The administrative costs of insuring a group may be significantly less than the cost of insuring members individually (since selling and advertising costs are usually nominal and often the employer or organization arranging for the group insurance takes over some of the administrative costs). Second, the risk characteristics for the group in question may be more favorable than for the population generally. For example, a group of accountants may be able to obtain term insurance at more favorable group rates than as individuals because the accountants as a group have a better life expectancy than the population as a whole: They eat better, they are not subjected to employment-related risks that most blue collar workers face, and they are probably less likely to engage in hazardous activities such as motorcycle racing or skydiving. Third, in some cases the insurer may be willing to quote lower rates because the volume of term policies generated improves its diversification of risk or because it wishes to retain important business relationships with the employer.

While group life insurance is usually cheaper than commercial term policies, it is not always cheaper. Premiums for group plans may be computed as an actuarial blend of a variety of risks; a single individual may be in a low risk category and may make a substantial saving by buying a commercial term policy rather than a group policy. In some instances, the employer subsidizes a portion of the cost of group insurance; where this is the case it is unlikely that commercial policies will be competitively priced. But the only way to determine whether a group policy is a good deal is to price similar term policies in the insurance market.

§11.9 WHOLE LIFE INSURANCE

The most common type of traditional life insurance sold today is known by a variety of different names, such as ordinary life, permanent life, or whole life. These policies, unlike the tax-oriented variable or universal life insurance policies described in later sections, provide a fixed benefit on the death of the insured. Further, unlike term insurance, the premiums remain level from the date of the inception of the policy until the maturation of the policy upon the death of the insured. They differ significantly from term insurance in three important, indeed fundamental, respects.

First, the premiums for whole life policies for relatively young adults (or rarely, young children) are initially much higher than for term insurance for the amount of insurance protection for a person of the same age. This difference in premiums may be by a factor of ten or more when the insured is in his or her 30s or 40s. For example, a 35-year-old man will typically pay an annual premium of $15 or $20 per $1,000 of coverage for a whole life policy while a comparable one-year renewable term policy would cost somewhere between $2 and $5 per $1,000. The premiums on term insurance, of course, increase with the age of the insured. If our hypothetical 35-year-old man retained the same amount of term insurance year after year, he would be in his early 60s before the annual term insurance premium equaled the annual premium for his whole life policy.

Second, even though the premiums remain constant, the face amount of insurance provided by a whole life policy also remains constant. Whole life insurance is unlike declining balance term insurance in this respect.

Third, whole life policies develop cash values or cash surrender values each year after the policy has been in existence for a couple of years. Much of the initial excess premium over the cost of term insurance goes to building up this value.

The logic underlying a whole life policy is basically very simple. The premiums during the early years of such a policy are much higher than the amount needed to buy only death protection (i.e., term insurance). A portion of this excess is set aside in a kind of savings account for later use by the owner of the policy. A whole life policy, unlike a term policy, thus combines a savings element as well as a life insurance element. This savings element gradually increases as the years go by and more premiums are paid. As described below, this cash value may be borrowed by the owner of the policy and will be paid to him or her if the policy is surrendered and the insurance lapses. When the insured dies, however, the company pays only the face value of the policy, not the face value plus the cash value. Thus, the payment of the face value of the whole life policy upon the death of the insured comes in part from the savings account inherent in the cash value concept and in part from true life insurance. As the years go by and the cash surrender value increases, the company needs to provide a decreasing amount of pure life insurance protection. Indeed, by the time the insured reaches the ripe age of approximately 85, the savings account reaches the amount of the face value of the policy and the obligation to pay premiums ends. Such a policy is fully paid up since the savings account equals the face value of the policy, and there is no remaining component of life insurance to be paid from premiums.

This description is in some ways an oversimplification. Typically, cash values in a whole life policy build very slowly: There is usually no cash value after one or two years of premiums, and it may be three or four years before the entire cash value equals the amount of the premium due in any single year. Thereafter, the cash value builds more rapidly, fueled in part by the premium payments and in part by earnings on the money already invested. Cancellation of the policy during its first years therefore may involve a substantial financial loss. Furthermore, if a policy lapses and an attempt is made to replace it at a later date, the insured will find that the premium is increased because he or she is placed in an older age group when applying for the new insurance. These costs are often used by insurance agents as arguments against canceling a whole life policy or allowing it to lapse, when they learn that an insured is having difficulty making the payments.

At first glance it may seem backward that the buildup of cash value in the earliest years is the lowest, since the pure insurance cost for protection in the earliest years is also the lowest. Several factors help to explain this structure: the administrative costs of writing a policy, including the cost of a medical examination; the commission structure for life insurance agents (described in section 11.15); and the desire to establish a premium structure that encourages retention of a policy rather than surrendering it.

As indicated above, the cash value of a whole life policy increases gradually each year after the first year the policy is in effect. A whole life policy is an investment, an asset of the owner of the policy, much like a bank account or a deposit in a mutual fund. A whole life policy may be assigned to a creditor as security for a loan; the creditor may name itself as beneficiary so that it will receive the proceeds from the policy upon the death of the insured and repay the loan from the proceeds. The remaining balance, if any, presumably belongs to the estate of the insured or his or her heirs. During the lifetime of the insured, the creditor may also surrender the policy for its cash surrender value if a default on the obligation occurs. While loans secured by assignments of life insurance are not uncommon, it is a mark of some desperation by the borrower, since he or she may be depriving the family of needed insurance protection in order to arrange a loan.

Before the policy matures by the death of the insured, the owner of the policy can also borrow all or part of the cash value from the insurance company. A loan of the cash surrender value does not increase the insurance risk from the standpoint of the insurer, since if the insured dies while a loan is outstanding, the insurer simply subtracts the outstanding loan from the face amount of the policy and pays the beneficiary the difference. Traditionally, the interest rate on such loans is very low, often 5 percent in the case of older policies. Newer policies may have an interest rate of 8 percent or more. It is important to recognize that this is a very peculiar loan because the insurance company is already holding the cash surrender value in order to make a death payment at some future time. Loans of the cash surrender value are more like advances than loans. In one respect, loans of the cash surrender value may adversely affect the insurance company. Its cash flow comes from two sources: premium payments and the return from investments. Loans of cash surrender values reduce the amount available for investment by the insurance company and may reduce its cash flow. This occurs on every such loan whenever the market interest rate on investments is higher than the interest rate charged to the policyowner.

During the period of high interest rates in the 1970s and 1980s, it was attractive to borrow all or part of the cash surrender value of existing whole life policies at 5 percent per year and invest the proceeds in riskless investments that earned 12 or 14 percent per year. However, by the early 1990s, interest rates had dropped significantly so that riskless investments were earning 3 percent or less per year. For many owners of whole life insurance policies who had taken out cash surrender value loans at an earlier time, it was sensible to reverse the strategy and pay off the cash surrender value loans, using funds that were currently invested in savings accounts or other riskless investments. This strategy, of course, is attractive only if the policyholder does not have even more expensive loans outstanding. It would be silly, for example, to use funds to pay off a 5 percent life insurance policy loan if the policyholder is carrying credit card balances that involve service charges at a rate of 18 or 20 percent per year.

After a whole life policy has been in effect for several years, loans from the cash surrender value may be used to pay future premiums. This practice may permit an insured to keep a policy in effect over long periods without paying premiums, but subject to a gradual reduction of the death benefit that will ultimately be paid. Do you see how this might work?

254

A study prepared by the Federal Trade Commission in 1979 attempted to estimate the rate of return on a whole life policy viewing its cash value as an investment. This is not a simple computation because a portion of each premium must be allocated to the insurance feature of the whole life policy. The study concluded that the return was negative — that is, the cash value was less than the amount invested — for over 10 years, and after 20 years the rate of return was only 2 percent. Thus, as a savings vehicle, the whole life policy is inferior to any modern insured savings account. Indeed, a strategy of "buying term and investing the difference" — a phrase used by critics of the traditional insurance industry — usually yields a significantly larger investment after 20 years than buying a whole life policy. This strategy is somewhat similar to the do-it-yourself annuities discussed in the previous chapter, and both suffer from some of the same problems. For example, while buying term and investing the difference yields superior results, the specific results are based on the assumption that a savings account will yield a definite return, and this cannot be guaranteed. A decline in the rate of interest on the savings component (such as the one that actually occurred in the early 1990s) may make the differences much less dramatic. Also, savings through life insurance premium payments is convenient, and there is a built-in incentive not to let the insurance lapse. Many persons might lack the discipline to make the same payments into a savings account absent the need to preserve their insurance. Whole life policies also contain some significant options that cannot be replicated in a do-it-yourself plan: A waiver of premiums in the event of disability, for example, is generally available at no additional cost and is tremendously valuable in the rare situation where disability occurs. Other valuable rights may include options to purchase annuity rights, the ability to use the cash surrender value to buy additional paid-up insurance without a medical examination, and so forth. Finally, accumulations in a "buying term and invest the rest" plan are subject to federal income taxes each year while the growth of cash value within a whole life policy (like the buildup of an annuity) is tax deferred.

Another way of evaluating the "buy term and invest the rest" strategy is to consider the following example. A 45-year-old male buying $350,000 of whole life insurance would gradually acquire an asset consisting of the cash surrender value of the policy. If that individual bought term insurance and invested the difference in premiums, he would in effect create a taxable savings account. On the assumptions — realistic in early 1991 but quite unrealistic one year later — that the fund is invested each year in taxable Treasury notes yielding 8.35 percent per year, and the individual is in the 31 percent bracket (see section 19.6), the cash surrender value of the whole life policy would equal the value of the savings account only at the end of 14 years and would exceed it thereafter. There are two basic variables in this calculation: The cash surrender value grows on a tax deferred basis, and the cost of the term insurance increases dramatically as the individual ages. See Table 11-3. These calculations assume that the whole life policy was purchased from a regular large insurance company.

An argument can be made that it is unrealistic to analyze a whole life policy as being divided into an insurance component and a savings component. One can argue that the whole life insurance contract should be viewed as an undifferentiated whole, and that it consists of buying insurance protection on a level-premium installment plan in which young people prepay their premiums in the earlier years for protection they will receive many years later when the actual insurance costs greatly exceed the premium then being paid. One basic problem with this analysis is that it gives little weight to the phenomenon of the growth of the cash value within a whole life policy, which is a central feature of whole life insurance. Furthermore, this approach toward whole life raises new questions: It ignores the time value of the money that is prepaid and also gives no weight to the possibility of inflation and increased earning capacity in later years. If this were the sole explanation of whole life insurance offered to most persons, it is likely that they would opt for term insurance and invest the difference.

§11.10 IS TERM OR WHOLE LIFE INSURANCE BETTER FOR ME?

The question whether to purchase term or whole life insurance cannot be answered in the abstract; the needs of the speaker must be carefully considered. It seems clear that for most young persons with family responsibilities but no significant assets, term insurance — particularly group insurance — meets a basic need of providing protection at the lowest possible cost. The consequences of an untimely and unexpected death may be so devastating that any trade-off that involves a smaller amount of protection at the same cost would seem unwise. It is surprising that many people in this situation are persuaded to buy whole life policies even though such policies provide significantly less protection for the dollar invested, and the savings account feature of whole life may strain the family's budget in order to provide benefits many years later when they do not need the money as badly. The reason many people are persuaded to buy whole life policies is apparently more a function of the persuasiveness of insurance agents, whose commissions are much higher on whole life policies than they are on term policies (see section 11.15), than on rational examination of the alternatives available.

For couples having children relatively late in life — during their late thirties and early forties — the choice between term and whole life is more difficult than it is for a couple having children in their twenties. Typically, the younger couple will have completed the education of their children by the time they are in their early fifties and can afford to let their term insurance lapse. A $250,000 term policy for a 30-year-old nonsmoking male costs about $315 per year; for a 60-year-old, the cost is between $1,800 and $2,300, but it increases dramatically thereafter. A couple having children in their forties may discover that the cost of term insurance while they are still educating their children in their sixties is prohibitive. Whole life therefore may be a desirable purchase.

Perhaps the most sound general statement is that term insurance is the best investment if one expects to maintain insurance at a stable level for only a few years, but whole life is more advantageous if one is relatively young and plans to keep the insurance in effect for the long haul.

Many term policies permit conversion to whole life at a later date without a medical evaluation. For young adults unsure of their future life style, convertible term insurance may provide the maximum flexibility.

Many people of modest means may buy whole life insurance to ensure that there will be readily available funds for burial and to discharge debts and obligations. Others may purchase whole life because of the savings and tax deferral features of such policies. When all is said and done, however, probably more whole life insurance is sold than objective analysis would justify.

One indication that too much whole life insurance is purchased is the fact that about one half of all whole life policies purchased are dropped within seven years. These "early surrenders" are a windfall to insurance companies and insurance agents and usually a negative investment for the insureds.

Even though life insurance companies offer reasonably standardized products, there are significant differences in costs from company to company with the larger, better known, most widely advertised companies usually being at the higher end. Many people apparently do not comparison shop for insurance; rather, they apparently deal with a specific life insurance agent and buy what he or she sells them.

These comments relate only to the traditional products of term and whole life insurance sold by companies. The development of variable life insurance products (discussed in sections 11.21) is not addressed in this basic choice.

§11.11 HOW MUCH LIFE INSURANCE DO I NEED?

The question of "how much?" is as open-ended and uncertain as "what kind"? The Wall Street Journal in 1991 asked ten advisers and insurance brokers how much life insurance should be purchased by a hypothetical 45-year-old male corporate manager. The facts specified that he earns

$75,000 per year and has group insurance provided by his employer equal to twice his annual salary. His children are 15 and 12, and his wife, age 42, earns $25,000 per year with no group insurance provided by her employer. Suggestions ranged from as little as $250,000 to as much as $1,250,000. Several persons responding pointed out that any plan should include insurance on the wife's life as well as on the husband's.

An old rule of thumb — perhaps as good as any — is that life insurance should equal five to seven times one's annual salary. A somewhat more sophisticated approach is to provide sufficient insurance to permit the family to pay off debts and mortgages and have a remaining nest egg that will provide 75 percent of the family's pre-death income. In this calculation, account should be taken of death benefits available under the social security system as well as benefits that may be available under employee retirement plans. Income from other employed members of the family as well as income from investments and other sources should also be taken into account in determining how much insurance is appropriate.

Many individuals are approached by life insurance salesmen who offer to do free analyses of the family's financial position in the event of death or serious illness. Since these individuals are compensated on a commission basis, it should not be surprising that almost invariably the conclusion is that additional insurance should be purchased. More reliable advice may be obtained from professional family planners who are compensated by fees not dependent on the purchase of insurance.

The computer age has seen a profusion of plans and worksheets that provide assistance in considering all variables for estimating insurance needs. Like all plans and worksheets, however, they should be viewed as suggestive rather than definitive.

§11.12 INDIVIDUAL RISK ASSESSMENT IN GENERAL

Of course, insurance companies must assess individual risks before writing life insurance to make sure that the risk is an average one and not unique in some way. An insurance company must always be careful that risks are randomly obtained and are not self-selected. For example, a life insurance company could easily go broke if it wrote standard insurance policies on a large number of persons with serious heart disease and a large number of persons engaged in ultra hazardous activities like motorcycle racing, skydiving, and bomb disposal. For exactly the same reason, property casualty companies generally refuse to write flood insurance since only persons living in flood-prone areas are likely to request such insurance, while persons living on top of the hill realize that they do not need the insurance and do not apply for it. It is impossible when writing flood insurance for the persons at risk to avoid self-selection.

The major ways used by an insurance company to ensure that risks are randomly selected are: questions on the application form relating to medical histories, occupations, and hobbies (discussed in section 11.13); and physical examinations, which are not always required (discussed in section 11.14). A person who can demonstrate that he or she is in reasonably good health and engages in activities of average risk is said to be insurable, while a person who cannot is said to be uninsurable. Approximately 3 percent of all insurance applicants each year find themselves in the position of being rejected for standard insurance coverage. These are not black and white categories, however. Insurance companies routinely write extra-risk insurance policies at higher premiums for persons with many known medical problems, such as apparently controlled cardiovascular disease, or a history of successful treatment for cancer. At the extreme, people with severe medical problems that create limited life expectancies — AIDS or pancreatic cancer, for example — probably cannot get life insurance at any price. But insurance is available today at an additional cost for many individuals with even serious medical problems.

Persons engaged in hazardous occupations or dangerous hobbies may also be rejected for standard insurance coverage but may be able to obtain life insurance only upon the payment of a higher premium.

Extra risk insurance policies are written only after careful assessment of the applicant's medical condition. In a sense, a person with controlled high blood pressure is insurable on an extra-risk basis because insurance companies have had sufficient experience with mortality rates of persons with that medical condition to permit the writing of actuarially sound insurance. Many insurance companies now give discounts for nonsmokers; a "discount" in this situation is simply a reduction in premiums for nonsmokers or, phrased differently, the establishment of a somewhat higher premium rate for insurance applicants who smoke.

Insurance companies have schedules (or tables) of increasing premiums for various medical problems. These applicants are referred to as "being rated." Furthermore, there are specialists whose livelihood consists of placing impaired risk insurance for such individuals. Fees of these specialists may be paid from the agent's commission rather than directly by the applicant for insurance.

How much more must an individual with medical problems pay? If one uses as a standard an insurance application for $250,000 of life insurance for a 45-year-old nonsmoking male, the standard premium is about $600 per year for a term policy and about $4,473 for a whole life policy. One insurance company quoted the premium rates set forth in Table 11-4 for the same insured who fell within the specific risk categories listed there. This table should be viewed as being illustrative only; many companies have as many as 16 tables covering a wide variety of medical conditions, and there is no assurance at all that different companies will place a rated individual in the same category.

Some rated policies require an extra premium for only a specified

Table 11-4
Sample Premiums for Health-related Individuals

	Term insurance premium	Whole life insurance premium
Table 1 (mildly overweight)	$ 758	$ 5,086
Table 2 (controlled diabetes)	$ 915	$ 5,683
Table 4 (uncontrolled hypertension)	$1,230	$ 6,878
Table 8 (liver problems)	$1,860	$ 9,268
Table 12 (uncontrolled diabetes; abnormal EKG)	$2,490	$11,658

period—seven years, for example. Other policies may provide a limited death benefit for the first two or three years of the policy with the full amount becoming payable only after the expiration of the preliminary period.

All of this indicates the importance of obtaining professional assistance when one learns that he or she is "rated" and is not entitled to insurance at standard premium rates.

§11.13 INDIVIDUAL RISK ASSESSMENT: QUESTIONS ON THE APPLICATION FORM

Questions on the application form for life insurance are carefully devised to provide the insurer accurate information as to the risks involved. Questions usually relate not only to medical histories and known medical conditions but also involve open-ended inquiries that may lead to further investigation, such as whether the applicant has been denied life insurance in the past or whether the applicant has been under the care of a physician for any reason in the recent past. An applicant for life insurance has every incentive to "fudge" on the application form or to omit reference to medical facts or hazardous activities in order to obtain insurance at favorable rates (or in some cases, to obtain insurance at all). Material omissions or misstatements constitute fraud and, if discovered, usually lead to the cancellation of the policy.

On the other hand, insurance companies may be tempted to welsh on policies that have been in effect for a long period of time for nondisclosure of material facts in the original application form. Such a practice might deprive insureds of the benefits of protection and liquidity even though they had dutifully paid premiums for several years and had not sought substitute insurance because they thought the original policy was valid. Modern life insurance regulation prevents insurance companies from canceling policies for nondisclosure after the lapse of a specified period of time. These so-called incontestability clauses are a kind of statute of limitations. They permit life insurance companies only a limited time to raise defenses; after that time has expired, the obligation to insure is binding and cannot be avoided for misrepresentation or nondisclosure in the application.

Incontestability clauses are mandated by state law: The Texas statute, for example, states that each life insurance policy must contain provisions that it and the application form "shall constitute the entire contract between the parties and shall be incontestable after it has been in force during the lifetime of the insured for two years from its date, except for nonpayment of premiums, and which provisions may, at the option of the company, contain an exception for violation of the conditions of the policy relating to naval and military service in time of war."

§11.14 INDIVIDUAL RISK ASSESSMENT: THE MEDICAL EXAMINATION

All newspapers carried the dramatic story that the famous basketball player, Magic Johnson, was HIV positive. Mr. Johnson's infection was discovered as a result of an insurance medical examination. Today, blood testing is required by insurers for most insurance applicants.

When the AIDS epidemic was first discovered, there were widespread predictions that AIDS would cause an insurance disaster: Predictions were made that as much as $50 billion in premature death benefits would become payable on individual policies because of AIDS. In fact, claims based on AIDS have been quite manageable: The industry as a whole has paid out only $640 million to insured persons dying of AIDS. Prudential, for example, a major writer of life insurance, expects claims based on AIDS-related deaths to be less than 7 percent of all claims; in 1990, Prudential paid out only $14.2 million, or 2 percent of all insurance claims, to AIDS victims. The industry as a whole, has largely escaped a widely predicted disaster primarily because of its use of blood testing to screen applicants carrying the AIDS virus and its refusal to insure any HIV positive persons.

Companies began using blood tests as early as 1985. While HIV testing was subjected to strenuous legal challenge, by 1989 both federal and state courts had upheld the insurers' right to demand blood testing for AIDS before issuing life insurance policies. Today, medical testing enters into insurance decisions on an unprecedented scale. Before AIDS, an insurance company might issue a $500,000 policy to a 35-year-old male with minimal underwriting and no medical examination. No more. Prudential originally began using blood tests for life policies of $500,000 or over. As the tests became less expensive the level at which testing is required has been lowered. Prudential now requires tests for policies as small as $50,000 or $60,000.

The AIDS situation illustrates how tenaciously insurers defend their right to deny insurance to individuals based upon medical information; insurance decisions based on genetic information may well be the next step. Of course this creates serious problems for the unfortunate person who is totally unable to obtain insurance at any price when he or she needs it the most.

HIV positive individuals often feel they are locked into current employment to preserve whatever insurance and health benefits they now have, and a job change may mean being rejected for all health and insurance coverage. Indeed, fearing that they may be dropped from insurance coverage even without a job change, HIV positive individuals often hide the fact of their infection, possibly seeking treatment under pseudonyms and paying for treatment out of their own pockets.

Practices of health insurers with respect to blood testing vary widely; self insurers such as Blue Cross and Blue Shield normally do not test. But smaller employers and private insurers usually do. Employers as a matter of policy usually try not to hire HIV positive people because of the possible impact on premiums in future.

It has been argued that insurers should be required by governmental edict to provide life and medical insurance for all persons who request it. In effect, this would prohibit classifications of risk categories through medical testing and require insurers to treat the entire population as a single risk category. The premiums for everyone would obviously increase but persons in need of insurance would be assured of having it. The insurance industry has argued that if the government wishes to provide life and medical insurance for persons who are uninsurable under industry criteria, it should do so through a governmentally financed program rather than seeking to do so indirectly by manipulating current insurance practices.

§11.15 THE MARKETING OF LIFE INSURANCE

Because whole life policies involve savings as well as insurance components, a "policy illustration" is usually an important component of the sales plan. This illustration shows how the investment portion of a policy may perform over the next 20 or 30 years with a particular set of assumptions about the investment options that may be selected, future interest or earnings rates and the like. The policy illustration should also disclose the mortality charge (the estimated payments the company must meet to cover death benefits) and the estimated charge for administrative expenses as well as the estimated earnings rate applicable to the investment portion of the policy.

The agent's commission on the sale of an ordinary life policy is typically 50 percent of the first year's premium plus a much smaller commission when subsequent premiums are paid. Distribution costs of ordinary life policies run 20 to 25 percent over the full life of the policy; distribution costs of term policies are much lower, running perhaps 6 percent of premiums. Because of this difference in premiums, it is not uncommon for insurance agents to recommend and seek to sell whole life policies rather than term policies.

Most states prohibit the rebating or sharing of commissions on whole life policies with the insured. In Florida and California it is legal for the agent to rebate a portion of the first year's commission back to the insured; however, insurers frown on this practice and may refuse to deal with agents who rebate commissions.

A few insurance companies offer "low load" or "low commission" insurance that is sold without the services of an insurance agent. Distribution costs run 5 to 10 percent in the case of these low load policies. Low load policies include whole life insurance, second-to-die policies, and annuity contracts. Companies offering low load policies tend to be small, and it is not easy to locate them since they are, for obvious reasons, not touted by life insurance agents. A list of such companies may be obtained from the International Publishing Corporation in Chicago, Illinois. A group of independent financial planners, called the Life Insurance Advisers Association (800-521-4578), will provide a list of independent insurance advisers who are available for consultation (at a fee of $250 to $1,000) with respect to available no-load insurance products.

§11.16 BLENDED DESIGN LIFE INSURANCE

Agents who refuse to give direct rebates of commissions may package together two or more different life insurance policies to create lower aggregate premiums than would be payable on the typical policy. This practice is known as the creation of "blended design" policies. Blended design policies also may sometimes be created that give insureds greater growth in cash surrender value at the same premium than would occur under the typical policy.

The components of a blended design policy may consist of whole life, term insurance, and paid-up additions. A paid-up addition is a little whole life policy on which all the premiums are prepaid in one lump sum. Paid-up additions may gradually increase the death benefit of a whole life policy by having the policy's annual dividends buy some additional paid-up insurance. Sales commissions on paid-up additions are much lower than on regular whole life so that more of each premium dollar flows into the policy's cash value component. Because of the paid-up additions, a blended policy has a significant cash value in the first year of the policy. On the other hand, the death benefit provided by these blended policies may rise more slowly than the death benefit of comparable whole life policies if the cash surrender value additions are used to purchase additional paid-up insurance.

The addition of term insurance to the blend creates a much greater death benefit per dollar of premium than can be obtained from a straight whole life policy. Because the cost of term rises as a person ages, the addition of term to the blend increases the possibility that premiums may increase at a later date if projected interest rates do not materialize or the general cost of term coverage increases.

In a well designed blend with accurate projections, there is a balancing act. The growth of the whole life component pays the term premiums and gradually replaces the term with whole life. If the projections turn out to be inaccurate, the policy may come up short on cash at a later date, requiring a much higher premium or many more payments than first contemplated.

§11.17 REINSURANCE

Individual insurance companies may diversify their portfolio of risks by the widespread practice of reinsurance. Reinsurance involves the transfer of certain risks to other insurance companies in exchange for a sharing of the premium. Through this process, imbalances of risks may be distributed throughout the life insurance industry. A specific insured is unlikely to be aware that his or her policy has been transferred through reinsurance to another company.

Insurance companies routinely pass off part of the risk of rated individuals (see section 11.12) through reinsurance. In evaluating a specific risk, an insurance company may inquire about the availability of reinsurance before agreeing to write a life insurance policy. Simultaneous applications for insurance with several different companies may therefore result in a number of different inquiries to a single reinsurer, which may in turn create a suspicion of fraud or that the health conditions are more serious than appear on the face of the application.

§11.18 ASSIGNMENTS OF INSURANCE POLICIES BY INSURERS

In addition to the practice of reinsurance (discussed in section 11.17), the practice of "assumption reinsurance" has become widespread. An insurance company may acquire hundreds or thousands of policies from another insurer, taking on the entire insurance obligation and transferring the policies to its books. Ordinary life, health, and investment-type policies, such as annuities, are the types most often transferred because they are longer term and usually cannot be canceled by insurers. The insureds are usually advised that the policies have been assumed by a new insurer and are requested to make payments to the assuming insurance company, though in some instances no notice has been given.

Policy transfers of this type affect the insureds if the acquiring life insurance company becomes insolvent and disclaims further responsibility on the policies. The original issuing company in these circumstances is likely to argue that its liability under the policies ended with the assumption of the policies. The standard legal argument made by policyholders in response is that they did not consent to the assignment or the release of the original insurer who therefore remains liable on its original obligation. In short, the argument is over the scope of the legal doctrine known as "novation." An inference that a novation occurred may be drawn if the insured has knowledge of the transfer, does not object to it, and thereafter makes payments to the assignee, particularly if the notice of assignment gives accurate information as to the financial condition of both the assigning and the assuming companies. There has been no definitive resolution of these competing arguments.

Assumption reinsurance may be subject to regulation by state insurance regulatory agencies. Insureds who are adversely affected may also have claims against state insurance guaranty funds. However, until the rights of insureds in this situation are adequately protected, it may be sensible to object to any assignment of policies in writing, stating that the insured will make payments to the assuming company but does not release the assigning company from liability under the policy. This precaution seems particularly justified where the credit rating of the assuming company is lower than the credit rating of the assigning company.

§11.19 LIFE INSURANCE AND ANNUITIES BASED ON THE SAME LIFE

The previous chapter on annuities pointed out that life insurance and annuities to some extent involve opposite risks, one ceasing on the death of the annuitant and the other commencing on the death of the insured. Much or all of the individual risk assumed by an insurance company when writing insurance on the life of an individual disappears if the insurance company at the same time is asked to write an annuity for the life of that person. This is well illustrated by the early tax case of Helvering v. Le Gierse, 312 U.S. 531 (1941). An 80-year-old woman executed two contracts with the Connecticut General Life Insurance Company less than a month before her death. The first was an annuity contract that entitled the applicant to annual payments of $589.80 for her lifetime; the consideration for this contract was a payment of $4,179. The second was a "single premium life policy — non participating" that provided for a payment of $25,000 to the applicant's daughter on the death of the applicant; the premium for this policy was $22,125. The applicant was not required to take a physical exam or to answer the questions on the insurance application form that other applicants were required to answer.

As one reflects on the position of the insurance company on these facts, it seems clear that it was assuming virtually no risk at all. It had the immediate use of $27,125 (the total of the two premiums), subject to the obligation to pay a relatively small annuity during the remaining life of an 80-year-old person plus a single $25,000 payment upon her death. It was a matter of virtual indifference to the company whether the applicant died immediately or lived for another decade. There was no risk. The issue raised by the case was whether the estate of the applicant could exclude the $25,000 life insurance payment from the applicant's estate for federal estate tax purposes. The Supreme Court concluded that this amount was not "receivable as insurance" by the daughter, and therefore was includable in the decedent's estate tax return. It is interesting that the principal argument made by the taxpayer in this case was that the two policies were entirely separate, and that the annuity was written only because it was difficult for Connecticut General to get a sufficient number of 80-year-old females to apply for similar insurance policies "and thus be brought into the broad average for underwriting purposes."

§11.20 ENDOWMENT, "VANISHING PREMIUM," AND PAID-UP-AT-65 POLICIES

In addition to the traditional whole life policy, many other life insurance policies are offered that combine savings and life insurance protection in varying degrees. An endowment policy, for example, involves payments for a specified period, perhaps 20 or 30 years; at that point the cash value equals the policy face amount and the insurance is fully paid up. A "paid-up-at-65" policy is similar except that the period during which payments must be made ends at age 65. Obviously, substantially higher premium payments are required for all types of endowment or "paid-up" policies than for a whole life policy. As a result, these policies enjoy limited attractiveness.

During the 1980s, when interest rates were high, a variation upon endowment policies was popular. Many middle-aged and older individuals were persuaded to purchase "vanishing premium" life insurance. These policies called for very substantial premiums for a limited number of years; thereafter the insurer projected (on the assumption that interest rates would remain at then current levels) that earnings from the cash value of the insurance would cover the premiums, which would then "vanish." The advertising for these policies generally disclosed in small print that the performance of the policy was based on projections and that performance was not guaranteed. Unfortunately, the projections used assumptions that turn out to have been unrealistic: The high interest rates of the 1980s on which projections were based declined steadily in the early 1990s. The result was predictable. The premiums did not "vanish" but continued or resumed as the earnings fell short of covering the premium. For persons expecting to buy permanent life insurance in a relatively few years, the decline in interest rates must have come as a sore disappointment.

An individual called upon to resume premium payments in order to preserve the insurance policy may be able to exercise other policy options, such as reducing the death benefit, to permit the policy to continue in existence without additional investment. It is generally undesirable to cancel a whole life policy and either take the cash surrender value or create a new policy at a lower death benefit because of policy terms that make cancellation financially less attractive than restructuring the policy by exercising available options.

§11.21 VARIABLE LIFE INSURANCE

The chaotic economic conditions of the late 1960s and 1970s were marked by high inflation rates and rapidly increasing interest rates. These developments created unprecedented pressures on the traditional forms of life insurance, particularly the whole life policy, the mainstay of the domestic life insurance industry. The prospect of high inflation rates made the savings account feature of cash surrender values relatively unattractive. People realized that they were investing current dollars in exchange for repayments many years later in dollars worth much less because of inflation. Further, the relatively low effective rates of return on the cash surrender value made whole life unattractive when compared with competing, riskless investments. The earliest indication of difficult times ahead for the insurance industry was the increase in cash surrender value loans as policy owners borrowed against cash surrender values at 5 percent per year in order to invest the proceeds in much higher yielding investments in the open market. Furthermore, between 1977 and 1981, whole life policies, while still the largest single selling type of insurance, declined significantly as a percentage of the total amount of ordinary life insurance outstanding, with growth in term insurance accounting for most of the increase. It was apparent from these trends that the insurance industry would have to come up with new products if it wished to prosper.

The first new products developed by the insurance industry were relatively modest. A variable premium life policy was offered, which provided that future premiums would be decreased if the company's investment income increased from rising interest rates and inflation. In effect, the company offered to share a portion of the windfall generated by rising interest rates with policyholders by reducing the premium in later years. An adjustable life insurance policy was also developed that allowed an individual to switch protection from term to whole life, or back. The policies also offered some flexibility in the timing and amount of premium payments, and provided for periodic readjustments to take into account mortality charges and expenses.

More recently, the insurance industry struck a popular chord when it developed a new life insurance policy that is now generally known as single-premium variable life insurance. This policy has significant tax deferral benefits and is sold more for the tax and investment benefits than for the insurance benefits. The policy can be analyzed as containing two interrelated components: a term life insurance component and an accumulation component analogous to the traditional cash surrender value of a whole life policy. At the outset the applicant must deposit a certain amount in an accumulation account to finance the insurance component and may make a larger initial deposit or may thereafter make additional deposits. The accumulation account is virtually an investment account. The applicant may direct how the accumulation account is to be invested within four or five limited alternatives provided by the insurance company or an associated brokerage firm. The choices cover the most popular investment strategies in terms of type of security, degree of risk, and diversification of investments, for example, a stock mutual fund, a bond fund, or a capital appreciation fund. As the accumulation account increases, the amount of insurance that must be purchased also increases, but at a much slower rate. The owner of the policy may also borrow the amount of the excess accumulation account, though since 1988 this has adverse income tax consequences.

The driving principle behind this insurance policy is that, like the accumulation of cash surrender values in a traditional whole life policy, the growth of the accumulation account is not subject to federal income tax so long as the policy remains outstanding. Hundreds of thousands of dollars may be deposited in the accumulation account to grow on a tax-exempt basis. Further, the accumulation is exempt from income taxation upon the death of the insured. In other words, this policy is really a tax deferred or tax sheltered investment vehicle packaged as life insurance.

The amount of term insurance provided in the package is the minimum amount required by Internal Revenue Code provisions to ensure that the package is taxed as an insurance policy rather than as an investment account. However, in practice the amount of insurance is not the dominant or driving factor but is incidental, determined by the tax laws and the amount the applicant has invested in the accumulation account.

It may be recalled that single-premium annuities also may serve as tax sheltered investment vehicles. (See section 10.8.) In 1986, Congress restricted the tax advantages of the annuity by providing that lifetime loans or distributions are deemed to be from the income component of the fund, and therefore taxable to the annuitant when made. In 1988, Congress extended the same treatment to loans and distributions from life insurance contracts. In addition, Congress imposed the 10 percent surtax on distributions made before the taxpayer reaches the age of fifty-nine and one-half (though there are exceptions that may avoid application of this penalty).

In addition, upon the death of the insured the proceeds may be excludable from the insured's estate for federal estate tax purposes, much as any other type of insurance; that is, if the policy is not owned by the deceased and is not payable to his or her estate.

The disadvantages of this novel type of insurance policy largely revolve around the fees and charges imposed by the insurance company. In addition, premature termination of the policy may result in a significant investment loss. Restrictions are also placed on what percentage of the value of an accumulation account may be borrowed by the insured. A further consequence is that the plan necessarily entails the purchase of increasing amounts of term life insurance as the accumulation account increases even though that purchase might not be justified in the absence of the tax deferral aspect of the plan. Finally, there is some lingering concern that Congress may decide to limit even further the tax deferral advantages of these life insurance policies. Certainly, Congress has consistently tried to limit tax shelters that are believed to be abusive or involve the loss of substantial revenue: The single premium variable life insurance policy may be found to fall within this category in the future.

The popularity of variable insurance products declined in the early 1990s along with interest rates and investment returns on relatively riskless investments. The decline in investment returns increased the possibility that a greater portion of the income from the investment would have to be allocated to the insurance component of the package. In addition, there was increased concern about the future solvency of insurance companies and less interest in the tax avoidance features of these policies. Life insurance companies responded by combining various options into new policies: for example, permitting the cash surrender value to be placed in a separate fund and invested as directed by the policyholder, allowing the policyholder to elect to accept a lower face value rather than an increase in premiums. These new policies are sometimes referred to as "universal life insurance" rather than variable rate insurance.

§11.22 "SECOND TO DIE" INSURANCE

"Second to die" insurance is life insurance that becomes payable when the second of two named insureds dies. It is used primarily as an estate tax planning device to assure the availability of funds to pay estate taxes when the surviving spouse of a wealthy couple dies. Whether or not second to die insurance is desirable is itself highly controversial since the premiums for insurance on the lives of elderly parents are high, and it may be more sensible simply to make direct gifts of amounts otherwise payable as premiums each year to potential heirs.

The annual cost of a second to die policy is lower than the cost of insuring either of two individuals separately. If it costs $10,000 per year to insure H and $7,500 per year to insure W, it might cost only $5,000 per year to insure the second to die. Annual premiums are smaller, but they go on for a longer time. Consider, for example, a 50-year-old man with a wife who is also 50 years old; the annual premium for a $1 million policy on the husband alone is $10,150 per year based on a projected life expectancy of 30 years and rate of return 6.9 percent; a second to die policy on the couple costs $5,070 because it is projected on a 40-year life expectancy and a 6.7 rate of return.

In making calculations about second to die insurance, one starts with the paradigm situation of the affluent couple who is concerned about estate taxes and desires to pass the maximum wealth to the next generation. If the combined estate exceeds $1.2 million, there are estate tax liabilities to consider: the rate starts at 38 percent and may go as high as 55 percent of the taxable estate. Because of the unlimited marital deduction it is possible to avoid the tax entirely upon the first to die, but the entire estate then is taxed when the second dies. Second to die insurance seems ideally suited to this situation because the policy provides cash to pay estate taxes when it is needed, and it may be kept out of the estate by the device of an insurance trust.

The alternative choice is to distribute the premiums directly to the heirs and pay the estate tax that may be due on the death of the first to die. This strategic decision involves a complex calculation that depends on unknown variables such as the time period between the deaths and the amount of appreciation in the value of the assets that should be assumed to occur between the two deaths. It may be sensible to pay estate tax on the death of the first to die if one assumes assets will appreciate and the deaths are likely to be far apart. For example, a $4 million estate taxed at the first death would pay $416,000 less in taxes than if it grew at 8 percent per year and it is held until the death of the second to die ten years later. If the deaths are 20 years apart, the tax difference would be $1.3 million.

A second to die policy may be sensible if one spouse is ill and the other healthy since the cost will be about the same as insuring the healthy spouse alone. It may also be sensible if the wife is considerably younger than her husband (since her longer life expectancy will make the policy relatively inexpensive).

Second to die policies have proved reasonably popular. In 1990, it was estimated that there were 10,000 such policies in existence with an average face amount of $1.3 million.

§11.23 "SPLIT-DOLLAR" INSURANCE

"Split-dollar" life insurance is an executive perk designed to permit the employer to provide life insurance benefits to executives at the lowest possible tax cost. Under current tax rules, an employer may provide up to $50,000 of group life insurance on a nondiscriminatory basis to its employees on a tax-free basis (that is, the premiums are deductible by the employer, but the value of the insurance is not includable in the income of covered employees for tax purposes). Fifty thousand dollars is not very much for an executive, and "split-dollar" insurance is widely used to increase the amount of life insurance provided by the employer as a perk to senior executives.

Under a split-dollar plan, the employer provides, and pays the premiums on, a whole life policy complete with a tax-deferred savings component normally provided by such policies. The executive owns the policy, but the employer and executive split the ownership, including both the cash surrender value and the death benefits. The employer is entitled to receive back at some time the premium payments, with interest, and has a lien on the cash surrender value until this obligation is repaid. Originally, the executive owns only the death benefit, and if he or she dies shortly after the policy is taken out, a portion of the death benefit must be used to repay the employer for the premiums. However, as the cash surrender value increases with time, the executive's ownership interest in the policy increases. Through this device, the employee not only obtains a significant death benefit immediately but also is taxed only on approximately what the premium on a term policy would be while having the benefits of tax deferral and growth of cash surrender value that a whole life policy provides.

§11.24 LIFE INSURANCE FOR THE NEWBORN

Because ordinary life insurance is tax deferred, one might consider giving a newborn child or grandchild a life insurance policy. A $175,000 ordinary life policy might require only a single premium of $5,000 payable on the birth of the child. This policy will have a cash surrender value of $15,000 by the time the child is ready for college; its cash surrender value should be near $675,000 by age 65, and $1.5 million by age 75.

Insurance contracts guarantee interest of 4.5 percent or less. Hence a life insurance policy is not a very good device to provide funds for college education. Giving the same amount to the child in the form of zero coupon treasuries should do better — by perhaps $10,000 — than the life insurance policy for this purpose. (Zero coupon bonds are described in section 16.17.) Tax free municipals (described in section 16.18) should also produce a better yield than the insurance policy. But, of course, these do not provide a lot of life insurance on the infant's life.

§11.25 LIFE INSURANCE AND TERMINALLY ILL PATIENTS

Many individuals owning life insurance have later become infected with the HIV virus and subsequently have become terminally ill with full-blown AIDS. In many instances, death has been preceded by prolonged illnesses, for months or even years, during which the individual has been unable to work and has rapidly exhausted whatever financial resources he or she had. It would appear reasonable that a person in this position should be able to utilize life insurance benefits to cover medical and housing expenses before he or she dies. Based on this reasoning, many traditional life insurance companies offer customers who are terminally ill with AIDS the chance to get their death benefits while they are still alive. Most companies, however, will advance death benefit payments only if the prognosis is that the patient has less than six months or, at most, a year to live. Prudential Insurance Company, for example, offers to pay 90 percent of the face value of a life insurance policy if the patient's physician certifies that he or she will not live more than six months.

A number of smaller companies have also entered this field. These companies offer to buy the life insurance policies of AIDS patients at reduced values so the patients can use the cash that will become payable upon their inevitable death during their last illnesses. Unlike the program of the larger insurer, these companies pay the patient anywhere from 50 to 90 percent of the face value of the policy, depending on how long the patient is expected to live. By 1992, about two dozen companies were in this rather ghoulish business, having bought about $100 million in insurance policies from terminally ill individuals. While most of the patients taking advantage of this new industry have been AIDS patients, the program is available to any terminally ill individual.

Some of the companies have raised funds from the general public by arranging to sell life insurance policies on individual patients to investors who then become the beneficiaries of the policy. In effect, an investor can reap varying amounts of profits depending on how soon a specific patient dies. The sooner the patient dies, the more profitable the arrangement from the standpoint of the investor. Some companies, moreover, provide a selection of patients to choose from, along with medical information on each. Apart from obvious questions of privacy, the legality of this arrangement must be viewed as doubtful, at best, under traditional concepts of insurable interest. It also raises serious questions of adequate disclosure under the securities laws. A number of companies involved in the purchase of life insurance policies from terminally ill patients do not sell policies to outside investors but raise capital in more traditional ways.

The Laid Off White Collar Employee

§12.1 INTRODUCTION

This brief chapter discusses the problems, concerns, rights, and strategies of the laid off white collar employee.

The recession that is occurring during the early 1990s (when this is being written) has created patterns of unemployment that are different from those of any other recession since World War II. In earlier recessions, unemployment was concentrated among hourly wage earners, particularly blue collar and unskilled or semi-skilled employees. Persons in these occupational groups were laid off when work dried up in a recession, but jobs would open up again when economic conditions improved. White collar office workers, particularly at the managerial and professional levels, were largely immune from concerns about unemployment.

In the recession of the early 1990s, large numbers of white collar workers became unemployed for the first time in their careers. The Labor Department estimated that the number of white collar unemployed increased from 2.2 million in July 1990 to 3.4 million in July 1992. That increase in unemployment was nearly 50 percent of the total increase in unemployment over that period and was spread throughout managerial and professional workers. Even associates and partners in law firms were not entirely immune from layoffs though the numbers were tiny in comparison to other industries. Furthermore, it appears unlikely that the positions that have been lost will reappear when economic conditions improve. Many higher level jobs seem to have disappeared permanently.

The causes of this development are varied and to some extent controversial. Certainly, a major factor has been reorganization of management levels within large enterprises in order to improve efficiency and profitability. Many companies had developed layers of managers, who, in retrospect, appeared to be not really necessary for efficient operations; elimination of one or more layers of managers resulted in numerous layoffs or early retirements of high income white collar workers with many years' seniority. Another factor was foreign competition that caused American companies to downsize their operations simply by closing one or more divisions or production lines. Further, there was the lingering effect of the leveraged buyouts of the 1980s, which saddled many companies with excessive debt that required rigorous control over expenses if the corporation were to avoid default on loans. One way to control expenses is to lay off nonessential white collar workers. There was also massive technological change in some areas, such as the computer industry, that resulted in many companies being left behind and simply unable to compete in a quickly changing market. These companies also laid off thousands of employees at all levels as they sought to preserve a much smaller company concentrated on the components that appeared to have a chance for continued commercial success. Yet another factor was the end of the cold war and the "peace dividend" that caused the cancellation or cutback of defense contracts and the layoffs of many highly skilled engineers and scientists.

Typical examples of white collar workers laid off during this period: a 40-year-old "manager of information systems" from a job that paid $75,000 per year, a 48-year-old "senior writer in corporate communications" from a job paying $55,000 per year, and a 49-year-old research scientist also making $55,000 per year. Each of these individuals survived an extensive period of unemployment and was ultimately successful in finding other employment after several months of searching but at significant reductions in pay and benefits.

This pattern of reduced income and benefits is typical in the 1990s. In one survey of laid off white collar workers who had found new jobs, 40 percent of those surveyed reported that the new job paid substantially less than their previous one — 25 percent or more. Further, the new jobs often carried fewer benefits, were with less secure employers, and were in distant locations, requiring an expensive uprooting of a settled family. It is not surprising that white collar workers with apparently secure jobs felt more insecure and vulnerable during the recession of the early 1990s than at any other time since World War II.

§12.2 PREPARING FOR THE WORST

The growth in white collar layoffs during the early 1990s created a feeling of pessimism and uncertainty even among employees who believed that their jobs were secure. These feelings doubtless contributed to the duration of the recession of the early 1990s, since they led to the cautious use of funds — saving or reducing debts — rather than optimistic purchases on credit of expensive products, goods, and services.

The general rule of thumb is that an employee who fears that he or she may face a layoff should strive to accumulate sufficient funds in the form of cash or cash-equivalents to cover a minimum of six months of living expenses. Typical cash equivalents are money market funds, bank deposits, and short term treasury securities. See Chapters 13 and 14. Other suggestions typically made include a review of household expenditures to preserve cash by reducing inessential expenditures and to increase cash flow from existing assets such as renting out a summer home if one owns one. A family might be able to get along with one automobile rather than two, for example.

Financial related recommendations include opening (but not using) a line of credit home equity loan (see section 7.13), improving cash flow by closing down discretionary contributions deducted automatically from paychecks, such as contributions to IRAs or section 401(k) programs or the purchase of United States savings bonds, and paying off (but not replacing) credit card and other high interest loans.

Relying on a home equity loan to provide additional cash during periods of unemployment is risky because monthly payments will shortly come due on that line of credit, and one is then faced with two monthly payments rather than one in order to keep the residence.

One suspects that even with these "batten down the hatches" strategies, many white collar workers fearing unemployment find it difficult to accumulate six months of living expenses.

§12.3 WHAT TO DO WHEN THE WORST HAPPENS

The receipt of a pink slip by a white collar worker is a traumatic event under the best of circumstances. The first reaction is often shocked disbelief, of deep anger against an employer who has been served faithfully for a number of years but is willing to cast off an employee without qualms. This is usually followed by a period of depression as one reviews the new, grim world of unemployment, COBRA, and severance rights. Serious consideration may be given to filing a lawsuit on the grounds of age discrimination or breach of contract.

After the initial shock, the next reaction is usually a resolve to burnish up the resume and immediately find another job. It is unusual, however, for a person who has been laid off to find a new job immediately. In 1992, a national outplacement company estimated that it was taking the average laid off white collar worker 7.3 months to find another job, up from 5.3 months in 1989. Thus, when a person is laid off, he or she should consider the problems of financial survival for the next few months. A typical guide for the laid off white collar worker might go something like this:

1. *Unemployment Benefits.* If the employee has truly been laid off (as contrasted with accepting early retirement or resigning after negotiating severance benefits), he or she is almost certainly entitled to unemployment benefits under state unemployment compensation statutes. Many employees consider that there is a stigma attached to applying for these benefits, but they are a matter of right and in a sense have been paid for by the employee during his or her years of employment. These benefits should be applied for promptly, but the amounts are usually meager. While unemployment benefits are computed as a percentage of wages for 26 weeks, there is a dollar maximum in most states, typically of $300 per week. In some states, the maximum is even lower.

Unemployment benefits are taxable as income under the federal income tax laws.

2. *Severance Pay.* Severance pay is provided by the employer to ease the shock of unemployment and provide a transition for the former employee. Severance pay is a fringe benefit that may not be widely advertised; the most typical rule is one week's pay for each year of service. Where the number of layoffs is large, however, severance benefits may be more generous, for example, two or three weeks' pay for each year of service with a minimum of three months regardless of years of service.

Senior management may have significantly better severance rights than mid-level management employees. At the very top, management may have "golden parachutes" and consulting arrangements that involve millions of dollars of severance benefits. Below that, upper level management may have "tin parachutes" that provide substantial but less generous severance benefits. These severance plans for the very top are designed to deter unwanted takeovers and to free upper level managers from fear about financial and job security concerns when making decisions that affect the continued independence of the employer.

In some instances, the amount of severance pay may be negotiable within limits even at lower levels. If it is negotiable, the employer will almost certainly insist that the employee resign voluntarily as the price of increased severance pay. The employee may also be required to sign a promise not to sue for age discrimination under the Older Workers Benefit Protection Act of 1990. A person who resigns voluntarily is not entitled to unemployment benefits. Whether increased severance pay is worth it, therefore, obviously depends on an analysis of the numbers involved.

More commonly, however, the amount is not negotiable, but the employee is given the option of taking the severance pay either in a single lump sum or in installments at regular salary levels for whatever period the pay is available. Which is better depends on hidden costs. While a lump sum payment is worth more than spread out payments because of the basic principle of the time value of money, there may be hidden costs to acceptance of a lump sum. The continuation of salary option may result also in the continuation of health and medical insurance for several months and may let additional time be credited to retirement programs. All of these benefits are likely to be terminated immediately if a lump sum payment is elected. Again, the choice obviously depends on an analysis of the numbers involved.

3. *Contract Consulting with Former Employer.* In some instances, an employee who is laid off may be able to provide services to the former employer for a temporary period on a contract basis. Not uncommonly, the employee has knowledge or experience that the employer may find difficult to replicate quickly and inexpensively. At the very least, there is no harm in asking, though, again, such an arrangement will usually involve the employer insisting that the employee resign voluntarily and sign a waiver against suing for age discrimination as conditions to the consulting contract.

4. *Health Insurance.* A federal statute, the Consolidated Omnibus Reconciliation Act ("COBRA"), requires employers to allow employees who are losing group health coverage to buy into that coverage so that it is continued for another 18 months (unless the employer is going out of business). The cost of continued insurance under COBRA is more expensive than the group rates usually applicable during employment but significantly lower than an individual would be charged for an individual or family policy. As a result, the COBRA insurance should usually be purchased.

Since COBRA insurance expires in 18 months, it may be sensible to seek alternative insurance during that period in the event new employment does not materialize or a new employer's medical plan is not attractive or will not cover existing conditions.

5. *Life and Disability Insurance.* If the employer provides these insurance coverages, it may be possible for a former employee to take over the premium payments as an individual insured. Whether or not this is attractive can be determined only by shopping for independent coverage and comparing costs.

6. *Retirement Plans.* Payments to retirement plans usually cease when salary payments cease. The full amount credited to the employee may become payable in a lump sum to the terminated employee at that time.

In addition, the employee may have been making payments to individual retirement plans, 401(k) plans, or other tax preferred savings plans. It is obviously tempting to retain and spend a large, lump sum payment of retirement benefits or to dip into IRAs and other retirement funds to tide one over the period of unemployment. The cost of doing this, however, is substantial. Not only are the funds subject to income tax if used for personal purposes (and thereby permanently reduced by a significant amount), there is an additional 10 percent penalty if the laid off employee is under the age of fifty-nine and one-half. This penalty may be waived only if the funds are used to pay unreimbursed medical expenses exceeding 7.5 percent of adjusted gross income, permanent disability, or the individual is over the age of 55 and retires. The combination of the income tax treatment of these funds and the 10 percent penalty causes a 40 percent depletion of the fund off the top. Typical advice therefore is to withdraw these funds only as a very last resort when all other sources of funds have been exhausted. See also section 10.17.

In some plans, the employee may be able to borrow a portion of the retirement funds without incurring a tax penalty. However, if the loans are not repaid pursuant to the terms of the plan, adverse income tax consequences will be imposed.

The usual advice is to roll over lump sum payments from retirement plans into a conduit IRA so that the funds may be added to other retirement funds at a later date without adverse income tax consequences.

§12.4. FINDING A NEW JOB

The secret to finding a new job usually lies in having a strong network of professional contacts and friends in other jobs who are willing to help. Also, flexibility is important: A new job in the same community involving similar work and similar pay is probably unrealistic. The unemployed professional who is willing to move to a new community and accept a position at a lower salary is more likely to find a job promptly than one who insists on replicating his former position.

Many employers laying off senior white collar workers provide them assistance in finding new jobs. "Out-placement programs," as they are usually called, may provide counseling, access to recruiters, and lists of available jobs. Many companies provide an office, minimal secretarial services, and access to a telephone for a limited period. Other employers, however, provide little or no assistance to their former employees.

When one is negotiating seriously for a new job after a period of unemployment, a dicey question is whether to attempt to negotiate desirable severance benefits as part of the new employment package. While sensible (and understandable) from the standpoint of a recently laid off white collar manager, a discussion of this issue may not sit well with a prospective employer who is well aware that the potential employee was involuntarily laid off from his or her earlier job.

§12.5 OPENING ONE'S OWN BUSINESS

An alternative sometimes considered by senior white collar workers who have been laid off is opening one's own business. The new business may be related to one's former professional area or in a totally new line of work, for example, the software engineer who decides to open up a garden nursery. Such a step is usually a very high risk response to temporary unemployment, though obviously individual circumstances vary widely. This strategy is much less risky if the unemployed worker's spouse has a steady and apparently secure job that is sufficient to meet the family's basic financial needs.

Many out-of-work executives and middle managers jump into franchising as their new careers. Having risen within the ranks of a corporate enterprise, they feel that they understand business principles and should be able to make a success with the assistance of a national franchised chain. Their severance benefits also permit them to make the very substantial investment required in many franchise operations. Sad experiences by many executives make clear, however, that the management of a franchise is quite unlike the corporate front office, involving long hours, self-resolution of problems, and lower incomes, and that many executives, who were successful in the corporate bureaucracy, are disasters as entrepreneurs. And failure may be disastrous from an economic standpoint, since severance and retirement benefits may be consumed in disentangling oneself from the franchising experiment.

The word "consulting" has become a virtual euphemism for "unemployed" and should be avoided to the maximum extent possible.

One important factor in considering self-employment is the need for expensive health and medical insurance. Employers typically provide these types of insurance for white collar workers, either as a fringe benefit or by subsidizing their cost so that the charge to employees represent only a fraction of their true cost. As a result, the loss of these benefits may be felt particularly keenly when a person leaves employment and strikes out on one's own. The cost of personal insurance has been increasing steadily and is one of the major problems of current American society since many individuals are unable to provide on their own even minimally adequate protection against illness, disease, or unexpected death.

As of early 1992, a 35-year-old male with three dependents to support, all of whom are healthy and have no long-term medical "problem," might find that full coverage health insurance will cost as much as $700 per month in some areas. However, the cost of this insurance may usually be reduced significantly by accepting deductibles so that insurance pays only medical expenses that exceed some specified amount. If one member of the family has serious and continuing health problems, insurance covering that individual may not be obtainable at any price or at premiums that may exceed $1,500 or $2,000 per month. This problem may be so severe as to compel the laid off white collar worker to give up plans to go into business as an entrepreneur and seek new employment.

The amount of disability and life insurance that is required by a new entrepreneur depends to some extent on the salary level and lifestyle of the individual involved. If a 35-year-old expects to earn $75,000 per year and wishes to purchase term insurance of twice that amount, the cost will be relatively modest, perhaps $200 per year. However, $150,000 in insurance is likely to be considered quite inadequate if there are dependents and no other source of family income; insurance equal to seven or ten times the needed salary may be desirable under these circumstances. See Chapter 11.

Disability insurance to preserve 60 percent of take-home income until the age of 65 with a 90-day waiting period (and an option to increase future coverage as price levels rise) may cost $1,500 per year. The cumulative cost of insurance is obviously a matter to be taken into account in deciding whether to seek another job or join the ranks of the self-employed.

In many instances, a white collar worker may be permitted to retain life and disability insurance provided by the former employer by assuming the obligation to pay the premiums thereafter. See section 12.3. This is in addition to the right of every laid off employee under COBRA to retain temporarily employer-provided health insurance after being laid off.

§12.6　PAYING OFF THE MORTGAGE

A white collar worker fearing or facing unemployment may have accumulated a cash nest egg that is sufficient to pay off the mortgage on the family residence. Faced with a potentially traumatic period of unemployment and job searches, the employee may get considerable psychological satisfaction from realizing that the family residence is secure and fully paid off.

The wisdom of using funds for this purpose, however, is doubtful. A person facing unemployment needs liquidity to be able to meet unexpected problems as they arise; paying off the mortgage on the family home usually minimizes liquidity since the house may have to be sold to obtain the use of the equity in the home. It may be possible in some instances to arrange for a line of credit home equity loan (or to increase an existing line of credit) to permit access to the funds invested in the home, but this will usually not be on a dollar-for-dollar basis and also requires the assumption of additional monthly payment on any home equity loans actually taken out.

The mortgage on the family home is generally more desirable than alternative loans since it is usually at a low interest rate, and the interest is tax deductible.

PART III

INVESTMENTS FOR INDIVIDUALS

13

Investment Strategy: Of Risk and Return

§13.1 INTRODUCTION

Part III generally discusses investment opportunities for individuals with excess funds. It concentrates not on the investment strategies and goals of the extremely wealthy (who are likely to have the benefits of professional investment advice and professional management) but on the moderately successful class of individuals who have some additional money — perhaps ranging from a few tens of thousands of dollars to a hundred thousand dollars or so — but not enough to justify expensive professional help. These funds may arise from inheritance, gift, the sale of appreciated property, the receipt of the proceeds of a life insurance policy or a lump sum payment of retirement funds from a former employer, collecting upon a judgment following litigation, or a fortuitous event such as winning a lottery. Probably the most common source of excess funds is a successful plan of systematic savings over a period of time.

This chapter discusses general concepts and alternatives while the following chapters discuss specific types of investments that are generally suitable for persons with moderate amounts of funds to invest.

§13.2 TYPES OF INVESTMENTS

Fifty years ago, if one were writing a treatise on investments for the moderately affluent, attention would have been focused on three basic types of investments: (1) deposits in savings accounts with banks, savings and loan institutions and credit unions; (2) the purchase of marketable debt instruments such as bonds, treasury bills, and the like; and (3) the purchase of "equity" investments consisting of common or preferred stock issued by the country's largest corporations. A fourth category might have been added: (4) investments in "mutual funds" or other investment companies that owned a portfolio of common stocks, though investment companies were somewhat out of fashion with most investors as a result of events that occurred during the depression of the 1930s.

While these various types of investments continue to be the principal investment alternatives today and are discussed in detail in the following chapters, the investment world has become much more complicated. Distinctions among these categories have become so blurred as to make the classification much less useful than it was 50 years ago. Furthermore, a number of new types of investment vehicles have become popular that are similar to, but not identical with, these more traditional investments. Indeed, today there are a bewildering number of types of investment vehicles available in financial markets, all competing for the individual's investment dollars. In addition, there is an immense market for "derivative" securities whose value is determined by or based on the values of more traditional securities and which may vary widely in risk and appropriateness for relatively unsophisticated investors. New types of derivative securities are being invented almost daily by financial theorists and others in an effort to attract investors' dollars.

Earlier chapters have discussed annuity contracts (Chapter 10) and life insurance (Chapter 11). For many individuals, modern versions of these traditional products may be suitable alternative investments for excess funds.

Today, the investments suitable for an individual with a moderate amount of excess funds and who is willing to take some risk in order to increase the return fall within the following categories, all discussed in the following chapters:

1) Common stocks issued by large publicly held corporations that are traded on the New York or American Stock Exchanges, the NASDAQ National Market, or a regional market. Chapter 14.
2) Preferred stocks issued by those companies. Chapter 17.
3) Fixed income investments which may fluctuate in value with interest rates but on which there is little or no risk of default: for example, United States Treasury notes and bonds. Chapter 16.

4) Fixed income investments issued by large publicly held corporations. Chapter 16.
5) Tax-exempt bonds issued by states or municipalities. Chapter 16.
6) Mutual funds or investment trusts that invest in portfolios of various kinds of equity or fixed income investments. Chapter 15.
7) Asset backed securities, sometimes called collateralized mortgage obligations (CMOS), of various types. Chapter 16.

Rarely — nay, very rarely — may an individual trade in the exotic market of commodities futures or in the market for derivative securities such as puts, calls, index futures, and like. These types of investments are described briefly in Chapter 18.

It is important to recognize that in many of these categories there exist hundreds or thousands of possible investments with widely varying risk and return. The choice of which security within a category to invest in may be more important than the selection of the most appropriate category or categories for an individual investor. A later section of this chapter sets forth a pragmatic description of investments classed in according with ascending risk, without regard to the classification of the particular investment.

§13.3 THE RELATIONSHIP BETWEEN RISK AND RETURN

In general terms, the greater the risk of an investment the higher its yield. This is vividly illustrated by the problems faced by many self-reliant retirees in the early 1990s. Beginning in the late 1980s, interest rates dropped precipitously on riskless certificates of deposit, which during the 1980s had been a favorite investment vehicle for retirees and others who were dependent on interest income to cover living costs. In order to maintain their lifestyles they had to search for higher yielding investments. Many of these individuals doubtless selected higher yielding investments in ignorance of the fact that they were necessarily taking greater risks than before. Quite possibly in some cases the risks being assumed would have been viewed as unacceptable if they had been clearly pointed out to the investor before the investment was made. Of course, the opposite may be true also: Investors for whom additional risk might be desirable in order to earn a higher return may, because of ignorance or lack of sophistication, choose a category of low yield/low risk investment, such as a riskless savings account, rather than a higher yielding investment, such as a mutual fund or unit investment trust investing in corporate bonds. Such an investment might be quite suitable for that individual's economic position and yield a return perhaps three times as great as the going return on riskless savings accounts.

This point is fundamental: In investing there is no such thing as a free lunch. Markets generally price investments efficiently; an investment that has a significantly higher yield than another must, somewhere, carry with it some additional element of risk. This is neatly illustrated by Figure 13-1, which presents in chart form the relationship between risk and return for the most common classes of investment securities.

Figure 13-1 Investment Vehicles

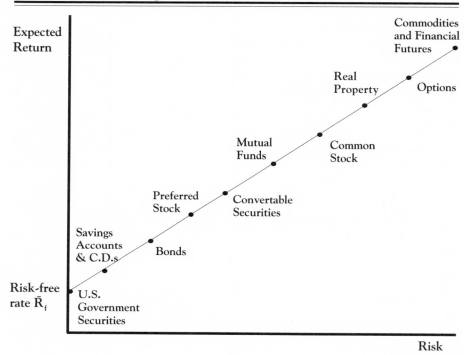

In deciding where to invest funds, an individual must look not only to the return he or she wishes to obtain but also to whether the risk that that yield requires is acceptable to the investor.

Figure 13-2 presents in chart form a risk-return classification for types of investors. Which of the designated categories most closely fits you?

Figure 13-2 Investor Types

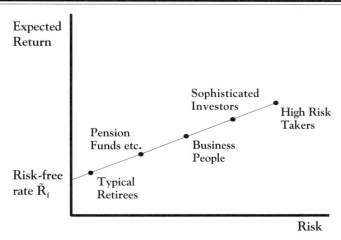

There are several types of investment risk. A naive conception of risk limits it to the possibility of declines in value of the investment because of adverse market movements when one has invested in common stocks, or in declining yields when one has invested in short term certificates of deposit and interest rates have dropped. Those are certainly the principal types of risk but not the only ones. There is also the risk, for example, that a corporation may decide to reduce or eliminate its annual dividend. The market for modern fixed income investments has its own set of risks, which are discussed in section 16.2.

§13.4 A RANKING OF INVESTMENTS BY RISK

In the 1992 world of low interest rates, a great deal of attention has been paid to investments that have yields significantly higher than the essentially riskless federally insured bank account or certificate of deposit. One classification of alternative investments sets up four basic categories of risk ranging from "conservative" to "even riskier." The investments described below are all discussed in the following chapters; the listing here is incomplete and impressionistic but clearly shows the relationship between risk and return.

1) CATEGORY 1: CONSERVATIVE

Investments in this category include treasury notes due in two to seven years and intermediate municipals, bonds maturing in two to ten years.

With riskless investments in the 2 to 3 percent range, yields in this category range from the 4 to 6 percent range for taxable investments.

2) CATEGORY 2: MODERATE RISK

Investments in this category include utility common stocks, preferred stocks, adjustable rate mortgage funds, and debt securities issued by the Government National Mortgage Agency (Ginnie Maes). Yields in this category range from a low of about 6 percent to about 8 percent per year.

3) CATEGORY 3: MORE ADVENTURESOME

Investments in this category include most high grade common stocks, equity mutual funds, collateralized mortgage obligations (CMOs) and European short-term and intermediate-term bonds. If all goes well, these investments should yield 9 or 10 percent per year.

4) CATEGORY 4: EVEN RISKIER

Investments in this category include common stocks of small speculative companies, junk bonds, limited partnerships, and smaller equity investments. Depending on luck and timing, yields in this category may be as high as 30 or 35 percent, or even higher in rare cases.

One suspects that many of the self-reliant retirees, having fled from low yielding riskless investments, placed their retirement dollars in investments that rank fairly high in the risk category.

§13.5 THE BASIC STRATEGY OF INVESTING: DIVERSIFICATION

The most sensible strategy for investors is to diversify investments and not place one's entire resources at the individualized risk of a single business or single type of investment. The reason is obvious: One should not put all of one's financial eggs into a single basket. Diversification largely eliminates the risk of massive losses when a single investment goes down the tube but does not provide protection against a system-wide or systemic decline in values.

A "portfolio" is simply the total of all the different investments held by a single investor. A diversified portfolio is less subject to risk than a portfolio that is concentrated in a single investment or a single class of investments.

Individual investors should also diversify among different types of investments in order to minimize systematic declines in values in any one category of investments. A plausible balanced portfolio for an investor with capital in the range of $100,000 might include 25 percent in riskless insured investments, 25 percent in long-term bonds or mutual funds specializing in longer term bonds, 40 percent in conservative stocks with some growth potential, and 10 percent in individual growth stock or strongly growth-oriented mutual funds. These percentages may change significantly, of course, with specific investment goals and with changes in economic conditions. A relatively young investor, for example, may have a higher percentage of a portfolio in growth stocks and a smaller percentage in the lower yielding category of long-term bonds or bond funds. This type of diversification, when followed by large institutional investors with hundreds of millions or billions of dollars to invest is called "tactical asset allocation."

The theory of risktaking in connection with investment strategy is known as portfolio theory. In business schools, portfolio theory is a highly theoretical, mathematically oriented subject. However, the basic lesson of this theory is simple: Diversify one's investments.

A relatively small investor cannot diversify effectively by purchasing small amounts of different publicly traded bonds or securities issued by different companies. The standard trading units (called "round lots") for most securities are simply too large to permit a small amount of money to be invested efficiently in a sufficiently diverse number of investments. The purchase of smaller numbers of specific securities (called "odd lots") is undesirable because brokers' commissions on odd lot transactions are higher per dollar of investment than round lot transactions and also because odd lots of securities discount due to the inconvenience of handling the odd lot. Fortunately there exist a large number of funds or investment companies that permit a small investor in effect to make a small investment in a portfolio of hundreds or thousands of securities without incurring excessive brokerage commissions or involving odd lot difficulties. The best known type of investment company is the mutual fund discussed in Chapter 15, but other types of diverse-portfolio investments also exist. Diversification for the small investor usually involves a combination of types of investment companies and other investments in his or her portfolio.

If a person has $50,000 or more available for investment, a diverse portfolio may be created by a judicious purchase of lower priced individual stocks or bonds. With very careful planning a considerable amount of diversification may be obtained in a portfolio as small as $25,000. This requires study and a considerable degree of sophistication; the problems of doing so are so great that it does not seem to be worth the effort for most individual investors, given the widespread availability of investment opportunities in already diversified portfolios.

§13.6 INVESTMENT GOALS

In order to make sensible investment decisions one must have an established goal or objective. One brokerage firm with a small investor orientation suggests that investors classify themselves in accordance with the following profiles based on investment objectives and risk tolerance:

1. *Conservative risk (growth oriented).* Security of principal is the primary concern for this investor, but some price volatility is acceptable if the potential for growth is increased.
2. *Conservative risk (income oriented).* Safety of principal and security of dividends and interest are the primary objectives for this investor. Growth of capital may be a secondary objective.
3. *Moderate risk.* The primary objective for this investor is achieving the highest return possible while controlling risk. This investor is willing to shift between asset classes as risk/reward trade-offs change.
4. *Aggressive risk.* This investor is willing to move aggressively among asset classes to take advantage of relative value or superior growth opportunities. This investor is also willing to commit a substantial portion of the portfolio to a single asset class if unusual investment opportunities emerge.

When establishing an investment portfolio, future inflation and the effect of income taxes must always be taken into account. During the 1980s and early 1990s, the inflation rate was between 3 and 4 percent per year. It is likely that the future will see inflation at roughly the same rate. The income from most investments is subject to federal and state taxation. An extremely conservative, all fixed-income strategy that yields less than 4 percent per year is at best a zero sum game in terms of growth of earning power and a net money loser if taxes are taken into account. Portfolios for everyone except for the most risk-adverse investor should have some mix of higher yielding (and therefore more risky) investments, such as mutual funds investing in common stocks (where the historic yield taking into account both capital appreciation and dividends approaches 10 percent per year) or long-term bonds.

§13.7 COMMON TACTICAL MISTAKES IN INVESTING

Persons making their initial forays in the world of investing should be aware of common mistakes made by unsophisticated investors (as seen through the eyes of a professional):

First, assembling a portfolio without an investment objective. Following the advice of a broker, one may buy a bit of this and a bit of that without any overall plan or scheme. The result is a smorgasbord of investments with no overall plan or scheme.

Second, investing too late in last year's favorite. One is likely to make the purchase just before the trend changes and the hot investment falls. One should make investment decisions on the basis of estimates of the future, not what was trendy in the past.

Third, taking profits too quickly. Timing, of course, is everything when speculating, but a common error is to become nervous that a paper profit will disappear overnight and sell the investment prematurely.

Fourth, failing to cut losses. What someone paid for a security is irrelevant; the question is whether the person would make the investment today. If the answer is no, sell it. A common misconception is to hold a losing investment waiting for it to go back up "so I can get even."

Fifth, believing one can time the market. The long term trend in investment values has been basically upward; moving totally out of the market when it is thought to be "too high" and coming back in when it is "low enough" is not likely to be as successful a strategy as simply staying in for the long haul. Cost averaging by making purchases at regular intervals such as the beginning of each month is likely to be more successful than holding back funds as they accumulate, trying to time the market's low point.

Sixth, relying too heavily on the advice of brokers (who have a financial interest in encouraging transactions). Brokerage firms make four or five "buy" recommendations for every "sell" recommendation. Most "sell" recommendations are made only after the investment has declined significantly in price and when it is too late. Brokerage firms are reluctant to make "sell" recommendations in part because of concern about relationships with the issuer, including participating in subsequent financings and having a reliable source of information. Also, most investors are buy oriented rather than sell oriented, so that "buy" recommendations generate more business than "sell" recommendations. This "buy" orientation of most investors has led to the following, partly humorous, interpretation of brokers' recommendations:

(a) A "strong buy" recommendation means buy it.

(b) A "weak buy" or "buy/hold" recommendation means that the price is too high now, definitely no more should be purchased, and perhaps this is a good time to sell.

(c) A "hold" or "neutral" recommendation means that one should dispose of the investment immediately since most of the growth has already occurred.

(d) A "sell" recommendation means it is too late; the issuer is about to go into Chapter 11 reorganization.

§13.8 THE IMPLICATIONS OF THE EFFICIENT CAPITAL MARKET HYPOTHESIS ON INVESTMENT STRATEGY

Many investors believe that successful investment strategy requires intelligence, mathematical skill, and a willingness to spend long hours determining which investments are likely to perform most satisfactorily. Rather surprisingly, modern financial theory tends to reject this widely held, intuitive belief.

Modern economic analysis has developed a theory that markets for securities are efficient: The implications of this theory are both far-reaching and startling. In brief, the efficient capital market hypothesis states that securities prices reflect everything publicly known about the prospect of individual companies and the economy as a whole at any point in time. When new information becomes available, the market absorbs and discounts it instantaneously and efficiently. Furthermore, the market accurately assesses the known information and is not put off or misled, for example, by announced changes in accounting principles that affect book earnings but not the real worth of a business. The efficiency of the market can be traced to the efforts of large numbers of analysts and speculators working independently, who follow the market extremely closely and exploit any opportunity to make a profit from temporary deviations of market prices from the prices that reflect all known information. These temporary deviations provide an incentive for analysts and speculators to continue to search for them, but the deviations are small and their existence is fleeting. The combined and systematic efforts of hundreds or thousands of persons to make profits in the market make the market efficient.

There are several different levels of the efficient capital market hypothesis. The version described above is called the "semi-strong version" and has the widest degree of acceptance. Under the semi-strong version, market prices do not encapsulate information that is not publicly available, for example, inside information about the issuer or the unexpected possibility that a specific takeover offer may be made in the future. The hypothesis, therefore, does not deny that profits may be made on inside information about the issuer or about planned takeover moves so long as the information is acted upon before it becomes public. Where leaks occur, persons acting on such information are part of the mechanism by which the information is absorbed quickly and accurately into the securities price; if this occurs before the time the information is officially announced, the market is said to have "fully discounted" the information in advance of the announcement.

The efficient capital market hypothesis, in its semi-strong version, has a number of important and counter-intuitive implications. First of all, if this theory is correct, one cannot predict the future movement of stock prices based on presently available information; since all current information is already embedded in a security's price, that price will be changed only by events or information that cannot now be foreseen. (If it could be foreseen, it would have been already embedded in the current price.) Second, at any instant in time, the next price movement of a stock is as likely to be down as to be up, irrespective of the direction of the previous price movement. Stock prices move randomly, showing no historical pattern. Third, all historical or technical analysis of previous stock price movements is useless for the prediction of future prices, since all that technical analysis is already embedded in current prices. It is true that many persons successfully charge substantial fees for making precisely this kind of historical or technical analysis, but, according to this theory, they are either charlatans or just plain lucky. Fourth, extensive reading and study of historical information about a company is also a waste of time — that information is already embedded in the price. The notion that a very smart and sophisticated person can improve the profitability of one's trading by studying historical information and trends is therefore essentially erroneous. Fifth, in-and-out trading is a losing strategy since one cannot beat the market in the long run, and such strategy simply runs up brokerage costs. Finally, the goal of many money managers and institutional investors to beat the averages in the long run is impossible: An investor can only do as well as the market as a whole.

For several years the *Wall Street Journal* has been running a low-key contest to test some of the implications of the efficient capital market hypothesis. Every month it compares the performance of investments recommended by professional investment advisers with the performance of investments chosen randomly by throwing darts at the New York Stock Exchange page of the *Journal*. While the professional advisers are somewhat ahead (as this is written), the contest is virtually even, and the difference may easily be attributed to randomness rather than a significant difference in ability to chose profitable investments.

There is little doubt that many Wall Street traders do not agree with the efficient capital market hypothesis in all of its implications. There are always numerous stories making the rounds of how X has devised a strategy that consistently beats the market. Economic theorists tend to reject such anecdotal evidence on the ground that it merely reflects the laws of chance in operation: After all, someone may be able to guess how ten coin flips will come out once in a while but will stumble on the eleventh. There are, however, some anomalies that create conceptual difficulties for the theory: investment strategies that have been empirically tested and appear to produce consistently above average market returns over long periods. Another serious problem for the theory was the sharp market break that occurred in October 1987. There appear to have been no developments during that period that can account for a decline of nearly one-third in the value of many stocks. Nevertheless, the amount of evidence supporting the efficient capital market theory, at least during periods of normal market activity, is overwhelming.

Despite some anomalies, the efficient capital market hypothesis is accepted as a reasonably accurate description of modern securities markets by many sophisticated people. For example, as described in the chapter on mutual funds, the basic premise of many institutional investors has gradually shifted in the direction of accepting the conclusion that their goal should be to try to equal the performance of the market as a whole, not to try consistently to beat it.

One important point about the efficient market hypothesis that is not always appreciated is that the studies tending to show the efficiency of the securities markets are largely based on examination of securities that are widely traded on the largest markets, particularly trading in shares of the largest companies registered on the New York Stock Exchange. Some parts of other markets also attract a large amount of interest and probably rival the NYSE markets in efficiency. See Chapter 14, part 3. When one moves into other parts of the over-the-counter market or into local securities traded on regional exchanges, however, there are many fewer analysts following specific stocks, and one would expect the efficiency of the market to be significantly lower than the market for the most widely traded stocks. Indeed, the market for many publicly held securities may be "thin," with trades occurring infrequently and only one or two brokers (whose primary interest is with other stocks) regularly quoting prices. In the market for such a stock, there may be virtually no efficiency in the theoretical sense.

Modern finance theory has cast some doubt on the fundamental precepts that underlie the efficient captial market hypothesis, particularly as it relates to the ability of markets to value efficiently whole enterprises. Everyone agrees, however, that modern markets are highly efficient in assimilating and pricing information. When one reads about new developments affecting a publicly traded stock, it is too late; the market has already discounted it.

14

An Overview of the Public Market for Equity Securities

PART I.   BASIC CONCEPTS

§14.1   INTRODUCTION

This chapter describes the market for common shares. Shares of common stock are the fundamental units into which the proprietary interest of the corporation is divided. If a corporation issues only one class of shares, they may be referred to by a variety of similar names: "common shares," "common stock," "capital stock," or, possibly, simply "shares" or "stock." Whatever the name, they are the basic proprietary units of ownership and are referred to here as simply common shares.

The two fundamental characteristics of common shares are: (1) They are entitled to vote for the election of directors and on other matters coming before the shareholders; and (2) they are entitled to the net assets of the corporation (after making allowance for debts and senior securities) when distributions are to be made, either during the course of the life of the corporation or upon its dissolution.

Common shares are "equity securities," a term that includes preferred shares as well, but excludes debt instruments such as bonds, debentures, and miscellaneous other evidences of debt. Equity securities theoretically involve ownership interests in the corporations themselves, while debt instruments reflect a debtor/creditor relationship. A person who owns equity securities is called a "shareholder" not a "creditor." Since equity securities reflect ownership interests, they may remain in existence for the duration of the corporation, which in most cases means indefinitely.

Preferred shares are quite different from common shares in economic and legal incidents, and a separate chapter (Chapter 17) is devoted to describing them.

An investor in common shares issued by a publicly held corporation receives a return on his or her investment principally in the form of (a) dividends paid by the corporation out of its current or prior earnings and (b) hopefully, on appreciation in the market value of the shares themselves. However, neither type of return is assured or guaranteed.

From an investment standpoint, common shares are generally viewed as involving greater risk and greater potential reward than debt securities. Unlike debt securities, the upward potential of an investment in common shares, at least in theory, is unlimited; if a corporation's business is extremely successful, an investor who purchases common shares before this success is evident may see dividends begin and increase and the value of his or her investment multiply manyfold. Correspondingly, if a corporation falls onto hard times, dividends may be reduced or omitted and the market value of the investor's shares may decline to a fraction of what he or she paid for them or, in the worst scenario, to zero.

Before discussing the markets in which common shares are traded, it is useful to describe in broad terms the management structure of modern publicly held corporations and the role of shareholders in corporate governance.

§14.2 PUBLICLY HELD AND CLOSELY HELD CORPORATIONS

Most economic activity in the United States is conducted in corporate form. Everyone is aware of the existence of the giant corporations that dominate the American economy; this chapter deals exclusively with securities issued by such corporations.

Corporations differ widely in form and structure; they are not all cast from a single mold. Throughout the legal literature relating to corporations there are references to two different corporate forms: "publicly held" corporations and "closely held" corporations. These two corporate forms are quite dissimilar in most important attributes. The only aspects that they have in common are that both are created under the same set of state statutes (the state corporation laws, which, in the case of publicly held corporations usually means the Delaware General Corporation Law), and both have the same internal tripartite structure: shareholders, a board of directors, and corporate officers. As a result, they share a common core of legal principles despite the very different economic and social environments in which they operate.

A "publicly held corporation" is one that has outstanding shares held by a large number of people. Corporations with shares traded on the securities exchanges, or shares for which there are published price quotations are all publicly held. Many publicly held companies are quite large. The so-called "Fortune 500" — the 500 largest corporations as determined by Fortune magazine — is composed almost entirely of publicly held companies. These companies each have billions of dollars of assets and annual sales, thousands of employees, and usually tens or hundreds of thousands of shareholders. They possess tremendous economic and political power merely from their size and their importance to the economy of communities, cities, and indeed, whole states. However, size alone is not a reliable criterion for the definition of a publicly held corporation: A few closely held corporations rival publicly held corporations in size.

A second important distinguishing feature of publicly held corporations is the general availability of relatively current information about their activities. As a consequence of requirements imposed by the federal Securities and Exchange Commission and the securities exchanges on which shares are traded, publicly held corporations are required to make prompt disclosure of material developments and to make periodic disclosure of financial information. There are generally no similar requirements applicable to closely held corporations.

A "closely held" corporation is one with relatively few shareholders. "Relatively few" is not a very precise term. Typically a closely held corporation is one in which: (1) The number of shareholders is small; (2) there is no outside market for its shares; (3) all or most of the principal shareholders participate in its management; and (4) the free transferability of shares is restricted by agreement. From the standpoint of potential outside investors, the absence of a market for shares is the most important single characteristic of a closely held corporation. Because there is no market for shares, there is a substantial risk that minority shareholders may be locked in with no avenue to sell their shares if they become alienated from the majority shareholders. As a result, sophisticated investors are reluctant to make equity investments in closely held corporations and do so only if contractual commitments are entered into under which their shares will be purchased by the corporation (or more rarely, by the other shareholders) under specified circumstances.

An investor of the type being discussed in these chapters should not even consider making an investment in a friend's, neighbor's, or family member's closely held corporation without competent legal advice.

§14.3 THE ROLE OF SHAREHOLDERS IN PUBLICLY HELD CORPORATIONS

The corporate model that appears in state incorporation statutes assumes that the internal organization of a corporation consists of three levels or tiers: shareholders, directors, and officers.

(1) Shareholders are persons who own shares in a corporation. Shares represent the ultimate ownership interests in the corporation. There is no state-imposed limit on the number of shareholders or the number of shares that may be issued by a corporation so that a corporation may have thousands or even millions of shareholders and millions or even billions of outstanding shares.

(2) The major managerial function of shareholders is the periodic

selection of a board of directors. Theoretically, the board of directors selected by the shareholders has the responsibility of managing, or overseeing the management of, the corporation's business. Management is divided from ownership in a corporation.

(3) The board of directors in turn theoretically selects corporate officers to execute the decisions of the board of directors and conduct the business on a day-to-day basis. The theory is that the ultimate power of management and control rests in the board of directors, not the officers of the corporation.

The reality of management in both publicly held corporations and closely held corporations is quite different from the theory.

In a closely held corporation, the principal shareholders are usually actively involved in management. The principal shareholders elect themselves and persons they trust to the board of directors, and then as directors they elect themselves as the officers of the corporation. Closely held corporations therefore usually are owner-run businesses.

In contrast, publicly held corporations are manager-run rather than owner-run businesses. In a publicly held corporation, things are turned completely upside-down. The affairs of the business are run by professional managers who usually own 1 percent or less of the outstanding shares; their remuneration is primarily in the form of compensation for managing rather than from owning shares. Moreover, they usually designate who is to be nominated to serve as directors, and those choices are then presented to the shareholders for approval or disapproval. The shareholders typically ratify these selections. The result is that power in a publicly held corporation tends to flow down from management to the board of directors rather than up from the shareholders to the board of directors. The top manager, usually called the Chief Executive Officer (CEO), is the most powerful force in the typical publicly held corporation.

Because managers of the corporation are not major shareholders, their selfish interests are not automatically aligned with the interests of the shareholders. From a selfish standpoint, the managers are more interested in generous compensation levels than in making sure the shareholders' return is maximized. The costs of monitoring managers to make sure they work to benefit the shareholders are called "agency costs." Much of modern corporation theory addresses the problems and concerns created by such costs, including development of strategies that more closely align the economic interests of managers with those of shareholders.

Shareholders in publicly held corporations are large in number, disorganized, and diffuse; usually no individual or group has direct voting control. While shareholders are entitled to vote on the election of directors and on a limited number of other important matters, this right is not very important to them. Consider, for example, the role of the small shareholder in selecting directors in a corporation. He or she is presented with a list of candidates selected and recommended by the current managers of the corporation. Since the shareholder presumably holds a diversified portfolio of stocks, her interest in any one corporation is relatively small, and it is not worthwhile to expend time and resources in investigating how best to vote. Further, the shareholder may only vote either for proposed candidates or may withhold his or her vote entirely; rarely does a shareholder have a choice among competing directoral candidates. Since the overwhelming majority of the shareholders are going to vote in favor of the persons proposed by management, it really does not make much difference whether or not the small shareholder exercises the franchise or pitches the proxy solicitation form into the nearest trash basket.

For purposes of locating the real source of selection of directors, one must usually look not to the election process, but to some earlier point where an internal decision within the corporation is made as to which names should be presented to the shareholders as the management's candidates. Until relatively recently, this decision was almost always made by the CEO individually. Today, it is more common to have a committee composed of members of the board of directors nominate candidates for directors. The CEO is usually a member, and often the chairman, of this committee. However, even when he is not, directors realize the importance of having board members who can work effectively with management so that the views of the CEO are carefully taken into account. In any event, the candidates proposed by a modern nominating committee are likely to be those recommended by, or at least acceptable to, management. However the slate is made up, this is usually the critical point at which the actual selection of directors occurs. The actual role of shareholders in publicly held corporations is merely to ratify this slate of directors.

Even though the CEO — the head of the management team that in fact runs the corporate business — traditionally has an important voice in the selection of directors, the CEO nevertheless serves at the pleasure of the board of directors. In 1992 and 1993, several boards of directors forced the resignations of long-term CEOs in highly publicized actions when the CEOs proved to be unable to redirect the energies of the corporation to meet rapidly changing business conditions. This occurred, for example, in General Motors, American Express, Digital Equipment Corporation, and IBM. The fact that these incidents were highly publicized indicates both that they are not very common and that boards of directors selected in the current fashion are quite capable of acting independently of management.

Even though shareholders have little incentive to vote their shares, the presence of an active market in shares means that shareholders dissatisfied with the management of a corporation may exercise the "Wall Street option" and sell their shares and invest the proceeds elsewhere. The exercise of the Wall Street option is, in a sense, a vote. A poor operating performance by management results in depressed share prices and may lead to the ouster of incumbent management. Thus, even though voting in elections is viewed as a meaningless formality by most shareholders, their investment decisions must be taken into account by the managers of the corporation.

§14.4 THE IMPORTANCE OF INSTITUTIONAL INVESTORS

For many years the small shareholder described in the previous section was thought to epitomize the public shareholder. The predominant view was that share ownership of publicly held corporations was almost atomistic and that, as a result, management had virtually a free hand subject only to the negative control imposed by the market for shares. "Ownership" had truly become separated from "control." This was the position put forth by A. Berle and G. Means in their influential book of 1932, "The Modern Corporation and Private Property" and was not seriously questioned until relatively recently. It is doubtful that this view was ever entirely correct, but since World War II a development has occurred that puts quite a different complexion on share ownership patterns.

Since World War II, a new type of public investor has grown tremendously in importance — the institutional investor. Institutional investors mainly collect and invest other people's money. They include insurance companies, retirement funds, investment companies (mutual funds), bank trust departments, university endowments, and similar organizations. Certainly a major factor in the growth of institutional investors has been the growth of private retirement plans discussed in an earlier chapter. Another major factor is the spectacular growth of mutual funds as investment vehicles; this development is described in Chapter 15.

Assets managed by institutional investors have grown by a factor of 100 or more in the last 40 years. These institutional investors typically invest primarily or exclusively in publicly held corporations and often only in the largest and most widely traded companies. Overall, they invest huge amounts of capital in a large variety of securities traded on the major securities exchanges. As a group they are now the largest single owner of publicly held corporations; they own nearly 50 percent of all the shares issued by the 1,000 largest corporations and their holdings in the aggregate are in excess of 40 percent of all the outstanding shares issued by all listed publicly held corporations. In many corporations, institutional investors now own 80 percent or more of the voting shares.

There are several thousand institutional investors, and they do not act as a single unit. Hence, even though their aggregate holdings may represent voting control in many corporations, it does not follow that institutional investors actually exercise control over such corporations. Indeed, many institutional investors view their roles as purely investors and eschew any interest in managing or exercising control over the business and affairs of corporations. Before changes in the proxy regulations in 1992, legal constraints also made it difficult for institutional investors to communicate directly with each other and vote cooperatively. In any event, institutional investors usually vote their shares in favor of management: If they are dissatisfied with management, they prefer to sell their shares rather than engage in a struggle for control. However, some institutional investors have felt compelled to take affirmative action in opposition to management on issues such as management compensation and the adoption of defenses against takeover attempts by outsiders.

Even though institutional investors generally view themselves as passive investors, their sheer size raises unique market problems. For example, if an institutional investor decides to exercise its Wall Street option and sell its shares, the block may be so large that only other institutional investors have the capacity to absorb the shares. Block trading by institutional investors is described briefly in section 14.17. Large institutional holdings may increase the volatility of share prices since an independent decision by several large institutional investors to dispose of their shares may markedly depress short-run prices because there is not enough demand to absorb the shares being dumped on the market.

Since the bulk of funds invested by institutional investors ultimately belongs to members of the general public in the form of potential retirement benefits, investments in life insurance policies, savings, or financial investments, the growth of institutional investor share holdings can be viewed as increasing the broad base of ownership of the means of production in modern society. A person with no savings, who lives in rented housing, may nevertheless be an indirect shareholder in American enterprise because he or she owns a life insurance policy or has an interest in his or her employer's retirement plan. However, in terms of power and potential control, the growth of institutional investors represents a concentration of the base particularly in the investment area. Now only a relatively few persons — the managers of and investment advisers for the institutional investors — determine where huge investments are to be placed or moved as well as how large blocks of shares are to be voted.

Institutional investors often owe fiduciary duties to retirement beneficiaries or beneficial owners of investment company shares, which require that the institutional investor maximize its short-run market gains. It has been feared that this concern for short-run return by the largest and most important shareholders may in turn compel corporate management to concentrate on maximizing its short-term earnings to the possible detriment of longer-range profitability. Whether or not this fear is justified is uncertain.

§14.5 CLASSES OF COMMON SHARES; WARRANTS AND RIGHTS

As discussed earlier, shares of common stock are the fundamental units of ownership of a corporation. Actually, state statutes give corporations broad power to create classes of common shares with different rights or privileges. For example, the rights of two classes of shares may be identical except that one class is entitled to twice the dividend per share of the second class. Or, shares of each class may have identical financial rights per share, but one class of common shares may have ten votes per share while another class has one vote per share or has no right to vote at all. Classes of shares are widely used in closely held corporations to govern the control relationships between two or more shareholders. Such classes are usually designated by alphabetical notations: Class A common, Class B common, and so forth.

Classes of common shares are created by provisions in the articles of incorporation of the corporation. Under modern corporation statutes it is relatively easy to amend articles of incorporation, and therefore also relatively easy to change or adjust the capital structure of a corporation when that is thought to be desirable.

Classified common shares are more widely used in closely held corporations than in publicly held ones. Nevertheless, there are a number of examples of publicly held corporations that have two or more classes of common shares outstanding; some of these classes may be publicly traded while others are held by only a few shareholders and are not publicly traded. The New York Stock Exchange has historically refused to list for trading shares of a corporation if the corporation also has a class of non-voting shares or one or more classes with fractional or multiple votes per share. In the 1980s, several publicly held corporations in which specific families had long been associated in a control capacity sought to combat potential takeover attempts by creating special classes of shares with "super" voting rights per share to be issued solely to family members. The terms of these special classes provided, for example, that they had ten votes per share but lost their special voting privilege if they were sold or conveyed to a person who was not a family member. In 1988, the SEC adopted Rule 19c-4, which in effect outlawed new classes of such shares for publicly traded corporations (with some exceptions), but that rule was invalidated by judicial decision. With the decline of takeover attempts during the

1990s, this issue has apparently ceased to be a burning one but continues to be discussed on a voluntary basis by the securities exchanges and the National Association of Securities Dealers. Rule 19c-4 was often referred to as the "one share one vote" rule.

Most publicly held corporations also may issue options, warrants, or rights to purchase common shares from time to time. Stock options granted to senior management are a common incentive compensation device designed to align the interests of managers with those of shareholders. Options to purchase shares may also be issued in connection with acquisitions of assets or other business-related transactions. These options are often nontransferable. However, options to purchase common shares of publicly held corporations may also be publicly traded and listed on securities exchanges. When they are publicly traded, they are usually referred to as "warrants" or "rights." The owner of a warrant or right has fewer rights than the holder of shares since an option holder has no voting right or right to dividends or distributions before the option is exercised. Warrants or rights to purchase shares are usually granted at prices that are fixed for the life of the option. Usually, the exercise price is set at a level below the market price of the common shares, so that a warrant or right becomes increasingly valuable as the market price of the common stock increases above the exercise price. When warrants or rights are exercised at a price that is lower than the current market price, the financial interests of then existing common shareholders are diluted.

Warrants are transferable options to acquire shares from the corporation at a fixed price that have a life of more than one year. Warrants have many of the market qualities of an equity security since their price is a function of the market price of the underlying shares and the specified issuance price. Of course, warrants (like options generally) have no dividend rights, while the underlying shares on which their value is based normally receive some dividend. Warrants frequently are issued as a sweetener in connection with the distribution of a debt or preferred stock issue: They may be issued in connection with a public exchange offer or as compensation for handling the public distribution of other shares. Sometimes they are issued in a reorganization to holders of a class of security not otherwise recognized in the reorganization. Warrants issued by a number of corporations are traded on the New York Stock Exchange or other exchanges.

Rights are short-term warrants expiring within one year. They may also be publicly traded and listed on securities exchanges. Rights are often issued in lieu of a dividend or in an effort to raise capital from existing shareholders.

The price relationship between a publicly traded warrant or right and the underlying common shares is a rather complex one. For example, if the underlying security is selling at $10 per share, but the warrant can be exercised (and the underlying security purchased) only for $12 per share, one might expect that the warrant would have no value. After all, who wants a right to purchase for $12 per share what can be bought immediately on the open market for $10? In fact, it would have some value (perhaps less than $1 per warrant) because of the possibility that the underlying security may rise in price above $12 during the life of the warrant. If the security does rise above $12 per share, the warrant can still be exercised at $12 per share for an instantaneous profit; when the market price of the underlying securities increases in value above the exercise price, the warrant will also rise in value virtually on a dollar-for-dollar basis. Whether it would be sensible to exercise such a warrant before its expiration depends on the income foregone on the capital necessary to exercise the warrant compared with the dividends likely to be declared on the underlying security. Of course, it should be exercised shortly before the expiration date if the price of the underlying security is above the exercise price. Rather than exercising the warrant, a holder may simply sell the warrant into the market and realize essentially the same profit that could be obtained by exercising the warrant and immediately selling the underlying security. See also the discussion of options trading in sections 18.2 through 18.6.

The value of a warrant or right may be divided into two components: an "intrinsic" value and a "time" value. In the foregoing example, the $12 warrant when the stock is selling at $10 per share has no intrinsic value but has some time value. When the underlying stock is selling at $14 per share, the warrant has an intrinsic value of $2 per share as well as a time value.

§14.6 STOCK CERTIFICATES AND RECORD OWNERSHIP

Until about 1970, ownership of equity securities was reflected by stock certificates. This is still true in closely held corporations, but it has largely been abandoned in publicly held corporations. Corporation statutes nevertheless still assume that owners of shares record their identities in the share transfer records of the corporation, and thereby become "record owners." The theory was that a purchaser of shares would obtain a stock certificate from the seller of the shares and submit that certificate to the corporation for cancellation and the issue of a new certificate that showed the purchaser was now the holder of record of the shares. The broker handling the transaction for the buyer would normally assume the responsibility of making sure that a stock certificate was received from the seller or his broker reflecting his ownership of the shares sold and accompanied by a power of attorney that authorized a new stock certificate to be issued in the name of the purchaser. If a purchaser did not become a record owner he or she was a mere "beneficial owner" and would not be recognized by the corporation as a shareholder for dividend, voting, and other purposes. While a beneficial owner has legally enforceable rights to compel the record owner (who has no financial interest in the shares) to vote the shares as the beneficial owner demands and to turn over any distributions received by the record owner, it might be expensive to enforce these rights.

The practice described in the previous paragraph was not universally followed by traders in publicly held securities, particularly speculators who expected to own the shares for only a brief period. Large numbers of shares were never registered at all in the name of the beneficial owners. Rather they were registered in "street name," that is, the name of a brokerage firm on Wall Street, and endorsed in blank by the brokerage firm. These certificates thereby became in effect bearer shares, transferable by delivery of the certificates themselves. Street name shares often remained in "street name" for extended periods, in effect being traded back and forth to satisfy transactions between customers of brokerage firms.

The practice of record ownership for publicly held shares and the widespread use of street name shares created horrendous back office problems in brokerage firms as trading volume increased in the late 1960s. The firms were awash in certificates and uncompleted transactions. The problem was solved by the development of a new system of registration by "book entry" for publicly held shares and trading through central clearing corporations. It is unnecessary to describe this new system in detail. From the standpoint of an investor, in the book entry system, shares purchased are not reflected by certificates but simply by a confirmation of the transaction from the investor's brokerage firm. Shares owned by an investor are thereafter listed in the monthly statements sent by the brokerage firm to the customer. Dividends appear in the account on the day they are payable, and the investor automatically receives proxy statements, annual reports, and other communications from the issuer through the broker. Sales of stock may be made simply by a telephone call to the broker who regularly deals with the investor, and there is no apparent red tape at all. Finally, there is no risk that the brokerage firm will become insolvent and be unable to honor the obligations inherent in their monthly statements since investors leaving securities with brokerage firms are insured by the Securities Investor Protection Corporation, a federal agency, against loss up to a very large amount.

When shares were represented by certificates, there was always the problem of physically protecting the certificates from destruction, theft, or loss. An investor usually placed certificates in bank safe deposit boxes, but a fair number used desk drawers, file cabinets, or the like. Others left the certificates with brokerage firms for safekeeping. The book entry system also has the incidental advantage of eliminating the risk of losing the certificates or having them stolen, forged, destroyed in a fire, and so forth.

Despite the ease and simplicity of book entry registration, a significant number of small investors still request that they receive certificates for their shares. These requests create paperwork for brokerage firms, issuers, and intermediaries, and some organizations impose a charge for this service. Presumably, investors who request certificates today recall the pre-1970 system and are uncomfortable with relying solely on a monthly statement from the brokerage firm that the securities are "really there." In fact, in the book entry system there are no certificates allocated to specific customers of a brokerage firm anywhere.

§14.7 PERIODIC REPORTING OF EARNINGS

Publicly held corporations report publicly their earnings each year on an aggregate and per-share basis. In addition, corporations report unaudited quarterly results also on an aggregate and per share basis. These earnings are closely watched since they show how individual corporations are faring in the competitive domestic environment.

Earnings per share are more meaningful to the individual investor than aggregate earnings. Earnings per share equal net earnings divided by the number of shares outstanding at the end of the reporting period.

Publicly held corporations almost always have outstanding commitments to third persons that permit those persons to acquire shares either by purchase, option exercise, or conversion of convertible securities. These are potential common shares since the privilege of acquiring the shares has not yet been exercised. The number of potential shares may be large in comparison with the number of actually issued and outstanding shares. The question then arises, what should be done about potential shares when reporting earnings per share? Should earnings per share be calculated on shares actually outstanding or on shares potentially outstanding? The solution adopted by the Securities and Exchange Commission is sensible. When the number of potential shares is material, earnings per share must be reported on both an actual share basis and a "fully diluted" basis, that is, on the assumption that all options and rights to acquire additional shares have been exercised.

Table 14-1 is an example of such reporting for the annual and quarterly earnings of three corporations, Spaghetti Warehouse, Spartech Corpora-

Table 14-1

DIGEST OF EARNINGS REPORTS

SPAGHETTI WAREHOUSE (N)

Year Jun 4:	a1992	1991
Revenues	$56,056,485	$43,033,433
Income	5,687,187	4,146,587
Extrd cred	....	(187,166)
Net income	5,687,187	3,959,421
Avg shares	6,494,751	5,164,614
Shr earns:		
Income	.88	.80
Net income .	.88	.77
Quarter:		
Revenues	15,794,923	11,789,862
Income	1,645,346	1,311,882
Extrd cred	....	(187,166)
Net income	1,645,346	1,124,716
Avg shares	6,457,932	5,542,253
Shr earns:		
Income	.25	.24
Net income .	.25	.21

a-For 53 and 13 weeks.
Figures in parentheses are losses.

SPARTECH CORP. (A)

13 wk Aug 1:	1992	1991
Revenues	$44,305,000	$40,482,000
Inco cnt op	1,204,000	(1,973,000)
Inco dis op	....	(7,000,000)
Net income	1,204,000	(8,973,000)
Shr earns (primary):		
Inco cnt op ..	.10	(.61)
Net income .	.10	(2.46)
Shr earns (fully diluted):		
Inco cnt op ..	.06	(.61)
Net income .	.06	(2.46)
39 weeks:		
Revenues	124,416,000	115,931,000
Inco cnt op	3,123,000	(2,161,000)
Inco dis op	....	(7,000,000)
Net income	3,123,000	(9,161,000)
Shr earns (primary):		
Inco cnt op ..	.33	(.83)
Net income .	.33	(2.68)
Shr earns (fully diluted):		
Inco cnt op ..	.16	(.83)
Net income .	.16	(2.68)

Figures in parentheses are losses.

TELEVIDEO SYSTEMS INC. (O)

Quar July 26:	1992	1991
Sales	$4,732,000	$5,680,000
Net income	(94,000)	(507,000)
Avg shares	44,548,000	44,376,000
Shr earns:		
Net income .	....	(.01)
9 months:		
Sales	15,786,000	20,120,000
Net income	(8,000)	(1,930,000)
Avg shares	44,476,000	44,376,000
Shr earns:		
Net income .	....	(.04)

Figures in parentheses are losses.

tion, and Televideo Systems. The (N) indicates a corporation whose common shares are traded on the New York Stock Exchange; the (A) indicates a corporation traded on the American Stock Exchange, and the (O) a corporation whose shares are traded over-the-counter. See sections 14.12 through 14.22.

PART II.   DIVIDENDS AND DISTRIBUTIONS

§14.8   DIVIDENDS AND DISTRIBUTIONS IN GENERAL

The word "distribution" in corporation law is a general term referring to any kind of payment (in cash, property, or obligations of indebtedness) by the corporation to one or more shareholders on account of the ownership of shares. The word "dividend" is usually understood to be a narrower term referring to a special type of distribution—a payment to shareholders by the corporation out of its current or retained earnings. An example of a distribution that is not a dividend is a partial payment to shareholders by a solvent corporation in the process of liquidation. In that situation, one would naturally refer to a liquidating distribution, not a liquidating dividend.

All state statutes contain provisions governing and restricting the power of corporations to make distributions or to pay dividends. Modern statutes contain two different types of prohibitions: (1) a capital protection provision that prohibits distributions, which in some sense invade or reduce the permanent capital of the corporation; and (2) a provision prohibiting distributions that have the effect of rendering the corporation insolvent in the sense of being unable to meet its obligations as they mature. The first test is usually referred to as the "balance sheet" test and the second as the "equity insolvency" test. These statutory provisions vary widely from state-to-state; they are confusing, sometimes internally inconsistent or self-contradictory, and often incomplete in the sense of not addressing at all some recurring issues relating to distributions. They are not, however, major limitations on distribution policies by publicly held corporations. Rather, they are of importance primarily in connection with distributions by closely held corporations.

A critical aspect of dividends or distributions is that they are discretionary with the board of directors. Thus, there is not the same degree of confidence that dividends will be paid as there is that a required payment of interest will be made. Omission of an interest payment is a "default" on a legal obligation; omission of a dividend usually has no legal repercussions and is simply a newsworthy item. That is a major difference between a "debt" security and an "equity" security.

§14.9   COMMON STOCK DIVIDEND POLICIES

Dividend policies adopted by a publicly held corporation are quite different from the policies normally followed by closely held corporations. The standard operating procedure for a publicly held corporation is to establish

313

an announced, or regular, dividend and maintain it indefinitely, or at least over several accounting periods. A regular dividend may be paid even though the corporation has suffered a loss in that year; the dividend is paid out of earnings accumulated from prior years. Most shareholders in a publicly held corporation, of course, are inactive investors who may come to rely on the regular dividend as part of their regular income or budget. However, the reluctance to change an announced dividend — particularly the reluctance to reduce the dividend in periods of adversity — is not based on concern about shareholders' cash flow. Rather, it is a market signal. A change in dividend policy is widely viewed in the securities markets as a signal about management's future expectations with respect to the company. An increase in the announced dividend is viewed as signaling improved prospects. It is a strong sign since it in effect states that the corporate prospects have improved to the point where management feels that an increased dividend rate can be maintained indefinitely. On the other hand, a reduction in the dividend rate is a warning of rough seas ahead. The communication of bad news has a potential for serious adverse market repercussions and is not to be made before management is reasonably certain that it is imprudent to continue the present dividend. Such a signal would not normally be given if management felt that the dip in earnings was temporary.

The "dividend yield" of a stock is the announced dividend divided by the price of the stock. In the early 1990s, many investors fled certificates of deposit because of their dramatically reduced yields and looked for higher yielding investments. They were naturally drawn to high dividend yield stocks, particularly utility stocks. Unfortunately, many investors blindly purchased such stocks on the basis of the dividend yield without carefully investigating whether the high dividends were likely to be maintained. A number of issues of these stocks have thereafter announced dividend cuts. The dividend yield of a stock is a treacherous indication of value. A declining stock price automatically improves the dividend yield, but a declining stock price also may well be an indication that knowledgeable investors expect a dividend cut. A dividend yield that is unusually high — higher than other stocks in the same industry group — may also be an indication not of a bargain but of a probable trap for the unwary investor.

An important measure of the probability that a dividend will be continued is the "pay-out ratio," that is, the dividend as a percentage of earnings per share. The pay-out ratio may exceed 100 percent if the corporation maintains its announced dividend rate in the face of a decline in earnings. But a pay-out ratio close to or above 100 percent is clearly an ominous sign of a possible impending cut in the announced dividend since it is unlikely that such a ratio may be maintained indefinitely. Such a ratio does not necessarily lead to a dividend cut because the decline in earnings may be temporary or because non-cash expenses may be depressing earnings without affecting the corporation's underlying cash flow. A normal payout ratio is 50 percent or less, and anything above that is cause for concern.

Another indication of a possible dividend cut is a high debt load being carried by the corporation in question. If a company's debt is more than 60 percent of its total capital, it may be hard pressed to maintain its dividend stream.

Corporations usually do not signal an impending cut in a dividend. Rather, the cut is simply announced after the board of directors decides that it should be made; at that point the price of the stock usually declines to the consternation of the investor, who assumed he or she was buying into a secure, high yielding investment.

If a corporation has an unusually good year or has the good fortune to receive a nonrecurring windfall, it may wish to distribute additional funds to shareholders but may be reluctant to announce a simple increase in the regular dividend because management may be unsure that the rate can be maintained in the future. In this circumstance it usually declares a "special" or "nonrecurring" dividend, which is paid on a onetime basis and does not create an expectation that a similar payment will be forthcoming in future years. Some corporations have adopted a policy of declaring "extras" above the announced rate almost every year, but that is not the customary practice.

Rather paradoxically, some corporations as a matter of policy pay no cash dividends at all. Assume that a corporation, recently gone public, has positive (and growing) earnings but needs all available cash for internal growth purposes. Even though a shareholder receives no immediate cash return, the series of glowing annual reports is likely to cause a steady increase in the market price of the stock. In effect, the market accepts and approves of the policy adopted of deferring cash dividends to foster internal growth and expects that sometime in the future substantial cash flows will be generated. An investment in that stock may yield substantial returns in the future even though it pays no dividend today. Persons may invest in that stock in order to benefit from increases in the market price of the stock, planning to sell it before dividend payments begin.

Until 1986, there were tax advantages in speculating in nondividend-paying growth stocks since market appreciation was taxed at favorable capital gains rates when the stock was sold, but dividends were taxed at ordinary income rates. See sections 19.22, 19.23. Some economic analysts even suggested that it was uneconomic for corporations ever to pay dividends under the tax structure then in effect. They argued that a policy by the corporation of reinvesting earnings coupled with a policy by the investor of selling appreciated nondividend-paying shares from time to time would yield a superior return than investing in a dividend-paying security. If the corporation has excess cash, it should be used to buy back its own shares on the open market. There are difficulties with this logic since at some point stocks have market value only because of anticipated future cash flows. Nor is it at all clear that the market price of nondividend-paying stocks increase sufficiently rapidly to outperform equivalent stocks that do pay dividends, even with a corporate buy-back program. However, even if the premises of the argument are accepted, the 1986 Tax Act eliminated one of the basic assumptions underlying this argument when it abolished the special capital gain tax rate for long-term capital gains. Even though special treatment for capital gains was partially restored in 1991 (see section 19.6), the benefit is so small that this tax treatment is unlikely to affect the dividend paying versus nondividend-paying controversy.

The financial press routinely reports dividend announcements of various types. Examples of these reports are set forth in section 14.11.

§14.10 SHARE DIVIDENDS AND SPLITS

Publicly held corporations often pay share dividends or announce share splits with respect to their common stock. These two transactions are very similar in principle and effect and are sometimes not fully understood by investors.

A share "dividend" is a distribution of shares of common stock by a corporation to its shareholders in proportion to their share holdings. Thus, a 10 percent share dividend means that the corporation issues one new share to each shareholder for every ten shares held; a holder of 100 shares will receive 10 new shares when the distribution is made, owning 110 shares in all. Fractional shares are usually distributed in cash. From a purely economic or logical point of view, this is not a dividend at all because the number of shares owned by each shareholder has been increased by exactly the same percentage, and each shareholder's proportional interest in the corporation has not been changed. In other words, a shareholder owning 1 percent of the outstanding shares before the share dividend is paid will own precisely 1 percent of the outstanding shares after it is paid as well: The percentage ownership has not changed even though the number of shares has increased. Despite this inescapable logic, many small shareholders welcome share dividends, and many sell them shortly after they are received, perhaps not realizing or caring that by doing so they have reduced slightly their (already infinitesimally small) interest in the corporation. For tax purposes, the gain upon the sale of a share dividend is determined by reallocating the original basis of the shares proportionally over the new shares and the old. It should thus be evident to every shareholder at some point that, at least for tax purposes, a sale of shares received as a dividend constitutes a net reduction of one's investment in the corporation.

A share dividend does have one favorable consequence if the corporation has a regular or stated cash dividend policy. It is customary to leave the regular or stated dividend unaffected after a share dividend so that following the dividend, the corporation's total dividend pay-out is increased. This results from the fact that the same rate is applied to a somewhat larger number of shares.

Why do corporations pay share dividends at all? The usual reason is that it is a tangible signal to shareholders that the corporation is profitable (despite the absence of a cash dividend) and is investing all available funds into the growth of the business. While unsophisticated shareholders may view such a dividend as a little something that can be sold without reducing one's investment in the corporation, in fact it is nothing but a signal.

A share "split" closely resembles a large share dividend. In a 2 for 1 split, for example, the corporation issues one new share for every share held by each shareholder so that each shareholder now owns two shares where before he or she owned only one share. It is customary to reduce the regular or stated dividend rate when a share split is completed; if the regular dividend is halved in connection with a 2 for 1 split, one would expect the market price of each new share would be approximately one-half of the market price of the pre-split shares. Often, however, the effective dividend rate is increased in connection with a share split: Thus, in a 3 for 1 split where the old dividend rate was $0.90 per share, the dividend rate on the split shares may be set, for example, at $0.35, equal to a rate of $1.05 on the pre-split shares.

Many corporations feel that there is an appropriate trading range for its common shares. The common stock of a corporation may have historically traded in the $20 to $30 range, for example. If the price gradually rises, to $40 say, the corporation may split the stock 2 for 1 in order to return the price to its historic range. One justification for maintaining traditional trading ranges is that if the price of a stock rises significantly to a new plateau but the stock is not split, trading volume may decline from previous levels as a result of the fact that most investors trade in round lots and may feel they cannot afford to invest in higher priced stocks. On the other hand, a stock split may slightly increase brokerage commissions on economically equivalent transactions. One major brokerage firm in 1992, for example, charged a commission of about $97 on a transaction involving 100 shares of a $40 stock. On a transaction involving 200 shares of a $20 stock, the commission was about $115.

Except for the marginal trading and commission differences discussed in the previous paragraph, a stock split is not economically meaningful if there is no dividend increase. "A stock split unaccompanied by a cash dividend increase is like giving somebody five singles for a $5 bill. You've got a thicker billfold, but it has no economic significance whatsoever," stated a partner at a leading investment firm. In part, it is a marketing tool and a source of free publicity, as financial newspapers dutifully report stock dividends or splits.

A corporation may also split its stock to reduce the number of shares outstanding. This is called a "reverse stock split" and is not really a split at all. Rather, the corporation amends its articles of incorporation to reduce the number of authorized shares. The amendment provides that each 10 (or 100 or 1,000) old shares are to be exchanged for 1 new share. Reverse stock splits often create fractional shares and may be used to liquidate the interests of small shareholders by establishing a procedure (authorized in many state statutes) to eliminate all fractional shares thereby created for cash. A few corporations have utilized reverse stock splits to eliminate all public shareholders by establishing the split ratio at a level sufficiently high that all nonmanagement shareholders become owners of fractional interests in a single share, and then by acquiring all fractional interests for a designated amount of cash. In these instances, a reverse stock split is functionally equivalent to a statutory merger.

§14.11 WHO IS ENTITLED TO A DISTRIBUTION?

Whenever a dividend or cash or stock distribution is declared or paid, the question may arise as to who is entitled to the distribution if the shares have been sold or transferred around the time of the declaration or payment. This problem is particularly acute in publicly held corporations where many thousands of shares are traded each day among anonymous persons. The New York Stock Exchange has adopted an "ex-dividend policy" to establish whether the buyer or seller of publicly traded shares is entitled to a distribution.

Table 14-2 is taken from The Wall Street Journal of February 25, 1993. It is an excerpt from the standard chart showing dividend announcements made on the previous business day. An examination of this table reveals much about the dividend practices of publicly held corporations and the law relating to dividend declarations. First of all, the table distinguishes between various types of dividends:

1. Regular (pursuant to a publicly announced dividend policy);
2. Irregular (occasional or erratic payments not pursuant to an announced policy);
3. Funds, real estate investment trusts, investment companies, limited partnerships (these are special types of investment vehicles, some of which are discussed in Chapter 15);
4. Stock (discussed in previous sections);
5. Foreign;
6. Initial (discussed in previous sections); and
7. Special (an announcement of a one-time "extra" or "special" dividend in addition to its regular dividend).

Table 14-2

CORPORATE DIVIDEND NEWS

Dividends Reported February 12

Company	Period	Amt.	Payable date	Record date
REGULAR				
AlaTenn Resources	Q	.30	3— 1—93	2—22
Alex & Alex Svcs	Q	.25	3—31—93	3— 2
BanPonce Corp	Q	.20	4— 1—93	3—12
Cabot Corp	Q	.26	3—12—93	2—26
Calgon Carbon	Q	.04	4— 1—93	3—12
Chicago Rivet&Mach	Q	.30	4—20—93	4— 5
Consol Papers	Q	.32	3— 5—93	2—22
Coors (Adolph) clB	Q	.12½	3—15—93	2—28
Cyprus Minerals	Q	.20	5— 1—93	4—12
Daniel Industries	Q	.04½	3—26—93	3— 5
DeKalb Genetic clB	Q	.20	3—12—93	2—26
Du Pont Canada A	Q	b.17½	4—30—93	4— 1
Eastman Kodak Co	Q	.50	4— 1—93	3— 1
Federal-Mogul	Q	.12	3—10—93	2—23
General Electric	Q	.63	4—26—93	3— 9
Goulds Pumps Inc	Q	.20	4—15—93	4— 5
Helix Technology	Q	.19	3—18—93	2—25
Huffy Corp	Q	.07½	5— 3—93	4—15
Integon Corp	Q	.08	3—15—93	2—23
Intermet Corp	Q	.04	3—11—93	2—25
Intl Aluminum Corp	Q	.25	4—12—93	3—22
James River	Q	.15	3—31—93	3—13
JamesRiver depsh O	Q	.515⅝	4— 1—93	3—18
James River deppf	Q	.87½	4— 1—93	3—18
James River pfK	Q	.84⅜	3— 3—93	4—19
Kinetic Concepts	Q	.03¾	3— 1—93	2—22
Natl Commerce Bncp	Q	.20	4— 1—93	3— 5
Nike Inc clB	Q	.20	4— 2—93	3—12
Noranda Inc	Q	b.25	3—15—93	2—26
Old Republic pfH	Q	.547	4— 1—93	3—22
Phoenix Re Corp	Q	.05	3—12—93	2—26
Pulaski Furniture	Q	.13	3—15—93	3— 1
Reynolds&Reyn clA	Q	.13	4—13—93	3—19
Scotsman Ind	Q	.02½	4—15—93	3—31
Thomas Industries	Q	.10	4— 1—93	3— 5
Union Electric Co	Q	.58	3—31—93	3— 9
Unitd Dominion Ind	Q	.05	3—31—93	3— 5
US Shoe Corp	Q	.13	4— 5—93	3—15
IRREGULAR				
1st Interstate Bk	—	.37	3—15—93	2—26
NFS Finl Corp	—	.07	3— 9—93	2—26

FUNDS - REITS - INVESTMENT COS - LPS

Company	Period	Amt.	Payable date	Record date
2002 Target Term	—	n.09½	2—26—93	n2—22
n-Revised record date on initial distribution.				
Amer Balanced Fd	Q	h.15	2—22—93	2—19
Cigna Hi Inco Shrs	M	.07½	3—10—93	2—26
ColonialHiIncoMuni	M	.057	3—12—93	2—28
Colonial Interm Hi	M	.06	3—12—93	2—28
Colonial Muni Inco	M	.053	3—12—93	2—28
Nich Applgt Grwth	—	k.144	2—26—93	2—19
Patriot PremDiv II	M	.07½	3—15—93	3— 1
Prud Hi Yld Plus	M	h.07	3—12—93	2—26
Santa Anita Rlty	Q	.34	4— 9—93	3— 8

STOCK

Company		Payable date	Record date
AirSensors Inc	v	2—22—93	2—22
v-One-for-six reverse stock split.			
Credit Accept	nn	3—17—93	3— 3
nn-Two-for-one stock split.			
DS Bancor Inc	5%	3—12—93	2—26
Duff&Phelps Corp	r	3—10—93	2—22
r-Three-for-two stock split.			
Millfeld Trading	pp	2—16—93	2—16
pp-One-for-4.5 reverse stock split.			
Nth Atlantic Indus	4%	3—26—93	2—26
Ocean Optique	rr	3—15—93	3— 1
rr-Six-for-five stock split.			
Sands Regent	vv	3—12—93	2—26
vv-Two-for-one stock split.			

INCREASED

Company	Period	New	Old	Payable date	Record date
		--Amounts--			
Abbott Labs	Q	.17	.15	5—15—93	4—15
HoraceMann Educatr	Q	.06	.05	3—15—93	3— 1
Vulcan Materials	Q	.31½	.30	3—10—93	2—24

REDUCED

Company	Period	New	Old	Payable date	Record date
		--Amounts--			
Food Lion clA	Q	.022	.028	3—16—93	2—25
Food Lion clB	Q	.021½	.0276	3—16—93	2—2!

FOREIGN

Company			Payable date	Record date
DankaBusnSys ADR	—	p	3— 2—93	2—26
p-Two-for-one stock split.				
Hghvld Steel ADR	—	t.077	5—10—93	3—12
Lydnbrg Plat ADR	—	t.12	4—12—93	2—26
Reuters Hldngs ADR	—	t.8776	5— 7—93	4— 1

RESUMED

Company			Payable date	Record date
Foothill Group A	—	.03	4—20—93	3—20

INITIAL

Company		Amt.	Payable date	Record date
Duff&Phelps Corp	—	.06	3—10—93	2—22
Monk-Austin Inc	—	.04	4— 7—93	3—15

A-Annual; b-Payable in Canadian funds; h-From Income; k-From capital gains; M-Monthly; Q-Quarterly; S-Semiannual; t-Approximate U.S. dollar amount per American Depositary Receipt/Share.

* * *

Stocks Ex-Dividend February 17

Company	Amount	Company	Amount
Airborne Freight	.07½	Integon Corp	.08
BankAmerica Corp	.35	LeaRonal Inc	.13
Federal-Mogul	.12	Perini Corp deppf	.53⅛
GulfStUtil deppf	1.07½	Piper Jaffray	.25
GulfStUtil $4.52pf	1.13	Unifi Inc	vv
GulfStUtil $5.08pf	1.27	vv-Three-for-two stock	
GulfStUtil $8.80pf	2.20	split.	
GulfStUt $4.40pref	1.10	WashingtonWaterPwr	.62

In addition, other self-explanatory categories, "increased," "reduced," or "omitted," may appear in some dividend tables if a company omits a dividend entirely or announces a reduction in its previously established dividend rate.

There are three dates established by the corporation with respect to each dividend or distribution:

(1) The *announcement date* is basically the date of the press release that a cash or stock dividend is to be paid or a distribution is to be made.

(2) The *record date* is a historical remnant of the time when shares were routinely issued in the names or record owners. (See section 14.6.) The record date still determines in whose name specific checks or share certificates are to be issued where the shares on which a dividend are declared are held of record by individual investors: The check is made out to the order of (or the certificate is made out in the name of) the person or pesons who are the holders of record on the books of the corporation at the close of business on the record date. For shares held in book entry form, the record date determines the "ex-dividend" date (described below) which in turn determines whether the buyer or seller of securities is entitled to the dividend.

(3) The *payable date* is the date the checks or certificates are actually mailed; the customary delay of between two to four weeks is necessary for the corporation to go through the mechanical process of making the distribution in the proper amounts to the thousands or millions of recordholders and holders of shares in book entry form.

The New York Stock Exchange ex-dividend policy is based on the record date. The ex-dividend date is set five business days before the record date. See the very bottom entries in Table 14-2. "Ex-dividend" means without the dividend. The ex-dividend date convention assigns the dividend to the buyer if a transaction occurs before the ex-dividend date and to the seller if a transaction occurs on or after the ex-dividend date. The theory behind the five-day gap between the ex-dividend date and the record date is based on the old standard settlement practice for stock exchange transactions, which was settlement five business days after the transaction on the exchange. On the settlement date the buyer must pay the purchase price and the seller must deliver the appropriate certificates appropriately indorsed. A buyer who was entitled to the certificates on or before the ex-dividend date was theoretically able to register the transfer with the corporation and become the record owner before the close of business on the record date for the dividend or distribution. The ex-dividend date was thus established as the last day on which that was possible. As a practical matter, of course, with book entry shares there is no need to actually register the transfer or have a settlement date, but the ex-dividend practice has continued.

The day a stock goes ex-dividend, its market price should decline by approximately the amount of the dividend, other things being equal, since the day before, every buyer of the stock was entitled to the dividend but on and after the ex-dividend date, buyers of the stock do not receive the dividend. Of course, this relationship may not be precise because market conditions can change overnight.

The ex-dividend date is a convention that is not dependent on whether a buyer actually arranges for certificates to be issued in his or her name on or before the record date. If a record owner of shares sells them after a dividend has been declared but before the ex-dividend date, he or she will thereafter receive a check for the dividend, but under the ex-dividend convention he or she is not entitled to retain it and must turn it over to the buyer. (As a practical matter, the seller's broker is responsible for withholding from the sales proceeds the amount of this dividend that must be paid to the buyer upon the dividend payable date.) The ex-dividend convention applies no matter what the buyer actually does with respect to the shares he or she is entitled to receive.

The ex-dividend convention is not automatically applicable to shares sold directly by one person to another not using the facilities of an exchange or the over-the-counter market. In a face-to-face transaction, the parties may make any agreement they wish with respect to entitlement to declared, but unpaid, dividends or distributions. The five-day settlement convention for publicly traded shares is also not applicable in a face-to-face transaction: Settlement may be on any date mutually agreed upon. In face-to-face transactions, in the absence of an express agreement as to who is entitled to a dividend, it is likely that a court would conclude that beneficial ownership on the record date determines who is entitled to the dividend. In other words, if the sale has been completed on or before the record date, the buyer would probably be held to be entitled to the dividend; if the sale occurs after the record date, the seller probably would be held to be entitled to retain the dividend. Case law on this issue is rather scant since in most cases the entitlement to a pending dividend or distribution is a matter of direct negotiation.

PART III.   THE MARKETS FOR EQUITY SECURITIES

§14.12 THE ORGANIZED MARKETS FOR TRADING IN EQUITY SECURITIES

The markets discussed in this chapter are primarily secondary markets in which persons who already own outstanding shares and wish to sell them deal with persons who wish to buy them. These markets provide basic liquidity so that persons who invest in publicly traded securities can be confident that they can dispose of them if and when they wish. The principal market in which equity securities are traded is the New York Stock Exchange. More than 2,500 stocks are regularly traded on the New York Stock Exchange. The American Stock Exchange is a much smaller exchange, also located in New York, that generally lists the stocks of smaller publicly held corporations. In addition, there are even smaller regional exchanges located in a number of cities: Philadelphia, Boston, the Pacific Coast Exchange in San Francisco, and so forth. All of these markets are organized and operate in a similar manner.

The second most important market today is the "over-the-counter" market, particularly the National Market System operated by the National Association of Securities Dealers. This market is organized on a totally different basis than the traditional securities exchanges described in the previous paragraph. The National Market System alone lists more than 5,000 different issues of shares, and its volume approaches that of the New York Stock Exchange.

These markets for equity securities are usually not the place where a corporation desiring to raise new capital through the sale of new securities to the public is likely to go (though in a few recent instances, the facilities of the New York Stock Exchange have been used to float new securities). Raising capital through the sale of new issues is accomplished through one or more investment bankers and chains of brokerage firms offering customers the opportunity to invest in the new issues. These chains of distribution for new issues are usually informal, based on a series of continuing business relationships, and do not involve negotiation over price.

In this and the following chapters, the New York Stock Exchange is also referred to as the NYSE; the American Stock Exchange as the AMEX; and the over-the-counter market as the OTC market.

§14.13 THE NEW YORK STOCK EXCHANGE AND RELATED EXCHANGES

The New York Stock Exchange is a place—a building located in the central part of the financial district on Wall Street in New York City. All transactions in shares occurring on that Exchange take place in a large room in this building. This room is called the trading floor, or simply the floor of the exchange. The reader may have seen pictures of the trading floor or even visited the NYSE as a tourist and watched from the balcony the beehive of activity that occurs on the floor during trading hours. The floor consists of a series of desks (or posts, as they are called) at which specific securities are traded and around which members interested in specific stocks congregate. Each security traded on the NYSE is assigned to a post. There are also numerous computer screens being watched, an electronic ticker that displays a continuous record of trading in more than 2,000 stocks more or less simultaneously with the transactions themselves, and news tickers running full blast.

Only stocks that are listed on the New York Stock Exchange are traded on that market. To be listed, a company must meet specific size and share ownership requirements; in addition, such a company must enter into a standard listing agreement with the Exchange, which imposes certain procedural and substantive obligations on the listing company. Among these obligations is a commitment to make publicly available on a timely basis information about developments affecting the company.

The listing requirements ensure that only the largest and most successful of the publicly held corporations are traded on the NYSE. This is the market for the blue chip stocks that are household names: General Motors, IBM, and so forth. However, among the more than 2,500 stocks currently actively traded on the NYSE, there are many that are not widely known.

Not anyone can go to the New York Stock Exchange building on Wall Street in New York and decide to buy or sell some shares: Only members of the Exchange have the privilege of trading on the Exchange floor. Most members are brokerage firms that deal with the general public; transactions are executed on behalf of members of the general public on the floor of the Exchange by representatives of those brokerage firms. Some individuals (called floor traders) also are members of the Exchange. To be entitled to membership, an individual or firm must buy a seat on the Exchange that entitles the member (or a broker employed by a member firm) to go onto the floor of the Exchange during trading hours and execute transactions. The number of seats is limited, and a trading market of sorts exists for seats. Since most Exchange members trade on behalf of the public, the value of a seat is partially dependent on market activity in securities. In recent years, seats have sold for several hundred thousand dollars each.

Transactions on the floor of the Exchange may take place between brokers with opposing orders to fill, or they may take place between a broker on the floor and the "specialist" in the particular security. The role of specialists is discussed in the following section.

The NYSE retains a hefty share of the order flow and volume of securities trading. Its success is based on several factors: (1) It is the most prestigious exchange, and many companies desire to be listed there and have their shares traded there; (2) the NYSE has historically provided a highly successful continuous and orderly market for securities traded there; and (3), perhaps most significantly, the Exchange prohibits members from executing transactions in listed securities other than on the floor of the Exchange. Today the Exchange is a highly computerized operation capable of handling trades of hundreds of millions of shares per day.

Several other exchanges are organized in a manner similar to the NYSE. A second important trading market located in the New York area is the American Stock Exchange (AMEX). The AMEX is considerably smaller than the NYSE. It operates in essentially the same way as the NYSE, but there is no cross-listing of individual stocks between the AMEX and NYSE. Listing standards for the AMEX are lower than for the NYSE, and most companies listed on the AMEX are smaller and the securities lower priced on the average than for companies on the NYSE. Most NYSE stocks sell for more than $20 per share while most AMEX stocks sell for less than $10 per share. These ranges are maintained over long periods by individual stocks through the device of splitting the stock if it rises in price beyond its traditional trading range.

It is relatively common for corporations, as they grow, to be first listed on the AMEX and later, as they continue to grow, to move up to the NYSE. This is a mark of some prestige: One sometimes sees advertisements placed by such companies announcing that in the future their stock will be traded on the more prestigious NYSE.

In addition to the NYSE and AMEX, several regional securities exchanges exist that operate in a similar manner: Philadelphia, Boston, Midwest, and Pacific being the largest and best known. Regional exchanges may list and freely trade in stocks listed on the NYSE and the AMEX. Over 1,000 NYSE stocks are traded on one or more regional exchanges. A computer system called ITS (Intermarket Trading System) provides automated price quotations on these stocks traded in multiple markets and an automated routing system so that orders are sent to the market providing the most favorable price. The regional exchanges also may actively trade in stocks of companies of local interest and with a regional following.

§14.14 THE ROLE OF THE SPECIALIST

Specialists play a central role in the market operations of the NYSE and related exchanges. They have existed on the New York Stock Exchange throughout most of its history. They are charged with the responsibility of making an orderly market for the shares they work with. They (or rather their representatives, since specialists are corporations) sit behind the post at which a stock is traded and may trade actively in fulfilling their market roles. They have access to highly sensitive market information in the form of orders to buy or sell securities at different prices. See section 14.16.

Specialists are expected to maintain inventories of the shares they are responsible for and to buy when the market is declining or to sell when the market is rising to assure a smooth trading pattern. In the absence of specialists, the price of a stock — even a stock as widely traded as IBM — might have erratic fluctuations due to temporary blips in demand or supply arriving at the post from floor orders placed by investors around the country. Indeed, it might be possible that there will be brief periods when there might be only buyers and no sellers, or only sellers and no buyers. In the absence of a specialist filling gaps, prices might fluctuate excessively in a manner unrelated to the essential supply and demand for the stock. Specialists are thus supposed to hew to their posts, smoothing out artificial fluctuations by trading against the market when necessary to ensure that the market remains orderly.

Specialists are not expected to try to prevent market declines (and indeed usually could not possibly do so, even if they tried) or encourage market rises. Their objective is to let the market find its proper level, given the supply and demand for the stock that then exists, in an orderly way. The obligation of the specialists to maintain an orderly market is qualified by the phrase "so far as is practical." During the sharp market break that occurred in October 1987, some specialists concluded that buying stock in the face of the massive decline then occurring was futile and could only bankrupt the specialist without improving the orderly flow of the market. Therefore they withdrew from the market for brief periods and requested halts in trading until an "acceptable" price to reopen trading could be established. A price is acceptable in this context when it clears the market, that is, when it leads to a balance between shares offered for purchase and shares offered for sale at that price without intervention by the specialist.

At first blush it might seem that specialists are sure to lose money in their trading activities when they trade against the trend. In fact, this is not the case. Specialists carry substantial inventories of their stock, much of which may have been purchased at significantly lower price levels in the past. Similarly, while they may purchase stock for their own account during a price decline, they may ultimately profit if the market recovers and they dispose of that stock at higher price levels. Specialists consistently show net trading profits from these activities. Indeed, over 60 percent of specialist net revenue comes from dealer-type transactions for their own accounts.

The second major source of income for specialists is commissions for acting as agent for brokers who place limit orders with them for execution. Limit orders are described in section 14.16. The specialist earns a commission on the execution of each such order. These commissions aggregate tens of millions of dollars per year since over 12 percent of all NYSE transactions involve limit orders on at least one side.

Over 50 firms are designated as specialists by the NYSE. Some 400 individuals actually perform the functions of specialists on behalf of these firms. There is only one specialist per stock but with 2,100 listed stocks, obviously specialist firms serve for many stocks. The largest firm acts as specialist for more than 100 stocks. The individuals who actually perform the specialist functions handle an average of 3.7 stocks each. Specialist firms must meet specified capital requirements and their performance is monitored, particularly during times of market turmoil.

Specialists are "downstairs" brokers since they deal only with members of the NYSE and not with members of the general public. The brokerage firms that deal with the public are known as "upstairs" brokers because their offices are physically located above the trading floor. Upstairs brokers are often many times larger than the downstairs specialist firms, and the question has arisen whether upstairs firms should be permitted to acquire specialists. The major concern is the fear of leakage of sensitive market information to the upstairs firm. Several upstairs firms, however, own specialists on regional exchanges without any apparent leakage of information.

§14.15 COMPUTERIZED ORDER EXECUTION

In the 1960s, the NYSE began the computerization of many aspects of its operations. Indeed, the tremendous growth in trading that has occurred in the last 30 years — in the 1960s a routine trading day involved a volume of about 10 million shares while in the 1990s the average volume was in the neighborhood of 150 million or 200 million shares per day — would not have been possible.

The computerized order execution system of the NYSE is known as Designated Order Turnaround or DOT. It permits member brokers to transmit orders electronically directly to the specialists' posts without the intervention of a floor broker. If the order is a market order and is smaller than a designated number of shares of a single stock, the order is automatically executed by computer either from other computerized orders or with the specialist. DOT also automatically notifies the member firm placing the order and the specialist of the price at which the transaction was executed.

DOT also permits much larger orders to be transmitted electronically to the specialist. These larger orders are not executed automatically but must be handled manually by the specialist. DOT also has a market order feature that is primarily used by program traders. It permits member firms to use DOT to electronically transmit orders to purchase or sell up to 500 different stocks simultaneously for automatic execution.

DOT order routing accounts for approximately two-thirds of all orders executed on the NYSE. Similar computerized systems also exist in the other exchanges.

§14.16 LIMIT ORDERS

Orders to purchase or sell securities are transmitted from investors through brokers to the floor of the exchange where they are executed. There are two basic types of orders: "Market orders" are orders to execute the transaction, either to buy or to sell, at the market price in effect at the time the order reaches the floor. A market order is executed almost instantaneously, usually through DOT. A second type of order is called a "limit order," which directs the broker to buy or sell at a specified price rather than at whatever price the stock is currently trading at. At a time when IBM is trading at about $85 per share, typical limit orders might be ones that specify a purchase of 100 shares of IBM "at 82 or lower" or a sale of IBM at "87 or higher." These are limit orders because the authority of the executing broker is limited as to the price at which the transaction may be executed.

Limit orders are handled quite differently from market orders. While they are largely entered through the DOT system, they are given to the specialist who records each limit order in a special book called the limit order book. The limit order book for each stock has a page for each price; orders to buy at that price are entered on one side and orders to sell at that price are entered on the other. In the above example, the specialist would enter the buy order on the $82 page and the sell order on the $87 page. If the price of IBM drops to $82, the purchase orders in the limit order book are filled in the order that they were received by the specialist. Because of this priority in execution, it is possible that the price of IBM may drop briefly to $82 and then rise again, and yet some limit orders at that price might not have been executed.

As indicated above, the limit order books record both offers to buy and offers to sell at various prices. An investor is normally interested in buying at a low price and selling at a high price. Thus, most limit orders are of the two types described above, that is, "buy at 82 or lower," or "sell at 87 or higher." Not all limit orders are of these types, however. Another type of limit order is a "day order," for example, "buy at $114 or better but in any event buy at the close of trading at the market." Still another type of limit order is a "stop order," which is an order to sell when the price has declined to a particular point or to buy when the price has increased to a particular point. A stop order to sell when a stock declines to a specific price may be placed by a person who wishes to save a profit or cut a loss by selling when a stock breaks in price. Similarly, a person may feel that a stock will continue to go up if it breaks through a particular price; hence a stop order to buy the stock if it reaches or exceeds a specified price may be utilized.

Limit orders (other than day orders) are good until canceled. In other words they remain on the specialist's books awaiting execution until they are canceled by the person placing the order. Brokers usually recommend that limit orders that are unlikely to be executed promptly or that have lost their original justification be canceled.

Originally limit order books were maintained by manual entries. Gradually these books have been replaced by electronic limit order books, which permit DOT-placed limit orders to be printed out directly in the specialists' records.

Limit order books contain important price-sensitive information relating to likely future movements of securities prices. They are therefore carefully guarded against improper disclosure. This is as true of electronic limit order books as it is of traditional physical limit order books.

§14.17 BLOCK TRADES

Block trades are trades involving large blocks of shares, a minimum of 10,000 shares and often much larger. They are of interest to small investors because they reflect a large part of trading each day and may have material effects on prices. Even though these trades are individually negotiated, NYSE rules require that they be transacted on the floor of the exchange so that at least theoretically any trader has the chance of participating in a transaction at a favorable price.

Only a relatively small number of potential buyers and sellers exist for trades of this magnitude, and almost all of them are institutional investors. However, block trades are an extremely important part of NYSE activity. In 1986, there were over 665,000 such trades that represented nearly 50 percent of total NYSE trading volume and a much smaller volume on other exchanges. These startling figures reflect the increasing dominance of institutional traders in the NYSE: In 1965 there were only 2,171 such trades, representing about 3 percent of NYSE volume.

The floor of the Exchange is touted as a place where the public can buy stock at the same price as the biggest players. This comes about because virtually all trades, even block trades, make a pass before the specialist prior to execution. If the specialist sees that a big block order has been negotiated at a better price than what is available on the floor at that time, the block can be picked apart and portions given over to satisfy orders from the investing public—both on the big board and on the regional exchanges. In the first possible retreat from this position, the NYSE in 1992 adopted a policy that prevents block trades from being picked apart when the price of the block trade is the same as the market price. Block trades at prices more favorable than the current market price may still be picked apart. This "clean cross" rule was adopted by the NYSE since it was losing block trade executions to regional exchanges or to electronic matching systems available only to institutional investors.

§14.18 MARGIN TRANSACTIONS

A margin transaction simply involves borrowing money from one's broker usually in order to enable an investor to buy more shares of marketable securities. By obtaining such a loan, an investor may make a larger investment than he or she could have without the loan. Since the loan is secured by a lien on the securities in the investor's portfolio, it is a riskless loan as a practical matter from the point of view of the broker.

Margin trading is subject to federal regulation because it is believed that excessive margin trading before the collapse of the securities markets in 1929 contributed significantly to the magnitude and severity of that collapse. An analysis of the way margin trading may have contributed to the dramatic collapse of securities prices in 1929 is instructive since it both reflects the dangers of leverage and explains how margined securities transactions work.

The late 1920s was a period of unparalleled optimism in the securities markets. Securities prices were going up and seemed to have no way to go but up even further. (The 1980s had a similar mentality.) Many brokers provided purchasers of shares with 90 percent or higher margin privileges. A person buying 1,000 shares of $10 stock could therefore buy $10,000 worth of stock simply by putting up $1,000 in cash and borrowing $9,000 from the broker. When the price of the stock went from $10 to $12, the investor more than doubled his money: He sold for $12,000 the stock he had purchased for $10,000, returned the $9,000 to the broker and kept $3,000 (minus brokerage commissions and interest) for himself. These transactions occurred time and time again during the 1920s: Buying stock on margin was like finding money. Furthermore, many people pyramided: They would take the potential gain from the run-up in price (without actually selling the stock and liquidating the position) and use that equity to borrow additional margin to buy additional stocks on the 90 percent debt to 10 percent equity ratio. To make matters even more dangerous, many persons of very modest means were speculating on margined stocks and pyramiding. When prices are going up, profits roll in at a fast clip; when prices decline, disaster strikes.

When the first breaks in price occurred in the summer of 1929, many margin purchasers found themselves facing margin calls, that is, requests from the broker to put up more collateral since the price of the stock had declined and the broker's loan was not fully secured by the stock. For example, in connection with the $10 stock described above, when the price declined to, say $9 per share, the broker was seriously at risk: The collateral was worth only $9,000 and declining, while the loan was at $9,000 plus accrued interest and increasing steadily (from additional interest charges). Most margin purchasers had no additional capital to deposit with the broker (even if they wished to do so) since all of their resources were already out "on margin" supporting other margin purchases (which were also seriously at risk because of the decline in price). To cut the potential losses, brokers began selling margined shares on a distress basis, if necessary, to recoup as much as they could. The decline began to feed on itself; panic resulted, driving down prices even further as more margin calls were triggered and increasing the sharpness of the market break. In October 1929, a break in prices of the same order of magnitude as that of 1987 occurred. In the process many brokerage firms were wiped out along with their customers since the customers were insolvent and the firms were unable to cover all of their customers' commitments. Brokerage firm failures then wiped out the assets of solvent customers since all accounts were uninsured, and the customers became unsecured creditors in the broker's bankruptcy proceeding. The bottom of the market collapse did not occur until 1931 and 1932, when many securities prices had declined by over 70 percent. It was not uncommon for the $10 stock sold in 1929 to be selling for $2 per share or less in 1931.

One lesson learned from the 1929 market debacle was that limits should be placed on the amount of margin customers can borrow on the security of marketable securities of fluctuating value. This regulatory power is vested in the Federal Reserve Board. Over the years, the required margin has varied; for over a decade, however, the requirement has been stable at 50 percent. This means that today an investor may borrow no more than 50 percent of the cost of his purchase. If one has $10,000 and wants to buy a $100 stock, one can borrow an additional $10,000 from a broker and buy 200 shares — $20,000 worth of the stock. From the broker's standpoint the risk is not very great since the $10,000 loan is secured by stock worth $20,000. Since the stock is collateral for the loan, the broker will, of course, not let the customer sell the stock or even obtain possession of certificates without discharging the loan. In a margin account the securities are restricted to protect the broker. Interest charged on loans in a margin account is relatively inexpensive: about two or three points above the prime, or 8 to 9 percent in 1992. Larger margin loans may be made at even more favorable rates. This interest charge in effect provides a spur to margin investors to close out margined positions if the stock does not move upward promptly.

Of course, when stocks go down, persons who have bought on margin are hurting. The effect of the 50 percent margin requirement is to double the consequence of each dollar of decline in the stock over what the consequence would have been in an unmargined investment. As was true in 1929, at some point the decline may be large enough that the broker will feel compelled to make a margin call. Indeed, many speculators were badly burned by margin calls during the 1987 market crash. As a result, the level of margined purchases in the early 1990s has never fully recovered to the level of the early 1980s.

A rule of the New York Stock Exchange requires additional margin when the value of the collateral has declined to the point that the amount the investor would have left after selling the shares (and paying off the loan) represents less than 25 percent of the value of the shares. In other words, if one bought 200 shares of a $100 stock on margin (putting up $10,000 in cash and borrowing the remaining $10,000), a margin call would be made when the stock declined to a value of $12,500. The stock would have to decline from $10 to $6.25 for this to occur, a major decline certainly. Many brokers, however, make margin calls before this level is reached; several leading brokerage firms, for example, require additional margin at 30 percent or 35 percent coverage rather than at the 25 percent level. Brokerage firms may also urge the investor to close out the position (by selling the stock) before it reaches this level. Many brokers have published brochures that set forth their policies as to when additional margin will be required.

Technically, margin is the amount that must be put up on the original purchase (50 percent currently) while maintenance is the point at which a margin call is made to preserve an outstanding position. Both margin and maintenance, however, are usually referred to as margin.

Margin calls are made on the basis of the value of the entire portfolio of securities maintained with the broker by the customer, not on each individual stock. When the value of the portfolio has dropped so that a margin call is necessary, the broker is expected to telephone the customer no later than the next day; depending on the brokerage firm's policies (and the perceived creditworthiness of the customer) the customer may be allowed a day or two, or as long as a week, to supply the additional capital in the form of either cash or marketable securities. If the additional capital is not received, the securities in the account are sold and the proceeds used to repay the outstanding margin loan.

Margin regulations are also applicable to banks. When a person borrows money from a bank secured by a lien on shares of stock, for example, he or she must sign a statement that the purpose of the loan itself is not to invest in marketable securities.

Margin loans do not have to be used for the purchase of securities. See section 7.5. Some brokerage firms encourage customers to use margin loans to consolidate credit card obligations or to pay for big ticket items. From the standpoint of the customer, the interest rate on margin loans is somewhat below the rates applicable to consumer loans generally. (One brokerage firm pointedly advertises its margin loans in the 8 percent range by comparing them with unsecured personal bank loans (16 percent), auto loans (10 percent), and credit card loans (18.5 percent).) On the other hand, individuals with securities accounts are unlikely to have extensive credit card obligations and may have sufficient cash resources to make direct purchases of consumer items using cash. There also may be some feeling that it is undesirable to mix personal transactions with a stock brokerage account; in any event it is apparently uncommon to use margin loans for personal purposes, and they are usually used for the purchase of shares or other investments.

With the development of standardized options trading (discussed in Chapter 18), one can obtain the same (or greater) leverage by the purchase of call options as can be obtained by margin trading.

§14.19 SHORT SELLING

Short selling is a well-known practice that enables an investor to speculate in a price decline to the same extent as the purchase of shares constitutes speculation in a price increase.

The idea is basically very simple: A short seller borrows shares from his or her broker and sells them immediately. When the price declines, the short seller buys shares in the market in order to replace the shares that he or she borrowed. The difference between the higher sales price and lower purchase price, less commissions, interest, and any dividends paid on the borrowed stock (all of which are the short seller's obligation), is the short seller's profit. At first blush, it may seem unethical to profit on a decline in prices or to sell something one does not actually own. However, that is a bit naive. As long as the person from whom the shares are borrowed consents to the transaction and gets the shares back, who is hurt?

Between 1929 and 1932, several fortunes were made by a systematic campaign of short selling (or "shorting") many common stocks. These campaigns are known as "bear raids." People borrowed shares and sold them, further driving down prices on an already soft market. Profits from successful short sales were used as collateral to borrow more shares and sell them to drive the price down further. In a way this appears to be predatory behavior. In another perspective, these people were simply more accurate in their foresight of what the short-term future would bring than the people who bought shares during this period believing that the worse was over and prices would be going up.

The mechanics of short selling are rather interesting. First of all, where does the borrowed stock come from? There is a large supply of marketable securities floating around the brokerage community that is available for borrowing. Stock loan departments of big brokerage firms routinely lend securities to short sellers as well as matching lenders and borrowers of stock. These departments may generate millions of dollars of interest income each year for brokerage firms. Big institutional investors also regularly lend stock in their portfolio. The incentive for lending shares is that these loans are collateralized with cash on which no interest is customarily paid to the stock borrower but on which the lender may earn interest. Institutional investors regularly lend shares in their portfolios simply to earn interest on the cash collateral. There is no downside risk of loss, and the short seller — the person borrowing the stock and selling it — is responsible to the owner of the stock for any dividends that may be declared on the stock while it is borrowed.

In periods of high interest rates, the lender, who obtains the use of the proceeds of the short sale, may pay the borrower a rebate or fee for agreeing to enter into the transaction. When a firm lending stock wishes it back, it issues a "call notice" to the borrower who then has five business days to return the stock. Typically, other shares in the floating supply are returned to the lender to close out the transaction.

From the standpoint of the short seller, the borrowing of stock is viewed as a margin transaction. The borrower must provide collateral equal to 50 percent of the value of the stock being borrowed. Upon receiving the borrowed stock and selling it, the proceeds are retained in the customer's account and cannot be drawn on if that would reduce the margin protection to the broker.

If the short seller guesses wrong, and the price of the stock goes up, he or she may face a margin call much as a margin buyer faces a margin call when the stock price goes down. Indeed, in most respects purchases on margin and short sales are mirror images of the same type of transaction. Theoretically, the liability of a short seller is infinite since there is no maximum limit on the rise of a stock price, while the most a margin buyer can lose is twice the amount of capital invested if the stock drops to zero (assuming a 50 percent margin requirement). These are theoretical maximum losses, however, not realistic ones.

The only situation in which a short seller is really at serious risk is when someone seeks to obtain a "corner" on the outstanding floating shares so that it becomes increasingly difficult for short sellers to find shares to buy back to cover their short positions. A corner requires the availability of very large amounts of capital to buy up the bulk of the outstanding floating supply of stock, absorbing the short sales made by persons after the run up in price has begun in the expectation that the price thereafter will go down. There have been no attempted corners in recent years in the securities markets though there have been attempts in the commodities markets. An attempt to corner the floating supply of a stock is sometimes called a "squeeze" or "squeezing the shorts."

Financial newspapers publish the short positions for many widely traded stocks on a monthly basis. Table 14-3 is an excerpt from such reporting for September 22, 1992. It is therefore relatively easy to determine whether the number of shares sold short (and not covered by repurchases) increased during the current month. An interesting question is this: Assuming that uncovered short sales did increase the previous month, is that a bullish or bearish sign? (A *bullish* sign indicates that prices are

Table 14-3

SHORT INTEREST HIGHLIGHTS

Largest Short Positions

Rank	Sep. 15	Aug. 14	Change
NYSE			
1 Disney Walt	14,244,605	14,549,921	−305,316
2 Blockbuster Enter	11,497,389	10,088,105	1,409,284
3 Unisys	9,870,662	11,200,971	−1,330,309
4 Chrysler	9,066,229	8,861,076	205,153
5 Banc One	8,785,924	8,651,415	134,509
6 Wal-Mart Stores	7,842,609	7,324,952	517,657
7 Home Depot	7,781,271	8,108,011	−326,740
8 Ford Motor	6,952,652	7,174,945	−222,293
9 Coca-Cola Co	6,927,063	6,653,561	273,502
10 Sysco Corp	6,649,354	5,885,819	763,535
11 Freeport-Mc C&G	6,399,009	5,978,953	420,056
12 CUC Int'l	6,272,458	6,284,294	−11,836
13 Conner Peripherals	6,225,196	6,304,584	−79,388
14 GM E	6,224,162	6,168,912	55,250
15 Citicorp	6,158,435	6,531,923	−373,488
16 Bell Atlantic	5,910,802	5,542,694	368,108
17 Marriott	5,717,361	6,703,609	−986,248
18 Alza Corp A	5,670,271	4,945,755	724,516
19 McDonnell Douglas	5,450,587	3,557,691	1,892,896
20 Intl Game Tech	5,439,141	4,433,298	1,005,843

NEW YORK STOCK EXCHANGE

The following tables show the Big Board and Amex issues in which a short interest position of at least 100,000 shares existed at mid-September or in which the short position had changed by at least 50,000 shares since mid-August.

	9/15/92	8/14/92	% Chg	Avg Dly Volume
A.L. Labs A	2,907,097	2,898,576	0.3	27,133
Abbott Labs	1,800,671	1,433,055	25.7	627,790
ACM Govt Sec F	88,768	4,300	1,964.4	42,047
ACM Man Incm Fnd .	101,169	173,047	−41.5	37,319
Acuson Corp	771,728	546,681	41.2	104,457
Adams Express	466,764	451,671	3.3	9,085
ADT (com shs)	1,210,000	1,888,854	−35.9	107,433
Advanced Micro	2,546,359	1,502,638	69.5	528,638
Aetna Life Cas	1,069,950	917,712	16.6	217,423
Affil Pub Ser A	770,996	764,644	0.8	47,890
Aflac Inc.	281,081	198,984	41.3	76,776
Ahmanson HF	658,143	607,820	8.3	228,219
Aileen Incorp	108,900	112,300	−3.0	11,490
Air Products	360,099	246,928	45.8	173,195
Airborne Freight	723,937	520,217	39.2	63,480
Alaska Air	513,938	654,624	−21.5	26,166
Albany Int'l A	362,764	375,392	−3.4	9,390
Alberto-Culv A	262,600	281,377	−6.7	11,923
Albertson's Inc	888,143	899,436	−1.3	169,552
Alcan Alumin	928,242	787,870	17.8	174,323
Alex. Brown	719,049	546,656	31.5	52,071
Alexander & Alex	141,085	138,349	2.0	57,090
Alexanders Inc	589,101	558,119	5.6	15,400
Allegheny Pwr	877,601	481,800	82.2	58,023
Allen Group Inc	150,816	144,390	4.5	18,990
Allergan, Inc.	207,612	257,111	−19.3	56,447
Allied-Signal	533,100	688,362	−22.6	255,395
Alltel Corp	158,033	116,344	35.8	111,057
Aluminum Co Am	1,101,744	1,281,873	−14.1	309,790
Alza Corp A	5,670,271	4,945,755	14.6	199,071
AM Internatl	881,106	894,379	−1.5	30,752
Amax Inc	736,141	611,922	20.3	131,352
Ambac Inc	129,332	126,500	2.2	68,614
Ambase Corp	554,173	480,200	15.4	43,033
Amer Brands	1,591,080	1,474,388	7.9	141,057
Amer Elec Pwr	402,628	762,306	−47.2	247,266
Amer Express	2,000,624	1,633,180	22.5	785,428
Amer General	249,324	206,237	20.9	105,319
Amer Health Prop	116,002	1,600	7,150.1	118,323
Amer Home Prod	1,561,098	1,616,677	−3.4	321,209
Amer Stores Co	1,932,868	1,805,784	7.0	84,652
Amer Tel & Tel	4,380,919	5,112,040	−14.3	812,766
Amer Water Works	62,980	5,689	1,007.0	19,604
Amerada Hess	624,064	541,449	15.3	182,971
American Barrick	3,584,099	3,125,260	14.7	244,914
American Cyan	315,220	401,644	−21.5	123,042
American Intl	631,794	573,833	10.1	285,519
Ameritech Corp	1,298,513	1,363,219	−4.7	149,857
Amoco Corp	1,673,358	1,455,413	15.0	603,847
AMP Inc	545,669	491,706	11.0	142,485
AMR Corp	1,252,131	1,349,165	−7.2	765,947
Amsouth Bancorp	512,106	483,049	6.0	40,809
Anacomp, Inc.	1,757,959	1,825,358	−3.7	70,761
Anadarko Petrol	456,062	565,286	−19.3	266,866
Anheuser Busch	501,829	489,663	2.5	364,552

likely to move up; a *bearish* sign indicates a downward movement.) An increase in uncovered short positions obviously means that many investors thought prices were going down; that should be bearish. However, most analysts put an opposite twist on the data. All the uncovered short sales reported for the month have been made and absorbed by the market; they will have to be covered in the future. Thus, an increase in uncovered short sales represents a potential increase in demand and is a bullish sign.

In some instances, an investor may enter into a short sale by borrowing the stock and selling it even though the investor already owns the stock. This is called a "short sale against the box," the "box" being a hypothetical safe deposit box in which the certificate is stored. This is primarily a tax-oriented maneuver.

Among securities traders, selling shares short while planning to cover in the near future by purchasing shares is as common a market strategy as purchasing shares and planning to resell them in the near future. Indeed, the terminology of traders suggests equivalence: A trader who owns shares is said to be "long" while one who owes shares to the market is said to be "short."

SEC regulations distinguish between regular security sales from a long position and true short sales in one respect. Aggressive short selling has the capacity to depress a security's price to unrealistically low levels, particularly in an already declining market. The SEC requires that short sales be made only on an uptick (that is, only after a market transaction that was at a higher price than the preceding transaction) or on a zero uptick (that is, only after one or more transactions at a level price if the previous price movement was an uptick). This provision, dating from the 1930s, is designed to prevent the depressing effect of an unrelieved series of short sales at steadily decreasing prices. During the market decline in October 1987, however, it appears that some short sales were made in violation of this rule—some short sales were executed despite the fact that the previous transaction was a downtick (that is, executed at a price lower than the transaction preceding it) or a zero downtick.

In 1991, the SEC proposed that short holdings of major investors be disclosed when they exceed 5 percent of the outstanding issue. This proposal was in response to an increase in volume of short selling, primarily by securities firms. It was estimated at the time that some $30 billion in stocks had been sold short, a significant increase from the early 1980s. (In contrast, the aggregate of long positions in stocks is about $3 trillion.) In its proposal to require disclosure of large short positions, the SEC described the following advantages of permitting short selling:

> Short selling provides the market with two important benefits: market liquidity and pricing efficiency. Substantial market liquidity is provided through short selling by market professionals. . . . To the extent that short sales are effected in the market by securities professionals, such short sale

activities in effect add to the trading supply of stock available to purchasers and reduce the risk that the price paid by investors is artificially high because of a temporary contraction of supply. An exchange specialist, for example, is required to maintain price continuity and to minimize the effects of temporary disparities between supply and demand, i.e. to maintain a fair and orderly market. Thus, the specialist may sell short in order to supply stock to satisfy purchase orders. . . .

Short selling also contributes to the pricing efficiency of the equities markets. Efficient markets require that prices fully reflect all buy and sell interest. When a short seller speculates on a downward movement in a security, his transaction is a mirror image of the person who purchases the security based upon speculation that the security's price will rise. Both the purchaser and the short seller hope to profit by buying the security at one price and selling at a higher price — the primary difference being that the sequence of transactions is reversed. Market participants who believe a stock is "overvalued" may engage in short sales in an attempt to profit from the perceived divergence of prices from true economic values. Such short sellers add to stock pricing efficiency because their transactions assure that their perception of future stock price performance (and, inferentially, issuer performance) is reflected in the market price.

Some short selling may be effected for manipulative purposes. . . . It appears, however, that historically downward price manipulations have been less frequent than upward manipulations. (Stock market manipulations may involve efforts to achieve an illegal profit by depressing the price of securities through (i) selling activity, including short sales, made for the purpose of inducing the sale of the security by others; or (ii) establishing a short position coupled with publicizing negative, materially misleading statements concerning the issuer.)

§14.20 THE OVER-THE-COUNTER MARKETS IN GENERAL

The over-the-counter market (OTC market) is quite unlike the organized exchanges described in the previous sections, though the trading strategies discussed in sections 14.16 through 14.19 may be readily executed in this market as well. There is no single location of the over-the-counter market. Rather, it consists of a large number of brokers and dealers who deal with each other by computer or telephone, buying and selling securities for themselves and for their customers.

Dealers and brokers involved in the OTC market are organized into a semi-public association called the National Association of Securities Dealers (NASD).

A "dealer" is a securities firm trading for its own account while a "broker" is executing an order for a customer. Large securities firms commonly act both as broker and dealer in OTC securities and may act as both broker and dealer in the same transaction if suitable notice is given to the customer. In other words, a broker executing a purchase transaction for a customer may supply the security out of its own inventory, in effect acting as a dealer. The NASD has developed guidelines for pricing of securities in transactions in which the securities firm the customer is dealing with executes the transaction out of its own inventory as a dealer. Similarly, a brokerage firm may buy a customer's securities for its own inventory when the customer decides to sell the security.

The OTC had very modest beginnings, but the development of the modern computer has made it into a major competitor to the NYSE for the trading of equity securities issued by large publicly held corporations. Indeed, many observers believe that in the long run the OTC will continue to grow while the NYSE and other traditional securities exchanges will decline.

The core of the OTC market is the market maker in an individual security. A "market maker" is a dealer who announces its continued willingness to both buy and sell a specific security; the price at which a market maker is willing to sell is, of course, somewhat higher than the price at which it is willing to buy. The difference — called the spread — is the source of the dealer's profit in in-and-out trading. Price quotations by market makers are referred to as bid-and-asked quotations, the "bid" price being what the dealer is willing to pay for the stock and the "asked" price what the dealer is willing to sell the security for.

The OTC market is a vast market, comprising thousands of brokers and dealers in securities of all types. It is the principal market in which marketable debt securities — corporate bonds, treasuries, municipals, convertibles, mortgage backed securities, and so forth — are traded. See Chapter 16. It is also an important market for various types of exotic or unusual securities. The balance of this chapter, however, deals only with the over-the-counter market for equity securities.

Today most bid-and-asked quotations for OTC stocks appear in a computerized quotation system called NASDAQ (National Association of Securities Dealers Automated Quotations), but many bids and asked quotations for less heavily traded stocks continue to appear in an overnight publication known as "the sheets." A broker with an order to buy or sell an OTC stock finds the best price quotation from a market maker, either from the NASDAQ screen or by using the telephone, and then places the order with the one with the best price. There may be more than one price in the OTC market since for most stocks there are several market makers. The OTC market thus consists of a web of brokers and dealers who deal with each other by telephone or computer. Essentially the same pattern is true for over-the-counter trading in securities other than common stocks.

A bit of history is instructive. The over-the-counter market for equity securities was originally completely unregulated and unorganized. Dealers would make a market in specific stocks simply by announcing price quotations in that stock. The accepted method of communication was through the insertion of representative bid-and-asked quotations in a daily publication called the "pink sheets." A broker with an order to fill would check the pink sheets to see which dealers were making a market and would then telephone one or more of them seeking the best price. For many years, this market functioned quietly, with virtually no information available as to actual prices at which trades occurred or to actual volumes of transactions in specific shares. Of course, this was before the age of computerization so that a technology to record transactions and prices in such a large and diffuse market simply did not exist.

With the development of the modern computer, a much more systematic and regularized OTC market for equity securities evolved, which is described in the following sections.

§14.21 NASDAQ AND THE NATIONAL MARKET SYSTEM

As described above, NASDAQ is the computerized quotation system at the heart of the modern OTC market. NASDAQ offers subscribers three levels of quotes: Level I provides representative bid-and-asked quotations that enable a person to get a feel for the market. Level II provides access to actual quotations by every market maker in each security listed. Level III allows market makers to input the machine and enter or change quotations.

A second major development in the OTC market was the creation of the National Market System for widely traded securities. The principal market makers for these securities now report actual trades and prices, and the reporting of such transactions is superficially indistinguishable from that of the formally organized exchanges. There are over 5,000 stocks in the National Market System. Many companies whose shares are traded in the National Market System rival in size and economic importance the companies listed on the New York Stock Exchange. The volume of trading in the national market system is reported daily in the Wall Street Journal along with — and on a par with — trading on the NYSE. See section 14.28. The average national market stock has over 7 market makers, and the most heavily traded ones may have 20 or more.

The large national securities firms are major market makers in OTC securities. Some may make markets in more than 1,000 different securities at any one time, ranging from securities traded in the National Market System to securities primarily of regional or local interest.

The National Association of Securities Dealers maintains an automated small order execution system (SOES), which permits automatic execution at the best available price quotation of orders for national market securities of up to 1,000 shares. SOES accounts for less than 2 percent of the volume of the National Market System but is involved in about 15 percent of its trades. In addition to SOES, several proprietary automatic execution systems are available on a subscription basis.

Reporting members of NASD who are not members of the NYSE may trade in NYSE-listed stocks. These trades, and some block trades arranged by NASD members, are reported in the NYSE composite trading list as NASD trades. See Table 14-5 set forth on page 342.

§14.22 OTHER LEVELS OF THE OVER-THE-COUNTER MARKET

There are several levels of the OTC market for equity securities. The first level is the National Market System described above, for which the National Association of Securities Dealers provides daily information on actual trades and volumes.

The second level is the so-called NASDAQ Small-Capital List, for which NASD provides representative volume figures but not actual prices. Bid and asked figures are dealers' quotations of prices, not transaction prices. Securities on the NASDAQ Small Capital List are widely traded, active issues that fall below the standards for listing in the National Market System. Table 14-4 shows representative quotations for the National Small-Capital List for August 31, 1992. They are in traditional "bid" and "asked" format but partial volume figures are shown.

The third level is the OTC Bulletin Board. This service provides members with electronic quotations for many stocks previously listed only in the pink sheets. Unlike NASDAQ quotations, Bulletin Board price quotations are not firm, and indeed, may be omitted entirely by a dealer indicating an interest in a specific stock. The Bulletin Board has been in existence since 1990, and it is possible that the Bulletin Board may be subsequently broadened to more closely resemble the two NASDAQ automated quotation services.

The fourth level of the OTC market is the quotations in the daily pink sheets of inactively traded OTC securities. Absent some special interest, it is very unlikely that any reader of this book would have an interest in investing in inactive securities listed in "the sheets." They may range from insolvent shells to solid, old-line companies that have barely enough outside holdings of shares to justify a listing in the sheets. Better quality companies may be quoted only with a bid quotation (possibly the company's own) and no asked prices — no shares offered for sale. Many of the companies listed in the sheets have so few shares publicly held that they are

Table 14-4

NASDAQ SMALL-CAP ISSUES

Issue	Div	Vol 100s	Last	Chg
A&A Fd g		30	2 1/8	+1/16
AAON		205	11/32	+1/16
ACTV		402	1 11/16	+1/16
AFN		50	21/32	...
AFP		5	29/32	+1/8
AGBag		315	2 5/8	-1/8
APA		8	3 3/4	+1/4
API		385	11/16	...
ASA Int		112	1 15/16	-1/16
ATC Env		34	2 9/16	...
ATC wtB		7	13/32	-1/8
ATC		175	2 5/16	...
Abatix		50	15/16	-1/8
Accuhlt		2	5 1/4	-1/4
AcrnVn		3	2 1/2	-1/16
ActnPr		53	2	+1/4
Adelph h		70	18	-5/8
Admar		433	2	+1/8
AdvEnv		661	1 3/4	...
AdvEn wt		45	1/2	-1/8
AdvFin		35	4 1/4	-3/4
AdvFn pf		7	4 1/4	...
AdvMed		1	3 1/2	...
AdNMR		862	2 11/16	+1/16
AdvLfe		48	13/16	-3/16
AerSyE		5	1 3/4	-1/4
Aerody		4	5 1/8	-3/8
Aeroson		19	2 1/8	...
Agristr		111	5/8	-1/16
AirSen		305	3/4	...
AirInt		4626	1 5/32	-1/32
AirIn wtA		1479	1/8	-1/16
Ajay		1870	11/16	-1/32
Ajay wt		20	7/32	...
Ajay un		10	3 3/4	-3/4
AlskAp		134	5/32	...
Alcide		150	9/16	+1/32
Alcoln s		782	3 1/2	-1/16
AldWste s		32	5 3/8	...
Alpha1		200	10 3/4	+1/4
Alph1 wtB		15	3 1/4	-1/4
Alphr un		20	4 1/4	...
Alpnet		20	3/4	-1/16
AltrSl s		228	11 1/4	+3/4
vjAWAirl		274	1/2	...
AAcft		545	15/32	-1/32
AmBcpNV t		14	9	-1/2
AmBiom		5	11 1/4	-1/8
AmBio wt		20	3 1/4	...
ABsCpt		783	1	-3/16
ACty pf	1.50	1	21 1/2	+1/2
AmDrg		159	1 1/2	...
AmEduc		2	4 1/4	...
AmEnt		161	1 1/16	-1/16
AmFB		1	6 1/2	...
AMdAlt		6	1 13/16	-1/16
AmMdTc		80	3	+1/8
ANtPt		2	3 3/8	-1/8
AmNwk s		28	8 1/2	-1/8
APacBk		344	2 3/8	...
ASfty h		250	7/16	+1/32
ASvFL		562	1 1/2	+1/8
AmtyBc		1	1 3/4	+1/4
Amnex		112	7/32	+1/32
Amtech		20	3/4	+1/16
AnlySur		35	2 3/4	...
Angecn		208	2 3/8	-1/8
AngSwis s		962	15/32	-3/8
Anuhco		535	2 5/8	...
AorTch		528	2 7/8	-1/8
Apco	1.35e	6	15 3/4	...
Aphton		41	20 1/4	...
AplRecy		43	11 1/4	-1
Ap DNA		90	15/32	+1/32
ApldLsr		345	4 1/8	-1/4
ApLsr wtA		10	2 3/16	-1/16
ApdLsr un		33	12 1/2	...
AquaBy		25	3 3/8	+1/8
Aquant		54	1 3/8	-1/16
ArchPt		101	4 5/8	-1/8
ArdenIn		70	2	+1/8
ArizInst		5	2 1/4	+1/2
Chapral		60	9/32	...
ChrtFdl		105	4 1/4	...
ChefInt		860	7/32	...
Chemex s		100	2 3/4	...
ChLea		1	19	-3/4
ChcEn h		41	17/32	...
ChchTc s		600	3/8	-3/16
Ciattis		145	3/8	-1/4
CircRs		10	7/32	-1/32
Ciro		10	3 1/2	+1
CtzSec	.04j	30	3 1/4	+1/8
CtyLTr		72	13/16	...
ClinHm		61	3 7/8	-1/8
Clinicom		111	5 5/8	-3/8
Clinicp		151	15 3/8	+1/8
ColCmc		200	3/16	+1/32
ComCent		75	5	...
ComndCr		350	7/32	+1/32
CmndSc		61	4 1/8	...
CmcBVA		2	15	-1
CmceG		27	1 1/2	...
CmclPr		5	3/4	...
ComIntl		352	3 7/8	-1/8
CmtyBTn	.24	15	5	+1/2
Comprt		1752	1/16	...
CmpMed		787	9/32	-1/32
CmpM un		230	3/8	+1/32
Cmpflt		4	21/32	-7/32
Cmputn		35	1 3/4	...
Comvrse		12171	27/32	+1/32
Concept		88	1 9/16	...
ConCm s		17	3 1/8	+3/8
CnqAir		262	3 3/8	+1/16
ConRch		80	4	+1/4
Consulr		30	5/16	...
Consumt		26	3/4	-1/8
Convoy		50	17/32	-1/16
Cornucp		10	3/4	...
Cortex		636	1 11/16	+1/16
Cortx wt		20	7/8	...
CreatvC		56	1 3/32	+1/32
CreatL		1693	4	+1/16
CrdDept		10	4 3/4	+1/4
CredoPt		20	1 1/2	-1/8
CrstCp		400	3/16	-1/32
Cryotch h		20	7/16	...
Cucos		11	1 1/8	...
CurrTec		30	3	...
Cusac g		295	11/32	+1/32
Cyanotc		10	1 1/4	+1/8
Cybmed		45	1	+1/8
Cybrnet		17	1	...
Cybrn wt		2	5/16	...
DCX		626	2 1/8	...
DRS Ind s		11	1 13/16	+1/8
DSI Ind		1001	13/32	-1/32
DSP		20	4 3/4	-1/8
DTI Md		204	2 1/16	+3/16
Daleco		10	1 1/16	+1/32
Danngr		890	2 1/16	...
DtBdcst		26	1 5/8	...
Dtaimg		2	6	+3/4
Daylgt		2	1/2	-1/8
Decora		358	2 3/16	-1/32
DeprAn		7	3 3/8	+1/8
DepA wt		51	7/8	-1/8
DiamEnt		1933	11/16	-1/16
DiamE wtA		10	1/8	...
DiamEn un		280	3 3/4	-1/4
DigBi		12	8 1/8	-1/8
DigPd un		11	6 1/4	+1 1/4
DigtlSol		20	7/8	+1/16
DrctCon		1617	1 1/8	-1/8
DrcCn wt		415	1/2	...
DixieN		5	1 1/8	-3/16
DocuCn		347	1 1/4	+1/8
DocuTcn		10	1 7/8	...
Dolco		8	4 1/8	+1/4
Dghtie	.16	67	4 1/4	...
Drivfn s		522	2	+1/16
DrgScr		21	3	+1/4
Duratek		96	3 1/4	-3/4
DynaGp		57	27/32	-3/32
Dynagn		580	5	-1/4
HartInds		2	3/4	...
HwkEn		4	11/16	...
Hawks		64	1/16	-1/32
HlthAdv s		15	2 1/16	-1/16
HltCre		64	13/32	+1/32
HlthClb		35	2 3/4	...
HltcrTc		1	1 3/16	-1/16
Hltplx		63	25/32	-3/32
HemaC		259	6 1/8	+3/8
Hickok	.15e	2	16	...
Hughes		608	2 1/8	+7/16
ICC Tch		276	2 7/8	+1/8
IEH Cp		31	5/32	-1/16
I-Flow s		20	2 3/4	...
IMRE		23	2 5/8	-1/16
IdanSft		40	1	...
ImgMgt		110	15/16	-3/32
Imex		5	1 13/16	...
Imucel h		2	1 9/16	-1/16
Imtec		1	3 1/2	+3/8
Imutec		1	1 3/8	-5/8
Inamed		415	2 7/8	-1/8
Incomnt		30	4 9/16	+1/8
IndSqS	1.44	3	18	...
IndEnt		842	11/32	...
Infonow		443	3 1/4	-1/8
Infonw wtB		10	1	+1/8
InfMgt		38	3	...
InfMg wt		50	2 3/8	-1/4
InfSolu		20	11/16	...
InnoVet		700	1 9/16	-5/16
InnoV wt		45	1	...
InnoV un		10	2 3/4	...
Inovo		30	8 1/4	+5/8
Insignia		57	2 3/4	...
InstaCl		222	11/16	...
Integral		27	11 1/2	+1/4
ItgPrc un		375	8 5/8	...
Intek		888	1 5/16	+3/8
IntLfe		16	11 3/4	+5/8
IntAbs		106	5 7/8	...
IntgRsc s		11	3	...
IntBas		26	1 3/8	...
IntlBus		208	1 13/16	+5/16
IntBu wt		1793	1 1/16	...
IntDst s		31	2 1/4	-1/8
IntlEl		52	9/16	-1/16
IntFast		20	5 7/8	...
Intphrm		10	29 7/8	+2 3/8
IntrLb		15	3 1/2	...
InvtDsg		11	1 7/8	...
Invitr		530	9/16	-5/16
Irvine		481	4	...
IrwnFn s	.80	8	64	+2
Isramc		75	1 1/2	...
JckCarl		1635	1/16	...
Jackpt wt		279	5 1/8	...
JackCty		13	18	...
Jako s		27	2 3/16	-1/4
JillEnt		116	1 1/16	-1/16
JimHi		140	15/16	+3/16
JonesSp		57	7/8	+1/8
Judicte		164	2 3/16	...
JuniprF		10	4	-1/8
KLH Eng		235	6	-1/8
KeithG		130	1 9/32	...
KdyWils		992	7 5/8	-1/4
KiddePd	.50e	3	39	...
KndrLr h		226	13/32	...
KngsRd		122	21/32	-3/32
KooKR		129	15/16	-5/16
L Rex		150	3 1/2	-1/2
LA Ent		9608	1/8	...
LSB SC	.60	16	18 1/4	+1 1/4
LaTeko		188	1	-1/8
Lamonts h		15	5/8	-1/16
Lancit		214	4	...
Lanc wt96		40	1 3/32	+1/32
LarDav		612	2 1/2	+1/4
LasVDsc		300	1 3/8	+1/8
LasVEnt		361	3 3/8	+1/4
LasVE wtA		496	1 11/16	...
LasVEE wtB		126	13/16	...
LasVE un		15	10 3/4	+5/8
Q Med		10	2	...
Qdrax		506	31/32	+1/32
QualPd t		155	1 1/8	...
QualSy		1	1 1/4	...
Questa		1	2 1/2	+1/2
RCLAcq		43	4 7/16	-1/16
RCL wtA		50	3/4	-1/16
RCL wtB		820	9/16	...
RCL un		88	5 5/8	...
RCM		50	3/8	+1/16
RT Inds		5	3 3/8	-1/8
RTI		4	1 1/16	-5/16
Ramtek		3	3/8	...
RandCa s		10	7	+5/8
RndAcc		171	1 1/2	-1/16
RawsnKo		150	7/16	-1/16
Raycom		703	1/4	+3/32
ReaGld		2	3/16	-1/8
RedRck		50	1 3/4	-1/4
RelbLfe	1.32a	6	40 1/4	+1 3/4
RenoA un		130	7	-1/8
Rentch		54	3 3/8	+1/16
RschFr		8	7 3/4	-1/4
Roadmst		855	1 3/8	...
Robern		371	2 1/16	-5/16
Robn wtB		44	5/16	-3/16
RochMd s		69	7 3/8	+3/8
RoyGld		333	1	+3/16
RoyInOp		20	1 1/8	-3/8
RoylInv	.45e	5	10 1/4	...
RoyceLb		1929	1 11/16	-1/16
Royce wt		50	11/32	...
Rubicn		40	3/8	-1/16
RyanMu		423	9/16	...
Ryka		651	1 5/16	+1/32
Ryka wt		145	5/16	+3/32
SA Hold s		28	13/16	-1/16
SBS En		111	5 1/4	-1/2
SGI Int		920	5 3/4	+1/4
SK Tch		157	15/16	-1/16
SMT un		326	3 3/8	-3/8
SOI Ind		1077	9/16	+1/32
SSE Tl		62	3 3/4	...
S2 Glf		1	4 3/8	+1/8
SageAlt		20	4 1/16	-3/8
SageA wt		120	1 7/16	+1/16
SageAnl		400	1 5/8	+1/4
SartgBd		31	1 1/8	...
SrtgB wt		70	1/4	-1/8
ScanGr		150	2 1/8	-3/16
Scnfrm		2	3/16	...
SchieldM		385	3/8	+1/32
Scorpn s		6585	31/32	-3/16
ScotLiq		40	1 3/8	...
ScriptSy		40	1 11/16	+1/16
SehwkD s		38	1 5/8	+1/16
Search		58	1 3/16	-1/16
Sector		927	1 5/8	+1/4
SecAsc wt		1236	1 3/16	...
SecEnv		100	9/16	-1/16
Seismd h		57	1 15/16	-3/16
Selvac		12	3/8	...
Sentex		2896	1/32	...
SrvSft		37	4	-3/16
Servtx pf		10	2 1/4	+3/4
Sherwd		52	21/32	+1/8
SlvMin g		3890	19/32	+1/16
SiteBas		3055	2 3/8	+1/8
Skoln wt		215	5/16	...
Skolnk pf		85	5 3/8	+1/4
Skolniks		27	5 5/8	+3/8
Skoln un		195	13	+1/2
Skylink		12	15/32	-5/32
Smtl wtB		10	1 3/8	+1/4
SftwrDv		201	3	...
Solitec s		10	3/4	-1/16
SolvEx h		110	1 5/16	-1/8
SonexR		130	1 5/16	+1/16
SouEdc		6	7	+1/2
SouldCp h		3453	1 11/16	+1/16
SprtSu		511	23/32	-1/16
SptSu wt		110	7/32	...
SptSu pf		10	3	...
SportK		450	1 15/32	+1/32
SptHero		95	9 3/8	-1/8

not registered with the Securities and Exchange Commission. The pink sheets are the last remnant of the good old days of the freewheeling and unregulated over-the-counter market.

PART IV.   THE PUBLIC REPORTING OF STOCK PRICES, INDEXES, AND TRADING

§14.23 HOW TO READ NEWSPAPER REPORTS OF SHARE TRADING

The financial pages of many newspapers give considerable information about the trading activity each day on the various exchanges and over-the-counter. Depending on the newspaper and the locale of its readership, information may be given about the trading in specific stocks of local interest as well as the most important stocks traded on the NYSE. The Wall Street Journal is the most widely distributed national financial newspaper today, and it contains a wealth of information about trading activity, the investment characteristics of specific stocks traded on the various exchanges and over-the-counter, and other information about investments. The sections that follow introduce the reader to the major tables published regularly in the Journal.

§14.24 THE LEVEL OF NYSE TRADING GENERALLY

Table 14-5 on page 342 shows the breakdown of trading in NYSE listed stocks by market, and on a half hourly basis, for Wednesday, September 9, 1992 (a routine day chosen more or less at random). About 211,000,000 shares were traded, a slightly higher than average trading day for that period. Trades executed on the regional exchanges are included in the composite figures and are broken down separately. While the NYSE still accounts for the great bulk of trading, the regional exchanges' share of the market for trades involving less than 3,000 shares has gradually increased to close to 30 percent of the trades of that size. Of course, when trades of all sizes are concerned, the NYSE still predominates since it executes trades for more than 80 percent of the stock traded on any day.

Table 14-6 is part of The Wall Street Journal daily diary that shows overall price movements for all stocks traded on Wednesday, September 9, Tuesday, September 8, and Wednesday, September 2. Block trades, the last entry, are single trades of 10,000 shares or more discussed in section

Table 14-5

BREAKDOWN OF TRADING IN NYSE STOCKS (9:30 a.m. to 4 p.m. EST)							
BY MARKET	Wed	Tues	WK AGO	½-HOURLY	Wed	Tues	WK AGO
New York	172,890,000	160,930,000	187,010,000	9:30-10	21,830,000	19,440,000	22,770,000
Midwest	8,608,900	8,871,000	9,741,400	10-10:30	15,550,000	13,480,000	15,510,000
Pacific	5,596,200	5,275,600	7,062,900	10:30-11	14,430,000	13,310,000	14,360,000
NASD	14,588,110	13,330,980	15,684,560	11-11:30	15,640,000	11,450,000	13,580,000
Phila	4,005,800	2,579,900	5,732,800	11:30-12	11,740,000	8,800,000	13,080,000
Boston	2,900,600	2,783,300	9,037,900	12-12:30	11,440,000	10,750,000	10,720,000
Cincinnati	2,454,000	2,118,800	2,473,000	12:30-1	9,250,000	8,270,000	10,060,000
Instinet	128,600	385,100	653,600	1-1:30	7,830,000	9,740,000	8,790,000
Composite	211,172,210	196,274,680	237,396,160	1:30-2	8,180,000	9,730,000	10,200,000
				2-2:30	9,100,000	11,480,000	12,750,000
				2:30-3	10,590,000	8,660,000	13,820,000
				3-3:30	16,990,000	15,680,000	19,350,000
				3:30-4	20,320,000	20,140,000	22,020,000

14.17. They are, of course, indicative of the degree of institutional investors' market activities.

The "closing tick" is the number of advancing stocks minus the number of declining stocks. The Closing ARMs (trin) is a comparison of the number of advancing and declining issues with the volume of shares rising and falling. Generally, a trin of less than 1.00 indicates buying demand; above 1.00 indicates selling pressure.

§14.25 INFORMATION ABOUT ACTIVE STOCKS

Tables 14.7 and 14.8 give information about the most active stocks traded on the NYSE on Wednesday, September 9, 1992, both from the standpoint of the most active issues and of the largest percentage gainers and losers. It may be noted that none of the volume leaders in Table 14-7 made the list of percentage gainers or percentage losers. This is to be expected because almost all large percentage gainers or losers are relatively low-priced stocks.

§14.26 INFORMATION ABOUT SPECIFIC NYSE STOCKS

Table 14-9 sets forth an excerpt from The Wall Street Journal NYSE table for trading in NYSE stocks that covers about two-thirds of the stocks that begin with the letter "I" for Thursday, September 10, 1992. The letter abbreviations, underlining, and bold facing in Table 14-9 are explained in Table 14-10, the Explanatory Notes that accompany this table. It may be

Table 14-6   Table 14-7

DIARIES

NYSE	WED	TUE	WK AGO
Issues traded	2,359	2,335	2,326
Advances	964	585	1,110
Declines	801	1,120	617
Unchanged	594	630	599
New highs	58	61	65
New lows	26	26	17
zAdv vol (000)	90,521	36,257	114,642
zDecl vol (000)	57,192	91,404	45,563
zTotal vol (000)	172,890	160,930	187,010
Closing tick[1]	+152	−204	+300
Closing Arms[2] (trin)	.76	1.32	.71
zBlock trades	3,927	3,319	4,417

MOST ACTIVE ISSUES

NYSE	VOLUME	CLOSE	CHANGE	
GenMotor	3,286,000	34	......	
ChemBank	2,250,600	31	−	$\frac{1}{2}$
Citicorp	2,214,000	$15\frac{3}{8}$	−	$\frac{1}{8}$
PhilipMor	1,696,600	$x84\frac{1}{8}$	−	$\frac{1}{4}$
TelefMex	1,671,900	$43\frac{1}{4}$	−	$1\frac{5}{8}$
RJR Nabisco	1,634,600	$8\frac{7}{8}$	−	$\frac{1}{8}$
GTE	1,602,200	$33\frac{1}{4}$	+	$\frac{1}{2}$
Compaq	1,576,000	$32\frac{3}{4}$	−	$\frac{3}{8}$
CocaCola	1,399,400	$x44\frac{1}{8}$	+	$\frac{3}{4}$
GlaxoHldg	1,390,000	$29\frac{3}{8}$	−	$\frac{1}{4}$
Limited Inc	1,384,500	$23\frac{1}{8}$	......	
Merck	1,365,400	$48\frac{1}{8}$	−	$\frac{1}{8}$
WasteMgt	1,328,200	$34\frac{3}{8}$	+	$\frac{3}{4}$
NtlSemi	1,317,900	$11\frac{1}{8}$	+	$\frac{1}{2}$
AmT&T	1,214,800	$42\frac{5}{8}$	+	$\frac{1}{2}$

Table 14-8

PRICE PERCENTAGE GAINERS ...

NYSE	VOL	CLOSE	CHANGE		% CHG
Live Entmt.pf	5,400	$5\frac{1}{4}$	+	$\frac{3}{4}$	+ 16.7
DataGen	288,200	$9\frac{1}{4}$	+	1	+ 12.1
LSILogic	103,200	$6\frac{1}{8}$	+	$\frac{5}{8}$	+ 11.4
AmMedRespns	71,200	$9\frac{7}{8}$	+	$\frac{7}{8}$	+ 9.7
ConvexCptr	195,800	6	+	$\frac{1}{2}$	+ 9.1
DycomInd	14,200	$6\frac{1}{8}$	+	$\frac{1}{2}$	+ 8.9
ConStore	258,100	$13\frac{3}{8}$	+	1	+ 8.1
EuroWtFd	73,000	$7\frac{3}{8}$	+	$\frac{1}{2}$	+ 7.3
T2Medical	122,500	$x26\frac{7}{8}$	+	$1\frac{3}{4}$	+ 7.0
GitanoGp	449,100	6	+	$\frac{3}{8}$	+ 6.7
RollinsEnvr	283,400	12	+	$\frac{3}{4}$	+ 6.7
NtlMedia	154,900	6	+	$\frac{3}{8}$	+ 6.7
NoSta$7pf	7,520	$98\frac{1}{8}$	+	$6\frac{1}{8}$	+ 6.7
NorthForkBcp	57,500	$6\frac{1}{4}$	+	$\frac{3}{8}$	+ 6.4
BurlgtnCoat	84,200	$16\frac{3}{4}$	+	1	+ 6.3
AlliedPdts	2,400	$2\frac{1}{8}$	+	$\frac{1}{8}$	+ 6.3
RecogEqpt	46,600	$10\frac{3}{4}$	+	$\frac{5}{8}$	+ 6.2
CampblSoup	708,800	$39\frac{1}{4}$	+	$2\frac{1}{4}$	+ 6.1
DigitalEqp	465,500	$37\frac{3}{4}$	+	$2\frac{1}{8}$	+ 6.0
EQKRlty	4,500	$2\frac{1}{4}$	+	$\frac{1}{8}$	+ 5.9

AND LOSERS

NYSE	VOL	CLOSE	CHANGE		% CHG
EngChina	40,000	$22\frac{5}{8}$	−	$5\frac{5}{8}$	− 19.9
GulfUSA	27,800	$2\frac{1}{8}$	−	$\frac{1}{4}$	− 10.5
vjSalant	5,400	$4\frac{7}{8}$	−	$\frac{1}{2}$	− 9.3
ICNPharm	325,200	$7\frac{3}{8}$	−	$\frac{5}{8}$	− 7.8
Patten	8,200	$1\frac{7}{8}$	−	$\frac{1}{8}$	− 6.3
LandsEnd	102,200	25	−	$1\frac{5}{8}$	− 6.1
Showboat	128,600	x10	−	$\frac{5}{8}$	− 5.9
CooperCo	18,400	2	−	$\frac{1}{8}$	− 5.9
AtlasCp	14,100	$4\frac{1}{8}$	−	$\frac{1}{4}$	− 5.7
Repsol	369,500	$25\frac{1}{2}$	−	$1\frac{1}{2}$	− 5.6
WillcoxGbs	43,800	$10\frac{1}{2}$	−	$\frac{5}{8}$	− 5.6
BET	33,100	$8\frac{1}{2}$	−	$\frac{1}{2}$	− 5.6
EmersRadio	8,100	$2\frac{1}{8}$	−	$\frac{1}{8}$	− 5.6
Craig	8,000	$8\frac{1}{2}$	−	$\frac{1}{2}$	− 5.6
WestnWaste	6,400	$10\frac{1}{2}$	−	$\frac{5}{8}$	− 5.6
Vencor	479,500	$32\frac{1}{4}$	−	$1\frac{7}{8}$	− 5.5
GiantInd	15,000	$4\frac{5}{8}$	−	$\frac{1}{4}$	− 5.4
Avalon	14,500	$2\frac{1}{4}$	−	$\frac{1}{8}$	− 5.3
DyersburgCp	6,600	7	−	$\frac{3}{8}$	− 5.1
UnitCp	10,200	$2\frac{3}{8}$	−	$\frac{1}{8}$	− 5.0

useful to consider the information about each stock that appears in the headings of this table.

Each stock is identified by an abbreviated name, for example, International Paper Company is identified as IntPaper, and the ticker symbol used to identify the stock in trading (IP). Preferred stocks (discussed in Chapter 17) use the trading symbol of the common stock with a further identification symbol.

Table 14-9

NEW YORK STOCK EXCHANGE COMPOSITE TRANSACTIONS

	52 Weeks Hi	52 Weeks Lo	Stock	Sym	Div	Yld %	PE	Vol 100s	Hi	Lo	Close	Net Chg
			-I-I-I-									
	19⅛	12⅞	IBP Inc	IBP	.20	1.2	15	2092	17½	17	17	– ⅛
	3⅞	2	ICM Prop	ICM		...	...	17	3½	3⅜	3½	...
	25⅜	**5½**	**ICN Pharm**	**ICN**		**...**	**10**	**1655**	**8**	**7½**	**7¾**	**+ ⅜**
	31⅜	26⅜	IES Ind	IES	2.10	6.8	16	178	30¾	30⅝	30¾	...
x	68	37½	IMC Fertlzr	IFL	1.08	2.4	11	x479	45	44⅜	44⅜	– ¼
	14½	6	IMCO Recyc	IMR		...	20	61	11¾	11½	11¾	+ ¼
	19⅛	16⅞	INA Invest	IIS	1.52	8.2	...	63	18¾	18⅜	18⅝	...
	27⅜	20¼	IP Timber	IPT	2.88	10.8	9	100	26¾	26¼	26¾	+ ⅛
▲	11	8⅜	IRT Prop	IRT	.80	7.4	35	114	11⅛	10⅞	10⅞	– ⅛
	70⅝	50	ITT Cp	ITT	1.84	2.8	13	5011	65¾	64¾	65	– ¼
	28¾	24⅜	IdahoPwr	IDA	1.86	6.9	18	178	27	26¾	27	+ ⅛
	21¾	14⅞	IdexCp	IEX		...	13	144	18⅜	18¼	18⅜	+ ⅛
s	25½	16½	IllCentl	IC	.20i	1.0	11	2829	19⅞	19⅜	19½	+ ¼
	25⅛	19¼	IllPwr	IPC	.80e	3.8	18	1556	21½	21⅛	21¼	– ⅜
	27	23⅜	IllPwr pf		2.04	7.6	...	z100	26¾	26¾	26¾	+ ¾
	27	23¼	IllPwr pf		2.10	8.4	...	z300	25¼	25	25	– ½
	28½	25	IllPwr pf		2.21	8.0	...	z900	28	27⅝	27⅝	– ⅞
	30	25¾	IllPwr pf		2.35	7.8	...	z200	30	30	30	+ ½
	51	45½	IllPwr pf		4.12	8.2	...	z1120	50½	49½	50	...
	48	41⅝	IllPwr pf		3.78	8.0	...	z13980	47½	47⅜	47⅜	...
	53¾	50	IllPwr pf		4.26	8.4	...	326	51	50⅞	51	+ ½
	51	42¾	IllPwr pf		3.50	7.0	...	2	50	50	50	+1¼
	44½	34¾	IllPwr pf		3.00	7.4	...	170	41½	40½	40½	– ½
	51	44½	IllPwr pf		4.00	8.3	...	5	48⅜	48⅜	48⅜	+ ⅛
	70⅝	54½	Ill Tool	ITW	.88	1.3	20	300	65¼	63⅝	65¼	+1⅝
sx	46⅝	28⅞	IMCERA	IMA	.40	1.1	22	x820	36	35¾	35⅞	+ ⅛
▲x	63	50¼	IMCERA pf		4.00	6.3	...	x1	64	64	64	+2
	14⅝	9⅜	ImoInd	IMD	.50	4.5	21	568	11⅛	11	11	– ⅛
	101⅜	81⅜	ICI	ICI	5.35e	6.4	15	305	84⅛	83¾	84	+ ½
	34⅜	25¼	Inco Ltd	N	1.00	3.9	...	1302	25⅝	25¼	25⅝	...
	26	12¾	IndiaGrFd	IGF	.93e	4.9	...	196	19	18¾	19	+ ⅛
▲	97	87	IndiMich pf		7.76	7.9	...	z9310	98¾	96	98¾	+4¼
	27¼	24⅜	IndiMich pf		2.15	8.3	...	21	26	25⅝	25⅞	...
	27½	24½	IndiMich pf		2.25	8.4	...	11	26¾	26½	26¾	+ ¼
	30¾	24¼	IndiEngy	IEI	1.48	5.1	17	28	29⅜	29	29¼	...
	11⅛	7¼	IndonesiaFd	IF	.10e	1.1	...	5	9	9	9	– ¼
n	**9⅜**	**6⅜**	**Indresco**	**ID**		**...**	**...**	**10113**	**7⅜**	**6½**	**7¼**	**+ ¾**
s	33⅛	21	IngersolRand	IR	.70	2.6	18	4928	27¼	26⅝	27⅛	+ ⅜
	27	17⅜	InlandStl	IAD		...	...	538	20⅛	19⅝	19¾	– ⅜
n	22⅞	14⅞	Integon	IN	.10e	.5	12	47	21¼	20¾	21	...
	7¾	3	Intellicall	ICL		...	...	118	3⅛	3	3⅛	...
	1⅛	**½**	**IntlogcTra**	**IT**		**...**	**...**	**45**	**¾**	**11/16**	**¾**	**+ 1/16**
	19½	13½	IntrRgnlFnl	IFG	.20e	1.4	4	774	15	14¼	14½	– ¾
	22⅞	20	IntcapSec	ICB	1.86	8.4	...	82	22½	22¼	22¼	– ⅜
	17¾	14¾	IntcapMnBd	IMB	1.05a	6.3	...	18	16¾	16⅝	16¾	+ ¼
n	15⅞	14⅞	IntercpMuniTr	IMT	.98	6.3	...	395	15½	15⅜	15½	+ ⅛
n	16	14¼	IntcapQual	IQT	1.08	7.0	...	55	15⅝	15⅜	15½	...
n	8⅝	6⅝	Interco	ISS		...	...	15	7¼	7⅛	7¼	+ ¼
	9⅜	3	Intlake	IK		...	...	210	4¼	4	4⅛	...
	25	18⅜	IntAlum	IAL	1.00	4.9	96	46	20¼	19¾	20¼	+ ⅝
	106⅜	81⅝	IBM	IBM	4.84	5.5	11	10967	87½	86⅝	87½	+ ⅝
n	15⅜	10⅝	IntlFamEntn B	FAM		...	...	154	11⅜	11⅛	11¼	– ⅛
	111¼	81½	IntFlavor	IFF	2.72	2.5	23	613	109	108⅜	109	+ ¼
▲	40	12	IntGameTech	IGT		...	46	4420	40⅝	39⅞	40⅜	+ ⅝
	31¼	23¼	IntMultfood	IMC	.80	3.1	13	854	25⅝	25¼	25⅝	+ ¼
	78½	61	IntPaper	IP	1.68	2.6	19	8498	65	62½	64¾	+2⅛
	26	11⅛	IntRecvry	INT		...	13	16	14	13¾	14	...
	20¼	7⅜	IntRect	IRF		...	21	314	9⅞	9½	9¾	+ ⅛
	24⅞	17	IntShiphld	ISH	.20	1.0	10	2	19½	19½	19½	– ⅛
n	**16⅛**	**9⅝**	**IntSpcPdt**	**ISP**	**.03e**	**.2**	**22**	**1102**	**13¼**	**12½**	**13⅛**	**+ ⅝**
	9⅛	4⅝	IntTech	ITX		...	14	725	5¼	5	5⅛	– ⅛
s	**34½**	**22⅛**	**IntpubGp**	**IPG**	**.46**	**1.3**	**24**	**902**	**34¼**	**32⅞**	**34¼**	**+1¾**
	19⅜	14⅜	IntstBaker	IBC	.44	2.4	10	1761	18½	17¾	18⅜	+ ½
	8⅛	3	IntstJhnsn	IS		...	6	150	6¾	6⅝	6⅝	– ⅛
	35¼	29⅞	IntstPwr	IPW	2.08	6.6	13	34	31⅞	31⅝	31¾	...
	31	26	IntstPwr pr		2.28	8.0	...	z200	29	28⅝	28⅝	– ⅜
	26¾	11½	IntertanInc	ITN		...	21	61	12⅞	12¾	12⅞	+ ⅛
	67½	39¾	Ionics	ION		...	31	13	52½	52	52⅛	– ⅛
	26⅜	23½	IowaIllGas	IWG	1.73	7.1	14	205	24½	24¼	24½	+ ⅛

Table 14-10

EXPLANATORY NOTES

The following explanations apply to New York and American exchange listed issues and the National Association of Securities Dealers Automated Quotations system's over-the-counter securities. Exchange prices are composite quotations that include trades on the Midwest, Pacific, Philadelphia, Boston and Cincinnati exchanges and reported by the NASD and Instinet.

Boldfaced quotations highlight those issues whose price changed by 5% or more from their previous closing price.

Underlined quotations are those stocks with large changes in volume, per exchange, compared with the issue's average trading volume. The calculation includes common stocks of $5 a share or more with an average volume over 65 trading days of at least 5,000 shares. The underlined quotations are for the 40 largest volume percentage leaders on the NYSE and the NASD's National Market System. It includes the 20 largest volume percentage gainers on the Amex.

The 52-week high and low columns show the highest and lowest price of the issue during the preceding 52 weeks plus the current week, but not the latest trading day. These ranges are adjusted to reflect stock payouts of 1% or more, and cash dividends of 10% or more.

Dividend rates, unless noted, are annual disbursements based on the last quarterly, semiannual, or annual declaration. Special or extra dividends, special situations or payments not designated as regular are identified by footnotes.

Yield is defined as the dividends paid by a company on its securities, expressed as a percentage of price.

The P/E ratio is determined by dividing the price of a share of stock by its company's earnings per share of that stock. These earnings are the primary per-share earnings reported by the company for the most recent four quarters. Extraordinary items are usually excluded.

Sales figures are the unofficial daily total of shares traded, quoted in hundreds (two zeros omitted).

Exchange ticker symbols are shown for all New York and American exchange common stocks, and Dow Jones News/Retrieval symbols are listed for Class A and Class B shares listed on both markets. Nasdaq symbols are listed for all Nasdaq NMS issues. A more detailed explanation of Nasdaq ticker symbols appears with the NMS listings.

FOOTNOTES: ▲-New 52-week high. ▼-New 52-week low. a-Extra dividend or extras in addition to the regular dividend. b-Indicates annual rate of the cash dividend and that a stock dividend was paid. c-Liquidating dividend. e-Indicates a dividend was declared or paid in the preceding 12 months, but that there isn't a regular dividend rate. g-Indicates the dividend and earnings are expressed in Canadian money. The stock trades in U.S. dollars. No yield or P/E ratio is shown. h-Indicates a temporary exception to Nasdaq qualifications. i-Indicates amount declared or paid after a stock dividend or split. j-Indicates dividend was paid this year, and that at the last dividend meeting a dividend was omitted or deferred. k-Indicates dividend declared or paid this year on cumulative issues with dividends in arrears. n-Newly issued in the past 52 weeks. The high-low range begins with the start of trading and doesn't cover the entire period. pf-Preferred. pp-Holder owes installment(s) of purchase price. pr-Preference. r-Indicates a cash dividend declared or paid in the preceding 12 months, plus a stock dividend. rt-Rights. s-Stock split or stock dividend amounting to 20% or more in the past 52 weeks. The high-low price is adjusted from the old stock. Dividend calculations begin with the date the split was paid or the stock dividend occurred. t-Paid in stock in the preceding 12 months, estimated cash value on ex-dividend or ex-distribution date, except Nasdaq listings where payments are in stock. un-Units. v-Trading halted on primary market. vi-In bankruptcy or receivership or being reorganized under the Bankruptcy Code, or securities assumed by such companies. wd-When distributed. wi-When issued. wt-Warrants. ww-With warrants. x-Ex-dividend or ex-rights. xw-Without warrants. y-Ex-dividend and sales in full, not in hundreds. z-Sales in full, not in hundreds.

1. The "52 Weeks: Hi-Lo" data to the left of the names simply reflect the highest and lowest prices during the previous 52 weeks. Prices of the last day's trading are not reflected in the 52-week figure.

2. The "High-Low-Close-Net Change" data to the far right of the table reflect the latest day's trading, in this case Thursday, September 10, 1992. For example, International Paper traded in the range between 62½ and 65, closing at 64¾, closing 2⅛ points above yesterday's close. In the previous 52 weeks, International Paper had traded in the range 61 to 78½; while the price rose significantly on September 10, the stock is still trading near its low for the year. If the price had broken through either the 52-week high or 52-week low figure (it did not on September 10) an upward carat

(for up) or a downward carat (for down) would have been added in the left margin, and the 52-week figures to the left would have been changed the following day.

A special daily table of new highs and new lows is also printed by The Wall Street Journal. See Table 14-11.

The "Net Change" figure represents the change between the closing price on September 10 and the closing price on the previous trading day, which in this case was September 9. The net change figure thus is unrelated to the high and low trading prices during the day.

3. The entry under "Div" is simply the dividend paid by International Paper. As described in section 14.9, most NYSE companies maintain a stable dividend over time; International Paper pays $1.68 per year, or $0.42 per quarter.

4. The entry under "Yld" ("Yield") is the approximate current sales price of a share of stock divided into the regular dividend per share. Thus, International Paper's dividend of $1.68 per share is a 2.6 percent return on a $64 investment. This number, of course, can be calculated directly from other information shown on this page.

5. The "Sales 100s" column describes the number of round lots traded on September 10. On that date 849,800 shares of International Paper were traded. The approximate value of International Paper

---

Table 14-11

NYSE HIGHS/LOWS

Thursday, September 10, 1992

NEW HIGHS — 76

ACMSpect	EnronLiq n	Kysor	Rollins
Albtsn	EnronOG	LeeEnt	SFER pf
AlcatlAsh n	EuroWtFd	LeucadiaNtl	ScieAtl
AmMedResp n	FtCmwFC n	MGMG rt	Singer
ApacheCp	FlowerInd	MarshInd	SmthBck s
BeckmanIns	FutureGer	MarvelEnt s	SpringsInd
BosE 8.88pf	GenCinema	Motorola	SunMed s
BroadInc pfP	GenMotE prC	MunihncFd	Tadrian n
BurlCt s	GtyNatl n	Mylan s	TexasInst
CBS	Haemonet	NatSemi	TexInst pf
CNA IncShr	HlthCP s	NICOR Inc	ThomBett
Circus s	HelmrPayne	NorStaPw	20CentInd s
ColgP	Irt prop	OklaGE pf	UnilvrNV
CwE 8.40pfF	Imcera pf	OldRep pf	UnEl 6.40pf
ConAgr pf E	IndM 7.76pf	PattenCp	Wellcome n
CyprusMn	IntGame	PhilVnH s	WstnGasRs
CypresMn pf	JonesApp	Polaroid s	WinnDixie
DPL wi	Kellogg s	PromusCo	Wrigley
EnglhrdCp	Kohls n	QuestValCap	Wrigley wi

NEW LOWS — 22

ASA Ltd	Craig	KanebSvc	Sizzler
Boeing	DiagPrd	Kennemetal	Tesoro Pet
CdnPac g	EngChina	LatAmDlr n	Tiphook ADR
Chase pfL	FstIntrstA	Mestek	Tremnt
Chyron n	HCA Hosp n	PatrtGlbl n	Valhi
CooperCo	HuntgIntl		

s-Split or stock dividend of 25 per cent or more in the past 52 weeks. High-low range is adjusted from old stock. n-New issue in past 52 weeks and does not cover the entire 52 week period.

traded in just one routine day was approximately 8,498 × 100 × $64, or something over $54,387,000. And International Paper represents only one of the "I"s, and the "I"s represent only a small fraction of all listed stocks; clearly billions of dollars of stocks are traded on the NYSE each day.

6. The entry under "P-E Ratio" (price/earnings ratio) is the ratio the current stock price for International Paper bears to its earnings per share for the prior reporting period. International Paper's price of $64 is 19 times its earnings per share last year. This number, unlike the yield, cannot be calculated from other information appearing on this page; earnings per share for International Paper were reported in The Wall Street Journal some time earlier and that number is essential for calculating the P-E ratio.

   The calculations of yield and P-E ratio are not adjusted daily and are indications of range. Because physical space is at a premium on this page, calculations are not carried out to any degree of precision.

   If one looks through the "I"s, one sees that there are companies that show a positive yield but have no P-E ratio. An example is Inco Limited. How can that be? Another company, IMCO Recycling has a P-E ratio of 20 but no yield. How can that be? Hint: Can a company pay a dividend even though it has no current earnings? Can a company have current earnings and pay no dividend?

§14.27 INFORMATION ABOUT SPECIFIC AMEX STOCKS

As indicated above the American Stock Exchange is considerably smaller than the NYSE and generally trades in smaller companies with lower priced stocks. Tables 14-12, 14-13, 14-14, 14-15, and 14-16 summarize operations and trading in this market on September 10, 1992. It will be noted that the stocks beginning with "I" traded on this Exchange are much fewer and generally lower priced than stocks traded on the NYSE.

§14.28 INFORMATION ABOUT SPECIFIC NASDAQ NATIONAL MARKET STOCKS

Tables 14-17, 14-18, 14-19, and 14-20 reflect the Friday, September 11, 1992 activity in the National Market System, and Table 14-21 shows the price quotations for a portion of the "I"s in that market. From these tables, it would be impossible to tell that the method of completing trades in this

Table 14-12   Table 14-13

DIARIES

AMEX	WED	TUE	WK AGO
Issues traded	717	729	888
Advances	267	284	357
Declines	222	223	357
Unchanged	228	222	174
New highs	13	17	39
New lows	8	8	37
zAdv vol (000)	4,296	5,593	16,860
zDecl vol (000)	2,419	3,302	15,368
zTotal vol (000)	8,917	11,487	40,987
Comp vol (000)	11,138	13,796	50,915
zBlock trades	n.a.	202	y487

MOST ACTIVE ISSUES

AMEX	VOLUME	CLOSE	CHANGE	
WangLab B	510,400	$\frac{1}{2}$	+	$\frac{1}{16}$
Amdahl	383,600	$14\frac{1}{2}$	+	$\frac{1}{4}$
NaborsInd	374,400	8	+	$\frac{1}{4}$
FruitLoom	350,900	$41\frac{5}{8}$	+	$\frac{1}{2}$
CitiznFst rt	331,400	$\frac{3}{16}$	......	

Table 14-14

PRICE PERCENTAGE GAINERS ...

AMEX	VOL	CLOSE	CHANGE		% CHG	
AmFructse B	125,500	$22\frac{3}{4}$	+	$3\frac{3}{4}$	+	19.7
FarragutMtg	107,400	$6\frac{1}{2}$	+	$\frac{5}{8}$	+	10.6
ICH	119,900	$4\frac{1}{8}$	+	$\frac{3}{8}$	+	10.0
WstbrdgeCap	21,700	$4\frac{1}{8}$	+	$\frac{3}{8}$	+	10.0
KitMfg	5,000	$5\frac{1}{2}$	+	$\frac{1}{2}$	+	10.0

AND LOSERS

AMEX	VOL	CLOSE	CHANGE		% CHG
IncstarCp	20,000	5	−	$\frac{1}{2}$	− 9.1
FountnPwrbt	2,000	$2\frac{1}{4}$	−	$\frac{3}{16}$	− 7.7
WaterhsInv	67,100	$12\frac{1}{8}$	−	1	− 7.6
SystemInd	10,100	$2\frac{11}{16}$	−	$\frac{3}{16}$	− 6.5
Teleflex	83,300	$29\frac{3}{4}$	−	2	− 6.3

Table 14-15

VOLUME PERCENTAGE LEADERS

AMEX	VOL	%DIF*	CLOSE	CHANGE	
BSN	113,200	1074.3	7	......	
FarragutMtg	107,400	1013.9	$6\frac{1}{2}$	+	$\frac{5}{8}$
AmRelnce	34,600	560.9	$14\frac{1}{2}$	−	$\frac{1}{2}$
AirExprss	127,800	396.1	$22\frac{7}{8}$	−	$\frac{1}{8}$
ConversnInd	194,300	388.3	8	−	$\frac{1}{8}$

market is quite different from that of the NYSE and other traditional exchanges.

The National Market lists many types of securities in addition to common stocks. They are identified by the distinctive "fifth letter" approach described in the note to Table 14-21.

Table 14-4 (see page 340) is a sample of the small capital market tabulation for that portion of the over-the-counter market.

Table 14-16

AMERICAN STOCK EXCHANGE COMPOSITE TRANSACTIONS

	52 Weeks Hi	52 Weeks Lo	Stock	Sym	Div	Yld %	PE	Vol 100s	Hi	Lo	Close	Net Chg
			-I-I-I-									
	6 3/8	**2 1/2**	**ICH**	**ICH**		...	...	**1199**	**4 1/8**	**3 3/4**	**4 1/8**	**+ 3/8**
	16	11 1/4	ICH pf		1.75	11.4	...	100	15 3/8	15	15 3/8	+ 1/4
	11 1/4	4	ICN Biomed	BIM	.15	3.5	39	27	4 1/4	4 1/8	4 1/4	...
	23	8 7/8	IGI Inc	IG		...	106	123	10 5/8	10 1/2	10 5/8	+ 1/8
	2 1/4	9/16	IRT Cp	IX		...	20	14	1	1	1	...
	4 1/2	**2 1/4**	**Identix**	**IDX**		...	...	**138**	**2 15/16**	**2 11/16**	**2 15/16**	**+ 3/16**
	17 1/2	11	ImperlHly	IHK	.48	3.9	...	17	12 3/8	12 3/8	12 3/8	...
	47 7/8	31 7/8	ImperOil g	IMO	1.80	...	...	311	39 3/8	39 1/8	39 1/4	− 1/8
s	6 5/8	4 7/8	IncoOpRlty	IOT		...	...	5	5 1/4	5 1/4	5 1/4	− 1/8
	9	**4 1/2**	**IncstarCp**	**ISR**		...	**19**	**200**	**5 1/2**	**5**	**5**	**− 1/2**
	11 1/4	8 1/4	InefMktFd	IMF	.67e	7.1	...	49	9 3/8	9 3/8	9 3/8	...
	2 7/8	5/8	InfoDisplay	IDT		...	7	5	7/8	7/8	7/8	...
	10 1/2	6 1/4	Insteellnd	III	.24b	2.6	15	44	9 3/8	9 1/4	9 3/8	+ 1/8
	13 3/4	8 1/2	InstronCp	ISN	.12a	1.3	12	8	9 1/2	9 1/4	9 1/2	+ 1/4
	8 1/4	4	InstrSys pf		.25t	4.4	...	10	5 5/8	5 5/8	5 5/8	...
	8 1/4	3 3/4	InstrSys	ISY		...	8	435	5 1/4	5 1/8	5 1/8	...
	15 1/4	9 1/2	IntchangeFnl	ISB	.70	4.9	9	10	14 5/8	14 3/8	14 3/8	− 3/8
	13 1/4	5 1/4	IntrmagGen	IMG	.31t	4.6	13	156	6 7/8	6 5/8	6 3/4	...
	1	**1/8**	**Intmark**	**IMI**		...	...	**179**	**5/16**	**5/16**	**5/16**	**+ 1/16**
	10 3/8	3 3/8	IntColnEngy	KCN		...	...	162	10 3/8	10	10 1/4	+ 1/8
	10 5/8	4 3/4	IntMoblMach	IMM		...	...	619	5 1/4	5 1/8	5 1/4	...
	2 7/8	**3/4**	**IntMovieGp**	**IMV**		...	**10**	**302**	**1**	**1**	**1**	**+ 1/8**
▼	**17 3/8**	**6 5/8**	**IntMurex**	**MXX**		...	...	**1869**	**7 1/8**	**6 1/2**	**6 5/8**	**− 3/8**
	8 1/2	1	IntMurex wt			...	...	147	1 1/8	1	1 1/8	...
	9 3/4	**2 7/8**	**IntTestSvc**	**ITS**		...	...	**18**	**3**	**2 7/8**	**2 7/8**	**− 1/4**
	7 1/2	1 7/8	IntThrgbrd	ITB		...	...	4	2 11/16	2 5/8	2 5/8	...
▲	5 7/8	1 7/8	IntThrgbrd pf			...	...	9	6 1/8	6	6	+ 1/4
	6 1/8	2 1/4	IntrvisBk	IBI		...	...	233	3 5/8	3 1/4	3 1/4	...
s	41 3/8	18 3/4	IvaxCp	IVX		...	115	1394	27 5/8	27	27 1/2	+ 1/4

PART V. STOCK MARKET INDEXES

§14.29 THE DOW JONES INDUSTRIAL AVERAGE

Stock market indexes or averages attempt to measure the general level of stock prices over time. Of these the best known is the Dow Jones average, which is actually four different averages: of 30 industrial companies, 20 transportation stocks, 15 utilities, and a composite average of the 65 stocks. The Dow Jones dates back to the end of the nineteenth century, and the index numbers purport to be comparable to those in earlier years.

Table 14-22 is the September 8, 1992 "Stock Market Data Bank" as they appear in the September 9, 1992 Wall Street Journal. The first entries show the daily entries for the Dow Jones averages. Dow Jones not only owns the averages but also the Wall Street Journal itself and the broad tape, which is the major Teletype news service covering financial, business, and national news.

The 65 stocks that make up this average are set forth in Table 14-23, as is the method of calculation of the averages themselves. The divisor shown next to the titles of the hourly data is divided into the total value

Table 14-17   Table 14-18

DIARIES

NASDAQ	FRI	THUR	WK AGO
Issues traded	4,181	4,180	4,181
Advances	1,288	1,356	1,608
Declines	1,096	1,011	1,513
Unchanged	1,797	1,813	1,060
New highs	105	92	217
New lows	42	58	186
Adv vol (000)	108,579	134,808	379,042
Decl vol (000)	55,947	40,382	207,430
Total vol (000)	188,327	200,938	683,426
Block trades	3,728	4,079	13,052

MOST ACTIVE ISSUES

NASDAQ	VOLUME	CLOSE	CHANGE
Biomet	3,811,000	18	− 3½
MCI Comm	3,128,600	35¼	+ ⅜
3ComCp	2,354,700	13⅝	+ ⅜
AST Rsrch	2,179,500	15¼	+ 1
SunMicrsys	2,171,700	31⅛	+ ⅜
OracleSys	2,024,800	19¾	+ ⅜
SequentCptr	1,743,400	16⅝	+ ⅝
TeleComm A	1,643,900	19⅛	+ ⅜
DellCptr	1,642,100	26¼	− ¼
AppleCptr	1,606,100	47⅝	− 1⅝
Novell	1,515,200	54⅛	+ ⅝
Borland	1,462,100	46⅜	− 1⅛
Intel	1,459,900	64	− ¼

Table 14-19

PRICE PERCENTAGE GAINERS . . .

NASDAQ	VOL	CLOSE	CHANGE		% CHG	
ConsumFnl	4,500	2¾	+	¾	+	37.5
PonderInd	196,000	4¼	+	1	+	30.8
GtCountryBk	15,100	2¾	+	⅝	+	29.4
TodaysMan	261,600	14¼	+	2½	+	21.3
Ciprico	8,000	3⅝	+	⅝	+	20.8
Acxiom	117,500	22⅞	+	3⅞	+	20.4
SpearFnl	105,300	8½	+	1⅜	+	19.3
InvestTitl	11,800	4¾	+	¾	+	18.8
F&CInt	93,300	7	+	1	+	16.7
Vestar	276,800	11	+	1½	+	15.8
NewmilBcp	2,700	2¾	+	⅜	+	15.8
AllncPhar	651,400	11½	+	1½	+	15.0
IntelElec	857,400	10⅝	+	1⅜	+	14.9
ServcFractr	226,000	3⅞	+	½	+	14.8

AND LOSERS

NASDAQ	VOL	CLOSE	CHANGE		% CHG	
WalkerPwr	64,500	2⅝	−	⅝	−	19.2
CincMicrw	95,200	3⅞	−	⅞	−	18.4
IntResrch	5,500	2¼	−	½	−	18.2
PoughkpSvg	6,100	1¾	−	⅜	−	17.6
Biomet	3,811,000	18	−	3½	−	16.3
NuclrSpt	21,700	4⅝	−	⅞	−	15.9
Trimark	24,800	4	−	¾	−	15.8
ErlyInd	6,300	2	−	⅜	−	15.8
CalStBank	6,300	8½	−	1½	−	15.0
TransInd	5,300	1⅞	−	5/16	−	14.3
MagainPharm	51,900	4⅞	−	¾	−	13.3
IntegSys	4,600	6½	−	1	−	13.3
EMCON	128,800	10¾	−	1½	−	12.2
AmIndemFnl	3,000	5	−	⅝	−	11.1

Table 14-20

VOLUME PERCENTAGE LEADERS

NASDAQ	VOL	%DIF*	CLOSE	CHANGE	
JonesIntcbl A	709,100	3827.4	11¼	+	½
SftwrEtc	1,198,500	3493.8	11	−	½
Aramedun	287,000	1742.3	38⅞	−	⅝
Atmel	1,098,800	1696.7	11	+	1
AgridyneTch	129,800	1293.6	4¾	−	½
HandexEnvr	258,100	1132.7	7½	......	
Curaflex	233,600	952.0	10½	+	¼
Varitrnic	53,100	928.1	5⅝	......	
Proteon	709,600	846.0	15	+	¼
FischrImag	193,600	815.7	14¾	−	¼
AmFuneral	281,200	661.4	14½	+	¾
Biomet	3,811,000	643.3	18	−	3½
CoastlHlthcr	285,300	624.1	21¾	+	⅝
KarchrCarl	439,600	605.7	9⅝	+	⅛
Acxiom	117,500	599.3	22⅞	+	3⅞
PoolEngySvcs	298,900	598.5	8¼	+	¾

Table 14-21

NASDAQ NATIONAL MARKET ISSUES

-I-I-I-

52 Weeks Hi	Lo	Stock	Sym	Div	Yld %	PE	Vol 100s	Hi	Lo	Close	Net Chg
19½	9¾	iSTAT	STAT		...	...	217	10½	10¼	10½	+ ¼
14	7¼	ISG Tch	ISGTF		...	...	10	8⅜	8¼	8¼	− ⅜
11	4½	ICF Int	ICFI		...	...	715	5¼	4½	5⅛	+ ⅛
19¾	5½	ICOS Cp	ICOS		...	...	1040	7	6½	6⅞	+ ¼
12	6¾	ICU Med	ICUI		...	...	21	10½	9¾	9¾	− ½
19½	11¾	IDB Comm	IDBX	t	...	47	2898	16	15½	15⅞	+ ¼
21¼	6¼	IDEC Pharm	IDPH		...	...	72	7¼	6¾	7¼	...
29	15⅜	IdexxLab	IDXX		...	41	706	26¾	25½	26¼	+ ¾
8¾	4¼	IFR Sys	IFRS		...	10	295	5	4¼	4½	+ ¼
17	7	IG Labs	IGLI		...	...	167	10½	9¾	10½	− ¼
20¼	11⅜	IHOP Cp	IHOP		...	20	151	15½	15	15	− ½
4¼	2⅛	II-VI	IIVI		...	8	1	2⅛	2⅛	2⅛	− ⅛
27¼	15¾	IISIntell	IISLF		...	17	216	26¼	25½	25½	− ⅛
23	8	ILC Tech	ILCT		...	10	142	11	10¼	10¼	− ¾
22	12	IMRS	IMRS		...	24	40	14½	13¾	14½	...
48	26½	INB Fnl	INBF	1.20	2.7	16	299	45¼	45	45⅛	+ ⅛
34¾	10¼	IPL Sys	IPLSA		...	9	613	13½	11¼	13	+1¼
22¾	16¼	IWC Res	IWCR	1.40	6.2	22	50	22¾	22¼	22¾	...
5	15/16	Icot	ICOT		...	8	275	1⅞	1⅝	1¾	− ⅛
3¼	1 1/16	IKOS Sys	IKOS		...	...	740	1¾	1⅝	1¾	+ ⅛
5⅝	2	Ilio	ILIO		...	...	10	2⅛	2⅛	2⅛	...
12¾	4⅛	ImageEntn	DISK		...	169	105	7⅛	6¾	6¾	− ⅛
12¼	7	ImagnFilm	IFEI		...	20	5	7⅝	7⅝	7⅝	− ⅜
3	29/32	Imatron	IMAT		...	...	1310	1 23/32	1 21/32	1 23/32	+ 1/16
28	7	ImCloneSys	IMCL		...	...	130	7¾	7¼	7¾	+ ½
26	6¾	Imucor	BLUD		...	21	193	7¾	7¼	7½	− ¼
25	8	ImmuLogPhrm	IMUL		...	...	113	9¾	9½	9½	...
25¼	8¼	Imunogen	IMGN		...	...	216	12	11	11¾	+ ¼
62¾	14¾	ImmunResp	IMNR		...	...	1389	19¼	18½	18½	− ¼
68	22½	Imunex	IMNX		...	...	6641	41¼	39	39⅞	+ ⅝
48¾	13¾	Imunex wt			...	...	156	24	23	23½	+ ½
17	5½	Imunomed	IMMU		...	...	411	7½	7⅛	7⅜	+ ⅛
15½	7¼	ImperlBcp	IBAN	t	...	117	17	10½	9¾	10½	...
16¼	7¼	ImperlCred	ICII		...	...	533	13¾	13¼	13⅝	+ ⅜
13½	5½	InFocusSys	INFS		...	38	150	9¼	8¾	9	− ¼
7⅛	3 5/32	InHomeHlth	IHHI		...	...	720	4⅞	4⅝	4¾	...
4⅛	½	InStoreAdv	ISAN		...	...	51	⅞	¾	¾	− ⅛
14¾	7	InaCom	INAC		...	22	63	12¼	11⅞	12¼	+ ½
24½	16¼	IndepndBcpPA	INBC	1.16	5.2	13	11	23¼	22½	22½	...
2½	¾	IndepnHldg	INHO	.02e	1.0	...	6	2	2	2	+ ⅛
17	9¾	IndepndBkMI	IBCP	.52	3.4	8	1	15¼	15¼	15¼	− ½
5	1¼	IndepndBkMA	INDB		...	...	2	3	3	3	+ ¼
22¾	14½	IndepndIns	INDHK	.88	5.7	7	70	15¾	15	15½	+ ¼
19¾	14	IndiFed	IFSL	.80	4.6	9	119	18¼	17¼	17¼	− ¾
18¼	12¾	IndUtd	IUBC	.40	2.2	8	31	18½	18¼	18½	+ ¼
1¾	⅝	IndusFdg	IFDCA		...	...	10	1⅛	1⅛	1⅛	− ⅛
5	2⅝	IndlHldgs	IHII		...	...	65	4⅛	4⅛	4⅛	+ ⅛
1	⅜	IndlHldgs wtA			...	...	10	11/16	11/16	11/16	− 1/16
½	3/32	IndlHldgs wtB			...	...	10	¼	¼	¼	− 1/16
21¼	15¾	InfinBdcst	INFTA		...	...	619	20¼	20	20	...
5½	1¼	Infodata	INFD		...	...	89	1⅞	1¾	1¾	− ⅛
8⅝	3⅞	InfoAm	INFO		...	27	108	5⅛	4¾	5⅛	+ ⅛
11½	6½	InfoInt	IINT	.22	2.3	...	13	10¼	9¾	9¾	− ½
36¼	18½	InfoRes	IRIC		...	37	6892	25¼	23¼	25¼	+2½
40	6	Informix	IFMX		...	19	5713	41½	39½	40⅞	+1⅝
17½	10½	Inforum	INFM		...	46	24	14	13¾	13¾	...
13⅝	6	Infrasonc	IFRA		...	33	1206	6½	6⅛	6¼	+ ⅛
8⅝	5⅝	InglsMkt	IMKTA	.22	3.5	16	35	6¼	5⅞	6¼	+ ¼

NASDAQ SYMBOL EXPLANATION

All securities listed in the Nasdaq system are identified by a four letter or five letter symbol. The fifth letter indicates the issues that aren't common or capital shares, or are subject to restrictions or special conditions. Below is a rundown of fifth letter identifiers and a description of what they represent:

A-Class A. **B**-Class B. **C**-Exempt from Nasdaq listing qualifications for a limited period. **D**-New issue of an exisitng stock. **E**-Delinquent in required filings with SEC, as determined by the NASD. **F**-Foreign. **G**-First convertible bond. **H**-Second convertible bond, same company. **I**-Third convertible bond, same company. **J**-Voting. **K**-Non-voting. **L**-Miscellaneous situations, including second class units, third class of warrants or sixth class of preferred stock. **M**-Fourth preferred, same company. **N**-Third preferred, same company. **O**-Second preferred, same company. **P**-First preferred, same company. **Q**-In bankruptcy proceedings. **R**-Rights. **S**-Shares of beneficial interest. **T**-With warrants or rights. **U**-Units. **V**-When issued and when distributed. **W**-Warrants. **Y**-American Depositary Receipt (ADR). **Z**-Miscellaneous situations, including second class of warrants, fifth class of preferred stock and any unit, receipt or certificate representing a limited partnership interest.

Table 14-22

STOCK MARKET DATA BANK		9/8/92

MAJOR INDEXES

HIGH	LOW (†365 DAY)		CLOSE	NET CHG	% CHG	†365 DAY CHG	% CHG	FROM 12/31	% CHG
DOW JONES AVERAGES									
3413.21	2863.82	**30 Industrials**	3260.59	− 21.34	− 0.65	+ 278.03	+ 9.32	+ 91.76	+ 2.90
1467.68	1160.50	**20 Transportation**	1243.68	− 4.41	− 0.35	+ 81.30	+ 6.99	− 114.32	− 8.42
226.15	200.74	**15 Utilities**	220.21	− 0.25	− 0.11	+ 14.28	+ 6.93	− 5.94	− 2.63
1205.95	1040.27	**65 Composite**	1142.20	− 5.49	− 0.48	+ 87.08	+ 8.25	− 14.62	− 1.26
399.95	352.36	**Equity Mkt. Index**	390.13	− 2.47	− 0.63	+ 30.76	+ 8.56	− 1.77	− 0.45
NEW YORK STOCK EXCHANGE									
233.66	207.57	**Composite**	228.37	− 1.38	− 0.60	+ 17.37	+ 8.23	− 1.07	− 0.47
290.02	257.77	**Industrials**	283.17	− 1.51	− 0.53	+ 18.70	+ 7.07	− 2.65	− 0.93
104.21	91.57	**Utilities**	102.71	− 0.49	− 0.47	+ 9.73	+ 10.46	+ 0.58	+ 0.57
212.83	175.52	**Transportation**	188.47	− 1.18	− 0.62	+ 12.95	+ 7.38	− 13.40	− 6.64
183.74	154.11	**Finance**	176.35	− 1.98	− 1.11	+ 20.25	+ 12.97	+ 3.67	+ 2.13
STANDARD & POOR'S INDEXES									
425.09	375.22	**500 Index**	414.44	− 2.64	− 0.63	+ 29.88	+ 7.77	− 2.65	− 0.64
499.51	442.42	**Industrials**	488.42	− 2.57	− 0.52	+ 32.23	+ 7.07	− 4.30	− 0.87
366.54	289.27	**Transportation**	315.76	− 1.83	− 0.58	+ 26.49	+ 9.16	− 25.70	− 7.53
159.03	135.59	**Utilities**	155.98	− 0.87	− 0.55	+ 14.25	+ 10.05	+ 0.82	+ 0.53
36.66	29.77	**Financials**	34.60	− 0.59	− 1.68	+ 3.39	+ 10.86	+ 0.50	+ 1.47
154.74	127.31	**400 MidCap**	143.58	− 0.85	− 0.59	+ 16.27	+ 12.78	− 3.01	− 2.05
NASDAQ									
644.92	511.28	**Composite**	571.17	− 2.27	− 0.40	+ 59.89	+ 11.71	− 15.17	− 2.59
741.92	570.34	**Industrials**	610.01	− 1.64	− 0.27	+ 39.67	+ 6.96	− 58.94	− 8.81
688.91	522.07	**Insurance**	677.09	− 0.69	− 0.10	+ 139.64	+ 25.98	+ 76.00	+ 12.64
468.68	318.54	**Banks**	455.44	− 0.91	− 0.20	+ 115.48	+ 33.97	+ 104.88	+ 29.92
285.08	225.43	**Nat. Mkt. Comp.**	253.11	− 0.99	− 0.39	+ 27.68	+ 12.28	− 6.63	− 2.55
296.32	226.90	**Nat. Mkt. Indus.**	244.73	− 0.59	− 0.24	+ 17.83	+ 7.86	− 23.06	− 8.61
OTHERS									
418.99	364.68	**Amex**	383.36	− 1.49	− 0.39	+ 17.17	+ 4.69	− 11.69	− 2.96
266.85	228.21	**Value-Line(geom.)**	246.73	− 1.58	− 0.64	+ 7.06	+ 2.95	− 2.61	− 1.05
212.61	174.71	**Russell 2000**	190.19	− 1.13	− 0.59	+ 14.48	+ 8.24	+ 0.26	+ 0.14
4121.28	3645.57	**Wilshire 5000**	3996.95	− 24.04	− 0.60	+ 306.35	+ 8.30	− 44.15	− 1.09

†-Based on comparable trading day in preceding year.

of the shares in each category to determine the appropriate average. The Dow Jones Industrial Average is narrowly based, reflecting the price movements of only 30 stocks; it is a "blue chip" average since the 30 companies are among the largest and most influential in the country. Because of this emphasis on the largest companies, it is not uncommon for the Dow Jones Industrial Average to move in one direction while the broader-based indexes appearing in Table 14-22 and described in the following section are moving in the opposite direction.

It is not entirely clear why the Dow Jones Industrial Average has achieved the prominence that it has. One advantage is its relative antiquity, going back for more than 100 years. (The first Dow Jones average

Table 14-23

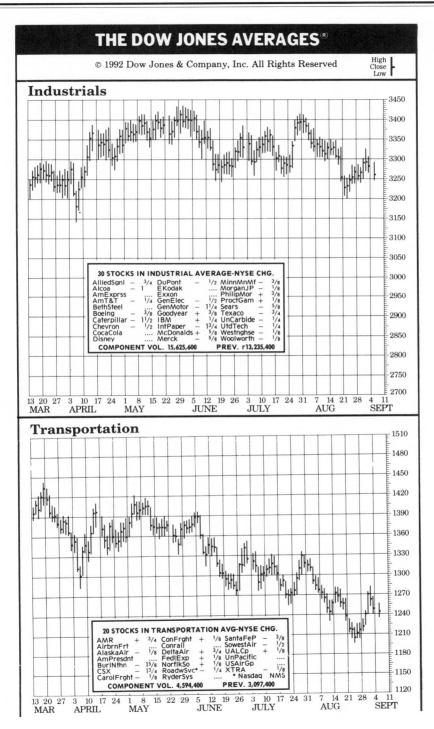

THE DOW JONES AVERAGES®

© 1992 Dow Jones & Company, Inc. All Rights Reserved

High
Close
Low

Industrials

30 STOCKS IN INDUSTRIAL AVERAGE-NYSE CHG.

AlliedSgnl	− 3/4	DuPont	− 1/2	MinnMnMf	− 3/8
Alcoa	− 1	EKodak	....	MorganJP	− 1/8
AmExprss	....	Exxon	....	PhilipMor	+ 3/8
AmT&T	− 1/4	GenElec	− 1/2	ProctGam	+ 1/8
BethSteel	....	GenMotor	− 1 1/4	Sears	− 5/8
Boeing	− 3/8	Goodyear	+ 3/8	Texaco	− 1/4
Caterpillar	− 1 1/2	IBM	+ 1/4	UnCarbide	− 1/4
Chevron	− 1/2	IntPaper	− 1 3/4	UtdTech	− 1/4
CocaCola	....	McDonalds	+ 5/8	Westnghse	− 1/8
Disney	....	Merck	− 5/8	Woolworth	− 1/8

COMPONENT VOL. 15,625,600   PREV. r13,235,400

13	20	27	3	10	17	24	1	8	15	22	29	5	12	19	26	3	10	17	24	31	7	14	21	28	4 11
MAR			APRIL				MAY					JUNE				JULY					AUG				SEPT

Transportation

20 STOCKS IN TRANSPORTATION AVG-NYSE CHG.

AMR	+ 3/4	ConFrght	+ 1/8	SantaFeP	− 3/8
AirbrnFrt	....	Conrail	....	SowestAir	− 1/2
AlaskaAir	− 1/8	DeltaAir	+ 3/4	UALCp	− 1/8
AmPresdnt	....	FedlExp	+ 1/8	UnPacific	....
BurlNthn	− 1 5/8	NorflkSo	+ 1/8	USAirGp	....
CSX	− 1 3/4	RoadwSvc*	− 1/4	XTRA	− 1/8
CarolFrght	− 1/8	RyderSys	....	* Nasdaq	NMS

COMPONENT VOL. 4,594,400   PREV. 3,097,400

13	20	27	3	10	17	24	1	8	15	22	29	5	12	19	26	3	10	17	24	31	7	14	21	28	4 11
MAR			APRIL				MAY					JUNE				JULY					AUG				SEPT

353

Table 14-23 (*continued*)

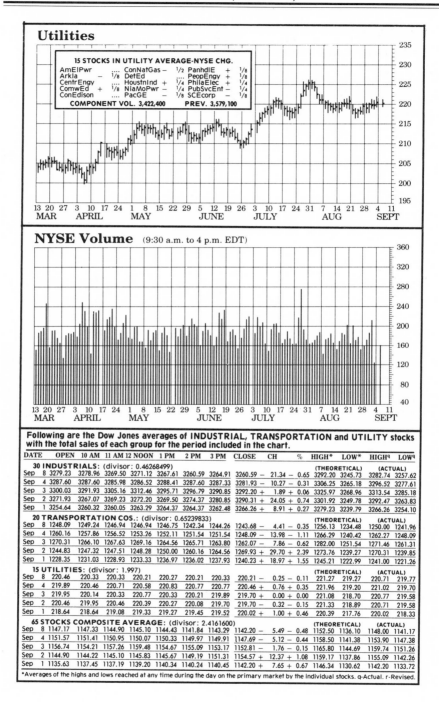

Utilities

15 STOCKS IN UTILITY AVERAGE-NYSE CHG.

AmElPwr	....	ConNatGas	−	1/2	PanhdlE	+	1/8
Arkla	−	1/8	DetEd	....	PeopEngy	+	1/8
CentrEngy	....	HoustnInd	+	1/4	PhilaElec	+	1/4
ComwEd	+	1/8	NiaMoPwr	−	1/4	PubSvcEnt	−	1/8
ConEdison	....	PacGE	−	1/8	SCEcorp	+	1/8

COMPONENT VOL. 3,422,400   PREV. 3,579,100

13 20 27 3 10 17 24 1 8 15 22 29 5 12 19 26 3 10 17 24 31 7 14 21 28 4 11
MAR   APRIL   MAY   JUNE   JULY   AUG   SEPT

NYSE Volume   (9:30 a.m. to 4 p.m. EDT)

13 20 27 3 10 17 24 1 8 15 22 29 5 12 19 26 3 10 17 24 31 7 14 21 28 4 11
MAR   APRIL   MAY   JUNE   JULY   AUG   SEPT

Following are the Dow Jones averages of INDUSTRIAL, TRANSPORTATION and UTILITY stocks with the total sales of each group for the period included in the chart.

DATE	OPEN	10 AM	11 AM	12 NOON	1 PM	2 PM	3 PM	CLOSE	CH	%	HIGH*	LOW*	HIGHq	LOWq
30 INDUSTRIALS: (divisor: 0.46268499)											(THEORETICAL)		(ACTUAL)	
Sep 8	3279.23	3278.96	3269.50	3271.12	3267.61	3260.59	3264.91	3260.59	− 21.34	− 0.65	3292.20	3245.73	3282.74	3257.62
Sep 4	3287.60	3287.60	3285.98	3286.52	3288.41	3287.60	3287.33	3281.93	− 10.27	− 0.31	3306.25	3265.18	3296.52	3277.61
Sep 3	3300.03	3291.93	3305.16	3312.46	3295.71	3296.79	3290.85	3292.20	+ 1.89	+ 0.06	3325.97	3268.96	3313.54	3285.18
Sep 2	3271.93	3267.07	3269.23	3272.20	3269.50	3274.37	3280.85	3290.31	+ 24.05	+ 0.74	3301.92	3249.78	3292.47	3263.83
Sep 1	3254.64	3260.32	3260.05	3263.29	3264.37	3264.37	3262.48	3266.26	+ 8.91	+ 0.27	3279.23	3239.79	3266.26	3254.10
20 TRANSPORTATION COS.: (divisor: 0.65239833)											(THEORETICAL)		(ACTUAL)	
Sep 8	1248.09	1249.24	1246.94	1246.94	1246.75	1242.34	1244.26	1243.68	− 4.41	− 0.35	1256.13	1234.48	1250.00	1241.96
Sep 4	1260.16	1257.86	1256.52	1253.26	1252.11	1251.54	1251.54	1248.09	− 13.98	− 1.11	1266.29	1240.42	1262.27	1248.09
Sep 3	1270.31	1266.10	1267.63	1269.16	1264.56	1265.71	1263.80	1262.07	− 7.86	− 0.62	1282.00	1251.54	1271.46	1261.31
Sep 2	1244.83	1247.32	1247.51	1248.28	1250.00	1260.16	1264.56	1269.93	+ 29.70	+ 2.39	1273.76	1239.27	1270.31	1239.85
Sep 1	1228.35	1231.03	1228.93	1233.33	1236.97	1236.02	1237.93	1240.23	+ 18.97	+ 1.55	1245.21	1222.99	1241.00	1221.26
15 UTILITIES: (divisor: 1.997)											(THEORETICAL)		(ACTUAL)	
Sep 8	220.46	220.33	220.33	220.21	220.27	220.21	220.33	220.21	− 0.25	− 0.11	221.27	219.27	220.71	219.77
Sep 4	219.89	220.46	220.71	220.58	220.83	220.77	220.77	220.46	+ 0.76	+ 0.35	221.96	219.20	221.02	219.70
Sep 3	219.95	220.14	220.33	220.77	220.33	220.21	219.89	219.70	+ 0.00	+ 0.00	221.08	218.70	220.77	219.58
Sep 2	220.46	219.95	220.46	220.39	220.27	220.08	219.70	219.70	− 0.32	− 0.15	221.33	218.89	220.71	219.58
Sep 1	218.64	218.64	219.08	219.33	219.27	219.45	219.52	220.02	+ 1.00	+ 0.46	220.39	217.76	220.02	218.33
65 STOCKS COMPOSITE AVERAGE: (divisor: 2.4161600)											(THEORETICAL)		(ACTUAL)	
Sep 8	1147.17	1147.33	1144.90	1145.10	1144.43	1141.84	1143.29	1142.20	− 5.49	− 0.48	1152.50	1136.10	1148.00	1141.17
Sep 4	1151.57	1151.41	1150.95	1150.07	1150.33	1149.97	1149.91	1147.69	− 5.12	− 0.44	1158.50	1141.38	1153.90	1147.38
Sep 3	1156.74	1154.21	1157.26	1159.48	1154.67	1155.09	1153.17	1152.81	− 1.76	− 0.15	1165.80	1144.69	1159.74	1151.26
Sep 2	1144.90	1144.22	1145.10	1145.83	1145.67	1149.19	1151.31	1154.57	+ 12.37	+ 1.08	1159.17	1137.86	1155.09	1142.26
Sep 1	1135.63	1137.45	1137.19	1139.20	1140.34	1140.24	1140.45	1142.20	+ 7.65	+ 0.67	1146.34	1130.62	1142.20	1133.72

*Averages of the highs and lows reached at any time during the day on the primary market by the individual stocks. q-Actual. r-Revised.

was published in 1884 when the prices of 11 stocks were added up and divided by 11; the 30 industrials format was adopted in 1928. Only 13 of the original companies are still in the average; gone are such former household names as Nash Motors, Mack Trucks, Wright Aeronautical, Victor Talking Machine, and General Railway Signaling. The Dow also has attracted a following because it involves rather dramatic price moves —during the first part of 1987, for example, it rose steadily, breaking "barriers" at 2,300, 2,400, and so forth reaching an all-time high of 2,722.42 on August 25, 1987. Alas, the 1987 "crash" described in the following paragraph occurred shortly thereafter, and the Dow did not recover for more than a year. It did not break the 3,000 "barrier" until the middle of 1991. These numbers, of course, have only psychological meaning since they are composite numbers with no intrinsic significance. Nevertheless there is a wide following of the Dow Jones average as it continues to break new barriers and set new records.

The Dow Jones average also has been widely used to describe the collapse of securities prices that occurred in October 1987, following the August 25 high. After a period of increasingly volatile prices, the second week of October was marked by several trading days of increases in trading volume accompanied by moderate decreases in the Dow Jones average. On Monday, October 19, however, the NYSE suffered its largest one-day loss in history as measured by the Dow—508.32 points. It closed on October 19 at 1,738.40, down one-third from its historic high in August. During the two-week period in October when most of this decline occurred, less than 3 percent of all the outstanding shares registered on the NYSE were traded, but the aggregate loss in value of all NYSE shares was approximately $1 trillion. While much of this loss reflected only the disappearance of appreciation in values during the long price run-up that had never been realized (so-called paper profits), many traders and investors suffered devastating losses of capital. All losses, whether of paper profits or of capital, are, of course, felt keenly and have a psychological effect on future economic behavior.

§14.30 OTHER INDEXES

There are several widely followed market indexes other than the Dow Jones average. Table 14-22 sets them forth as presented by The Wall Street Journal. Several of these are broad-based indexes covering hundreds or thousands of stocks. None of them, however, have achieved the wide following of the Dow Jones Industrial Average. All of them reflected the market break that occurred in 1987 indicating that the decline was market-wide and not limited to the 60 blue chip stocks that comprise the Dow Jones averages.

The two most widely followed alternative indexes are the New York Stock Exchange Composite and Standard & Poor's 500 indexes. These indexes differ conceptually from the Dow Jones average. In the Dow, a dollar change in the price of a single stock in the average has the same effect as a change of one dollar in the price of any other stock in the average. There is no weighting of the individual stocks by the size of the company, the number of shares outstanding, or the volume of trading. Both the S&P and NYSE Composite are true indexes. They measure changes in total market value of the stocks that make up the index, and the index number is the percentage change compared with a base period. The NYSE Composite is indexed to December 31, 1965 (when the base was 50), while the S&P 500 is indexed to the period from 1941 to 1943 (when the base was 10). The NYSE Composite is based on 1,632 companies traded on that Exchange; S&P 500 is based on 500 stocks, primarily on the NYSE.

The Value Line Composite Index is based on 1,650 stocks, 300 of which are traded OTC and 100 of which are AMEX stocks. The Wilshire 5,000 is even broader, covering 5,000 stocks traded on all the principal securities markets.

An important function of these alternative indexes is to serve as the basis for options and futures trading on indexes. This subject is described briefly in Chapter 18.

15

Investment Companies

§15.1 INTRODUCTION

As discussed in Chapter 13, the most sensible investment strategy is to diversify investments and not place one's entire resources at the individualized risk of a single business or single type of investment. Further, a relatively small investor cannot diversify effectively by purchasing small amounts of different publicly traded securities issued by different corporations. The obvious alternative is to invest in one or more investment companies or mutual funds, the subject of this chapter.

An investment company is simply a corporation or business trust that invests only in marketable securities of other corporations. An investment company therefore has at any given time a portfolio of securities and usually some trivial amount of cash or cash-equivalent assets awaiting investment. Because of the nature of the holdings of an investment company, it is relatively easy to determine the aggregate value of its holdings at any point in time. Valuation is not usually a problem for investment companies.

Historically, investment company portfolios were limited to common shares. But there is nothing inherent in the investment company concept that limits portfolios to this class of investment, and many investment company portfolios today are invested entirely in corporate bonds, while others invest only in United States treasuries, in tax-exempt state or municipal bonds, in bonds issued by the Government National Mortgage Company (Ginny Mae), in short-term cash-equivalent investments, in foreign securities, and so forth. Indeed, the number and diversity of investment vehicles offered is one of the more remarkable aspects of this remarkable growth industry.

And a growth industry it is. The investment company industry had assets of about $2.5 billion in 1950. By 1977 it had grown to $50 billion and by 1990 to $1.0 trillion. Since then, growth has increased. In just two years it grew by $600 billion to $1.6 trillion. During 1992, the industry was growing at the rate of over $1 billion per day. Since 1990, investment companies have invested more than $300 billion in publicly traded common shares; over 95 percent of the "new money" coming into the stock markets for equities has been provided by the investment company. With the growth of tax-exempt mutual funds, investment companies have become the principal market for municipal debt, as well as major investors in United States Treasury securities of various types.

In June 1992, it was estimated that investment companies controlled 11.4 percent of all financial assets in the United States. By comparison, pension funds controlled 21.1 percent, insurance companies, 16.6 percent, commercial banks, 26.8 percent, thrift institutions of various types 10.5 percent, and others, 13.6 percent.

One important type of investment company is the money market fund, which invests only in short-term cash-equivalent securities and is structured so that it is more similar to a bank account than an investment in securities. Money market funds are discussed in Chapter 16 along with other fixed income, cash-equivalent investments. See section 16.8.

Most investment companies are themselves corporations that issue shares. Some are business trusts organized under special Massachusetts or Delaware statutes that permit trusts to issue shares. Investors may purchase these shares and thereby obtain instant diversification since the shares issued by an investment company in effect constitute investment in the portfolio owned by the investment company. Because the value of the investment company's portfolio is known, it is also relatively easy to determine the net asset value of each share of the investment company's stock. One simply values all the holdings in the investment company's portfolio and divides by the number of outstanding shares.

Not all companies that invest in marketable securities are investment companies. A company that invests exclusively in controlling interests in several operating companies and itself has no other business is usually called a "holding company" and is not an investment company. A holding company that is held by a few persons is called a "personal holding company." A company that itself has business operations and also invests in marketable securities is also not viewed as an investment company.

The investment companies discussed in the balance of this chapter are all publicly held corporations or trusts. Publicly held investment companies are subject to a substantial degree of regulation by the Securities and Exchange Commission under the Securities Act of 1933, the Securities and Exchange Act of 1934, and particularly the Investment Company Act of 1940, a statute that has been the predominant force in shaping the modern investment company into the forms it presently has. The hallmark of an investment company, for purposes of this chapter, is that it is registered under the Investment Company Act of 1940.

§15.2 PUBLIC INVESTMENT COMPANIES IN GENERAL

The investment goals of a publicly held investment company — the objective of its portfolio activities — must be publicly stated. They may be to maximize long-term capital appreciation, to maximize current income, to invest in a diversified portfolio of public utility stocks, to invest in long-term investment grade bonds, to invest in foreign securities or the securities of companies from a specific foreign country or from several countries, or some combination of these various goals. Modern investment companies do not seek controlling or even influential stock positions; most are diversified investors, who limit their investments in any one corporation to a small fraction (for example, less than 1 percent) of the voting shares of each operating company.

Investment companies earn profits from two principal sources: trading profits from buying and selling portfolio securities, and dividends or interest from investments. Investment companies that distribute substantially all of their earnings each year (after expenses) to shareholders are subject to special income tax treatment. They are not themselves subject to tax; rather, they are conduits whose income — for example, capital gains, tax-exempt municipal bond interest — is passed through to its shareholders in the same form as it is received. Thus, an investor who seeks only federal income tax exempt municipal bond income may invest in an investment company that invests only in such bonds, and the dividends received by the shareholder are exempt from income tax to the extent they represent interest on tax-exempt municipal bonds. An investor who seeks income that is exempt from both federal income taxation and from New York state and New York City income taxation also has a choice of alternative investments in the investment company field since several funds specialize in "triple exempt" New York City bonds. Management fees and other expenses are subtracted from income prior to their distribution to shareholders and usually are not separately itemized in the distribution process, a practice that tends to make investors feel they are getting a better bargain than they actually are.

An investment company itself has shareholders. It must hold shareholders' meetings, elect directors and officers, and so forth as required by the governing statute. The corporation statutes of the state of Maryland are particularly suited for investment companies, and many of these companies are incorporated in that state. Most investment companies contract with a brokerage firm or investment banker to obtain investment advice for a fee: The brokerage firm or investment banker may also handle share transfer and other related costs of the investment company operation. Of course, fees are also charged for these services.

Publicly held investment companies are broken down into two broad categories discussed in the two sections immediately following: "closed-end companies" and "open-end companies." Open-end companies are usually called "mutual funds."

§15.3 CLOSED-END INVESTMENT COMPANIES

Closed-end companies are the oldest type of investment companies. Their unique characteristic is that they have outstanding a fixed number of their own shares that are traded either on a securities exchange or over-the-counter. Before World War II, investment companies were generally closed-end; after World War II they fell into a period of eclipse, but in the last decade a large number of new closed-end funds have been created. Many of these new closed-end funds concentrate in foreign securities of specific countries. Closed-end companies are also known as "publicly traded funds" since their shares are listed on securities exchanges or traded in the OTC market like any other securities.

An investor who decides to invest in a closed-end fund simply places an order with a broker to purchase the desired number of shares wherever the shares are traded. A shareholder who decides to liquidate her interest in the closed-end company places an order to sell the shares in the appropriate market. In either event, investing in a closed-end fund or disposing of such an investment involves merely the payment of the standard brokerage fees for executing the transactions.

The market price for shares issued by closed-end investment companies fluctuates according to market conditions and may be either higher or lower than the net asset value of the shares. Shares of a closed-end fund are said to trade at a discount if the market price for its shares is less than the net asset value per share. Closed-end fund shares are said to trade at a premium if the market price of the fund shares is higher than the net asset value. Table 15-1 is a table of the major publicly traded closed-end funds that invest in common shares, and Table 15-2 is a table of a portion of the publicly traded closed-end funds that invest solely in corporation bonds. In both tables "N.A. Value" is net asset value per share and "Stock

Table 15-1

PUBLICLY TRADED FUNDS

Friday, September 4, 1992

Following is a weekly listing of unaudited net asset values of publicly traded investment fund shares, reported by the companies as of Friday's close. Also shown is the closing listed market price or a dealer-to-dealer asked price of each fund's shares, with the percentage of difference.

Fund Name	Stock Exch.	N.A. Value	Stock Price	% Diff.
Diversified Common Stock Funds				
Adams Express	NYSE	20.05	19 1/4 −	3.99
Allmon Trust	NYSE	10.48	9 3/4 −	6.97
Baker Fentress	NYSE	21.34	18 1/4 −	14.48
Blue Chip Value	NYSE	7.50	7 3/4 +	3.33
Clemente Global Gro	NYSE	b10.14	8 7/8 −	12.48
Gemini II Capital	NYSE	17.46	14 1/8 −	19.10
Gemini II Income	NYSE	9.76	13 3/8 +	37.04
General Amer Invest	NYSE	28.23	28 5/8 +	1.40
Jundt Growth Fd	NYSE	14.14	13 −	8.06
Liberty All-Star Eqty	NYSE	a10.32	10 7/8 +	5.38
Quest For Value Cap	NYSE	26.88	22 3/4 −	15.36
Quest For Value Inco	NYSE	11.69	13 1/2 +	15.48
Royce Value Trust	NYSE	12.02	11 1/8 −	7.45
Salomon Fd	NYSE	15.12	14 −	7.41
Source Capital	NYSE	41.63	46 7/8 +	12.60
Tri-Continental Corp.	NYSE	28.41	27 7/8 −	1.88
Worldwide Value	NYSE	15.76	13 3/8 −	15.13
Zweig Fund	NYSE	11.16	12 7/8 +	15.37
Closed End Bond Funds				
CIM High Yield Secs	AMEX	7.79	7 3/4 −	0.51
Franklin Multi Inc Tr	NYSE	b10.74	10 5/8 −	1.07
Franklin Prin Mat Tr	NYSE	b8.33	7 3/4 −	6.96
Franklin Universal Tr	NYSE	b8.94	8 5/8 −	3.52
Flexible Portfolio Funds				
America's All Seasn	OTC	5.35	4 3/4 −	11.21
European Warrant Fd	NYSE	7.28	6 5/8 −	9.00
Zweig Total Return Fd	NYSE	a9.15	10 3/8 +	13.39
Loan Participation Funds				
Pilgrim Prime Rate	NYSE	9.98	9 3/8 −	6.06
Specialized Equity and Convertible Funds				
Alliance Global Env Fd	NYSE	11.29	9 1/2 −	15.85
American Capital Conv	NYSE	22.33	19 1/2 −	12.67
Argentina Fd	NYSE	10.55	11 +	4.27
ASA Ltd	NYSE	bc35.98	36 3/8 +	1.10
Asia Pacific	NYSE	12.63	13 7/8 +	9.86
Austria Fund	NYSE	8.88	8 −	9.91
Bancroft Convertible	AMEX	a22.51	20 1/2 −	8.93
Bergstrom Capital	AMEX	98.23	116 3/4 +	18.85
BGR Precious Metals	TOR	be8.33	6 7/8 −	17.47
Brazil	NYSE	b14.51	16 5/8 +	14.58
Brazilian Equity Fd	NYSE	b9.31	10 3/4 +	15.47
CNV Holdings Capital	NYSE	11.86	7 3/4 −	34.65
CNV Holdings Income	NYSE	9.46	12 1/4 +	29.49
Castle Convertible	AMEX	25.29	22 3/4 −	11.53
Central Fund Canada	AMEX	b4.08	3 7/8 −	5.02
Central Securities	AMEX	12.72	10 5/8 −	16.47
Chile Fund	NYSE	35.26	33 7/8 −	3.93
China Fd	NYSE	13.89	13 1/4 −	4.61
Couns Tandem Secs	NYSE	15.94	13 5/8 −	14.52
Duff&Phelps Utils Inc.	NYSE	9.82	10 1/2 +	6.92
Ellsw Conv Gr&Inc	AMEX	9.22	8 1/4 −	10.52
Emerging Ger Fd	NYSE	8.87	7 7/8 −	11.22
Emerging Mark Tele Fd	NYSE	13.40	13 1/2 +	0.75
Emerging Mexico Fd	NYSE	b18.13	17 3/8 −	4.16
Engex	AMEX	10.62	8 3/8 −	21.14
Europe Fund	NYSE	12.75	12 1/4 −	3.92
1stAustralia	AMEX	9.41	8 1/2 −	9.67
First Financial Fund	NYSE	13.27	11 5/8 −	12.40
First Iberian	AMEX	8.78	7 1/2 −	14.58
First Philippine Fund	NYSE	14.94	11 3/8 −	23.86
France Growth Fund	NYSE	12.18	10 3/8 −	14.82
Future Germany Fund	NYSE	15.02	13 5/8 −	9.29
Gabelli Equity Trust	NYSE	a10.37	10 7/8 +	4.87
Germany Fund	NYSE	11.40	11 1/2 +	0.88
Global Health Sciences Fd	NYSE	12.59	11 7/8 −	5.68
Greater China Fd	NYSE	13.46	13 −	3.42
Growth Fund Spain	NYSE	10.59	8 7/8 −	16.19
GT Greater Europe Fd	NYSE	11.56	10 3/8 −	10.25
H&Q Healthcare Inv	NYSE	18.69	21 +	12.36
H&Q Life Sciences Inv Fd	NYSE	13.39	14 3/4 +	10.16
Hampton Utils Tr Cap	AMEX	b15.76	14 1/4 −	9.58
Hampton Utils Tr Pref	AMEX	b50.20	51 5/8 +	2.84
India Growth Fund	NYSE	f18.65	18 5/8 −	0.13
Indonesia Fund	NYSE	8.45	9 5/8 +	13.91
Inefficient Market Fund	AMEX	10.67	9 1/2 −	10.97
Irish Investment Fd	NYSE	9.48	7 3/4 −	18.25
Italy Fund	NYSE	8.62	7 7/8 −	8.64
Jakarta Growth Fd	NYSE	6.89	7 7/8 +	14.30
Japan OTC Equity Fund	NYSE	8.26	9 3/4 +	18.04
Japan Equity Fd	NYSE	10.63	10 1/4 −	3.57
Jardine Fleming China Fd	NYSE	13.94	13 5/8 −	2.26
Korea Fund	NYSE	10.24	11 1/2 +	12.30
Korean Investment Fd	NYSE	9.50	10 1/2 +	10.53
Latin America Disc Fd	NYSE	13.26	12 3/8 −	6.67
Latin America Income Fd	NYSE	13.94	15 1/8 +	8.50
Latin America Equity Fd	NYSE	15.44	14 7/8 −	3.66
Latin America Inv Fd	NYSE	25.20	26 +	3.17
Malaysia Fund	NYSE	14.71	12 5/8 −	14.17
Mexico Equity Inc Fd	NYSE	b15.11	13 3/4 −	9.00
Mexico Fund	NYSE	b22.81	21 3/4 −	4.65
Morgan Grenf SmCap	NYSE	11.11	11 −	0.99
Morgan Stan Em Mks Fd	NYSE	16.55	16 3/4 +	1.21
New Germany Fund	NYSE	12.89	11 7/8 −	7.87
Patriot Prem Div Fd	NYSE	10.52	10 1/4 −	2.57
Patriot Prem Div Fd II	NYSE	12.67	12 1/8 −	4.30
Patriot Select Div Trust	NYSE	16.45	17 1/4 +	4.86
Petrol & Resources	NYSE	29.48	27 1/8 −	7.99
Pilgrim Regional	NYSE	11.37	10 3/4 −	5.45
Portugal Fund	NYSE	12.07	10 1/4 −	15.08
Preferred Income Fd	NYSE	18.82	19 1/4 +	2.28
Preferred Inc Opport Fd	NYSE	12.85	13 1/2 +	5.06
Putnam Dividend Inc Fd	NYSE	11.80	12 1/2 +	5.93
RI Estate Sec Inco Fd	AMEX	7.59	7 5/8 +	0.46
ROC Taiwan Fund	NYSE	b8.69	9 +	3.57
Scudder New Asia	NYSE	15.18	15 7/8 +	4.58
Scudder New Europe	NYSE	10.24	9 −	9.67
SE Thrift & Bank Fd	OTC	b13.68	12 −	12.28
Singapore Fd	NYSE	b10.52	10 −	4.94
Spain Fund	NYSE	10.59	9 3/4 −	7.93
Swiss Helvetia Fd	NYSE	15.43	14 3/8 −	6.84
Taiwan Fund	NYSE	b19.53	18 3/8 −	5.91
TCW Convertible Secs	NYSE	8.15	8 7/8 +	8.90
Templeton Em Mkts	NYSE	b18.52	22 7/8 +	23.52
Templeton Global Util	AMEX	b13.42	13 3/4 +	2.46
Thai Capital Fund	NYSE	9.89	8 1/2 −	14.05
Thai Fund	NYSE	16.83	15 5/8 −	7.16
Turkish Inv Fund	NYSE	6.09	6 1/2 +	6.73
United Kingdom Fund	NYSE	11.13	10 1/8 −	9.03
Z-Seven	OTC	14.32	16 3/4 +	16.97

a-Ex-dividend. b-As of Thursday's close. c-Translated at Commercial Rand exchange rate. e-In Canadian Dollars. f-As of Wednesday's close, using the Free − Market Spot Rate.

Table 15-2

CLOSED-END BOND FUNDS

Friday, September 4, 1992
Unaudited net asset values of closed-end bond fund shares, reported by the companies as of Friday's close. Also shown is the closing listed market price or a dealer-to-dealer asked price of each fund's shares, with percentage of difference.

Fund Name	Stock Exch.	N.A. Value	Stock Price	% Diff.
Bond Funds				
ACM Govt Inco Fund	NYSE	a10.87	11 1/4	+ 3.50
ACM Govt Oppor Fd	NYSE	a9.72	9 3/4	+ 0.31
ACM Govt Securities	NYSE	10.88	11 1/4	+ 3.40
ACM Govt Spectrum	NYSE	a9.20	9 3/8	+ 1.90
ACM Mgd Inco Fd	NYSE	a9.40	10 1/4	+ 9.04
AIM Strategic Inco	AMEX	9.32	9	− 3.43
American Adj Rate '95	NYSE	ac9.95	10 3/8	+ 4.27
American Adj Rate '96	NYSE	ac9.71	10 1/4	+ 5.56
American Adj Rate '97	NYSE	ac9.65	10 1/8	+ 4.92
American Adj Rate '98	NYSE	ac9.70	10	+ 3.09
American Capital Bond	NYSE	ab 20.30	20 3/4	+ 2.22
American Capital Inco	NYSE	8.11	8 3/8	+ 3.27
American Govt Income	NYSE	ac8.54	8 3/4	+ 2.46
American Gov't Portf	NYSE	ac 11.09	10 7/8	− 1.94
American Govt Term	NYSE	ac9.78	10 5/8	+ 8.64
American Opp Inco Fund	NYSE	ac 11.28	11 5/8	+ 3.06
American Strat Inc	NYSE	ac 14.90	16	+ 7.38
American Strat Inc II	NYSE	a14.15	15 1/4	+ 7.77
AMEV Securities	NYSE	10.18	11 3/8	+ 11.74
Blackrock 1998 Term	NYSE	c10.51	10 3/8	− 1.28
BlackRock 2001 Term	NYSE	c 9.41	10	+ 6.27
Blackrock Advtg Trm	NYSE	c10.71	10 7/8	+ 1.54
Blackrock Income	NYSE	c 9.24	9 5/8	+ 4.17
Blackrock Inv Qual Term	NYSE	c 9.98	10 1/8	+ 1.45
Blackrock Strat Term	NYSE	c10.07	10 1/4	+ 1.79
Blackrock Target Term	NYSE	c10.56	10 5/8	+ 0.62
Bunker Hill Income	NYSE	16.40	16 3/4	+ 2.13
CIGNA High Income Shs	NYSE	7.29	7 7/8	+ 8.02
CNA Income Shares	NYSE	c11.11	12 5/8	+ 13.64
Colonial Int High Inco	NYSE	6.58	6 3/4	+ 2.58
Colonial Intrmkt Inco I	NYSE	11.67	12	+ 2.83
Current Income Shares	NYSE	13.48	13 3/8	− 0.78
Dean Witter Govt Inco	NYSE	a9.68	9 1/8	− 5.73
Dreyfus Strt Gov Inco	NYSE	11.42	12	+ 5.08
1838 Bond-Deb Trading	NYSE	22.29	25 3/8	+ 13.84
Excelsior Inco Shares	NYSE	c19.07	18 1/2	− 2.99
First Boston Inco Fd	NYSE	8.68	8 7/8	+ 2.25
First Boston Strategic	NYSE	9.93	10 5/8	+ 7.00
Ft Dearborn Income	NYSE	16.58	16 1/2	− 0.48
John Hancock Income	NYSE	16.86	17 1/4	+ 2.31
John Hancock Invest	NYSE	22.37	23 5/8	+ 5.61
Hatteras Income Secs	NYSE	16.54	18 1/4	+ 10.34
High Income Adv Tr	NYSE	a5.79	5 3/4	− 0.69
High Income Adv II	NYSE	a6.38	6 1/8	− 4.00
High Income Adv III	NYSE	a6.96	7	+ 0.57
High Yield Income Fd	NYSE	7.47	7 7/8	+ 5.42
High Yield Plus Fund	NYSE	8.17	8 3/8	+ 2.51
Hyperion 1999 Term Tr	NYSE	9.19	10 1/4	+ 11.53
Hyperion Total Ret	NYSE	a11.10	11 5/8	+ 4.73
INA Investments	NYSE	19.23	18 1/4	− 5.10
Independence Sq	OTC	18.16	18 3/4	+ 3.25
Convertible Bond Funds				
Lincoln Natl Convert	NYSE	c18.44	17 1/2	− 5.10
Putnam Hi Inco Conv	NYSE	8.54	9 1/8	+ 6.85
World Income Funds				
ACM Mgd Multi-Market	NYSE	a10.37	10 7/8	+ 4.87
Blackrock No Am	NYSE	c14.04	14 5/8	+ 4.17
Dreyfus Strt Gov Inco	NYSE	11.42	12	+ 5.08
First Australia Prime	AMEX	10.19	11 1/4	+ 10.40
First Commonwealth	NYSE	14.48	15	+ 3.59
Global Government	NYSE	8.15	8	− 1.84
Global Income Plus	NYSE	9.93	10 5/8	+ 7.00
Global Yield Fund	NYSE	8.82	8 7/8	+ 0.62
Kleinwort Benson Aust	NYSE	a10.99	10 5/8	− 3.32
Latin Amer Dollar Inc	NYSE	13.94	15 1/8	+ 8.50
Strat Global Income	NYSE	14.51	14 7/8	+ 2.52
Templeton Global Govt	NYSE	9.11	10	+ 9.77
Templeton Global Inco	NYSE	8.90	9 1/2	+ 6.74
Municipal Bond Funds				
Allstate Mun Inc Op	NYSE	a8.81	8 3/4	− 0.68
Allstate Mun Inc Op II	NYSE	a8.97	8 3/4	− 2.45
Allstate Mun Inc Op III	NYSE	a9.45	9 5/8	+ 1.85
Allstate Mun Inc	NYSE	a10.67	10 3/4	+ 0.75
Allstate Mun Inc II	NYSE	a10.43	10 1/4	− 1.73
Allstate Mun Inc III	NYSE	a9.81	9 5/8	− 1.89
Allstate Muni Pr Inco	NYSE	a10.39	10 3/4	+ 3.46
Amer Muni Term Tr	NYSE	ac 10.50	10 3/4	+ 2.38
Amer Muni Term Tr II	NYSE	ac 10.20	10 1/4	+ 0.49
Apex Muni Fund	NYSE	10.26	10 1/8	− 1.32
Blackrock Insured Muni	NYSE	9.99	9 7/8	− 1.15
Blackrock Muni Tar Trm	NYSE	10.07	10	− 0.70
Colonial Hi Inco Muni	NYSE	8.86	9 1/8	+ 2.99
Colonial Inv Gr Muni	NYSE	11.05	11 3/4	+ 6.33
Colonial Muni Inco Tr	NYSE	7.97	8 3/8	+ 5.08
Dreyfus Cal Muni Inco	AMEX	9.47	9 5/8	+ 1.64
Dreyfus Muni Inco	AMEX	10.14	10 5/8	+ 4.78
Dreyfus NY Muni Inco	AMEX	10.17	10 5/8	+ 4.47
Dreyfus Strat Muni Bd	NYSE	9.90	10 3/8	+ 4.80
Dreyfus Strat Munis	NYSE	10.15	11	+ 8.37

a-Ex-dividend. b-Fully diluted. c-As of Thursday's close. d-Assumes rights offering fully subscribed.
Source: Lipper Analytical Services, Denver Colorado.

Price" is the market price of the shares issued by the closed-end company. The "% Diff." is the premium or discount between the stock price and the net asset value calculated as follows:

$$\text{Discount} = \frac{\text{stock price} - \text{net asset value}}{\text{net asset value}}$$

These tables reveal that most common stock closed-end funds trade at a discount, while bond funds are more mixed. Where closed-end funds trade at significant discounts, enterprising speculators have sometimes purchased large amounts of the shares on the open market and then successfully forced the closed-end fund to amend its articles of incorporation or declaration of trust to become an "open-end" fund (thereby automatically eliminating the discount from net asset value). See section 15.4.

Some closed-end bond funds are "leveraged," that is, they borrow money to purchase additional bonds. As bond prices improved with declining interest rates (see section 16.12), these funds have done much better than unleveraged funds, and many traded at a premium in the summer of 1992. However, when bond prices ultimately decline (as they will when interest rates begin to climb), these closed-end leveraged funds may be expected to do considerably worse than their unleveraged counterparts.

Experience demonstrates that it rarely pays to subscribe to a brand new issue of a closed-end fund at net asset value. After a period of price stabilization at or above the issue price (during which the issue is marketed), the fund shares are permitted to seek their own level in the market, which usually is significantly lower than net asset value. Investors, who originally subscribed, suffer the loss caused by the market's discounting of the shares.

The attractiveness of many closed-end funds is that they sometimes trade at deep discounts from net asset value, and the discount varies over time. If the discount narrows, an investor may show substantial capital appreciation. Since many closed-end companies trade at discounts over long periods, a seemingly advantageous investment may turn out disadvantageous if the discount remains stable or even widens. On the other hand, a number of new country-oriented or region-oriented closed-end funds consistently trade at significant premiums over net asset value, apparently a result of limited investment opportunities in attractive developing economies in countries such as South Korea.

"Playing the discount" involves buying when the discounts widen and selling or selling short when the discounts narrow or when prices creep up so that the shares are trading at a premium over net asset value. One trader suggests the following strategy: One should buy when: (1) The discount is 75 percent greater than the average discount over the previous six months; and (2) the discount exceeds 3 percent for a balanced fund, 5 percent for a junk bond fund, and 10 percent for a country fund.

§15.4 OPEN-END INVESTMENT COMPANIES (MUTUAL FUNDS) IN GENERAL

Open-end investment companies are usually called mutual funds. They are unlike closed-end funds in two respects: First, they do not have a fixed number of shares outstanding but stand ready at any time to issue new shares to persons desiring to invest in the fund; and, second, they stand ready to redeem any shares at net asset value (or in some cases at a small discount from net asset value) at any time for investors who wish to liquidate their positions. Open-end companies are open-ended because there is no fixed capitalization of the investment company: As an open-end fund grows in size, the number of outstanding shares grows also.

Open-end funds are not publicly traded on the NYSE or other securities markets. Rather, a person who wishes to invest in a mutual fund deals directly with the fund itself and receives newly issued shares. When a person decides to liquidate his or her interest in such a fund, the investor again contacts the mutual fund and arranges to have his or her shares redeemed. Mutual funds are sold directly or through brokers who may push such investments for small investors.

Most of the investment company growth since 1950 has been centered in mutual funds. Much of the growth before 1992 was in money market funds (see section 16.7) and in funds investing in fixed income securities. However, equity mutual funds continued to grow throughout this period and then really took off when interest rates declined in the early 1990s. Equity funds have had explosive growth since 1991 as money has flowed out of all types of fixed income investments and into mutual funds investing in equity securities.

Several additional factors have contributed to the phenomenal growth of mutual funds. They include the growth in popularity of defined contribution retirement plans that offer mutual fund investment alternatives, the increased willingness of institutional investors to place their funds in so-called index funds that seek to match the performance of broad stock market indexes, the increase in securitization type investments (see sections 16.18, 16.19), and the growth in interest in foreign investments that may be pooled into country funds.

About 95 percent of all investment company assets today are accounted for by mutual funds. Closed-end funds account for the remaining 5 percent.

Increasingly, mutual funds are organized into investment company "families" or "complexes," that is, large groups of mutual funds associated with common advisers and underwriters, typically with liberal exchange privileges among the funds within the family. The goal is to provide a fund that meets the investment objectives of numerous diverse groups of investors with different short- and long-term goals. Most fund families permit free transfer of investments from one fund in the family to another fund in the same family without service charge. In this way, the managers hope to retain control over investment funds even when the goal of the investor changes because of changes in individual circumstances. The largest fund families (in terms of assets) are managed by the Fidelity Group, Merrill Lynch, Vanguard, Dreyfus, and Franklin.

Most mutual funds are actively managed. This means the fund manager shifts investments aggressively in order to maximize the return to investors. This is not always beneficial. One mutual fund "bailed out" on October 19, 1987, the day of the market crash and dumped $800 million of stocks on the market, undoubtedly contributing to the market collapse. Some fund managers have the reputation of making portfolio changes to capture a relatively small amount of appreciation, thereby increasing both trading volume and trading volatility. The usual yardstick for performance of a stock fund is whether the fund exceeds the market performance of one of the broad market averages, usually either Standard & Poor's 500 stock index or the New York Stock Exchange Composite Index. The efficient capital market hypothesis (see section 13.8) states that fund managers cannot hope to beat the market averages consistently, and indeed most mutual funds have not been able to consistently exceed these market averages. One study in the late 1970s showed, for example, that 90 percent of the managed funds fared worse than the Standard & Poor 500 index over a ten-year period. In recent years there has been a strong trend toward "index funds" that are not actively managed but hold a portfolio, which is structured so that it closely mimics the mix of stocks in one or more broad market indexes. Index funds have become attractive to sophisticated institutional investors since they involve significantly less trading than a managed fund, and brokerage commissions, investment advice, and other costs are significantly reduced. The growth in mutual funds in recent years is in part the result of the increased use of index funds by pension plans and other institutional investors who are seeking only a market level return on their investments.

Mutual funds provide instant diversification for the small investor at relatively nominal cost. The major problems with the use of this investment vehicle by the small investor are, first, the difficulty of ascertaining the actual cost of alternative mutual fund investments, and second, the bewildering variety of different families of funds and the equally bewildering variety of funds with varying investment objectives within each family.

With mutual funds, one cannot always trust the label. Popular words — growth, value, aggressive growth, and balanced — do not have clear content and may include a variety of different portfolios. "Growth" typically refers to the purchase of stocks whose earnings are expected to grow faster than average over time while "value" refers to stocks that are attractively priced on the basis of traditional value measures such as dividend yield (see section 14.9) or price-earnings ratios (see section 14.26). However, many growth funds have extensive holdings of income producing stock while value funds may have pricey stocks based on traditional measures. A person who desires a low risk investment may inadvertently end up with a fund that has a much higher degree of risk than expected. A "balanced" fund may have average price/earnings ratios (see section 14.26) as high as

33, which is an astronomical number when compared to the S&P index with a P-E ratio of 19.

Additional evidence of the slippery nature of names of mutual funds is the development of "hub and spoke" funds. A fund manager creates a "hub" portfolio of securities into which a number of "spoke" mutual funds invest all their assets. Even though each spoke fund has an interest in the common portfolio, they may have different names, different sales charges (see section 15.5), and different distribution systems, so that one investor may end up paying considerably more for a mutual fund investment than another investing in the identical portfolio. Individual spoke funds may be advertised as being designed as investment vehicles for retirement funds, for institutional investors, for bank-sold funds, for broker-sold funds, for "no-load" funds, and so forth. In 1992, there were approximately 40 "hub" funds with 60 "spokes" and about $12 billion in assets.

§15.5 OF MUTUAL FUND "LOADS" AND CHARGES

Table 15-3 is an excerpt from the Wednesday, September 9, 1992 Wall Street Journal showing quotations for many of the mutual funds beginning with "A" for Tuesday , September 8, 1992. In this table, NAV stands for net asset value; since there is no market trading in open-end fund shares (shares are "sold" by submitting them for redemption to the fund), there are no share price quotations as is the case with closed-end funds. NAV Chg. shows the change in net asset value from the previous day.

On February 1, 1993, the Wall Street Journal made significant changes in its form of reporting mutual fund quotations. Table 15-4 is from the February 2, 1993 Journal. These changes give considerably more information about the results of operations of the listed mutual funds and reflect the increased importance of mutual funds in the portfolios of investors of all types.

The entry under "Offer Price" and the enigmatic entry "N.L." require some explanation. Until relatively recently, the fees charged by mutual funds were strictly regulated by the SEC. There were two types of funds: "load" funds and "no-load" funds. A load is an additional charge imposed on an investor when he or she invests in the fund; it is sometimes called a "front-end" load since it is imposed at the time of the purchase of the mutual fund shares. Historically, the load was about 8 percent above the net asset value for small investments and decreased gradually for larger investments. Today, only a small handful of funds have front-end loads in excess of 5 percent. Load funds can be easily identified from Table 15-3 since they are the funds that show a dollar entry under the "Offer Price" category. Load funds are heavily advertised and recommended by brokers

MUTUAL FUND QUOTATIONS

Table 15-3

	NAV	Offer Price	NAV Chg.
AAL Mutual:			
Bond p	10.62	11.15	+.03
CaGr p	14.17	14.88	−.08
MuBd p	10.75	11.29	+.01
AARP Invst:			
CaGr	30.48	NL	−.21
GiniM	16.24	NL	+.05
Gthlnc	28.67	NL	−.15
HQ Bd	16.58	NL	+.07
TxFBd	18.13	NL	+.07
ABT Funds:			
Emrg p	10.62	11.15	−.07
FL TF	10.97	11.52	+.03
Gthln p	10.11	10.61	−.06
Utilln p	12.83	13.47	−.05
AHA Funds:			
Balan	12.29	NL	−.02
Full	10.88	NL	+.06
Lim	10.60	NL	+.01
AIM Funds:			
AdjGv p	9.93	10.24	+.01
Chart p	8.23	8.71	−.05
Const p	12.21	12.92	−.07
CvYld p	12.85	13.49	−.06
HiYld p	5.75	6.04	+.01
IntlE p	9.35	9.89	...
LimM p	10.26	10.36	+.01
Sumit	9.41	....	−.08
TF Int	10.58	10.91	+.01
Weing p	16.23	17.17	−.09
AIM Funds C:			
AgrsvC p	14.81	15.67	−.03
GoScC p	10.48	11.00	+.04
GrthC p	13.67	14.47	−.08
HYldC p	9.63	10.11	...
IncoC p	8.34	8.76	+.05
MuBC p	8.42	8.84	+.03
TeCfC p	10.74	11.28	+.02
UtilC p	13.96	14.77	−.02
ValuC p	18.09	19.14	−.03
AMF Funds:			
AdjMtg	10.02	NL	...
IntMtg	10.05	NL	+.02
IntlLiq	11.03	NL	+.02
MtgSc	11.47	NL	+.04
ASO Funds:			
Balance	11.03	11.55	−.01
Bond	11.57	12.12	+.06
Equity	12.90	13.51	−.09
LtdMat	10.92	11.20	+.02
AcornF	49.10	49.10	+.03
AdsnCa p	19.08	19.67	−.15
Advest Advant:			
Govt p	9.26	9.26	+.05
Gwth p	16.13	16.13	−.11
HY Bd p	8.90	8.90	...
Inco p	11.85	11.85	−.03
Spcl p	14.85	14.85	−.09
Aetna Funds:			
Aetna	10.16	NL	−.02
Bond	10.35	NL	+.04
GrwIncm	10.03	NL	−.04
IntlGr	9.35	NL	−.03
Afuture	8.82	9.64	−.01
Alger Funds:			
Growth t	16.39	16.39	−.03
IncGr r	11.98	11.98	−.06
SmCap t	18.98	18.98	−.11
Alliance Cap:			
Alian p	6.37	6.74	−.04
Balan p	13.23	14.00	−.04
Canad p	5.06	5.35	−.03
Count p	19.47	20.60	−.10
GlbSA p	9.58	10.14	+.02
GovtB p	8.66	8.66	+.04
Govt p	8.66	8.93	+.04
GrInc p	2.46	2.60	−.01
HiYld p	5.75	6.04	+.01
ICalT p	13.38	14.01	+.03
InsMu p	10.24	10.72	+.02

	NAV	Offer Price	NAV Chg.
MonIn p	12.89	13.53	+.09
MrtgA p	9.28	9.57	+.04
MrtgB p	9.28	9.28	+.04
MrtgTrB p	10.00	10.00	+.02
MltlG	9.90	10.00	−.08
Mltln t	1.93	1.93	−.02
MMSA p	9.17	9.45	−.16
MMSB t	9.17	9.17	−.16
MuCA p	10.25	10.73	+.01
MuNY p	9.79	10.25	...
NtlMu p	10.46	10.95	+.02
NEur p	10.01	10.59	+.05
NAGvB p	10.18	10.18	+.01
QusrA p	19.33	20.46	−.08
ST Mia p	9.46	9.75	−.10
ST Mib t	9.46	9.46	−.10
Tech p	24.28	25.69	−.04
Wldln p	1.93	1.93	−.01
Ambassador Fds:			
Bond	10.35	NL	+.01
Grwth	10.77	10.77	−.05
IdxStk	11.06	11.06	−.07
IntBd	10.47	10.47	+.04
IntlStk	10.09	10.09	−.09
SmCoG	11.09	11.09	−.02
Amer AAdvant:			
Balan	12.08	NL	−.02
Equity	10.91	NL	−.09
IntlEq	9.79	NL	−.10
LtdTr	10.28	NL	+.02
Amer Capital:			
Cmstk	17.35	18.96	−.12
CpBd p	7.07	7.42	+.03
EmGr p	19.33	20.51	−.14
EntA p	13.18	13.98	−.09
EntB p	13.12	13.12	−.09
EqInc p	4.95	5.25	−.01
Exch	100.77	...	−.41
FMgA p	12.71	13.24	−.01
FMgB p	12.72	12.72	−.01
GlEqA p	10.08	10.69	−.04
GlGvA p	9.43	9.90	+.10
GlGvB p	9.46	9.46	+.10
GlEqB p	10.07	10.07	−.03
GvScB p	10.94	10.94	+.05
GvScA p	10.94	11.49	+.06
GvT97 p	12.82	13.22	+.07
GrInc p	12.85	13.63	−.06
HarbA p	14.94	15.85	−.04
HiYld p	6.43	6.75	+.01
MunB p	10.06	10.56	+.02
PaceB p	13.28	13.28	−.09
Pace p	13.37	14.19	−.10
TxE I p	11.39	11.96	+.01
TXMS p	9.82	10.31	+.01
TEHY p	11.02	11.57	+.01
American Funds:			
A Bal p	12.28	13.03	...
Amcp p	12.51	13.27	−.07
AMutl p	21.41	22.72	−.09
Bond p	14.31	15.02	+.05
CapIB p	31.53	33.45	−.02
CapW p	16.26	17.07	+.01
Eupac p	34.08	36.16	+.01
FdInv p	17.38	18.44	−.11
Govt p	14.31	15.02	+.06
Gwth p	22.31	23.67	−.13
HI Tr p	14.54	15.27	+.01
Inco p	13.87	14.72	−.02
IntBd p	14.45	15.17	+.04
ICA p	17.58	18.65	−.08
NEco p	23.76	25.21	−.01
N Per p	12.41	13.17	−.05
SmCp p	18.09	19.19	...
TxEx p	11.84	12.43	+.01
TECA p	15.30	16.06	+.02
TEMd p	15.06	15.81	+.02
TEVA p	15.53	16.30	+.01
Wsh p	16.15	17.14	−.10
A GthFd	8.16	8.92	−.07
A Heritg	1.05	NL	...
A Invst	5.50	5.76	−.05
A Inv In	5.49	5.75	−.01

	NAV	Offer Price	NAV Chg.
Amer Natl Funds:			
Grth	4.68	5.11	−.04
Inco	22.44	24.52	−.17
Triflex	15.92	17.21	−.05
API Gr fp	10.66	10.66	+.01
Am Perform:			
Bond	11.18	11.65	+.05
Equity	11.36	11.83	−.13
IntBd	11.07	11.41	+.05
AmUtlFd	22.01	NL	−.01
Amway f	7.29	7.52	−.02
Analyt	12.56	NL	−.05
AnchrCa f	24.11	24.11	−.05
Aquila Funds:			
AZ TF	10.58	11.02	+.03
CO TF	10.42	10.85	+.02
HI TF	11.44	11.92	+.01
KY TF	10.67	11.11	+.02
OR TF	10.57	11.01	+.02
Arch Funds:			
CapApp	13.69	14.34	−.11
Div Fl	10.58	11.08	+.03
MoTF	11.28	11.81	+.02
US Gov	11.15	11.68	+.03
Amstng	7.27	NL	−.04
AtlantaGr p	10.04	10.43	+.01
Atlas Funds:			
CaMuni	10.91	11.25	+.03
GvtSc	11.15	11.08	+.02
GroInc	12.76	13.15	−.08
NaMuni	10.97	11.31	+.03
BFMShDu	....	...	...
BJB GInc p	12.34	NL	+.02
Babson Group:			
Bond L	1.67	NL	+.01
Bond S	10.62	NL	+.02
Enterp2	13.06	NL	−.16
Enterp	15.50	NL	−.03
Gwth	11.93	NL	−.08
Intl	13.59	NL	...
Shadw	10.49	NL	...
TaxFr	9.19	NL	+.03
UMB B	11.44	NL	+.03
UMB St	15.39	NL	−.07
Value	21.18	NL	−.11
BairdBl p	18.07	19.17	−.10
BairdCa p	21.12	22.41	−.03
BakerGv	....	...	...
BaronA r	16.14	16.14	−.04
Bartlett Funds:			
BasVl	14.00	NL	−.06
FixedI	10.44	NL	+.03
VI Intl	10.10	NL	−.03
Bascom	23.00	23.00	−.05
Beac Hill	32.79	NL	−.24
Benham Group:			
AdjGov	10.11	NL	...
CaTFI	10.95	NL	+.03
CatfIn	10.03	NL	+.02
CaTFS	10.11	NL	+.01
CatfH	9.19	NL	+.02
CatfL	11.54	NL	+.03
EqGro	10.95	NL	−.08
EurBd	11.54	NL	+.11
GNMA	10.92	NL	+.03
GoldIn	8.25	NL	−.03
IncGro	13.11	NL	−.09
NITFI	10.80	NL	+.03
NITFL	11.71	NL	+.03
Tg1995	88.95	NL	+.27
Tg2000	62.39	NL	+.61
Tg2005	41.48	NL	+.46
Tg2010	29.02	NL	+.40
Tg2015	21.27	NL	+.28
Tg2020	14.47	NL	+.16
TNote	11.16	NL	+.03
Berger Group:			
100	11.53	NL	−.07
101	9.06	NL	−.05

e-Ex-distribution. f-Previous day's quotation. s-Stock split or dividend. x-Ex-dividend. NL-No load. p-Distribution costs apply, 12b-1 plan. r-Redemption charge may apply. t-Both p and r footnotes apply.

Table 15-4

MUTUAL FUND QUOTATIONS

What These Listings Provide...

		NASD DATA			LIPPER ANALYTICAL DATA			
Monday	Inv. Obj.	NAV	Offer Price	NAV Chg.	%Ret YTD	Max Initl Chrg.	Total Exp Ratio	..
TUESDAY	Inv. Obj.	NAV	Offer Price	NAV Chg.	YTD	——Total Return—— 4 wk	1 yr	Rank
Wednesday	Inv. Obj.	NAV	Offer Price	NAV Chg.	YTD	–Annualized Total Return– 13 wk	3 yr	Rank
Thursday	Inv. Obj.	NAV	Offer Price	NAV Chg.	YTD	–Annualized Total Return– 26 wk	4 yr	Rank
Friday	Inv. Obj.	NAV	Offer Price	NAV Chg.	YTD	–Annualized Total Return– 39 wk	5 yr	Rank

EXPLANATORY NOTES

Mutual fund data are supplied by two organizations. The daily Net Asset Value (NAV), Offer Price and Net Change calculations are supplied by the National Association of Securities Dealers (NASD) through Nasdaq, its automated quotation system. Performance and cost data are supplied by Lipper Analytical Services Inc.

Daily price data are entered into Nasdaq by the fund, its management company or agent. Performance and cost calculations are percentages provided by Lipper Analytical Services, based on prospectuses filed with the Securities and Exchange Commission, fund reports, financial reporting services and other sources believed to be authoritative, accurate and timely. Though verified, the data cannot be guaranteed by Lipper or its data sources and should be double-checked with the funds before making any investment decisions.

Performance figures are on a total return basis without regard to sales, deferred sales or redemption charges.

INVESTMENT OBJECTIVE (Inv. Obj.) – Based on stated investment goals outlined in the prospectus. The Journal assembled 10 groups based on classifications used by Lipper Analytical in the daily Mutual Fund Scorecard and other calculations. A detailed breakdown of classifications appears at the bottom of this page.

NET ASSET VALUE (NAV) – Per share value prepared by the fund, based on closing quotes unless noted, and supplied to the NASD by 5:30 p.m. Eastern time.

OFFER PRICE – Net asset value plus sales commission, if any.

NAV CHG. – Gain or loss, based on the previous NAV quotation.

TOTAL RETURN – Performance calculations, as percentages, assuming reinvestment of all distributions. Sales charges aren't reflected. Percentages are annualized for periods greater than one year. For funds declaring dividends daily, calculations are based on the most current data supplied by the fund within publication deadlines. A YEAR TO DATE (YTD) change is listed daily, with results ranging from 4 weeks to 5 years offered throughout the week. See chart on this page for specific schedule.

MAXIMUM INITIAL SALES COMMISSION (Max Initl Chrg) – Based on prospectus; the sales charge may be modified or suspended temporarily by the fund, but any percentage change requires formal notification to the shareholders.

TOTAL EXPENSE RATIO (Total Exp Ratio) – Based on the fund's annual report, the ratio is total operating expenses for the fiscal year divided by the fund's average net assets. It includes all asset based charges such as advisory fees, other non-advisory fees and distribution expenses (12b-1).

RANKING (R) – Funds are grouped by investment objectives defined by The Wall Street Journal and ranked on longest time period listed each day. Performance measurement begins at either the closest Thursday or month-end for periods of more than one year. Gains of 100% or more are shown as a whole number, not carried out one decimal place. A=top 20%; B=next 20%; C=middle 20%; D=next 20%; E=bottom 20%.

QUOTATIONS FOOTNOTES

e-Ex-distribution. f-Previous day's quotation. s-Stock split or dividend. x-Ex – dividend.

p-Distribution costs apply, 12b-1 plan. r-Redemption charge may apply. t – Footnotes p and r apply.

NA-Not available due to incomplete price, performance or cost data. NE-Deleted by Lipper editor; data in question. NL-No Load (sales commission). NN-Fund doesn't wish to be tracked. NS-Fund didn't exist at start of period.

k-Recalculated by Lipper, using updated data. n-No valid comparison with other funds because of expense structure.

who receive a commission from the load. For example, the ABT family of funds in Table 15-3 are all load funds. One can purchase shares in the "Emerging Growth Fund" that have a net asset value of $10.62 per share for $11.15 per share; that is about a 5 percent load. An investment in this fund would have to increase about 5 percent before the investment could be liquidated without loss to the investor. The net asset value of this fund declined by 7 cents from its closing net asset value of the previous day.

Front-end loads are used to compensate the various participants in the transaction. The broker actually placing the order for the investor may get 30 to 45 percent of the load; the sponsor of the fund may receive 20 percent, and the brokerage firm employing the selling broker gets the remaining 35 to 50 percent. Thus, on a $10,000 investment in a fund with a 4.5 percent front-end load, $9,550 is actually invested, and $450 is distributed to the broker, the sponsor, and the brokerage firm. The selling broker might receive a commission of $144 on this transaction.

No-load funds are funds that offer to sell shares at net asset value. They are sold without extensive advertising and usually without the intervention of a broker so that the investor has to locate the desired investment on his or her own and contact the manager of the no-load fund directly. Many investment advisers recommend that investors invest in no-load funds suitable for their investment needs in order to avoid paying the sales load. However, the actual investment performance of the two types of funds does not unambiguously indicate that this strategy leads to a higher net return.

Most mutual funds have minimum investment amounts for the initial investment. Most major groups require an initial investment of $2,500, but many funds permit initial investments of as little as $500 or $200. Usually, no minimum is imposed if the investor signs up for an automatic investment plan that assures a steady flow of investments into the fund. Also, a transfer from one fund to another within a group normally is done at net asset value with the loads or charges being imposed.

In recent years, the SEC has relaxed the rules relating to the types of sales charges that may be imposed, and many mutual funds have switched to more complex pricing structures. Some funds have reduced their front-end loads but imposed a back-end redemption charge on redemptions occurring shortly after the investment is made. A first year redemption charge may be as high as 6 percent but ratchets down thereafter. A number of former no-load funds now levy redemption charges. These redemption charges have been the subject of numerous investor complaints since they are generally not disclosed when the investor is persuaded to invest. They raise significantly the cost of transfer of funds from one mutual fund family to another or from one brokerage firm to another. Funds that impose a redemption charge in Table 15-3 are marked with an "r."

In addition, an SEC rule allows mutual funds to deduct certain marketing and distribution costs directly from assets and earnings; in effect this imposes the costs of distribution on existing fund holders rather than on new investors. Such charges are called "12b-1 fees" based on the number of the regulation authorizing such fees. A number of former no load funds now levy 12b-1 fees. Funds imposing 12b-1 fees in Table 15-3 are marked with a "p." When rule 12b-1 was originally approved, the assumption of the SEC was that these charges would permit more selling effort, more growth in the size of funds, and a concomitant reduction in fees and charges to investors. Everything has appeared to happen as expected, except the reduction in charges.

Funds may impose both a redemption fee and a 12b-1 fee for marketing and distribution costs. These funds are marked with a "t" in Table 15-3. Most load funds impose fees of all three types. A sales load may also be charged indirectly on reinvested dividends. Some no load funds may charge 12b-1 fees and exit fees; some may charge a small front-end load. With a variety of costs being imposed (some in a hidden manner without complete disclosure) and the distinction between load and no load blurred, the comparison of costs between alternative mutual fund investments has become treacherous.

Most funds that charge both 12b-1 fees and a front-end sales load have reduced the latter from the traditional 8½ percent to 3 or 4 percent, further blurring the distinction between load and no load funds. Only about 30 major funds currently charge the maximum allowable front-end load.

To complicate matters even further, mutual funds are increasingly offering investors a choice as to how fees are to be paid: either a traditional front-end load or an exit fee coupled with a 12b-1 fee drawn from annual earnings. Alliance Capital Management's Multi-Market Trust, for example, issues Class A shares with a 3 percent front-end load plus a three-tenths of one percent 12b-1 fee; class B shares have no front-end load but carry a 1 percent 12b-1 fee plus a declining exit fee that begins at 3 percent. In the long run, these should come out to pretty much the same thing, but there may be a significant difference in various short run scenarios. This choice may seem particularly baffling to an investor since a rational solution depends on unknowable future events, in particular, how long will the investor wish to stay in the investment?

The following table, based on a $10,000 investment in a basic value fund assuming a 10 percent return by the fund and payment of various sales charges shows that the difference in fees is time sensitive:

Table 15-5
Comparison of Mutual Fund Charges Value
if Liquidated at End of Year

Year	Class A 6.5% front-end load	Class B 1% 12b-1 fee plus 4% declining exit fee
1	$10,285	$10,459
2	$11,314	$11,514
3	$12,445	$12,674
4	$13,689	$13,949
5	$15,058	$15,351
6	$16,564	$16,725
7	$18,221	$18,222
8	$20,043	$19,853
9	$22,047	$21,629

In this example, the hefty up-front charge applied to Class A shares keep the Class B shares $610 ahead of the Class A after one year; however, the exit fee cuts this advantage of the Class B if they were liquidated after one year. This advantage of the Class B nevertheless continues for seven years; after that time the 12b-1 fee pushes the Class B shares below the Class A shares.

As a rule of thumb, in funds with a load of 4.5 percent or less, it is usually cheaper to pay the load than a 1 percent 12b-1 fee. For investors with high loads that may cash out early, it is usually cheaper to pay the 12b-1 charge unless there is a heavy exit fee.

The controversy over fees and charges is largely limited to stock funds. In 1992, the SEC proposed major changes in the regulation of investment companies, largely directed to the issues of fees and charges. The SEC proposed a cap on annual 12b-1 fees at 0.75 percent per year and a new 0.25 percent service fee. Sales charges were proposed to be capped at 6.25 percent for a fund that charges the service fee and at 7.25 percent for funds that charge a 12b-1 fee but not a service fee. In addition, a single fee structure would be authorized instead of the complex of fees presently permitted. In part, these proposals are a result of the unwillingness of large funds to reduce their fees despite the economies of scale that should occur as funds grow in size. Indeed, on stock funds the average expense ratio on equity funds grew from 1.19 percent in 1980 to 1.57 percent in 1991. Since equity funds have assets of over $375 billion, this difference equals $1.4 billion per year in fees. In contrast, bond funds have lower expense ratios ranging from 0.90 percent to 1.06 percent per year. However, some individual bond funds have expense ratios of 2 percent or more. With current yields running between 6 and 8 percent, as much as one-third of total earnings of some funds now flow into expenses.

The SEC also proposed that a mix of closed-end and open end funds, called "interval funds," be authorized. An interval fund would be closed-end except for specified times or intervals when shareholders could opt to redeem shares at net asset value. It is unlikely that an interval fund would trade at a significant discount as most closed-end funds do.

The SEC also proposed to permit "off-the-page" sales. Investors would be permitted to buy fund shares simply by clipping a newspaper ad and sending a check. The expensive prospectus procedure currently followed would be eliminated. This proposal, like most of the others proposed in 1992, will require legislation to implement.

§15.6 UNIT INVESTMENT TRUSTS

Unit investment trusts are somewhat similar to investment companies. They usually are vehicles for fixed income investments, particularly municipal bonds, though some unit investment trusts hold mortgage-backed securities and corporate bonds. A unit investment trust has a fixed portfolio of securities, all with the same or similar maturities. They are "unmanaged" in the sense that they hold the securities until they mature, are sold, or are called for redemption. Unit investment trusts have fixed life spans that may vary from one to 30 years. When the unit investment trust receive payments of principal or interest, the amounts are paid to the investors and not reinvested. Unit investment trusts are created by a "sponsor," which is usually a brokerage firm. Units are sold publicly, and a secondary market is usually maintained by the sponsor so that investors may liquidate their investment short of maturity.

Unit investment trust units are sold on a "dollar price" basis that includes a sales charge of 3 to 5 percent. The longer the trust units are held, the lower the impact of the sales charge on the yield.

Unit investment trusts are attractive investments for small investors since one may invest modest amounts in a diversified or predictable portfolio. Because bonds held by unit investment trusts may be callable (see section 16.15), advertised high yields are not guaranteed. In the case of older investment trusts, it is likely that high yielding securities will in fact be called before they mature, thereby reducing the yield available on the balance of the investment.

§15.7 REAL ESTATE INVESTMENT TRUSTS

Real estate investment trusts (usually called REITs) are not strictly investment companies, but they are similar in some respects. They invest in income-producing real estate rather than in stocks, bonds, or other securities. They compete directly with investment companies for the small investor's dollars since they provide a fair amount of instant diversification in relatively conservative real estate investments and a return that is typically competitive with mutual fund returns. A number of real estate investment trusts are publicly held; about 85 of them are publicly traded on securities exchanges. As a result, interests in REITs are easy to buy and easy to sell and provide the benefits of owning income-producing real estate without management responsibilities.

REITs have had a checkered career. In the 1970s and 1980s, they were sometimes formed as tax shelters or to develop and construct commercial real estate ventures, ventures that usually failed. The form that is popular in the 1990s is called an "equity REIT" and is a conservative manager of completed and operating income-producing properties. Such a REIT may own 15 or 30 properties in a number of different communities. While the managers take a cut of the income, the yield on well managed REITs is between 5 and 10 percent per year, an attractive return given the yields generally available on other conservative investments in the 1990s. If a REIT distributes substantially all its income to its investors, it is treated as a conduit in exactly the same way as investment companies.

Care must be taken in the selection of a safe REIT. Some REITs are still saddled with problem properties carried over from the real estate boom-and-bust era of the 1980s; others have invested heavily in office buildings, which are a drag on the market in many communities.

Equity REITs are not related to mortgage-backed securities or CMOs, both of which are discussed in section 16.19. Mortgage-backed securities and CMOs are investments in pools of mortgages, while equity REITs invest directly in commercial real estate.

16

Fixed Income Securities

§16.1 INTRODUCTION

This chapter deals with investments (1) that are generally viewed as fixed income securities or (2) that have many of the characteristics of fixed income securities. A fixed income security involves the receipt of fixed or determinable amounts of money by the investor in the future. The amounts to be received may be fixed for the life of the security or may be adjusted from time to time during the life of the security. Some types of fixed income securities do not provide for periodic payments at all but simply for a fixed final payment upon maturity; these securities are sold at a discount from the final payment with the difference representing interest earned on the sales price.

Fixed income securities typically represent a loan by the investor to some enterprise or an interest in a loan previously made to some enterprise. They are "debt" securities as contrasted with the "equity" securities that are the subject of Chapters 14, 15, and 17. Unlike equity securities, they usually have a time of maturity or for repayment and thus do not exist indefinitely. The classic debt security is a marketable "bond" or "debenture" issued by a governmental or private commercial entity.

Some investment companies have portfolios that consist entirely of fixed income securities; closed-end bond funds are a good example. See Chapter 15. The shares of such companies are technically equity securities even though they have many of the characteristics of fixed income securities because of the "pass through" nature of distributions by investment companies which is a hallmark of that type of investment. However, the "money market fund," an extremely popular type of investment company that invests in short-term, virtually riskless, fixed income obligations, is so closely related to bank deposits that it is discussed in this chapter rather than in Chapter 15.

Fixed income securities discussed in this chapter also include securities created out of undivided interests in assets such as real estate mortgages or credit card receivables.

Investments in fixed income securities are attractive to individual investors because they are relatively secure (usually), provide a predictable return (usually), throw off cash at regular intervals (usually), may readily be sold or exchanged for cash (usually), and carry an attractive mix of risk and return (usually). However, fixed income investments come in many varieties and are tricky because they may carry different kinds of risk that may be hidden and not immediately evident to an unsophisticated investor.

Fixed income securities are issued in huge amounts by the federal government, by private corporations, and by state and local governments. Fixed income securities issued by the United States Treasury have no credit or default risk, but carry other types of risk. The interest from fixed income securities issued by state and local governments ("municipals") is usually exempt from federal income tax and may also be exempt from state and local income taxes. Municipals, however, carry some degree of credit or default risk. Because of the attractive tax exempt feature of municipals, their yield is lower than other securities of equivalent risk. In July 1992, investment quality municipals yielded about 83 to 85 percent of the yield on equivalent taxables; in other periods this spread has been greater.

Marketable fixed income securities are also issued by thousands of private and public issuers. Many issuers have hundreds of different fixed income securities outstanding, many of which may be very similar to each other, varying only in the date of issue or maturity, or in some other minor detail. Identification of individual issues is by CUSIP number, a unique number assigned to each public issue of debt or equity securities. CUSIP is an acronym for the Committee on Uniform Securities Identification Procedures.

§16.2 RISK FACTORS IN FIXED INCOME INVESTMENTS

Chapter 13 points out that there generally is a direct relationship between risk and return or yield. There are four basic types of risk associated with modern fixed income securities. Not all four types of risk are customarily present in a single investment, but at least one or more are present in every fixed income investment. Comparison of the amount of risk in different fixed income investments may be difficult because the four types of risk are to a large extent independent of each other and may be difficult to measure or compare with each other.

1) *Interest rate risk.* If interest rates rise, the value of marketable debt bonds or debentures goes down. Section 16.13 explains this phenomenon and shows why this is a particularly serious risk for long-term debt instruments that mature many years in the future and pay a fixed dollar amount of interest each year.

2) *Credit risk.* Credit risk (also called default or nonpayment risk) is the risk that the debtor will not be able to make the payments called for by the investment when they are due. The only types of debt securities that have no credit risk are securities issued or guaranteed by the United States Government. (It is virtually inconceivable that the United States Government might default on a financial obligation since it has the power to print money; if it did, the economy would be in such turmoil that peace and tranquillity itself would be in doubt and all prior estimates of risk would be obsolete.)

Credit risk arises because there is always a slight chance that every company or governmental entity (other than the United States Treasury) that issues fixed income securities (no matter how large and secure it appears to be when the securities are issued) may later fall on hard times, default, and be unable to meet its obligations when they mature. A few years ago, several major retailers, including Macy's and Federated Department Stores, issued bonds paying extremely attractive rates of interest. They were unable to meet their obligations and filed for reorganization under Chapter 11 of the Bankruptcy Code. Holders of their bonds have lost (or are in the process of losing) a major portion of their investment. During the 1980s, many well-known and respected companies borrowed large amounts of money in connection with transactions called leveraged buyouts; when times became more difficult in the early 1990s, a significant number of these companies found that they could not repay their loans;

the holders of securities representing all long-term loans by these companies suffered significant losses. That is credit risk. It is possible that the holders of debt issued by a defaulting company will get nothing back, or at some future time they may receive back a portion of their investment. But they certainly lose the benefit of interest payments they expected to receive and may never recoup more than a fraction of their investment. That is credit risk.

Credit risk also exists in the case of debt securities issued by foreign governments (for example, Russian bonds issued before 1917) or by state or municipal governments (for example, Bridgeport, Connecticut). While defaults on government obligations are relatively rare, the risk nevertheless exists.

Credit risk is usually measured through one or more rating companies that estimate the risk involved in investing in specific debt instruments and then "rate" the investment, using a code consisting of alphabetical (or alphabetical and numerical) ratings. The two principal rating systems and their codes are set forth in Table 16-1.

Table 16-1
Fixed Income Investment Grades

	Moody's	Standard and Poor's
Highest quality	Aaa	AAA
High grade	Aa	AA
Upper medium grade	A	A
Medium grade	Baa	BBB
Speculative	Ba	BB
Uncertain position	B	B
Poor	Caa	CCC
Speculative to a high degree	Ca	CC
Extremely poor prospects	C	C
In default	—	D

Moody's applies numerical modifiers, 1, 2, and 3, in the generic classifications Aa through B, where 1 indicates that the security ranks in the higher end of the rating category, while 3 indicates that the issue ranks in the lower end. Standard and Poor's uses a plus (+) or minus (−) for ratings of AA through CCC to provide further gradations of quality within a specific grade.

"High quality" bonds are generally rated AAA through AA in Standard and Poor's, while "medium quality" bonds are ranked as A through BBB. "Junk" or "high yield" bonds are assigned ratings of BB through C, if they are rated at all.

Ratings of state and municipal bonds are particularly uncertain. See section 16.16.

3) *Prepayment risk.* Corporations, governments, or other commercial entities that borrow money during periods of high interest rates must obviously pay high rates of interest on those loans. Many such borrowers have the right to prepay (or "call") the securities representing these loans before the due date. If interest rates thereafter decline, these borrowers may decide to refinance their high interest loans for the same reason that a homeowner decides to refinance a high interest rate mortgage.

When a business decides to call an issue of debt securities, it may borrow money by selling new debt securities at lower interest rates into the market, using the proceeds to retire the outstanding high interest rate securities. The process of borrowing money to repay old loans is usually referred to as "rolling over" a loan or "refinancing" an issue. The owners of the old securities, basking in the high interest payments they are receiving, suddenly learn that their securities have been called and they are to receive cash immediately that can be invested only at much lower current rates (assuming the same category of risk). That is prepayment risk.

Many debt obligations permit prepayment only after the lapse of a certain specified period. Such securities provide an assured return during the period prepayment is prohibited. Debt securities also often provide that a slightly higher price may have to be paid as a penalty to call outstanding securities before the maturity date, but that simply requires a somewhat more favorable reduction in the interest rate before prepayment becomes attractive. For example, a bond that has a face value of $1,000 may provide that it may be called only after five years and only if the issuer will pay each holder $1,050 for each $1,000 face value of the bond. The interest yield on those bonds is guaranteed for five years; thereafter, whether or not it is sensible to call those bonds at $1,050 depends entirely on how much interest rates have moved during the interim.

Whenever a debt security is paying an attractive above-market return and does not have a significant credit risk, one should examine the terms of the security closely to make sure that the issuer cannot call or prepay the obligations in the near future. A good example of investments in which the prepayment risk largely determines the value of specific securities are mortgage-backed securities discussed in section 16.19.

4) *Currency risk.* Investors who consider high returns available from investments in foreign countries should take into account the possibility that foreign currencies might decline in value or be formally devalued, with the consequence that a portion of the investment may be lost. Mexico treasury bills may yield 15 percent, for example, but if the peso is devalued there will be an automatic reduction in the value of the principal of the investment that may well eclipse any gain from the high yield. Even investments in European countries face a credit risk, as witnessed by the volatile nature of many European currencies during late 1992; investment

companies concentrating on investments in specific European countries saw the value of their portfolios measured in American dollars decline by as much as 3 percent in a single day because of currency rate fluctuations. That is currency risk.

§16.3 INTEREST-BEARING CHECKING/SAVINGS ACCOUNTS

For small investors, at least a part of every portfolio should be invested in interest-bearing deposits with financial institutions. Some funds should be readily available in riskless investments in the case of emergency, yet it is possible that these funds may not be needed over long periods. Since excess funds should never remain idle but should always be invested productively in income generating investments, at the minimum an interest-earning bank account is an essential part of every portfolio. Interest-bearing deposits are discussed in Chapter 3. Alternative investments to interest-bearing deposits — certificates of deposit and money market funds — are discussed briefly in this chapter because they compete directly with other types of fixed income investments.

Interest-bearing deposits in commercial banks and savings and loans institutions are truly riskless investments to the extent they are insured by the Federal Deposit Insurance Corporation or other federal agency. The maximum deposit currently covered by this insurance is $100,000, and virtually all banks and saving and loans institutions are covered.

Until the 1980s, the United States Government regulated the maximum interest rates that federally insured commercial banks and savings and loan associations could pay on savings accounts. For many years, the maximum rate was 5.5 percent per year. Furthermore, the payment of interest on checking accounts was prohibited. This regulation was thought to be necessary to ensure the financial solvency of financial institutions and created no real problem until the early 1980s when competitive interest rates rose to 12 percent or higher in some areas. At first, regulated banks and savings and loan associations grew fat, as they paid 5.5 percent interest on deposits that they could lend out to borrowers at rates as high as 15 or 16 percent. That joy proved to be very short-lived, however, as mutual fund managers, investment bankers, and brokerage firms developed a type of mutual fund, called money market funds, that gave even small investors high market rates of interest in a virtually risk-free investment. Money market funds are discussed in section 16.8. As a result, since about 1980, federally insured financial institutions have been free of rate regulation and permitted to offer investment type accounts paying market rates of interest.

Further, as described in section 3.3, the formerly sharp line between savings accounts (which paid interest) and checking accounts (which did not) offered by banks has been obliterated under this new freedom. Banks now offer savings accounts on which checks may be written and checking accounts on which interest is paid on balances over some minimum amount. Financial institutions may use different fancy names to describe its various accounts and certificates. An interest-bearing account on which checks may be written may be called a money market account, a money market checking account, or a variety of other names to emphasize that it provides a floating interest rate based on market rates; it is the traditional banking institutions' response to the money market fund. See section 16.8. A depositor may be entitled to write a limited number of checks on the account without penalty or service charge, or he or she may be able to write an unlimited number of checks if the account's balance remains above some arbitrary limit. Some institutions may also provide free transferability from a savings account to a checking account at the same institution, or vice versa. Some accounts provide an automatic periodic transfer of excess funds in a checking account to a savings account. This is called a "sweep."

Checking and savings accounts are called "demand deposits" because they may be drawn upon at any time without penalty.

Interest-bearing demand deposits pay low rates of interest. In 1992, interest rates on these accounts were below 3 percent and in many institutions below 2 percent. This is less than the rate of inflation, which is running close to 4 percent per year. Further, if income taxes due on interest received on these deposits is taken into account, the actual return on these accounts is clearly negative.

The rate of interest is so low on these accounts in 1992 that more money can be saved by the judicious selection of the type of account to be used and by avoiding additional bank charges for such things as use of automatic teller machines ($1 per use by some banks) and bounced checks (from $3 to $40 per check, depending on the bank) than whether or not interest is being paid on the account. For example, many banks offer free checks in a checking account that does not bear interest (and that maintains a relatively low minimum balance) but only a limited number of free checks in an account that does pay interest; the cost for additional checks in the interest-bearing account usually exceeds the amount of interest earned; one would be better off selecting the non-interest-bearing checking account and maintaining the required minimum balance.

Additional savings may also sometimes be obtained by combining all accounts in a single bank, if that bank gives additional free services to large depositors and has a relational system that bases eligibility on the total amounts in all accounts with the bank. Again, the cost saving of combining accounts may exceed the amount of interest being paid on demand deposits.

§16.4 CERTIFICATES OF DEPOSIT

Banks and savings institutions offer competitive interest rates on certificates of deposit (CDs) that pay somewhat higher interest rates than on demand deposits. CDs are usually issued in round-number denominations, say, $1,000, $5,000, $10,000, and larger amounts up to $100,000. Large CDs are sometimes called Jumbos. Interest rates on larger denomination and longer term CDs are somewhat higher than on smaller denominations and shorter terms. A CD differs from a traditional demand deposit in that the investor agrees to leave the investment with the bank for a specified period (for example, one month, six months, a year, or longer). Withdrawals before the expiration of the period are usually permitted subject to forfeiture of a substantial portion of the interest otherwise earned on the CD.

Interest-bearing checking or savings accounts generally pay interest at a rate that is set by the financial institution on a month-to-month basis. Interest rates on certificates of deposit, on the other hand, are fixed for the term of the certificate; thus a five-year CD "locks in" the rate offered at the time the CD is acquired.

CDs issued by financial institutions are insured by the FDIC. Brokerage firms also sell CDs issued by financial institutions to their customers; these CDs are also insured by the FDIC. Thus, an investment account with a brokerage firm may conveniently be invested in short-term CDs if that offers an attractive rate of interest.

The 1990s has seen a spectacular decline in interest rates paid on both interest-bearing deposits and CDs. In the late 1980s six-month CDs might pay interest at the rate of 7 percent or more in some instances; by 1991, rates had declined to 5 percent, and a year later to between 2 and 3 percent, with the trend continuing downward. Table 16-2 shows average yields of CDs on September 15, 1992, as published by Banxquote of

Table 16-2

BANXQUOTE® INDEX
Tuesday, September 15, 1992

AVERAGE YIELDS OF 18 LEADING BANKS

	Savings Yield	Wkly Chg.	Jumbo Yield	Wkly Chg.
Money Market	2.82	− 0.05	3.00	− 0.07
1 Month CD	....	....	2.60	− 0.12
2 Month CD	....	....	2.62	− 0.12
3 Month CD	2.67	− 0.10	2.68	− 0.11
6 Month CD	2.86	− 0.12	2.80	− 0.12
1 Year CD	3.03	− 0.14	2.95	− 0.13
2 Year CD	3.62	− 0.14	3.62	− 0.13
5 Year CD	5.09	− 0.13	5.17	− 0.12

AVERAGE YIELDS OF LEADING BROKERS

	3 Mo.	6 Mo.	1 Yr.	2 Yr.	5 Yr.
Savings CD	2.50	2.60	3.00	3.48	5.00
Weekly Change	− 0.40	....	− 0.10	+ 0.04	+ 0.05

Source: BANXQUOTE, WILMINGTON De.

Wilmington, Delaware. The low rate of return on CDs in 1992 in part reflects sluggish demand for loans in a recessionary economy, and interest rate trends may reverse in the future when the demand for bank loans improves. However, these very low rates have made CDs unattractive as investments in the short run. Billions of dollars of maturing CDs are not being renewed; the money may be placed temporarily in interest-bearing demand deposits and then moved to alternative uninsured investments — stocks, bonds, mutual funds, and annuities — in which the yield is higher. Indeed, this trend out of CDs is so strong that many banks have set up in-house brokerage services in an effort to capture the funds represented by maturing CDs that are being placed in alternative investments. While these brokerage firms may be closely affiliated with specific banks, the investments offered by them are traditional mutual funds and the like, which are both uninsured and more risky than the CD in which the funds were previously invested.

The average yield of broker-sold CDs is usually somewhat below those offered by financial institutions. Table 16-2 shows that in September 1992, for example, the average yield of 18 leading banks on a small six-month CD was 2.86 percent while six-month CDs sold by brokerage firms yielded an average of 2.60 percent; a bank five-year CD yielded an average of 5.09 percent while broker-sold five-year CDs yielded 5.0 percent. A $90,000 "jumbo" five-year CD issued directly by financial institutions yielded an average of 5.17 percent during this period.

There is a fair amount of confusion as to how yields on certificates of deposits should be calculated. In addition to differences in compounding periods and the methods of calculating how long a year is (see section 7.4), there are several different plausible calculations, and different terms may be used to describe them. When interest rates on CDs were in the 8 to 10 percent range, these differences were more important than in 1992, when this is being written. For example:

1. *Annual effective yield* (or "annual yield") represents actual annual return after compounding of interest on the assumption that the investment is held for precisely one year. Assuming an investment of $10,000 in a one-year CD with a 9.5 percent interest rate compounded quarterly, after one year the investment will grow to $10,984.38 (because of the quarterly compounding), for an annual effective yield of 9.84 percent. Annual effective yield may be misleading for investments of less than a year because it assumes reinvestment of principal and interest at the same rate for the full 12 months, which is unlikely to occur if the investment matures or the interest rate used in the calculation of interest changes within a year.

2. *Average annual yield* is a more accurate measure than annual effec-

tive yield for investments that continue for more than one year. It is calculated by allocating the aggregate yield over the entire period of the investment. For example, if $10,000 were invested in a five-year CD paying 9.5 percent interest compounded quarterly, after five years there would be $15,991.08 in the account; dividing the $5,991.08 aggregate return by five yields the average annual return of 11.98 percent.

3. *CD basis* is a method of calculating annual effective yield that assumes the year consists of 360 days for purposes of determining the daily rate but then applies it over a 365-day period. This results in a somewhat higher apparent daily yield: In the case of the one-year 9.5 percent CD with quarterly compounding, the "annual effective yield on a CD basis" would be 9.99 percent rather than the 9.84 percent set forth in paragraph (1).

4. *Bond equivalent basis* is a method of calculating annual effective yield similar to CD basis except that it consistently views the year as being one length (either 360 days or 365 days).

5. *Time-weighted return* is what one dollar invested in an investment account yields over a period of time. When dollars are added to or taken from the account from time to time, the actual number of dollars earned in the account are not an accurate reflection of the yield because the number of dollars earned are also affected by the deposits and withdrawals. To get an accurate estimate of the yield on such an account, one should use a time-weighted return. The actual change in the value of an account, taking into account the deposits and withdrawals is sometimes called the "dollar-weighted return."

These various methods of calculating yields do not have a material effect on the amount a CD will actually yield. They were often used in advertising, however, without clear indication of the method of calculation. As a result, highly advertised small differences in return tended to be more in the method of calculation than in the actual return on the investment.

§16.5 MARKET LINKED CERTIFICATES OF DEPOSIT

As interest rates on traditional certificates of deposit declined in the 1990s, some banks offered a synthetic investment that has some of the characteristics of a certificate of deposit with a return tied to the growth of a stock index, usually the S&P 500. A basic "market linked CD" might consist of a package of zero coupon bank debt maturing on a specified date in five years that will equal the investor's initial investment, coupled with long-term put or call options on the S&P 500 index. (See Chapter 18.) If the S&P index goes up over the five-year period, the investor gets most of the profit on the option plus a return of the initial investment as the zero coupon bank debt matures. If the S&P index does not go up, the option on the index expires valueless, but the investor gets back the initial investment when the zero coupon bank debt matures. By changing the terms of this composite derivative security slightly, the risk can be increased: For example, more of the initial investment may be invested in options so that the yield is greater if the market goes up; in this event the zero coupon debt part of the package is reduced so that it may yield only 90 percent, say, of the initial investment. The zero coupon bank debt component of this security is guaranteed by the FDIC.

When first offered, these market linked "certificates of deposit" were offered only in large denominations: $100,000 or more. By the summer of 1992, however, they were being offered in denominations as low as $2,000, though $10,000 units were more common.

§16.6 CREDIT UNIONS

Credit unions come from a different tradition than banks and savings and loan institutions. Their history is from the nineteenth century tradition of people pooling their money and making loans to one another. Credit unions have "members" rather than "customers." They accept deposits from, and make loans to, their members.

Membership is usually based on employment with a specific employer or membership in professional organizations, labor unions, or other groups. About 25 percent of the population was eligible for membership in credit unions in 1992, but this was expanding as larger credit unions increasingly allow relatives of members to join and actively seek to increase their membership.

Credit unions have largely avoided the pitfalls that have placed other financial institutions at risk. They completely avoid loans to third world countries and real estate syndications, investments that have troubled large banks. The wild real estate loans and questionable investments that virtually destroyed the savings and loan industry also have little counterpart in credit unions.

Approximately 95 percent of all credit unions are covered by federal deposit insurance, and it is essential to be sure of this before depositing funds in a credit union. Rhode Island had long had a system of state-organized insurance to which Rhode Island credit unions paid premiums and received "insurance." However, the collapse of one major credit union in 1990 revealed that the insurance available was in fact woefully inadequate, and the governor of the state was compelled to declare a moratorium on withdrawals until the mess could be straightened out, a process that took two years, during which time many investors could not obtain access to their funds.

§16.7 AVOIDING CREDIT RISK ON LARGE BANK DEPOSITS

Bank failure is an event that has occurred with sufficient frequency in the recent past that plans should be made to avoid loss when depositing sums that exceed the maximum amount of federal insurance, currently $100,000. While bank failures may seem to be a remote possibility, even remote risks should be avoided when dealing with sums of this magnitude. If the amount involved is not too large, complete protection can be obtained by making separate $100,000 deposits to different insured institutions or to accounts under different names in a single institution. Care must be taken in this regard, however, because the rules of the FDIC as to when accounts are viewed as separate accounts are rather technical.

When the amount is so large that it is unwieldy to break it into $100,000 units, there are alternative investments that are either riskless or carry such slight risk of default that they are viewed as riskless. These investments include treasury bills or notes (see section 16.10) and high quality commercial paper. Commercial paper is unsecured debt maturing on a specific day in the future, usually 30 days or less. Commercial paper issued by large finance companies or major industrial corporations is generally viewed as being essentially a risk-free short-term investment. The yield on commercial paper is somewhat higher than for treasury bills, which are entirely risk-free.

Another essentially riskless investment is "bankers' acceptances" — short-term interestbearing notes whose payment has been guaranteed by a major commercial bank. Acceptances arise out of commercial transactions, usually large international sales transactions. Payment may also be guaranteed by the parties to the underlying transaction and possibly by a lien on the goods themselves. Like high-quality commercial paper, bankers' acceptances are generally viewed as essentially risk-free investments; again the yield is slightly higher than for entirely risk-free treasury bills.

A person investing very large sums of money on a short-term basis (over $100,000) may consider repurchase agreements (usually called "repos"). A repo is a loan structured as a sale; a bank "sells" an investor riskless securities — Treasury notes usually — while simultaneously agreeing to buy them back at a later date for a higher price. The difference in price represents interest to the investor. Repos may be overnight transactions or may continue for as long as a year.

The theory underlying repos is that if the bank fails while a repo is open, the customer simply keeps the securities sold to it. In this kind of transaction it is therefore essential that the securities involved be in some way set aside for the investor, usually through a third-party escrow account. The investor should also get a list of the securities sold, including certificate numbers. Otherwise, the transaction may be attacked as an unsecured loan by a bankruptcy trustee or receiver. Repos generally earn somewhat more than banks pay on insured certificates of deposit for the same period. A "reverse repo" is a repo from the standpoint of the dealer who is seeking to borrow securities in order to sell them, in other words to engage in a short sale. Short sales are discussed in section 14.19.

§16.8 MONEY MARKET FUNDS

One unusual type of mutual fund, which became extremely popular during the 1980s, is the virtual equivalent of an uninsured savings account: the money market fund. The development of this type of mutual fund is a good illustration of the problems of government regulation when faced with free market forces. As described above, for many years the United States regulated the maximum interest rates that commercial banks and savings and loan associations could pay on savings accounts. This created no real problem until the early 1980s, when competitive interest rates rose to 12 percent or even higher in some areas, while the highest lawful rate was set at 5.5 percent. Mutual fund managers, investment banks, and brokerage firms devised a new type of mutual fund that promised market rates of interest for even small depositors in a virtually risk-free investment. The federal government quickly realized that if long-standing financial institutions were to survive at all, they would have to be permitted to compete effectively with the newfangled money market funds for savings.

A money market fund is a mutual fund that invests only in short-term, virtually riskless investments. They bear names such as "cash management accounts" or "liquid assets funds." Most money market funds are very large, with hundreds of millions or billions of dollars of assets. They traditionally invest in such items as negotiable bank certificates of deposit maturing within six months issued by large commercial banks, bankers' acceptances, commercial paper, short-term time deposits with foreign banks, and U.S. treasury notes and bills. Investments by money market funds are usually in units of at least $10,000,000, and often in amounts of $100,000,000 or more. Since all of these investments have very short maturities, measured in days rather than months or years, the risk of default or collapse is very low.

With the general decline in interest rates in the 1990s, yields on money market funds declined to unattractive levels. This has had two effects. First, like bank CDs, there has been a steady net outflow of funds from these money market accounts, presumably to be reinvested in higher risk investments. Second, the money market funds have broadened the nature of their investments in an effort to improve yield. In addition to the traditional securities found in money market fund portfolios, some managers are adding repos (see section 16.7), asset-backed securities (see section 16.20), and a variety of exotic short-term securities with floating yields linked to foreign currency exchange rates and foreign interest rates. While these investments improve yield, they may also increase risk to an uncertain extent. However, the most serious problem is likely to be that some of these exotic investments may be difficult to dispose of quickly for cash should the need arise.

One unique aspect of money market funds is that the trading unit is one dollar and earnings are reflected not by increases in the value of the trading unit but by adding more trading units to the account. The result is that an investor who holds, for example, 3,456 shares of a money market fund thinks in terms of having a deposit of $3,456. And the money market fund does what it can to further that impression. Additional trading units are added to the fund in proportion to its size in one dollar units. Depositors are permitted to write checks on the account without limitation, though small checks under $100 may be prohibited. Whenever a check is presented, the required number of trading units are redeemed in dollars. The whole arrangement is indeed very close to a bank account.

Money market funds are not insured against loss by the United States government. There is at least a theoretical default risk, but none has actually materialized. Perhaps the closest default risk occurred in 1990, when a major publicly held company, Integrated Resources, defaulted on its commercial paper, leaving two money market funds facing potential losses that could have reduced the net asset value of each share below one dollar. In both cases, the parent companies immediately rushed in to make up the losses, leaving intact the money market funds' record of never varying from the one dollar per share price. Following this incident, the SEC required money market funds to upgrade the quality of the commercial paper in their portfolios. A secondary consequence was that issuers of commercial paper with lower credit ratings found it increasingly difficult to raise working capital by issuing commercial paper.

An extremely risk-adverse investor might consider investing in government-only money market funds. These funds are of two types: (1) those that invest exclusively in securities issued by the United States and its agencies, such as Federal Home Loan Mortgage Corporation or Student Loan Marketing Association, and (2) those that invest only in securities issued by the United States Treasury. These government-only funds virtually eliminate the credit risk at some cost in yield. The difference in yield between a money market fund of the first type and a traditional mixed money market fund is about 0.25 percent of yield; because there is a remote risk that an agency of the government might default, money market funds of the second type lose about another 0.10 percent of yield. These differences in yield may narrow or increase from time to time.

Table 16-3 is an excerpt from The Wall Street Journal of September 17, 1992, reporting the results of operations of a number of large money market funds. Because of the short-term nature of the investments, yields are reported on alternative annualized "seven-day yield" bases: (1) on the actual yield over the prior seven-day period (the "7 day Yld") and (2) the same yield on a compounded basis (the "7 day EFF" or "e 7 Day yield"). The latter is usually called the "seven-day compounded yield" and assumes the reinvestment of all dividends at the same rate for one year. See section 16.14 for a further discussion of the complex subject of yield calculations. The table also gives the average maturity of the portfolio investments in days and the approximate size of the fund's portfolio. The portfolio size is reported in millions of dollars: AARP Money Fund, for example, has assets of $213,700,000 while the Active Asset Government Securities Fund has assets of $241,100,000.

Money market funds may also have specialized portfolios to a limited extent. Some funds invest solely in short-term tax-exempt municipal anticipation notes or similar securities in order to provide a tax-exempt yield on a pure money market fund investment. In 1992, an SEC ruling required the maximum date of maturity of tax-exempt investments to be limited to 90 days or less; before that time many tax-exempt mutual funds invested in securities with maturity dates of several months. Of course, the yield on tax-exempt funds is lower than the yield on taxable money market funds, though depending on the supply of short-term paper of each type, the difference in yield may at times be less than the tax benefit to investors in the highest tax bracket. See also section 16.18.

§16.9 UNITED STATES SAVINGS BONDS

United States Savings Bonds developed a stodgy image during the period when interest rates on riskless investments were at or above 10 percent while savings bonds were paying about one half that. However, these bonds are priced on a basis different from interest rates for other short-term riskless investments and therefore they may become more attractive as returns on other riskless investments drop. The early 1990s was such a period, and the sale of savings bonds soared to more than $9 billion in 1991.

The bonds available in the 1990s are Series EE bonds. For such a

Table 16-3

MONEY MARKET MUTUAL FUNDS

The following quotations, collected by the National Association of Securities Dealers Inc., represent the average of annualized yields and dollar-weighted portfolio maturities ending Wednesday, September 16, 1992. Yields don't include capital gains or losses.

Fund	Avg. Mat.	7Day Yld.	e7Day Yld.	Assets
AALMny	53	2.63	2.66	108
AARP HQ	45	2.31	2.34	326
AIMCshC	60	2.65	2.69	78
AIM MM	32	2.46	2.49	113
AIMMMC	62	2.65	2.68	93
ASO Pr	65	3.02	3.06	472
ASO US	73	2.89	2.93	310
ActAsGv	72	2.87	2.91	572
ActAsMny	69	3.05	3.09	3795
Aetna MM	53	3.61	3.61	31
AlexBwn	47	2.81	2.85	1092
AlxBTr	49	2.80	2.84	637
AlgerMM	67	3.51	3.57	139
AliMuCT	62	2.38	2.41	52
AlliaCpRs	69	2.81	2.85	1946
AliaGvR	76	2.69	2.73	1583
AlliMny	73	2.78	2.82	1464
AmAAdTr	55	3.11	3.15	106
AmAAdMM	86	3.49	3.55	2823
AmCRes	52	2.37	2.40	306
AmExDDiv	87	3.08	3.13	16982
AmExGv	85	3.01	3.05	3857
AmPerCsh	84	3.05	3.09	164
AmPerTrs	58	2.74	2.78	145
AmbMM	46	2.86	2.90	299
AmbTreas	68	2.70	2.74	93
ArchUSTr	49	2.69	2.72	185
ArchFd	55	2.63	2.66	540
AMF St Lq	10	2.79	2.83	185
AutCsh	61	3.03	3.07	1220
AutGvt	41	2.88	2.93	3251
AuGvSvc	40	2.83	2.87	372
AutTreasC	40	2.65	2.68	14
Babson	55	2.64	2.67	57
BartCsR	85	2.93	3.08	65
BayFdMM	78	3.03	3.07	293
BedfdGv	43	2.51	2.54	234
BdfdMM	52	2.65	2.69	748
BenhGvAg	57	2.76	2.80	779
BiltTF	47	2.85	2.89	52
BiltTrea	38	3.13	3.18	62
BILTmm	48	3.29	3.34	86
WmBlrRdy	40	2.87	2.91	422
BlnchGv	58	3.39	3.44	75
BostCo	82	2.86	2.90	268
BostGvt	55	2.67	2.70	115
BradGovObl	43	2.51	2.54	42
Bradfd	35	2.60	2.63	658
BullBDlr	50	2.76	2.80	70
CBC Cn Pr	87	2.99	3.03	284
CBC Cn Tr	52	2.69	2.73	936
CIMCO	27	2.30	2.32	9
CalvSoc f	53	2.73	2.77	172
CapCash	19	3.27	3.32	2
CapPre II	2	2.37	2.40	343
CapPrsv	54	2.74	2.78	3072
CapitolMM	62	3.11	3.16	96
CardGvt	26	2.39	2.42	477
Carillon	40	3.18	3.23	17
Carnegie	22	2.41	2.44	33
CascdCs	47	2.56	2.59	136
CshActMM	53	2.40	2.42	47
CshAcctGv	26	2.45	2.48	33
CshAset	59	3.11	3.16	291
CashEqv	43	2.67	2.71	4080
CshEqGv	25	2.61	2.64	2999
CashMgt	20	2.63	2.66	2050
CshTrGv	42	2.49	2.52	562
CshTrPr	63	2.61	2.64	764
CshTrTreas	41	2.48	2.51	618
CshTrII	39	2.59	2.62	231
Centn Csh	64	2.75	2.79	93
CentnGv	52	3.02	3.07	627
Centen	70	3.07	3.12	1484
ChchCsh	30	2.71	2.75	129
ColonIMM A	29	2.39	2.42	48

a-Actual return to shareholders may vary due to capital gain or losses. b-Account size varies due to fixed charges. c-Primarily federally tax exempt securities. e-Effective (compounded) 7-day yield. f-As of previous day. z-Unavailable.

bond held for five years, the interest rate equals 85 percent of the rate on five-year Treasury notes (see section 16.10) or 6 percent, whichever is higher. It is the latter feature that permits savings bonds to pay higher than alternative market investments. In early 1992, savings bonds held for five years paid the minimum 6 percent while the average 5-year certificate of deposit (see section 16.4) paid only about 5 percent. The interest rate on savings bonds is reset every six months. In early 1993, the minimum guaranteed note was reduced to 4 percent for bonds held for five years.

Savings bonds held for periods of less than five years pay interest at reduced rates. At the 6 percent minimum rate for bonds held for five years, the rates for bonds held for shorter periods as of August 1992 are set forth in Table 16-4.

Table 16-4
Relative Yields of Savings Bonds and CDs

	Savings bonds	*Rate on Insured Certificates of Deposit for same period*
6 months	4.16%	3.01%
1 year	4.27	3.24
2 years	4.64	3.86
5 years	6.00	5.29

Bonds are issued in face amount denominations ranging from $50 to $10,000 and are sold at one half of their face value. At the minimum 4 percent rate, a bond will double in value and reach its face value in 18 years. Interest continues to accrue until the bond is redeemed, which may be as long as 30 years. However, no interest is actually paid to the holder until the bond is redeemed, and no income tax is due on the growth of value until that time. If the owner of the bond uses the proceeds to pay the costs of higher education the tax on the interest is forgiven if the owner's adjusted gross income is less than $40,000 for individual taxpayers and $60,000 for taxpayers filing joint returns. These various features increase the attractiveness of United States savings bonds for the small investor.

Proposals have been made in Congress to exempt all interest on savings bonds used to pay higher education costs regardless of the owner's income. If enacted, this would greatly enhance the attractiveness of these bonds in the eyes of affluent individuals with young children who may be expected to go to college.

Savings bonds are not a good choice for investors who may need to dip into investments for current cash since they cannot be redeemed for a minimum period of six months except in cases of extreme hardship.

Savings bonds may be purchased at most banks and thrift institutions, at branches of the Federal Reserve Bank, and through payroll deductions at many corporations, educational institutions, and the like. The purchaser fills out an application form and the bond is delivered by mail about three weeks later. Interest begins to accrue on the first day of the month that payment is received. Bonds intended as gifts may be evidenced by certificates that the donee may turn in in order to have the bonds issued in his or her name.

§16.10 SHORT-TERM MARKETABLE DEBT INSTRUMENTS

Some short-term debt obligations do not carry an affirmative obligation to pay interest by the borrower. Rather, the borrower simply agrees to pay a specific amount — say, $10,000 in 30 days — and then sells this obligation at whatever price it can get at an auction or by a negotiated sale. A person may buy such an obligation for, say, $9,970. The $30 difference in price in effect represents both the interest earned by the purchaser and the cost of the borrowing to the debtor. The effective interest rate for the 30-day period is a little less than 4 percent per year. That interest is computed by comparing the amount invested ($9,970) and the interest earned ($30) on an annualized basis. Rather confusingly, interest rates on transactions of this type are often quoted as the percentage the discount bears to the face amount — $30 as a fraction of $10,000 rather than as a fraction of $9,970. The difference is usually not great, but the latter quotation understates slightly the true rate of interest on the investment. Quoted interest rates on short-term discounted debt are usually annualized for convenience of making comparisons.

The "effective" interest rate based on the purchase price is sometimes called the "coupon-equivalent yield," the "bond equivalent yield," or the "investment yield." The calculation normally reported (that compares the interest received to the face amount of the bill) is usually called the "discount rate."

A major issuer of debt instruments at a discount is the United States government. The United States Treasury issues discount instruments — known as treasury bills (also called "T-bills" or simply "bills") — with maturities as short as three months. Large volumes of discounted bills due in six months or one year are also sold each month. The minimum purchase is $10,000 of face value and a round lot is $5 million of face value. These instruments are viewed as entirely riskless and the price is established solely on the basis of market interest rates in the economy. The higher the interest rates, the greater the discount and, hence, the lower the price a $10,000 bill would command.

Secondary markets in discounted securities are made by securities dealers and brokers in all maturities of Treasury issues so that holders may sell securities before they mature. This secondary market also enables persons to make investments in these short-term interests through brokerage firms at times when the Treasury is not making a direct offering in the primary market. Fees and commissions generally make such investments attractive only for persons with large amounts of liquid funds.

Treasury bills and notes also may be purchased at banks or directly from the United States Treasury through its "Treasury Direct" program. If purchased directly, no commissions or fees are paid. The price and yield of securities purchased through the Treasury Direct program are established by the results of auctions conducted by the government on a regular basis. Information about this program may be obtained from the nearest Federal Reserve Bank or directly from the Treasury's Bureau of the Public Debt. The telephone number is 202-287-1414.

Table 16-5 on page 394 consists of excerpts from the daily report of trading of Treasury Bills as reported by the Wall Street Journal for April 5, 1993.

Short-term discounted instruments are also sold by state and local governments, corporations, and other entities.

§16.11 LONG-TERM MARKETABLE DEBT INSTRUMENTS

The two traditional types of fixed income instruments issued by private corporations are debentures and bonds. These types of securities may be publicly traded, and they have close economic similarities to publicly traded preferred stock, a security discussed in the following chapter. Bonds and debentures are described in section 16.12.

Federal and state governments also issue similar securities in large amounts, as do agencies of the federal government, municipalities, water districts, school districts, and a wide variety of local independent governmental agencies. Interest received upon municipal debt obligations is generally exempt from federal income taxation. See section 16.18. Securities issued by federal agencies such as GNMA, FHLMC, and FNMA are discussed in sections 16.19 and 16.20. In general terms, securities issued by these agencies are generally assumed to be guaranteed against default by the United States Government. However, this guarantee is not express, and, as a result, these securities carry a higher yield, reflecting this credit risk.

Table 16-5

TREASURY BONDS, NOTES & BILLS

Friday, April 2, 1993

Representative Over-the-Counter quotations based on transactions of $1 million or more.

Treasury bond, note and bill quotes are as of mid-afternoon. Colons in bid-and-asked quotes represent 32nds; 101:01 means 101 1/32. Net changes in 32nds. n-Treasury note. Treasury bill quotes in hundredths, quoted on terms of a rate of discount. Days to maturity calculated from settlement date. All yields are to maturity and based on the asked quote. Latest 13-week and 26-week bills are boldfaced. For bonds callable prior to maturity, yields are computed to the earliest call date for issues quoted above par and to the maturity date for issues below par. *-When issued.

Source: Federal Reserve Bank of New York.

TREASURY BILLS

Maturity	Days to Mat.	Bid	Asked	Chg.	Ask Yld.
Apr 07 '93	1	3.07	2.97	+0.01	3.01
Apr 08 '93	2	2.97	2.87	....	2.91
Apr 15 '93	9	2.94	2.84	+0.03	2.88
Apr 22 '93	16	2.95	2.85	+0.02	2.89
Apr 29 '93	23	2.75	2.65	−0.01	2.69
May 06 '93	30	2.86	2.82	....	2.87
May 13 '93	37	2.84	2.80	−0.01	2.85
May 20 '93	44	2.85	2.81	....	2.86
May 27 '93	51	2.85	2.81	−0.02	2.86
Jun 03 '93	58	2.90	2.88	....	2.93
Jun 10 '93	65	2.90	2.88	....	2.94
Jun 17 '93	72	2.90	2.88	....	2.94
Jun 24 '93	79	2.87	2.85	....	2.91
Jul 01 '93	**86**	**2.91**	**2.89**	**+0.01**	**2.95**
Jul 08 '93	93	2.91	2.89	....	2.95
Jul 15 '93	100	2.91	2.89	....	2.95
Jul 22 '93	107	2.93	2.91	+0.01	2.98
Jul 29 '93	114	2.94	2.92	....	2.99
Aug 05 '93	121	2.94	2.92	+0.01	2.99
Aug 12 '93	128	2.94	2.92	−0.03	2.99
Aug 19 '93	135	2.96	2.94	....	3.01
Aug 26 '93	142	2.98	2.96	....	3.04
Sep 02 '93	149	2.99	2.97	....	3.05
Sep 09 '93	156	3.00	2.98	....	3.06
Sep 16 '93	163	3.01	2.99	....	3.07
Sep 23 '93	170	3.00	2.98	....	3.06
Sep 30 '93	**177**	**3.00**	**2.98**	**....**	**3.07**
Oct 21 '93	198	3.04	3.02	+0.01	3.11
Nov 18 '93	226	3.08	3.06	....	3.15
Dec 16 '93	254	3.09	3.07	+0.01	3.17
Jan 13 '94	282	3.12	3.10	....	3.20
Feb 10 '94	310	3.15	3.13	+0.01	3.24
Mar 10 '94	338	3.17	3.15	....	3.27

Table 16-6 sets forth the Bond Market Data Bank entries for a wide variety of taxable and tax exempt securities for September 16, 1992, and representative quotations on such securities. This table is published daily in the Wall Street Journal and sets forth indexes reflecting price movements of the major types of debt securities. Incidentally, "Yankee bonds" referred to in this table are dollar denominated, SEC-registered bonds of foreign issuers sold in the United States.

Table 16-6

BOND MARKET DATA BANK 9/15/92

MAJOR INDEXES

HIGH	LOW (12 MOS)		CLOSE	NET CHG		% CHG	12-MO CHG		% CHG	FROM 12/31		% CHG
U.S. TREASURY SECURITIES	(Lehman Brothers indexes)											
3812.88	3365.51	Intermediate	3804.74	− 8.14	−	0.21	+ 439.18	+	13.05	+ 249.77	+	7.03
4695.41	4001.89	Long-term	4662.47	− 26.54	−	0.57	+ 641.70	+	15.96	+ 310.59	+	7.14
1472.90	1345.19	Long-term(price)	1460.46	− 8.61	−	0.59	+ 96.63	+	7.09	+ 18.10	+	1.25
4013.95	3513.85	Composite	4000.17	− 12.48	−	0.31	+ 486.09	+	13.83	+ 263.20	+	7.04
U.S. CORPORATE DEBT ISSUES	(Merrill Lynch)											
619.65	535.68	Corporate Master	617.84	− 1.81	−	0.29	+ 82.16	+	15.34	+ 49.11	+	8.64
462.05	401.96	1-10 Yr Maturities	460.94	− 1.11	−	0.24	+ 58.98	+	14.67	+ 36.42	+	8.58
464.34	398.36	10+ Yr Maturities	462.90	− 1.44	−	0.31	+ 63.83	+	15.99	+ 37.41	+	8.79
272.30	222.39	High Yield	272.30	+ 0.03	+	0.01	+ 49.91	+	22.44	+ 37.62	+	16.03
450.80	386.77	Yankee Bonds	448.57	− 1.96	−	0.44	+ 61.80	+	15.98	+ 34.60	+	8.36
TAX-EXEMPT SECURITIES	(Bond Buyer; Merrill Lynch: Dec. 31, 1986 = 100)											
101-7	94-7	Bond Buyer Municipal	97-27	− 31	−	0.98	+ 3-16	+	3.71	+ 1-11	+	1.39
150.01	133.64	New 10-yr G.O.(AA)	148.63	+ 0.02	+	0.01	+ 14.99	+	11.22	+ 9.13	+	6.54
160.39	136.95	New 20-yr G.O.(AA)	156.32	+ 0.02	+	0.01	+ 19.37	+	14.14	+ 11.88	+	8.22
186.61	155.43	New 30-yr revenue(A)	181.66	+ 0.03	+	0.02	+ 26.23	+	16.88	+ 16.73	+	10.14
MORTGAGE-BACKED SECURITIES	(current coupon; Merrill Lynch: Dec. 31, 1986 = 100)											
184.40	159.24	Ginnie Mae(GNMA)	182.52	− 0.94	−	0.51	+ 23.28	+	14.62	+ 9.92	+	5.75
186.23	158.94	Fannie Mae(FNMA)	184.84	− 0.73	−	0.39	+ 25.90	+	16.30	+ 13.55	+	7.91
182.86	158.57	Freddie Mac(FHLMC)	181.98	− 0.46	−	0.25	+ 23.41	+	14.76	+ 11.97	+	7.04
CONVERTIBLE BONDS	(Merrill Lynch: Dec. 31, 1986 = 100)											
159.08	141.02	Investment Grade	159.08	+ 0.13	+	0.08	+ 18.06	+	12.81	+ 9.95	+	6.67
160.19	131.69	High Yield	160.19	+ 0.37	+	0.23	+ 28.50	+	21.64	+ 21.39	+	15.41

CORPORATE BONDS

Quotes of representative taxable issues at mid-afternoon New York time, provided by First Boston/CSFB Ltd.

ISSUE (RATING: MOODY'S/S&P)	COUPON	MATURITY	PRICE	CHANGE		YIELD	CHANGE
FINANCIAL							
Chase Manhattan Corp (Baa2/BBB)	9.750	11/01/01	113.072	−	0.530	7.725	0.075
Citicorp (Baa3/BBB+)	9.500	02/01/02	109.575	−	0.522	8.025	0.075
Ford Credit Co (A2/A)	8.875	06/15/99	112.070	−	0.438	6.625	0.075
GMAC (Baa1/A−)	8.250	08/01/96	107.671	−	0.274	6.000	0.075
Household Fin (A3/A)	7.625	06/15/99	104.534	−	0.277	6.774	0.050
UTILITY							
Commonwlth Ed (Baa2/BBB)	9.625	07/01/19	107.169	−	0.811	8.915	0.075
Pacific G&E (A1/A)	8.125	01/01/97	102.560	−	0.278	7.415	0.075
Sou Bell Tel (Aaa/AAA)	8.500	08/01/29	103.993	−	0.910	8.155	0.075
Sou Cal Ed (Aa3/A+)	9.375	02/15/17	107.361	−	0.809	8.645	0.075
US West Commun (Aa3/AA−)	8.875	06/01/31	107.781	−	0.942	8.205	0.075
INDUSTRIAL							
Amoco (Aaa/AAA)	8.625	12/15/16	107.357	−	0.855	7.935	0.075
Capital Cities (A1/A+)	8.750	03/15/16	106.290	−	0.823	8.145	0.075
Du Pont & Co (Aa2/AA)	6.000	12/01/01	94.089	−	0.487	6.875	0.075
Exxon Shipping (Aaa/AAA)	Zero	09/01/12	20.828	−	0.298	8.016	0.075
East Kodak (A3/A−)	9.125	03/01/98	108.150	−	0.354	7.288	0.075
Mobil (Aa2/AA)	8.625	07/01/94	107.741	−	0.148	4.100	0.075
FOREIGN							
Hydro-Quebec (Aa3/AA−)	8.500	12/01/29	102.565	−	0.889	8.275	0.075
Int Bk Recon Dev (Aaa/AAA)	9.875	10/01/97	117.431	−	0.366	5.835	0.075
Sweden (Aa1/AAA)	8.125	11/01/96	105.682	−	0.281	6.529	0.075
Victoria Finance (Aa2/AA)	8.450	10/01/01	111.506	−	0.542	6.730	0.075

Table 16-6 (*continued*)

TAX-EXEMPT BONDS

Representative prices for several active tax-exempt revenue and refunding bonds, based on institutional trades. Changes rounded to the nearest one-eighth. Yield is to maturity. n-New. Source: The Bond Buyer.

ISSUE	COUPON	MAT	PRICE	CHG	BID YLD
Bass Brook Minn	6.000	07-01-22	96½	– 1	6.26
Calif Dept of Wtr Res	6.125	12-01-13	98½	– 1	6.25
Charlotte Hosp Auth NC	6.250	01-01-20	98¾	– ¾	6.35
Chgo GO Ser 92 Proj A	5.875	01-01-22	94	– 1	6.33
Chgo Ill Arpt Ser 92A	6.000	01-01-18	94	– ¾	6.49
Citrus Co Fla Ser92B	6.350	02-01-22	99¼	– ⅞	6.40
Clark Co Nev Ser92A	6.000	07-01-22	95⅞	– ⅞	6.31
Farmngtn NM Util Sys	5.750	05-15-13	94⅜	– ⅞	6.23
Fla Mun Pwr Agcy	5.500	10-01-12	92	– ⅞	6.20
Fla Mun Pwr Agcy	5.700	10-01-16	93⅝	– ¾	6.21
Fla St Bd of Ed	6.000	06-01-22	96⅜	– 2	6.27
Jacksonville Elec Fla	5.750	10-01-12	94½	– ¾	6.23
Kans Dept Trans Ser92	6.500	03-01-12	102⅛	– ¾	6.31
LA Dept Wtr & Pwr	6.000	08-15-32	95⅞	– 1⅜	6.28
Metro Seattle Swr	6.200	01-01-32	97⅛	– ¾	6.40
N.J. Turnpike Au Ser 91	6.200	01-01-18	99½	– ¾	6.24
NJ Hwy Auth Ser 9	6.250	01-01-14	100	– ⅞	6.25
NY Tnsp Auth commuter	6.125	07-01-12	98⅜	– ⅞	6.27
NY Tnsp Auth commuter	6.250	07-01-17	99⅝	– ⅝	6.28
NYC Muni Wtr Fin Auth	5.750	06-15-18	93⅞	– ⅞	6.22
NYC Muni Wtr Fin Auth	6.000	06-15-17	94⅛	– 1¼	6.48
NYS Med Care Fin Agcy	6.200	08-15-22	98	– 1⅛	6.35
NYS Pwr Auth	6.250	01-01-23	99¼	– ¾	6.30
NYS Thruway Auth SerA	5.750	01-01-19	92⅛	– 1⅛	6.37
Osceola Co Fla Transp	6.100	04-01-17	98⅛	– ⅞	6.25
P R Hwy & Transp Auth	6.500	07-01-22	100⅜	– 1	6.48
P R Hwy & Transp Auth	6.625	07-01-18	101½	– ⅞	6.51
P R Various G O	6.000	07-01-14	95¼	– 1¼	6.40
P.R. G.O. Pub Imprvmt	6.800	07-01-21	102⅞	– 1	6.58
P.R. Pub Bldg Auth	6.875	07-01-21	103½	– ⅞	6.60
Penna Tpke Comm	5.750	12-01-12	95	– ⅞	6.18
Penna Tpke Comm	6.000	12-01-12	98	– ⅞	6.18
S.C. Pub Serv Rev	6.625	07-01-31	101¾	– ¾	6.50
Salt Lake City Utah 92	6.250	02-15-23	97⅞	– ⅞	6.41
Salt River Agri Impvmt	6.000	01-01-13	97	– 1	6.26
San Antonio Texas	5.750	08-01-13	94⅛	– 1⅛	6.26
Sikeston Mo Elec Sys	6.250	06-01-22	99¾	– ⅝	6.27
TBTA Ser 92	6.000	01-01-15	97⅛	– 1	6.23
Univ of Pittsburgh	6.125	06-01-21	98⅜	– 1	6.24
Washn Hlth Care Fac	5.750	08-15-22	92¼	– 1	6.33

MORTGAGE-BACKED SECURITIES

Representative issues, quoted by Salomon Brothers Inc.

	REMAINING TERM (Years)	WTD-AVG LIFE (Years)	PRICE (OCT) (Pts.-32ds)	PRICE CHANGE (32ds)	CASH FLOW YIELD*	YIELD CHANGE (Basis pts.)
30-YEAR						
GNMA 8.0%	29.6	10.3	103-22	– 8	7.47%	+ 5
FHLMC Gold 8.0%	29.1	6.3	103-23	– 8	7.20	+ 8
FNMA 8.0%	29.3	6.6	103-17	– 10	7.22	+ 9
GNMA 9.0%	29.3	5.4	107-02	– 6	7.22	+ 38
FHLMC Gold 9.0%	29.2	3.2	106-03	– 6	6.63	+ 17
FNMA 9.0%	28.3	3.1	106-07	– 5	6.45	+ 17
GNMA 10.0%	29.0	3.1	109-16	– 4	6.31	+ 29
FHLMC Gold 10.0%	27.4	1.7	107-28	– 4	4.67	+ 16
FNMA 10.0%	27.6	1.7	108-00	– 4	4.47	+ 16
15-YEAR						
GNMA 8.0%	14.5	6.3	106-09	+ 6	6.71%	– 3
FHLMC Gold 8.0%	14.7	5.0	106-00	+ 6	6.49	– 4
FNMA 8.0%	14.7	5.2	105-22	+ 6	6.57	– 2

*Based on projections from Salomon's prepayment model, assuming interest rates remain unchanged from current levels

COLLATERALIZED MORTGAGE OBLIGATIONS

Spread of CMO yields above U.S. Treasury securities of comparable maturity, in basis points (100 basis points = 1 percentage point of interest)

MAT	SPREAD	CHG FROM PREV DAY
NEW ISSUES		
2-year	115	unch
5-year	110	unch
10-year	115	unch
20-year	95	unch
SEASONED ISSUES		
2-year	105	unch
5-year	100	unch
10-year	105	unch
20-year	90	unch

GUARANTEED INVESTMENT CONTRACTS

Source: T. Rowe Price GIC Index

	1 YEAR		2 YEARS		3 YEARS		4 YEARS		5 YEARS	
	RATE	CHG	RATE	CHG	RATE	CHG	RATE	CHG	RATE	CHG
High	3.56%	–0.05	4.62%	+0.04	5.15%	+0.02	5.80%	unch	6.15%	–0.02
Low	2.60	unch	3.42	+0.02	4.18	+0.07	4.65	+0.05	5.22	+0.08
INDEX	3.06	–0.01	4.07	+0.02	4.73	+0.01	5.29	+0.02	5.82	+0.02
TOP QUARTILE RANGE	3.56% - 3.33%		4.62% - 4.29%		5.15% - 4.91%		5.80% - 5.50%		6.15% - 5.98%	
SPREAD vs. TREASURYS	–0.10		+0.27		+0.35		+0.31		+0.47	

GIC rates quoted prior to 3 pm (Eastern) net of all expenses, no broker commissions. Rates represent best quote for a $2-$5 million immediate lump sum deposit with annual interest payments. Yield spreads based on U.S. Treasury yields, as of 3 pm (Eastern), versus the index rate unadjusted for semi vs. annual interest payments. CHG reflects change in rate from previous day. INDEX is average of all rates quoted. Universe is investment grade.

Table 16-6 (continued)

INTERNATIONAL GOVERNMENT BONDS
Prices in local currencies, provided by Salomon Brothers Inc.

COUPON	MATURITY (Mo./yr.)	PRICE	CHANGE	YIELD*	COUPON	MATURITY (Mo./yr.)	PRICE	CHANGE	YIELD*
JAPAN (Closed)					**GERMANY** (5 p.m. London)				
					8.00%	1/02	102.024	− 0.026	7.54%
					8.50	9/96	101.465	+ 0.221	7.90
					8.88	7/95	101.137	+ 0.240	8.22
					8.38	1/97	101.216	+ 0.194	7.86
					6.75	1/99	93.944	+ 0.104	7.84
UNITED KINGDOM (5 p.m. London)					**CANADA** (3 p.m. EDT)				
10.00%	4/93	99.859	− 0.250	10.32%	9.50%	6/10	111.450	− 1.600	8.25%
9.00	10/08	100.594	− 1.281	8.93	8.50	4/02	106.900	− 1.200	7.47
10.00	11/96	100.344	− 1.188	9.87	9.25	6/22	110.150	− 1.600	8.32
9.75	8/02	102.969	− 1.344	9.28	7.00	9/94	102.200	− 0.600	5.82
10.00	6/94	99.875	− 0.625	10.06	7.50	7/97	103.150	− 0.900	6.72

*Equivalent to semi-annual compounded yields to maturity

Total Rates of Return on International Bonds
In percent, based on Salomon Brothers' world government benchmark bond indexes

	— LOCAL CURRENCY TERMS —				SINCE 12/31	— U.S. DOLLAR TERMS —				SINCE 12/31
	1 DAY	1 MO	3 MOS	12 MOS		1 DAY	1 MO	3 MOS	12 MOS	
Japan	Closed									
Britain	− 0.88	+ 0.19	+ 1.43	+ 9.72	+ 7.64	− 2.35	− 3.09	+ 1.70	+ 17.55	+ 7.18
Germany	+ 0.17	+ 1.32	+ 2.45	+ 4.57	+ 5.42	− 0.10	− 0.52	+ 7.84	+ 17.40	+ 7.12
France	− 0.13	+ 1.56	+ 2.25	+ 7.97	+ 4.80	− 0.50	− 0.36	+ 6.88	+ 21.73	+ 7.25
Canada	− 1.04	− 0.25	+ 5.72	+ 18.62	+ 9.16	− 1.39	− 2.12	+ 3.50	+ 10.67	+ 3:59
Netherlands	+ 0.10	+ 1.71	+ 1.55	+ 9.33	+ 5.98	− 0.09	+ 0.04	+ 7.02	+ 23.00	+ 7.83
Non-U.S.	NA	NA	NA	NA	NA	− 0.74	− 0.78	+ 5.66	+ 18.59	+ 6.76
World*	− 0.32	+ 0.84	+ 2.78	+ 9.11	+ 5.90	− 0.70	− 0.53	+ 5.00	+ 16.10	+ 5.94

*Includes U.S. Treasury benchmark index   NA=not applicable

EURODOLLAR BONDS
Provided by First Boston/CSFB Ltd.

ISSUE (RATING: MOODY'S/S&P)	COUPON	MATURITY	PRICE	CHANGE	YIELD	CHANGE
Canada (Aaa/AAA)	9.000	02/27/96	112.170	unch	4.988	− 0.003
Quebec (Aa3/AA−)	9.125	08/22/01	113.766	unch	6.904	− 0.001
Belgium (Aa1/NR)	9.625	07/10/98	114.936	unch	6.355	− 0.001
Italy (Aaa/NR)	9.000	07/28/93	104.219	unch	3.897	− 0.016

The United States Treasury issues "notes" rather than "bonds" for maturities of less than ten years. Notes are usually sold by competitive bid at auctions based on yield or interest rate rather than on price. A round lot for Treasury notes and bonds is usually $1,000,000 of face value.

Table 16-7 describes trading in Treasury notes of varying maturities; this table is truncated and omits intermediate quotations.

Long-term commercial loans may also be privately negotiated and evidenced by promissory notes; such loans typically are not represented by certificates or evidences of indebtedness and are not publicly traded. Most long-term commercial bank loans are of this character. Even though debt

TREASURY BONDS, NOTES & BILLS

Friday, February 12, 1993

Representative Over-the-Counter quotations based on transactions of $1 million or more.

Treasury bond, note and bill quotes are as of mid-afternoon. Colons in bid-and-asked quotes represent 32nds; 101:01 means 101 1/32. Net changes in 32nds. n-Treasury note. Treasury bill quotes in hundredths, quoted on terms of a rate of discount. Days to maturity calculated from settlement date. All yields are to maturity and based on the asked quote. Latest 13-week and 26-week bills are boldfaced. For bonds callable prior to maturity, yields are computed to the earliest call date for issues quoted above par and to the maturity date for issues below par. *-When issued.

Source: Federal Reserve Bank of New York.

GOVT. BONDS & NOTES

Rate	Maturity Mo/Yr	Bid	Asked	Chg.	Ask Yld.
6 3/4	Feb 93n	100:03	100:05	− 2	1.56
7 1/8	Mar 93n	100:15	100:17	− 2	2.44
9 5/8	Mar 93n	100:24	100:26	− 3	2.47
7 3/8	Apr 93n	100:21	100:23	− 2	2.70
7	Apr 93n	100:25	100:27	− 2	2.68
7 5/8	May 93n	101:02	101:04	− 2	2.86
8 5/8	May 93n	101:10	101:12	− 2	2.80
10 1/8	May 93n	101:21	101:23	− 2	2.85
6 3/4	May 93n	101:00	101:02	− 2	2.92
7	Jun 93n	101:13	101:15	− 2	2.93
8 1/8	Jun 93n	101:26	101:28	− 2	2.93
7 1/4	Jul 93n	101:20	101:22	− 2	3.05
6 7/8	Jul 93n	101:20	101:22	− 1	3.09
8	Aug 93n	102:10	102:12	− 2	3.12
8 5/8	Aug 93	102:20	102:22	− 2	3.11
8 3/4	Aug 93n	102:22	102:24	− 2	3.10
11 7/8	Aug 93n	104:07	104:09	− 3	3.08
6 3/8	Aug 93n	101:20	101:22	− 1	3.14
6 1/8	Sep 93n	101:23	101:25	− 1	3.18
8 1/4	Sep 93n	103:01	103:03	− 1	3.14
7 1/8	Oct 93n	102:14	102:16	− 2	3.25
6	Oct 93n	101:26	101:28	....	3.27
7 3/4	Nov 93n	103:05	103:07	− 2	3.32
8 5/8	Nov 93	103:25	103:27	− 1	3.33
9	Nov 93n	104:02	104:04	− 2	3.32
11 3/4	Nov 93n	106:02	106:04	− 3	3.32
5 1/2	Nov 93n	101:19	101:21	− 1	3.34
5	Dec 93n	101:10	101:12	− 1	3.38
7 5/8	Dec 93n	103:18	103:20	− 1	3.35
7	Jan 94n	103:04	103:06	....	3.41
4 7/8	Jan 94n	101:09	101:11	− 1	3.43
6 7/8	Feb 94n	103:07	103:09	− 1	3.49
8 7/8	Feb 94n	105:05	105:07	− 2	3.49
9	Feb 94	105:09	105:11	− 1	3.49
5 3/8	Feb 94n	101:27	101:29	....	3.48
5 3/4	Mar 94n	102:11	102:13	....	3.53
8 1/2	Mar 94n	105:09	105:11	− 2	3.57
7	Apr 94n	103:24	103:26	− 1	3.61
5 3/8	Apr 94n	101:31	102:01	....	3.63
4 1/8	May 89-94	100:13	100:29	....	0.35
7	May 94n	103:30	104:00	....	3.67
9 1/2	May 94n	106:30	107:00	− 1	3.68
13 1/8	May 94n	111:09	111:11	− 3	3.69
5 1/8	May 94n	101:23	101:25	....	3.69
5	Jun 94n	101:19	101:21	....	3.75
8 1/2	Jun 94n	106:06	106:08	− 1	3.77
8	Jul 94n	105:20	105:22	− 1	3.82
4 1/4	Jul 94n	100:17	100:19	....	3.83
6 7/8	Aug 94n	104:09	104:11	....	3.86
8 5/8	Aug 94n	106:26	106:28	− 1	3.85
8 3/4	Aug 94	106:30	107:02	− 4	3.84
12 5/8	Aug 94n	112:18	112:20	− 1	3.85
4 1/4	Aug 94n	100:16	100:18	+ 1	3.87
4	Sep 94n	100:02	100:04	....	3.92
8 1/2	Sep 94n	107:02	107:04	....	3.91
9 1/2	Oct 94n	108:22	108:24	− 1	3.99
4 1/4	Oct 94n	100:11	100:13	....	4.00
6	Nov 94n	103:07	103:09	....	4.03
8 1/4	Nov 94n	106:30	107:00	− 1	4.05
10 1/8	Nov 94	110:02	110:04	− 1	4.05
11 5/8	Nov 94n	112:19	112:21	− 2	4.03
4 5/8	Nov 94n	100:29	100:31	....	4.06
4 5/8	Dec 94n	100:27	100:29	+ 1	4.12
7 5/8	Dec 94n	106:08	106:10	....	4.08
8 5/8	Jan 95n	108:04	108:06	....	4.12
4 1/4	Jan 95n	100:04	100:06	....	4.15
3	Feb 95	98:30	99:30	+ 9	3.03
5 1/2	Feb 95n	102:15	102:17	+ 1	4.16
7 3/4	Feb 95n	106:24	106:26	....	4.16
10 1/2	Feb 95	111:31	112:01	....	4.15
11 1/4	Feb 95n	113:13	113:15	− 2	4.14
6 3/8	Jan 99n	102:18	102:20	+ 2	5.84
8 7/8	Feb 99n	114:31	115:01	+ 1	5.86
7	Apr 99n	105:16	105:18	+ 2	5.91
8 1/2	May 94-99	105:18	105:26	+ 2	3.67
9 1/8	May 99n	116:14	116:16	+ 2	5.92
6 3/8	Jul 99n	102:06	102:08	+ 2	5.95
8	Aug 99n	110:24	110:26	+ 2	5.97
6	Oct 99n	99:31	100:01	+ 2	5.99
7 7/8	Nov 99n	110:04	110:06	+ 3	6.01
6 3/8	Jan 00n	102:05	102:07	+ 3	5.98
7 7/8	Feb 95-00	106:06	106:10	....	4.53
8 1/2	Feb 00n	113:21	113:23	+ 4	6.06
8 7/8	May 00n	115:28	115:30	+ 3	6.12
8 3/8	Aug 95-00	108:10	108:14	+ 1	4.75
8 3/4	Aug 00n	115:07	115:09	+ 3	6.17
8 1/2	Nov 00n	113:24	113:26	+ 4	6.22
7 3/4	Feb 01n	109:07	109:09	+ 5	6.26
11 3/4	Feb 01	133:29	134:01	+ 7	6.27
8	May 01n	110:23	110:25	+ 3	6.30
13 1/8	May 01	143:10	143:14	+ 3	6.29
7 7/8	Aug 01n	109:29	109:31	+ 2	6.34
8	Aug 96-01	107:07	107:11	− 3	5.65
13 3/8	Aug 01	145:27	145:31	+ 2	6.30
7 1/2	Nov 01n	107:15	107:17	+ 13	6.36
15 3/4	Nov 01	162:14	162:18	+ 1	6.32
14 1/4	Feb 02	153:13	153:17	+ 3	6.35
7 1/2	May 02n	107:21	107:23	+ 1	6.38
6 3/8	Aug 02n	99:23	99:25	+ 1	6.41
11 5/8	Nov 02	137:07	137:11	+ 4	6.41
6 1/4	Feb 03n*	99:09	99:11	+ 5	6.34
10 3/4	Feb 03	131:07	131:11	+ 4	6.45
10 3/4	May 03	131:16	131:20	+ 5	6.48
11 1/8	Aug 03	134:21	134:25	+ 5	6.50
11 7/8	Nov 03	140:25	140:29	+ 5	6.52
12 3/8	May 04	145:29	146:01	+ 5	6.53
13 3/4	Aug 04	157:12	157:16	+ 1	6.55
11 5/8	Nov 04	140:08	140:12	+ 3	6.62
8 1/4	May 00-05	110:01	110:05	+ 2	6.47
12	May 05	144:02	144:06	+ 3	6.66
10 3/4	Aug 05	133:27	133:31	+ 2	6.69
9 3/8	Feb 06	122:28	123:00	+ 4	6.70
7 5/8	Feb 02-07	106:11	106:15	+ 3	6.66
7 7/8	Nov 02-07	108:03	108:07	....	6.71
8 3/8	Aug 03-08	112:05	112:09	+ 3	6.72
8 3/4	Nov 03-08	115:03	115:07	+ 3	6.74
9 1/8	May 04-09	118:12	118:16	+ 5	6.75
10 3/8	Nov 04-09	128:30	129:02	+ 6	6.75
11 3/4	Feb 05-10	140:14	140:18	+ 5	6.76
10	May 05-10	126:14	126:18	+ 5	6.77
12 3/4	Nov 05-10	150:09	150:13	+ 1	6.78
13 7/8	May 06-11	161:01	161:05	+ 5	6.80
14	Nov 06-11	163:14	163:18	+ 5	6.81
10 3/8	Nov 07-12	131:08	131:12	+ 4	6.94
12	Aug 08-13	147:11	147:15	+ 2	6.95
13 1/4	May 09-14	160:13	160:17	+ 2	6.97
12 1/2	Aug 09-14	153:13	153:17	+ 2	6.98
11 3/4	Nov 09-14	146:09	146:13	+ 4	7.00
11 1/4	Feb 15	144:31	145:01	+ 7	7.16
10 5/8	Aug 15	138:07	138:09	+ 7	7.17
9 7/8	Nov 15	129:28	129:30	+ 6	7.18
9 1/4	Feb 16	122:25	122:27	+ 7	7.20
7 1/4	May 16	100:14	100:16	+ 5	7.21
7 1/2	Nov 16	103:04	103:06	+ 6	7.22
8 3/4	May 17	117:10	117:12	+ 5	7.22
8 7/8	Aug 17	118:25	118:27	+ 6	7.22
9 1/8	May 18	122:00	122:02	+ 7	7.21
9	Nov 18	120:20	120:22	+ 7	7.22
8 7/8	Feb 19	119:04	119:06	+ 7	7.23
8 1/8	Aug 19	110:10	110:12	+ 6	7.24
8 1/2	Feb 20	114:28	114:30	+ 7	7.23
8 3/4	May 20	118:00	118:02	+ 7	7.22
8 3/4	Aug 20	118:01	118:03	+ 7	7.23

obligations are not represented by certificates, they may later be "bundled" together in separate packages and interests in the packages may be represented by certificates and be publicly traded. This process is known as "securitization" and is discussed in section 16.19.

§16.12 BONDS AND DEBENTURES IN GENERAL

Both bonds and debentures are true debt instruments: They reflect unconditional obligations to pay specific sums at a date in the future and usually to pay interest in specified amounts at specified times in the interim. Technically a "debenture" is an unsecured corporate obligation while a "bond" is secured by a lien or mortgage on specific corporate property. However, the word "bond" is often used to refer to both bonds and debentures and is so used hereafter. The presence or absence of security for these marketable debt interests is not as important as might be first supposed because if a secured holder actually seeks to foreclose on corporate property, the corporation will immediately obtain protection from the federal bankruptcy court.

A bond is usually a long-term debt security: Long-term may mean 50 years or more in some cases, though many marketable bonds and debentures mature in ten years or less. By history and tradition, bonds are bearer instruments, negotiable by delivery, with interest payments represented by coupons that are periodically clipped and submitted to the issuer for payment. Registered bonds, however, have long existed side-by-side with bearer bonds: They are bonds issued without coupons in the name of, and made payable to the order of, a specific payee. Interest is payable to the registered owner of such a bond in much the same way as dividends are payable to the registered owner of shares of stock. Transfer of a registered bond is effected by endorsement rather than by mere physical delivery of the piece of paper. Article 8 of the Uniform Commercial Code makes registered bonds negotiable just like any other security. Bearer bonds have historically been a convenient place to invest funds the source and identity of which the owner would prefer to remain confidential. The Internal Revenue Code now requires virtually all new bonds to be registered securities, transferable only by endorsement, so that in future years, it is likely that registered bonds will become more common and bearer bonds rarer.

Many debt instruments are now held in "book entry" form, similar to shares of stock. (See section 14.6) Bonds held in book entry form are not certificated; they may be sold simply by ordering the brokerage firm to do so.

Interest payments on debt securities are usually fixed obligations, due in any event, and expressed as a percentage of the face amount of the security. However, a number of variations exist. So-called income bonds, in which the obligation to pay interest is conditioned on adequate corporate earnings, also exist, as do participating bonds, where the amount of interest payable on the bonds increases with corporate earnings. Such securities are known as hybrid securities since they have some characteristics of an equity security. In the 1980s another variation, debt securities with variable interest rates — based on market interest rates — was also created.

Bonds and debentures, like preferred stock discussed in the next chapter, may be made convertible into common shares, thereby giving them some of the market characteristics of equity securities. The following sections deal with prices and yields of "straight" bonds and debentures, followed by a brief discussion of convertibles and the interrelationship between the power to redeem debt securities and the conversion privilege.

§16.13 BOND PRICING

Before turning to pricing, it is necessary to first describe the characteristics of the instrument under discussion. Bonds are issued in $1,000 denominations or in multiples of $1,000. Each bond carries with it a right to receive a stated amount of interest every half year (or full year, in some cases). The ratio between this fixed amount and the $1,000 face value is called the "coupon rate." This usage is still common despite the fact that bonds increasingly are issued in registered or book entry form and the interest payments are not represented by negotiable coupons. Rather than the owner "clipping coupons," the issuer simply sends a check to the registered owner or the brokerage firm every six months for the maturing interest obligation.

The coupon rate is set when the bond is created and is an integral part of the description of the bond. For example, a bond that commits the issuer to pay $45 every six months has a coupon rate of 9 percent: $90 per year is 9 percent of the face value of $1,000. This coupon rate is constant for the life of the bond, and the bond is usually described as a 9 percent bond.

When bonds are originally issued, the coupon rate is usually fixed at or very close to the then going market interest rate so that the bond initially sells for approximately $1,000. Sales at the face amount of the bond are said to be "at par" or at "face value." Once the bonds are issued and sold to the public, a market in them develops. As interest rates and risk of nonpayment change, the bonds sell at various prices determined by the market for debt instruments. The market price is unrelated to par or face value. If interest rates are higher than the coupon rate, the bond sells at a discount from par, that is, for less than $1,000. The actual market price is the price that makes the return obtained by a purchaser of the bond at that price equal to the higher market rate of interest on investments with the same degree of risk associated with that bond. If market interest rates are lower than the coupon rate, the bond sells at a premium, that is, at a price higher than the par value of $1,000.

An illustration may be useful. A small volume of bonds is traded each day on the New York Stock Exchange. Table 16-8 is an excerpt from this table for trading that occurred on September, 15 1992. First, one must learn to read the descriptions of the bonds themselves: The first entry, "AMR 9s16" means that these are bonds issued by AMR, the parent of American Air Lines, maturing in the year 2016 (the "16" following the "s" indicates the date of maturity); the coupon rate is 9 percent per year (the "9" before the "s" indicates the coupon rate), or, in other words, the holder of each bond receives $45 every six months. The "s" means that the interest is paid semiannually; bonds that pay interest annually appear without an "s," for example, "ATT 5 1/8 01" makes a single annual payment of $51.25 in interest each year. Trading prices for bonds are quoted without one zero for reasons of space (or what amounts to the same thing, are quoted in $10 units); the five and one-eighth ATT bond closed at ninety and one/eighth, or $901.25 for each $1,000 face value bond. How could it be that a bond with a face amount of $1,000 and paying $51.25 per year in interest sells for only $901.25? That is the market compensating for the fact that the current market interest rate for a bond with this bond's financial return, risk characteristics, and date of maturity is higher than five and one-eighth percent.

What is the actual market interest rate for this bond? The column "Cur Yld" (current yield) gives a strong clue: That shows an entry of 5.7 percent for the AT&T bond under discussion. It turns out that the 5.7 percent figure is only an approximation. All interest-bearing bonds have two features. For example, the purchaser who buys the five and one-eighth percent AT&T bond for $901.25 is entitled to receive two things: (1) $51.25 every year from now until the year 2001; and (2) on a specified day in the year 2001, $1,000 in cash as the bond matures. For this combination of two benefits, a purchaser today pays $901.25. The 5.7 percent current yield in the table reflects only the return on $901.25 that the $51.25 annual payments yield; no account is taken of the fact that some nine years from now the holder will also receive $1,000 while investing only $901.25.

The notation "cv" in the current yield column of Table 16-8 is discussed in section 16.15.

The true measure of yield that takes into account both factors is called the yield-to-maturity. The yield-to-maturity is the interest or discount rate that in a present value calculation would make all the cash payments over the remaining life of a bond — both interest payments and repayment of principal at maturity — equal to the bond's market value. This calculation assumes that interim interest payments are reinvested at the same yield-to-maturity rate.

Calculations of yield-to-maturity are obviously closely related to pres-

NEW YORK EXCHANGE BONDS

CORPORATION BONDS

Volume, $47,930,000

Bonds	Cur Yld	Vol	Close	Net Chg.
AMR 9s16	9.0	212	100⅜	– ⅛
AMR zr06	...	1	43⅜	– ⅜
AMR 8.10s98	7.8	60	104	+ ⅛
Advst 9s08	cv	8	89	...
AirbF 6¾01	cv	31	89½	...
AlaP 9⅜16	9.1	10	103¼	– 1⅝
AlskAr 6⅞14	cv	20	83¾	– ¾
AlldC zr92	...	4	99 11/32	...
AlldC zr95	...	20	86	+ 1
AlldC zr97	...	15	72⅜	+ ¼
AlldC zr03	...	10	42½	– 1¾
AlldC zr09	...	120	25⅞	+ ½
AlegCp 6½14	cv	30	87½	– ½
AldSig 9⅞97	9.4	188	104⅞	...
Allwst 7¼14	cv	26	89	– 1
AAir dc6¼96	6.2	1	100¼	+ ¼
ABrnd 8½03	7.8	50	109⅛	– ⅞
ACyan 7⅜01	7.2	3	102	+ 1¼
AmStor 01	cv	25	109	– 1¼
ATT 5½97	5.5	128	99¾	– ⅛
ATT 6s00	6.1	451	98⅜	– ⅛
ATT 5⅛01	5.7	72	90⅛	...
ATT 7s01	6.9	194	101	– ⅛
ATT 7⅛03	7.1	976	100⅜	– ¼
ATT 8⅝26	8.3	1216	104⅜	– ½
ATT 8⅝31	8.1	120	106	– ¾
ATT 7⅛02	6.9	30	103⅜	– ¼
ATT 8⅛22	7.9	537	102¼	– ¼
ATT 8⅛24	8.0	312	101⅞	– ⅝
Amoco 6s98	6.0	140	100¼	+ ⅛
Amoco 7⅞07	7.5	3	104⅜	+ 2⅛
Amoco 8⅝16	7.9	20	109⅜	+ ⅛
AmocoCda 7⅜13	6.4	13	115	– ½
Ancp 13⅞02f	cv	2	106	– 2
Andarko 6¼14	5.8	199	108½	– 1½
Anhr 8⅝16	8.2	2	105½	+ ½
Apache 7½00	cv	10	121	– 1½
Aristr 14¼94	12.0	3	119	...
ArizP 7.45s02	7.3	33	101⅝	+ ⅝
Arml 9.2s00	9.7	10	94½	...
Arml 8½01	9.1	10	93	+ ½
Arml 13½94	12.6	1	107¼	– ¼
Asar 9¾2000	9.3	3	105	+ 3
AshO 8.8s00	8.6	7	101¾	...
AshO 8.2s02	8.0	3	103	+ 1⅛
AshO 6¾14	cv	50	87¼	– ¼
ARch 9½96	9.3	331	101⅞	– ⅛
AubrnHl 16⅞20f	...	233	135¾	...
AutDt zr12	...	1582	37¾	+ ½
Avnet 8cld	cv	5	100¾	...
Avnet 6s12	cv	5	95½	– ½
BRE 9½08	cv	15	107½	– ½
Ballys 6s98f	cv	50	76½	+ ½
Bally 10s06f	cv	532	98	– ⅛
BalGE 9⅜08	8.9	15	105	– ½
BncFla 9s03	cv	20	92⅛	– ⅞
BkNY 7½01	cv	15	127⅜	– ⅛
Banka 7⅞03	7.8	69	101¼	– 1
Banka 8⅞05	8.6	20	102¾	– ½
Bkam 8.35s07	8.2	10	102¼	– ⅛
Bkam zr92	...	69	99½	+ 3/32
Barnt 8½99	7.9	18	108	+ ¼
BearStr 8⅛97	7.7	3	105	+ 5
BellCn 9s08	8.6	10	104¼	– ⅜
BellPa 8⅝06	8.4	15	102⅞	...
BellPa 7⅛12	7.2	15	98¾	– ⅛
BellPa 7½13	7.5	163	99¾	– ¼
BellPa 8¾15	8.3	7	105¼	...
BellPa 9¼19	8.7	10	105¾	+ ½
BenCp 7.45s00	7.4	15	100	...
BenCp 7½02	7.5	10	100	+ 2½
BrkHa zr04	...	10	52⅛	...
BethSt 9s00	9.1	26	99	– ¼
BethSt 8.45s05	9.0	51	94⅜	+ ½
BethSt 8⅜01	8.8	15	95½	+ 1¼
Bevrly 7⅝03	cv	44	92½	...
BlkBst zr04	...	4	41	...
BoisC 7s16	cv	134	87	...
BoltBer 6s12	cv	100	62½	– 1¼
Bordn 8⅜16	7.8	3	107	+ 4
BwnSh 9¼05	cv	63	97	– 1½
BwnFer 6¼12	cv	130	92½	– ¾
BurN 6.55s20 O	7.7	41	85	+ 3½
BurNo 3.20s45	7.6	25	42	– 1
BurNo 9⅝96	9.3	50	103⅞	+ 1⅛
BurNo 9s16	8.6	7	105	+ 2
CBS 7.85s01	7.5	3	105	+ 5⅞
CIGNA 8.2s10	cv	151	103	– 1½
CPC 4sr	8.0	20	50	– 1
CaroT 7¾01	7.6	1	101½	+ 1½
CarnCr 4½97	cv	6	100¼	+ 1¼
Carolco 14s93	21.5	5	65⅛	– ⅞
CaroFrt 6¼11	cv	1	79	+ 1
CarPL 7¾02	7.6	4	102½	...

Bonds	Cur Yld	Vol	Close	Net Chg.
Chvrn 8¾96	8.5	2	102⅜	– ¼
Chvrn 9⅜16	8.5	378	110¾	– ⅛
Chiquta 11⅞03	11.4	157	104½	– ½
Chiquta 10½04	10.5	240	100	...
ChNY 8¼02	8.0	3	103	+ 1
ChckFul 7s12	cv	6	91	...
ChryF 9.30s94	9.2	151	101⅛	+ ⅛
ChryF 13¼99	11.4	30	116¼	...
ChryF 7¼95t	8.0	5	90¾	– 2½
ChryF 8⅜97	8.6	100	97⅝	– ¼
ChryF 8⅛94	8.1	280	100¾	– ⅛
ChryF 8½18	9.2	10	92	...
Chryslr 8s98	8.2	10	97½	– 1
Chryslr 13s97	12.1	197	107	– 1
Chryslr 12s15	11.5	166	104½	...
Chryslr 9.6s94	9.2	179	104	– ¼
Chryslr 10.95s17	10.7	86	102½	– ¼
Chryslr 10.4s99	10.3	142	101¼	– ½
ChvrnC 7⅞97	7.5	50	104⅜	...
vjCircK 12¾97f	...	35	9½	+ ½
vjCircK 13s97f	...	38	2⅛	+ ⅛
CitiPP 12½96	cv	145	102½	– ⅜
Citicp 8.45s07	8.4	55	100⅝	– ⅛
Citicp 8⅛07	8.2	325	99⅜	– ⅜
Clmt zr94	...	2	85¾	+ ¾
Clmt zrD00	...	10	46⅝	+ 1⅜
ClevEl 9¼09	8.9	20	103½	...
ClevEl 8⅜11	8.4	137	100¼	– ⅜
Coastl 11¼96	10.8	42	104	...
Coastl 11¾06	10.1	165	116⅝	...
Coastl 11⅛98	10.2	71	109	+ ⅜
vjColG 9s94f	...	10	101⅝	...
vjColuG 8¾s95f	...	4	101⅛	...
vjColuG 9⅛s95f	...	6	103	+ 2
vjColuG 7½97M f	...	14	98	+ ¾
vjColuG 7½97J f	...	39	96⅝	– ⅛
vjColuG 7½97O f	...	76	98¼	+ ⅞
vjColuG 9⅞99f	...	30	103¼	– 1¼
vjColuG 10⅛95f	...	3	104⅝	...
vjColuG 10¼99f	...	33	105⅜	+ 1
vjColuG 9s93f	...	28	105¼	+ ⅞
CmwE 8s03	7.8	5	102½	...
CmwE 8¾05	8.5	25	103	– ⅞
CmwE 9⅜04	9.0	16	103⅝	– ⅜
CmwE 8⅛07J	8.0	5	101¾	+ 1¼
CmwE 8⅛07D	8.0	10	102	– ½
CmwE 8¼07	8.1	10	102¼	+ ¾
CmwE 9⅛08	8.8	21	103¾	+ ⅛
ConrPer 6¾01	cv	79	95½	– 1⅛
Consec 12¾97	12.1	10	105⅝	+ ⅛
ConEd 4⅝93	4.6	15	100	– ½
ConEd 7.9s01	7.7	30	102⅞	+ ⅛
ConEd 7.9s02	7.7	9	102⅜	– ¼
CnNG 9s95	8.8	3	102¼	...
ConNG 7¼15	cv	15	112	...
CnPw 7⅝99	7.6	23	100¾	– ¼
CnPw 8⅝00	8.4	25	102¾	– ⅛
CnPw 7½01	7.5	7	99½	– 1¼
CnPw 7½02J	7.5	87	99¾	– ¼
CnPw 7½02O	7.5	23	99⅞	...
CnPw 9s08	8.7	17	103½	+ ¼
CrayRs 6⅛11	cv	90	80	– ½
CrocN 8.6s02	8.5	60	101½	+ ⅛
CumE zr05	...	5	37½	– ½
Dana dc5⅞06	cv	3	90	...
DatGen 8⅜02	9.5	49	88	+ ½
DataGn 01	cv	45	91	+ 6½
Datpnt 8⅞06	cv	281	64	– 1
DetEd 7⅜01	7.3	10	101	+ 1
Disney zr05	...	555	47	...
duPnt 8½06	8.2	37	103⅝	– ⅛
duPnt dc6s01	6.3	345	95¼	– ¼
duPnt 8½16	8.1	33	104⅝	– ½
DukeP 7¾03	7.5	18	102⅞	...
DukeP 8⅛cld	...	48	102⅞	...
DukeP 8⅜cld	...	10	103⅝	+ ⅛
DuqL 8¾00	8.3	26	105	+ 1½
DuqL 8⅜07	8.0	12	104⅝	+ ½
EMC 6¼02	cv	10	120	...
EKod 8⅝16	8.3	443	104⅛	– ⅞
EKod zr11	...	126	29¼	– ⅛
EmbSuit 10½94	10.1	8	103⅝	– ⅛
EmbSuit 11s99	10.4	5	105½	...
EmbSuit 10⅞02	10.2	35	106¼	+ ¾
EBP 6¾06	cv	22	65¾	– 1
Exxon 6s97	6.0	35	100½	– ⅛
Exxon 6½98	6.4	67	100⅞	+ ¼
FMC 9½2000	9.3	25	101¾	– 1
FairCp 13⅛06	13.5	20	97	...
FairCp 13s07	13.2	1	98¼	+ 1½
FedN zr19s	...	70	11⅛	...
FedDS 10s00	9.9	274	101	...
Fldcst 6s12	cv	29	71	– 1
FUnRE 8⅜94	8.4	5	100	+ ¼
Flemg 6½96	cv	10	100¼	– ½
FrdC 8⅜01	8.2	43	101⅝	+ ⅛
FrdC 8½02	8.3	3	102⅞	...

EXPLANATORY NOTES

(For New York and American Bonds)

Yield is current yield.

cv-Convertible bond. cf-Certificates cld-Called. dc-Deep discount. ec-European currency units. f-Dealt in flat. il-Italian lire. kd-Danish kroner. m-Matured bonds, negotiability impaired by maturity. na-No accrual. r-Registered. rp-Reduced principal. st-Stamped. t-Floating rate. wd-When distributed. ww-With warrants. x-Ex interest. xw-Without warrants. zr-Zero coupon.

vj-In bankruptcy or receivership or being reorganized under the Bankruptcy Act, or securities assumed by such companies.

ent value calculations of the type described in Chapter 2. For many years these calculations were made by the use of "basis books" that show yield-to-maturity when coupon, bond price, and time remaining until maturity were known. Today these calculations may be most efficiently performed by preprogrammed handheld calculators.

Two debt securities with the same yield-to-maturity may trade at very different prices, depending on coupon rates and maturity dates. To facilitate price comparisons in active trading in debt securities, traders usually refer to "basis points" rather than price. A basis point is one one-hundredth of 1 percent in yield. A price movement of 25 basis points is a change in price sufficient to change the yield-to-maturity of a security by one fourth of 1 percent.

The current yield is widely used because: (a) It is much easier to calculate than the yield-to-maturity; and (b) when the payment date is far in the future, the difference between the current yield and the yield-to-maturity will rarely be significant. Recall how small the present values of payments due in the distant future are. See Chapter 2.

The method of calculation of current yield probably explains some apparent anomalies in Table 16-8. For example, why does the AT&T 5 1/2 97 carries a current yield of only 5.5 percent while the 5 1/8 bond carries a current yield of 5.7 percent? The risk is presumably about the same for both bonds. The reason is that the final payment of $1,000 due in 1997 — approximately four years from the date of the quotation — is a significant component in calculating the yield-to-maturity of the five and one-half percent bond. A person buying this bond pays about $997.50 for (1) annual payments of $55.00 for four years plus (2) $1,000 at the end of the four-year period. Clearly the current yield, which takes into account only component (1) significantly understates the true yield-to-maturity of this investment.

When bonds are bought and sold, it is customary to apportion the interest due as of the date of closing. Bonds that are in default, or are significantly below investment grade, may be "dealt in flat," that is, there is no apportionment of interest, and each holder is entitled to any payments received without regard to the period those payments represent.

Most bond trading occurs over-the-counter rather than on the New York Stock Exchange. In the over-the-counter market a round lot is $25,000 of face value, and most trades are in much larger units. The NYSE has a "nine bond rule" which states that transactions involving more than nine bonds may be executed off the Exchange floor. Thus the published quotations in Table 16-8 do not reflect the prices at which the vast majority of bond trades actually occurred: Indeed most publicly traded bonds are not even listed on the NYSE. A much better indication of bond trading appears in Table 16-6, the "Bond Market Data Bank" for September 16,

1992. Of particular interest in the private bond quotations in this table are the descriptions of the issues traded that prominently set forth the credit rating given each bond by the two major bond credit rating organizations, Moody's and Standard and Poor's.

Investments in corporate bonds by individual investors may appear attractive because of their relatively high interest rate and relatively low risk of default. There are potential pitfalls for individual investors, however. Corporate bonds carry, in addition to the credit risk inherent in those bond ratings by Standard and Poor's and Moody's, a significant interest rate risk as well. A rise in interest rates by itself immediately erodes the value of the investment significantly; there is usually no downside price protection for the investor in the event of a rise in interest rates. Further, the price erosion caused by an increase in interest rates is felt more heavily by holders of bonds with longer maturities than those with shorter maturities. For example, a rise of 200 basis points (2 percent in yield) reduces the price of a ten-year bond with a 7 percent coupon rate by about 13 percent. If this bond had a 30-year maturity, the decline in price as a result of a 200 basis point price movement would be nearly 20 percent.

The very worst thing to do is to buy long-term fixed income investments at the low point in the interest rate cycle. One can minimize interest rate risks by going short-term and avoiding long-term investments. For example, a bond with a 7 percent coupon purchased at par ($1,000) will decline by the following amounts with a 1 percent rise in interest rates:

a) A three-year bond will decline to $973.80;
b) A five-year bond will decline to $959.40;
c) A seven-year bond will decline to $947.20;
d) A ten-year bond will decline to $932; and
e) A thirty-year bond will decline to $886.90.

Going "long" is dangerous, too, because there is also a prepayment risk that when interest rates drop (and the value of the bond therefore goes up), the bonds will be called or redeemed, and the investor will not realize the benefits of the higher-than-market coupon rate. See section 6.13.

The "yield curve" is a diagram that shows the yields of Treasury debt securities of various maturities. Usually, the yield rises as the maturity rises, so the yield curve slopes upward. When short-term yields drop, as they have done in the early 1990s, investors are tempted to invest in longer term debt securities to improve the yield — in other words to move "up the yield curve." The trick is to find a spot on the yield curve where the yield is high but the exposure to rising interest rates is limited. At the end of 1992, advisers were suggesting that most risk adverse investors should be comfortable at about five years, where the current yield was about 6 percent, about 82 percent of the yield on the clearly risky 30 year bond.

The inherent credit risk in long-term corporate bonds may be magnified by corporate changes over which the bondholder has no control. Such changes may lead to a lowering of the credit rating given to the bonds by Standard & Poor's or Moody's and an immediate price decline as the market prices the bond as a higher risk security. Whether or not corporate management may lawfully enter into a transaction that adversely affects bondholders depends on the terms of a complex document called the bond indenture. Generally, protection against dilution or loss of credit rating must be found in this document if the bondholders have any protection at all. During the 1980s, several major leveraged buyouts were accomplished that had significant adverse effects on current bondholders because the bond indenture did not prohibit or limit the addition of large amounts of new debt to the corporation's capital structure which was on a parity with the corporation's existing publicly held debt. In 1992 Marriott proposed a corporate restructuring that split the corporation into two smaller corporations: Virtually all of the corporation's long-term debts were placed in one corporation with a fraction of the former corporation's assets while the remaining assets were placed in a second corporation that was virtually debt free and had no residual reponsibility with respect to the corporation's bonds. Needless to say, the bond ratings declined precipitously, and the holders suffered significant losses of capital.

Finally, there may be a lack of liquidity when the number of bonds (less than $25,000 of face value) being purchased is small; over-the-counter traders may not be interested in purchasing bonds in units of less than $25,000 of face value except at a deep discount.

A common strategy when investing in bonds is "laddering," which simply means buying bonds and notes of different maturities so that they mature in different years rather than all at one time. When planning for the education of several children, for example, one might match the maturities to the years in which tuition obligations are likely to be the greatest so that money will be available for that purpose. Retirees may do the same by moving part of their savings into laddered longer-term securities that offer significantly better yields than shorter term debt securities or money market funds or savings accounts. A laddered portfolio mixes together bonds with short and long maturities so that the overall yield is better than the yields of short-term investments. If the longer term bonds and notes are selected carefully, the risk is only slighter greater than the risk in the short-term investments.

Rather than investing in one or a few bond issues, the small investor is generally better served by investing in mutual bond funds (see Chapter

15) or in investment trusts that hold large amounts of bonds and provide a fair degree of liquidity.

§16.14　OF REDEMPTIONS AND YIELDS

In evaluating fixed income investments, section 16.13 points out that a distinction must be drawn between yield (or "current yield") and total return. Yield or current yield refers only to the interim interest payments on the investment while it is being held. Total return takes into account not only the interest earned on an investment but also interest earned on that interest during the period the investment is outstanding and the profit or loss incurred when the investment is redeemed or disposed of. On very long term investments—for example, a 30-year noncallable bond that the investor plans to hold until maturity—the interest earned on the reinvested interest will be the single major contributor to the total return on the investment. On an investment not held to maturity, the profit or loss on the sale of the investment will be a primary determinant of the total return, and that usually will be largely dependent on whether interest rates rise or fall while the investment is held. Only in interestbearing short-term investments does the yield closely follow the total return on the investment.

Yield to maturity is calculated on the assumption that future interest payments are invested at a constant rate. This assumption is necessary if yields to maturity are to be calculated on a consistent basis when comparing bonds of different maturities and different coupon rates. However, the assumption is unrealistic since future interest rates are not stable, and a bondholder is likely to receive future interest payments, but during periods of low interest rates be unable to invest them at a constant rate. If interest rates decline, the bondholder will be unable to achieve the original estimated yield to maturity since she will be unable to invest interest payments at the assumed rate.

In general, yields and interest rates are higher for bonds with longer maturities. For example, 20-year Treasury bonds yielded 1.9 percent more than two and one-half year bonds on November 11, 1991. By September 1992, this spread had increased to more than 2 percent. The longer a bond's maturity, the greater its price volatility with respect to changes in interest rates. This should be evident from the discussion in section 16.13 of the price movement of a 7 percent bond when interest rates increase by 1 percent. Prices are equally volatile when interest rates decline: With a 2 percent decline in interest rates, a 7.5 percent bond, maturing in eight years, will increase in value by 13 percent, while a similar 20-year bond will increase by 24 percent.

Yields to maturity are likely to be unrealistic for another reason as well. Bonds are usually subject to redemption, which means that the corporation has reserved the power to call in and pay off the obligation before it is due, often at a slight premium over the face value of the debt security. The most common mistake unsophisticated bondbuyers make is to buy a bond on the basis of current yield or yield to maturity without regard to callability. In low interest periods, such as the early 1990s, the most reliable and conservative indication of value of high coupon bonds is "yield to call" since high coupon bonds will almost certainly be called as soon as legally possible. The general rule of thumb is that if an older bond has a coupon rate 1.5 percent above a new bond, the odds are strong that the old issue of bonds will shortly be called in its entirety, if it is legal to do so, in a transaction financed by the issue of new bonds.

Calls may also occur in contexts other than a complete refinancing of an issue. Typically individual bonds may be redeemed without redeeming the entire issue. Bonds chosen for redemption may be chosen by lot or by some other system. In the case of coupon bonds (that are not registered in the name of the owner), the only legally required notice that a bondholder is entitled to receive is a published advertisement in the financial press identifying the issue of bonds being redeemed and a list of certificate numbers of individual bonds that have been redeemed. As a practical matter, the bondholder is likely to learn of the redemption only when a coupon is submitted for payment at some later date, and the coupon is returned with a notice that the bond has previously been called, and funds to pay off the bond have been deposited in some bank. The investor generally is not entitled to interest on the amount that has been deposited.

During long periods of relatively stable interest rates, calls are not something to be feared. Indeed, many older debt securities require the corporation to create sinking funds, to redeem a part of the issue each year or to accumulate to pay off the entire issue when it matures. A sinking fund is simply a fund created by the issuer and added to periodically to assure the holders of the issue that the corporation will have adequate funds to pay off the remainder of the issue when it matures. Sinking fund provisions are also common in connection with issues of preferred stock.

Not all issues of debt securities are callable. In the case of privately issued bonds, most are callable. One simply has to check before completing the purchase, typically by requesting information from the broker handling the purchase. The United States Treasury stopped issuing callable bonds in 1985. Currently only 78 billion of 2.3 trillion Treasury bonds are subject to call. Again, one simply has to check before purchasing specific Treasury bonds. Municipals typically have an optional call date beginning ten years after the issue date. They may also contain an extraordinary call provision if they were issued to finance a project such as housing, which itself may

generate funds to pay off the issue early (usually by refinancings by purchasers). Municipals often pay $1,020 for each $1,000 of face value when
called, except that extraordinary calls pay off at par.

§16.15 CONVERTIBLE AND CALLABLE DEBT SECURITIES

Debt securities, like preferred shares, may also be made convertible into
equity securities, almost always common shares, on some predetermined
ratio. Convertible debt securities are almost always unsecured debentures
rather than secured bonds.

The conversion privilege for bonds operates in a very similar manner
to conversion privilege for preferred shares, which is discussed at length in
the following chapter. See sections 17.6 to 17.11. Like convertible preferred, the conversion ratio is set by the creating documents and is usually
protected against dilution by adjustments for share splits, dividends, etc.
When convertible debentures are converted, they, and the debt they
represent, disappear, and new equity securities (the conversion securities)
are issued in their place. Convertible debentures themselves are treated as
equity securities for some purposes; in calculating fully diluted earnings per
share, for example, the common shares that would be issued upon conversion are taken into account in the calculation.

Convertible debentures are priced differently than straight debentures
since they carry the potential for sharing in the appreciation of value of
the common stock. For this reason, convertibles cannot be directly compared with the market price for straight debt instruments. Convertibles are
identified in Table 16-8 by the notation "cv" in the current yield column
of the NYSE traded bonds with no calculation of a current yield. If the
value of the securities into which a convertible may be converted is greater
than the value of a straight debenture with the same terms but without
the conversion right, the convertible debenture will be priced at or above
its conversion value rather than at its value as a debt instrument. (Since
the coupon rate on a convertible is usually greater than the dividend rate
on the conversion securities, holders of convertibles trading at or above
their conversion value usually will not exercise the conversion privilege
until "forced" to do so (see section 17.9), and the convertible will in fact
trade at a small premium over its conversion value to reflect the additional
income.) Because convertibles may trade on the basis of their conversion
value, rather than their value as a debt security, prices of convertibles may
soar to very high levels. This point is made graphically in Table 16-9, a
listing of representative convertible debentures traded on NASDAQ on
September 24, 1992. The price, for example, of the "BBTFn8 3/4 05" is

Table 16-9

NASDAQ

Convertible Debentures

Thursday, September 24, 1992

Issue	Sales	Bid	Asked	Net Chg.
AirWtr 8s15	2000	77½	79	...
BBT Fn 8¾05	70	165½	171	...
Brunos 6½09	3000	106½	108	− ½
BuildT 8s05	500	83½	85	...
BuildT 6½11	300	66½	68½	...
CandgWn 7s11	100	92	94	...
Cellulr 6¾09	530	75	78	...
Chirn 7¼15	100	109	111	+ 2
DSC 7¾14	940	83½	86½	+ ½
DSC 8s03	50	82½	85½	...
Diceon 5½12	50	38	40	...
DrgEmp 7¾14	100	71	73	− 1
DurrF 7s06	10000	100	100⅝	...
Encln 7½01	3000	73	75	...
Hechng 5½12	670	69½	71½	...
Intfce 8s13	110	100	102½	...
Kaman 6s12	370	76½	77½	...
LTX 13½11	100	75	81	+ 1
LaPetit 6½11	250	77	79	...
MCI Cm zr04	40	45	46	...
Medco 6s01	14000	123	126	+ 1
Microp 6s12	2000	57	60	− 1½
MoblTel 6¾02	2000	114½	116½	...
SCI Sy 5⅝12	2000	77	80	+ ½
SCI Sy 9s15	9000	112½	114	+ 1
Sanifll 7½06	13000	82½	84	...
Seagte 6¾12	1000	72	73	− 1½
Sungd 8¼15	700	117½	119	...
Synetic 7s01	100	109½	111½	− ½
TPI El 02	2000	122	124	...
VLSI 7s12	50	79	81¾	...
WestwdOn 9s02	180	80½	84½	...

EXPLANATORY NOTES

(For New York and American Bonds) Yield is current yield.

cv-Convertible bond. cf-Certificates. cld-Called. dc-Deep discount. ec-European currency units. f-Dealt in flat. il-Italian lire. kd-Danish kroner. m-Matured bonds, negotiability impaired by maturity. na-No accrual. r-Registered. rp-Reduced principal. st-Stamped. t-Floating rate. wd-When distributed. ww-With warrants. x-Ex interest. xw-Without warrants. zr-Zero coupon.

vj-In bankruptcy or receivership or being reorganized under the Bankruptcy Act, or securities assumed by such companies.

$1,655 for a $1,000 debenture that has a normal or average coupon rate; the price of $1,655 must be based on its conversion value rather than its value as a debenture.

The interaction between the power of the corporation to call convertible debentures and the power of the holder to exercise the conversion privilege is similar to that of preferred shares. If a convertible debenture is called for redemption, the conversion privilege continues until the debentures are actually redeemed. If the value of the conversion securities exceeds the redemption price, it is obviously to the holders' advantage to convert following an announcement that the debentures will be called for redemption on a specified date. Such a conversion is usually described as "forced." A conversion of debentures cleans up the balance sheet of the issuer by substituting equity for debt, reducing the debt/equity ratio and otherwise appearing to improve the financial health of the business.

§16.16 "HIGH YIELD" BONDS

"High yield" bonds is a euphemistic name for bonds that are below investment grade as determined by an investment rating service. They are perhaps better known as "junk bonds." They are bonds that are rated below BBB- by Standard and Poor's Corporation and below Baa-3 by Moody's Investor's Service. Some receive no rating at all. Originally, high yield bonds were "fallen angels," bonds that were at one time of investment grade but because of financial adversity the risk of default has loomed large. However, they are now generally issued as "junk" and expect to remain forever in that category.

During the 1980s, junk bonds were widely used to raise very large amounts of capital — billions of dollars in many cases — for takeover bids by outsiders. To increase the attractiveness of the most risky of these bonds, novel terms were included, such as "reset provisions," which required the interest rate to be increased at periodic intervals if necessary to preserve or restore the market price of the bonds. In these highly leveraged takeover situations, the cash flow generated by the corporation being acquired was usually the sole source of funds to service the debt represented by the junk bonds. Many — but by no means most — of these issues of junk bonds went into default (or were rescued from default by large infusions of additional capital) when the acquired corporation was unable to generate sufficient funds to service the additional debt. Defaults on these bonds peaked in 1990 at $28.5 billion, and investments in them were an important contributing factor in the widespread collapse of savings and loan institutions. The widely predicted collapse of most of these high risk securities did not materialize, however, and since then junk bonds have made a modest comeback both in price and in popularity. A number of new junk bond issues have been floated; while they are still in the "junk" category, they generally are not in the high-risk or exotic class that epitomized the era of the 1980s.

As interest rates declined in the 1990s, junk bonds became more attractive. Rather than the 17 percent or higher yields of the 1980s, these bonds were yielding a "modest" 10 percent. But these bonds were attractive to investors faced with alternative yields of 3 to 6 percent paid on money market funds, savings accounts, and investment-grade corporate bonds.

The safest way to invest in junk bonds is through one or more mutual funds that limit their investments to high yield debt securities. In this way the risk of default is minimized because these funds invest in a large number of different issues. Nevertheless, one should realize that the high yield of these investments carry with it a significant risk. As in all investments, higher yield means higher risk.

Table 16-10 on page 412 sets forth information about high yield bonds drawn from the Wall Street Journal of September 17, 1992.

§16.17 ZERO COUPON AND SIMILAR BONDS

The bonds issued by Allied Corporation described in Table 16-8("AlldC") are examples of zero coupon bonds. These are bonds that are issued at deep discounts from par value and do not pay interest. A "zero" issued by Allied Corporation and due in 2003 can be purchased for about $425 for a $1,000 bond. The entire difference of $575 represents interest that is in effect paid in a lump sum in 2003 when the bond matures. Since zeros by definition do not pay current interest, there is no current yield.

The Allied Corporation zero due in 2003 actually yields a little over 8 percent per year. Again, at first blush, this would appear to be an attractive investment for individuals. However, the tax rules applicable to such investments are unfavorable: An individual buying a zero must include in his or her tax return each year the amount of imputed interest payable on the investment even though it is not received until maturity. As a result, zeros are attractive investments only for tax-exempt entities, particularly Keogh plans and IRAs owned by individuals. Of course, the risk of default may also be increased by reason of the long period between the time the investment is made and the time of maturity of the obligation.

Deep discount bonds are similar to zeros except that they pay current interest rates well below effective market interest rates.

Brokerage firms create zeros by stripping interest-bearing coupons from United States long-term bonds. They are usually offered under feline acronyms: CATS (certificates of accrual on treasury securities) or TIGRs (treasury investment growth receipts). In response, the United States Treasury has issued its own zeros called STRIPS (Separate Trading of Registered Interest and Principal of Securities). Table 16-11 is drawn from the "Treasury Bonds, Notes and Bills" table from the Wall Street Journal of February 16, 1993. One may purchase either the stripped "coupon interest," that is, the stream of interest payments, or the stripped principal; these are identified by the cryptic notations "np" (or "bp") and "ci." Zeros based on United States securities are attractive because there is no risk of nonpayment at maturity. The same cannot be said for corporate zeros, such as those issued by Allied Chemical Corporation.

Zeros that are publicly traded, of course, fluctuate in price in response to changes in interest rates. Zeros are very volatile. For example, a 20-year bond selling at par might be stripped of its coupons and sold at $146 per $1,000 bond to yield 9.55 percent to maturity. If the price of the

Table 16-10

HIGH YIELD BONDS

Wednesday September 16, 1992

	Total Daily Return	Index Value	Average Price Change	Vol.
Flash Index	+ 0.04%	138.51	+ 0.01	L
Cash Pay	+ 0.02	135.71	− 0.01	L
Deferred Int	+ 0.06	149.34	+ 0.06	L
Distressed	+ 0.04	146.02	unch	L
Bankrupt	+ 0.23	119.97	+ 0.09	L

Volume Key: H = Heavy, M = Moderate, L = Light

Index value = 100 on July 1, 1990

Key Gainers

	Type/ Coup.	Mat.	3:00P.M. Bid Price	Price Change	Principal Return	Yld to Mat.
USG	e/13.250	7/00	34 1/2 +	2 1/2 +	7.81	z
PennTraff	b/13.500	6/98	107 3/4 +	3/4 +	0.68	11.60
E-II Hldgs	e/12.850	3/97	110 1/4 +	1/2 +	0.46	z
Fieldcrest	e/11.250	6/04	104 1/4 +	1/4 +	0.23	10.60

Key Losers

RH Macy	b/14.500	11/01	11 1/2 −	1/2 −	2.96	z
OrNda	e/12.250	5/02	102 −	1/2 −	0.47	11.89
ChryslrAubH	a/16.875	5/20	129 −	3/8 −	0.28	z
ICH Corp	e/11.250	12/96	92 3/4 −	1/4 −	0.26	13.55

Name	Type/Rating	Coup.	Mat.	Close	Net Chg.	% Yld. to Mat.
ARA Services	a /BB	10.625	8/00	108	unch	9.17
AdelphComm	a /B	12.500	5/02	104 1/8	unch	11.77
AmerStandard	a /B	10.875	5/99	103 1/2	unch	10.13
ChryslrAubH	a /B+	16.875	5/20	129	− 3/8	z
CokeBotSW	b /B	12.000	5/97	102	unch	11.42
EPIC Hldgs	c /CCC+	12.000	3/02	59	unch	12.05
FedDeptSerB	d /NR	10.000	2/00	100	unch	10.00
Grand Union	a /B+	11.250	7/00	101 1/2	unch	10.95
HookSupeRx	a /BB-	10.125	6/02	103 1/2	unch	9.56
Kroger	e /B	9.750	2/04	100 1/4	unch	9.71
MagmaCopper	e /BB-	11.500	1/02	105 1/4	unch	10.59
Magnetek	e /B	10.750	11/98	104 1/2	unch	9.76
McCawCell	e /CCC+	12.950	8/99	106	unch	11.66
News Corp	a /BB-	12.000	12/01	110 3/8 −	1/8	10.23
QuantumChem	e /B-	12.500	3/99	98 −	1/4	12.96
RH Macy	e /D	14.500	10/98	25 1/2	unch	z
RJR Nabisco	f /BB+	15.000	5/01	125 1/2	unch	11.98
Safeway	d /B+	9.650	1/04	102 3/4	unch	9.25
Southland	a /B+	12.000	12/96	101 1/4	unch	11.61
StoneCont	e /B+	10.750	4/02	94 1/4 −	1/2	11.77
Stop & Shop	e /B+	9.750	2/02	103 1/4 −	1/4	9.22
SupermktGenl	b /B-	11.625	6/02	104	unch	10.94
UnisysCrSns	a /B	15.000	7/97	109 1/2	unch	12.30
ViacomIntl	e /B+	9.125	8/99	102 1/2	unch	8.63
VonsCompany	e /BB-	9.625	4/02	105 1/2 −	1/4	8.76

Volume indicators are based solely on the traders' subjective judgment given the relative level of inquiry and trading activity on any given day.

a-Senior. b-Subordinated. c-Senior, Split Cpn. d-Secured. e-Senior Sub. f-Subordinated, PIK. z-omitted for reset or bankrupt bonds, or yields above 35%.

Source: Salomon Brothers

Table 16-11

TREASURY BONDS, NOTES & BILLS

U.S. Treasury strips as of 3 p.m. Eastern time, also based on transactions of $1 million or more. Colons in bid-and-asked quotes represent 32nds; 101:01 means 101 1/32. Net changes in 32nds. Yields calculated on the asked quotation. ci-stripped coupon interest. bp-Treasury bond, stripped principal. np-Treasury note, stripped principal. For bonds callable prior to maturity, yields are computed to the earliest call date for issues quoted above par and to the maturity date for issues below par.
Source: Bear, Stearns & Co. via Street Software Technology Inc.

U.S. TREASURY STRIPS

Mat.	Type	Bid	Asked	Chg.	Ask Yld.
May 93	ci	99:08	99:08	....	3.09
Aug 93	ci	98:14	98:14	+ 1	3.21
Nov 93	ci	97:20	97:20	+ 1	3.26
Feb 94	ci	96:21	96:22	....	3.42
May 94	ci	95:20	95:21	+ 1	3.62
Aug 94	ci	94:13	94:15	....	3.85
Nov 94	ci	93:06	93:08	....	4.06
Nov 94	np	93:05	93:06	+ 2	4.09
Feb 95	ci	92:00	92:02	....	4.19
Feb 95	np	92:00	92:01	+ 2	4.20
May 95	ci	90:24	90:26	+ 1	4.35
May 95	np	90:22	90:24	+ 2	4.38
Aug 95	ci	89:18	89:20	+ 2	4.44
Aug 95	np	89:14	89:16	+ 2	4.50
Nov 95	ci	88:09	88:11	+ 2	4.57
Nov 95	np	88:07	88:09	+ 2	4.60
Feb 96	ci	86:24	86:27	+ 2	4.77
Feb 96	np	86:23	86:25	+ 3	4.79
May 96	ci	85:10	85:13	+ 2	4.93
May 96	np	85:09	85:12	+ 2	4.94
Aug 96	ci	83:29	84:00	+ 2	5.05
Nov 96	ci	82:19	82:22	+ 3	5.15
Nov 96	np	82:14	82:17	+ 3	5.20
Feb 97	ci	80:29	81:00	− 1	5.35
May 97	ci	79:20	79:23	....	5.42
May 97	np	79:17	79:21	+ 2	5.44
Aug 97	ci	78:06	78:09	− 2	5.52
Aug 97	np	78:04	78:07	+ 2	5.54
Nov 97	ci	76:26	76:30	....	5.61
Nov 97	np	76:20	76:23	+ 2	5.67
Feb 98	ci	75:14	75:18	+ 2	5.69
Feb 98	np	75:10	75:13	− 1	5.73
May 98	ci	74:01	74:05	+ 1	5.79
May 98	np	73:28	74:00	− 1	5.83
Aug 98	ci	72:22	72:26	+ 2	5.86
Aug 98	np	72:17	72:21	− 1	5.90
Nov 98	ci	71:08	71:12	− 5	5.96
Nov 98	np	71:03	71:07	− 4	6.00
Feb 99	ci	69:25	69:29	+ 1	6.06
Feb 99	np	69:25	69:29	+ 2	6.06
May 99	ci	68:18	68:22	+ 4	6.11
May 99	np	68:18	68:22	+ 5	6.11
Aug 99	ci	67:11	67:15	+ 4	6.15
Aug 99	np	67:17	67:21	+ 10	6.11
Nov 99	ci	66:08	66:13	+ 2	6.17
Nov 99	np	66:21	66:25	+ 4	6.08
Feb 00	ci	64:20	64:24	+ 3	6.31
Feb 00	np	64:23	64:27	+ 3	6.29
May 00	ci	63:15	63:19	+ 3	6.35
May 00	np	63:13	63:18	+ 2	6.36
Aug 00	ci	62:06	62:10	+ 3	6.41
Aug 00	np	62:03	62:07	+ 3	6.43
Nov 00	ci	61:00	61:04	+ 3	6.46
Nov 00	np	60:30	61:03	+ 3	6.47
Feb 01	ci	59:15	59:19	....	6.58

unstripped bond rises from $1,000 to $1,010, the price of the stripped zero would rise about $28, or a price increase of nearly 20 percent over the original $146 purchase price.

The yield to maturity of a zero can be calculated mathematically and precisely since it is not affected by subsequent changes in the levels of interest rates. Since most United States Treasury bonds and notes are not callable, there is no call risk when buying a stripped treasury. (The same may not be true of zeroes issued by municipalities and states; see section 16.18.) The yield to maturity of a regular treasury—a treasury bond that still has the right to interest payments—is, of course, calculated on the assumption that future interest payments are invested at a constant rate. Future interest rates are not stable, so one cannot be sure of actually obtaining the yield to maturity of regular bonds. However, the yield to maturity of a stripped treasury is assured. Variations in the differences between the yields to maturity of zero treasuries and regular treasuries may therefore reflect a market estimate of the future trends in interest rates. If it is believed that rates are likely to go down, the yield to maturity of the zero should be slightly above the yield to maturity of the interestbearing treasury, and vice versa if it is expected that interest rates are likely to rise.

§16.18 TAX-EXEMPT BONDS

Bonds issued by states, municipalities, and state-created taxing authorities are called municipal bonds. They are attractive investments primarily because interest on them is exempt from federal income taxation. Because of this tax-exempt feature, municipals carry significantly lower interest rates than taxable bonds of approximately the same risk.

Some municipals issued by a specific state may also be exempt from state income taxes and from municipal income taxes as well. These bonds are referred to as "double-exempt" or "triple-exempt" bonds. Double- or triple-exempt bonds should be purchased only by persons who can take full advantage of the multiple tax exemptions.

In the 1986 Tax Act, Congress restricted the purposes for which municipal bonds that are entitled to federal tax exemption may be used. Since tax exemption is an important part of the value of municipals, reliable advice as to the tax status of specific municipals should be obtained before any investment is made. There is another risk in investing in individual municipals as well. Municipalities may issue "certificates of participation" ("COPs") that superficially appear to be municipal bonds but in fact are not legal obligations of the issuing municipalities and are not secured by the promise of repayment by the municipality. Upon default (which may conceivably occur simply by the decision of the voters of the municipality to stop making payments on the debts), the only remedy the holders of COPs have is to seize whatever property secures the obligation. If the collateral is something that is not readily salable—for example, used police cars—the investor is uncompensated.

Tax-exempt municipal bonds are predominantly investments for the affluent taxpayer in high tax brackets. The lower tax rates applicable in

1987 and later years under the 1986 Act may limit the attractiveness of holding municipal bonds in the future.

Table 16-6 shows representative quotations for tax-exempt bonds drawn from the September 16, 1992 "Bond Market Data Bank."

Zero coupon municipal bonds are an increasingly popular financing device for state and local government entities. They are also popular with individual investors because the growth in value is tax-exempt, and there is no imputation of taxable income as occurs with most zeros. There are, however, pitfalls for individuals directly investing in these bonds because most such bonds are callable at defined prices during the period before maturity. In a period of low interest rates, there is a chance that the zeroes will be called, and much of the anticipated growth in value lost. Furthermore, an early call may compound problems for investors who inadvertently paid a premium when making the initial investment. Since zeroes are sold at a discount from face value, the concept of a "premium" requires some explanation. Zero coupon bonds, if callable at all, are callable at their accreted value as defined in the indenture. *Accreted value* usually is defined to equal the original issue price plus interest compounded semiannually at the announced yield until the time of the call. If an investor purchases a zero for more than the accreted value at the time of the purchase, he has paid a premium. If the zero is later called at the accreted value, the investor receives that amount, not the purchase price plus interest compounded at the original yield. It is unlikely that most investors are aware that they are paying premiums or that a subsequent call may result in a significant loss of apparent accumulated interest as well as future interest.

Municipal zeroes that are not callable are more attractive investments than those that are and, as a result, command a premium.

Municipal governments also issue large amounts of short-term municipal notes with maturities of less than one year. These may be called "tax anticipation notes" or similar names. These notes share the tax-exempt feature of longer term municipals and carry yields below those of short-term Treasury bills and notes (because of the tax-exempt feature of the municipals). However, the volume of short-term municipal notes may be so great that the lower yield is offset by the tax-exempt feature of the notes. Short-term municipal notes are held in large quantities by tax-exempt money market funds.

The principal market for municipal bonds is over-the-counter; there is no central system of reporting prices of actual transactions. As a result, price quotations for the identical security may vary from dealer to dealer. There is no single consensus price. Further, there are literally thousands of outstanding issues of tax-exempt bonds, many of which carry significant credit risk. Defaults by municipalities (let alone specialized tax districts in rural areas) are not as uncommon as might be supposed. While credit ratings for many tax exempts are available from Moody's and Standard &

Poor's (and from a third rating agency, Fitch Investor Services, Inc.), these ratings appear to be more subjective and less reliable than ratings on privately issued bonds. Perhaps this is due to the inherent difficulty of predicting the future debt-paying willingness of organizations that rely on taxes as their principal source of income. One indication of this lack of reliability is that bonds with the same credit rating not uncommonly have apparently inexplicable significant variations in yield to maturity. In this market, it pays to comparison shop among different dealers to locate the best price when either buying or selling municipals.

§16.19 MORTGAGE-BACKED SECURITIES AND CMOs

This and the following section discuss a new type of security called "asset-backed securities," which have become immensely popular: More than $1.2 trillion of asset-backed securities were outstanding in September 1991. Increasingly, beginning in the late 1980s, these securities have been packaged in relatively small denominations and marketed for sale to the general public as appropriate investments for the small investor seeking a riskless but attractive yield. They are generally known as "mortgage-backed bonds," or "collateralized mortgage obligations." The process by which these new securities are created is called "securitization of assets."

The first asset-backed securities were created in the 1970s by federal agencies charged with broadening the real estate market by providing loans for development: particularly, Ginnie Mae (the nickname for the Government National Mortgage Association), Fannie Mae (the nickname for the Federal National Mortgage Association), and the Federal Home Loan Mortgage Corporation. In an effort to increase the supply of lendable funds, these agencies developed the concept of bundling together thousands of home real estate mortgages from around the country into a single pool and selling undivided interests in the pool. In effect a new security was created consisting of undivided interests in a large pool of assets. The proceeds of the sales of these securities were recycled into further home mortgage loans. These new securities are called "mortgage-backed securities" or "mortgage-backed bonds."

Mortgage-backed bonds carry almost no default risk. They are made up of thousands of home mortgages on which individual defaults are relatively rare; further, the pool is "over collateralized" so that individual defaults should not affect the overall return; as a result, mortgage-backed bonds regularly obtain the highest triple-A bond ratings. Further, since real estate mortgages carry relatively high interest rates, the yield of these securities has always been attractive. Table 16-6 contains a representative quotation of mortgage backed securities prices drawn from the Wall Street Journal's "Bond Market Data Bank" for September 15, 1992.

Even though conservative in orientation, mortgage-backed securities are peculiar investments in some ways and may contain unexpected risks for the unsophisticated investor. Even though the default risk is minimal, the prepayment or call risk is substantial and difficult to evaluate.

Since these are fixed income investments, their market value should decline as interest rates increase and should increase as interest rates decline. This is classic interest rate risk that all fixed income bonds and debentures face and is not particularly unusual. In fact, many mortgage-backed securities behave perversely to interest rate changes. During the market interest rate decline of the early 1990s, many mortgage-backed securities did not increase in value at all and even declined in value. The explanation lies in the fact that these securities have an unusual prepayment risk. They do not have a true maturity date. The expected maturity date is an average of the thousands of maturity dates of the underlying individual mortgages, but relatively few of those mortgages will remain outstanding until their maturity. As interest rates decline, more and more mortgages are refinanced at lower interest rates. As more mortgages are refinanced, the expected maturity date of the pool of mortgages that are represented by the mortgage-backed securities shortens. When interest rates rise, fewer and fewer expected refinancings occur, and the effective expected maturity dates of mortgage-backed securities increase. As a result, investors can never be sure how short-term or long-term their bonds really are. This uncertainty about the timing of principal repayments is perhaps the most extreme example of prepayment risk in the public securities markets today.

The high yields of mortgage-backed securities have led to the creation of mutual funds whose portfolios consist primarily or exclusively of those investments. The prices of these mutual funds reflect the prepayment risk of the underlying portfolios. The prepayment rates on all mortgage-backed securities issued by the Federal National Mortgage Association in 1991 jumped to 17.36 percent from 7.67 percent in 1990. The yields of funds such as Franklin US Government, Vanguard Fixed Income GNMA, and Kemper US Government that in earlier years were well over 12 percent, necessarily declined as more and more high rate mortgages were refinanced. The result was significant (and unexpected) erosion in the net asset values of these funds. To some extent, prepayment risk in mortgage-backed securities may be hedged by investing in offsetting equity-backed securities, but that may increase the overall default risk.

In 1983, the Federal Home Loan Bank Board created a new variation of mortgage-backed securities called "collateralized mortgage obligations" or "CMOs." A CMO is a debt obligation whose structure allows the cash flows on the underlying mortgage pool to be carved into separate classes of securities called "tranches," each with a specified coupon and stated maturity. Scheduled payments and prepayments from the mortgage pool are allocated to retire the tranches in the order of stated priorities. Favorable tax treatment of CMOs was assured by the inclusion in the Tax Reform Act of 1986 of provisions permitting the creation of "Real Estate Mortgage Investment Conduits" (REMICS), which allowed the allocation of income and principal to participants to be accepted for tax purposes.

A typical CMO issues at least four tranches with each tranche typically having a different maturity, interest rate, and prepayment risk. Like most sequential pay securities, the first tranche on which principal is paid typically is the class with the shortest maturity, and that class generally bears the highest prepayment risk. However, that risk may be ameliorated by assigning to that tranche a segment of fixed amortization rights. For instance, some tranches, called "Planned Amortization Classes," (PACs) have less-than-average exposure to call risk because that risk is assumed by other tranches called "companions." But the call risk that is squeezed out of low-risk PAC trances, like nuclear waste, can't be eliminated; instead, it is off-loaded to the "companions." The more low-risk PACs in the deal, the more volatile the "companions." If companions are closed out by prepayments, the risk of future prepayments then falls on the more conservative PACs. Thus, in CMOs, call risk can be increased to levels much higher than with normal mortgage-backed securities. The most extreme examples are "interest only" (IO) and "principal only" (PO) CMOs. An IO is entitled to receive all the interest on a certain pool of mortgages; a PO all the principal payments. Obviously, IOs and POs offset each other and represent the totality of the value and the risk of the pool. Because an increase in prepayments reduces dramatically the amount of interest that will be earned on the pool, some IOs lost more than 35 percent of their value within a few weeks as interest rates fell rapidly in the early 1990s. Ultimately the loss could be much higher. In contrast, the PO holders received their funds much more rapidly than they expected, thereby getting a much higher rate of return than originally projected.

In effect, the creator of CMOs isolates the interest and principal payments from the underlying mortgage-backed securities, and rechannels the interest and principal payments into different cash-flow tranches. Basically, the idea is to prioritize the cash flows among many different tranches of CMOs, each with its own custom-made dose of call risk.

As indicated above, CMOs have "estimated" or "projected" maturity dates that may be wildly inaccurate as interest rates fluctuate and prepayments rise. This is graphically illustrated by Table 16-12, which compares three tranches marketed for sale to individual investors.

Table 16-12
Estimated and Actual Maturities for CMOs

CMO Issue	Projected Yield	Projected Maturity	Actual Return	Actual Maturity
FNMA 91-37 L	9.00	15 yrs	7.92	16 mos
FHLMC 1143 N	9.00	9 yrs	7.81	10 mos
FNMA 91-29 Q	8.75	5 yrs	7.56	15 mos

The structures of different CMO issues obviously vary widely, and comparison shopping is a difficult task for the ordinary investor. The most useful information may be obtained from so-called "scenario analyses" that describe how a CMO is likely to behave if interest rates rise or fall. Such analyses should be requested from brokers who sell the securities.

Consider, for example, a CMO designed by the Federal Home Loan Mortgage Corporation, specifically for small investors, called the FHLMC Remic Gold Series 1113-0. When issued in the summer of 1991, it had an average life of 21.4 years and a 9.3 percent yield, a full percentage point above comparable Treasuries. Very good, one might say. However, a scenario analysis for this CMO showed that if interest rates drop one percentage point and stay there, this CMO turns from a 21-year bond to a short-term note with an average life of 1.4 years; if rates drop two percentage points, the average life becomes 18 days. On the other hand, the estimated maturity of the 1113-0 does not extend very much if rates rise; even under extreme scenarios, the average length of maturity does not rise much beyond 23 years. But that still means the investor is locked into a 9.3 percent yield for more than 20 years.

This Remic (the 1113-0) would fail to do as well as plain old Treasury bonds in five out of seven scenarios—the only situations where it does better are where rates are posited as being flat or down by less than one percentage point. This is because the Remic was originally priced at 93.75 percent of face value, so it gets a boost from higher homeowner refinancings when rates fall (because principal is paid back at full face value). If rates fell by one percentage point, the Remic would have total return (principal value plus interest) of about 12 percent, considerably better than treasuries. If rates fall two percentage points, however, the Remic becomes too short to be worth as much to investors; the return would be about 9 percent— lagging behind treasuries for the same period.

If rates rise and prepayments slow down, the price of this Remic falls faster than comparable Treasuries. Investors who decide to sell these bonds may face real losses of about 13 percent after interest payments on a two point drop in rates.

Obviously, a scenario analysis can be complex. This example, drawn from a Wall Street Journal sponsored analysis of a specific Remic, shows the complexity and risk involved in what may well be touted as a conservative investment.

§16.20 OTHER ASSET-BACKED SECURITIES

The success of securitization of real estate mortgages by the federal lending agencies described in section 16.19, has led many private Wall Street securities firms, national retailers, and banks and thrifts to pool together other kinds of illiquid assets, such as credit card receivables, boat loans, railway car leases, aircraft leases, or what have you, and sell undivided interests in the pool. Like mortgage securities, these undivided interests are then purchased by institutions and other investors as fixed-income investments that pay interest and assure return of principal on a relatively riskless basis. The proceeds of the sales of these interests to investors are cycled into new mortgages, credit card loans, boat loans, and so forth. Novel new securitized products are regularly being proposed.

At the end of 1991, it was estimated that asset-backed securities (exclusive of mortgage-backed bonds) totaled $158.3 billion; of this, credit card receivables and automobile loans amounted to $129.4 billion.

From the standpoint of the owner of assets to be securitized, the process has significant advantages. Illiquid assets are changed into liquid ones and are removed from the owner's balance sheet. Risk of loss or nonpayment is also transferred from the owner to the investor.

Asset-backed securities outside of the mortgage area regularly receive triple-A ratings from major credit rating companies. They may carry significant investor protection in the form of bond insurance, letters of credit, over-collateralization, and prepayment obligations if the risk unexpectedly increases. For example, credit card receivable-backed securities may require payment of the entire obligation in full if the default rate on the underlying credit card loans exceeds a certain specified percentage.

Despite these high ratings, novel securitized investments may carry risks. The process works best when the packaged loans are homogeneous and have predictable risks and income streams. There is little information available about some of the new securitized products, and therefore problems may arise when assessing the risks of specific investments. In addition, investments in these new securities may turn out to be difficult to dispose of because the market for such securities may not be as liquid as the market for mortgage-backed bonds and CMOs.

17

Preferred Shares

§17.1 INTRODUCTION

Preferred shares are an alternative investment that lies somewhere between common shares and debt. Preferred shares are equity securities. They are created by provisions in the articles of incorporation (or in other publicly filed documents). In effect, preferred shareholders are granted limited economic rights that are carved out of the rights of common shareholders; "preferred" simply means that some economic right of the preferred shareholders — a right to distributions or a right to share in the surplus on dissolution, or both — must be "preferred," that is, satisfied ahead of the rights of common shareholders. Preferred shareholders, however, are "shareholders" not "creditors." Their dividend right is not guaranteed and remains at the discretion of the board of directors in the same way that dividends on common shares are not guaranteed; traditional legal restraints on distributions to common shareholders (see section 14.8) also may limit

421

the power of a corporation to pay dividends on preferred shares. In the event of liquidation, preferred shares rank behind debt securities but ahead of common shares in priority of payment. Dividend rights of preferred shares are traditionally limited to a fixed amount and no more, no matter how profitable the corporation: In this respect preferred shares are more similar to fixed income securities than to common shares. From an investment point of view, these securities seem to have the worst of both worlds. However, because of these various limitations, the yields on preferred shares are usually higher than on either common shares or debt securities. For a person interested in high current income with little prospect of capital appreciation, preferred shares should be considered as a possible investment.

As a practical matter, the risk that a preferred dividend will be omitted is very low on most publicly traded preferreds. The restraints on possible dividends discussed in the preceding paragraph have little or no application to most publicly traded preferreds, and, as described below, boards of directors have strong incentives to maintain the dividend on preferred shares.

In the early 1990s, during a period of low interest rates on fixed income investments, preferred shares have become increasingly attractive. Yields of 8 or 9 percent are common on high quality preferred stock investments. Given this popularity, a number of companies have made large public offerings of preferred shares in 1992 — for example, Ford Motor Company sold 2.3 billion of preferred shares at a yield of 8.4 percent.

Modern corporate practice has blurred the distinction between common and preferred shares on the one hand, and between preferred shares and debt securities on the other. The nature of these hybrid securities is discussed briefly in section 17.6.

Preferred shares differ from common shares in that (1) they usually have limited dividend and liquidation rights, (2) they have an economic preference over the rights of common shares, and (3) they are usually nonvoting. Most preferred shares have preferential rights over common shares both in connection with the payment of dividends and in connection with distributions of assets in voluntary or involuntary dissolution of the corporation. A "dividend preference" means that the preferred shares are entitled to receive a specified dividend each year before any dividend may be paid on the common shares; a "liquidation preference" means that the preferred shares are entitled to receive a specified distribution from corporate assets in liquidation (after provision has been made for corporate debts) before the common shares are entitled to receive anything. However, some preferred shares may have only a dividend preference and no liquidation preference, or vice versa.

Publicly traded preferred shares usually are nonvoting shares, though a limited voting right may be granted under specified circumstances, for example, upon the omission of a preferred dividend for a specified period.

And, there is no inherent reason why preferred shares may not be given the right to vote either on other matters or generally on all matters coming before the shareholders.

The rights of preferred shareholders are defined in the corporation's articles of incorporation, or in directors' resolutions filed with the articles of incorporation (in the case of series of preferred shares). If an existing corporation wishes to create a new class of preferred shares, usually it must formally amend its articles of incorporation. Collectively the provisions in these basic corporate documents describing and defining the terms and rights of preferred shareholders are referred to as the "preferred shareholders' contract" with the corporation. Basically, this usage reflects that rights of preferred shareholders are generally limited to those set forth in this "contract" and that preferred shareholders have relatively few rights outside of those granted expressly to them by that contract.

A single corporation may have outstanding several different classes of preferred shares with varying rights and preferences. While a specific class of preferred may have subordinate rights to another class of preferred, both are still preferred shares since they both have preferences over the common shares.

§17.2 DIVIDEND RIGHTS

Most classes of preferred shares are entitled to a limited preferential dividend, and no more. The dividend preference may be described either in terms of dollars per share (the "$3.20 preferred") or as a percentage of par or stated value (the "5 percent preferred"). A dividend preference does not mean that the preferred is entitled to the payment in the same way that a creditor is entitled to payment from his or her debtor. A preferred dividend is still a dividend and may be made only if the corporation has available surplus from which a dividend may be made. Further, even if there are funds legally available from which a preferred dividend may be paid, the directors may decide to omit all dividends, common and preferred. The incentive to pay a preferential dividend comes from the principle that if it is omitted all dividends on the common shares must also be omitted. The preference feature of preferred shares technically means that they are entitled to the dividend first from any amount set aside by the board of directors for the payment of dividends.

§17.3 CUMULATIVE AND NONCUMULATIVE DIVIDENDS

Shares preferred as to dividends may be "cumulative," "noncumulative," or "partially cumulative." If cumulative dividends are not paid in some years, they are carried forward, and both they and the current year's preferred dividends must be paid in full before any common dividends may be declared. Non cumulative dividends disappear each year if they are not paid. Partially cumulative dividends are usually cumulative to the extent of earnings, that is, the dividend is cumulative in any year only to the extent of actual earnings during that year. Unpaid cumulative dividends are not debts of the corporation but a continued right to priority in future earnings.

An example may help to illustrate the concept of cumulative, non-cumulative, and partially cumulative dividends. Assume that a preferred stock has a preferential right to a dividend of $5 per share per year, but the directors, as is their right, decide to omit all dividends for two consecutive years. In the third year they conclude that the corporation is able to resume the payment of dividends. If the preferred shares' preferential right is cumulative, the board of directors must pay $15 on each preferred share ($5 per share for each of the two years missed plus $5 per share for the current year) before any dividend may be paid on the common shares in the third year. If the preferred shares' preferential right is noncumulative, the preferences for the two omitted years disappear entirely, and a dividend on the common shares may be paid after the $5 preferred dividend for the third year is paid. If the dividend is cumulative to the extent earned, the earnings of the corporation in each of the two years in which dividends were omitted must be examined, and the dividend is cumulative each year only to the extent the earnings cover the $5 preferred dividend. If the corporation had a loss in one of those years, the preferred dividend for that year would be lost much as though the dividend were entirely non-cumulative.

Publicly traded preferred shares traditionally have fully cumulative dividends.

§17.4 DIVIDEND POLICIES IN GENERAL

In evaluating dividend policies with respect to preferred shares, one starts with the basic principle that distribution rights of most preferred shares are limited to specific preferential amounts set forth in the preferred share-holders' contract. Preferred shareholders are thus entitled to the specified dividend before anything is paid on the common, but they will never be paid anything more than the amount specified in their contract irrespective of how large the earnings of the corporation become. Indeed, an attempt by directors to pay a dividend to preferred shareholders in excess of their limited dividend right may be enjoined by common shareholders as a violation of their rights.

Preferred shareholders should also work on the assumption that the board of directors is elected by the common shareholders and will normally maximize the dividends payable on common shares at the expense of preferred shareholders to the extent they lawfully may do so. A board of directors may seek to minimize the preferred shareholders' rights without violating contractual rights. A noncumulative preferential dividend right, in particular, leaves the preferred shareholders quite exposed to strategic maneuvers, because the common shareholders' position is improved in the future whenever a preferred dividend is omitted. Indeed, a policy of paying dividends erratically once every few years materially improves the position of the common with respect to the noncumulative preferred. Do you see why? Such a policy, however, may be subject to legal attack as a breach of the directors' fiduciary duty to treat fairly all classes of outstanding shares.

Cumulative dividends provide preferred shareholders considerably greater protection than noncumulative or partially cumulative dividends. But cumulative dividends are not a complete answer either because the board of directors may defer the payment of all dividends indefinitely in an effort to depress the price of the preferred which may then be acquired on the open market. On the other hand, it is customary to provide that preferred shares may elect a specified number of directors if preferred dividends have been omitted for a specified period, and the presence of one or more directors elected by the preferred shareholders may be unappealing to the incumbent management and such a provision therefore tends to minimize the possibility of such overtly unfair strategies.

Preferred shares may be given the right to participate in earnings equally with common shares by contract, that is, by specific provision in the document creating the class of preferred shares. Such shares are usually called "participating preferred shares" to reflect the unusual character of their dividend right. A typical pattern is that the preferred shares are entitled to the original preferential dividend, the common is entitled to receive a specified amount, and then the preferred and common share in any additional distributions on some predetermined ratio. Such shares are quite rare; they are sometimes referred to as "Class A common" or a similar designation reflecting that their right to participate is open-ended. Preferred shares are participating shares only if their rights are expressly so defined in the "preferred shareholders' contract."

§17.5 MARKET PRICE OF PREFERRED SHARES

Preferred shares may be publicly traded on the NYSE or over the counter. In general terms, publicly traded preferreds are high quality preferreds on which continued dividend payments are highly probable. As a result, risk of omitted dividends is relatively low, and yields and prices are more highly sensitive to interest rates and relative rights than to changes in earnings or prices of common shares. Values are based on discounted cash flow analysis of the stream of payments that the dividend right reflects. The differences in yields of preferreds of about the same degree of risk are usually based on differences in rights. For example, an unfavorable redemption privilege from the standpoint of shareholders may depress the yield on that preferred.

Most publicly traded preferred shares have no right to participate in the earnings of the corporation except to the extent of a fixed dividend per year. Most also do not have a conversion right, which, if it exists, may dramatically affect the pricing of the shares. The discussion below relates only to "straight" preferreds; convertibles are discussed in section 17.8.

Many utility companies have outstanding several issues of publicly traded preferred shares carrying varying rates of dividends. Illinois Power is a good example; it has ten different classes of preferreds that were traded on the NYSE on September 10, 1992. See Table 14-9, at page 344. On September 24, 1992, Illinois Power announced the payment of dividends on 13 different publicly traded preferreds, some of which are traded over the counter. Presumably these preferreds reflect different financing by Illinois Power at different times. Some of the New York Stock Exchange traded preferreds are not traded in round lots of 100 shares (the entries marked with a "z" in the sales column). A round lot for these classes of preferred is usually ten shares. It will be noted that no P-E ratio is set forth for preferreds; this is because they are limited participation securities with no claim to increased dividends based on increases in earnings. Their value therefore is determined largely by their distribution rights. The yields for these preferreds issued by a single company may vary substantially depending on their relative priorities to distributions and other rights of the specific class, including conversion and call rights. The yields on the Illinois Power preferreds vary from 7.0 percent to as high as 8.4 percent — significantly higher than the yields obtainable on investment grade, fixed income investments. At the same time, investment grade industrial bonds were yielding about 1 percent less.

§17.6 CONVERTIBILITY

Preferred shares may be made convertible at the option of the preferred shareholder into common shares at a specified price or a specified ratio. When convertible shares are converted, the original preferred shares are turned in and canceled, and new common shares are issued. The conversion price or ratio is fixed and defined in the preferred shareholders' contract: The conversion ratio is usually made adjustable for share dividends, share splits, the issuance of additional common shares, and similar transactions affecting the underlying common shares. The provisions requiring such adjustments are usually called anti-dilution provisions. See section 17.10.

Convertible preferred shares represent potential dilution of the voting power of the common shares since, by exercise of the conversion right, preferred shareholders may become common shareholders. The cost of doing this is that the preferred shareholder loses his or her preferential dividend right and may be entitled to receive only a smaller dividend being paid on common shares.

Convertible preferred stock may also be publicly traded. Such stock may be an attractive investment because it combines the stability of the preferred stock dividend with the possibility of appreciation in value that characterizes an investment in common stock. Typically, when both the common and the convertible preferred are publicly traded, the original conversion ratio is established so that the common must appreciate substantially in price before it becomes attractive to convert the preferred into common. A rather detailed illustration of the application of these principles appears in section 17.8 of this chapter.

§17.7 REDEEMABILITY

Preferred shares are usually made redeemable at the option of the corporation upon the payment of a fixed amount for each share. Such shares are called "callable" or "redeemable" shares. Redemption prices are established in the preferred shareholders' contract; they are usually established at a level somewhat higher than the consideration originally paid by the investor for the preferred shares. The redemption right is of particular importance in connection with convertible preferred shares since its exercise may in effect require holders of these shares to elect to become shareholders or be cashed out at the redemption price.

The power to redeem preferred shares is usually applicable only to the entire class or series of preferred as a unit. However, the preferred shareholders' contract sometimes provides that redemptions of a portion of a class or series are permitted; such provisions may also include rules for determining which shares are to be redeemed. If a convertible preferred is called for redemption, the conversion privilege continues after the announcement that the shares will be called for redemption until the shares are actually redeemed.

§17.8 MARKET PRICE OF CONVERTIBLE PREFERRED SHARES

The pricing of a convertible preferred is considerably more interesting and more complex than the pricing of a straight preferred. A rather involved example should be useful. Assume that in 1988 a publicly held corporation had outstanding several million shares of common stock traded on the New York Stock Exchange. The current market price of the common was $20 per share, and management believed that it was likely to trade in the $20 to $30 range for the indefinite future. A regular dividend of $1 per share had been paid on the common shares for the three prior years and management anticipated that this regular dividend would be continued at that rate for the indefinite future. In order to raise additional working capital, the corporation decided to make a public offering of a new convertible preferred stock with the following rights: It was entitled to a cumulative dividend of $6 per share per year; and it was offered initially to the public at $54 per share in order to yield an initial investor an 11 percent return, the approximate yield of similar convertible preferred shares at the time. There was no appreciable risk that the $6 dividend would be omitted in any year in the foreseeable future. Each preferred share was convertible into two shares of common stock at any time at the option of the holder and was callable by the corporation at any time for $65 per share. The basic financial characteristics described in this paragraph may be summarized

Table 17-1

	Preferred shares	Common shares
Market price	$54	$20
Dividend	$ 6	$ 1
Convertibility	Into common 2:1	no
Callability	$65	no

When the preferred was issued, it was listed on the New York Stock Exchange where it traded at between $52 and $60 per share while the common continued to trade at about $20 per share. At that price, no one exercised the conversion privilege: After all, why give up something worth between $52 and $60 in order to acquire two shares of stock that can be bought on the New York Stock Exchange for $40? Similarly, the corporation did not give serious consideration to calling the preferred at $65: If the corporation wishes to retire some preferred shares, it may buy them on the open market for $52 to $60; why pay $65 for them?

Now consider what happened to the price of the preferred when the price of the common began to creep up in 1991. When it reached $27.50 per share, the value of the conversion security (the security into which the preferred may be converted) had risen to $55, and the preferred immediately rose in price and remained at or above $55 per share. If it dropped below $55 (to $53, say), speculators who closely followed the market immediately bought the preferred at $53 and converted it into common shares that were immediately sold for $55 per share, making an instant $2 riskless profit. This type of transaction is known as "arbitrage," a fancy term for the process of profiting on small differences in market prices of two different but equivalent securities (as here) or in the market prices of the same security in two different markets or available at two different times.

By early 1992, the price of the common has risen further to $32 per share. The conversion value of the preferred is now $64, and every purchaser of the initial preferred at $54 has made a tidy paper profit of at least $10 per share. (It is only a paper profit because it has not been realized either by the sale of the preferred or by its conversion into common and the sale of the common.) More importantly, once the common reached $32, the preferred was no longer priced in the market as a straight preferred. Rather, its price was now directly tied to the price of the common in accordance with the conversion ratio: If the common declined in price by $1 per share, the preferred automatically declined by about $2 per share; if the common went up by $3 per share to $35, the preferred went up by about $6 per share. If there was a major market sell-off and the price of the common plummeted, the preferred would follow the common down (at a $2 decline per preferred share for each $1 decline in value of the common) until the preferred reached a price that reflected its market value as a pure preferred stock; at that point it again began to trade much as a straight preferred.

Assuming that the common was at $32 per share in early 1992, what price would the market place on the preferred? Would it be $64, or would it be even higher? A moment's thought should indicate that it must be higher than $64: If two shares of common with an aggregate $2 dividend sell for $64, a stock with the same market characteristics but with a $6 dividend is going to be worth more. How much more? One might expect it would be the present value of the stream of the $4 difference between the two dividends. However, it was much less than that because the market recognized that it was unlikely that the corporation would permit the difference in dividend rates to continue indefinitely: The corporation may always call the preferred at any time in the future. This differential may also be affected by the possibility that the $32 price of the common may itself reflect the market anticipating an increase in the common dividend rate. (The second factor is relevant because the preferred's dividend can never exceed $6 per share so that an increase in the common dividend reduces the $4 advantage the preferred enjoyed.) The market, in its impenetrable way, considered these variables, and a price of between $67 or $68 resulted.

Another interesting question is this: Should a holder of the preferred have converted in early 1992 when the common was at $32 if he believed that the price of the common was going to go even higher? A moment's thought should reveal that that would be an unwise decision. Why give up a $6 cumulative dividend in order to obtain two common shares with a combined dividend of $2 per share? There was no risk that the expected increase in price of the common might escape the owner of the preferred because, as described above, the price of the preferred was now directly tied to the price of the common, and therefore there was nothing to be gained and much to be lost by converting immediately.

§17.9 FORCED CONVERSIONS

Finally, in August 1992, the corporation called the preferred shares for redemption at $65 per share. Let us consider the strategic considerations that caused the corporation to exercise that power at that time. A critical point in the redemption process is that the corporation must announce an impending redemption in advance, and the privilege to convert continues to exist after the announcement and up until the instant the redemption becomes effective; only at that point does the shareholder cease to be a shareholder and become entitled to the $65 redemption price.

What happens after a call for redemption is issued depends essentially on the price of the underlying common shares at the time the redemption actually occurs. If the market price of two shares of common stock is less than $65 per share at that time, shareholders should not convert their preferred shares into common stock, but rather permit the shares to be called at $65 per share. Thus, if the corporation calls the shares for redemption at a time when the price of the underlying common is $32.50 or less, it should end up redeeming the entire issue for cash and having to pay $65 per share for every share of preferred. On the other hand, if the market price of the common is above $32.50 per share at the time of redemption, the shareholders should exercise the conversion privilege shortly before the call becomes effective and convert the preferred into the more valuable common. For example, if the common is at $35 per share, the choice is between permitting the shares to be called for a payment of $65 or converting them into shares of common stock worth $70. Such a conversion is called "forced" since the economics are such that a rational investor has no choice but to exercise her power to convert (or to sell the preferred, in which case the purchaser will convert). Thus, in August 1992, when the corporation called the preferred for redemption, the common stock was at about $33 per share, and essentially all holders of the preferred elected to convert their shares to common shares before the effective date of the redemption.

Of course, in the real world, things do not work perfectly. Preferred shareholders are scattered around the country and may not be able to select the best option at the very last minute. Some must decide several days in advance of the final date, and a last minute price movement of the common may mean that they make the wrong decision. Also, a few may simply act too late and find that their shares were redeemed when they intended to exercise the conversion privilege. Still others may be ill, out of the country, or unaware that they own the shares of preferred stock and make no decision at all. Their shares, of course, are all redeemed. But the great bulk of shares will be handled in a rational fashion.

Why do corporations compel forced conversions? From the standpoint of the cash flow of the corporation, the substitution of two shares of common for every share of preferred causes a reduction in dividend payments from $6 to $2 for every share of preferred. This reduction in dividend payments is pure gravy since there is no capital outflow to eliminate the more expensive preferred shares. A forced conversion may also appeal to notions of equity between holders of the common and of the preferred, since the preferred was receiving the full benefit of run-ups in the price of the common but was enjoying three times the dividend and has some protection against price declines on the downside. Also, the elimination of the preferred shares simplifies the capital structure of the corporation and improves the appearance of the corporation's balance sheet.

If the directors call a convertible preferred for redemption, they are required to give the holders of the preferred accurate information about the reasons for the redemption. The corporation may not withhold from the preferred shareholders information as to developments that might affect the price of the underlying common and thereby affect the decision whether or not to convert the shares.

§17.10 PROTECTION AND CONVERSION PRIVILEGE AGAINST DILUTION

In the example discussed in the last section, each share of the preferred stock was entitled to be converted at any time into two shares of common stock. What happens if the board of directors decides, before the preferred is called for redemption, to split the common shares three-to-one — that is, it decides to issue each common shareholder a new certificate for two additional shares for every share he or she originally owns so that now each shareholder has three shares where before he or she had one? Let us further assume that the dividend rate on each new share is one-third the rate on each old share so that each new share sells for almost exactly one-third of the price of each old share — about $10 per share if before the split the old shares sold for approximately $30 per share. See section 14.10. What does this do to the conversion privilege of the preferred?

The black letter rule is very simple: If the drafters of the preferred shareholders' contract did not take this possibility into account, the conversion privilege is not adjusted for the share split. Each preferred share continues to be convertible into only two shares of common stock and the conversion privilege has lost two-thirds of its potential value. Provisions guarding the conversion privilege against changes of this type in the conversion security are called anti-dilution provisions and should always be included in preferred shareholders' contracts when there is a conversion privilege. Drafting an anti-dilution clause is tricky because the courts are not going to help the draftsman out if he or she overlooks some possibility. Significant dilution may occur because of a variety of transactions, such as mergers, share dividends, executive compensation plans, and the like, and it is often controversial as to which issuances of new common shares the anti-dilution clause should protect against. Nevertheless, the basic principle seems clear and straightforward, at least so far as share splits are concerned: The drafters of the preferred shareholders contract should insert a clause providing that if the common stock is split, the conversion privilege should be adjusted so that each share of preferred is convertible into the number of new common shares that two shares of the old common stock became upon the split.

§17.11 SINKING FUND PROVISIONS

Some classes of preferred may have the benefit of sinking fund provisions. Such provisions require the issuer to set aside a specified amount each year to retire a portion of the shares of the class that are outstanding. The retirement usually may be made by redemption or by the repurchase of the shares on the open market. Similar sinking fund provisions often appear in trust indentures for debt securities.

§17.12 SERIES AND CLASSES OF PREFERRED SHARES

Articles of incorporation may authorize the board of directors to issue preferred shares from time to time in "series." The articles of incorporation in effect create a class of preferred shares without any substantive terms and authorize the board of directors to carve out series from within that class from time to time and to establish the substantive terms of each series without formal shareholder approval. The theory is that where preferred shares are to be sold by a corporation occasionally to raise capital in substantial amounts, the privilege of allowing the board of directors to set financial terms simplifies financing since the price, dividend, liquidation preference, sinking fund provision, voting rights, and other terms of each series may be tailored to then current market conditions without incurring the expense of a proxy solicitation and the holding of a special shareholders' meeting to approve the terms of the class. Shares of different series have identical rights except for the specified business terms, which may be varied.

During the 1980s the power to create series of preferred shares was utilized by boards of directors of publicly held corporations fearing a take-over to create "poison pills" without shareholder approval.

There is little between a series or a class of shares except their manner of creation — by amendment to the articles of incorporation in the case of a class and by action of the board of directors, acting alone, in the case of a series. Series of preferred shares may be publicly traded in the same way as classes of such shares.

§17.13 NOVEL TYPES OF PREFERRED SHARES

The high interest rates of the early 1980s led to the development of novel financing devices, many of which involved preferred shares. For example, many corporations issued preferred stock that was redeemable at the option of the holder or that became redeemable upon the occurrence of some external event, such as a change in interest rates or the lapse of a specified period of time. Still other corporations issued preferred shares with floating or adjustable dividend rates that depended on interest rates or some similar measure. Most of these novel preferreds were designed for sophisticated lenders, but they illustrate that the line between "equity" and "debt" can be blurred.

Market-quality preferred shares are particularly attractive investments for corporations because of the intercorporate dividend-received deduction, which permits a corporation receiving a dividend to deduct 70 percent of it from its taxable income (80 percent if the receiving corporation owns more than 20 percent of the paying corporation). The dividend-received deduction often makes an investment in preferred stock more attractive than a straight loan of funds by one corporation to another. In the case of a straight loan, the interest paid by the debtor is a deductible business expense, and the interest is ordinary income to the creditor. A corporate creditor, desiring to minimize the tax cost of the transaction to it, may insist that "loans" by it to another corporation be cast in the form of a purchase of a special class of preferred stock rather than a loan. This special class of preferred stock may have a variable dividend rate tied to an interest rate index and a contractual obligation on the part of the issuing corpo-ration to redeem the special class of preferred upon demand. The redemp-tion price may be a matter of negotiation between the corporation and an investor. In other words, the loan transaction is dressed up as a sale of preferred stock with the identical economic terms as the contemplated loan transaction.

Since a lender who is an individual is not entitled to a dividend-received deduction, there is no incentive to transmute a loan transaction into a preferred stock purchase in the case of individual lenders.

§17.14 PERCS

The decline in interest rates in the early 1990s led to the development of a "capped" preferred stock that has obtained some degree of popularity. These stocks are called "preferred equity redemption cumulative shares," or PERCS. By 1992, nearly $9 billion of such shares have been publicly sold by a variety of companies, including General Motors, Sears, KMart, and RJR Nabisco. A PERC is issued at the same price as the then market price of the common. The PERC pays a dividend that is significantly higher than the dividend on the company's company stock; PERC yields may be 8 or 9 percent per year. But the price that the PERCS can reach is sharply limited because at the end of three years the PERCS automatically convert into the lower of either the current price of the common stock or an amount of cash or stock equal to the original issue price of the PERCS plus a specified percentage of that value — 30 percent or 40 percent are the most popular percentages. This latter provision is the "cap." Usually, the redemption is in common stock rather than cash: If the "cap" controls the redemption price, the holder of a PERC will receive less than one full share of the common stock.

For example, Citicorp issued PERCS at $14.75 per share, the price of its common stock on the date of issue. Two years later, the common had risen to $19 but the PERCS were selling at $16.25 because of the impending cap. Investors would have been better off giving up the yield on the PERCS and buying common stock directly. On the other hand, when the common stock does not go up, the PERCS may do relatively well, buoyed by the higher dividend. For example, Westinghouse issued PERCS when its common stock was at $17. Even though the common stock then declined to $12.60, the PERCS traded at more than $16.

18
Exotic Investments

§18.1 INTRODUCTION

This chapter introduces the reader to a variety of investment vehicles, including standardized option contracts for securities and futures contracts for commodities, currencies, and financial indexes. Many of these vehicles are extremely high-risk investments: They are attractive to the high roller from a speculative standpoint primarily because they combine relatively small initial investments with a substantial potential for gain or loss. They are therefore unsuitable investments for the average reader of this book. In some situations, however, — and this is the principal reason this chapter is included — is that these investment devices may also be used to "hedge" established positions, that is, to protect existing investments from unacceptable declines in value. When used in this manner, they are conservative rather than speculative in character. In addition, some of the securities described in this chapter are packaged for sale to small investors and undoubtedly from time to time unsophisticated investors are persuaded to invest in some of these securities.

Some of the securities discussed in this chapter are "derivative securities," that is, their value may be based on price movements in individual stocks (usually NYSE stocks) or on changes in stock indexes that themselves reflect a hypothetical portfolio of publicly traded stocks. These indexes are described in sections 14.29 and 14.30. Elaborate computer-based trading strategies have been developed to take advantage of these new securities. These strategies link the new markets for these derivative securities with the traditional markets for securities and have greatly increased the volatility and volume of trading in those traditional markets. This was vividly demonstrated in April 1992 when a break in underground tunnels under the Chicago financial district resulted in massive underground flooding and the loss of electricity in several major buildings, including the buildings housing the Chicago Board of Trade, the Chicago Mercantile Exchange, the Chicago Board of Options Exchange, the Midwest Stock Exchange, and the Mid-America Commodities Exchange. Trading in financial futures and options was suspended for several days, and there was immediately a marked reduction in trading volume and a noticeable decrease in volatility of prices on the New York Stock Exchange.

Some of the investment vehicles described in this chapter are of comparatively recent origin. Others, such as trading in commodities futures, have existed for more than a century. They all share the common characteristic of being dynamic and arcane tools primarily for professional traders and speculators. Traditional stocks and bonds described in earlier chapters are sometimes referred to as "plain vanilla" securities by speculators to distinguish them from the securities discussed in this chapter.

This chapter deals only with the standard options and futures that are traded on established markets. This is the tip of an iceberg. There also exists a vast, and largely unregulated, over-the-counter market for a variety of individually created options or rights with respect to securities or currencies. Some of these securities are so new that the risks involved in them may not be well understood even by the persons who create them. No attempt is made in this chapter to describe the numerous varieties of newly created options or rights that may be available, or indeed, to describe the complex trading strategies that may be utilized with the standard options and futures described here.

§18.2 SECURITIES OPTIONS: PUTS AND CALLS

Perhaps the easiest way to describe how standardized securities options work is to use a real-life example. Table 18-1 is the portion of the listed options quotations page of The Wall Street Journal for September 30, 1992 that contains the Chicago Board of Trade's listed options for IBM common stock for September 29, 1992.

There are two types of publicly traded options: (1) *Call* options are options to purchase IBM stock at a fixed price for a limited period; and (2) *put* options are options to sell IBM stock at a fixed price for a limited period. The left-hand column of Table 18-1 simply names the stock in question (IBM) and the closing price of $81 per share for that stock on the New York Stock Exchange for reference purposes. The second column, "Strike Price," is the price at which a specific option in question is exercisable. For this reason it is also sometimes called the exercise price. The strike price is fixed when the option is created and remains unchanged during the life of the option. IBM options in Table 18-1 are in the October-November-January expiration cycle, which means that separate options expire at the close of trading on the third Friday of the months of October, November, and January. Options on other publicly traded securities are on a variety of monthly cycles so as to avoid simultaneous maturity dates for all options.

The columns under "Calls-Last" and "Puts-Last" are closing market prices for IBM options at the listed strike prices expiring in the month in question. Thus for IBM there are options potentially being traded at eight different strike prices at 5-dollar intervals between 70 and 105, expiring at 3 different times, or 24 different potential call options on IBM stock. Similarly, there are 24 different potential put options, or a total of 48 different options on IBM in all (though neither put nor call options are traded or written for all the various possible variations). It must be conceded that information about a large number of different options is crammed into a small amount of space in Table 18-1.

Table 18-1

LISTED OPTIONS QUOTATIONS

Tuesday, September 29, 1992

Options closing prices. Sales unit usually is 100 shares.
Stock close is New York or American exchange final price.

CHICAGO BOARD

Option & Strike NY Close Price		Calls-Last			Puts-Last		
		Oct	Nov	Dec	Oct	Nov	Dec
I B M	70	s	s	$12\frac{1}{8}$	s	s	$\frac{11}{16}$
81	75	r	$7\frac{3}{4}$	$7\frac{1}{2}$	$\frac{1}{4}$	1	$1\frac{11}{16}$
81	80	$2\frac{5}{16}$	$3\frac{1}{4}$	$4\frac{1}{2}$	$1\frac{3}{16}$	$2\frac{1}{2}$	$3\frac{1}{2}$
81	85	$\frac{7}{16}$	$1\frac{1}{16}$	$2\frac{5}{16}$	$4\frac{1}{4}$	$5\frac{3}{4}$	$6\frac{1}{2}$
81	90	$\frac{1}{8}$	$\frac{5}{16}$	1	$9\frac{1}{8}$	$9\frac{5}{8}$	$10\frac{3}{8}$
81	95	$\frac{1}{16}$	s	$\frac{7}{16}$	13	s	15
81	100	$\frac{1}{16}$	s	$\frac{1}{4}$	r	s	r
81	105	r	s	$\frac{1}{8}$	$23\frac{3}{8}$	s	$25\frac{1}{4}$

r-Not Traded. s-No Option.

In January 1993, the Wall Street Journal simplified its manner of reporting trading in puts and calls. Table 18-2 is the new tabular format for reporting the option trading in puts and calls on IBM stock on February 12, 1993. At this time IBM was trading at about 50.

Puts and calls are traded in units or blocks of options on 100 shares; the option unit on 100 shares is called a "contract." The quotations in Table 18-1, however, are on a per-share rather than a per-contract basis.

Put and call options are referred to by the name of the stock, the strike price, the month of expiration, and the nature of the option (i.e., a put or a call). For example, the "IBM January 80 call option" refers to the option in the third row, fifth column, of Table 18-1, priced at $4.50 at the close on September 29.

§18.3 CALL OPTIONS

On September 29, 1992, the price of the IBM October 95 call option was 1/16, or $0.0625 per option. Obviously, for any significant speculation, a purchase of several hundred contracts would be feasible for even a person with modest means.

Table 18-2

LISTED OPTIONS QUOTATIONS

Friday, February 12, 1993

Volume, close, net change and open interest of the 1,400 most active equity and 100 most active long-term contracts. Volume figures are unofficial. Open interest is total outstanding for all exchanges and reflects previous trading day. **CB**-Chicago Board Options Exchange. **AM**-American Stock Exchange. **PB**-Philadelphia Stock Exchange. **PC**-Pacific Stock Exchange. **NY**-New York Stock Exchange. **a**-Underlying stock on primary market. **c**-Call. **p**-Put.

Option/Strike				Vol	Exch	Last	Net Chg	a-Close	Open Int
IBM	Apr	40	p	528	CB	5/16	- 1/16	50 5/8	2,261
IBM	Mar	45	p	636	CB	1/2	...	50 5/8	3,903
IBM	Apr	45		79	CB	7	- 1/4	50 5/8	3,632
IBM	Apr	45	p	552	CB	15/16	- 1/16	50 5/8	9,238
IBM	Jul	45	p	133	CB	1 7/8	...	50 5/8	4,626
IBM	Feb	50		1,652	CB	1 3/16	- 9/16	50 5/8	16,680
IBM	Feb	50	p	1,594	CB	9/16	- 1/8	50 5/8	14,523
IBM	Mar	50		1,067	CB	2 11/16	- 5/16	50 5/8	11,429
IBM	Mar	50	p	681	CB	1 3/4	...	50 5/8	6,527
IBM	Apr	50		901	CB	3 1/2	- 1/4	50 5/8	15,133
IBM	Apr	50	p	265	CB	2 9/16	+ 3/16	50 5/8	8,833
IBM	Jul	50		688	CB	4 3/4	- 3/8	50 5/8	7,095
IBM	Jul	50	p	650	CB	3 7/8	+ 1/8	50 5/8	6,477
IBM	Feb	55		1,712	CB	1/8	- 1/16	50 5/8	21,887
IBM	Feb	55	p	321	CB	4 3/8	+ 3/8	50 5/8	3,458
IBM	Mar	55		1,416	CB	13/16	- 3/16	50 5/8	10,890
IBM	Mar	55	p	211	CB	5	+ 1/4	50 5/8	778
IBM	Apr	55		965	CB	1 1/2	- 1/4	50 5/8	21,711
IBM	Jul	55		217	CB	2 7/8	- 1/8	50 5/8	8,118
IBM	Jul	55	p	176	CB	6 7/8	+ 1/8	50 5/8	2,947
IBM	Mar	60		322	CB	1/4	...	50 5/8	304
IBM	Apr	60		1,105	CB	5/8	- 1/16	50 5/8	17,094
IBM	Jul	60		117	CB	1 9/16	- 1/8	50 5/8	6,487
IBM	Apr	65		781	CB	1/4	- 1/16	50 5/8	9,175
IBM	Jul	65		169	CB	13/16	- 1/8	50 5/8	3,741
IBM	Apr	70		322	CB	3/16	...	50 5/8	12,021
IBM	Apr	80		95	CB	1/16	...	50 5/8	4,190
IBM	Apr	85		100	CB	1/16	...	50 5/8	4,928

A person who purchased an IBM October 95 call option would have acquired, at a cost of $6.25, the right to purchase 100 shares of IBM at 95 dollars per share at any time between the date of acquisition and the date of expiration on Friday, October 16, 1992. In this particular case, the expiration date is a little over two weeks after the date of acquisition. A call option gets its name from the power of the purchaser to "call away" the stock from whoever granted or "wrote" the option.

Let us assume for the moment that a speculator has reason to believe that there will be a substantial run-up in IBM in the next two weeks. Indeed, she fully expects that the price of IBM will rise 25 points in the next two weeks — from 81 to 106. This may sound unlikely, and indeed it is given the problems IBM was having in 1992, but it is not impossible since IBM traded as high as 104 within the preceding 52 weeks (see Table 14-9 in Chapter 14), and similar increases in price commonly occur in takeover-candidate stocks in very short periods of time.

Assume also that our speculator has only about $8,100 to invest. If she were to buy IBM common stock, she can afford to purchase only 100 shares at cost of 81 (for simplicity this discussion ignores commissions and interest). If she can arrange a margin purchase, she can buy an extra 100 shares with funds borrowed from her broker (see section 14.18) for a total of 200 shares. If the price of IBM in fact rises to 106 as expected and the speculator sells at this price, she will have made $2,500 ($10,600 − $8,100) on a straight purchase; if she makes a margin purchase, she will make about $5,000 ($21,200 − $16,200). These are certainly tidy profits for a two-week investment.

But consider what happens if the speculator takes $8,100 and buys IBM October 95 call options: She can buy 1,264 contracts ($8,100 divided by 6.25) for 100 shares each, and thereby control 126,400 shares with those 1,264 contracts. Now, when the price goes up 25 points to 106 our speculator is able to exercise the call option and buy 126,400 shares at $95 per share and immediately sell them in the open market for $106. The gross profit is about $1,390,400, all on a two-week speculation involving a $8,100 investment.

One can obviously get rich quickly on call options if one can correctly predict when a big run-up in price will occur. People who made fantastic profits on inside information during the insider trading scandals regularly used call options to maximize their gains from reliable inside information.

It is not necessary for the speculator to actually exercise the option to purchase the shares at 95 and then immediately resell them; the options themselves are publicly traded, and as the options become valuable (usually described as being "in the money"), they can be sold by themselves. Thus, the $1,390,400 gross profit on IBM is obtainable by the speculator whether or not she has the capital to exercise options on 126,400 shares of IBM at 95. Nor is there any danger that the option writer will welsh upon this calamitous run-up in price of IBM; his or her performance is guaranteed by both the Chicago Board of Trade and the broker who arranged for the option to be written. Nor is there any danger that someone will goof up and a valuable option will go unexercised on the last day; brokerage firms regularly sweep option customers accounts and exercise all options that are "in the money."

There obviously has to be a downside risk to all of this get-rich-quick stuff. And indeed there is. A price run-up of 25 points is pretty unusual for IBM, particularly when the price of the stock has been sliding steadily for nearly two years because of continuing problems faced by IBM within the computer industry. That is about a 25 percent increase in price within two weeks in direct opposition to the long-term trend in the stock's price. What happens if the speculator is wrong on her timing, and the price run-up does not occur, and the price of IBM stock remains stable? If the speculator bought the stock itself, she is about even: IBM has remained stable in price (or at most declined somewhat), and most of her $8,100 investment can be recovered simply by selling the stock. Even if the speculator had bought an extra 100 shares on margin, she still would come out basically all right. She is paying interest on the margin loan and her risk has doubled in comparison to the straight purchase of 100 shares, but the bulk of the $8,100 investment is still intact. But if the speculator had bought call options, they would have expired valueless near the end of October, and she would have lost the entire $8,100.

The October 95 IBM call option used in the last example is an "out of the money" option, since IBM would have to rise 14 points in price before it has any inherent value. The October 80 IBM option, on the other hand, is "in the money," since the stock is selling at 81 and the option has an intrinsic value of $1.00. This option sold for two and five-sixteenths dollars on September 29: The difference between the intrinsic value and the option price is a premium for the possibility that IBM common stock may increase in price over the next two weeks before the option expires. The difference between the intrinsic value and the option price is sometimes called the "time value" of the option to distinguish it from the option's intrinsic value. The purchase of the 80 option gives the buyer a great deal of upward leverage: if the price of IBM rises from 81 to 82 in one day, that is a tiny fractional rise in the stock of a little more than 1 percent. However, the 80 option will probably rise by a full point also; going from two and five-sixteenths to perhaps three and one-half; that is about a 38 percent increase in a single day. A decline of IBM from 81 to 80 will also cause a much larger percentage decline in the 80 option, but it probably would be less than a full point. Do you see why? Hint: Why is there any value at all in any out-of-the-money option?

As one would intuitively expect, call options that expire in later months sell for more than options that expire in earlier months. While the IBM October 80 call option traded at two and five-sixteenths dollars on September 29, 1992, the IBM November call option traded at $3.25 and the January 1993 call option was priced at $4.50. Do you see why call options with later expiration dates are more valuable than otherwise identical options with earlier expiration dates?

The person who commits himself or herself to sell IBM shares upon the call of the option purchaser is called the writer of the option. Who writes call options? Any investor who owns 100 shares of IBM can write a call option on those shares but, as a practical matter, most call options are written by substantial investors managing large portfolios. When a person writes an option and sells it on the Chicago Board of Trade, the writer receives the sales price of the option: The writer of the 1,264 contracts for IBM October 95 calls described above pockets the $8,100 sales price for the options (less a brokerage commission). If the option expires valueless, the writer keeps the $8,100, thereby improving the yield on the portfolio. If IBM unexpectedly moves up in price and the option is exercised, the writer will, of course, have to sell the shares at 95 (the strike price). The writer still has a profit to the extent of the difference between 81 and 95, but all profits above the strike price inure to the purchaser of the call option. That is what the purchaser of the call options buys for $8,100. Writing call options at above-market strike prices is generally profitable in stable or declining markets, since few or none of them will be exercised. If the market rises, the writer receives the strike price and the option purchaser the entire value of the stock above the strike price.

Some investors write call options without actually owning the shares. This is called "going naked" or "writing naked options," and obviously is considerably more risky than writing covered options, namely options for which the writer already owns the shares. Writing a naked call option on IBM common stock is analogous, in terms of risk, to a short sale of IBM stock. If the price moves in an unfavorable direction, both the short seller and the writer of the uncovered call are required to go into the market to buy IBM stock on unfavorable terms to close out the transaction. Since the broker selling the uncovered call option on behalf of the writer is responsible for the production of the shares if the call is exercised, from its standpoint it is essential that the writer of an uncovered call post margin and that that margin be increased if the price of the underlying IBM stock rises during the life of the option.

Most writers of uncovered calls are securities firms or professional investors.

Call options may be purchased in order to hedge short sale positions. It will be recalled that a short seller borrows shares and sells them, hoping prices will decline so that he or she can replace the borrowed shares at a lower price. See section 14.19. A short seller gets squeezed when prices move up rather than down; if the short seller is concerned about this prospect he or she can cover most of the risk by buying a call option on the same stock. (It is important to recognize that the discussion about the naked option writer above deals with the risk of the writer of the option not the purchaser; the present paragraph deals with a purchaser of the option who is exposed to a price rise because he or she previously sold the stock short.) If the price goes up, the loss on the short sale position will be largely offset by the gain on the call. Whether or not this is desirable depends in part on how expensive the purchase of the call is, since that is the "premium" for this type of insurance.

§18.4 PUT OPTIONS

A put option enables the purchaser of the put to profit on market declines. A put is the mirror image of a call option. The writer of a put option commits to buy the stock at the strike price for the specified period at the option of the buyer of the option. In a call, the writer commits to sell, and the buyer of the call has the option whether or not to buy. In a put, the writer commits to buy and the buyer of the put has the option whether or not to sell.

For example, from Table 18-1 (on page 437) it will be seen that the IBM October 80 put option sold at one and three-sixteenths dollars per option on September 29. If a person bought this put, and the price of IBM declined to 75, say, the holder of the put would show a profit equal to the difference between 80 and 75, minus the cost of the put option. In the vernacular, the holder of the put could "buy IBM at 75 and put it to the writer at 80." That is why it is called a put. In Table 18-2, the new format for option trading tables, puts are identified by the letter "p."

An examination of Table 18-1 shows the inverse relationship between puts and calls. When a call is in the money and has intrinsic value, the corresponding put must, by definition, be out of the money, and vice versa. Thus, the IBM 95 October call is out of the money since the stock price is 81; the IBM 95 October put is in the money selling for $13 per share. It may be noted that this option apparently has an intrinsic value of $14 (95 minus 81) while it is priced at $13. That is, of course, not possible; there is no easy free lunch of that type in the securities markets. The explanation is that the option price and closing price are not reported at the identical time; if one checks both option price and trading price at the same time, the apparent discrepancy disappears.

Since the writer of a put option only commits to purchase a stock at a specified price, there is no precisely analogous concept to writing naked call options on the put side. The writing of puts, however, can create devastating losses if there is a sudden strong downward movement in the price of the stock. The risk involved in writing put options is not apparent in a generally rising market (since relatively few out of the money puts are exercised and "in the money" puts are usually exercised to cut losses rather than to make a profit). A rising market existed from early 1982 through August 1987. Many brokers recommended to relatively unsophisticated clients during this period that the clients write put options to increase the investment yield of their portfolios. It seemed to be a relatively riskless way of increasing investment return. In the abrupt market decline that occurred in October 1987, many of these investors' savings were wiped out as brokerage firms liquidated entire portfolios in order to meet obligations under put contracts and some ended up owing their brokerage firms substantial amounts as well. The writing of put options in excess of available at-risk capital is sometimes referred to as writing naked put options as an analogy to the risk involved in writing naked call options in a rising market.

It may be noted that the writer of a put option can limit future losses by buying an offsetting put option with the same maturity and strike price. Considerable protection may also be obtained by purchasing any "in the money" put option; partial protection may sometimes be obtained by writing call options. In a period of sharp market decline such as occurred in October 1987, however, the prices of puts advanced so rapidly (and the process of communicating securities orders was often so constricted) that these strategies were, as a practical matter, unavailable to at-risk put writers.

Puts may be purchased to shield portfolio positions from price declines; for example, a person with 100 shares of IBM who fears a short-term decline in the stock but who does not want to sell the shares, may purchase a put option for 100 shares. If the price does decline, the loss of value in the underlying stock will be largely offset by the rise in value of the put.

§18.5 LONG OPTIONS

In 1990, the Chicago Board Options Exchange began trading in long-term put and call options, called "long-term equity anticipation securities" (LEAPS). These options have expiration periods of as long as two years. They have been reasonably popular and similar options are now traded by several exchanges. Table 18-3 is the CBOE quotations for long-term IBM options on September 29, 1992.

The strike prices for LEAPS usually parallel those for regular short-term options, but the cost is significantly higher than for short-term options. This is, of course, to be expected since the longer time span greatly increases the risk of the option writer. The January 1994 85 call was priced at nearly $6.50 per option while the put at the same strike price was quoted at nearly $12 per option; corresponding prices for the longest short-term

Table 18-3

LONG TERM OPTIONS

CBOE

Option/Exp/Strike	Last
IBM Jan 94 70	14
IBM Jan 94 70 p	4
IBM Jan 94 85	6½
IBM Jan 94 85 p	11⅞
IBM Jan 94 95	3⅝
IBM Jan 94 105	2
IBM Jan 94 105 p	27
IBM Jan 95 70	16
IBM Jan 95 70 p	6½
IBM Jan 95 85	9
IBM Jan 95 85 p	14
IBM Jan 95 105	3⅝

options expiring in January 1993 (see Table 18-1) on the same day was $2.50 for the call option and $6.50 for the put option. This pricing mechanism means that big price swings must occur for LEAPS to be profitable for the purchaser; price swings replace the time pressure that exists for regular short-term options.

§18.6 EXAMPLES OF OPTION TRADING STRATEGIES

It is important to note that in options trading, the purchaser of a put or call option risks only the money he or she has invested in the option. If the price moves in the wrong direction, the holder of the option simply allows the option to expire unexercised. The writer of an option, on the other hand, is much more at the mercy of market forces.

One can speculate simultaneously on upward and downward movements (a strategy known as a "straddle") by the purchase of options. One may buy, for example, a put on IBM at 80 for one and three-sixteenths ($1.1875) per share and a call on IBM at 85 for seven-sixteenths ($0.4375) per share. The straddle thus costs $1.625 per share plus commissions. One makes money on this straddle if the price of IBM drops below about 78 or rises above about 87. One loses only if IBM steadily trades in the range between 78 and 87 for the balance of the option period.

One can also create a "synthetic security" from put and call options. For example, one might purchase an IBM 80 call option and simultaneously write an IBM 80 put option. This combination of options roughly parallels the price movement of IBM stock itself, but the total cost of the position is significantly less than buying the stock itself.

Option trading requires a good sense of timing. In order to be profitable, an anticipated movement in stock prices must occur during the period of the option. Similarly, when one has a profit on an options position one must decide whether to take the profit or let the position run (i.e., remain open) to improve the profitability. The danger, of course, is that the price movement may reverse itself and the profitable opportunity lost.

Table 18-4 summarizes profitable strategies in options trading.

Table 18-4
Trading Strategies

	Increasing Prices	*Declining Prices*
1)	buy the stock	sell the stock
2)	buy on margin	sell short
3)	buy calls	buy puts
4)	write puts	write calls

§18.7 OPTIONS ON INDEXES AND INTEREST RATES

Options trading — the writing and buying of puts and calls — can be extended to any product that fluctuates in price. Rather than writing an option on a single stock, one can write an option on a bundle of stocks. One can write an option on a stock index. One can write an option on foreign currencies (whose values fluctuate with respect to U.S. dollars). One can write options on treasury notes or treasury bonds (whose values fluctuate solely in response to interest rate changes since they are viewed as riskless investments). The only real requirement is that the price moves.

Indeed, marketable options are traded on all of the non-stock interests referred to in the previous paragraph. Table 18-5 is a partial listing of trading in these non-stock options as reported by The Wall Street Journal for September 29, 1992. The variety of indexes and currencies for which options are currently traded is interesting. The only real difference in operation between traditional securities options described in the previous section and these non-stock options is that one cannot usually receive or deliver the underlying indexes when the option is exercised; one has to settle up in cash.

It will be noted that LEAPS (see section 18.5) have been created on some index options.

Options on indexes are extremely popular. They have flourished while options on particular stocks have seen only incremental growth. Table 18-6 shows the most active options traded on the Chicago Board and the American and New York exchanges as of September 29, 1992. These include both stock and non-stock options. It will be noted that, in terms of volume, most options trading is in index options, and that the S&P 100 index option traded on the Chicago Board has the widest following of any single option.

Table 18-5

INDEX TRADING

Tuesday, September 29, 1992

OPTIONS

Chicago Board

S&P 100 INDEX (OEX)-$100 times index

Strike Price	Calls—Last Oct	Nov	Dec	Puts—Last Oct	Nov	Dec
350	....	....	....	1/4	1 7/16	2 1/2
355	....	....	....	3/8	1 11/16	3 1/8
360	26	....	....	7/16	2 1/4	3 3/8
365	....	....	24 1/2	3/4	2 15/16	4 3/8
370	16 1/8	18 1/2	20 1/2	1 1/8	3 7/8	5 5/8
375	11 1/2	14 1/4	16	1 3/4	5 1/8	7
380	7 5/8	10 1/2	12 3/4	2 7/8	6 5/8	8 3/4
385	4 1/4	7 1/2	9 3/4	4 5/8	8 1/2	10 1/2
390	2 3/16	5 1/4	7 1/4	7 5/8	11 3/8	12 7/8
395	1	3 1/4	5 1/4	11 1/2	14 3/8	16 1/4
400	7/16	1 15/16	3 3/8	15 3/4	18 3/4	....
405	3/16	1 1/16	2 1/8	....	....	....
410	1/8	9/16	1 1/2	....	....	....
415	1/16	5/16	13/16	....	....	....

Total call volume 87,330   Total call open int. 392,073
Total put volume 84,795   Total put open int. 402,939
The index: High 385.01; Low 382.68; Close 383.84, −0.42

S&P 500 INDEX (NSX)-$100 times index

Strike Price	Calls—Last Oct	Dec	Mar	Puts—Last Oct	Dec	Mar
365	....	....	....	....	1 3/8	....
375	....	....	....	....	2 1/8	5 1/2
380	....	....	....	....	2 5/8	....
385	....	....	....	3/8	....	....
390	....	....	....	3/8	4 1/8	....
395	23 1/2	....	....	5/8	5 1/8	....
400	....	22 1/2	27 5/8	1	5 5/8	....
405	13 1/4	19	....	1 9/16	7	....
410	9 1/2	15 1/2	....	2 1/4	8 3/4	14 3/8
415	5 5/8	....	17 1/2	3 3/4	10 7/8	16
420	3 3/8	9 1/2	....	6 1/2	12 1/2	....
425	1 1/2	6 3/4	....	9 7/8	15	....
430	9/16	....	....	13 7/8	18 1/4	....
435	1/4	....	....	17 3/4	....	....
440	1/8	....	....	....	....	....
450	....	3/4	....	....	33 1/2	....

Total call volume 10,707   Total call open int. 334,161
Total put volume 8,475   Total put open int. 534,752
The index: High 417.38; Low 415.34; Close 416.80, +0.18

S&P 500 INDEX (SPX)-$100 times index

Strike Price	Calls—Last Nov	Dec	Mar	Puts—Last Nov	Dec	Mar
375	....	....	....	....	....	5 1/2
385	....	....	....	....	3	....
390	....	....	....	2 7/16	....	....
395	25	....	....	2 7/8	5	....
400	....	22 7/8	27 5/8	3 3/4	5 3/4	....
405	....	....	....	4 5/8	....	....
410	....	....	....	6	8 5/8	14
415	9 1/2	11 3/4	17 1/2	7 1/2	11	15 3/4
420	6 5/8	9 1/4	15	9 7/8	12 1/4	....
425	4 1/2	6 3/8	....	....	....	....
430	3	5	....	....	....	....
435	1 9/16	....	....	....	....	....
440	1	....	....	....	....	....
445	....	....	4 3/4	....	....	....
450	....	....	3 5/8	....	....	....

Total call volume 6,124   Total call open int. 134,389
Total put volume 7,807   Total put open int. 108,420
The index: High 417.38; Low 415.34; Close 416.80, +0.18

LEAPS-S&P 100 INDEX

Strike Price	Calls—Last Dec 92	Dec 93	Dec 94	Puts—Last Dec 92	Dec 93	Dec 94
30	....	....	....	....	5/8	....
32 1/2	....	....	....	....	1	....
35	....	....	....	1/4	1 7/16	....
37 1/2	1 9/16	....	....	....	2 5/16	....
40	3/8	....	....	....	2	4 1/2

Total call volume 1,031   Total call open int. 33,893
Total put volume 937   Total put open int. 185,330
The index: High 38.50; Low 38.27; Close 38.38, −0.05

LEAPS-S&P 500 INDEX

Strike Price	Calls—Last Dec 92	Dec 93	Puts—Last Dec 92	Dec 93
40	....	....	5/8	2 1/8
42 1/2	11/16	....	1 1/2	....
45	....	....	....	4 1/2

Total call volume 5   Total call open int. 31,118
Total put volume 185   Total put open int. 148,931
The index: High 41.74; Low 41.53; Close 41.68, +0.02

CAPS-S&P 100 INDEX (CPO)

Strike Price	Calls—Last Oct 92	Dec 92	Puts—Last Oct 92	Dec 92
400	....	....	15 1/4	....

Total call volume 0   Total call open int. 370
Total put volume 10   Total put open int. 373
The index: High 385.01; Low 382.68; Close 383.84, −0.42

CAPS-S&P 500 INDEX (CPS)

Strike Price	Calls—Last Dec 92	Puts—Last Dec 92
410	14 1/4	....
430	....	14 1/4

Total call volume 4   Total call open int. 276
Total put volume 104   Total put open int. 1,301
The index: High 417.38; Low 415.34; Close 416.80, +0.18

American Exchange

S&P MIDCAP INDEX

Strike Price	Calls—Last Oct	Nov	Dec	Puts—Last Oct	Nov	Dec
145	1 1/4	....	....	2 1/2	4 1/4	4 3/4
147 1/2	1/2	....	....	....	....	....
150	....	1	....	....	....	....

Total call volume 45   Total call open int. 24,538
Total put volume 388   Total put open int. 41,749
The index: High 143.82; Low 142.99; Close 143.82, +0.59

MAJOR MARKET INDEX

Strike Price	Calls—Last Oct	Nov	Dec	Puts—Last Oct	Nov	Dec
305	....	....	....	1/16	....	....
310	....	....	....	1/8	....	....
320	....	....	....	3/16	....	....
325	....	....	29 3/4	....	....	....
330	....	....	....	3/8	....	....
335	....	....	....	5/8	....	....
340	12 3/4	15 1/8	....	1 1/8	....	....
345	8 3/4	10 3/4	....	1 15/16	....	7 3/4
350	4 7/8	8	10 3/4	3 1/4	7 1/4	....
355	2 7/16	5 3/4	7	5 1/2	9 1/4	....
360	15/16	3 1/4	....	8 5/8	11 7/8	....
365	7/16	1 3/4	....	13 1/2	....	....
370	3/16	1	1 3/4	....	....	....
375	1/16	....	....	....	....	....
380	....	....	....	....	28 3/8	....

Total call volume 2,618   Total call open int. 60,476
Total put volume 1,731   Total put open int. 83,245
The index: High 352.25; Low 349.46; Close 351.05, −0.36

The possibility of using puts and calls on individual stocks to hedge against price movements has previously been noted. Is there any social benefit to the trading of index options described in this section? Or are they pure gambling on price movements in abstract numbers? These questions have evoked some controversy. Basically, options package the risk components of investments in units that can be traded separately from the

Table 18-6

MOST ACTIVE OPTIONS

CHICAGO BOARD

	Sales	Last	Chg	N.Y. Close
CALLS				
SP100 Oct 385	24475	4¼	-⅛	383.83
SP100 Oct 390	19082	2 3/16	-1/16	383.83
SP100 Oct 380	11086	7⅝	...	383.83
SP100 Oct 395	9236	1	-⅛	383.83
TelMex Oct 45	5738	11/16	+5/16	43⅞
SP100 Oct 400	4728	7/16	...	383.83
Sears Oct 45	4185	15/16	+¾	44¾
SP100 Nov 395	3888	3¼	+⅛	383.83
I B M Oct 85	2907	7/16	-¼	81
I B M Oct 80	2554	2 5/16	-1 3/16	81
PUTS				
SP100 Oct 380	19375	2⅞	-1/16	383.83
SP100 Oct 385	17180	4⅝	-⅛	383.83
SP100 Oct 375	7737	1¾	...	383.83
SP100 Oct 390	4879	7⅝	...	383.83
SP100 Oct 365	4807	¾	...	383.83
SP100 Oct 360	4771	7/16	...	383.83
SP100 Oct 370	4073	1⅛	...	383.83
I B M Oct 80	3888	1 3/16	+9/16	81
SP100 Nov 365	3321	2 15/16	-3/16	383.83
SP100 Oct 355	3285	⅜	...	383.83

AMERICAN

	Sales	Last	Chg	N.Y. Close
CALLS				
Cooper Oct 50	1187	2⅛	+¾	51
Pfizer Nov 85	1000	3/16	-1/16	74½
US Surg Oct 65	983	1 7/16	-3/16	61⅝
JpnIdx Oct 185	936	4¼	-⅜	178.75
Glaxo Nov 30	903	5/16	+⅛	27⅛
Amgen Oct 65	887	1	-⅛	62¼
AppleC Oct 50	817	⅛	-1/16	44⅞
Motrla Oct 90	814	1 1/16	+3/16	87¼
MajMkt Oct 365	784	7/16	+⅛	351.04
PhilPt May 25	780	3⅝	+3⅝	28
PUTS				
JpnIdx Oct 165	905	1¾	-5/16	178.75
US Surg Oct 60	741	2⅛	+⅛	61⅝
Lilly Jan 65	714	4¾	+¼	62¼
Glaxo Nov 22½	645	⅛	-⅛	27⅛
Disney Oct 35	611	5/16	-1/16	36½
US Surg Oct 90	600	27	+½	61⅝
Amgen Oct 60	558	1¼	...	62¼
MajMkt Oct 350	522	3¼	...	351.04
JpnIdx Oct 175	458	4⅝	-⅛	178.75
Pfizer Dec 75	448	3½	-⅜	74½

PHILADELPHIA

	Sales	Last	Chg	N.Y. Close
CALLS				
MartnM Nov 60	1690	1 1/16	+1/16	58½
MorgSt Nov 50	1040	1¼	-⅝	48½
A Hess Nov 50	1011	1¼	-5/16	47⅞
Allwst Feb 7½	1000	3/16	-5/16	5⅝
BkBost May 22½	1000	1	-5/16	19⅜
TimeW Oct 25	827	⅜	-⅜	24
CML Nov 30	638	1¼	+⅛	28⅜
Primca Oct 40	500	2 7/16	-1 11/16	42¼
Comsat Oct 40	325	1⅜	+¼	41⅛
Waste Nov 40	305	¼	+1/16	35¾
PUTS				
TimeW Mar 22½	800	1 3/16	+¼	24
F N M Nov 65	660	2⅛	-⅛	65¾
Bard Oct 30	630	3¾	+½	26⅝
TimeW Dec 25	622	1⅞	...	24
Bard Oct 35	400	8⅜	+1⅛	26⅝
HomeDp Oct 55	339	1 3/16	+5/16	55⅛
Synrgn Oct 40	267	1	-1/16	43⅝
MBIA Oct 55	250	11/16	-1 3/16	56¼
Primca Oct 50	250	7⅝	+7⅝	42¼
TimeW Oct 27½	240	3¼	+1	24

PACIFIC

	Sales	Last	Chg	N.Y. Close
CALLS				
Micsft Oct 80	1063	1 7/16	+7/16	78¾
SwBell Apr 65	1060	4¾	+1¼	67⅜
Stride Jan 22½	1042	⅝	+⅛	18⅞
AdobeS Oct 30	726	⅝	...	27½
Micsft Oct 75	666	4⅝	+1⅛	78¾
GMills Jan 70	613	1⅝	+⅛	66⅛
SwBell Oct 60	592	7⅛	+¾	67⅜
Compaq Oct 35	498	11/16	+⅛	33⅞
MedCrA Oct 25	475	1	-⅛	23⅝
PacTel Oct 45	440	⅜	...	44⅜
PUTS				
AdobeS Oct 50	2001	23½	+2	27½
AdobeS Oct 55	2000	28½	+5½	27½
Micsft Oct 75	431	13/16	-½	78¾
Mc D D Feb 45	300	9⅛	...	38
Stratus Nov 40	300	1¼	+1¼	42
Stratus Oct 40	290	15/16	+13/16	42
Dole Dec 30	275	1½	-⅛	30
50-Off Oct 15	260	2⅜	+⅞	13
Stratus Oct 35	250	3/16	-½	42
AdobeS Oct 30	223	3⅛	+⅝	27½

NEW YORK

	Sales	Last	Chg	N.Y. Close
CALLS				
NY Idx Dec 225	550	8¼	+¼	228.89
Anthem Oct 40	510	⅝	-⅛	37⅝
NY Idx Dec 230	500	5¼	-⅝	228.89
TelMex Feb 45	280	2⅞	+⅜	43⅞
CSoup Oct 40	250	1 3/16	+3/16	41
TelMex Nov 45	244	1⅝	+5/16	43⅞
Chubb Apr 75	175	9⅝	+4⅝	82⅞
Chubb Jan 70	129	12⅞	+5⅞	82⅞
Novlus Mar 12½	100	2	-⅛	12⅜
TelMex Oct 45	100	½	+1/16	43⅞
PUTS				
TelMex Nov 40	876	⅞	-3/16	43⅞
NY Idx Dec 230	100	6½	-1⅛	228.89
BordCh Feb 15	50	⅞	+7/16	16¾
Chubb Oct 75	50	1/16	-1/16	82⅞
NY Idx Oct 235	50	6⅝	-¾	228.89
QntmCp Feb 12½	50	⅞	-⅛	13⅞
TimesM Dec 30	50	¾	-¼	31¼
SurgAf Oct 30	41	8½	+1½	21⅞
BordCh May 15	40	1¼	+1¼	16¾
Chubb Oct 80	40	⅝	-⅜	82⅞

underlying stocks. Index options permit investors with large and diversified portfolios to hedge against broad price movements. On the other hand, index options appear to many to be legalized gambling on price movements in stock prices generally.

§18.8 COMMODITIES TRADING

Commodities trading, primarily based in Chicago, and to a lesser extent in New York, has existed for more than a century. Until relatively recently, it did not involve trading in securities, but that has changed significantly in recent years. The options trading described in the previous sections illustrates the gradual broadening of the products traded on these traditional commodities exchanges, particularly the Chicago Board of Trade. This section deals with traditional commodities trading; the following section briefly discusses financial futures.

The traditional commodities market consists of two separate markets. The market for commodities available today—commodities located in warehouses or storage silos—is the "cash market" or "spot market." Table 18-7 shows cash market prices for September 30, 1992. These products may be sold by sample or quality designation or description. They are actual goods available for delivery. This market is used by suppliers, producers, and users of the various commodities that are traded. The prices

Table 18-7

CASH PRICES

Wednesday, September 30, 1992.
(Closing Market Quotations)

GRAINS AND FEEDS

	Wed	Tues	Yr.Ago
Barley, top-quality Mpls., bu	n2.20-.50	2.50	2.27½
Bran, wheat middlings, KC ton	74.-76.0	72.-74.0	59.00
Corn, No. 2 yel. Cent-Ill. bu	bp2.08	2.08½	2.41½
Corn Gluten Feed, Midwest, ton ..	95.-115.	95.-115.	100.00
Cottonseed Meal, Clksdle,Miss. ton	157½-160	157.-160.	1.33¾
Hominy Feed,Cent-Ill. ton	68.00	70.00	75.00
Meat-Bonemeal, 50% pro. Ill. ton.	230.00	230.00	237.50
Oats, No. 2 milling, Mpls., bu	z	155.00	1.37½
Sorghum, (Milo) No. 2 Gulf cwt ...	4.23	4.23	4.85
Soybean Meal, Decatur, Illinois ton..................	169.-172.	168.-172.	190.00
Soybeans, No. 1 yel Cent.-Ill. bu ..	bp5.27	5.28½	5.77½
Wheat, Spring 14%-pró Mpls. bu	4.03¾	3.92	3.50⅞
Wheat, No. 2 sft red, St.Lou. bu ...	bp3.38½	3.37½	2.82
Wheat, No. 2 hard KC lb.	3.65½	3.58½	3.44½
Wheat, No. 1 sft wht, del Port Ore	4.43	4.43	3.67

FOODS

Beef, Carcass, Equiv.Index Value, choice 1-3,550-700lbs.	110.90	c111.05	107.95
Beef, Carcass, Equiv.Index Value, select 1-3,550-700lbs.	106.70	c106.55	102.50
Broilers, Dressed "A" NY lb	x.5218	.5212	.5388
Broilers, 12-Cty Comp Wtd Av	.5248	.5248	.5311
*Comparable, but not exact.			
Butter, AA, Chgo., lb.	.85	.85	1.09½
Cocoa, Ivory Coast, $metric ton ...	g1,236	1,216	1,365
Coffee, Brazilian, NY lb.	n.42½	.42	.61½
Coffee, Colombian, NY lb.	n.59	.57¼	.84
Eggs, Lge white, Chgo doz.	.57-.63	.59-.65	.68
Flour, hard winter KC cwt	9.40	9.25	9.10
Hams, 17-20 lbs, Mid-US lb fob	.77	.77	.85
Hogs, Iowa-S.Minn. avg. cwt	42.75	42.75	47.75
Hogs, Omaha avg cwt	42.50	43.00	47.50
Pork Bellies, 12-14 lbs Mid-US lb ..	.27½-.30	.29-.32	.34½
Pork Loins, 14-18 lbs. Mid-US lb ..	.93-1.03	.95-1.00	1.05
Steers, Tex.-Okla. ch avg cwt	75.25	75.25	72.75
Steers, Feeder, Okl Cty, av cwt ...	89.80	90.25	94.25
Sugar, cane, raw, world, lb. fob ...	.0868	.0886	.0932

FATS AND OILS

Coconut Oil, crd, N. Orleans lb. ...	xxn.24	.24½	.23
Corn Oil, crd wet mill, Chgo. lb. ...	n.19¾	.19¾	.28¼
Corn Oil, crd dry mill, Chgo. lb. ...	n.20	.20	.29¾
Grease, choice white, Chgo lb.	.13½	.13½	.11¾
Lard, Chgo lb.	.15¼-½	.15½	.14¼
Palm Oil, ref. bl. deod. N.Orl. lb. ..	n.21½	.21½	.19
Soybean Oil, crd, Decatur, lb.	.1817	.1821	.2028

Tallow, bleachable, Chgo lb.	.15¼	.15¼	.13¼
Tallow, edible, Chgo lb.	.16¼	.16	.14½

FIBERS AND TEXTILES

Burlap, 10 oz 40-in NY yd	n.2450	.2450	.2725
Cotton 1 1/16 str lw-md Mphs lb ...	.4936	.4944	.5851
Wool, 64s, Staple, Terr. del. lb.	2.10	2.10	1.95

METALS

Aluminum ingot lb. del. Midwest	q57.8-58.5	57.8-58.5	.55
Copper cathodes lb.	p1.08	1.08-.11	1.12¼
Copper Scrap, No 2 wire NY lb	k.91	.92	.83
Lead, lb.	p.37-.40	.37-.40	.35
Mercury 76 lb. flask NY	q205.00	205.00	90.00
Steel Scrap 1 hvy mlt Chgo ton ...	89.-92.	78.-96.0	97.00
Tin composite lb.	q4.1713	4.2063	3.5994
Zinc Special High grade lb	p.64186	.64186	.51500

MISCELLANEOUS

Rubber, smoked sheets, NY lb. ...	n.47¼	.47	.44¼
Hides, hvy native steers lb., fob ...	.78	.78	.74

PRECIOUS METALS

Gold, troy oz			
Engelhard indust bullion	350.24	348.74	357.26
Engelhard fabric prods	367.75	366.18	375.12
Handy & Harman base price	349.00	347.50	356.00
London fixing AM 349.00 PM ...	349.00	347.50	356.00
Krugerrand, whol	a350.00	350.00	355.25
Maple Leaf, troy oz.	a361.00	360.00	367.50
American Eagle, troy oz.	a361.00	360.00	367.50
Platinum, (Free Mkt.)	367.50	364.50	355.00
Platinum, indust (Engelhard)	368.00	365.00	359.00
Platinum, fabric prd (Engelhard)	468.00	465.00	459.00
Palladium, indust (Engelhard) ...	96.00	94.00	85.00
Palladium, fabrc prd (Englhard)	111.00	109.00	100.00

Silver, troy ounce			
Engelhard indust bullion	3.750	3.745	4.210
Engelhard fabric prods	4.050	4.045	4.505
Handy & Harman base price	3.735	3.735	4.175
London Fixing (in pounds) Spot (U.S. equiv. $3.7660)	2.1105	2 1155	2.4050
3 months	2.1570†	2.1620	2.4665
6 months	2.2005	2.2050	2.5265
1 year	2.2870	2.2900	2.6485
Coins, whol $1,000 face val	a2,746	2,731	3,054

a-Asked. b-Bid. bp-Country elevator bids to producers. c-Corrected. d-Dealer market. e-Estimated. f-Dow Jones International Petroleum Report. g-Main crop, ex-dock, warehouses, Eastern Seaboard, north of Hatteras. j.-f.o.b. warehouse. k-Dealer selling prices in lots of 40,000 pounds or more, f.o.b. buyer's works. n-Nominal. p-Producer price. q-Metals Week. r-Rail bids. s-Thread count 78x54. x-Less than truckloads. z-Not quoted. xx-f.o.b. tankcars.

of many commodities are quite volatile and may change quickly. Most of the speculative interest in commodities is not in the cash market, however, but in the futures market described in the following paragraphs.

Table 18-8 shows the quotations for the futures markets for two staple agricultural commodities — corn and oats — for September 30, 1992. Unlike the spot market, the futures market reflects trading in hypothetical units of corn or oats for delivery at specific times in the future. The futures market for corn is a good example. Table 18-8 reflects trading on September 30, 1992 in hypothetical 5,000 bushel units of corn for future delivery: December 1992, and March, May, July, September, and December 1993. On September 30, 1992, one could buy or sell corn in 5,000-bushel units for future delivery in December 1992 for $2.15 per bushel, or corn for delivery in December 1993 for $2.38 a bushel. These transactions must be in the standard 5,000-bushel units. Let us assume that you decide on September 30, 1992 to purchase 5,000 bushels of corn for December 1992 delivery. For simplicity, let us further assume that the price of December 1992 corn when you actually entered into this transaction is $2.15 per bushel. As a result of this transaction you have made a commitment to buy 5,000 bushels of corn next December; if the purchase were actually carried out, the transaction would involve $10,750 ($2.15 × 5,000 = $10,750). On the other hand, it is essential to realize that you have not actually bought any corn in the physical sense: You have simply committed yourself to buy corn next December at $2.15 per bushel.

The price of December 1992 corn varies from day to day, hour to hour, and minute to minute during each trading day for reasons to be discussed shortly. Both the Chicago Board of Trade (where your purchase

Table 18-8

FUTURES PRICES

Wednesday, September 30, 1992

Open Interest Reflects Previous Trading Day.

GRAINS AND OILSEEDS

CORN (CBT) 5,000 bu.; cents per bu.

	Open	High	Low	Settle	Change	Lifetime High	Lifetime Low	Open Interest
Dec	215¼	217	215	215¼	− ¼	275¾	212¾	128,295
Mr93	225¼	226	224	224¼	− ½	281¼	221¾	44,376
May	230¾	232	229¾	230¼	− ½	284¾	228¼	19,065
July	235	235¾	233¾	234¼	− 1	286	232¾	20,345
Sept	236	237¼	235½	235½	− ½	271½	234	1,727
Dec	238½	239½	238	238¼	− ¼	268½	237	5,037

Est vol 35,000; vol Tues 37,377; open int 218,869, +3,018.

OATS (CBT) 5,000 bu.; cents per bu.

	Open	High	Low	Settle	Change	Lifetime High	Lifetime Low	Open Interest
Dec	140¼	140¾	136	136¾	− 2¼	198½	116½	7,241
Mr93	141½	141½	138	139	− 1¼	195¼	122	1,384
May	142	142	139	139¾	− 1	177½	126	408
July	140½	140½	140½	140¼	− 1	163½	129½	313

Est vol 1,200; vol Tues 873; open int 9,352, −12.

was executed) and the securities broker that placed your order are responsible for the performance of your obligation to buy the corn. Therefore, when you "buy the future," that is, when you enter into the contract to buy 5,000 bushels of corn at $2.15 per bushel next December, you must post some money to assure that you will carry out your commitment. When you buy the future you will be required to put up perhaps 10 percent of the total purchase price of $10,750, or $1,075 in cash. This up-front payment is called margin, but it differs in a fundamental way from a margin purchase of stock discussed in section 14.18. In a purchase of stock on margin, the broker is actually lending the investor funds to purchase shares, and the margin required is actually a down payment on the purchase price. In a margin transaction for stock, interest is charged on the unpaid balance. In the case of margin in a commodities future transaction, no credit is extended to buy anything; the margin in this context is somewhat analogous to a performance bond. Further, no interest is charged on a commodities future transaction since no funds have been advanced by the broker.

The futures market does not differentiate between buyers and sellers with respect to margin: If you believed on September 30, 1992 that corn prices were going down, you could sell the future, that is, enter into a contract to sell 5,000 bushels of corn in December, for $2.15 per bushel through your broker. The terms would be precisely the same as though you had purchased corn: You would have to post about $1,075 margin with your broker.

A speculator who expects the price of a commodity to go up purchases a futures contract for that commodity; a person who expects the price to go down sells a futures contract. One interesting aspect of futures trading is that a person can buy or sell commodities for future delivery in the futures market, speculating on the prices of commodities for years without ever acquiring, owning, or selling the commodities themselves. A speculator in corn, for example, never needs to own a single grain of real corn despite a lifetime of trading in corn futures.

Virtually none of the delivery obligations created by futures contracts actually leads to delivery of the commodity. In order to see how this works, let us follow through on the preceding hypotheticals to show a speculation in corn futures. Let us assume first that you buy a corn futures contract on September 30, 1992 for $2.15 per bushel. Over the summer, the drought continues to worsen, the potential corn harvest continues to decline, and the price of corn continues to spiral upwards. By November 10, the price of December 1992 corn has risen to $3.15 per bushel. Clearly, you have made a profit, but how do you realize upon it? In the world of commodities futures you do not "assign" or "turn in" or "sell" your contract to buy. Nor do you await delivery and then sell the corn itself on the spot market. Rather, you simply enter into another futures contract to sell December

1992 corn at \$3.15 per bushel on November 10. When this transaction is executed, you have netted out or closed out your position. Since you now have commitments both to buy and to sell the standard trading unit of December 1992 corn, you do not owe the market any corn and the market does not owe you any corn. At that point your account with your broker reflects only the purchase of December corn for \$10,750 and the sale of December corn for \$15,750 (\$3.15 × 5,000 = \$15,750) for a nifty two-month profit of \$5,000. You are neither long nor short in corn. Your cash account with the broker, available for future commodities speculation now contains \$6,425, the \$5,000 profit on the transaction in December corn plus the \$1,075 cash originally put up as the performance bond.

This process of netting out, of course, works equally well if you originally sold a corn future. You simply buy a corn future with the same maturity, and your position is netted out. This process is so well established, so universal, that it is reflected in the commission structure for commodities futures. Only a single commission is charged for the dual step of buying a future and then closing it out. Thus, in the normal and routine futures transaction, if a position has not been closed out and the date of delivery is drawing near, one avoids the nuisance of accepting or tendering delivery by entering into an offsetting contract. This is not to say that deliveries under futures contracts never occur. If a user of corn, a producer of corn oil, say, decides it needs the corn in December, it simply does not net out its position; then delivery of 5,000 bushels of real corn is required under the standardized futures contract. A speculator who fails to net out similarly would have to make or accept delivery. This transaction, however, would be in the form of a warehouse receipt: A speculator who is long in corn runs no risk of awakening one morning to see a truck pulling up with 5,000 bushels of corn to be dumped in his front yard.

For every futures transaction, there must be both a buyer and a seller. The process, however, is as totally anonymous as on a securities exchange: The buyer has no idea of the identity of the seller and vice versa. Indeed, since the Chicago Board of Trade guarantees each trade, it in effect becomes the buyer for each seller and the seller for each buyer, once the transaction has been verified. Because of the settlement process that is followed, there is also no limit on the number of futures contracts that can be written. Theoretically, there may be more open contracts to deliver grain in the future than all the grain that actually exists in the world. Usually, however, the numbers are more modest. Table 18-8 provides information as to the number of futures contracts opened on September 30, 1992: Approximately 35,000 futures contracts in corn. Further, the third item in the bottom line, "open int 218,869" indicates that there exist 218,869 contracts for future delivery of corn that have not yet been closed out by an offsetting purchase at the close of trading on that date.

As the date of delivery draws nearer, the open interest declines as more and more speculators net out. On the delivery date, the open interest is down virtually to zero.

§18.9 FUTURES TRADING IS HIGHLY SPECULATIVE

Futures trading may lead to huge speculative gains or losses on rather small investments. In the above example there was a return of $5,000 on a $1,075 investment in two months: That is an annualized return of over 500 percent per year. Of course, the buyer assumed a considerable risk by purchasing that December 1992 corn. If the price of corn had declined, the loss could easily have exceeded the initial $1,075 investment. If the price of December corn had declined to $1.50, for example, the buyer would have incurred a loss of $3,250 ($2.15 minus $1.50 equals $0.65 loss on each bushel; on 5,000 bushels, the standard trading unit, the loss is $3,250). Before a loss of this magnitude would occur, the broker would have had to be assured that the buyer had sufficient assets to cover the loss — either free capital or freshly posted additional margin made after a margin call — or the broker would close out the transaction on its own.

There is so much speculation possible in commodities futures because: (1) Commodities often exhibit substantial price movements; and (2) a purchaser's or seller's net gain or loss on a futures transaction is measured by the price movement of a large amount of the commodity, but the actual capital invested is approximately 10 percent of the total value of the commodity. Again, it is a species of leverage, though in this case there is no actual use of borrowed capital.

§18.10 MARKING TO MARKET

Margin calls are common in the commodities futures business since only a small payment is required to carry a much more substantial position. In the foregoing example, a $1,075 payment enables one to have the advantages or risks of price movements on 5,000 bushels of corn worth ten times the amount of the payment. In this market, each person's account is "marked to market" on a daily basis. Marked to market simply means that the margin position of the account is recalculated each day. The price used is the price set forth in the "Settle" column of Table 18-8. If the price moves in a favorable direction, the account, when marked to market, will show a surplus over the minimum needed to carry the position: That surplus may be withdrawn or used to buy additional futures contracts. In other words, one can "pyramid" a successful futures speculation very easily. If the price moves in an unfavorable direction, the margin in the account is marked down. The Chicago Board of Trade limits the maximum price movements that can occur in a single day in the futures market. Trading is suspended when the maximum change in a single day occurs. This enables all accounts to be marked to market before trading is resumed the next day.

§18.11 THE TRADING FLOOR FOR COMMODITIES FUTURES

Trading in commodities futures is quite unlike trading on the New York Stock Exchange and other securities exchanges. The Chicago Board of Trade is a place where traders come to trade. Trading for each commodity takes place in separate pits, which are large depressions in the floor: Persons trading contracts for a specified month stand on the same step or level within the pit. Trading is by outcry and hand signal, with purchasers and sellers of the futures often trading on small price movements. You may have seen photographs of this hectic process—traders screaming and shouting in the pits. Repeated outcries of price are necessary because prices remain valid only during the outcry. Because of price volatility and the small margins required to acquire futures positions, this trading is hectic, and fortunes may be made or wiped out in very short periods of time. Traders (unlike speculators) rarely carry overnight a net short or net long position.

§18.12 HEDGING TRANSACTIONS

Commodities futures are widely used by producers and users of commodities to hedge against future price changes. A farmer growing corn, for example, may know that his corn will be harvested and ready to market in July 1993. The futures price for July corn is about $2.35. If that price is acceptable to the farmer for his crop, he can lock in an approximate $2.35 price by selling one or more July corn futures in the approximate amount of his expected harvest. If the price of corn declines, he will sell his corn at a loss but recoup that loss on the profit on the futures contract (since he can close out the account by buying July corn for substantially less than $2.35). If the price goes up, the farmer has a loss on the futures contract but is able to sell his harvested corn above $2.35: Again the two transactions should largely offset each other. A manufacturer that uses corn in its manufacturing process may similarly ensure itself of reliable raw material prices for an extended period in the future by buying futures contracts.

Farmers or users of commodities may also hedge by buying or selling commodities "for forward delivery" at fixed prices without using the standardized futures market.

§18.13 FUTURES TRADING IS A "STACKED DECK"

Commodities futures trading is "stacked" against the small outside speculator. About 90 percent of all individual commodity speculators lose money; the average lifetime of an individual futures account is less than a year. There are numerous trading systems or strategies that are commercially available for a fee, but the results of these systems or strategies are indifferent, despite advertising claims to the contrary. An article in the Wall Street Journal describes the situation faced by the small investor in this market: "In the best of times, an individual futures-market speculator, like a casino gambler, has a less than even chance of making money in the futures markets. The odds always favor the house, or the markets." Also, other participants in this market are sophisticated, powerful, and have superior access to information in the market. Huge grain-trading companies or banks actively participate in this market; they have nearly instant access to market-moving information, and their multimillion-dollar trades may themselves dramatically effect future prices in seconds, usually when it is advantageous to them. Further, professional futures pit speculators are present on the trading floor and may make split-second trading decisions based on price changes before an individual speculator has time to pick up the phone and call a broker.

Active trading by the small speculator runs up commission costs, an expense that persons in the trading pit do not have to pay. Futures contracts expire every few months and positions are bought and sold, often on a daily basis. It is not unusual for an individual's futures account to be eaten up by commissions in less than a year.

An administrative law judge for the Commodities Futures Trading Commission summed matters up neatly when he said, "You've got to be out of your gourd to trade futures."

§18.14 PUBLIC COMMODITY TRADING FUNDS

In an effort to attract small traders into the futures market, a number of publicly offered commodity trading funds appeared in the 1980s. These funds make public offerings of securities and invest the funds raised in commodities futures with the benefit of "expert" trading advice. Some of these funds have assets of as much as $250 million, but most are considerably smaller — $30 million or less. These funds were among the fastest growing sectors of the investment scene, with assets of about $25 billion in 1991, up from $10 billion in 1989. However, the results of investments in these funds have been less than spectacular, and a number have become inactive as their funds were consumed by trading losses.

Some of these funds are "guaranteed" in the sense that the investor is guaranteed the return of his or her investment (usually without interest) after five years, no matter how poorly the fund performs. This repayment obligation is "funded" by the purchase of a zero coupon risk-free bond with the bulk of the funds provided by the investor, and with the balance devoted to commodity trading. Usually more than half — and sometimes as much as 80 percent — of the investor's capital is used to fund the repayment obligation. Since a rational investor may easily combine a riskless zero with a highly risky commodities fund speculation, this guarantee seems designed to seduce the unsophisticated investor.

Public commodity funds are "managed futures" — funds supplied by investors that are pooled and actively invested by "trading advisers" or "money managers" in commodity and financial futures. Other types of managed futures also exist, including affluent individuals who may place funds of $100,000 or more directly with a trading adviser, or private pools, usually limited to 35 or fewer investors, who may invest $20,000 or more each. In contrast, the public funds may accept investments as small as $5,000.

The risk in futures trading in pooled funds is somewhat reduced because investments are spread over a number of different types of futures contracts, and the investor has therefore reduced the odds of big losses in an extremely treacherous market. Many trading advisers use computerized programs involving price movements and trading volume, but the strategies are often unsuccessful. In early 1992, several funds had trading losses of as much as 35 percent. While the risk of loss is high, there can be whopping returns: Annual returns of 75 percent or more are not uncommon in good years.

§18.15 FUTURES TRADING DIFFERS FROM TRADING IN OPTIONS

Futures trading resembles option trading, but there are important differences. An option does not commit the purchaser of the option to do anything: If the price moves in the wrong direction the purchaser of the option simply lets it expire. A futures contract, on the other hand, commits the purchaser to close out the position: If the price moves in the wrong direction, the purchaser of the futures contract has to take a loss that grows steadily as the price moves further in the wrong direction. In the financial futures market discussed in the next section, we will see that that is a very significant difference indeed.

The margin required in a futures transaction is also superficially analogous to the purchase price of an option. Again, however, there is a difference. The price paid for an option is the cost of obtaining a power to enter into a transaction: The premium becomes the property of the writer of the option. On the other hand, the margin required in a futures contract is a guarantee of performance and remains the ultimate property of the person entering into the contract.

As was noted earlier, the writer of an option is totally at the risk of market forces. In a futures contract, both sides of every contract are totally at the risk of market forces.

§18.16 FINANCIAL FUTURES AND OPTIONS TO BUY FUTURES

Today, most of the excitement in the futures business is in financial and index futures, not commodities futures. Standardized contracts to buy or sell foreign currencies at stated times in the future — British pounds in 25,000 pound units, Canadian dollars in $100,000 units, Japanese yen in 12.5 million yen units — are actively traded. Interest rate futures in treasury bonds, and 5-year treasury notes are traded in $100,000 units; treasury bills are traded in $1 million dollar units. All of these financial futures can be bought or sold for approximately 10 percent down and constitute speculation on interest rates or foreign exchange rates.

From a dollar standpoint, the most active trading in all futures contracts today occurs in stock and bond indexes. Table 18-9 reflects a sampling of the September 30, 1992 trading in these indexes. A major difference between commodities futures and these financial futures is that it is impractical to deliver the financial futures on the delivery date: One must always settle in cash for the difference between the contract price and the present level of the index.

Because futures carry with them the risk of loss from adverse price movements in excess of the amount initially invested, a logical development is the creation of put and call options on financial or commodities futures. Indeed, some instruments of these types have been created, but they have not been as popular as the straight financial futures trading on the S&P 500 index. This lack of popularity has probably been a result of the complexity of the security thereby created and the difficulty of relating its value to the value of the underlying commodities or indexes.

Table 18-9

FUTURES PRICES

INTEREST RATE

TREASURY BONDS (CBT)–$100,000; pts. 32nds of 100%

	Open	High	Low	Settle	Chg	Yield Settle	Yield Chg	Open Interest
Dec	105-13	105-19	105-08	105-10	– 6	7.484	+ .018	320,014
Mr93	104-01	104-09	103-31	104-01	– 4	7.605	+ .012	25,088
June	102-28	102-28	102-21	102-22	– 4	7.734	+ .012	13,034
Sp93	101-19	101-19	101-13	101-13	– 4	7.859	+ .012	1,122
Dec	100-06	100-07	100-06	100-06	– 4	7.981	+ .013	460
Sp94	97-10	97-10	97-03	97-03	– 4	8.300	+ .013	52

Est vol 175,000; vol Tues 162,577; op int 359,879, –5,427.

TREASURY BONDS (MCE)–$50,000; pts. 32nds of 100%

	Open	High	Low	Settle	Chg	Yield Settle	Yield Chg	Open Interest
Dec	105-11	105-19	105-05	105-07	– 6	7.492	+ .017	12,116

Est vol 4,100; vol Tues 4,616; open int 12,133, –907.

T–BONDS (LIFFE) U.S. $100,000; pts of 100%

	Open	High	Low	Settle	Chg	Lifetime High	Lifetime Low	Open Interest
Dec	105-10	105-19	105-08	105-14	– 0-14	106-31	104-04	1,972

Est vol 225; vol Tues 121; open int 1,972, –57.

GERMAN GOV'T. BOND (LIFFE)
250,000 marks; $ per mark (.01)

	Open	High	Low	Settle	Chg	Lifetime High	Lifetime Low	Open Interest
Dec	90.55	90.96	90.38	90.94	+ .44	91.17	87.12	133,869
Mr93	90.62	91.07	90.62	91.08	+ .45	91.20	89.62	4,803

Est vol 85,101; vol Tues 58,087; open int 138,672, +8,735.

TREASURY NOTES (CBT)–$100,000; pts. 32nds of 100%

	Open	High	Low	Settle	Chg	Yield Settle	Yield Chg	Open Interest
Dec	109-06	109-12	109-04	109-07	– 2	6.719	+ .008	176,099
Mr93	107-26	107-29	107-26	107-27	– 2	6.901	+ .008	654

Est vol 35,000; vol Tues 35,600; open int 176,763, –19,761.

5 YR TREAS NOTES (CBT)–$100,000; pts. 32nds of 100%

	Open	High	Low	Settle	Chg	Yield Settle	Yield Chg	Open Interest
Dec	110-00	10-025	09-295	10-005	– 1.5	5.672	+ .011	120,800
Mr93	108-27	08-285	108-25	08-275	– 1.5	5.927	+ .011	1,538

Est vol 21,000; vol Tues 20,232; open int 124,338, –8,229.

2 YR TREAS NOTES (CBT)–$200,000, pts. 32nds of 100%

	Open	High	Low	Settle	Chg	Yield Settle	Yield Chg	Open Interest
Dec	06-235	06-245	106-22	06-232	– 1	4.448	+ .016	13,271

Est vol 300; vol Tues 651; open int 13,271, –3,380.

CURRENCY

JAPAN YEN (IMM)–12.5 million yen; $ per yen (.00)

	Open	High	Low	Settle	Change	Lifetime High	Lifetime Low	Open Interest
Dec	.8380	.8419	.8300	.8322	– .0046	.8419	.7410	45,659
Mr93	.8338	.8338	.8296	.8314	– .0046	.8368	.7445	1,448

Est vol 15,320; vol Tues 14,597; open int 47,117, –1,751.

DEUTSCHEMARK (IMM)–125,000 marks; $ per mark

	Open	High	Low	Settle	Change	Lifetime High	Lifetime Low	Open Interest
Dec	.6990	.7072	.6954	.6990	– .0008	.7083	.5645	60,389
Mr93	.6920	.6920	.6860	.6896	– .0008	.6968	.5724	3,184
June	.6815	.6820	.6790	.6813	– .0008	.6850	.6280	844
Sept	....	....	....	.6733	– .0008	.6720	.6720	300

Est vol 60,953; vol Tues 76,660; open int 64,743, +341.

CANADIAN DOLLAR (IMM)–100,000 dlrs.; $ per Can $

	Open	High	Low	Settle	Change	Lifetime High	Lifetime Low	Open Interest
Dec	.7919	.7952	.7892	.7951	+ .0042	.8740	.7866	25,584
Mr93	.7820	.7885	.7820	.7881	+ .0047	.8712	.7780	993
June	.7799	.7820	.7799	.7816	+ .0054	.8360	.7750	1,282
Sept	.7765	.7765	.7765	.7761	+ .0069	.8335	.7720	622
Dec	....	....	....	.7706	+ .0082	.8310	.7640	294

Est vol 5,524; vol Tues 8,855; open int 28,775, –500.

BRITISH POUND (IMM)–62,500 pds.; $ per pound

	Open	High	Low	Settle	Change	Lifetime High	Lifetime Low	Open Interest
Dec	1.7670	1.7820	1.7488	1.7556	– .0052	1.9746	1.6280	28,427
Mr93	1.7360	1.7430	1.7280	1.7342	– .0054	1.9400	1.6500	902

Est vol 10,508; vol Tues 10,807; open int 29,384, +500.

SWISS FRANC (IMM)–125,000 francs; $ per franc

	Open	High	Low	Settle	Change	Lifetime High	Lifetime Low	Open Interest
Dec	.8070	.8129	.7988	.8023	– .0047	.8076	.6280	28,859
Mr93	.8000	.8012	.7922	.7953	– .0048	.8005	.6790	313

Est vol 25,061; vol Tues 31,020; open int 29,244, –79.

AUSTRALIAN DOLLAR (IMM)–100,000 dlrs.; $ per A.$

	Open	High	Low	Settle	Change	Lifetime High	Lifetime Low	Open Interest
Dec	.7095	.7115	.7079	.7082	– .0016	.7462	.7058	3,045

Est vol 171; vol Tues 325; open int 3,063, –11.

U.S. DOLLAR INDEX (FINEX)–1,000 times USDX

	Open	High	Low	Settle	Change	Lifetime High	Lifetime Low	Open Interest
Dec	82.50	83.39	82.00	83.10	+ .51	94.93	79.85	3,536
Mr93	83.66	84.58	84.41	84.36	+ .70	91.00	81.45	673

Est vol 3,690; vol Tues 3,740; open int 4,212, +406.
The index: High 81.71; Low 80.58 ; Close 81.34 +.30

INDEX

S&P 500 INDEX (CME) 500 times index

	Open	High	Low	Settle	Chg	High	Low	Open Interest
Dec	416.80	418.80	416.45	418.35	+ .80	427.25	391.40	156,757
Mr93	417.15	418.90	416.70	418.40	+ .75	426.20	397.50	2,984
June	419.00	419.00	417.00	418.50	+ .80	427.10	404.60	930

Est vol 33,163; vol Tues 37,288; open int 160,691, +1,356.
Indx prelim High 418.58; Low 416.67; Close 417.80 +1.00

NIKKEI 225 Stock Average (CME)–$5 times Prem.

	Open	High	Low	Settle	Chg	High	Low	Open Interest
Dec	17380.	17450.	17370.	17445.	– 445.0	21100.	14270.	12,553

Est vol 1,344; vol Tues 631; open int 12,570, +4.
The index: High 17909.71; Low 17398.98; Close 17399.08 –349.01

EURODOLLAR (IMM)–$1 million; pts of 100%

	Open	High	Low	Settle	Chg	Yield Settle	Yield Chg	Open Interest
Dec	96.86	96.89	96.85	96.86	....	3.14	....	372,794
Mr93	96.82	96.85	96.81	96.81	....	3.19	....	288,212
June	96.53	96.56	96.51	96.51	– .02	3.49	+ .02	198,167
Sept	96.19	96.21	96.15	96.15	– .03	3.85	+ .03	131,600
Dec	95.60	95.61	95.54	95.54	– .05	4.46	+ .05	91,348
Mr94	95.28	95.29	95.21	95.22	– .06	4.78	+ .06	78,116
June	94.84	94.87	94.79	94.80	– .05	5.20	+ .05	61,364
Sept	94.51	94.51	94.44	94.46	– .04	5.54	+ .04	46,871
Dec	94.08	94.08	94.04	94.04	– .02	5.96	+ .04	41,173
Mr95	93.95	93.95	93.90	93.92	– .02	6.08	+ .02	40,248
June	93.67	93.68	93.63	93.64	– .02	6.36	+ .02	30,107
Sept	93.46	93.47	93.43	93.44	– .01	6.56	+ .01	24,201
Dec	93.14	93.15	93.12	93.13	....	6.87	....	22,382
Mr96	93.10	93.11	93.07	93.09	....	6.91	....	21,198
June	92.91	92.93	92.90	92.90	– .01	7.10	+ .01	11,969
Sept	92.77	92.78	92.74	92.75	– .02	7.25	+ .02	7,458
Dec	92.53	92.53	92.50	92.50	– .02	7.50	+ .02	5,106
Mr97	92.51	92.52	92.50	92.51	– .02	7.49	+ .02	4,938
June	92.42	92.42	92.37	92.39	– .02	7.31	+ .02	6,838
Sept	92.27	92.29	92.27	92.28	– .02	7.72	+ .02	1,636

Est vol 144,578; vol Tues 147,841; open int 1,485,726, –3,053.

OTHER FUTURES

Settlement prices of selected contracts. Actual volume (from previous session) and open interest of all contract months.

	Vol.	High	Low	Close	Net Change	Lifetime High	Lifetime Low	Open Interest
BRITISH POUND (MCE) 12,500 pounds; $ per pound								
Dec	494	1.7630	1.7490	1.7540	– .0060	1.9734	1.7024	864
BROILERS (CME) 40,000 lb.; ¢ per lb.								
Oct	0	....	....	49.10	....	52.25	49.25	80
CATTLE-LIVE (MCE) 20,000 lb.; ¢ per lb.								
Oct	52	75.35	75.07	75.30	+ .12	76.15	66.25	252
CORN (MCE) 1,000 bu.; cents per bu.								
Dec	3,533	217	215	215¼	– ¼	275¾	212¾	11,035
CRB INDEX (NYFE)–500 times Index								
Dec	125	201.45	200.10	201.35	+ 1.15	218.70	199.50	1,187
The index: High 200.41; Low 199.28; Close 200.36 +.84								
DEUTSCHEMARK (MCE) 62,500 marks; $ per mark								
Dec	627	.7018	.6954	.6987	– .0011	.7085	.5773	690
DEUTSCHEMARK (PBOT) 125,000 marks; ¢ per mark								
Nov	100	....	....	.7010	– .0004	.7071	.7071	1,308
DIAMMONIUM PHOSPHATE (CBT 100 tons; $ per ton								
Dec	103	120.00	119.50	119.90	– .10	146.00	119.50	1,348
5-YR. INT. SWAP (CBT)–$25 per ½ b.p.; pts of 100%								
Dec	0	na	....	....	....	....	....	0
FRENCH FRANC (PBOT) 500,000 francs; tenths of a ¢ per unit								
Nov	4	....	....	2.0565	– .0065	2.0775	1.9170	15,560
GSCI (CME) $250 X GSCI nearby index;								
Oct	292	187.20	186.10	187.10	+ .30	189.50	182.30	448
The index: High 187.27; Low 185.87; Close 187.05 +.30								
GOLD-KILO (CBT) 32.15 troy oz.; $ per troy oz.								
Dec	58	350.00	348.20	348.30	+ .10	385.00	334.00	278
HOGS (MCE) 20,000 lb.; ¢ per lb.								
Oct	153	42.42	41.85	42.32	+ .32	42.42	37.60	551
JAPANESE YEN (MCE) 6.25 million yen; $ per yen (.00)								
Dec	157	.8349	.8299	.8320	– .0050	.8376	.7785	251
JAPANESE YEN (PBOT) 12,500,000 yen; hundredths of a ¢ per unit								
Nov	72	....	....	.8300	– .0068	.8235	.7980	83
KC MINI VALUE LINE (KC)–100 times index								
Dec	150	349.20	347.10	349.20	+ 1.35	361.50	340.40	282
KC VALUE LINE INDEX (KC)–500 times Index								
Dec	141	349.15	347.00	349.15	+ 1.65	366.00	340.30	966
The index: High 350.63; Low 348.86; Close 350.63 +1.57								
LUMBER (CME) 160,000 bd .ft., $ per 1,000 bd.ft.								
Nov	633	214.30	211.70	213.00	+ .80	248.50	207.00	1,380
MARK/YEN Cross Rate (CME) DM 125,000; JY per DM								
Dec	0	84.10	83.80	83.95	+ .33	87.65	76.20	192
PROPANE (NYM) 42,000 gal.; ¢ per gal.								
Nov	255	37.25	37.00	37.50	– .45	38.75	29.75	3,184
RICE-ROUGH (MCE) 2000 cwt; $ per cwt								
Nov	26	6.720	6.690	6.720	....	7.980	6.590	1,321
SILVER (MCE) 1,000 troy oz.; cents per troy oz.								
Oct	8	....	....	376.2	+ 1.4	382.5	377.5	1,248
SOYBEANS (MCE) 1,000 bu.; cents per bu.								
Nov	3,678	543½	540¼	540¾	– 1	651	527½	19,363
SOYBEAN MEAL (MCE) 20 tons; $ per ton								
Oct	3	186.20	185.10	185.90	+ .90	208.80	182.30	62
S&P MIDCAP 400 (CME)–$500 x S&P 400 Stock Index								
Dec	121	144.80	144.00	144.70	+ .60	154.20	136.60	4,180
The index: High 144.48; Low 143.80; Close 144.48 +.66								
SWISS FRANC (MCE) 62,500 francs; $ per franc								
Dec	317	.8082	.7991	.8023	– .0047	.8082	.6560	724
WHEAT (MCE) 1,000 bu.; cents per bu.								
Dec	507	350½	347½	350¼	+ 2½	440	312½	4,458
WHITE WHEAT (MPLS) 5,000 bu.; cents per bu.								
Dec	79	450	448	449	+ 1	457	383	338

§18.17 ARBITRAGE: PROGRAM TRADING

The development of index options and index futures described in this chapter open up a variety of new computerized trading strategies involving arbitrage. Arbitrage is the process of taking advantage of small price differences in equivalent securities. Such differences may arise from different maturity dates on equivalent securities, trading in different geographical markets, or trading in securities with different forms but equivalent or interrelated values. At the present time, index options, index futures, and the underlying securities that comprise the indexes all trade simultaneously in different markets. It is almost impossible for an individual to determine whether the prices of the 500 stocks that make up the S&P 500 stock index are selling at a price below what their value should be in the futures market for the S&P index. Computers, however, now permit arbitrage transactions across markets of this type. Computerized trading programs may involve simultaneous purchases of long positions in a package of several hundred securities (in round lots) that mimic the S&P 500 index with the simultaneous sales of S&P 500 index futures on the Chicago Board of Trade futures market. This kind of trading is known as "program trading." Because there are many arbitrageurs involved in program trading, and because all programs may dictate the simultaneous purchase or liquidation of long positions on the New York Stock Exchange in very large amounts, program trading undoubtedly contributed to the October 1987 market collapse, to the increase in volume of trading on the NYSE, and to the wild trading swings that sometimes occur in that market. Indeed, concern has sometimes been expressed about the possibility of manipulation of the underlying prices of securities on the NYSE in order to profit in the index futures or options markets.

§18.18 OTHER TRADING STRATEGIES

An institutional investor that holds a portfolio of securities similar to that reflected in the Standard & Poor 500 index may hedge that position by selling S&P 500 index futures in much the same way that a farmer with a long position in the form of a crop in the ground can hedge against a price decline. See section 18.12.

The creation of a variety of new derivative securities has revolutionized the traditional securities markets for large investors. It is usually cheaper in terms of commissions and brokerage fees to effect major changes in portfolio strategies by transactions in the futures markets than by the sale and repurchase of an entire portfolio of securities. For example, a predominantly debt portfolio can be converted rapidly to equity by simultaneously selling bond futures and buying stock index futures. Of course, commission costs will be incurred if the underlying debt portfolio is ultimately liquidated and equity investment substituted. However, these transactions may be delayed indefinitely through the use of index futures.

Tactical Asset Allocation (TAA) is the name given to an investment strategy that concentrates on classes of investments — for example, equities, debt securities, and money market funds or cash equivalents — rather than on specific securities. Large institutional investors use computer-driven programs to effectuate changes in asset allocations within large portfolios by the purchase and sale of financial futures rather than on transactions in the underlying securities themselves.

PART IV

TAXATION

19

The Taxation of Individual Incomes

§19.1 INTRODUCTION

This concluding chapter describes the modern tax structure applicable to individual incomes. Principal attention is given to the federal income tax. State income tax statutes are discussed more briefly.

An important goal of this chapter is to provide the reader with background information about the Internal Revenue Code and to describe how we have reached where we are in 1992.

During most of the twentieth century, federal income taxes have had a major influence on virtually all business and financial transactions. Indeed, the Internal Revenue Code probably is the single most important statute ever adopted by the United States in terms of its effect on commercial transactions, dwarfing other important statutes such as the antitrust laws, the securities acts, and the bankruptcy acts.

In 1986, Congress enacted sweeping changes in the tax laws. The core ideas behind these changes were: (1) to cut maximum tax rates; (2) to expand the tax base; and (3) to minimize or eliminate tax shelter-oriented transactions that are entered into primarily for their effect on one's tax bill. This revolutionary change in tax laws has contributed to some of the phenomena discussed elsewhere in this book, particularly the decline in residential and commercial real estate values. It also has affected investment strategies, particularly in its decision to eliminate favorable tax rates on long-term capital gains. As this is being written, six years later, it is clear that many of the changes made by the 1986 legislation remain controversial and continue to be actively debated in the political forum. Indeed, important tax changes were made by the Revenue Reconciliation Act of 1990, effective for 1991 and later years, and further, important changes in the tax laws will doubtless be made in future years under the Clinton Administration.

Because the rules of the tax game changed very significantly in 1986, many of the widely used pre-1986 strategies for reducing taxes on individual incomes and wealth are obsolete. Among those that remain effective are investments in tax-exempt municipal debt securities (see section 16.17), tax deferred United States Savings Bonds (see section 16.8), tax deferred retirement plans and annuities of various types (see Chapter 10), and single-premium variable life insurance policies (see section 11.21). The 1986 income tax statute also spawned new devices to minimize individual taxes, particularly the home equity loan (see section 7.13).

Because of the volatility of modern tax law, reliance on published texts or treatises (including this book) is risky. One should always check the current rules before making important financial decisions. This chapter basically describes the tax rules applicable to the year 1992.

The Tax Reform Act of 1986 renamed the Internal Revenue Code the "Internal Revenue Code of 1986" even though the 1986 Act was not a recodification in the true sense of the word. The balance of this chapter uses the phrase "the 1986 Act" to refer to the post-1986 tax law, often including the changes made in 1991; the pre-1986 statutes are referred to collectively as "the old Act" or as the "Internal Revenue Code of 1954." References to "the old Act" as a single entity are somewhat misleading since numerous substantive amendments to the tax laws were made over the years before 1986, particularly during the period between 1976 and 1984. Thus, there are numerous "old Acts," almost one for each year, at least after 1976. These references should therefore be viewed as being to general principles in effect before the enactment of the 1986 Act rather than to the galaxy of specific rules applicable in any one particular year.

The federal income tax laws are administered by the Internal Revenue Service (the IRS), an agency within the United States Department of the Treasury that, as a practical matter, has a considerable degree of independence. In addition to the statute, the IRS has published voluminous regulations that also have the force and effect of law. In addition, there are published revenue rulings and policy statements of various types by the IRS, as well as decisions by a specialized tax court, the United States Tax Court, and federal courts at all levels to provide guidance to taxpayers. In some circumstances, taxpayers may apply to the IRS for private letter rulings as to how specific transactions should be treated for tax purposes.

This chapter has only a limited and modest purpose. It introduces the reader to the broadest concepts, a summary overview as it were, and tries to explain how it is that the tax laws are as complex as they are.

§19.2 THE CENTRAL ROLE OF TAX LAW IN BUSINESS AND FINANCIAL TRANSACTIONS

The reasons for the preeminent importance of tax law on business and financial transactions can be set forth quite simply: The purpose of business and financial transactions is to earn a profit, and the federal income tax statutes (at least since World War II) require persons who earn income or profits to share a substantial portion of them — indeed, at times very substantial portions of them — with the United States government. Further, the federal income tax is not, and never was, a flat tax imposing the same percentage tax on all income and gains (assuming that were possible) but is composed of numerous distinctions imposing different levels of taxation on different amounts of income and different types of income. Different tax rates are also applicable to individuals with identical incomes depending on their marital or filing status. Under the old Act, some dollars of income were taxed at very high rates — as high as 90 percent at some periods shortly after World War II and as high as 70 percent as late as 1980. Tax rates at these levels provide a powerful incentive for devising techniques to avoid their full impact wherever possible. For many years, ingenious minds have been devoted to creating and perfecting such techniques. For example, at the same time that the maximum rates of 70 percent or more were in effect, the maximum tax rate on a different form of income — long-term capital gains arising from the sale or exchange of capital assets held for more than six months—was only 25 percent. This dramatic difference in rates created strong incentives to structure transactions or establish long-term strategies so as to transmute ordinary income into long-term capital gain in order to make the 25 percent rather than the 70 percent rate applicable. Several successful strategies were devised, but the 1986 Act invalidated them entirely by applying the same tax rate to both ordinary income and long-term capital gain.

There is, of course, always an incentive to structure transactions and devise strategies so as to reduce taxes no matter what the rates. Thus, the same incentive exists under the 1986 Act with its lower rates as existed under the old Act, though perhaps without the same degree of urgency. It is for this reason that the changes made by the 1986 Act are unlikely to affect the central importance of taxes and tax planning in business and financial transactions generally.

§19.3 ON TAX SPECIALISTS AND COMPLEX RULES

The income tax laws (including the regulations issued by the IRS to implement these laws) are exceedingly complex and difficult to understand. Anyone attempting to read the thousand-plus page statute for the first time is almost immediately lost in numerous cross references, defined terms, and opaque and elliptical provisions that appear to form a seamless web with no beginning and no end. The regulations are in many ways even worse: They consist of multiple volumes of fine print that are, if anything, even more opaque and difficult to get through than the statute. The IRS publishes proposed regulations for comment: Such regulations are often included in commercial compilations even though they have only been proposed and may be changed in substantial respects before they are finally adopted. In some instances, regulations may remain in "proposed" form for many years. The standard, multi-volume, loose-leaf tax services that are in every law library and most lawyers' offices attempt to describe and summarize the rules, but they contain even more detail than the statute and regulations. Merely using the index volume to these loose-leaf tax services may be a daunting task.

The tax laws have become much more complicated since World War II. Most of this complexity dates from about 1975 when new and often fundamental concepts began to be introduced into the tax laws almost every year. Probably more complexity was introduced between 1975 and 1985 than in the preceding 35 years. Regrettably, the 1986 Act did not improve either the simplicity or clarity of these statutes. Quite the contrary. It did not expressly eliminate or repeal; rather it added a new layer of complex provisions over what was there before. This is particularly true with respect to provisions relating to tax shelters and the deductibility of interest paid on personal (as contrasted with business) obligations. The special tax treatment of long-term capital gains was largely eliminated not by repealing the elaborate provisions that defined how they were to be calculated but by changing the applicable tax rates. The 1991 amendments accepted the 1986 Tax Act as the basic statute and added new provisions on top of the old. Thus, as a result of recent tax legislation, the Internal Revenue Code is even longer, thicker, and more difficult to understand than it was before 1985.

The natural consequence of complexity on important economic matters is the development of specialists to deal with problems and give advice. And so it has been with a vengeance in the tax area. Today, the complexity of the tax laws are such that sometimes even tax specialists despair of understanding the entire tax structure and fear that they are becoming unable to provide prompt and accurate advice to clients without expensive study and preparation. Twenty years ago most taxpayers filled out their own tax returns. Many lawyers who were not tax specialists advised clients on tax matters and often prepared tax returns for valued clients, either for a nominal fee or as a favor. Increasingly this work is done by accountants, "street front" commercial tax return preparers, and lawyers who specialize in tax law. The complexity of the tax laws has increased so substantially that most taxpayers today obtain professional assistance in filling out their tax returns if they involve the use of the "long form" (and quite often if they involve simple returns as well). Lawyers in general practice have become increasingly cautious about giving tax advice or preparing returns for clients. To be an effective tax lawyer today, one pretty much has to specialize in that subject.

Growth of specialization is in part a result of the increased specificity of Code provisions defining how certain transactions are to be handled. A generation ago much tax advice involved the application of general tax principles to a specific situation. Today there are often very specific provisions that must be located and carefully parsed in connection with each specific situation. The likelihood of overlooking relevant language or other applicable sections is obviously much greater under a very detailed statute than it is under a more general one.

§19.4 ON TAX AVOIDANCE AND TAX EVASION

It is obviously entirely proper to seek to minimize one's taxes by lawful means. Careful planning and judicious structuring and timing of receipts and transactions may permit the same income or gains to be taxed at much lower rates, to be deferred to a later tax year, or in some instances to escape income tax entirely. Thus was born the tax attorney, the tax planner, and the tax adviser. All engage in essentially the same planning activity — to structure transactions and economic activities in a way that takes the maximum legitimate advantage of the various provisions of the Internal Revenue Code — to structure transactions so as to minimize taxes due to Uncle Sam. Of course, these tax specialists engage in other activities as well: They may prepare returns, represent taxpayers before the IRS in administrative proceedings or in litigation against the Service, and so forth.

The services of the most sophisticated tax planners — usually lawyers and CPAs — are largely utilized only by the affluent individual taxpayer and by business. These are the only taxpayers that are regularly involved in transactions large enough to support the high fees normally charged for these services. Of course, many taxpayers engage in tax planning on a modest scale. The middle income taxpayer may use storefront tax return preparers, neighborhood accountants, or individuals who are licensed and hold themselves out as being tax advisers.

Every tax adviser and every individual taxpayer must constantly be aware of the basic distinction between legitimate tax avoidance and improper tax evasion. Tax avoidance is the structuring of transactions so as to take legitimate advantage of the provisions of the Internal Revenue Code and the regulations existing thereunder. Tax evasion, on the other hand, involves improper or unlawful reduction of tax liabilities by omission, misstatement, misrepresentation, or fraud. To take simple illustrations: For many years the special tax treatment for long-term capital gains was available only for capital assets held for more than six months. Gains from the sale or exchange of capital assets held for less than six months were taxed at the considerably higher rates applicable to ordinary income. A person planning to sell a capital asset at a profit might legitimately wait until the day after the six-month period expired to make the sale. That is simple tax avoidance: The taxpayer takes the economic risk, by deferring the sale, that the value of the capital asset may decline during that period. On the other hand, if the same transaction is agreed upon five months and twenty days after the taxpayer originally acquired the asset, possession of the asset is transferred immediately to the purchaser, and both the sale contract and the payment check are dated and delivered so that the sale appears to have occurred after the expiration of the six-month holding period, there is a significant risk that the IRS, if the circumstances become known, will treat the sale as occurring within the six-month holding period. More serious examples of improper evasion are situations involving "forgetting" to include items of income at all or claiming exemptions for six children when in fact the taxpayer only has three. If such transactions are discovered, civil fraud penalties are usually imposed, and in extreme cases, there may be criminal prosecution as well.

Often, however, the distinction is not as easy or sharp as these two hypotheticals suggest. Many transactions have as their principal purpose the reduction of taxes. The IRS may attack these transactions on very broad grounds—for example, that they are sham transactions without business purpose that should be ignored entirely, that they are step transactions that should be viewed as a single whole rather than as a series of independent transactions, or that the effect of the transactions should be recast so as to clearly reflect income. In some instances a taxpayer may be able to obtain an advance ruling as to how a specific transaction should be treated for tax purposes (a "private letter ruling" as it is usually called), but the IRS declines to give rulings in many sensitive or fact-specific areas.

Tax shelters have been a major target of the Service, and the tax returns of many thousands of taxpayers were ensnarled in this campaign during the late 1980s and early 1990s.

The giving of tax advice and the treatment of close questions is greatly affected by the fact that most returns are not fully audited, and the questionable treatment of a specific item may never be raised. Nevertheless, disclosure of the questionable item in the return is sensible in order to minimize the risk that the Service may later attempt to impose a fraud penalty on the taxpayer or, conceivably, penalties on the attorney involved or on the person who prepared the return. Also, relatively high-income persons with complex or tax-avoidance oriented transactions cannot rely on escaping an audit since the probability of an audit increases substantially as the taxpayer's income increases.

Until the 1980s, most of the taxpaying public was probably unaware of the full extent of the activity by the affluent to avoid or minimize taxes. Most Americans are employed and are subject to the tax withholding mechanism that in effect requires all employers to become tax collectors for Uncle Sam. For them, paying taxes involves little discretion (at least if they are honest) and usually is relatively painless. Indeed, since many taxpayers whose sole incomes are salaries or wages end up being entitled to a refund, the process is often almost pleasant.

§19.5 THE PRE-1986 PROGRESSIVE TAX RATE STRUCTURE

The pre-1986 tax rates for individuals combined high-percentage tax rates with a highly progressive rate structure. This tax structure directly or indirectly caused much of the complexity of the Internal Revenue Code and dissatisfaction with this pattern of tax rates led to the 1986 Act.

A *progressive rate structure* is one in which the rates are fixed so that as taxable income increases, the tax rate on additional dollars also increases. Under a progressive rate structure, additional or last dollars earned by a higher income person are taxed at a higher percentage rate than the same number of additional dollars earned by a lower income person. The progressive rate structures in the pre-1986 tax law can best be illustrated by the tax rates from the year 1980 (the last year before the "Reagan era") to persons filing joint returns:

Table 19-1
1980 Tax Rates

Taxable income	Tax
$3,400 or less	-0-
$3,400-5,499	14% of income in excess of $3,400
$5,500-7,599	$294 plus 16% of excess over $5,500
$7,600-11,899	$630 plus 18% of excess over $7,600
$11,900-15,999	$1,404 plus 21% of excess over $11,900
$16,000-20,199	$2,265 plus 24% of excess over $16,000
$20,200-24,599	$3,273 plus 28% of excess over $20,200
$24,600-29,899	$4,505 plus 32% of excess over $24,600
$29,900-35,199	$6,201 plus 37% of excess over $29,900
$35,200-45,799	$8,162 plus 43% of excess over $35,200
$45,800-59,999	$12,720 plus 49% of excess over $45,800
$60,000-85,599	$19,678 plus 54% of excess over $60,000
$85,600-109,399	$33,502 plus 59% of excess over $85,600
$109,400-162,399	$47,544 plus 64% of excess over $109,400
$162,400-215,399	$81,464 plus 68% of excess over $162,400
$215,400 or more	$117,504 plus 70% of excess

First, a brief description of how to read the above tables might be helpful. The tax brackets are additive or cumulative. For example, a couple with a taxable income of up to $5,500 filing a joint return and paying a tax under the above schedule would owe .14 × ($5,500 − $3,400) = .14 × ($2,100) = $294. If the couple's income were $7,600, they would owe the same $294 on the first $5,500 plus 16 percent of the excess over $5,500; the tax would be .16 × ($7,600 − $5,500) + $294 = .16 × ($2,100) + $294 = $630. As the hypothetical couple's taxable income continues to increase, the tax on the lower levels remains unaffected, but the additional income is subject to increasingly higher percentages. At the very top, the couple would owe 70 percent of each dollar of taxable income earned in excess of $215,400. Looking at this explanation of this table it should be clear that the odd-looking numbers at the beginning of the right hand column of the table are not mysterious at all; they are simply the amount of tax determined cumulatively from the rows of the table above the row in question. The different levels of income subject to different tax rates in the above table are universally referred to as "tax brackets." The percentage rates set forth in the above table (14 percent, 16 percent, etc. on up to 70 percent) are called "marginal rates" because they apply only to the additional dollars earned above the previous bracket. The marginal rate must be distinguished from the "effective rate" of taxation, which is the percentage that the total tax is of one's total taxable income (or of one's gross income before exemptions and deductions). To illustrate, in 1980 a couple filing a joint return with precisely $35,200 dollars of taxable income is in the 43 percent bracket. However, the amount of tax actually due on $35,200 of income is $8,162, or 23 percent of taxable income. Assuming that the person had an average amount of deductions and exemptions, his or her total income before deductions and exemptions was probably about $50,000, so that the effective tax rate on total income would be about 16 percent. That is a large percentage to be sure, but the actual effective tax rate is nowhere near the 43 percent that a superficial examination of the tax rates might indicate to be applicable. Of course, if our hypothetical taxpayer earned additional dollars of taxable income, each of those dollars would be taxed at the 43 percent rate until the couple reached $45,800 of taxable income when the marginal rate would increase from 43 percent to 49 percent.

The effective tax rate is never higher than the marginal rate (since the first dollars of income are always taxed at lower rates than the highest marginal rate), though at very high incomes the two tend to merge. For example, a couple with $300,000 of taxable income in 1980 was comfortably in the 70 percent bracket and owed $176,724 in taxes — 59 percent of taxable income. If the couple were really well off and had $10,000,000 of taxable income, their tax bill would be $6,966,724; this is an effective rate of 69.67 percent of taxable income, still lower than the marginal rate, but not by much.

For tax planning purposes, the marginal rate is usually more important than the effective rate. This is because most tax planning relates to specific transactions that take place "at the margin"; for example, a strategy that defers tax on a transaction defers the tax that would be due if the gain from that transaction were added to all the other taxable income of the taxpayer. The bulk of the taxpayer's other income, and the tax that will be due on that income, is unaffected by that tax planning.

Under even a progressive tax rate structure with very high marginal rates, it always pays to earn another dollar (so long as the highest bracket is less than 100 percent). Some high-income taxpayers in the past indicated that "it was not worth it" to earn more money because of the tax structure. Take these remarks with a grain of salt. Certainly, if a person earns another dollar, he or she will always keep a part of it even under a progressive tax structure. A more subtle question (which is the point the "not worth it" speakers may have had in mind) is whether a person will engage in risky, entrepreneurial conduct in an effort to earn an extra dollar when he or she is allowed to keep only 30 percent of it.

The high and progressive rate structure also created significant anomalies in treatment for essentially indistinguishable taxpayers. For example,

one major consequence of the rate structure described above was that
splitting income among two or more different taxpayers would often reduce
the total tax due from higher income taxpayers. Do you see why this was
usually so? When high progressive rates were first imposed during World
War II, most families consisted of a single, male income earner and a wife
who remained at home to care for the family. The first major controversy
arose when married couples with a single wage earner who resided in
community property states argued successfully that the nonworking spouse
should report one half of the community's earnings on the theory that
one-half of the earnings was hers under state law. If the couple's income
was substantial, this incomesplitting created obvious discrimination between otherwise identical families who happened to live in community
property and non-community property states. This dispute was resolved by
the development of different tax schedules for single individuals and for
married individuals filing a joint return, with the latter entitled to use a
tax schedule that in effect gave all married couples the advantage of
income-splitting that community property residents were entitled to for tax
purposes. The 1980 tax schedule set forth above was applicable to married
couples filing joint returns. Over the years, the number of separate tax
schedules gradually increased; the present pattern is described briefly in
section 19.10.

With the growth in the number of working wives, the income-splitting
tax schedules for families created a new type of discrimination. If one
spouse within a family was the sole wage earner, the rates applicable to
married taxpayers filing joint returns provided a significantly lower tax than
if that same wage earner were unmarried. However, if two persons had
equal amounts of income, their total tax bill was significantly higher if
they were married and required to file joint returns than it would have
been if they were not married and were filing separately. For example, in
1980, if two individuals living together each had precisely $25,000 of
taxable income, the tax on their joint return was $14,778 if they were
married. If they had remained single and each filed separate returns as
unmarried individuals, the tax would have been $5,952 each, or a total of
$11,904. This results from the fact that when the two taxpayers are
married, the second income is added to the first and is taxed only at the
higher brackets. When the two taxpayers are not married, each gets to
take advantage of the very low marginal rates on their first dollars of
income. The difference between $14,778 and $11,904 can be viewed as a
tax on marriage, or put another way, a bonus of nearly $3,000 per year for
living in sin. This discrimination against marriage even led a few married
couples to divorce but continue to live together, or to divorce on December
28 and remarry on January 3, in order to save on federal income taxes.
(While there is a filing category, "married couples filing separate returns,"
the tax schedule for this category was created to ensure that couples filing

separate returns were subject to the same tax brackets and rates as if they filed jointly; as a result the "marriage tax" could not be avoided simply by filing separate returns.) An attempt was made to lessen this discrimination during the 1980s by giving a special deduction of up to $3,000 per year for a married couple when both worked; this lessened but did not eliminate the discrimination. The 1986 Tax Act repealed this special deduction for two-income families on the theory that the changes in rates mandated by that Act minimized this discrimination, though it does not eliminate it entirely. This is one of the few instances in which the 1986 Tax Act actually simplified the system.

High-income taxpayers also found it profitable from a tax standpoint to give income-producing property to infant children in order to permit the income to accumulate for college expenses at lower tax brackets than if the parent retained the property, paid tax on the income from the property, and then used the remainder to pay for college. Indeed, a number of tax-oriented trust and custodial devices were invented in order to enable high-income taxpayers to minimize the effect of the sharp progressivism of rates. This strategy was largely foreclosed by provisions in the 1986 Act that basically require the bulk of unearned income of children under the age of 14 to be taxed at their parent's top rates. See section 19.17. Unlike the repeal of the working couple deduction, this change greatly complicates the tax structure, requiring many children to obtain social security numbers and file returns; it also creates potential complications and anomalies when the minor child works for all or, more likely, part of the year.

The progressive structure of rates also had one other significant effect. It caused tax revenues to increase automatically during periods of inflation. Whatever was happening at the high-income level of the spectrum, millions of taxpayers whose sole income was from wages and salary were paying taxes under a progressive tax structure that built in progressivism at a relatively low level. During periods of inflation, as individual incomes increased along with price increases, taxpayers were pushed into higher marginal brackets, and the revenues of the United States government increased dramatically even though the taxpayers were probably not better off economically from the increased wages. The large number of brackets at relatively low levels of income reflect the brackets originally established when income levels were perhaps one-third of what they were in 1981. As inflation continued, the progressive income tax rates became an effective money machine for government. Perhaps no feature of the progressive tax structure infuriated the Reagan administration more than this automatic increase in governmental revenues due purely to the interaction between inflation and progressive tax rates.

The 1986 Tax Act ended the period of high marginal rates. Table 19-2 shows the three-bracket tax rates applicable in 1992 to a married couple filing jointly:

Table 19-2
1992 Tax Rates
Married Persons Filing Jointly

Taxable Income	Amount of Tax	Rate on Excess
Up to $35,800	15% of income	
$35,800-$86,500	$5,370 plus	28% over $35,800
Over $86,500	$19,566 plus	31% over $86,500

§19.6 THE SUCCESSFUL ATTACK ON PROGRESSIVISM AND HIGH TAX RATES

The sharply progressive tax structure and relatively high marginal rates illustrated by the 1980 tax rates was a basic philosophical underpinning of tax policy for more than 50 years. The notion that a person who makes more could afford to, and should be required to, pay a higher portion of the extra dollars earned seemed so obvious as not to require extended discussion. The resulting anomalies that were necessarily created between married and cohabiting taxpayers, or between single and married one-income taxpayers, were viewed as an inevitable cost of a progressive system. However, as early as the 1950s, and increasingly during the 1960s and 1970s, serious criticism of the theory underlying high tax rates and a progressive rate structure in the Internal Revenue Code surfaced. Most of the criticism was based on a conservative political agenda embraced by President Reagan.

First and most broadly, there was the belief by conservatives that the federal government was too large and too heavily oriented toward ill-conceived welfare schemes. One naive way to attack big government is based on the quite erroneous belief that reduction of the growth of tax revenues would lead to a reduction in growth of governmental operations. In fact, reductions in the growth of tax revenues, when they occurred during the 1980s, did not produce a corresponding change in governmental activities but rather simply inflated the federal deficit.

A second, and entirely inconsistent, conservative argument was that high taxes and high tax rates were undesirable because they had adverse affects on the economy. Lower rates, it was argued, spur economic activity to such an extent that any loss of tax revenue from reduced rates would be more than offset by revenue increases from improved economic activity. This too has not been borne out by experience.

A more persuasive argument is that the high and progressive rate structure prompted inexorable political pressure by interest groups for special deductions, special exceptions, and special credits for favored activity. By 1980, the Internal Revenue Code, it may be argued, had become so riddled with special interest provisions that it had ceased to be a fair and progressive structure. One perverse result of this constant pressure was that the tax system enabled many high-income individuals quite legally to avoid paying taxes entirely or to pay only very small amounts — often less than a middle-class wage earner. Also, it quickly became clear that the tax changes made in 1981 to encourage and assist business to recover from the deep recession of that period had virtually eliminated the corporate income tax as a factor in raising revenue. Many very large companies ended up owing no tax or even being entitled to refunds of tax from earlier years despite the fact that they were reporting substantial earnings to their investors.

A related charge was that the combination of high progressive tax rates and complex rules led to the development of sophisticated avoidance techniques by affluent individual taxpayers. Congress responded to many of these techniques over the years by special provisions designed to close off specific avoidance techniques. This, however, increased the complexity of the Code and did not solve the underlying problem that was the motivation to create new avoidance techniques caused by the high and progressive rates.

During the early 1980s, particular attention was paid to the development and growth of "tax shelters," investments whose purpose was not so much to make money as to make tax deductions available to high-income persons to allow them to protect other income from federal income taxes. By 1983, the maximum tax bracket had been reduced from 70 percent to 50 percent, but even at that rate investments may be profitable solely because of the tax savings involved. If a taxpayer is in the 50 percent bracket, the impact of an investment that shows an economic loss before taxes is greatly reduced or even made profitable if the amount of the loss is deductible against other income, and that saving in tax is viewed as a consequence of the tax shelter. (Most tax shelter analysis during this period assumed that at some future time the property could be disposed of profitably at long-term capital gains rates so as to recoup the bulk of the original investment, but that was not an essential aspect of some tax shelters.) During the 1980s, public advertisements of tax shelters increased dramatically. Further, the liberalization of depreciation schedules in 1981 just about assured that every commercial real estate venture had some tax shelter benefits. All this led to the further charge that the Internal Revenue Code appeared to be warping economic activity by placing emphasis on less than maximal economic activity, particularly over-investment in real estate, oil wells, box cars, and other items. Such shelters were often widely advertised and purported to offer deductions three or four (or sometimes even more) times larger than the amount invested. While most of these publicly advertised shelters were later successfully attacked by the IRS, during the early 1980s it appeared likely that tax avoidance might become

commercially available to everyone. In other words, it appeared that the
high tax rates and sharp progressivism of the system had generated a
counterattack that blunted the force of the tax system.

Finally, there was the belief that the special tax treatment of long-
term capital gains gave unwarranted tax benefits to high-income taxpayers
who used complex strategies to transmute ordinary income into capital
gains, and who used capital gains treatment as the device ultimately to
bail out of tax shelters.

The 1986 Act made sweeping changes in the tax structure. The 14
or 15 brackets of prior law were swept away and a peculiar two-bracket
structure (15 percent and 28 percent with a limited 5 percent surcharge)
substituted; in the 1990 Revenue Reconciliation Act the limited surcharge
was removed and an additional tax bracket at 31 percent was added.
Because of the lower, more egalitarian rates applicable to income generally,
all special tax benefits for long-term capital gains were eliminated, and
such gains receive no special treatment under the 1986 Act. (The elimination of preferential treatment for capital gains was extremely controversial, and a small capital gains break was added back by the 1990 Act: The
maximum rate on net long-term capital gains cannot exceed 28 percent,
the intermediate rate in the 1992 schedule of rates.)

In order to avoid a massive revenue loss from the reduction in rates,
Congress made numerous changes in deductions and exemptions in the
1986 and 1990 statutes. Nevertheless, many individual taxpayers received
some reduction in income taxes as a result of this legislation, and in the
case of some affluent taxpayers, very significant reductions. The 1986 Act
tightened up dramatically the tax on corporations, which ended up paying
for most of the tax reductions. Further, a major attack on tax shelters was
mounted both by broadening the alternative minimum tax (see section
19.19) and by imposing restrictions on deductibility of losses from passive
investments by individuals. These passive loss limitations largely prevent
taxpayers in the post-1986 period from taking advantage of tax shelters
created in the pre-1986 period to shelter other income from tax. While
the fairness of such retroactive changes may perhaps be questioned, there
is no doubt that these changes, discussed in section 19.16, have effectively
stemmed what appeared to be a major erosion of the pre-1986 tax base.

§19.7 WHO WERE THE BENEFICIARIES OF THE RATE REDUCTIONS?

A comparison of the current rates with the 14 or 15 brackets of earlier law
shows that the progressivism of the tax structure has been dramatically
reduced. Now there are only three formal tax brackets with a maximum
rate of 31 percent (for taxable income on a joint return in excess of
$86,500) rather than a whole string of brackets with rates increasing as

high as 70 percent in 1980 and 50 percent in 1986 (the last tax year before the new rates began to go into effect). Looking at these rate changes alone, it would appear that the tax reduction benefits went primarily to the affluent, who were the only ones affected by the highest tax brackets. This, however, is not the case. On the average, the reductions in tax rates for high-income individuals were largely offset by elimination of deductions, the repeal of the preferential tax rate on long-term capital gains, and the broad attack on tax shelters. Overall, considering the high-income portion of the population as a group, the 1986 Tax Act's effect was relatively neutral, though the effect on specific wealthy individuals was spectacular in either a positive or negative direction depending on the extent to which those individuals had taken advantage of deductions and tax shelters in the past.

Further, many low-income taxpayers received tax cuts under the 1986 Act because of the greatly broadened 15 percent bracket, a more generous personal exemption, and a larger standard deduction. Indeed, one important consequence of the 1986 Act appeared to be that the more generous personal exemption and larger standard deduction would eliminate many individuals at or close to the poverty line from all liability for federal income taxes. Again, however, the effect was not as dramatic or far-reaching as expected. Even though many low-income taxpayers were removed entirely from the income tax rolls, significant increases in employment taxes were enacted during the Reagan administration that largely wiped out the income tax benefits. Employment taxes appear as "F.I.C.A." on W-2 forms and are a flat percentage (7.65 percent in 1992) of employment income up to $55,500. This regressive tax was increased because of concern about the long-term solvency of the Social Security System (a concern that continues today). The increase in employment taxes largely wiped out any reduction in taxes for lower income groups, and indeed in many instances may actually have increased the tax burden on those groups.

A study completed in 1992 concluded that with all these various offsetting changes, the average tax burden on the American taxpayer remained essentially constant since 1982 despite the major reductions in marginal rates. Of course, the same is not necessarily true of specific individuals, some of whom are worse off, and some better off, as a result of these massive tax changes.

§19.8 HOW PERMANENT IS THE PRESENT TAX STRUCTURE?

The federal income tax structure was a highly charged political issue in the late 1970s and early 1980s. Much to most people's astonishment, massive changes in structure and rates were enacted in 1986. The feat of getting this legislation enacted largely free of special interest influence was so difficult and remarkable that it seemed unlikely that major changes would be made in the near future. Yet, as this is written six years later, there is still uncertainty whether the changes made in 1986 will persist or whether they will be whittled away either directly or through exceptions, qualifications or even more ingenious stratagems. Already suggestions have been made in the political arena that some of the most wide-reaching changes should be reconsidered. The proposals with the widest support are that even higher marginal tax rates be reimposed on high-income persons, that the tax rate for long-term capital gains be further reduced particularly for investments held for more than five years, and that the 1986 provisions affecting real estate transactions be softened. Thus, what is described below may change in the near future and may change dramatically.

§19.9 THE CALCULATION OF INDIVIDUAL INCOME TAXES

The following sections give a broad and somewhat cursory analysis of the 1992 individual income tax. The discussion below assumes that the individual in question files Form 1040, the standard full-length individual income tax return and not one of the short forms, 1040A or 1040EZ, which are available to most lower-income taxpayers. In the event you have never seen a real Form 1040, the 1992 form appears at pages 479-480 as Form 19-1.

The process by which a taxpayer moves from his or her gross receipts to the amount of income subject to tax (or "taxable income") may be shown schematically as follows:

1) Gross receipts
   minus trade and business expenses and expenses directly connected with other gainful nonemployment activity, equals
2) Total income
   minus "adjustments to income" (employee business and moving expenses, pension plan deductions, and alimony), equals
3) Adjusted gross income
   minus allowable itemized personal deductions (or the standard deduction if one does not itemize) minus the allowance for personal exemptions, equals
4) Taxable income.

From taxable income one calculates the tax due on the taxable income reflected in the return either from tax tables (if taxable income is less than $100,000) or by the calculation described in the following section. See

Form 19-1

| Form **1040** | Department of the Treasury—Internal Revenue Service
U.S. Individual Income Tax Return | **1992** | (L) | IRS Use Only—Do not write or staple in this space. |

For the year Jan. 1–Dec. 31, 1992, or other tax year beginning _____ , 1992, ending _____ , 19 ____ | OMB No. 1545-0074

Label

(See instructions on page 10.)

Use the IRS label. Otherwise, please print or type.

L A B E L H E R E	Your first name and initial	Last name	Your social security number
	If a joint return, spouse's first name and initial	Last name	Spouse's social security number
	Home address (number and street). If you have a P.O. box, see page 10.	Apt. no.	**For Privacy Act and Paperwork Reduction Act Notice, see page 4.**
	City, town or post office, state, and ZIP code. If you have a foreign address, see page 10.		

Presidential Election Campaign (See page 10.)

Do you want $1 to go to this fund? . . . . | Yes | No

If a joint return, does your spouse want $1 to go to this fund? . | Yes | No

Note: Checking "Yes" will not change your tax or reduce your refund.

Filing Status

(See page 10.)

Check only one box.

1 ☐ Single

2 ☐ Married filing joint return (even if only one had income)

3 ☐ Married filing separate return. Enter spouse's social security no. above and full name here. ▶ _____

4 ☐ Head of household (with qualifying person). (See page 11.) If the qualifying person is a child but not your dependent, enter this child's name here. ▶ _____

5 ☐ Qualifying widow(er) with dependent child (year spouse died ▶ 19 ____). (See page 11.)

Exemptions

(See page 11.)

6a ☐ **Yourself.** If your parent (or someone else) can claim you as a dependent on his or her tax return, **do not** check box 6a. But be sure to check the box on line 33b on page 2

b ☐ **Spouse** . . . .

c **Dependents:**

If more than six dependents, see page 12.

(1) Name (first, initial, and last name)	(2) Check if under age 1	(3) If age 1 or older, dependent's social security number	(4) Dependent's relationship to you	(5) No. of months lived in your home in 1992

No. of boxes checked on 6a and 6b ____

No. of your children on 6c who:
● lived with you ____
● didn't live with you due to divorce or separation (see page 13) ____

No. of other dependents on 6c ____

d If your child didn't live with you but is claimed as your dependent under a pre-1985 agreement, check here ▶ ☐

e Total number of exemptions claimed . . . .

Add numbers entered on lines above ▶

Income

Attach Copy B of your Forms W-2, W-2G, and 1099-R here.

If you did not get a W-2, see page 9.

Attach check or money order on top of any Forms W-2, W-2G, or 1099-R.

7 Wages, salaries, tips, etc. Attach Form(s) W-2 . . . . | 7

8a **Taxable** interest income. Attach Schedule B if over $400 . . . . | 8a

b **Tax-exempt** interest income (see page 15). DON'T include on line 8a | 8b

9 Dividend income. Attach Schedule B if over $400 . . . . | 9

10 Taxable refunds, credits, or offsets of state and local income taxes from worksheet on page 16 | 10

11 Alimony received . . . . | 11

12 Business income or (loss). Attach Schedule C or C-EZ . . . . . | 12

13 Capital gain or (loss). Attach Schedule D . . . . | 13

14 Capital gain distributions not reported on line 13 (see page 15) . . | 14

15 Other gains or (losses). Attach Form 4797 . . . . | 15

16a Total IRA distributions . | 16a | b Taxable amount (see page 16) | 16b

17a Total pensions and annuities | 17a | b Taxable amount (see page 16) | 17b

18 Rents, royalties, partnerships, estates, trusts, etc. Attach Schedule E . . . . | 18

19 Farm income or (loss). Attach Schedule F . . . . | 19

20 Unemployment compensation (see page 17) . . . . | 20

21a Social security benefits | 21a | b Taxable amount (see page 17) | 21b

22 Other income. List type and amount—see page 18 .... | 22

23 Add the amounts in the far right column for lines 7 through 22. This is your **total income** . ▶ | 23

Adjustments to Income

(See page 18.)

24a Your IRA deduction from applicable worksheet on page 19 or 20 | 24a

b Spouse's IRA deduction from applicable worksheet on page 19 or 20 | 24b

25 One-half of self-employment tax (see page 20) . . . | 25

26 Self-employed health insurance deduction (see page 20) | 26

27 Keogh retirement plan and self-employed SEP deduction | 27

28 Penalty on early withdrawal of savings . . . . . | 28

29 Alimony paid. Recipient's SSN ▶ _____ | 29

30 Add lines 24a through 29. These are your **total adjustments** . . . . ▶ | 30

Adjusted Gross Income

31 Subtract line 30 from line 23. This is your **adjusted gross income.** *If this amount is less than $22,370 and a child lived with you, see page EIC-1 to find out if you can claim the "Earned Income Credit" on line 56* . . . . ▶ | 31

Cat. No. 12600W

Form **1040** (1992)

Form 19-1 (continued)

Form 1040 (1992)   Page 2

Tax Computation (See page 22.)	**32**	Amount from line 31 (adjusted gross income)	**32**
	33a	Check if: ☐ **You** were 65 or older, ☐ Blind; ☐ **Spouse** was 65 or older, ☐ Blind. Add the number of boxes checked above and enter the total here . . . . . ▶ **33a**	
	b	If your parent (or someone else) can claim you as a dependent, check here . ▶ **33b** ☐	
	c	If you are married filing separately and your spouse itemizes deductions or you are a dual-status alien, see page 22 and check here . . . . ▶ **33c** ☐	
	34	Enter the larger of your: { **Itemized deductions** from Schedule A, line 26, **OR** **Standard deduction** shown below for your filing status. **But if you checked any box on line 33a or b,** go to page 22 to find your standard deduction. **If you checked box 33c,** your standard deduction is zero. • Single—$3,600 • Head of household—$5,250 • Married filing jointly or Qualifying widow(er)—$6,000 • Married filing separately—$3,000 }	**34**
	35	Subtract line 34 from line 32	**35**
If you want the IRS to figure your tax, see page 23.	**36**	If line 32 is $78,950 or less, multiply $2,300 by the total number of exemptions claimed on line 6e. If line 32 is over $78,950, see the worksheet on page 23 for the amount to enter	**36**
	37	**Taxable income.** Subtract line 36 from line 35. If line 36 is more than line 35, enter -0-	**37**
	38	Enter tax. Check if from a ☐ Tax Table, b ☐ Tax Rate Schedules, c ☐ Schedule D, or d ☐ Form 8615 (see page 23). Amount, if any, from Form(s) 8814 ▶ e ____	**38**
	39	Additional taxes (see page 23). Check if from a ☐ Form 4970 b ☐ Form 4972	**39**
	40	Add lines 38 and 39 . . . . ▶	**40**

Credits (See page 23.)	**41**	Credit for child and dependent care expenses. Attach Form 2441	**41**	
	42	Credit for the elderly or the disabled. Attach Schedule R .	**42**	
	43	Foreign tax credit. Attach Form 1116	**43**	
	44	Other credits (see page 24). Check if from a ☐ Form 3800 b ☐ Form 8396 c ☐ Form 8801 d ☐ Form (specify)____	**44**	
	45	Add lines 41 through 44		**45**
	46	Subtract line 45 from line 40. If line 45 is more than line 40, enter -0- . . . . . . ▶		**46**

Other Taxes	**47**	Self-employment tax. Attach Schedule SE. Also, see line 25 .	**47**
	48	Alternative minimum tax. Attach Form 6251	**48**
	49	Recapture taxes (see page 25). Check if from a ☐ Form 4255 b ☐ Form 8611 c ☐ Form 8828	**49**
	50	Social security and Medicare tax on tip income not reported to employer. Attach Form 4137	**50**
	51	Tax on qualified retirement plans, including IRAs. Attach Form 5329	**51**
	52	Advance earned income credit payments from Form W-2	**52**
	53	Add lines 46 through 52. This is your **total tax** . . . . ▶	**53**

Payments Attach Forms W-2, W-2G, and 1099-R on the front.	**54**	Federal income tax withheld. If any is from Form(s) 1099, check ▶ ☐	**54**	
	55	1992 estimated tax payments and amount applied from 1991 return .	**55**	
	56	**Earned income credit.** Attach Schedule EIC	**56**	
	57	Amount paid with Form 4868 (extension request)	**57**	
	58	Excess social security, Medicare, and RRTA tax withheld (see page 26)	**58**	
	59	Other payments (see page 26). Check if from a ☐ Form 2439 b ☐ Form 4136	**59**	
	60	Add lines 54 through 59. These are your **total payments** . . . . . . ▶		**60**

Refund or Amount You Owe ▶ Attach check or money order on top of Form(s) W-2, etc., on the front.	**61**	If line 60 is more than line 53, subtract line 53 from line 60. This is the amount you **OVERPAID** . ▶		**61**
	62	Amount of line 61 you want **REFUNDED TO YOU** . . . . ▶		**62**
	63	Amount of line 61 you want **APPLIED TO YOUR 1993 ESTIMATED TAX** ▶	**63**	
	64	If line 53 is more than line 60, subtract line 60 from line 53. This is the **AMOUNT YOU OWE.** Attach check or money order for full amount payable to "Internal Revenue Service." Write your name, address, social security number, daytime phone number, and "1992 Form 1040" on it		**64**
	65	Estimated tax penalty (see page 27). Also include on line 64	**65**	

Sign Here Keep a copy of this return for your records.	Under penalties of perjury, I declare that I have examined this return and accompanying schedules and statements, and to the best of my knowledge and belief, they are true, correct, and complete. Declaration of preparer (other than taxpayer) is based on all information of which preparer has any knowledge.

	▶ Your signature	Date	Your occupation
	▶ Spouse's signature. If a joint return, BOTH must sign.	Date	Spouse's occupation

Paid Preparer's Use Only	Preparer's signature ▶	Date	Check if self-employed ☐ · Preparer's social security no.
	Firm's name (or yours if self-employed) and address ▶		E.I. No. · ZIP code

*U.S. Government Printing Office: 1992 — 315-038

Form 19-1 (continued)

SCHEDULES A&B
(Form 1040)

Department of the Treasury
Internal Revenue Service   (5)

Name(s) shown on Form 1040

Schedule A—Itemized Deductions

(Schedule B is on back)

▶ Attach to Form 1040. ▶ See Instructions for Schedules A and B (Form 1040).

OMB No. 1545-0074

1992

Attachment
Sequence No. **07**

Your social security number

Medical and Dental Expenses		**Caution:** *Do not include expenses reimbursed or paid by others.*	
	1	Medical and dental expenses (see page A-1)	1
	2	Enter amount from Form 1040, line 32 . **2**	
	3	Multiply line 2 above by 7.5% (.075)	3
	4	Subtract line 3 from line 1. If zero or less, enter -0- . . . . ▶	4
Taxes You Paid (See page A-1.)	5	State and local income taxes	5
	6	Real estate taxes (see page A-2)	6
	7	Other taxes. List—include personal property taxes . ▶	7
	8	Add lines 5 through 7 . . . . ▶	8
Interest You Paid (See page A-2.) **Note:** Personal interest is not deductible.	9a	Home mortgage interest and points reported to you on Form 1098	9a
	b	Home mortgage interest not reported to you on Form 1098. If paid to an individual, show that person's name and address. ▶	9b
	10	Points not reported to you on Form 1098. See page A-3 for special rules	10
	11	Investment interest. If required, attach Form 4952. (See page A-3.)	11
	12	Add lines 9a through 11 . . . . ▶	12
Gifts to Charity (See page A-3.)		**Caution:** *If you made a charitable contribution and received a benefit in return, see page A-3.*	
	13	Contributions by cash or check	13
	14	Other than by cash or check. If over $500, you **MUST** attach Form 8283	14
	15	Carryover from prior year	15
	16	Add lines 13 through 15 . . . . ▶	16
Casualty and Theft Losses	17	Casualty or theft loss(es). Attach Form 4684. (See page A-4.) . . . . ▶	17
Moving Expenses	18	Moving expenses. Attach Form 3903 or 3903F. (See page A-4.). . . . . . ▶	18
Job Expenses and Most Other Miscellaneous Deductions (See page A-5 for expenses to deduct here.)	19	Unreimbursed employee expenses—job travel, union dues, job education, etc. If required, you **MUST** attach Form 2106. (See page A-4.) ▶	19
	20	Other expenses—investment, tax preparation, safe deposit box, etc. List type and amount ▶	20
	21	Add lines 19 and 20	21
	22	Enter amount from Form 1040, line 32 . **22**	
	23	Multiply line 22 above by 2% (.02)	23
	24	Subtract line 23 from line 21. If zero or less, enter -0- . . . . ▶	24
Other Miscellaneous Deductions	25	Other—from list on page A-5. List type and amount ▶ .... ▶	25
Total Itemized Deductions	26	Is the amount on Form 1040, line 32, more than $105,250 (more than $52,625 if married filing separately)? • **NO.** Your deduction is not limited. Add lines 4, 8, 12, 16, 17, 18, 24, and 25. ▶ • **YES.** Your deduction may be limited. See page A-5 for the amount to enter.	26
		Caution: *Be sure to enter on Form 1040, line 34, the **LARGER** of the amount on line 26 above or your standard deduction.*	

For Paperwork Reduction Act Notice, see Form 1040 instructions.   Cat. No. 11330X   **Schedule A (Form 1040) 1992**

Form 19-1 (continued)

Schedules A&B (Form 1040) 1992   OMB No. 1545-0074   Page **2**

Name(s) shown on Form 1040. Do not enter name and social security number if shown on other side. | Your social security number

Schedule B—Interest and Dividend Income

Attachment Sequence No. **08**

Part I
Interest Income

(See pages 14 and B-1.)

If you had over $400 in taxable interest income OR are claiming the exclusion of interest from series EE U.S. savings bonds issued after 1989, you must complete this part. List ALL interest you received. If you had over $400 in taxable interest income, you must also complete Part III. If you received, as a nominee, interest that actually belongs to another person, or you received or paid accrued interest on securities transferred between interest payment dates, see page B-1.

Note: If you received a Form 1099-INT, Form 1099-OID, or substitute statement from a brokerage firm, list the firm's name as the payer and enter the total interest shown on that form.

Interest Income	Amount
1 List name of payer—if any interest income is from seller-financed mortgages, see page B-1 and list this interest first ▶	1

2 Add the amounts on line 1	2
3 Excludable interest on series EE U.S. savings bonds issued after 1989 from Form 8815, line 14. You MUST attach Form 8815 to Form 1040	3
4 Subtract line 3 from line 2. Enter the result here and on Form 1040, line 8a. ▶	4

Part II
Dividend Income

(See pages 15 and B-1.)

If you had over $400 in gross dividends and/or other distributions on stock, you must complete this part and Part III. If you received, as a nominee, dividends that actually belong to another person, see page B-1.

Note: If you received a Form 1099-DIV or substitute statement from a brokerage firm, list the firm's name as the payer and enter the total dividends shown on that form.

Dividend Income	Amount
5 List name of payer—include on this line capital gain distributions, nontaxable distributions, etc. ▶	5

6 Add the amounts on line 5	6
7 Capital gain distributions. Enter here and on Schedule D* .	7	
8 Nontaxable distributions. (See the inst. for Form 1040, line 9.)	8	
9 Add lines 7 and 8	9
10 Subtract line 9 from line 6. Enter the result here and on Form 1040, line 9 . ▶	10

*If you received capital gain distributions but do not need Schedule D to report any other gains or losses, see the instructions for Form 1040, lines 13 and 14.

Part III
Foreign Accounts and Foreign Trusts

(See page B-2.)

If you had over $400 of interest or dividends OR had a foreign account or were a grantor of, or a transferor to, a foreign trust, you must complete this part.

	Yes	No
11a At any time during 1992, did you have an interest in or a signature or other authority over a financial account in a foreign country, such as a bank account, securities account, or other financial account? See page B-2 for exceptions and filing requirements for Form TD F 90-22.1		
b If "Yes," enter the name of the foreign country ▶		
12 Were you the grantor of, or transferor to, a foreign trust that existed during 1992, whether or not you have any beneficial interest in it? If "Yes," you may have to file Form 3520, 3520-A, or 926 .		

For Paperwork Reduction Act Notice, see Form 1040 instructions.   Schedule B (Form 1040) 1992

Form 1040, lines 37-38, at page 480. Table 19-3 is a page taken from the tax tables applicable to persons with taxable income of less than $100,000.

Form 19-1 (continued)

SCHEDULE D (Form 1120S)	**Capital Gains and Losses and Built-In Gains**	OMB No. 1545-0130
Department of the Treasury Internal Revenue Service	► Attach to Form 1120S. ► See separate instructions.	19**92**
Name		Employer identification number

Part I Short-Term Capital Gains and Losses—Assets Held One Year or Less

(a) Kind of property and description (Example, 100 shares of "Z" Co.)	(b) Date acquired (mo., day, yr.)	(c) Date sold (mo., day, yr.)	(d) Gross sales price	(e) Cost or other basis, plus expense of sale	(f) Gain or (loss) ((d) less (e))
1					

2	Short-term capital gain from installment sales from Form 6252, line 26 or 37	**2**	
3	Short-term capital gain or (loss) from like-kind exchanges from Form 8824	**3**	
4	Combine lines 1 through 3 and enter here	**4**	
5	Tax on short-term capital gain included on line 31 below.	**5**	
6	**Net short-term capital gain or (loss).** Subtract line 5 from line 4. Enter here and on Form 1120S, Schedule K, line 4d or line 6	**6**	

Part II Long-Term Capital Gains and Losses—Assets Held More Than One Year

7					

8	Long-term capital gain from installment sales from Form 6252, line 26 or 37	**8**	
9	Long-term capital gain or (loss) from like-kind exchanges from Form 8824.	**9**	
10	Combine lines 7 through 9 and enter here	**10**	
11	Tax on long-term capital gain included on lines 23 and 31 below	**11**	
12	**Net long-term capital gain or (loss).** Subtract line 11 from line 10. Enter here and on Form 1120S, Schedule K, line 4e or line 6	**12**	

Part III Capital Gains Tax (See instructions before completing this part.)

13	Enter section 1231 gain from Form 4797, line 10	**13**	
14	Net long-term capital gain or (loss)—Combine lines 10 and 13	**14**	
	Note: If the corporation is liable for the excess net passive income tax (Form 1120S, page 1, line 22a) or the built-in gains tax (Part IV below), see the line 15 instructions before completing line 15.		
15	Net capital gain. Enter excess of net long-term capital gain (line 14) over net short-term capital loss (line 4) .	**15**	
16	Statutory minimum	**16**	$25,000
17	Subtract line 16 from line 15	**17**	
18	Enter 34% of line 17.	**18**	
19	Taxable income (see instructions and attach computation schedule)	**19**	
20	Enter tax on line 19 amount (see instructions and attach computation schedule)	**20**	
21	Net capital gain from substituted basis property (see instructions and attach computation schedule) . . .	**21**	
22	Enter 34% of line 21.	**22**	
23	**Tax.** Enter the smallest of line 18, 20, or 22 here and on Form 1120S, page 1, line 22b	**23**	

Part IV Built-In Gains Tax (See instructions before completing this part.)

24	Excess of recognized built-in gains over recognized built-in losses (see instructions and attach computation schedule)	**24**	
25	Taxable income (see instructions and attach computation schedule)	**25**	
26	Net recognized built-in gain. Enter smaller of line 24 or line 25 (see instructions)	**26**	
27	Section 1374(b)(2) deduction	**27**	
28	Subtract line 27 from line 26. (If zero or less, enter -0- here and on line 31.)	**28**	
29	Enter 34% of line 28.	**29**	
30	Business credit and minimum tax credit carryforwards under section 1374(b)(3) from C corporation years	**30**	
31	**Tax.** Subtract line 30 from line 29 (if zero or less, enter -0-). Enter here and on Form 1120S, page 1, line 22b	**31**	

For Paperwork Reduction Act Notice, see page 1 of Instructions for Form 1120S.   Cat. No. 11516V   Schedule D (Form 1120S) 1992

163

Following the calculation of the income tax due and its entry on line 38 of Form 1040, the second page of the Form 1040 systematically goes

Form 19-1 (continued)

Schedule D (Form 1040) 1992	Attachment Sequence No. **12A**		Page **2**
Name(s) shown on Form 1040. Do not enter name and social security number if shown on other side.	**Your social security number**		

Part III   Summary of Parts I and II

19	Combine lines 8 and 18 and enter the net gain or (loss). If a gain, also enter the gain on Form 1040, line 13	19
	Note: If both lines 18 and 19 are gains, see Part IV below.	
20	If line 19 is a (loss), enter here and as a (loss) on Form 1040, line 13, the **smaller** of:	
a	The (loss) on line 19; **or**	
b	($3,000) or, if married filing a separate return, ($1,500)	20 ( )
	Note: When figuring whether line 20a or 20b is **smaller,** treat both numbers as positive.	
	Complete Part V if the loss on line 19 is more than the loss on line 20 OR if Form 1040, line 37, is zero.	

Part IV   Tax Computation Using Maximum Capital Gains Rate

USE THIS PART TO FIGURE YOUR TAX ONLY IF BOTH LINES 18 AND 19 ARE GAINS, AND:

You checked filing status box:	AND	Form 1040, line 37, is over:	You checked filing status box:	AND	Form 1040, line 37, is over:
1		$51,900	3		$43,250
2 or 5		$86,500	4		$74,150

21	Enter the amount from Form 1040, line 37	21
22	Enter the **smaller** of line 18 or line 19	22
23	Subtract line 22 from line 21	23
24	Enter: $21,450 if you checked filing status box 1; $35,800 if you checked filing status box 2 or 5; $17,900 if you checked filing status box 3; or $28,750 if you checked filing status box 4	24
25	Enter the **greater** of line 23 or line 24	25
26	Subtract line 25 from line 21	26
27	Figure the tax on the amount on line 25. Use the Tax Table or Tax Rate Schedules, whichever applies	27
28	Multiply line 26 by 28% (.28)	28
29	Add lines 27 and 28. Enter here and on Form 1040, line 38, and check the box for Schedule D . .	29

Part V   Capital Loss Carryovers from 1992 to 1993

30	Enter the amount from Form 1040, line 35. If a loss, enclose the amount in parentheses	30
31	Enter the loss from line 20 as a positive amount	31
32	Combine lines 30 and 31. If zero or less, enter -0-	32
33	Enter the **smaller** of line 31 or line 32	33
	Note: If both lines 8 and 20 are losses, go to line 34; otherwise, skip lines 34-38.	
34	Enter the loss from line 8 as a positive amount	34
35	Enter the gain, if any, from line 18	35
36	Enter the amount from line 33	36
37	Add lines 35 and 36	37
38	**Short-term capital loss carryover to 1993.** Subtract line 37 from line 34. If zero or less, enter -0- .	38
	Note: If both lines 18 and 20 are losses, go to line 39; otherwise, skip lines 39-45.	
39	Enter the loss from line 18 as a positive amount	39
40	Enter the gain, if any, from line 8	40
41	Enter the amount from line 33	41
42	Enter the amount, if any, from line 34	42
43	Subtract line 42 from line 41. If zero or less, enter -0-	43
44	Add lines 40 and 43	44
45	**Long-term capital loss carryover to 1993.** Subtract line 44 from line 39. If zero or less, enter -0- .	45

Part VI   Election Not To Use the Installment Method. Complete this part **only** if you elect out of the installment method and report a note or other obligation at less than full face value.

46	Check here if you elect out of the installment method . . . . ▶ ☐	
47	Enter the face amount of the note or other obligation . . . . ▶	
48	Enter the percentage of valuation of the note or other obligation . . . . ▶	%

Part VII   Reconciliation of Forms 1099-B for Bartering Transactions.
Complete this part **only** if you received one or more Forms 1099-B or substitute statements reporting **bartering income.**

Amount of bartering income from Form 1099-B or substitute statement reported on form or schedule

49	Form 1040, line 22	49
50	Schedule C, C-EZ, D, E, or F (specify) ▶	50
51	Other form or schedule (identify). If nontaxable, indicate reason—attach additional sheets if necessary:	51
52	**Total.** Add lines 49 through 51. This amount should be the same as the total bartering income on all Forms 1099-B and substitute statements received for bartering transactions	52

through another set of calculations to determine the amount that should be paid with the return:

1) The tax due on the taxable income reflected in the return minus credits (lines 41-44) (i.e., amounts that are subtracted directly

Table 19-3

1992 Tax Table—Continued

If line 37 (taxable income) is— At least	But less than	Single	Married filing jointly	Married filing separately	Head of a household
			Your tax is—		
41,000					
41,000	41,050	8,699	6,833	9,160	7,750
41,050	41,100	8,713	6,847	9,174	7,764
41,100	41,150	8,727	6,861	9,188	7,778
41,150	41,200	8,741	6,875	9,202	7,792
41,200	41,250	8,755	6,889	9,216	7,806
41,250	41,300	8,769	6,903	9,230	7,820
41,300	41,350	8,783	6,917	9,244	7,834
41,350	41,400	8,797	6,931	9,258	7,848
41,400	41,450	8,811	6,945	9,272	7,862
41,450	41,500	8,825	6,959	9,286	7,876
41,500	41,550	8,839	6,973	9,300	7,890
41,550	41,600	8,853	6,987	9,314	7,904
41,600	41,650	8,867	7,001	9,328	7,918
41,650	41,700	8,881	7,015	9,342	7,932
41,700	41,750	8,895	7,029	9,356	7,946
41,750	41,800	8,909	7,043	9,370	7,960
41,800	41,850	8,923	7,057	9,384	7,974
41,850	41,900	8,937	7,071	9,398	7,988
41,900	41,950	8,951	7,085	9,412	8,002
41,950	42,000	8,965	7,099	9,426	8,016
42,000					
42,000	42,050	8,979	7,113	9,440	8,030
42,050	42,100	8,993	7,127	9,454	8,044
42,100	42,150	9,007	7,141	9,468	8,058
42,150	42,200	9,021	7,155	9,482	8,072
42,200	42,250	9,035	7,169	9,496	8,086
42,250	42,300	9,049	7,183	9,510	8,100
42,300	42,350	9,063	7,197	9,524	8,114
42,350	42,400	9,077	7,211	9,538	8,128
42,400	42,450	9,091	7,225	9,552	8,142
42,450	42,500	9,105	7,239	9,566	8,156
42,500	42,550	9,119	7,253	9,580	8,170
42,550	42,600	9,133	7,267	9,594	8,184
42,600	42,650	9,147	7,281	9,608	8,198
42,650	42,700	9,161	7,295	9,622	8,212
42,700	42,750	9,175	7,309	9,636	8,226
42,750	42,800	9,189	7,323	9,650	8,240
42,800	42,850	9,203	7,337	9,664	8,254
42,850	42,900	9,217	7,351	9,678	8,268
42,900	42,950	9,231	7,365	9,692	8,282
42,950	43,000	9,245	7,379	9,706	8,296
43,000					
43,000	43,050	9,259	7,393	9,720	8,310
43,050	43,100	9,273	7,407	9,734	8,324
43,100	43,150	9,287	7,421	9,748	8,338
43,150	43,200	9,301	7,435	9,762	8,352
43,200	43,250	9,315	7,449	9,776	8,366
43,250	43,300	9,329	7,463	9,791	8,380
43,300	43,350	9,343	7,477	9,806	8,394
43,350	43,400	9,357	7,491	9,821	8,408
43,400	43,450	9,371	7,505	9,837	8,422
43,450	43,500	9,385	7,519	9,853	8,436
43,500	43,550	9,399	7,533	9,868	8,450
43,550	43,600	9,413	7,547	9,884	8,464
43,600	43,650	9,427	7,561	9,899	8,478
43,650	43,700	9,441	7,575	9,915	8,492
43,700	43,750	9,455	7,589	9,930	8,506
43,750	43,800	9,469	7,603	9,946	8,520
43,800	43,850	9,483	7,617	9,961	8,534
43,850	43,900	9,497	7,631	9,977	8,548
43,900	43,950	9,511	7,645	9,992	8,562
43,950	44,000	9,525	7,659	10,008	8,576

If line 37 (taxable income) is— At least	But less than	Single	Married filing jointly	Married filing separately	Head of a household
			Your tax is—		
44,000					
44,000	44,050	9,539	7,673	10,023	8,590
44,050	44,100	9,553	7,687	10,039	8,604
44,100	44,150	9,567	7,701	10,054	8,618
44,150	44,200	9,581	7,715	10,070	8,632
44,200	44,250	9,595	7,729	10,085	8,646
44,250	44,300	9,609	7,743	10,101	8,660
44,300	44,350	9,623	7,757	10,116	8,674
44,350	44,400	9,637	7,771	10,132	8,688
44,400	44,450	9,651	7,785	10,147	8,702
44,450	44,500	9,665	7,799	10,163	8,716
44,500	44,550	9,679	7,813	10,178	8,730
44,550	44,600	9,693	7,827	10,194	8,744
44,600	44,650	9,707	7,841	10,209	8,758
44,650	44,700	9,721	7,855	10,225	8,772
44,700	44,750	9,735	7,869	10,240	8,786
44,750	44,800	9,749	7,883	10,256	8,800
44,800	44,850	9,763	7,897	10,271	8,814
44,850	44,900	9,777	7,911	10,287	8,828
44,900	44,950	9,791	7,925	10,302	8,842
44,950	45,000	9,805	7,939	10,318	8,856
45,000					
45,000	45,050	9,819	7,953	10,333	8,870
45,050	45,100	9,833	7,967	10,349	8,884
45,100	45,150	9,847	7,981	10,364	8,898
45,150	45,200	9,861	7,995	10,380	8,912
45,200	45,250	9,875	8,009	10,395	8,926
45,250	45,300	9,889	8,023	10,411	8,940
45,300	45,350	9,903	8,037	10,426	8,954
45,350	45,400	9,917	8,051	10,442	8,968
45,400	45,450	9,931	8,065	10,457	8,982
45,450	45,500	9,945	8,079	10,473	8,996
45,500	45,550	9,959	8,093	10,488	9,010
45,550	45,600	9,973	8,107	10,504	9,024
45,600	45,650	9,987	8,121	10,519	9,038
45,650	45,700	10,001	8,135	10,535	9,052
45,700	45,750	10,015	8,149	10,550	9,066
45,750	45,800	10,029	8,163	10,566	9,080
45,800	45,850	10,043	8,177	10,581	9,094
45,850	45,900	10,057	8,191	10,597	9,108
45,900	45,950	10,071	8,205	10,612	9,122
45,950	46,000	10,085	8,219	10,628	9,136
46,000					
46,000	46,050	10,099	8,233	10,643	9,150
46,050	46,100	10,113	8,247	10,659	9,164
46,100	46,150	10,127	8,261	10,674	9,178
46,150	46,200	10,141	8,275	10,690	9,192
46,200	46,250	10,155	8,289	10,705	9,206
46,250	46,300	10,169	8,303	10,721	9,220
46,300	46,350	10,183	8,317	10,736	9,234
46,350	46,400	10,197	8,331	10,752	9,248
46,400	46,450	10,211	8,345	10,767	9,262
46,450	46,500	10,225	8,359	10,783	9,276
46,500	46,550	10,239	8,373	10,798	9,290
46,550	46,600	10,253	8,387	10,814	9,304
46,600	46,650	10,267	8,401	10,829	9,318
46,650	46,700	10,281	8,415	10,845	9,332
46,700	46,750	10,295	8,429	10,860	9,346
46,750	46,800	10,309	8,443	10,876	9,360
46,800	46,850	10,323	8,457	10,891	9,374
46,850	46,900	10,337	8,471	10,907	9,388
46,900	46,950	10,351	8,485	10,922	9,402
46,950	47,000	10,365	8,499	10,938	9,416

If line 37 (taxable income) is— At least	But less than	Single	Married filing jointly	Married filing separately	Head of a household
			Your tax is—		
47,000					
47,000	47,050	10,379	8,513	10,953	9,430
47,050	47,100	10,393	8,527	10,969	9,444
47,100	47,150	10,407	8,541	10,984	9,458
47,150	47,200	10,421	8,555	11,000	9,472
47,200	47,250	10,435	8,569	11,015	9,486
47,250	47,300	10,449	8,583	11,031	9,500
47,300	47,350	10,463	8,597	11,046	9,514
47,350	47,400	10,477	8,611	11,062	9,528
47,400	47,450	10,491	8,625	11,077	9,542
47,450	47,500	10,505	8,639	11,093	9,556
47,500	47,550	10,519	8,653	11,108	9,570
47,550	47,600	10,533	8,667	11,124	9,584
47,600	47,650	10,547	8,681	11,139	9,598
47,650	47,700	10,561	8,695	11,155	9,612
47,700	47,750	10,575	8,709	11,170	9,626
47,750	47,800	10,589	8,723	11,186	9,640
47,800	47,850	10,603	8,737	11,201	9,654
47,850	47,900	10,617	8,751	11,217	9,668
47,900	47,950	10,631	8,765	11,232	9,682
47,950	48,000	10,645	8,779	11,248	9,696
48,000					
48,000	48,050	10,659	8,793	11,263	9,710
48,050	48,100	10,673	8,807	11,279	9,724
48,100	48,150	10,687	8,821	11,294	9,738
48,150	48,200	10,701	8,835	11,310	9,752
48,200	48,250	10,715	8,849	11,325	9,766
48,250	48,300	10,729	8,863	11,341	9,780
48,300	48,350	10,743	8,877	11,356	9,794
48,350	48,400	10,757	8,891	11,372	9,808
48,400	48,450	10,771	8,905	11,387	9,822
48,450	48,500	10,785	8,919	11,403	9,836
48,500	48,550	10,799	8,933	11,418	9,850
48,550	48,600	10,813	8,947	11,434	9,864
48,600	48,650	10,827	8,961	11,449	9,878
48,650	48,700	10,841	8,975	11,465	9,892
48,700	48,750	10,855	8,989	11,480	9,906
48,750	48,800	10,869	9,003	11,496	9,920
48,800	48,850	10,883	9,017	11,511	9,934
48,850	48,900	10,897	9,031	11,527	9,948
48,900	48,950	10,911	9,045	11,542	9,962
48,950	49,000	10,925	9,059	11,558	9,976
49,000					
49,000	49,050	10,939	9,073	11,573	9,990
49,050	49,100	10,953	9,087	11,589	10,004
49,100	49,150	10,967	9,101	11,604	10,018
49,150	49,200	10,981	9,115	11,620	10,032
49,200	49,250	10,995	9,129	11,635	10,046
49,250	49,300	11,009	9,143	11,651	10,060
49,300	49,350	11,023	9,157	11,666	10,074
49,350	49,400	11,037	9,171	11,682	10,088
49,400	49,450	11,051	9,185	11,697	10,102
49,450	49,500	11,065	9,199	11,713	10,116
49,500	49,550	11,079	9,213	11,728	10,130
49,550	49,600	11,093	9,227	11,744	10,144
49,600	49,650	11,107	9,241	11,759	10,158
49,650	49,700	11,121	9,255	11,775	10,172
49,700	49,750	11,135	9,269	11,790	10,186
49,750	49,800	11,149	9,283	11,806	10,200
49,800	49,850	11,163	9,297	11,821	10,214
49,850	49,900	11,177	9,311	11,837	10,228
49,900	49,950	11,191	9,325	11,852	10,242
49,950	50,000	11,205	9,339	11,868	10,256

* This column must also be used by a qualifying widow(er).

Continued on next page

from the tax bill as contrasted with "deductions" that are subtracted from gross income to determine taxable income)

2) plus "other taxes" due on income tax related taxes (lines 47-53)

3) minus payments made under the "pay as you go" system of tax collection described in section 19.13 and certain other payments that may be treated as payment of federal income tax (lines 54-60)

4) equals the amount of the additional payment that is due from the taxpayer or the amount of the refund the taxpayer is to receive (lines 61-64). In the case of a refund, the form also gives the taxpayer the option of receiving refund by check or having the amount credited against next year's estimated tax.

This logical structure of the Form 1040 can be most easily appreciated by examining carefully the front and back of the Form as set forth on pages 479-480. There is, however, a large amount of background and nuance in these lines of the Form 1040 that is described in the following sections.

§19.10 THE CALCULATION OF TOTAL INCOME

The federal income tax is a tax on income, not gross receipts. Thus, the costs and expenses of a business must be subtracted from receipts by the business in order to arrive at an income figure on which income taxes may be calculated. An individual engaged in an individual trade or business is thus entitled to these deductions to the same degree as a corporation. An individual who operates a retail hardware store, for example, may deduct the costs of inventory, rent, advertising, and so forth. These expenses are deductible on a separate schedule, Schedule C, which is similar to a profit and loss statement for any business. After deducting these expenses, only the net amount of income is transferred forward to line 12 of the first page of the Form 1040. A copy of Schedule C appears at pages 487-488 as Form 19-2. Much the same pattern of deduction of business expenses from gross receipts before the calculation of total income also appears in Schedule E (income from "rents, royalties, partnerships, trusts, etc.") and Schedule F (farm income), which are not reproduced in this book. In effect, Schedules C, E, and F permit deduction of trade and business expenses before the calculation of taxable income. The test for whether specific trade or business, rental or farming expenses are deductible is whether they are "ordinary and necessary" for the business and "paid or incurred" during the taxable year in question. Expenses that provide a benefit over several taxable years, (for example, the purchase of a truck) must be capitalized and depreciated (or amortized) over the useful life of the asset. Depreciation schedules for

Form 19-2

SCHEDULE C (Form 1040)	**Profit or Loss From Business** (Sole Proprietorship)	OMB No. 1545-0074
Department of the Treasury Internal Revenue Service (0)	▶ Partnerships, joint ventures, etc., must file Form 1065. ▶ Attach to Form 1040 or Form 1041. ▶ See Instructions for Schedule C (Form 1040).	19**92** Attachment Sequence No. **09**

Name of proprietor	Social security number (SSN)

A Principal business or profession, including product or service (see page C-1) | **B** Enter principal business code (from page 2) ▶

C Business name | **D** Employer ID number (Not SSN)

E Business address (including suite or room no.) ▶ ....
City, town or post office, state, and ZIP code

F Accounting method: **(1)** ☐ Cash   **(2)** ☐ Accrual   **(3)** ☐ Other (specify) ▶ ....

G Method(s) used to value closing inventory: **(1)** ☐ Cost   **(2)** ☐ Lower of cost or market   **(3)** ☐ Other (attach explanation)   **(4)** ☐ Does not apply (if checked, skip line H) | **Yes** | **No**

H Was there any change in determining quantities, costs, or valuations between opening and closing inventory? If "Yes," attach explanation

I Did you "materially participate" in the operation of this business during 1992? If "No," see page C-2 for limitations on losses . .

J Was this business in operation at the end of 1992? . . . .

K How many months was this business in operation during 1992? . . . . ▶

L If this is the first Schedule C filed for this business, check here . . . . ▶ ☐

Part I   Income

1	Gross receipts or sales. **Caution:** If this income was reported to you on Form W-2 and the "Statutory employee" box on that form was checked, see page C-2 and check here . . . . . . ▶ ☐	**1**	
2	Returns and allowances	**2**	
3	Subtract line 2 from line 1	**3**	
4	Cost of goods sold (from line 40 on page 2)	**4**	
5	**Gross profit.** Subtract line 4 from line 3	**5**	
6	Other income, including Federal and state gasoline or fuel tax credit or refund (see page C-2) . . . ▶	**6**	
7	**Gross income.** Add lines 5 and 6 . . . . ▶	**7**	

Part II   Expenses (Caution: *Do not enter expenses for business use of your home on lines 8–27. Instead, see line 30.*)

8	Advertising	**8**	**21** Repairs and maintenance . .	**21**	
9	Bad debts from sales or services (see page C-3) . .	**9**	**22** Supplies (not included in Part III) .	**22**	
10	Car and truck expenses (see page C-3—also attach **Form 4562**) . . .	**10**	**23** Taxes and licenses . . . . **24** Travel, meals, and entertainment:	**23**	
11	Commissions and fees . . .	**11**	**a** Travel	**24a**	
12	Depletion	**12**	**b** Meals and en-		
13	Depreciation and section 179 expense deduction (not included in Part III) (see page C-3) . .	**13**	tertainment . . **c** Enter 20% of line 24b subject to limitations (see page C-4) . .		
14	Employee benefit programs (other than on line 19) . .	**14**	**d** Subtract line 24c from line 24b .	**24d**	
15	Insurance (other than health) .	**15**	**25** Utilities	**25**	
16	Interest:		**26** Wages (less jobs credit) . .	**26**	
a	Mortgage (paid to banks, etc.) .	**16a**	**27a** Other expenses (**list type and amount**):		
b	Other	**16b**	....		
17	Legal and professional services .	**17**	....		
18	Office expense	**18**	....		
19	Pension and profit-sharing plans .	**19**	....		
20	Rent or lease (see page C-4):		....		
a	Vehicles, machinery, and equipment	**20a**			
b	Other business property . .	**20b**	**27b** Total other expenses . . .	**27b**	

28	**Total expenses** before expenses for business use of home. Add lines 8 through 27b in columns ▶	**28**	
29	Tentative profit (loss). Subtract line 28 from line 7	**29**	
30	Expenses for business use of your home. Attach **Form 8829**	**30**	
31	**Net profit or (loss).** Subtract line 30 from line 29. If a profit, enter here and on Form 1040, line 12. Also, enter the net profit on Schedule SE, line 2 (statutory employees, see page C-5). If a loss, you MUST go on to line 32 (fiduciaries, see page C-5)	**31**	
32	If you have a loss, you MUST check the box that describes your investment in this activity (see page C-5). If you checked 32a, enter the loss on Form 1040, line 12, and Schedule SE, line 2 (statutory employees, see page C-5). If you checked 32b, you MUST attach **Form 6198**.	**32a** ☐ All investment is at risk. **32b** ☐ Some investment is not at risk.	

For Paperwork Reduction Act Notice, see Form 1040 instructions.   Cat. No. 11334P   Schedule C (Form 1040) 1992

Form 19-2 (continued)

Schedule C (Form 1040) 1992   Page **2**

Part III   Cost of Goods Sold (see page C-5)

33	Inventory at beginning of year. If different from last year's closing inventory, attach explanation . .	33
34	Purchases less cost of items withdrawn for personal use	34
35	Cost of labor. Do not include salary paid to yourself	35
36	Materials and supplies	36
37	Other costs	37
38	Add lines 33 through 37	38
39	Inventory at end of year	39
40	**Cost of goods sold.** Subtract line 39 from line 38. Enter the result here and on page 1, line 4 .	40

Part IV   Principal Business or Professional Activity Codes

Locate the major category that best describes your activity. Within the major category, select the activity code that most closely identifies the business or profession that is the principal source of your sales or receipts. **Enter this 4-digit code on page 1, line B.** For example, real estate agent is under the major category of **"Real Estate,"** and the code is **"5520." Note:** If your principal source of income is from farming activities, you should file **Schedule F (Form 1040),** Profit or Loss From Farming.

Agricultural Services, Forestry, Fishing
Code
1990 Animal services, other than breeding
1933 Crop services
2113 Farm labor & management services
2246 Fishing, commercial
2238 Forestry, except logging
2212 Horticulture & landscaping
2469 Hunting & trapping
1974 Livestock breeding
0836 Logging
1958 Veterinary services, including pets

Construction
0018 Operative builders (for own account)
Building Trade Contractors, Including Repairs
0414 Carpentering & flooring
0455 Concrete work
0273 Electrical work
0299 Masonry, dry wall, stone, & tile
0257 Painting & paper hanging
0232 Plumbing, heating, & air conditioning
0430 Roofing, siding & sheet metal
0885 Other building trade contractors (excavation, glazing, etc.)
General Contractors
0075 Highway & street construction
0059 Nonresidential building
0034 Residential building
3889 Other heavy construction (pipe laying, bridge construction, etc.)

Finance, Insurance, & Related Services
6064 Brokers & dealers of securities
6080 Commodity contracts brokers & dealers; security & commodity exchanges
6148 Credit institutions & mortgage bankers
5702 Insurance agents or brokers
5744 Insurance services (appraisal, consulting, inspection, etc.)
6130 Investment advisors & services
5777 Other financial services

Manufacturing, Including Printing & Publishing
0679 Apparel & other textile products
1115 Electric & electronic equipment
1073 Fabricated metal products
0638 Food products & beverages
0810 Furniture & fixtures
0695 Leather footwear, handbags, etc.
0836 Lumber & other wood products
1099 Machinery & machine shops
0877 Paper & allied products
1057 Primary metal industries
0851 Printing & publishing
1032 Stone, clay, & glass products
0653 Textile mill products
1883 Other manufacturing industries

Mining & Mineral Extraction
1537 Coal mining
1511 Metal mining

1552 Oil & gas
1719 Quarrying & nonmetallic mining

Real Estate
5538 Operators & lessors of buildings, including residential
5553 Operators & lessors of other real property
5520 Real estate agents & brokers
5579 Real estate property managers
5710 Subdividers & developers, except cemeteries
6155 Title abstract offices

Services: Personal, Professional, & Business Services
Amusement & Recreational Services
9670 Bowling centers
9688 Motion picture & tape distribution & allied services
9597 Motion picture & video production
9639 Motion picture theaters
8557 Physical fitness facilities
9696 Professional sports & racing, including promoters & managers
9811 Theatrical performers, musicians, agents, producers & related services
9613 Video tape rental
9837 Other amusement & recreational services
Automotive Services
8813 Automotive rental or leasing, without driver
8953 Automotive repairs, general & specialized
8839 Parking, except valet
8896 Other automotive services (wash, towing, etc.)
Business & Personal Services
7658 Accounting & bookkeeping
7716 Advertising, except direct mail
7682 Architectural services
8318 Barber shop (or barber)
8110 Beauty shop (or beautician)
8714 Child day care
7872 Computer programming, processing, data preparation & related services
7922 Computer repair, maintenance, & leasing
7286 Consulting services
7799 Consumer credit reporting & collection services
8755 Counseling (except health practitioners)
7732 Employment agencies & personnel supply
7518 Engineering services
7773 Equipment rental & leasing (except computer or automotive)
8532 Funeral services & crematories
7633 Income tax preparation
7914 Investigative & protective services
7617 Legal services (or lawyer)
7856 Mailing, reproduction, commercial art, photography, & stenographic services
7245 Management services
8771 Ministers & chaplains
8334 Photographic studios
7260 Public relations
8733 Research services

7708 Surveying services
8730 Teaching or tutoring
7880 Other business services
6882 Other personal services

Hotels & Other Lodging Places
7237 Camps & camping parks
7096 Hotels, motels, & tourist homes
7211 Rooming & boarding houses

Laundry & Cleaning Services
7450 Carpet & upholstery cleaning
7419 Coin-operated laundries & dry cleaning
7435 Full-service laundry, dry cleaning, & garment service
7476 Janitorial & related services (building, house, & window cleaning)

Medical & Health Services
9274 Chiropractors
9233 Dentist's office or clinic
9217 Doctor's (M.D.) office or clinic
9456 Medical & dental laboratories
9472 Nursing & personal care facilities
9290 Optometrists
9258 Osteopathic physicians & surgeons
9241 Podiatrists
9415 Registered & practical nurses
9431 Offices & clinics of other health practitioners (dieticians, midwives, speech pathologists, etc.)
9886 Other health services

Miscellaneous Repair, Except Computers
9019 Audio equipment & TV repair
9035 Electrical & electronic equipment repair, except audio & TV
9050 Furniture repair & reupholstery
2881 Other equipment repair

Trade, Retail—Selling Goods to Individuals & Households
3038 Catalog or mail order
3012 Selling door to door, by telephone or party plan, or from mobile unit
3053 Vending machine selling
Selling From Showroom, Store, or Other Fixed Location
Apparel & Accessories
3921 Accessory & specialty stores & furriers for women
3939 Clothing, family
3772 Clothing, men's & boys'
3913 Clothing, women's
3756 Shoe stores
3954 Other apparel & accessory stores
Automotive & Service Stations
3558 Gasoline service stations
3319 New car dealers (franchised)
3533 Tires, accessories, & parts
3335 Used car dealers
3517 Other automotive dealers (motorcycles, recreational vehicles, etc.)
Building, Hardware, & Garden Supply
4416 Building materials dealers
4457 Hardware stores
4473 Nurseries & garden supply stores
4432 Paint, glass, & wallpaper stores

Food & Beverages
0612 Bakeries selling at retail
3086 Catering services
3095 Drinking places (bars, taverns, pubs, saloons, etc.)
3079 Eating places, meals & snacks
3210 Grocery stores (general line)
3251 Liquor stores
3236 Specialized food stores (meat, produce, candy, health food, etc.)

Furniture & General Merchandise
3988 Computer & software stores
3970 Furniture stores
4317 Home furnishings stores (china, floor coverings, drapes)
4119 Household appliance stores
4333 Music & record stores
3996 TV, audio & electronic stores
3715 Variety stores
3731 Other general merchandise stores

Miscellaneous Retail Stores
4812 Boat dealers
5017 Book stores, excluding newsstands
4853 Camera & photo supply stores
3277 Drug stores
5058 Fabric & needlework stores
4655 Florists
5090 Fuel dealers (except gasoline)
4630 Gift, novelty & souvenir shops
4838 Hobby, toy, & game shops
4671 Jewelry stores
4895 Luggage & leather goods stores
5074 Mobile home dealers
4879 Optical goods stores
4697 Sporting goods & bicycle shops
5033 Stationery stores
4614 Used merchandise & antique stores (except motor vehicle parts)
5884 Other retail stores

Trade, Wholesale—Selling Goods to Other Businesses, etc.
Durable Goods, Including Machinery Equipment, Wood, Metals, etc.
2634 Agent or broker for other firms— more than 50% of gross sales on commission
2618 Selling for your own account
Nondurable Goods, Including Food, Fiber, Chemicals, etc.
2675 Agent or broker for other firms— more than 50% of gross sales on commission
2659 Selling for your own account

Transportation, Communications, Public Utilities, & Related Services
6619 Air transportation
6312 Bus & limousine transportation
6676 Communication services
6395 Courier or package delivery
6361 Highway passenger transportation (except chartered service)
6536 Public warehousing
6114 Taxicabs
6510 Trash collection without own dump
6635 Travel agents & tour operators
6338 Trucking (except trash collection)
6692 Utilities (dumps, snow plowing, road cleaning, etc.)
6551 Water transportation
6650 Other transportation services
8888 **Unable to classify**

✭U.S. GPO: 1992-43-1410168/315-174

488

most major assets are set by the statute rather than by individualistic estimates of useful life.

The 1986 Act added a major wrinkle to the deductibility of business expenses when it created three classes of income — active business income, investment income, and passive income — and limited the deductibility of expenses to that from the last two categories. See section 19.16.

§19.11 THE CALCULATION OF ADJUSTED GROSS INCOME

A second category of business-related expenses that are treated differently from "trade or business" expenses involves certain business-related adjustments that Congress permits to be deducted directly from total income to determine adjusted gross income. These adjustments appear in lines 24 through 29 of form 1040. They include IRA and Keogh plan contributions (see sections 10.14 to 10.13, respectively), one-half of any self employment tax reported on Schedule SE (not reproduced in this book), penalties on early withdrawal of savings from retirement plans, and alimony. The recipient of alimony must include the amount in his or her taxable income; for this reason the 1040 requires disclosure of the recipient's social security number.

The taxpayer's total income minus these adjustments is the taxpayer's "adjusted gross income," one of the most important numbers on the return, since it is used in the calculation of a variety of limitations on deductions elsewhere in the return.

§19.12 OTHER BUSINESS-RELATED EXPENSES

A second category of business-related expenses that are treated differently from "trade or business" expenses reported on Schedule C and from "adjustments to income" reported on the front page of the form 1040 involves "employee business expenses" and "expenses for the production of income" that are not related to employment. These expenses share the common characteristic that they are related to the production of wages or income and Congress has decreed that they may be deducted from adjusted gross income. These expenses fall into two categories:

1. Expenses relating to the production of income or wages by an employee include unreimbursed moving expenses, union dues, uniforms (where required by the employer), unreimbursed travel expense, local transportation costs of salesmen, real estate brokers, and the like, the expense of maintaining an office in the home, and unreimbursed entertainment expense.

2. Expenses for the production of other income include rental fees for safe deposit boxes, accountants' fees for keeping books of income-producing property, insurance charges to protect merchandise held by the taxpayer for resale as an investment, investment advisers, and the like.

Historically, many of the expenses in these categories have been subject to abuse in the sense that taxpayers have claimed deductions to which they are arguably not entitled. These deductions were also claimed by millions of lower- and middle-income taxpayers so that widespread small cheating entailed a very substantial revenue loss. As a result, in 1986 Congress decreed that these income-generating expenses were to be deductible only to the extent that they exceed 2 percent of adjusted gross income. This calculation appears on lines 22, 23, and 24 of Schedule A (see page 481). This 2 percent limitation is called a "floor." It serves the purpose of preventing small scale cheating and simplifying the preparation of returns for many taxpayers whose income-related expenses may involve a couple of hundred dollars at the most and clearly do not exceed the floor.

The 2 percent floor was viewed as a simplifying change when it was enacted, and doubtless it is for many taxpayers. On the other hand (and this illustrates that many simplifying changes may unexpectedly cause increased complexity in individual returns), in the case of a joint return, this 2 percent floor is calculated on the combined income of husband and wife; when both spouses have income but only one has expenses subject to the floor, the filing of separate returns may yield a lower tax since the 2 percent floor is then calculated only on the income of the spouse who has the expenses subject to the floor. Only a calculation "each way" will show which is preferable.

These income related expenses, to the extent that they exceed the 2 percent floor, are not directly subtracted from adjusted gross income. Rather, they are reported in Schedule A and subject to a further limitation on deductibility discussed in the following section.

§19.13 THE CALCULATION OF TAXABLE INCOME

In addition to the business- or income-oriented expenses described in the previous sections, the Internal Revenue Code has always allowed, as a matter of policy, the deduction of certain types of personal expenses. Historically, the most important of these were state income, property and sales taxes, interest on personal debts and on real estate mortgages, medical and dental expenses, charitable contributions up to the specified maxima, and casualty losses (see Schedule A, page 481). The reasons for these deductions obviously vary: encouraging charitable contributions, lessening the financial burden on the unfortunate family struck by a major casualty loss or catastrophic medical expenses, and so forth.

The policies underlying some of these deductions are viewed as suspect by tax theorists since they involve personal rather than business expenditures; however, from a political standpoint some of them are immensely popular. These personal expenses have also involved a fair amount of petty cheating by large numbers of taxpayers. In the 1986 Act and the 1990 amendments, Congress took several steps to limit the widespread use and misuse of these deductions. The most important substantive changes were: limiting the deduction of state taxes to two categories: income and real estate taxes, excluding state sales taxes; and limiting the deduction of interest on personal and consumer loans basically to those arising from the purchase of residential real estate or, to a limited extent, home equity loans secured by liens on such real estate. See section 7.13 for a discussion of home equity loans.

The Internal Revenue Code has adopted several additional devices to limit the availability of personal deductions. First, the most important device is the availability to all taxpayers of the "standard deduction" that may be used in lieu of the itemization of all personal deductions. The size of the standard deduction varies with the filing status of the taxpayer discussed below. In 1992 the amounts are as follows:

Single persons, $3,600
Heads of households, $5,250
Married persons filing jointly, $6,000
Married persons filing separately, $3,000.

These amounts are set forth in line 34 of Form 1040. The standard deduction is increased for persons over the age of 65 and for persons who are blind. It is indexed for inflation, and thus slowly increases. The standard deduction applies only to personal deductions: It does not affect the deductibility of employee business expenses or expenses incurred in the production of income. Also, as indicated above, the standard deduction is not a floor (like that applied to employee business expenses) but an amount that is available to and may be claimed by every taxpayer as an alternative to itemization. If the standard deduction is generous enough, most persons, of course, do not itemize but simply elect to take the standard deduction. This has multiple advantages from the standpoint of the system: It eliminates petty cheating, it simplifies the preparation of returns for many taxpayers, and it improves general equity, since more taxpayers compute their taxes on precisely the same basis.

The second important device designed to limit personal deductions to extraordinary or unusual situations (and possibly also to prevent petty cheating) is the imposition of a floor on specific types of expenses similar to that imposed on employee business expenses. The oldest such floor is on medical expenses, where Congress originally attempted to distinguish between ordinary medical expenses and extraordinary ones by limiting their aggregate deductibility to medical expenses that exceed 3 percent of adjusted gross income. This floor was raised to 7.5 percent in the 1986 Act, thereby eliminating deductions in all but extraordinary situations given the amount of available income. A similar floor was placed on casualty losses in the 1960s because of perceived abuses of claimed losses that were minor in character and often not of the true "casualty" type. Currently, any claimed casualty loss must be reduced by (a) $100, and (b) 10 percent of adjusted gross income, and only the excess is deductible. Again the policy was to limit the deduction to extraordinary losses given the amount of available income. In both instances, only the deductible portion of medical or casualty losses is taken into account to determine whether the standard deduction is advantageous.

A third device is to require specific documentation about claimed deductions to be filed with the return. This is required, for example, for charitable deductions claimed for contributions of noncash property valued over $500, where valuations are likely to be overoptimistic.

The 1990 amendments added another restriction on itemized deductions. In order to raise revenue (rather than to prevent small-scale cheating), taxpayers having adjusted gross income in excess of $105,200 in 1992 must reduce itemized deductions by 3 percent of the excess over the threshold. However, the maximum reduction may not exceed 20 percent

Form 19-3

Itemized Deductions Worksheet—Line 26 (keep for your records)

1. Add the amounts on Schedule A, lines 4, 8, 12, 16, 17, 18, 24, and 25 . . . .   **1.** _____

2. Add the amounts on Schedule A, lines 4, 11, and 17, plus any gambling losses included on line 25 . . . .   **2.** _____

   Caution: *Be sure your total gambling losses are clearly identified on the dotted line next to line 25.*

3. Subtract line 2 from line 1. If the result is zero, **stop here;** enter the amount from line 1 above on Schedule A, line 26 . . .   **3.** _____

4. Multiply line 3 above by 80% (.80) . . .   **4.** _____

5. Enter the amount from Form 1040, line 32   **5.** _____

6. Enter $105,250 ($52,625 if married filing separately) . . . .   **6.** _____

7. Subtract line 6 from line 5. If the result is zero or less, **stop here;** enter the amount from line 1 above on Schedule A, line 26 . .   **7.** _____

8. Multiply line 7 above by 3% (.03) . . .   **8.** _____

9. Enter the **smaller** of line 4 or line 8 . . . .   **9.** _____

10. **Total itemized deductions.** Subtract line 9 from line 1. Enter the result here and on Schedule A, line 26 . . . .   **10.** _____

of total deductions. This calculation is made on line 26 of Schedule A. The instructions to Form 1040 include a worksheet to calculate the actual amount that is deductible. Form 19-3 is this worksheet, which is not filed as part of the tax return.

§19.14 PERSONAL EXEMPTIONS

Personal exemptions are entirely different from personal deductions. Exemptions permit the subtraction of arbitrary amounts for the taxpayer and spouse (if a joint return is filed) and for each dependent relative (defined precisely in the Code). Additional exemptions were long provided for persons over 65 and for blind people, but the 1986 Act eliminated these exemptions in favor of a limited increase in the standard deduction for the aged and blind. The personal exemption for the 1992 tax year is $2,300 for each allowable exemption.

As a result of the combination of personal exemptions and the standard deduction, a family of four pays no tax if its adjusted gross income is $14,200 or less ($9,200 of personal exemptions and $5,000 of standard deduction).

The 1986 Act added a new twist on personal exemptions by providing a gradual phase-out of the benefit of the exemptions for high-income taxpayers. This is accomplished by reducing the allowable exemptions by 2 percent for each $2,500 of income in excess of $157,900 on a joint return until the advantage of all personal exemptions is eliminated. In other words, the high-income taxpayer begins to lose tax benefits from personal exemptions when his or her income exceeds $157,900 and loses all benefit from them when the income exceeds $282,900 on a joint return. (The loss of 100 percent of the exemptions requires 50 2 percent increases; hence 50 × $2,500 = $125,000; $157,900 + $125,000 = $282,900.) This calculation is made in lines 34-36 and another worksheet in the instructions. This worksheet is set forth as Form 19-4.

§19.15 THE CALCULATION OF THE TAX DUE

Once taxable income is calculated, the next step is the calculation of the actual tax that is due. This is done either from a set of tables (for persons with incomes of less than $100,000) or by a mathematical calculation. Since the lower income tables are themselves simply a reflection of the mathematical calculation, this discussion concentrates on the formulas. The formulas set forth in Table 19-2 apply to the 1992 tax year.

There are four different categories of individual taxpayers with different sized brackets depending on marital or family status. These multiple

Form 19-4

Deduction for Exemptions Worksheet—Line 36 (keep for your records)

Use this worksheet **only** if the amount on Form 1040, line 32, is more than the dollar amount shown on line 3 below for your filing status. If the amount on Form 1040, line 32, is equal to or less than the dollar amount shown on line 3, multiply $2,300 by the total number of exemptions claimed on Form 1040, line 6e, and enter the result on line 36.

1. Multiply $2,300 by the total number of exemptions claimed on Form 1040, line 6e . . . .   1. _____

2. Enter the amount from Form 1040, line 32 . .   2. _____

3. Enter on line 3 the amount shown below for your filing status:
   - Married filing separately, enter $78,950
   - Single, enter $105,250
   - Head of household, enter $131,550   } 3. _____
   - Married filing jointly or Qualifying widow(er), enter $157,900

4. Subtract line 3 from line 2. If zero or less, **stop here;** enter the amount from line 1 above on Form 1040, line 36 . . . .   4. _____

   Note: *If line 4 is more than $122,500 (more than $61,250 if married filing separately),* **stop here;** *you* **cannot** *take a deduction for exemptions. Enter -0- on Form 1040, line 36.*

5. Divide line 4 by $2,500 ($1,250 if married filing separately). If the result is not a whole number, round it up to the next higher whole number .   5. _____

6. Multiply line 5 by 2% (.02) and enter the result as a decimal amount . . . .   6. ____.____

7. Multiply line 1 by line 6 . . . .   7. _____

8. **Deduction for exemptions.** Subtract line 7 from line 1. Enter the result here and on Form 1040, line 36 . . . .   8. _____

categories, of course, are an inheritance from the earlier era of 14 or 15 narrow brackets and are typical of the complexity of the modern tax law system and the failure of the 1986 Tax Act effectively to simplify the system. The three basic categories of taxpayers are: (1) a married couple filing jointly or a "surviving spouse" (defined as a person whose spouse has died within the previous two years); (2) a "head of household" (defined as an unmarried person who is not a surviving spouse and who maintains a home for a dependent child or relative); and (3) a single person. The fourth category, married taxpayers filing separately, is created by simply halving every entry in the joint return category, and thereby it ensures that married couples with two incomes cannot take advantage of the single person tax schedule but remain on a tax parity with families in which one spouse is the wage earner and the other is a homemaker. See section 19.5 for a further discussion of how these categories of individual taxpayers evolved.

§19.16 LIMITATIONS ON INVESTMENT OR PASSIVE LOSSES

The 1986 Act develops a classification of interest and passive loss deductions primarily to eliminate excessive deductions from tax shelters. See generally section 19.6. Unfortunately, in doing so, Congress again significantly increased the complexity of the individual income tax system.

The basic idea is not very complicated. "Investment interest," for example, is basically interest on obligations incurred to buy or carry investment property. That interest is deductible only to the extent the taxpayer has income from the investments. The purpose of this provision is to prevent a taxpayer from borrowing funds to acquire deferred income investments and deducting the interest immediately, thereby sheltering other current income from tax. If one does incur interest in a year when it is not deductible because of the absence of investment income, that deduction is not lost but may be carried over indefinitely and deducted in a later year when the taxpayer does have available investment income in excess of investment interest.

The 1986 Act also establishes a similar pattern by creating a class of losses and credits, called "passive losses," that can be deducted only to the extent that there is income from passive activities. "Passive activities" include essentially all rental activities and trade or business activities in which the taxpayer does not materially participate. Investment activity is not passive activity. The ownership and rental of commercial or residential property is expressly included in the definition of passive activities, and participation by owners in decisions on matters such as who should be tenants does not take the activity out of the passive category. Virtually the only nonpassive commercial real estate activity is owning and operating a hotel. The purpose of this provision is to eliminate most tax shelters, particularly tax shelters involving the direct ownership of commercial or rental residential real estate. However, there are exceptions to this rigid treatment of passive activity, including the right to deduct up to $25,000 of passive losses for taxpayers with adjusted gross incomes of less than $100,000. This deduction is itself gradually phased out at higher incomes until all deduction is prohibited for taxpayers with adjusted gross incomes in excess of $150,000. Passive losses that cannot be taken advantage of in any year because of the lack of passive income also do not disappear but may be carried over to later years in which there is passive income in excess of passive losses.

Losses and credits arising from a trade or business in which the taxpayer materially participates are fully deductible. "Materially" means that the taxpayer is involved in the operations of the activity on a regular, continuous, and substantial basis. If the activity is not material, the business becomes a passive activity. Thus, the 1986 Tax Act created a threefold

495

classification of individual profitmaking activity in order to eliminate tax shelters and related activities: (1) investment activities; (2) trade or business activities in which the taxpayer materially participates; and (3) passive activities. Except for real estate activities that are clearly defined as passive activities, difficult problems of classification at or near the boundaries between these three categories arise. Indeed, the mere reporting of activities in each category significantly increases the complexity of the schedules to Form 1040.

§19.17 TAXATION OF UNEARNED INCOME OF MINORS

As indicated above (see section 19.6), significant tax savings may be obtained by affluent taxpayers by making gifts of income-producing property to minor children, in effect splitting the income in future years and permitting the children to take advantage of the lower marginal rates for lower incomes. It is relatively easy to make gifts to minor children that effectively transfer the legal right to the income to the child and thus make the child an independent taxpayer, while the donor retains the power to manage and control the investment of the funds through the device of a custodial account created under the Uniform Gift to Minors Act, the Uniform Transfers to Minors Act (enacted in virtually all states), or through the device of a trust. Distributions to the child before the age of 18 in the case of a custodial account may also be controlled by the parent donor, though the funds must be turned over to the child when he or she reaches the age of 18.

The 1986 Tax Act sharply reduced the scope of this tax avoidance device (but did not eliminate it entirely) by imposing the "kiddie tax" on the unearned income of minor children. The first $600 of unearned income of a child under the age of 14 is not taxed as a standard deduction; the next $600 is taxed at the rate of 15 percent, which is the lowest individual tax bracket, but all income over $1,200 is taxed to the minor at the parent's highest bracket. This tax is not applicable to income earned by the child from his or her own employment or labor, and to income earned after the child reaches the age of 14. In some circumstances the parents may simply include the child's unearned income in their return rather than filing a separate tax return for the child.

One consequence of the "kiddie tax" is that many parents have to obtain social security numbers for their children and file income tax returns on their behalf.

§19.18 SOCIAL SECURITY RECIPIENTS

For many years, pensions from the Social Security System were viewed as being not includible in taxable income. Social security benefits, however, are reduced by either wages or self employment income earned while the recipient is entitled to social security benefits. The loss of benefits schedule for social security recipients in 1992 is set forth in Table 19-4.

Table 19-4
Loss of Social Security Benefits
by Receipt of Wages or Unearned Income

Age	Wages or earned income over	Loss of benefits
Under age 65	$7,440	$1 for each $2 over limit
65-69	$10,200	$1 for each $3 over limit
70 or over	Unlimited	no loss of benefits

In addition to the loss of benefits for wages or earned income, high income social security recipients are required to include a portion of their benefits in taxable income. The formula is rather complex. In 1992, a couple filing joint returns must include up to 50 percent of their benefits as taxable income if their adjusted gross income exceeds $32,000. It may be that relatively affluent social security recipients will be taxed on an even greater percentage of social security benefits in the future.

§19.19 THE ALTERNATIVE MINIMUM TAX

The alternative minimum tax is a special tax designed to prevent taxpayers from escaping their fair share of taxation by the judicious combination of tax benefits. The alternative minimum tax limits the ability of a taxpayer to avoid all taxes by using a variety of tax benefits, either singly or in combination. It is applicable only to taxpayers with taxable incomes in excess of $50,000. The alternative minimum tax essentially requires a second tax calculation on an entirely different set of computational rules. If the alternative minimum tax is greater than the tax computed in the normal manner, then the taxpayer must add to the tax due on the normal computation an amount equal to the difference between the normal tax and the alternative minimum tax. In simpler terms, if the alternative minimum tax exceeds the normal tax, the taxpayer's total tax liability is based on the alternative minimum tax rather than on the normal computation of tax.

The alternative minimum tax is a flat 24 percent of an amount computed as follows: One starts with the adjusted gross income of the taxpayer computed on the normal basis and adds back in specific "tax preference items" claimed by the taxpayer in the calculation of adjusted gross income. From this amount one subtracts: (1) $40,000; and (2) allowable deductions for charitable contributions, interest on mortgages on the personal residence of the taxpayers, and investment interest. The alternative minimum tax is 24 percent of the amount that remains.

The tax preference items that must be added back into income for the computation of the amount subject to the alternative minimum tax include accelerated depreciation on property, capital gain deductions, intangible drilling costs, excess itemized deductions, certain tax-exempt bonds, portions of incentive stock options excluded from income, and percentage depletion.

The alternative minimum tax provision is an effort to overcome the deficiencies of the normal income tax structure by overlaying a separate tax schedule to prevent the use of multiple tax benefits to reduce taxable income. As the alternative tax rate (24 percent) is close to the normal tax rate (28 percent or 31 percent), the normal rate dwindles in significance for upper-income taxpayers who take advantage of tax avoidance devices. The alternative minimum tax obviously complicates the tax returns of all high-income taxpayers.

§19.20 THE COLLECTION PROCESS

The Internal Revenue Service has the responsibility for collection of federal income, gift, estate, and excise taxes. The discussion here is limited to the process of collection of income taxes.

Income taxes are collected on a highly efficient "pay as you go" basis. For most Americans, the "pay as you go" system means simply that employers must withhold from each paycheck an amount that approximately covers the employee's tax liability by the end of the year. Probably every reader has had some contact with this withholding system, involving the filing of a W-4 Form with one's employer declaring the number of exemptions claimed, and the receipt from the employer each January of a W-2 Form showing the amounts actually withheld during the previous calendar year. The withholding schedules and tax rates are structured so that if a person accurately declares the number of exemptions and uses the standard deduction, he or she ends up having more deducted from paychecks than the amount of tax actually due. Most taxpayers therefore receive refunds every year. In 1992, President Bush ordered an adjustment of withholding schedules in an effort to put more spendable funds in the hands of taxpayers and help the country out of a recession. This adjustment did not change the ultimate amount of tax due, but it decreased the amount withheld and thereby reduced the refund many taxpayers expected to receive in early 1993. In some instances, it doubtless changed an expected refund into an unexpected additional payment.

Of course, year-end refunds caused by overwithholding are paid without interest in effect from funds painlessly collected over the course of the preceding year from the taxpayer by his or her employer. The fact that most people are entitled to refunds each year materially increases the political acceptability of the system. The arrangement is attractive to the federal government as well: The collection process is relatively painless and does not give rise to large amounts of resentment, the government has the interest-free use of funds for nearly a year, and tax collections are spread around the year and not bunched in a single month.

The employer is required to pay over to the IRS the amount withheld from employees at specified times dependent on the number of employees. Even though the Internal Revenue Code requires that these withheld funds be placed in a separate account, most employers do not segregate the funds but simply use them as part of general working capital until the check is written to the IRS. Of course, from time to time a business may become insolvent without having forwarded the money withheld from employees to the Service. There is a 100 percent penalty against an individual with the responsibility for these funds who fails to pay them over to the Service. In other words, the corporate treasurer or individual with analogous responsibilities is personally liable for the amount withheld if it is not in fact paid over. Like other claims arising under the Internal Revenue Code, this liability is not discharged in bankruptcy. Whether or not the Service successfully collects the withheld taxes from the employer, however, the employee is entitled to credit against his or her taxes of the amounts shown as withheld on statements reported to the IRS.

If persons have income or gains not subject to withholding, they may be required to file quarterly declarations of estimated tax, which are intended to provide a "pay as you go" system to taxpayers with substantial amounts of self-employment activity, personal investments, and other sources of nonwithheld income such as gambling or stock market trading. Quarterly declarations are due April 15, June 15, September 15, and January 15 for calendar year taxpayers, and must be accompanied by a proportional amount of the estimated tax that is shown to be due on the estimate. A person subject to withholding is theoretically required to file a quarterly declaration whenever taxes withheld are less than 90 percent of taxes due, but such persons may avoid this filing if they increase the amount of withholding so that the estimated tax for that quarter is shown to be zero. The obligation to file quarterly declarations of estimated tax and to pay the proportional amount of tax due is enforced by penalties applied when the final return is filed for the year showing substantial underpayment of tax. What is substantial in this context is defined in the Tax Code very specifically: There is a substantial underpayment if the amount paid by withholding and quarterly estimates is less than 90 percent of the actual tax shown to be due on the return. Before 1986, the penalty could be automatically avoided if estimated tax payments equaled the actual amount of the previous year's tax, but that "safe harbor" no longer exists for many taxpayers.

§19.21 CASH BASIS ACCOUNTING

Most individual taxpayers are on the cash basis, reporting income when it is received rather than when it is earned and taking advantage of deductions when they are paid rather than when they are incurred or when they are due. This permits some income and deduction shifting from one year to another. For example, a doctor who does not bill for November or December services until January takes the income arising from those services into his or her tax return for the second year, not the first. It is almost always advantageous to defer taxes even if tax rates are identical because of the time value of a deferred payment. Prior to 1986, year-end planning might also permit a taxpayer to shift income from a high-income year to a lower-income year to be taxed at lower marginal rates. Similarly, a taxpayer may be able to shift two years' real estate property taxes into a single year by paying one year's taxes in January and prepaying the next year's taxes in December of the same year. Combining two years' taxes into a single year may be advantageous if the standard deduction is claimed for the year in which no payments of real estate tax are made. While strategies of this type offer some modest degree of tax saving, they have become significantly less important since the 1986 Act with its lower overall tax rates and limited number of tax brackets.

There are some exceptions to the straight cash basis of individual taxpayer accounting. The doctrine of "constructive receipt" does not permit a taxpayer to defer reporting income items that are within his immediate control. One cannot defer an income item, for example, merely by not depositing a check until the following year. There are also special rules relating to receipt of interest: Interest on financial instruments such as zero coupon bonds purchased at a discount from face value (see section 16.17) must be reported as it is earned rather than being deferred until the instrument is paid. Similarly, interest paid by a taxpayer in a lump sum to cover several accounting periods cannot be deducted in the year of payment but must be accrued and deducted ratably over the relevant periods. Restrictions also are imposed on the deductibility of prepaid amounts. These various qualifications to the general cash method of accounting reflect pragmatic judgments designed to limit revenue loss from tax-minimizing transactions.

§19.22 SALES AND EXCHANGES OF PROPERTY IN GENERAL

A major area of tax law deals with gains and losses from the sale or exchange of property. At the most basic level, a sale or exchange of property gives rise to taxable income. Say a farmer swaps a side of beef for a bolt of cloth from the local dry goods store. The exchange is a taxable transaction and each participant should report gain or loss from the transaction on his or her federal income tax return. Obviously, in the barter economy that quietly exists in many communities there is a lot of tax evading going on, since it is likely that few, if any, transactions of this type are reported.

Of course, in the barter of the beef for the cloth, both parties are swapping goods that involve their trade or business. But that is not essential. If you sell your secondhand car at a profit, the gain should be reported to the IRS as income. Similarly, if you swap your car for a motorcycle or a used computer, the gain should be reported. (Losses from such personal transactions are not deductible at all and hence need not be reported.)

The calculation of the amount of the gain from sales or exchanges involves the use of technical language that is fundamental to any understanding of the tax laws:

a. *Basis* is the investment the seller of the property has in the property. It is the cost or purchase price of the property paid or incurred by the seller in acquiring the property. In the case of property acquired by gift, the basis in the hands of the donee is usually the same as the basis in the hands of the donor (a "substituted basis"); in the case of property acquired by inheritance, it is generally the fair market value of the assets on the death of decedent (a "stepped up basis").

b. *Adjusted basis* is the basis of the property (1) plus capital improvements made by the seller, purchase commissions originally paid by the seller, legal costs for defending or perfecting title, and so forth, and (2) minus returns of capital, particularly depreciation claimed as tax deductions, depletion, deducted casualty losses, insurance reimbursements, and the like.

c. The *amount realized* includes the cash received for the property on a sale or the fair market value of the property received in exchange for the property. Selling expenses, including brokerage commissions paid by the seller, reduce the amount realized. In the case of property subject to a mortgage, the amount realized also includes the amount of mortgage debt which the seller is relieved from paying as a result of the sale. For example, if an owner of real estate that is encumbered by a $50,000 mortgage sells the property for $10,000 cash over and above the mortgage, which the buyer agrees to assume and pay, the amount realized from the sale is $60,000, not $10,000. If the property is sold with the seller giving the buyer $5,000 for assuming the mortgage of $50,000, the amount realized is $45,000.

d. *Gain* on a transaction equals the amount realized minus the adjusted basis. If the adjusted basis is greater than the amount realized, the difference is the loss.

In order to be taxable, a gain or loss must be "recognized" as well as "realized." "Realized" means that the transaction is closed and the sale or exchange has occurred. "Recognized" means that the gain or loss is also to be taken into account as a taxable transaction. If a realized gain or loss is not recognized, it is deferred to a later year.

Generally, gain or loss is recognized whenever property is sold or exchanged, but there are significant exceptions: exchanges of like kinds of property, involuntary conversions of property, sales of residences followed by a rollover of the purchase price into a new residence, and sales between related persons.

A gain on the sale or exchange of the property may be recognized even though a loss on the sale of the same property is not deductible. This includes, for example, a sale of personal assets such as the family home. The loss is not recognized in the case of personal assets because it is considered a result of the personal consumption involved in living in a home rather than an economic loss.

19.23 SPECIAL TREATMENT OF LONG-TERM CAPITAL GAINS AND LOSSES

The 1986 Act imposed the same tax rate on long-term capital gains and losses as on income generally. This represented a major and controversial change in long-standing tax policy. In 1990, a maximum rate of 28 percent was established for such gains. It appears likely that a difference in treatment of long-term capital gains will remain in the tax laws in the future. Hence a description of the treatment of sales of assets is appropriate.

Under the 1954 Code, gains and losses from sales or exchanges of property were generally taxable in the same manner as any other income. However, gains and losses from the sale or exchange of "capital assets" were subject to special rules and limitations.

A "capital asset" is any property held by a taxpayer other than inventory, property held primarily for sale to customers, depreciable and real property used in a trade or business, and several other less important items. A taxpayer's personal residence is thus a capital asset, but if the same property were used in a trade or business it would not be a capital asset. Depreciable property used in a trade or business (such as the residence), however, was often entitled to special treatment under the 1954 Code that was even more favorable to the taxpayer than if it were a capital asset.

Shares of stock in a corporation are capital assets; interests in a partnership are also capital assets (except for designated assets such as accounts receivable and appreciated inventory). On the other hand, an interest in a proprietorship is not a capital asset but a composite of individual assets.

A "capital gain" or "capital loss" arises from the sale or exchange of a capital asset. Historically, a distinction was also made between long-term and short-term capital gains and losses, the dividing line usually being a holding period of six months. In some years between 1954 and 1986, the holding period was as long as 12 months. Under the 1954 Code, long-term capital gains were subject to special treatment that in effect imposed a maximum tax of 25 percent on them when other income was being taxed at progressive rates up to 70 percent. Long-term capital losses were also subject to special treatment, but that treatment was usually disadvantageous to the taxpayer since long-term losses were deductible against ordinary income only to a limited extent and in many years not on a dollar-for-dollar basis.

The actual calculation of the amount of gain or loss that qualified for long-term capital gain or loss treatment under the 1954 Code was complicated because a single taxpayer often had both short- and long-term gains or losses in a single tax year. Basically, the tax law required a netting of short-term gains and losses separately from long-term gains and losses, then netting the two categories, with only the ultimate difference being categorized as long- or short-term.

If a taxpayer's return showed a net long-term capital gain, that gain was entitled to special tax treatment under the 1954 Code. Mechanically, the taxpayer was permitted to exclude a specified percentage (50 or 60 percent, depending on the year the transaction occurred) of the net long-term gain entirely from the tax computation, and only the remaining portion of the net long-term gain was included in ordinary income. When the maximum tax bracket was 50 percent, exclusion of half of the gain in effect meant that the maximum tax rate applicable to long-term capital gains was 25 percent. When the exclusion was 60 percent, the maximum tax rate on long-term capital gains was 20 percent (only 50 percent of the remaining 40 percent was subject to tax). When the maximum tax bracket was 70 percent, the exclusion of half the gain might theoretically lead to a tax rate higher than the 25 percent applicable to long-term capital gains, but in those years, a maximum 25 percent rate on long-term capital gains was also specifically mandated.

Long-term capital losses were also treated differently from ordinary losses. Losses from capital assets that were for personal use (such as a residence or an automobile) were not deductible at all. Other long-term capital losses (after the netting process described above) were deductible against ordinary income only up to the amount of $3,000, and long-term capital losses counted for only one-half, so that $6,000 of long-term losses were needed to obtain a $3,000 deduction. The precise treatment of net capital losses varied somewhat depending on the year in question.

Short-term capital gains (after the netting process described above) were includible in ordinary income in their entirety, while short-term capital losses were deductible in full against ordinary income.

In these pre-1986 years, it was generally desirable to structure sales and exchanges so that the taxpayer showed either a net long-term capital gain or a short-term capital loss, or even better, an ordinary loss.

19.24 EVALUATION OF THE TREATMENT OF CAPITAL GAINS

As indicated above, the 1986 Tax Act eliminated all special treatment of long-term capital gains after 1987, a result which was partially ameliorated in 1991 when a 28 percent maximum rate was added. In the calculation of taxable income since 1986, the application of the $3,000 maximum deduction for long-term capital losses continues to apply, but the old two-for-one rule was eliminated. See section 19.23 and Schedule D of Form 1040 (pages 483-484).

The special treatment of capital gains is a highly political issue. Republicans generally support a special, lower tax on the theory that special tax treatment will encourage business and investment. Democrats generally oppose special tax treatment on the theory that it benefits only the wealthy and has little economic benefit.

One argument that a special rate for long-term capital gains is unnecessary under the 1986 Act tax rates is that the principal justification for the special rate was to avoid squeezing an incremental gain over several years into a single year when the capital asset was sold or exchanged. This was particularly unfair when the pre-1986 progressive tax structure was applicable, but it is less likely to be viewed as unfair under the three-bracket tax structure now mandated by the 1986 Tax Act.

On the other hand, it has been argued that the complete elimination of special tax treatment for long-term capital gains may cause investors to stress current income at the expense of risktaking in new ventures promising higher growth returns in the future. It is difficult to assess whether this argument is based on self-interest in a more favorable tax rate or on a genuine concern that the 1986 Tax Act may reduce economic risktaking.

Most industrial countries tax long-term capital gains at low rates or not at all. One commentator's initial examination of the 1986 tax reform was that it was somewhat pro-consumption and short-changes savings and investment. He concluded, however, that "only time will tell whether there is need for corrective action."

Raising the tax on capital gains in the transition year 1987 did cause a burst of sales at the end of 1986. Perhaps those that did not liquidate unrealized long-term capital gains in existing investments in 1986 may feel locked in to existing investments and hold them to await more favorable treatment of long-term capital gains in the future. If this "locking in" phenomenon occurs, it may slow the flow of capital to more efficient uses and, ironically, may reduce tax receipts in later years.

§19.25 EFFECT OF DEATH OF A TAXPAYER

When a person dies, the estate's representative must file a final return in the decedent's name for the period ending with death. The estate must then file an estate income tax return for the period beginning the day after the date of death and ending on a date selected by the fiduciary for the estate. Annual returns from the estate may be necessary thereafter. The income items included in the return of the estate may include investment income from assets owned by the estate, gains from the sale or exchange of estate property, and the receipt of post-death income items attributable to services of the decedent, such as fees for services provided by the decedent before death if payment is received after death. These latter items are called "income in respect of a decedent."

In calculating taxable income, an estate may claim expenses in much the same manner as an individual. An estate is also entitled to a single $600 personal exemption.

An important rule affecting the income tax consequences of the death of a person is the step-up in basis of property that automatically occurs upon the death of the owner. The basis of all property owned by the decedent automatically becomes its fair market value on the date of death. This principle often results in elderly or ill individuals refraining from selling or disposing of appreciated properties during their lifetimes. The appreciation in value during the lifetime of the decedent escapes taxation entirely.

§19.26 STATE INCOME TAXATION

State income taxation may be classified into several basic categories. Seven states — Alaska, Florida, Texas, Washington, Nevada, South Dakota, and Wyoming — have no income tax as of 1992. New Hampshire and Tennessee do not tax wages and salaries but do tax capital gains, dividends, and interest. All other states impose state income taxes. State income taxes may be as high as 11 percent (in California for taxpayers with income above $400,000), but rates in the 5 to 8 percent range are more typical. Most states today "piggyback" on the federal system by using adjusted gross income or taxable income as set forth in the taxpayer's federal income tax return. Several states, however, require an independent income calculation.

Rhode Island calculates its tax as a percentage of federal income tax liability; in 1991, Rhode Island increased its rate from 22.5 percent of federal income tax liability to 27.5 percent.

Some cities impose income taxes as well. New York City imposes a tax that ranges from 2.5 percent to 3.4 percent. Philadelphia imposes a tax of 4.96 percent on residents and 4.3125 percent on nonresidents who work in Philadelphia.

The general trend of state income tax rates is upward more rapidly than federal rates. For example, an income tax was imposed in Connecticut for the first time in 1992 with rates ranging from 1.5 percent to 4.5 percent. Pennsylvania increased its maximum tax rate to 3.1 percent from 2.1 percent in the same year. Some of these tax increases have been labeled as "temporary." State income taxes are clearly becoming an increasingly important consideration in tax planning as more governmental functions appear to be delegated to states by the federal government.

State income taxes are deductible on federal income tax return if the taxpayer itemizes deductions. A number of states return the favor by permitting taxpayers to deduct federal income taxes on their state returns.

Federal debt obligations are not subject to state income tax. Many states also exempt from state tax debt obligations issued by the state; cities that impose a separate income tax also may exempt debt obligations issued by the city and its agencies from city income tax. Mutual funds have been created that invest in obligations that are exempt from both federal and state income tax; these are advertised as double exempt funds. Mutual funds have also been created that invest only in triple exempt investments: exempt from federal, state, and city income taxation. As with all tax-exempt investments, the yield of these double and triple exempt funds must be compared with the higher yield obtainable on taxable investments.

Persons may be subject to income taxation in more than one state. States generally give a credit for taxes paid to other states on the same income. New York and California now seek to impose income taxes on pensions earned while the taxpayer was a resident of those states even though the taxpayer has retired and moved to a state, such as Florida, that does not have an income tax. The theory behind this action is obvious; whether it will survive legal challenge is an open question.

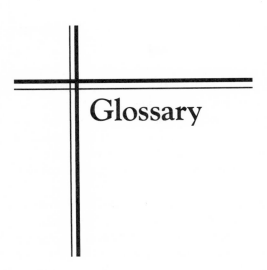

Glossary

401(k) Plan is a popular tax-oriented savings plan available to employees of private employers at the discretion of the employer.

403(b) Plan is a plan for governmental employees similar to section 401(k) plans for employees of private employers.

Abstract Company. *See* Title Company.

Abstracting a Judgment means filing a copy or summary of the judgment in the public records. Pursuant to state statute, such a judgment then becomes a lien on all the non-exempt real property owned by the judgment debtor in the state or locality. Abstracting a judgment is a simple and relatively inexpensive way to collect upon a judgment since the judgment debtor may not convey clear title to any of his or her real estate affected by the lien without obtaining a discharge of the lien.

ACH is an acronym for automated clearing house.

Actuaries determine rate, returns, and the like for life insurance policies or annuities for the lives of persons on the basis of average life expectancies. Life expectancies are determined from recorded data, particularly records of mortality that show numbers of persons of various ages and occupations who die each year.

Add-on Interest is the method used for computing interest on some small consumer loans (either cash loans or loans to finance the purchase of major consumer items). Add-on interest is calculated on the original loan amount for the entire period of the loan even though periodic payments reduce the unpaid principal.

Adjustable Life Insurance is life insurance that allows an individual to switch protection from term insurance to whole life insurance or back, subject to specified restrictions. *See* Term Insurance; Whole Life Insurance.

Adjustable-Rate Mortgage (ARM) in real estate parlance is a mortgage that provides for periodic adjustments to the effective interest rate on the mortgage based on changes in a market interest rate or index of interest rates. Usually, these adjustments are reflected by changes in the amount of the monthly payment on an annual or semiannual basis. An adjustable rate mortgage is also known as a variable rate mortgage or VRM. *See* Conventional Loan; Alternative Mortgage.

Adjusted Basis in tax parlance is the basis of property with adjustments: (1) *plus* capital improvements made by the seller, purchase commissions originally paid by the seller, legal costs for defending or perfecting title, and so forth, and (2) *minus* returns of capital, depreciation claimed as tax deductions, depletion, deducted casualty losses, insurance reimbursements, and the like. *See* Basis.

Adjusted Gross Income for federal income tax purposes equals total income minus adjustments to income (employee business and moving expenses, pension plan deductions, and alimony). *See* Total Income.

After-Tax Dollars refers to arrangements in which: a) Payments are made by an employer on behalf of an employee and the payments are includible in the taxable income of the employee; or b) payments are made by a person from personal assets which are not deductible from taxable income.

Alternative Minimum Tax in federal income tax parlance is a separate method of calculating a taxpayer's liability if the taxpayer has taken advantage of specified tax preference items. *See* Tax Preference Items.

Alternative Mortgage in real estate parlance refers to a mortgage that contains interest and/or payment terms that differ from the traditional conventional mortgage. *See* Fixed-Rate Conventional Mortgage.

American Stock Exchange (AMEX) is a securities exchange located in New York City that lists for trading securities issued by somewhat smaller companies than those traded on the New York Stock Exchange.

AMEX. *See* American Stock Exchange.

Amortize or **Amortization** means to reduce and ultimately pay off a debt or other obligation by periodic payments. In the classic level-payment real estate mortgage, for example, the loan is amortized over the period of the loan by monthly payments that are fixed in advance and remain constant throughout the life of the mortgage. A portion of each payment represents interest, and the remainder reduces (amortizes) the loan. Amortize may also be used in other contexts.

Amount Realized in tax parlance is part of the calculation of gain or loss on a sale or exchange of property. Amount realized includes the cash received for the property on a sale or the fair market value of the property received in exchange for the property. Selling expenses, including brokerage commissions paid by the seller, reduce the amount realized. In the case of property subject to a mortgage, the amount realized also includes the amount of mortgage debt that the seller is relieved from paying as a result of the sale. *See* Gain or Loss.

Annual Percentage Rate, in consumer transactions, is the interest rate calculated in accordance with the rules established by Regulation Z promulgated by the Federal Reserve Board under the federal Truth in Lending Act.

Annualized Interest is the basis on which many interest rates on discounted debt with maturities of less than one year are quoted. Annualized interest rates facilitate comparisons between different issues with different periods before maturity.

Annuitant is a person receiving an annuity. The annuitant may, but need not, be the same person as the creator of the annuity.

Annuity is a stream of constant payments to be made at fixed intervals in the future.

APR is an acronym for Annual Percentage Rate.

Arbitrage is a market strategy for profiting on small differences in market prices of two different but equivalent securities in the same or different markets, or in the market prices of the same security in two different markets, or the same securities available now for delivery at two different times in the future.

ARM is an acronym for Adjustable-Rate Mortgages.

Article 9 of the Uniform Commercial Code deals with security interests in personal property.

Assignee is a person who purchases or otherwise acquires tangible or intangible property from another. If the subject of the assignment is a claim, the assignee may enforce the claim against the debtor to the same but no greater extent than the original creditor (subject to whatever defenses arising out of the same transaction that the original debtor may have against the original creditor). An assignment is typically a voluntary transaction.

Assignment for Benefit of Creditors is a state law substitute for a bankruptcy proceeding. It proceeds on the theory that the debtor has recognized the hopelessness of his or her financial situation and has voluntarily decided to assign all available property to a trustee or receiver for the benefit of creditors to be administered and divided up on an equitable basis.

Assignment of a Note is a transfer to a third person by an instrument that states the note is assigned. If a transfer of a promissory note is cast as an "assignment" (rather than as an "indorsement"), the assignee does not become a holder in due course, no defenses are cut off (unless the maker agrees to waive them), and the holder of the note stands in precisely the same shoes as the original lender. *Compare* Holder in Due Course; Indorsement.

Assume a Mortgage in real estate parlance refers to an agreement by a purchaser of real estate to purchase a property subject to an existing mortgage and to promise to make the required payments on that mortgage.

Assumption of a Mortgage. *See* Assume a Mortgage.

Assumption Reinsurance involves the assignment of insurance policies from one insurer to another under which the assignee assumes full responsibility to provide the insurance protection. Whether or not the assignor is relieved from ultimate responsibility for that insurance protection if the assignee becomes insolvent may be unclear in many situations.

ATM is an acronym for automated teller machine. These machines accept deposits and provide cash up to designated amounts through the use of a plastic card (usually a debit card), and a personal identification number (PIN).

Automated Clearing Houses permit the electronic deposit of salary checks and the electronic payment of specified monthly bills.

Automatic Stay in bankruptcy law parlance refers to the stay on collection procedures by creditors that automatically follows the filing of a voluntary or involuntary bankruptcy petition.

Average Daily Balance is used to calculate the finance charge on credit cards. The average daily balance equals the sum of the amounts outstanding on each day of the period divided by the number of days in the period.

Back-End Load. *See* Load.

Badges of Fraud are transactions presumed to be in fraud of creditors under statutory or common law principles of fraudulent conveyances.

Balance Sheet Insolvency. *See* Insolvency.

Balloon Note is a note that requires periodic amortization payments, but the unpaid balance comes due before the payments amortize the full borrowed amount. The final, large payment is the "balloon," which may have to be refinanced. In some contexts, an interest-only note or even a note without periodic payments may be referred to as a balloon note.

Bankers Acceptances are short-term debt instruments the payment of which are guaranteed by a commercial bank. Bankers acceptances originate in commercial transactions and payment may also be guaranteed by the participants and by a lien on the goods involved.

Bankrupt has several varied and loose meanings. In the most technical sense, bankrupt means a person who is the subject of a federal bankruptcy proceeding. At one time it also meant a person who had committed one or more acts of bankruptcy (a concept that was eliminated from the Federal Bankruptcy Code in 1978 but continues to be referred to in the literature). It may also mean a commercial trader who is insolvent (either in the equity or balance sheet sense). It also may be used most generally as a synonym for insolvent.

Bankruptcy Judge is a federal official who presides at bankruptcy proceedings. A bankruptcy judge is not an Article III judge and has limited powers. Orders by a bankruptcy judge may be appealed to the presiding federal district judge.

Barter is a payment mechanism in which goods or services are exchanged without the use of currency.

Basis in tax parlance is the investment the seller of the property has in property. Basis is the cost or purchase price of the property paid or incurred by the seller in acquiring the property with appropriate adjustments. *See also* Adjusted Basis; Substituted Basis; Stepped-Up Basis.

Basis Book is a set of tables used to calculate yield-to-maturity for marketable debt securities at various prices, coupon rates, and dates of maturity.

Basis Point in debt securities trading parlance is a change in yield-to-maturity of 1/100th of 1 percent. Thus a change of price of 50 basis points equals a change in price sufficient to change the yield-to-maturity of a debt security by 1/2 of 1 percent, a major movement in price for most debt securities.

Bearer Note is a promissory note that is payable to bearer, that is, the person who has physical possession of the piece of paper. Such a note is transferred simply by physical transfer of the paper.

Bearer Paper refers to a negotiable instrument that may be negotiated merely by delivery of the paper itself. The alternative to bearer paper is a negotiable instrument payable to the order of a specific person.

Bearish Sign is a sign that market prices should move downward.

Before-Tax Dollars is a shorthand phrase for the concept that certain amounts may be set aside for the benefit of employees or others without the beneficiaries being required to include in their income tax returns the value of the amounts so set aside. Usually the benefits received by the beneficiaries will be taxable income when actually received, so the before-tax dollars do not escape taxation permanently. *See* After-Tax Dollars.

Beneficiary of a Life Insurance Policy is the person to whom the face value of the life insurance policy is paid upon the death of the insured. *See also* Owner of a Life Insurance Policy.

Bid and Asked Quotations are price quotations in securities markets set by market-makers in the over-the-counter market or specialists in the securities exchanges.

Binder in insurance parlance is a temporary policy of insurance covering the period while the insurance company assesses the risk of writing a regular policy. It is a preliminary commitment to insure against a risk. Insurance agents usually have authority to issue binders even though they may not have independent authority to bind the insurance company to a regular policy. In real estate parlance a binder issued by a title company is a preliminary report of the status of title to a property.

Block Trades are trades in securities involving blocks of 10,000 or more shares.

Blue Chip Shares are securities issued by the very largest and most secure domestic corporations, typically the leading firms within their industry. The Dow Jones Industrial Average of 30 stocks is the most accurate reflection of price movements in blue chip shares. Blue chip may also refer only to the 30 companies that make up the Dow Jones Industrial Average.

Bond is a long-term debt instrument that is secured by a lien or mortgage on specific corporate property. Many bonds are publicly traded. The word bond is also used more broadly to refer to all long-term marketable debt securities, whether secured or unsecured. *See* Debt Instrument; Debenture.

Book Entry is the most common method of holding ownership in publicly traded shares. The shares owned by an investor are reflected only by entries on the books of the brokerage firm and on monthly statements provided to the investor; the shares owned by the brokerage firm in turn are reflected by book entries on the books of a clearing house, and the record ownership of the shares are held by a nominee for the clearing house.

Bounce a check means to have a check dishonored usually because there are not sufficient funds in the account to cover the check.

Brackets. *See* Tax Brackets.

Broad Tape in securities trading parlance is the news service ticker operated by Dow Jones and Company.

Broker in securities trading parlance is a securities firm that is executing an order for a customer with a third person. A securities firm that buys or sells securities for its own account is a dealer. Large securities firms commonly act both as broker and as dealer in OTC securities and may act as both a broker and a dealer in the same transaction if suitable notice is given to the customer. *See* Dealer.

Buildup in the parlance of annuities is the amount by which the value of a deferred annuity increases from earnings on funds invested in the annuity before the annuity payments begin.

Bullish Sign is a sign that market prices should move upward.

Bunching of Income in tax parlance is including in one taxable year income or gain from activities or efforts over several years. Bunching has adverse tax consequences in any progressive rate structure.

Business in the broadest sense means any asset or group of assets that promises to produce a flow of cash or income in the future. It generally includes all gainful activity other than employment.

Buy a Future in securities law parlance means to enter into a contract to buy a futures contract, that is, a commitment to purchase standard amount of a commodity or financial contract at a specified date in the future.

Buy Down Option. *See* Pledged Account Mortgage.

Buy-Sell Agreement in corporation law parlance is a type of share transfer restriction that commits the shareholder to sell, and the corporation or other shareholders to purchase, the shares owned by the shareholder at a fixed or determinable price upon the occurrence of a specified event.

Buying Term and Investing the Difference is insurance law parlance for attempting to replicate the rights created by a whole life insurance policy by buying term insurance and investing the differential in premiums in an income-producing savings account.

Call is an option to purchase a designated security at a fixed price for a limited period. *See* Strike Price. In a different context, call means a demand to post additional capital. *See* Margin Call.

Cap is a maximum amount for a commitment, payment, liability, or transaction. For example, in commercial real estate financing, lenders often decline to provide more than 95 percent of the contemplated construction cost; the 95 percent figure is a cap.

Capital Asset in tax parlance means property held by a taxpayer other than inventory, property held primarily for sale to customers, depreciable and real property used in a trade or business, and several other less important categories of property.

Capital Gain in tax parlance means the gain from the sale or exchange of a capital asset. Long-term capital gains are taxed at a lower rate than other forms of. *See* Gain; Capital Asset.

Capital Loss in tax parlance means the loss from the sale or exchange of a capital asset.

Cash Market is an acronym for Spot Market.

Cash Sale Rule is a principle that permits retailers to avoid usury problems. It allows the seller to establish a higher price for credit sales than for cash sales of the identical goods without the difference being considered interest under the usury statute. This distinction is also known as the time-price differential.

Cash Surrender Value of a whole life insurance policy is the current value of the policy prior to the death of the insured. It is the amount that may be obtained from the insurance company if the policy is surrendered or the amount that may be borrowed by the owner from the insurance company. The cash surrender value is also referred to as the cash value of the policy.

Cash Value of a whole life policy is its cash surrender value. *See* Cash Surrender Value.

Cashier's Check is a check issued by the bank itself to a designated third party. A cashier's check is requested usually by a depositor; when the check is issued, the amount is immediately deducted from the depositor's account so that risk of dishonor is eliminated. A typical cashier's check is a two-party instrument: the bank and the payee, though the name of the depositor purchasing the cashier's check may appear on the face of the cashier's check as the "remitter."

CATS is an acronym for certificates of accrual on treasury securities; a treasury bond stripped of its interest coupons to create a zero. *See* STRIPS.

CCCS is an acronym for Consumer Credit Counseling Services.

CD is an acronym for certificate of deposit.

Cede and Company is the nominee used by the Depository Trust Company.

Certificate of Deposit is a document that evidences the deposit of funds with a bank or financial institution for a fixed term at a specified interest rate. Premature withdrawals usually involve forfeiture of some or all of the earned interest. Certificates of deposit are better known by their acronym CDs.

Certified Check is a check made out by the depositor who presents it for certification to the bank. The bank signifies its "acceptance" of the check by a stamp placed on the check itself. When a bank certifies a check, the amount is immediately deducted from the remitter's account. Risk of dishonor is therefore eliminated.

Chapter 11 refers to the chapter of the Bankruptcy Code that permits corporations and individuals who are not hopelessly insolvent to obtain protection from creditors in federal bankruptcy court in order to devise a plan of reorganization that enables the debtor to resume normal business operations. A plan of reorganization may involve the payment of some or all of the debtor's outstanding liabilities; the plan must be approved by certain categories or percentages of creditors as well as by the bankruptcy court. During the period of reorganization, the debtor usually continues to manage its business and assets. In the plan of reorganization, some creditors may be compelled to accept partial or deferred payments or equity interests in the debtor in lieu of previous current obligations. Many businesses that file for reorganization ultimately emerge as successful and profitable businesses.

Chapter 7 refers to the chapter of the Bankruptcy Code under which the assets of a hopelessly insolvent debtor are marshalled and liquidated to pay claims of creditors to the extent of those assets. Chapter 7 may lead to the discharge of an individual debtor from certain debts.

Chapter 13 refers to the chapter of the Bankruptcy Code that permits gainfully employed individuals to rearrange their debts without liquidation of assets. Chapter 13 is somewhat similar to Chapter 11. Major differences are that Chapter 13 reorganization is available only for individuals, approval of the plan of reorganization requires court but not creditor approval, and all debts must be paid in full.

Chattel Mortgage is a pre-UCC term to describe documents that create liens in personal property to secure the repayment of loans. Under the Uniform Commercial Code, the document creating this type of interest is called a "security agreement."

Check (or personal check) is a written order to a bank to transfer specific funds from the account of the writer of the check to a payee, who is usually a third person.

Check Cashing Firms are private firms that flourish in many cities, particularly in the poorer sections. These firms cash salary and government checks for a fee for persons who do not have a bank account. They also may provide other services, such as the sale of money orders.

Check Guaranty Programs are designed to permit local retailers to accept personal checks of customers without the risk of dishonor. These plans may require the retailer to make a telephone call to a designated bank office, or increasingly, to require the purchaser to present a plastic card similar to a credit card along with a personal check. National check guaranty programs maintained by private organizations also exist; these programs permit retailers to make an electronic inquiry about a proffered check. Since the private organizations do not have access to bank records or computerized credit histories, decisions are made on the basis of known credit history of the person proffering the check and similar information. It is quite possible that these programs may refuse to guarantee the payment of a check even though the writer has ample funds on deposit to cover that check.

Chicago Board of Trade is the principal commodities futures exchange. It provides trading markets for financial futures, options on shares, options on commodities futures, and options on financial futures.

CHIPS is an acronym for Clearinghouse Interbank Payment System, a wire transfer system operated by the New York Clearinghouse Association. *See* Wire Transfer.

Claims Made Insurance is liability insurance that provides protection only for claims made during the period the policy is in force. Most liability insurance is of this nature.

Clear the Market in securities trading parlance is a price in a market that causes the supply of the stock at that price to equal the demand for the stock at that price.

Clearing House is a device that simplifies the handling of numerous checks drawn on and presented by banks in a single city or federal reserve district: all checks drawn on and presented by a single bank are netted together each day, and the bank in effect pays only the net amount (or receives a credit for the net amount) into a specific account (called a clearing account) maintained for that bank with the clearing house. Clearing houses are also used for many securities transactions.

Closed-End Investment Company is an investment company that has outstanding a fixed number of shares that are traded either on a securities exchange or over-the-counter. *See also* Open-End Investment Company.

Closing is the second step in important commercial transactions, where the parties meet to formally complete the transaction: to make payments and deliver deeds, bills of sale, mortgages, or other documents. Ownership usually changes hands at the closing, though possession of the property may have been delivered at another time. A closing may or may not entail an escrow arrangement. If it does not, cash payments are in the form of certified or bank checks and documents are executed and delivered at the closing pursuant to a script prepared by the person in charge of the closing. A closing may also be called a "settlement" of the transaction.

Closing Costs in real estate parlance are a variety of fees, charges, and points that a purchaser or seller must pay in connection with the sale of the real estate. *See* Points.

Closing Officer is the person who is responsible for a real estate closing. Typically he or she makes sure that all necessary documents have been properly executed and received, receives and deposits checks, and so forth. Most real estate closings involve an escrow arrangement with the closing officer being responsible that the terms of the escrow are followed, ensuring that all documents are recorded in the proper order and that payments are made to the persons entitled to them.

Closing Out a Position in commodities futures trading means purchasing or selling an offsetting contract so that the speculator neither owes nor is owed any of the commodity. Closing out a position is also called netting out the position.

COBRA is the acronym for the Consolidated Omnibus Reconcilation Act.

Collateral is the property with respect to which a lien or security interest has been obtained by a creditor to assure repayment of a loan.

Collection Agency is a firm that seeks to collect unpaid debts owed to creditors for a fee.

Collection Practices generally refers to methods followed by creditors to collect upon consumer indebtedness. It is relatively uncommon to pursue traditional legal remedies of obtaining a judgment and levying on the debtor's property. More customary collection practices include cutting off future credit, reporting the default to credit agencies, and assigning the account for collection to a collection agency. Debts that cannot be collected in one of these ways are usually written off as part of the cost of doing business. *See* Collection Agency.

Commercial Annuities are annuities sold by life insurance companies or other financial institutions. Most commercial annuities are for the life of one or more persons and involve calculations based on mortality tables.

Commercial Credit Reporting Agency is an agency that compiles financial information and credit files about individuals and businesses and provides credit reports upon payment of a fee. Individuals and businesses are entitled under federal law to have access to the information in the agency's files. There are four national credit reporting agencies.

Commodities Markets consist of two interrelated markets: the spot market and the futures market. *See* Spot Market; Futures Market.

Comparables in real estate parlance are prices at which similar nearby properties sold in the recent past.

Composition is an agreement between a debtor and two or more creditors by which the creditors agree to accept a payment in partial satisfaction of their claims and forgive the balance.

Compound Interest is calculated over several periods on the assumption that earned interest that is not withdrawn during any period is treated as principal in subsequent periods, itself to earn interest in the future period. In most real-life situations, the assumptions underlying the compound interest calculation are more realistic than those underlying the simple interest calculation. *See also* Simple Interest.

Compound Interest Tables are tables that calculate the present or future value of payments, annuities, etc. for one dollar of investment over various periods and at various interest rates.

Compounded Quarterly means that interest is calculated at the end of every three months and the resulting interest is treated as principal in the following quarter.

Consolidated Omnibus Reconciliation Act (COBRA) requires employers to permit employees who are losing their employer-provided health coverage for any reason to continue that insurance for another 18 months by paying the full cost of that insurance during that period.

Consolidation of debts involves substituting a single loan, usually called a debt consolidation loan, for numerous consumer debts, using the proceeds of the debt consolidation loan to pay off those consumer debts.

Constructive Receipt in tax parlance is the principle that a cash-basis taxpayer must take into income amounts that are unqualifiedly available to him or her even though not actually reduced to the taxpayer's control.

Consulting is often an euphemism for recently unemployed.

Consumer Credit Counseling Services are nonprofit organizations that advise troubled debtors on handling of funds, credit, and assets and may negotiate payment plans on their behalf with creditors. Private organizations may also provide consumer credit counseling services for a fee.

Contract in securities trading parlance is the standard trading unit for options or futures. In the case of options on securities it is an option to purchase or sell 100 shares of the specified security.

Contract for Deed is a type of real estate transaction in which the purchaser enters into a contract agreeing to make specified payments over a period of years in return for entitlement to immediate possession and use of the property. Title, however, is conveyed to the purchaser only after the last required payment is made. Contract for deed is sometimes referred to as an installment sales contract for real estate.

Contributor to an Annuity. *See* Creator of an Annuity.

Contributory Plan is a qualified retirement plan in which employees are required to make contributions as well as the employer. The employees' contribution is with after-tax dollars; the employer's with before-tax dollars. *See* Qualified Retirement Plan; Before-Tax Dollars; After-Tax Dollars.

Conventional Loan in real estate parlance is a long-term loan at a fixed interest rate that is secured by a first mortgage on the real estate and is amortized by level payments over the duration of the loan. Depending on the context, conventional loan may also mean a loan made by a bank or savings and loan institution that is not insured by a governmental organization such as the Federal Housing Authority or the Veterans' Administration.

Conversion Ratio in convertible securities is the ratio between one share of the convertible security and the number of shares into which it may be converted. For example, a convertible preferred share that may be converted into two shares of common has a conversion ratio of 2:1.

Convertible Preferred Shares are preferred shares that are convertible at the option of the preferred shareholder into common shares at a specified price or at a specified ration. Upon conversion, the preferred shares disappear.

Corner in securities trading parlance is a market strategy in which one or more persons buy up most of the floating supply of shares in order to compel short sellers to cover at very high prices.

Coupon Bonds are long-term debt instruments that are transferred by delivery and have attached coupons representing future interest payments. *See* Coupons.

Coupon Clippers is a slang term for the owners of bearer bonds who clip coupons representing their periodic payments of interest.

Coupon Rate of a bond or debenture is the relationship between the face amount of the bond and the amount that is paid as interest each year on the bond or debenture. The name comes from the fact that at one time all bonds or debentures carried interest coupons to reflect the future interest payment obligation.

Coupons on long-term debt instruments represent future interest obligations of the issuer. Each coupon reflects a single interest payment due at some time in the future.

Creator of an Annuity is the person who makes the payments required to create an annuity. The creator of an annuity may also be described as the contributor to the annuity.

Credit Bureaus are local organizations supported by banks, retail stores, and other commercial organizations that maintain credit information about local residents. Credit bureaus may rely in part on credit reports prepared by national credit reporting organizations and may provide information to such organizations.

Credit Cards are the ubiquitous plastic cards, predominantly involving Mastercard or Visa. The use of credit cards involves the short-term extension of credit by the bank or organization issuing the card. *Compare* Debit Card.

Credit Life Insurance is declining-balance term insurance sold in connection with the making of a loan that provides that if the debtor dies, the loan will be paid off by the insurance proceeds.

Credit Report is a computer-based report of an individual's handling of credit transactions. Credit reports are assembled by one or more national organizations from information supplied routinely by stores, banks, and other creditors. In addition to reporting of credit transactions, credit reports may include information about bankruptcies, unsatisfied judgments, foreclosures, tax liens, and other publicly recorded information about the individual's financial status. A credit report may also be referred to as a credit history.

Credit Unions are lending and savings membership institutions. Most credit unions are covered by federal deposit insurance, and some of them are quite large.

Credits in federal tax parlance are amounts that may be subtracted from the tax due on a return in partial satisfaction of the liability shown on the return. *See also* Deductions.

Current Yield in securities parlance is the relationship between the current market price of a bond or debenture and the annual interest payments on that security. It differs from the true yield or yield-to-maturity in that no account is taken of whether the security is purchased at a premium or a discount over its value at maturity. *See* Yield-to-Maturity.

519

CUSIP is an acronym for the Committee on Uniform Securities Identification Procedures.

CUSIP Number is a unique number applied to each issue of publicly traded securities.

Day Order in NYSE trading parlance is a limit order that provides that if the order is not filled during the trading day, it is to be filled at the closing market price at the end of the day.

Dealer in securities trading parlance is a securities firm trading for its own account. Large securities firms commonly act both as broker and as dealer in OTC securities and new issues and may act as both a broker and a dealer in the same transaction if suitable notice is given to the customer. *See also* Broker.

Dealt in Flat in bond trading parlance means that no apportionment of interest is made between buyer and seller of the security. Bonds that are dealt in flat are either in default or of such speculative character that any interest payment is uncertain or unlikely.

Debenture is a negotiable long-term debt instrument that is unsecured. Debentures may be publicly traded. The word bonds is often used to refer to debentures as well as bonds in the narrower sense. *See* Debt Instrument; Bond.

Debit Cards are superficially indistinguishable from credit cards but involve an immediate deduction of the amount of the purchase from the account of the user rather than the extension of credit. Most ATM cards are debit cards.

Debt Collection Agencies are private organizations that assist creditors to obtain payment of debts through contact with the debtors.

Debt Consolidation Loan is a loan used for the consolidation of debts by a troubled debtor.

Debt Instrument is an instrument that reflects unconditional obligations to pay specific sums at a date in the future and usually to pay interest in specified amounts at specified times in the interim. Promissory notes, bonds, and debentures are all debt interests.

Debt Management Plan is a payment plan for a troubled debtor negotiated by a Consumer Credit Counseling Service or a private credit counseling service.

Debt Securities are traditionally viewed as bonds or debentures. Treasury bills and notes are also sometimes referred to as debt securities. Debt securities in theory must ultimately be repaid, though maturing debt may often be rolled over.

Declining Balance Insurance is term insurance with a face amount that gradually declines while the premium remains constant. Credit life insurance or mortgage life insurance are common examples of declining balance insurance. *See also* Face Amount Insurance.

Deductions in tax parlance are amounts that may lawfully be deducted from adjusted gross income in calculating taxable income. *See also* Credits.

Deep Discount Bonds in securities trading parlance are bonds that pay current interest at rates well below effective market interest rates and therefore trade at deep discounts. *See* Zero Coupon Bonds.

Deferred Annuity is an annuity in which payments begin only after the lapse of a period of time.

Deferred Interest Rate Mortgage is a graduated payment mortgage with a fixed payment and a fixed date of maturity. However, initial payments for the first several years are fixed at such a low level that they do not cover the interest cost of the loan. Such a mortgage involves negative amortization.

Deficiency in debit collection parlance arises when the proceeds of the sale of foreclosed property are not sufficient to discharge the loan (as is usually the case). The creditor continues to have an unsecured claim against the debtor for the amount of the deficiency and may reduce it to a judgment, a so-called deficiency judgment, and collect on it in the same manner as any other judgment.

Deficiency Judgments arise when a secured creditor forecloses upon the collateral, but that collateral does not yield an amount sufficient to satisfy the secured debt, and a subsequent judgment is entered for unpaid balance of the debt.

Defined Benefit Plan is a qualified retirement plan in which the size of the employer's contribution is determined on an actuarial basis to provide employees with designated benefits upon retirement (for example, a retirement benefit equal to 2 percent of the employee's average salary over the last three years of his or her employment multiplied by the number of years of employment). *See also* Defined Contribution Plan.

Defined Contribution Plan is a qualified retirement plan in which the size of the employer's contribution is determined each period on a basis unrelated to the size of promised retirement payments. For example, contributions may be established as a percentage of the employer's profits during the period in question or as a percentage of the actual salary paid to the employee during that period. *See also* Defined Benefit Plan.

Demand Deposits are deposits with financial institutions that may be withdrawn at any time without penalty.

Depository Trust Company is the clearinghouse for transactions on the New York Stock Exchange and some of the regional exchanges.

Derivative Securities are securities the value of which are based on or derived from price movements in individual shares (usually NYSE-traded), on changes in stock index levels that reflect a hypothetical portfolio of publicly traded securities, or price movements in commodities futures, or on other securities.

Designated Order Turnaround is the computerized trading system operated by the New York Stock Exchange. It is usually referred to by its acronym DOT.

DIM in real estate parlance is an acronym for deferred interest mortgage. A DIM involves negative amortization.

Discharge in Bankruptcy is the order entered by the bankruptcy court discharging an individual from pre-filing debts. A discharge in bankruptcy does not cover all debts and may be withheld entirely in the event of specified types of misconduct by the bankrupt.

Discount means generally a reduction or subtraction from a designated amount.

Discount Factors are decimals that represent the present values of one dollar payable at various time periods in the future at specified interest rates. Discount factors are convenient to use when determining the present value of future payments due at different times in the future. A discount factor is the reciprocal of the future value of one dollar over the same period and interest rate.

Discount Point. *See* Points.

Discount Rate is the interest rate used to determine the present value of a right to receive a specified payment at a specified time in the future. Discount rate is also the name of the rate set by the Federal Reserve System on loans to commercial banks. This is the wholesale cost of money from the perspective of banks; the retail rate is the prime rate. The discount rate is set by the Federal Reserve System partially on political and partially on economic considerations. Changes in this rate receive considerable publicity.

Discounting generally means reducing or subtracting from a designated amount.

Discounting Future Payments to Net Present Value refers to the process by which amounts payable at different times are made comparable by reducing all payments to their present value. *See* Discounting; Time Value of Money.

Dishonor of a check occurs when the bank on which the check is written refuses to pay the check. A check may be dishonored for a variety of reasons: for example, the depositor may not have sufficient funds to cover the check; the depositor may have entered a "stop payment order" directing the bank not to pay the check; or the account may have been closed in the meantime.

Diversification is the principal investment strategy suggested by modern portfolio theory. It involves investing in a variety of different investments rather than placing one's entire resources at the individualized risk of a single business or single type of investment.

Diversified Investment Company is an investment company that limits its investments in any one corporation to a small fraction of its total assets. Diversified investment companies may also limit the percentage of assets that may be invested in any one industry.

Dividend in corporation law parlance means a distribution by a corporation to its shareholders out of its current or retained earnings.

Dividend Yield is the regular dividend paid by a publicly held corporation divided by the price of the stock.

Do-It-Yourself Annuity is a plan by which a person desiring an annuity decides to replicate the desired payments from investments without actually purchasing an annuity from a writer of commercial annuities.

DOT is an acronym for Designated Order Turn-around.

Double Exempt Municipal Bonds are bonds that are exempt from state income taxes as well as federal income taxes.

Dow Jones Average is an average of the stock prices of 65 major blue chip stocks. It is subdivided into industrial, transportation, and utility sub-components, and averages for each of the sub-components are also maintained.

Downstairs Brokers in NYSE trading parlance are brokerage firms who only deal with other brokers on the floor of the New York Stock Exchange. *See also* Upstairs Brokers.

Downtick in securities trading parlance means that the current price quotation is below the price at which the last transaction occurred. *See also* Uptick.

Due on Sale Clause in mortgages provides that the face amount of the mortgage comes due upon the sale of the property. Due on sale clauses are used to prevent trafficking in below-market interest rate mortgages and to require the buyer to refinance upon a purchase.

Earnest Money is a payment that usually accompanies a proposed contract of sale presented by the hopeful buyer to the seller of real estate.

Effective Rate of Interest is the actual return on loans for the period the loan is outstanding. The effective rate of interest is sometimes called the Yield. *Compare* Nominal Rate of Interest.

Effective Tax Rate in a progressive income tax rate structure is the ratio between the amount payable as tax on the return and the amount of income shown on the return. Income in this calculation is usually measured as taxable income as shown on the return but may also be calculated on adjusted gross income or total income. *See* Adjusted Gross Income; Taxable Income; Total Income.

Employee Business Expenses for tax purposes are ordinary and necessary expenses incurred by an employee in connection with his or her employment. Such expenses are deductible subject to a floor of 2 percent of total income.

Employee Retirement Plans are retirement annuity plans created by employers for the benefit of their employees.

Encashment Fees are charges imposed by some foreign stores, hotels, and restaurants to accept traveler's checks. These fees may range from 2 to 10 percent of the face value of the check and reflect the preference of foreign establishments to deal with plastic credit cards and electronic communication rather than paper.

Endorsement. *See* Indorsement.

Endowment Life Insurance is an insurance policy that provides for premiums greater than those required for a whole life policy so that the policy becomes fully paid up at an earlier time. An endowment policy may be created so that it is fully paid up after a specified period (for example, 20 years) or when the insured reaches a specified age (for example, 65). *See* Fully Paid Up Policy; Whole Life Insurance.

Equity Insolvency. *See* Insolvency.

ERISA stands for Employee Retirement Income Security Act. ERISA is the basic federal statute that defines and regulates Qualified Retirement Plans.

Escrow means that payments and documents relating to a transaction have been placed in the custody of an independent third person with instructions to take steps to complete the transaction when specific actions have been taken and specific conditions have been met. Payments and executed but undelivered documents held by the third person are said to be held in escrow.

Estimated Tax is tax parlance for that portion of the Pay As You Go tax collection system that requires taxpayers with significant amounts of income not subject to withholding to file quarterly declarations of estimated tax and to make a payment with respect to estimated taxes with the declaration.

Exact Interest is calculated by treating the year as consisting of 365 or 366 days, as the case may be, and ignoring weeks or months. With the development of modern calculating devices, the computation of exact interest, like the calculation of compound interest, has been greatly simplified. *See also* Ordinary Interest.

Excess Liability Insurance. *See* Umbrella Insurance Policies.

Exclusion Ratio for deferred annuities is the ratio applied to each annuity payment to determine what portion is a tax-free return of capital to the annuitant and what portion is taxable income. *See* Tax Deferral.

Exclusive Listing in real estate parlance means that a real estate broker has been given the sole right to sell the property for a specified period and is entitled to a commission if the property sells during that period whether from its efforts or from the efforts of the owner or others.

Execution Sale is a public sale of part or all of a judgment debtor's non-exempt assets by a public official in order to satisfy the judgment.

Exempt Property refers to property of a debtor which by state or federal law cannot be levied upon to satisfy a judgment.

Expenses for the Production of Income in tax parlance are ordinary and necessary expenses incurred by a taxpayer in connection with his or her income-producing activities.

Extension Agreement is an agreement between creditors and a debtor that gives the debtor additional time to pay debts but does not forgive them. Extension agreement may also refer to a variety of other contracts, such as agreements extending a relationship beyond a stated termination date or agreements extending the period of an applicable statute of limitations. *See also* Composition.

Extra Risk Life Insurance Policies are policies written for persons with known medical problems, such as apparently controlled cardiovascular disease or a history of successful treatment for cancer.

Face Amount Insurance is term insurance for a fixed amount payable upon the death of the insured during the period the policy is in effect. Premiums for face amount insurance increase gradually as the insured gets older. *See also* Declining Balance Insurance.

Fed in securities trading and banking parlance is a shorthand reference to the Federal Reserve Board.

Federal Estate Tax is a tax due on the estate of a decedent upon his or her death. It is not an income tax but is levied upon the value of the assets includable in the taxable estate of the decedent.

FEDWIRE is the name of the wire transfer system operated by the Federal Reserve System.

FHA Mortgages are residential real estate mortgages the payment of which are insured by the Federal Government. FHA insurance is not available for large mortgages.

Finance Charges are interest and other charges imposed by a lender in a consumer transaction for the loan of funds. The federal Truth In Lending Act requires disclosure of the aggregate amount of the finance charges imposed as well as the "annual percentage rate" of interest being charged on the transaction.

Financial Futures are futures contracts in a variety of financial instruments, for example, foreign currencies, United States Treasury debt securities, and stock and bond indexes.

First Mortgage. *See* Senior Mortgage.

Fixed-Rate Conventional Mortgage (FRCM) in real estate parlance is a long-term mortgage that provides for a fixed interest rate and level periodic payments that totally amortize the loan upon the final payment.

Flexible Premium Life Insurance is life insurance that permits the insured to increase or decrease premiums within a broad range. The cash surrender value or face amount of the policy is adjusted accordingly.

Float is the period of time in the check collection process during which the amount of a check appears as a deposit in the creditor's account and yet has not been subtracted from the debtor's account. In connection with traveler's checks, the float is the supply of funds that represent the proceeds of sales of traveler's checks that have not been redeemed.

Floor in tax parlance means a minimum amount below which no deduction for expenses is allowed. If expenses exceed the minimum amount, the excess amount is deductible.

Flyspeck in real estate parlance is a trivial defect in the title that is unlikely to have any practical significance or effect and does not make the title unmarketable.

For Sale by Owner when used in connection with residential real estate implies that the property has not been listed with a broker and no brokerage commission is involved.

Forced Conversion of a convertible security in securities trading parlance occurs when the convertible is called for redemption at a time when the price of the underlying conversion security, the conversion ratio, and the redemption price are such that it is profitable for all security holders to convert their convertible securities rather than to permit them to be called for redemption.

Foreclosure is the process by which a creditor having a lien or security interest in property owned by a debtor seizes the property. In the case of consumer goods, usually the property may be "repossessed" by the creditor without judicial process. The goods may thereafter be sold and the proceeds applied against the unpaid loan. In the case of real estate and intangible property, foreclosure may require judicial process, including a public sale of property that has been seized.

Form 1040 is the long tax return form used by individual taxpayers with substantial taxable income, with income not subject to withholding, or with substantial deductions. More simplified forms may be used by many taxpayers who have smaller incomes or who do not itemize deductions.

Fraud on Creditors. *See* Fraudulent Conveyance.

Fraudulent Conveyance is a state law doctrine designed to protect creditors from transactions entered into by debtors that have the purpose or effect of hindering or defeating the creditor's ability to collect on his or her indebtedness.

Fresh Start is the slang term often used to describe the discharge that is available under Chapter 7 of the federal bankruptcy laws for most individual debtors that enables one to be relieved of the obligations owed to unpaid creditors.

Front-End Load. *See* Load.

Fully Discounted Information is information about securities issues that the market is aware of and therefore price changes in securities affected by the information have already occurred.

Fully Paid-Up Policy is a whole life or endowment insurance policy in which the cash surrender value equals the face value of the policy, and there is no remaining component of life insurance to be paid from premiums.

Funds Availability Rule is the federal statute that sets specific time periods following the deposit of a check drawn on a different bank for the funds to be made available to the depositor of the check.

Future Value of a Present Sum is the amount by which a present sum will grow at a specified compound interest rate during a specified period.

Futures Contract is a contract to buy or sell a standardized amount of a commodity, currency, securities index, or debt security on a specified date in the future.

Futures Market is the market in which futures contracts are traded. *See also* Spot Market.

Gain or Loss on a transaction in tax parlance equals the amount realized minus the adjusted basis of the property.

Gap Insurance in automobile leasing transactions protects the lessor from economic loss in the event the car is "totaled" at a time when the lessor's investment in the car exceeds its fair market value.

Garbage is a slang term for the useless computational results obtained when inadequate, incomplete, or inaccurate data is manipulated by precise statistical or mathematical methods. The phrase "garbage in — garbage out" (GIGO) is often used in this context.

Garnishment is a procedure by which a judgment creditor may execute upon ("garnish") amounts owed to the judgment debtor. A writ of garnishment is served on a person who owes the judgment debtor money and commands that person to pay the amount owed to the garnishing creditor rather than to the judgment debtor. Bank accounts are the most common garnished property. Some states wholly or partially exempt certain types of payments from garnishment, such as wages or salaries.

General Warranty Deed is a deed for the conveyance of real estate that includes a general warranty by the seller that his or her title is valid as against the world. General warranty deeds may be known by different names in some localities. *See also* Special Warranty Deed; Quitclaim Deed.

GIC is an acronym for Guaranteed Investment Contract.

Going Naked. *See* Naked Options.

Good to Cancelled in NYSE trading is a limit order that is not a day order.

GPARM (or GP/ARM) is an acronym for Graduated Payment Adjustable-Rate Mortgage.

GPM is an acronym for Graduated Payment Mortgage.

Grace Periods in promissory notes or mortgages are provisions that allow the debtor to correct defaults or make up missed payments for specified periods after the default.

Graduated Payment Adjustable-Rate Mortgage (GPARM) is a mortgage that combines a graduated payment feature with an adjustable interest rate. This type of mortgage may also be referred to as a graduated payment/adjustable-rate mortgage (GP/ARM). *See* Adjustable-Rate Mortgage; Graduated Payment Mortgage.

Graduated Payment Mortgage (GPM) has a fixed interest rate and a fixed time for repayment like a fixed-rate conventional mortgage (FRCM). However, the monthly payments under a GPM start out at a lower level than those called for by the equivalent FRCM but thereafter rise periodically, usually in three or four steps. *See* Fixed-Rate Conventional Mortgage.

Group Life Insurance is term insurance that is made available, usually at special premium rates, to members of a group such as all employees of a specific employer, members of a social or professional organization, and so forth.

Guaranteed Investment Contract is a contract offered by insurance companies under which they agree to invest retirement funds at a guaranteed rate of return until retirement. Such contracts carry an insolvency risk since they constitute unsecured promises by the insurance company.

H.R. 10 Plans. *See* Keogh Plans.

Head of Household in tax parlance is an unmarried person who is not a surviving spouse and who maintains a home for a dependent child or relative.

Hedge in securities trading parlance is a general term that describes a transaction designed to protect an existing holding or position from adverse price movements. For example, a speculator who has sold a stock short may hedge the risk by purchasing a call option on the same stock. In commodities futures trading hedgers are persons, such as farmers or users of agricultural commodities, who fix future prices for commodities they will produce or will need by entering into commodities futures transactions. For example, a farmer with a corn crop in the ground may hedge his or her projected harvest against price decline by selling a corn futures contract. Similarly, a manufacturer using raw corn in its manufacturing processes may lock in acceptable prices by buying corn futures contracts roughly matching its needs for raw corn. The effect of hedging by the farmer and/or manufacturer usually is to transfer the risk of price movement to a market speculator willing to take that risk.

High Yield Bonds is another name for junk bonds.

Holder in Due Course is a person who acquires a negotiable instrument by endorsement for value and without knowledge of possible defenses. A holder in due course may enforce the promise of payment set forth in the negotiable instrument free of most defenses that the debtor might have had if suit had been brought directly by the party to the underlying transaction. The negotiation of a negotiable instrument to a holder in due course results in a debt becoming an article of commerce largely freed from the underlying transaction that gave rise to it and ceases to be a personal obligation between the creditor and debtor.

Home Equity Loan is a loan or line of credit secured by a mortgage on a person's residence that may be drawn upon for a variety of personal needs. Interest on home equity loans is generally tax deductible even if the proceeds are used for personal purposes.

Homestead is a person's personal residence. A homestead is exempt from execution in whole or in part in many states.

Immediate Annuity is an annuity in which the payments begin almost immediately.

Income Bonds are bonds on which the obligation to pay interest is limited to the amount of corporate earnings in each accounting period.

Income Splitting in tax parlance is the division of a single income among two or more persons for tax purposes. If the persons involved do not have additional outside income, income splitting results in a lower aggregate tax bill on the income, though the advantages of income splitting were reduced by the 1986 tax amendments.

Incontestability Clause in life insurance policies prohibits a life insurance company from cancelling a policy for fraud or non-disclosure after the lapse of a specified period. Following the expiration of this period the policy is said to be incontestable. Incontestability clauses are required in life insurance policies by state law.

Index Fund is a mutual fund that attempts to replicate the performance of the market as a whole, usually by investing in a pattern that is comparable to the mix of securities in a major market index such as Standard & Poor's 500 stock index.

Index Futures are futures contracts in a variety of widely followed securities indices, particularly the Standard & Poor's 500 share index.

Individual Retirement Accounts (IRAs) permit employees whose employers do not have a qualified retirement plan and employees with incomes below a specified amount to make retirement contributions to a tax deferred account.

Indorsement is a method of transfer of an instrument, such as a check or promissory note payable to the order of a person. The payee of the note or check writes on the back of the note or check, "Pay to the order of Y," signs his or her name, and delivers the note or check to Y. Y can then enforce the note or check as though he or she were the payee, or may indorse the note or check to Z by following the same process. As a practical matter, checks rarely carry multiple indorsements.

Insolvency (or Insolvent) has two quite different meanings. The most common meaning is that the debtor is unable to meet its obligations as they come due. This is usually referred to as "equity insolvency" or "insolvency in the equity sense." The second meaning is that a debtor's total liabilities are greater than the value of his or her non-exempt property taken at a fair valuation. This is usually referred to as "balance sheet insolvency" or "insolvency in the bankruptcy sense." Balance sheet insolvency requires reference to accounting principles in its application.

Institutional Investors are large investors who primarily invest other people's money. They include life insurance companies, pension funds, investment companies (divided into Closed-End and Open-End Funds), bank trust departments, charitable foundations, educational institutions, and similar organizations.

Insurable in life insurance parlance refers to a person who can demonstrate that he or she is in reasonably good health and engages in activities of average risk.

Insured in a life insurance policy is the person whose demise triggers the obligation of the insurance company to pay the face value of the policy.

Interest is the amount paid by a borrower for the use of the lender's money. It is the cost of a loan to a borrower; it is the return from owning capital to the lender. Interest may be called various names in consumer transactions, for example, "finance charge," "service charge," "points," and "transaction fee."

Interest-Only Mortgage is an alternative mortgage that provides that, for the first years of the loan, payments need only equal the interest payable on the loan. Principal is amortized beginning at the end of the interest-only period. *See* Alternative Mortgage.

Interim Financing in real estate parlance is short-term financing obtained during periods when permanent loans are expensive or difficult to obtain. The purchaser hopes that financing conditions will ease and a permanent loan may later be obtained to pay off the interim financing.

Intermarket Trading System (ITS) is a computerized trading system that links trading in specific securities on the regional and New York securities markets.

Internal Revenue Code of 1986 is the official name of the 1986 statute that made major changes in the federal income tax laws.

Intrinsic Value of a warrant, right, or option is the difference between the call, strike, or exercise price and the current market value of the security to which the warrant, right, or option relates. *See* Time Value.

Investment Company is a corporation that invests only in marketable securities of other corporations. *See* Closed-End Investment Company; Open-End Investment Company.

Investment Interest in tax parlance is interest on obligations incurred to buy or carry investment property. Under the 1986 amendments such interest is deductible only to the extent the taxpayer has income from the investments.

IOU is a written acknowledgment by the debtor that a debt exists. The initials "I.O.U." stands for "I owe you." An IOU may simplify the evidentiary requirements otherwise imposed on a creditor seeking to enforce a debt but it is not, by itself, a promise to repay the debt.

IRA is an acronym for Individual Retirement Account.

Judgment Debtor is a person against whom a final money judgment has been entered.

Jumbos are large certificates of deposit, usually $100,000.

Junior Mortgages are subordinated mortgages, for example, second or third mortgages. They carry higher interest rates than first mortgages because of the significantly higher risk of default.

Junk Bonds are below-investment grade bonds, as determined by one or more bond rating services, often issued in connection with takeover attempts.

Keogh Plans are self-employed retirement plans that in effect permit the self-employed to make retirement contributions with before-tax dollars. A self-employed individual may make contributions to a Keogh Plan (up to a specified maximum) and deduct the payment from his or her federal income tax return. Keogh Plans are also known as H.R. 10 Plans.

Kiddie Tax refers to the 1986 tax provisions that tax investment income of minor children at the maximum rate applicable to the income of the parents.

Laddered Portfolio is a portfolio of debt securities structured so that a specified amount of the securities will mature each year. A laddered portfolio may be created, for example, to pay for anticipated college tuition costs for children in the future.

Leveraged Buyout is a bootstrap transaction in which a corporation's assets are used to secure and pay loans, the proceeds of which are used to buy out all public shareholders.

Levy means to sell certain property at an execution sale.

LIBOR is an acronym for the London Interbank Offered Rate, an interbank lending rate on dollar denominated investments traded in London. LIBOR is used as an index in some adjustable-rate mortgages.

Lien is an intangible interest in property that secures the payment of a debt. A lien allows the creditor, if the loan is not repaid, to seize the property subject to the lien to satisfy the unpaid loan. Usually the property is sold and the proceeds applied against the unpaid loan. Liens may be created by consent or involuntarily as when a judgment creditor records the judgment in the land records to place a lien on real estate owned by the judgment debtor. Consensual liens created in property covered by the Uniform Commercial Code are called security interests. The process by which a creditor seizes property subject to a lien is called foreclosure.

Life Expectancy of a person is the actuarial determination of the period he or she is expected to live. The life expectancy of a person is an essential aspect of many insurance and annuity calculations.

Limit Order is an order to buy or to sell securities on an exchange at other than the market price when the order reaches the securities floor.

Limit Order Book is the book in which a record of limit orders is maintained by the specialist in a stock. It may either be a physical book or an electronic book.

Line of Credit is a common kind of open arrangement between a bank and a customer by which the customer may borrow money as needed up to a stated maximum. Interest is usually charged only on amounts actually borrowed, though fees may be charged when creating or renewing the arrangement.

LIST is the name of the part of the DOT computerized trading system operated by the New York Stock Exchange that allows arbitrageurs and others to trade lists of securities instantaneously.

Listed Shares on the New York Stock Exchange are the shares that are traded on the floor of the Exchange. To be listed, companies must meet certain size and securities holdings requirements and enter into a listing agreement with the Exchange.

Listings in real estate parlance are properties that have been listed for sale with a real estate broker.

Load in mutual fund parlance is an additional charge imposed on an investor when he or she invests in an open-end investment company (a front-end load) or when he or she redeems his or her shares in that investment company (a back-end load). Front-end loads are more common that back-end loads. A front-end load is also called a sales load while a back-end load may be called an exit fee.

Long Position in securities trading parlance means that the trader owns more of a security than he or she owes to the market.

Long Term in tax parlance, when used in the context of capital gains or losses, means the statutory holding period for capital assets. This period is six months but sometimes in the past has been one year.

Loss on a transaction in tax parlance equals the amount by which the adjusted basis of the property exceeds the amount realized.

Magnetic Ink Character Recognition (MICR) refers to the process of electronic recognition of numbers on checks. These numbers appear at the bottom left hand portion of each check and identify the Federal Reserve district, the bank, and the account on which the check is drawn.

Maintenance in securities trading parlance refers to the level of asset coverage in a margin account that triggers a call for additional capital to be added to the account. *See* Margin Call.

Margin is the amount of capital a customer must deposit with a broker to engage in margin transactions in securities under regulations established by the Federal Reserve Board. For many years the requirement has been 50 percent. Margin when used in connection with commodities futures by trading is a deposit — a performance bond — that provides assurance that a speculator in commodities futures has available assets to cover short-term losses if the market moves adversely to his or her interst. *See also* Maintenance.

Margin Account is an account with a broker in which purchases on margin or short sales are authorized.

Margin Call is the request by a broker for additional capital when the value of a portfolio containing margin transactions or short sales has dropped to the point at which an additional contribution of capital is necessary under applicable maintenance requirements.

Margin Loans are loans made by brokers on the security of marketable securities in the possession of the broker.

Margin Transactions in securities involves borrowing money from a broker to buy more shares of marketable securities. *See* Margin.

Marginal Tax Rate in a progressive income tax rate structure is the rate of tax applicable to the last dollar earned by the taxpayer. *See also* Effective Tax Rate.

Mark to Market refers to the process by which the value of an account or position is recalculated each day at a specified time. This price may be called the "settle price." If the value of the account is below a specified level, the speculator must deposit additional capital in the account or the position will be closed out by the broker. Commodity futures accounts are marked to market on a daily basis.

Market Linked Certificates of Deposit is a derivative security offered by some banks that is similar to a certificate of deposit, but its yield is tied to the performance of a stock index.

Market Maker in the over-the-counter securities market is a dealer who announces its continued willingness to both buy and sell a specific stock. The price at which a market maker is willing to sell (the asked price) is somewhat higher than the price at which it is willing to buy (the bid price).

Market Order is an order to buy or to sell securities at the market price when the order reaches the floor.

Marketable Securities are securities for which a regularly established trading market exists. Securities may be marketable even though the market is "thin" and trades occur relatively infrequently.

Medicaid is a federal program providing minimum medical benefits for the poorest members of society. Medicaid is available only for low income families.

Medicare is a federal program providing for limited medical benefits to all persons over the age of 65.

Medigap insurance is private health insurance designed to cover the amount of medical expenses that are not paid for by Medicare.

Members of the New York Stock Exchange are persons or firms that have acquired seats on the Exchange and are entitled to trade securities on the floor of the Exchange. *See Seats.*

MICR is the acronym for Magnetic Ink Character Recognition.

Money Market Account is an interest-bearing account in a bank or financial institution. Usually the depositor is permitted to write checks on the account, sometimes with restrictions as to size or number that may be written each month.

Money Market Fund is a mutual fund that invests only in short-term, virtually riskless investments. Money market funds bear names such as cash management accounts, liquid asset funds, and the like. Money market funds keep their net asset value at one dollar per share so that the fund appears to be similar to an interest-bearing bank account. Money market funds usually permit checks to be used to access funds invested in the account.

Money Orders are used by persons who do not maintain checking accounts to make payment to creditors. Both postal or bank money orders are available. The debtor takes currency to the issuer of the money order and receives a form that may be made payable to the debtor or to a creditor of the debtor.

Mortgage Life Insurance is declining-balance term insurance sold in connection with a mortgage that provides that if the borrower dies the mortgage will be paid off by the insurance proceeds. Mortgage life insurance is also called mortgagor life insurance.

Mortgagee Policy in real estate parlance is a title insurance policy that protects only the interest of a mortgagee. A mortgagee policy may leave the owner dangerously exposed if an unexpected title defect surfaces. *See also* Owner's Policy.

Multiple Listing Service in real estate parlance is a centralized listing system for residential real estate properties that have been listed with brokers for sale. A multiple listing service gives all participating brokers in the community access to all properties.

Multiple Payment Annuity is a deferred annuity for which the contributor makes periodic payments. Many employer-created pension plans in effect involve multiple payment annuities.

Municipal Bonds are bonds or debentures issued by states, municipalities, and state-created taxing authorities. They carry lower interest rates than other debt instruments because the interest is exempt from federal (and sometimes state) income taxes.

Municipals is a slang term for tax-exempt bonds issued by states and other taxing districts.

Mutual Fund is the common name for an Open-End Investment Company.

Mutual Life Insurance Company is an insurance company that does not have shareholders. Its board of directors is elected by its policyholders, and excess earnings of the company are paid to policyholders in the form of annual dividends. In a mutual company, policyholders are somewhat analogous to owners of the company. *See also* Stock Life Insurance Company.

Naked Options are standard put or call options written by a person who does not own the underlying securities (in the case of call options) or does not have the financial resources to purchase the shares if the options are exercised (in the case of put options). Such options are also called uncovered options. Writing naked options is also sometimes referred to as going naked.

Narrow Tape is the Dow Jones ticker tape that sets forth individual securities transactions.

NASD. *See* National Association of Securities Dealers.

NASDAQ. *See* National Association of Securities Dealers Automated Quotations.

National Association of Securities Dealers (NASD) is a semi-public association of securities dealers active in the over-the-counter market.

National Association of Securities Dealers Automated Quotations (NASDAQ) is the computerized trading system operated by the NASD that handles price quotations for securities traded in the national market and small-cap programs.

National Market System is the portion of the over-the-counter market in which the most active and widely held securities in that market are traded. The principal market makers for these securities report actual trades and prices so that the reporting of such transactions is indistinguishable from those of the formally organized exchanges. There are several market makers for each National Market System security. *See* Over-the Counter Market.

Negative Amortization in real estate parlance occurs when the payment terms of a mortgage provide for payments in early years of the mortgage that do not cover the interest charges. The difference is negative amortization. It is added to principal to be amortized in later years when payments have increased. Negative amortization may also occur in transactions involving property other than real estate.

Negative Amortization Mortgage is a mortgage that provides for negative amortization during the time the loan is outstanding. *See also* Fixed-Rate Conventional Mortgage; Alternative Mortgage.

Negotiable Form refers to an instrument — usually a promissory note or check — that meets minimal statutory requirements: It must (1) be signed by the maker; (2) contain only an unconditional promise or order to pay a certain sum in money; (3) be payable on demand or at a definite time; and (4) be payable to order or bearer. Most notes and checks used in commercial transactions are in negotiable form.

Negotiable Instrument is an instrument that is in negotiable form.

Negotiation of a negotiable instrument means that it is transferred to a holder in due course. *See* Negotiable Instrument; Holder in Due Course; Assignment of Note.

Net Asset Value of investment company shares equals the current market value of the investment company's portfolio divided by the number of outstanding shares of the investment company. *See* Investment Company.

Net Change in securities trading parlance is the change between the closing price of the security on the day in question and the closing price on the previous trading day.

Netting Out a Position. *See* Closing Out a Position.

New Money generally refers to additional capital contributions or payments that are being discussed.

New York Stock Exchange is the principal secondary market for trading in corporate securities

New York Stock Exchange Composite Index is an index of price movements of more than 1,600 securities listed on the New York Stock Exchange.

Nine Bond Rule in NYSE parlance is the rule that permits members of the exchange to deal with bonds in the over-the-counter market when the number of bonds involved exceeds nine units of $1,000 each.

No-Load Fund is a mutual fund that does not charge a sales load. *See* Load.

Nominal Rate of Interest is the quoted annual rate of interest on transactions that involve extensions of credit for periods shorter than one year. *Compare* Effective Rate of Interest.

Non-contributory Plan is a qualified retirement plan in which only the employer makes contributions. *See* Qualified Retirement Plan; After-Tax Dollars.

Non-current Loans. *See* Problem Loans.

Non-participating Life Insurance Policy is a policy that is not entitled to receive dividends. Such policies are usually written by stock companies. *See also* Participating Life Insurance Policy.

Non-recourse Loan is a loan secured by property in which it is agreed that in the event of default the holder may foreclose on the property but may not hold the maker personally liable for any deficiency.

Novation is the substitution of one debtor for another on an obligation with the consent of the creditor.

NYSE is an acronym for the New York Stock Exchange.

October 19 Collapse refers to the dramatic decline in securities prices and securities indices that occurred on October 19, 1987.

Odd Lot in securities trading parlance is a trading order that involves less than a round lot of securities. *See* Round Lot.

Open Account is an unsecured loan represented by an account maintained by the creditor. A purchase of gasoline on a credit card is a good example: When one fills up, one "pays" by the use of the credit card. The cost of the gasoline is electronically communicated to a central accounting office located someplace and added to the buyer's account. At the end of the month, the company selling the gasoline sends a bill for purchases made during the month.

Open-End Investment Company is usually called a mutual fund. An open-end investment company does not have a fixed number of shares outstanding, but rather, issues new shares to persons desiring to invest in the fund and redeems its own shares at net asset value (or in some cases at a small discount below net asset value) from investors who wish to liquidate their positions. An open-end company has no fixed capitalization; as it grows or declines in size, the number of its outstanding shares also grows or declines.

Open Interest in commodities futures trading parlance means the number of futures contracts that are outstanding and have not been netted out.

Ordinary Interest is calculated on the assumption that a year consists of

360 days divided into 12 months of 30 days each. Ordinary interest is still used by many banks and in the computation of interest on corporate, agency and municipal bonds. *See also* Exact Interest.

Ordinary Life Insurance. *See* Whole Life Insurance.

OTC (or O-T-C) stands for over-the-counter. *See* Over-the-Counter Market.

Out of the Money Option is an option that has no intrinsic value. *See* Intrinsic Value.

Out Placement Programs are provided by employers of laid-off senior employees to assist them in locating other employment. Not all employers provide out placement programs.

Out Years are years in the relatively far distant future in which payments are to be received or made. In estimating present values of a stream of payments, payments in out years make a relatively small contribution to the present value of that stream.

Over-the-Counter Market for securities consists of a large number of brokers and dealers who deal with each other via computer or telephone, buying and selling shares for customers or for their own accounts. Most brokers and dealers active in trading in the over-the-counter market are members of the National Association of Securities Dealers. The over-the-counter market is a vast and informal network of securities brokers and dealers that has become increasingly competitive with the traditional securities exchanges in handling securities trading.

Overdraft is a check that exceeds the funds on deposit. An overdraft may occur because of an error on the part of the depositor or because a deposit made recently has not been made available by the bank as permitted by Federal Reserve System regulation. Banks usually dishonor overdrafts but may honor overdrafts for its better customers up to some limit as a service to them. Banks may charge a fee for each overdraft it honors under this service.

Owner of a Life Insurance Policy is the person who has the power to exercise a number of important options with respect to the policy: to name or change the designation of the beneficiary, to borrow against the policy or pledge it as security for a loan (if it has a cash surrender value), and to surrender the policy or decide to let it lapse for nonpayment. The owner and the insured need not be the same person, and indeed it is often advantageous from an estate tax standpoint for them to be different persons.

Owner's Policy in real estate parlance is a title insurance policy that protects the title of the owner as well as the title of a mortgagee.

PAM. *See* Pledged Account Mortgage.

Parent Loans for Undergraduate Students (PLUS) is a major federal student loan program.

Participating Life Insurance Policy is a policy that is entitled to share in dividends declared by the life insurance company. Such policies are usually written by mutual companies. *See also* Non-participating Life Insurance Policy.

Passive Activities in tax parlance are all rental activities and trade or business activities in which the taxpayer does not materially participate. Investment activity is a separate category. The ownership and rental of commercial or residential property is a passive activity even if the owner participates in decisions on matters such as who should be tenants. Otherwise, material participation means that the taxpayer is involved in the operations of the activity on a regular, continuous, and substantial basis. Losses from passive activities are deductible only to the extent the taxpayer has income from passive activities.

Pawn Shops make short-term small loans to individuals on the security of personal property.

Pay As You Go in tax parlance refers to the tax withholding and estimated tax provisions of the Internal Revenue Code that are designed to ensure that all or most of the tax due is withheld by employers or paid by taxpayers as estimated tax payments during the taxable year as income is earned.

Payment Options for deferred annuities are the elections available to an annuitant prior to the time of the first payment. Common options are for the life of the annuitant, or the life of the annuitant with a specified number of payments guaranteed, or for the combined lives of the annuitant and his or her spouse.

Payout Ratio is the dividend of a corporation as a percentage of earnings per share.

Pell Grants is the name of a federal program that provides outright financial contributions to permit students from low income families to attend college.

Pension Max is a retirement strategy that combines the purchase of life insurance with a pension election in an effort to provide maximum retirement benefits for the retired employee and his or her spouse.

Pension Plan provides retirement benefits to employees. A pension plan is usually a qualified defined benefit plan, but the term pension plan is often used more broadly to refer to a defined contribution plan or even to any type of qualified or non-qualified retirement plan.

Perfection of a Security Interest refers to the process by which a security interest is made superior to other possible subsequent security interests and other subsequent claims, including that of a bankruptcy trustee. Perfection usually involves the public filing of a notice. For security interests in goods, a "financing statement" must usually be filed in the office of the Secretary of State, but security interests in some types of goods are perfected automatically or by the creditor obtaining possession of the collateral. In the case of real estate, filing of the mortgage or deed of trust in the land records is usually required. A failure to perfect means that subsequent creditors may obtain competing security interests senior to the unfiled interest and that a bankruptcy trustee may be able to avoid the unfiled security interest, reducing the holder of the unfiled secured interest to unsecured status.

Permanent Life Insurance. *See* Whole Life Insurance.

Perpetual Annuity is an annuity that continues forever. The present value of a perpetual annuity equals the reciprocal of the applicable discount rate.

Personal Exemptions in tax parlance means the flat amount that a taxpayer may deduct from adjusted gross income for him or herself, his or her spouse, and for dependent relatives in the taxpayer's family.

Personal Identification Number (PIN) is a security device designed to prevent the possessor of a stolen or lost credit card from using it to withdraw cash or cash equivalents from automated teller machines. This number must be entered manually by the user to effectuate the transaction.

PI stands for principal and interest. The PI payment on a real estate mortgage is the amount necessary each month to pay interest and amortize principal.

PIN is an acronym for personal identification number.

Pink Sheets. *See* Sheets.

PITI stands for principal, interest, taxes, insurance. The PITI payment on a real estate mortgage is the PI payment plus the required payments to be held in escrow by the lender in order to pay real estate taxes and casualty insurance premiums each year.

Pits are the trading areas for commodities and financial futures contracts. They are large depressions in the floor of the trading area with steps — persons trading contracts for a specified month stand on the same step or level within the pit.

PLAM. *See* Price Level Adjusted Mortgage.

Pledged Account Mortgage (PAM) is a deferred interest or graduated payment mortgage in which a fund is created at the closing to finance the lower initial payments. In creative financing, the seller may make a payment to this fund. If the seller makes a contribution, the arrangement is sometimes known as a buy down option.

PLUS is an acronym for the Parent Loan for Undergraduate Students loan program.

Points in real estate parlance are charges made at closing by the lender. A point is a charge equal to 1 percent of the loan amount; a lender who charges 3 points on a $100,000 loan in effect imposes an additional $3,000 fee at closing. A point is also sometimes called a discount point. In securities trading parlance a point means one dollar when discussing price movements of equity securities.

Policy Illustration is the typical selling tool for modern life insurance products that contain both tax deferred investment and insurance components. The policy illustration shows how the investment portion of the product will fare under various assumptions about investment options and assumed rates of return.

Portfolio in securities trading parlance is the total of the investments held by a single investor at any one time.

POS is an acronym for point of sale.

Posts on the New York Stock Exchange Floor are the locations at which trading in specific securities occur.

Preferences are transactions by debtors that favor one creditor over another and are voidable to a limited extent if the debtor thereafter becomes the subject of a federal bankruptcy proceeding.

Prepayment Penalty in real estate parlance is a charge for prepaying the principal of a mortgage before it is due. A prepayment penalty is nominally justified as a charge to help defray the cost of accepting a prepayment and re-deploying the funds into another mortgage. In fact, prepayment penalties are usually viewed by mortgagees simply as another way of increasing the profitability of the lending business during periods of stable interest rates since most mortgages are refinanced when properties are sold and prepayment penalties may be imposed.

Price Level Adjusted Mortgage (PLAM) is a mortgage in which the interest rate and the term of the mortgage are fixed, but the outstanding balance is adjusted periodically in accordance with changes in some agreed-upon price index.

Primary Markets in securities parlance are markets in which corporations who wish to raise capital sell their new securities. *See also* Secondary Market.

Prime Rate is the interest rate that is usually (and not always accurately) defined as the rate large commercial banks charge large borrowers that run essentially no risk of default. It is the "weather vane" rate for loans by banks and other institutions to individuals and businesses.

Private Annuity is created by the transfer of property by one person to another in exchange for a promise by the recipient to make fixed periodic payments for the life of the transferor. A private annuity is an annuity based on the credit of the recipient who is not in the business of writing annuities. A private annuity may be advantageous because it permits deferral of income taxation on gain realized upon the transfer of the property.

Private Letter Ruling in tax parlance is a ruling by the Internal Revenue Service on the tax consequences of a proposed transaction. Private letter rulings are not confidential.

Problem Loans in real estate parlance are loans that are in default but the owner has not given up, and the mortgages have not been foreclosed. Problem loans are also sometimes referred to as non-current loans.

Profit-Sharing Plan is a type of qualified defined contribution plan in which the amount of the annual contribution is based on the profits of the employer. *See* Qualified Retirement Plan.

Progressive Income Tax Rates are tax rates on income that themselves increase as income increases. For example, a rate structure that taxes income under $10,000 at 14 percent and all income in excess of $10,000 at 28 percent is progressive.

Promissory Note is a standard instrument that states that the debtor "promises to pay to the order of" the payee an amount set forth in the promissory note. A holder may sell or assign the underlying obligation simply by transferring the promissory note to a third person, who in some circumstances may take free of defenses that the maker has against the original payee.

Proposed Regulations in tax parlance are regulations that the Internal Revenue Service has published for comment but has not yet promulgated. Proposed regulations may be pending for many years and may be relied upon by taxpayers to a limited extent.

Public Land Records in real estate parlance are the documents recorded in the office of the appropriate public official and the indexes maintained by that official. These records are not widely used in most jurisdictions since they are not normally organized on a tract basis. *See* Title Company.

Public Sale is a sale at public auction.

Publicly Traded Fund is another name for a closed-end investment company.

Purchase Money Security Interest is the phrase used by the Uniform Commercial Code to describe the security interest obtained by a seller of goods for a loan of all or part of the purchase price of the goods.

Purchase on Margin. *See* Margin Transaction.

Put is a standardized option to purchase a designated security at a fixed price for a limited period. *See* Strike Price.

Qualified Retirement Plan is a pension plan that meets the requirements of the Employee Retirement Income Security Act (ERISA) and the Internal Revenue Code. Contributions may be made to a qualified plan by the employer for the employee's benefit without the contributions being included in the employee's tax return and without affecting the deductibility of the contributions from the standpoint of the employer.

Quarterly Declarations of Estimated Tax must be filed by taxpayers who have substantial amount of self-employment income, income from personal investments, or other sources not subject to withholding such as gambling or stock market trading. A payment of estimated tax may have to accompany a quarterly declaration if it reveals an estimated underpayment of tax.

Quitclaim Deed in real estate parlance is a deed that conveys whatever title the seller processes without any warranty of any kind. Quitclaim deeds may be known by different names in some localities. *See also* General Warranty Deed; Special Warranty Deed.

Ratings of risks is a process of evaluating individual risks in determining whether to insure against those risks and, if so, what premium should be charged.

Real Defenses are defenses such as forgery or duress that may be asserted by a maker of a note against a holder in due course. *See* Holder in Due Course.

Real Estate Investment Trusts (REIT) are companies that invest in a portfolio of real estate investments. Like investment companies, REITs are not subject to income tax if they distribute substantially all their earnings to investors.

Realization of Gain or Loss in tax parlance means that a transaction involving a sale or exchange is closed for the purpose of determining the gain or loss from the transaction. However, a realized gain or loss is includable in the taxpayer's return for the year in question only if the gain or loss is recognized.

Recognition of Gain or Loss in tax parlance means that a realized gain or loss is to be taken into account as a taxable transaction. If a realized gain or loss is not recognized, it is said to be deferred to a later year.

Refinancing of a Mortgage involves obtaining a new loan to pay off the old loan secured by the mortgage. A mortgage is usually refinanced when the property is sold. When interest rates decline significantly, a wave of refinancings follow.

Regional Exchanges are securities exchanges located outside of New York. The principal regional exchanges are Philadelphia, Cincinnati, Boston, Midwest, and Pacific.

Registered Bonds are debt securities that have been issued in the name of a specific person, called the registered owner. Registered bonds do not have interest coupons. Periodic interest payments are made to registered owners by check, much the same way as cash dividends are paid on shares of stock. Registered bonds are transferred by endorsement rather than merely by delivery as is the case with coupon bonds.

Regressive Tax Structure is a structure of tax rates that result in low income taxpayers being taxed at a higher effective tax rate than taxpayers with higher incomes.

Regulations in tax parlance refers to the regulations issued by the Internal Revenue Service to implement the Internal Revenue Code. Regulations often involve substantive tax issues and usually have the force of law.

Reinsurance is the process by which an insurance company transfers some of the risk of loss it incurs to other insurance companies. Reinsurance permits diversification of risk by insurance companies.

REIT is an acronym for Real Estate Investment Trust.

Rent to Own Stores lease consumer goods primarily to low income customers on terms that provide that the lessee owns the goods outright after a specified number of lease payments have been made. If payments are not made the goods may be repossessed, and the lessee is not liable for future payments. Rent to own stores are viewed by some persons as devices to avoid consumer protection laws and usury statutes.

Repo is a loan structured as a sale and repurchase obligation of a riskless instrument. The repurchase obligation is secured by control of the riskless instrument itself.

Reverse Annuity Mortgage in real estate parlance is a mortgage that provides monthly payments to the owner of the mortgaged property. These payments are secured by the mortgage in increasing amounts based on the accumulated equity in the residence.

Roll Over Mortgage (ROM) in real estate parlance is a long-term mortgage in which the interest rate and monthly payments are renegotiated periodically. Caps are provided on the maximum adjustment permitted in any single adjustment.

Rolling Over Debt means obtaining a new loan shortly before the maturation of older debt and using the proceeds of the new loan to pay off the maturing debt.

Rollovers are transfers of vested retirement plan benefits received by a former employee into individual retirement accounts (or other qualified retirement plans) in order to avoid income taxation on the receipt of the vested benefits. Rollovers must comply with federal income tax regulations.

ROM. *See* Roll Over Mortgage.

Round Lot in securities trading is a standard unit of 100 shares though in some lightly traded shares the unit may be 10 shares.

Rule of 78's is a method of calculating the unpaid balance of a long-term loan that requires periodic payments. The mechanics of the rule of 78's are discussed in section 7.8.

Rule of 72 is a simple way of estimating how long it will take an investment to double in value if it earns compound interest at a fixed rate. The rule of 72 states that such an investment will double in value in the number of years that equals 72 divided by the interest rate (ignoring the decimal). Thus, an 8 percent savings account doubles in nine years ($72 \div 8 = 9$).

Sale and Leaseback in real estate parlance is a transaction that is economically equivalent to a mortgage in that the financier buys a commercial property from the developer and then immediately leases it back for fixed or determinable rentals over a long period that usually exceeds the estimated life of the improvements.

Sales Load. *See* Load.

Schedule C in tax parlance is the form used by proprietors to reflect the income or loss of their business in their personal income tax returns.

Seats on the New York Stock Exchange authorize holders to go onto the trading floor of the Exchange and deal in securities. Most owners of seats today are brokerage firms.

Secondary Markets are markets in which persons who already own outstanding shares and wish to sell them deal with persons who wish to buy shares. *See also* Primary Markets.

Secured Credit Cards require the holder of the card to deposit in advance funds with the bank issuing the card. The maximum amount of "credit" available to the holder of the card thereafter usually does not exceed the amount on deposit.

Security Agreement in Uniform Commercial Code parlance is an agreement that creates a security interest.

Security Interest under the Uniform Commercial Code is a consensual interest obtained by a creditor in personal property owned by a debtor to assure repayment of the loan. A security interest permits the creditor to seize the property subject to the security interest if the loan is not repaid to satisfy the loan. Security interests may be created in various kinds of tangible or intangible property or rights, including accounts receivable, proceeds of transactions, insurance policies, an automobile, or anything else that may be reduced to cash if the borrower defaults. If the transaction involves the sale of goods on credit, the seller may obtain a "purchase money security interest" in the goods sold.

Sell a Future in commodities trading parlance means to enter into a contract to sell a standard amount of a commodity, such as corn, at a specified date in the future.

Seller of an Annuity is the entity that agrees to make the annuity payments. Sellers are usually life insurance companies in the business of selling annuities and life insurance. The seller of an annuity is also described as the writer of the annuity.

Senior Mortgage is a mortgage to which other mortgages are junior or have been subordinated. A senior mortgage is also called a first mortgage.

SEP is an acronym for simplified employee pension. These plans may also be referred to as SEP-IRA plans. *See* Simplified Employee Pension Plan.

Series EE Bonds are United States government bonds designed for investment by individuals with modest incomes.

Settle Price in commodities futures trading is the price that is used to mark all open positions in commodities futures trading accounts to market each day.

Settlement of a transaction means the closing of the transaction. *See* Closing.

Settlement Sheet in real estate parlance is the document that shows all the receipts and disbursements of money by the closing officer in connection with the sale of real estate.

Sham Transactions in tax parlance are transactions that appear to have no business purpose other than to reduce tax liabilities. The Internal Revenue Service may ignore such transactions in the computation of income tax liabilities.

Share Dividend (or Stock Dividend) is a distribution of shares of common stock by a corporation to its shareholders in proportion to their shareholdings. Thus, a 10 percent share dividend means that the corporation issues one new share to each shareholder for every ten shares held. A holder of 100 shares will receive ten new shares when the distribution is made, owning 110 shares in all.

Share Split is a distribution of shares of common stock by a corporation to its shareholders in proportion to their shareholdings. Thus a "2 for 1 split" involves the corporation issuing an additional share for each share already owned, so that a shareholder who owned 100 shares before the split owns 200 shares after the split. A share dividend and share split are usually treated differently for accounting purposes on the books of the corporation. However, a share split differs from a share dividend in degree more than in kind. A share split usually involves a substantial increase in the number of outstanding shares whereas a share dividend involves a smaller increase.

Share Transfer Restriction limits the power of a shareholder to dispose of his or her shares. Such restrictions are widely used in closely held corporations for purposes such as permitting other shareholders to determine with whom they are associated in the business and ensuring a minority shareholder of a market for his or her shares in specified circumstances. *See* Buy-Sell Agreement.

Shared Appreciation Mortgage in real estate parlance is a mortgage under which the lender shares in any increase in value of the project upon its sale or refinancing.

Shares of Stock are the fundamental units into which the proprietary interest of a corporation is divided. Shares of stock may also be referred to simply as shares or as stock.

Sheets (or Pink Sheets) is a daily overnight publication containing representative price quotations for less heavily traded stocks in the over-the-counter market.

Short Position in securities trading parlance means that the trader owes more share to the market than he owns. Short position may also refer to short sales that have been entered into but have not been covered by purchases.

Short Sale in securities trading parlance is a transaction that enables an investor to speculate on a price decline to the same extent as a purchase of shares constitutes speculation on a price increase. A short seller borrows shares from his or her broker and sells them immediately, planning to repurchase them and replace the borrowed shares after the price drops. A short sale is treated as a margin transaction.

Short sale "against the box" is a short sale at a time when the seller owns shares to cover the transaction but elects to borrow shares and sell them. The "box" referred to is a hypothetical safe deposit box in which the share certificates are stored. *See* Margin Transactions.

Signature Loan is an unsecured loan made solely on the borrower's signature.

Simple Interest is calculated over several periods on the assumption that the principal on a loan remains stable. In simple interest calculations, interest earned in earlier periods does not earn interest in subsequent periods even if that interest is not withdrawn by the creditor. *Compare* Compound Interest.

Simplified Employee Pension Plan (SEP) is a retirement plan designed for self-employed individuals and employees of small business enterprises. They are similar to Keogh plans but are less complex. Contributions for all participants must be made to an "individual retirement arrangement" that may be established in a manner similar to an Individual Retirement Account. The individual retirement arrangement may be referred to as a SEP-IRA. Contributions are deductible by the employer and not includible in the income of the employees in a manner similar to qualified pension or profit sharing plans.

Single Premium Deferred Annuity is an annuity purchased for a single payment today with annuity payments to begin at some future time.

Single Premium Life Insurance is a tax deferred investment account wrapped in a life insurance policy to assure tax deferral of the earnings in the investment account.

Single Premium Variable Life Insurance Policy is a life insurance policy created by a single payment or series of payments. The portion of the payment not needed immediately for insurance premiums is placed in an accumulation account. The owner of the policy usually may direct the manner in which the funds in the accumulation account are invested and may borrow from the account much as though it were the cash surrender value of a traditional whole life policy. The amount of the insurance provided under the variable life insurance policy is adjusted periodically to ensure that the earnings from the capital invested in the policy are not immediately taxable to the owner of the policy. Variable life insurance policies have significant tax deferral benefits and are sold more for the tax and investment benefits than for the insurance benefits.

Small Claims Courts provide judicial assistance for debt collection inexpensively and usually without hiring a lawyer. The jurisdiction of small claims courts is limited to claims involving less than a specified amount. A non-commercial creditor or claimant might resort to these courts for assistance in connection with disputes with other individuals or commercial enterprises; commercial lenders rarely use these courts to collect upon small claims against individuals.

Small Order Execution System (SOES) is an automated execution system maintained by the NASD for securities traded in the National Market System. This system permits automatic execution at the best available price quotation or orders for national market securities of up to 1,000 shares. *See* National Market System; Over-the-Counter Market; National Association of Securities Dealers.

Smart Cards are plastic cards that permit credit and personal information to be placed on the card itself. The purpose is to eliminate the delay caused by a call to the credit card center that is required when simple plastic debit or credit cards are used. Each transaction is recorded on the smart card when the card is used.

SOES. *See* Small Order Execution System.

Spec House in real estate parlance is a house or apartment complex built by a speculator who has no buyer for the property but who plans to find a buyer after it is improved.

Special Warranty Deed in real estate parlance is a deed with a warranty by the seller that his or her title is valid as against any act of the seller but does not warrant good title against the world. Special warranty deeds may be known by different names in some localities. *See also* General Warranty Deed; Quitclaim Deed.

Specialist is the market maker of securities on the New York Stock Exchange. A specialist is obligated to trade as a dealer in an effort to maintain an orderly market.

Split Dollar Life Insurance is a form of executive compensation that provides life insurance coverage to the executive at a low cost. It involves loans by the employer to the executive to pay premiums on a whole life insurance policy. While the loans must be repaid (either by the executive or out of the proceeds of the policy), all other attributes and benefits of ownership belong to the executive.

Spot Market in commodities trading is the market for commodities for current delivery. The spot market is also called the cash market, and prices in this market may be called cash prices.

Standard & Poor's 500 Index is an index that reflects the price movements in listed securities issued by 500 leading corporations.

Standard Deduction in tax parlance means a deduction that a taxpayer may take instead of itemizing personal expenses.

Step Transactions in tax parlance are apparently independent transactions that may be linked together for tax purposes. The Internal Revenue Service may treat step transactions as a single transaction for tax purposes.

Stepped-Up Basis in tax parlance arises upon the death of a person owning appreciated property. The basis of that property is automatically increased or "stepped up" to its fair market value on the death of the owner. The appreciation of property owned by a person at his or her death escapes taxation because of this step-up in basis.

Stock Bonus Plan is a qualified profit-sharing plan in which contributions are made in the form of shares of stock of the employer rather than in cash.

Stock Life Insurance Company is in form a traditional corporation with shareholders who purchase stock in the company and who are entitled to elect the company's board of directors. Dividends in a stock company are paid to the shareholders, not to the policyholders as in a mutual company. In a stock company, policyholders are more analogous to customers of the company than to owners. *See also* Mutual Life Insurance Company.

Stock. *See* Shares of Stock.

Stop Order in NYSE trading is a limit order to sell when the price has declined to a particular level or to buy when the price has increased to a particular level.

Stop Payment Order is an order given by the writer of a check to a bank to refuse to honor a specific check when it is presented for payment. A bank charges a fee for accepting a stop payment order.

Straddle in options trading parlance is the simultaneous purchase of a put option and a call option on the same security. In a straddle, the speculator profits if the price moves significantly in either direction.

Straight Bankruptcy is the traditional Chapter 7 bankruptcy proceeding that leads to the liquidation of assets owned by the bankrupt and possibly to an individual's discharge from unpaid debts. *See* Discharge in Bankruptcy.

Straw Party in real estate parlance is a person (or corporation) without substantial assets who enters into a contract on behalf of the developer of real estate in order to avoid imposing personal liability on the developer. Some straw parties provide this service for a fee. A straw party may also be used in transactions not involving real estate.

Street Name Shares in securities trading parlance refers to shares that are registered in the names of New York brokerage firms and are traded, primarily among brokers, simply by delivery. While significant numbers of shares are still held in street names in this sense, most shares are held in book entry form. The phrase "street name" may sometimes be used to refer to shares held in book entry form and registered in the name of a nominee for a clearing house. *See* Book Entry.

Strike Price of an option is the fixed price at which the specific option in question is exercisable. *See* Put; Call.

STRIPS are zero coupon bonds issued by the United States Treasury. Brokerage firms may create equivalent securities by removing the coupons from treasury bonds and depositing the stripped bonds with an appropriate depository. These securities are known by feline acronyms such as CATS or TIGRS. Strips is an acronym for Separate Trading of Registered Interest and Principal of Securities; a zero created by the United States Treasury.

Subordination of a Claim means that other creditors are entitled to collect the amounts due them before the holder of the subordinated claim. Subordination may be voluntary, as when a creditor agrees to accept a second mortgage with knowledge that the holder of the first mortgage has priority; or it may be involuntary, as when a bankruptcy court orders a loan subordinated because of inequitable conduct by the holder. A lien securing a subordinate loan may be described as a subordinate lien.

Subrogation means stepping into the shoes of another. For example, following the payment of a claim by an insurance company, the company is subrogated to the rights that the claimant may have against third parties and may pursue those rights.

Substantial Underpayment of Estimated Tax is tax parlance for the failure to make sufficient payments under the pay as you go tax collection procedure to avoid statutory penalties imposed after the filing of the final return for the year in question.

Substituted Basis in tax parlance is the principle that in the case of property acquired by gift, the basis in the hands of the donee is the same as the basis in the hands of the donor. *See* Basis; Stepped-Up Basis.

Sum of Digits method is another name for the rule of 78's. The mechanics of the rule of 78's are discussed in section 7.8.

Surviving Spouse in tax parlance is a person whose spouse has died within the previous two years. A surviving spouse is entitled to use the special tax rates applicable to married couples.

Sweep is an arrangement by a bank by which a customer's noninterest-bearing checking account is periodically examined (swept), and any excess funds are moved to an interest-bearing money market account. Similarly, a sweep of option accounts by brokerage firms occurs shortly before expiration to ensure that all options with value are exercised prior to expiration.

Take Back Mortgage is a mortgage taken by the seller of the property to enable the purchaser to complete the purchase.

Take Subject To in real estate parlance is an agreement by a purchaser of real estate to purchase subject to an existing mortgage. The purchaser must make the required payments under threat of losing the property but has no personal liability with respect to the mortgage.

Tape in securities trading parlance refers to the tape operated by Dow Jones which reports securities transactions. It is sometimes called the narrow tape. *See also* Broad Tape.

Tax Avoidance is the reduction of one's taxes by structuring or timing transactions in a legal way.

Tax Brackets are the different levels of income subject to different tax rates under federal or state income tax statutes.

Tax Deferral means delaying the reporting of income or gain on a transaction to a later period. For example, annuities provide tax deferral because the buildup is not subject to tax as it is earned. The tax is deferred until payments begin on the annuity itself. *See* Exclusion Ratio.

Tax Evasion is the improper or unlawful reduction of one's taxes by omission, misstatement, fraud, or misrepresentation.

Tax Preference Items in tax parlance are the items that must be taken into account by a taxpayer in connection with the calculation of the alternative minimum tax. Tax preference items include accelerated depreciation on property, capital gains deductions, portions of incentive stock options excluded from income, and percentage depletion.

Tax Shelters in tax parlance are investments whose primary purpose is to provide tax deductions for high-income persons to allow them to protect or shelter other income from tax. Most tax shelters were sharply limited or eliminated entirely by the 1986 tax amendments.

Taxable Income in tax parlance equals adjusted gross income minus allowable itemized personal deductions (or the standard deduction if one does not itemize) minus the allowance for personal exemptions.

Teaser Rates are heavily advertised low initial monthly payments for graduated payment mortgages (GPM). The ads may not warn that payments increase materially over the life of every GPM.

Term Insurance is life insurance that provides only basic life insurance protection. It provides for payment of the face amount of the policy upon the death of the insured during the term of the policy. Term insurance is based on actuarial data as to the probability of death occurring within the fixed period of the policy with no savings account feature. As a person gets older the cost of term insurance increases. *See also* Whole Life Insurance.

Thin Market is a market in which there are relatively few traders and relatively few securities offered for sale. The market for many over-the-counter securities and for debt securities are thin markets.

Thinly Traded Shares are shares issued by smaller companies that are publicly traded on the over-the-counter market, but by reason of their size or the number of shareholders, the volume of trading is small.

TIGRS is an acronym for treasury investment growth receipts; a treasury bond stripped of its interest coupons to create a zero. *See* STRIPS.

Time Value of a warrant, right, or option is the difference between the intrinsic value of the warrant, right, or option and its current market value. *See* Intrinsic Value.

Time Value of Money is the basic concept that dollars payable in the future are always worth less than dollars payable immediately.

Time-Price Differential. *See* Cash Sale Rule.

Title Assurance in real estate parlance is the process by which buyers are assured that they receive goods and marketable title free and clear of liens or title defects, including easements and intangible interests in property.

Title Company is a private company that has created an index for real estate records by tracts rather than by the names of grantors and grantees in order to facilitate searches of title. The records maintained by a title company are called a title plant. Title companies may also write title insurance. A title company is also called an abstract company.

Title Insurance is a method of title assurance that provides indemnification against defects in title not specifically excepted from coverage by a title insurance company.

Title Plant. *See* Title Company.

Title Report is a statement of the results of a title search conducted by an attorney or a title company.

Torrens System is a method of registration of land ownership provided by local governments in some areas of the United States.

Total Income in tax parlance equals gross receipts minus trade and business expenses and expenses directly connected with other gainful, non-employment activity.

Trade or Business Expenses in tax parlance are ordinary and necessary expenses incurred by a business in connection with the generation of revenues.

Trading Floor of an Exchange is the area where trading in listed securities takes place. The trading floor is often referred to simply as the floor of the Exchange or the floor.

Traveler's Checks are issued by banks and other companies, particularly American Express Company. Traveler's checks are purchased in advance, and the traveler is promised the convenience of world-wide acceptance of such checks as payment. Lost checks are replaced free. The purchaser of traveler's checks signs each check twice: once when they are purchased and a second time when they are actually used. In this way, it is difficult for a thief or finder of checks to negotiate them. But if they are stolen, the risk is on the organization issuing the checks and not the traveler. Traveler's checks are profitable to the issuer because of the "float," the free use of funds between the time traveler's checks are purchased and the time they are used.

Triple Exempt Municipal Bonds are municipal bonds that are exempt from state and city income taxes as well as federal income taxes.

True Yield in securities parlance means yield-to-maturity. More broadly, true yield means the mathematical calculation of the relationship between the total return from owning the security and the market price. *See* Yield-to-Maturity; Current Yield.

Truncated Checking Accounts are accounts that provide only a monthly statement describing checks that have cleared and do not return the checks themselves. The checks are destroyed after photocopies are made in the event of future disputes.

Trustee in Bankruptcy is a person with responsibility for ensuring that all assets subject to the bankruptcy proceeding are recovered and properly administered for the benefit of creditors.

Truth in Lending Act is a federal statute regulating consumer credit information. It is formally Title 1 of the Consumer Credit Protection Act.

UFCA (Uniform Fraudulent Conveyance Act) is a uniform statute relating to fraudulent conveyances. It has been superseded by the Uniform Fraudulent Transfers Act.

UFTA (Uniform Fraudulent Transfers Act) is a uniform statute relating to fraudulent conveyances.

Umbrella Insurance Policies provide excess liability coverage over and above the amount provided by a basic liability insurance policy. Such policies are sometimes called excess liability insurance policies. A person with $300,000 of liability insurance, for example, may be able to purchase an umbrella insurance policy providing protection between $300,000 and $10,000,000 at a relatively modest premium.

Uncovered Options. *See* Naked Options.

Uninsurable in life insurance parlance is a person who cannot demonstrate that he or she is in reasonably good health or who engages in activities of extraordinary risk. Many uninsurable persons may obtain some insurance by paying a higher premium.

Universal Life Insurance is another name for variable rate life insurance.

Unlisted Properties in real estate parlance usually refers to residential or other real estate that is for sale but has not been listed with a broker. In another context, it may also refer to properties that have been listed with a broker but have not yet appeared in the multiple listing service. *See* Multiple Listing Service.

Upstairs Brokers in NYSE trading parlance are brokerage firms that deal with the public. They transmit orders to the floor of the Exchange. Upstairs and Downstairs, when referring to brokers, describe the physical location of brokerage offices in the New York Stock Exchange building.

Uptick in securities trading parlance means that the current price quotation is above the price at which the last transaction occurred. Under SEC regulations a short sale may be effectuated only on an uptick or zero uptick. *See* Zero Uptick; Short Sale.

Usury Statutes purport to limit the maximum interest rate that may be charged on loans to individuals to a specified level.

VA (Veteran's Administration) Mortgages are residential real estate mortgages the payment of which is guaranteed by the federal government. VA insurance is available only for veterans and for modest transactions.

Value usually means the price established for an item by transactions in the item between willing buyers and sellers in a market. Value also may be used in the sense of the value of the asset to the user or the cost of reproducing or replacing the asset.

Value Line Composite Index is an index of price movements based on 1,650 stocks traded on the New York and American Stock Exchanges and over-the-counter.

Vanishing Premium Insurance is life insurance that requires substantial premiums at the outset to build up a sufficient cash surrender value to permit future premiums to be paid from investment income and/or loans from the cash surrender value.

Variable Annuity is a deferred annuity in which the amount of the annuity ultimately paid depends on the investment success of a fund managed by the writer of the annuity.

Variable Premium Life Insurance Policy is a life insurance policy that provides that premiums are decreased if the company's investment income increases to a specified amount as a result of rising interest rates and inflation.

Variable Rate Life Insurance is a modern life insurance product that

Glossary

permits the owner to direct the investment of the cash surrender value or change the face amount of the insurance in order to increase or decrease the annual premium. This type of insurance is also called universal life insurance.

Variable Rate Mortgage. *See* Adjustable Rate Mortgage.

VEBA in as acronym for voluntary employee benefit association.

Voluntary Employee Benefit Association is a tax deductible employee contribution plan to cover future medical insurance or health costs. Employers may also contribute to such associations.

W-4 is the form employers provide to employees to determine or adjust the amount of withholding of federal income taxes the employer must make from each periodic payment of wages or salary.

W-2 is the form employers provide to each employee to show the wages paid to the employee and the amount that has been withheld from the employee's wages for various purposes during the year. One copy of this form must be attached to the employee's federal income tax return and another copy to the employee's state income tax return.

Walk Away in real estate parlance is the ability of an owner or developer to abandon an unprofitable project, leaving the mortgagee to deal with it. The ability of a solvent developer to walk away from a project may depend on whether he or she is personally liable on the mortgage. A person who abandons a project is sometimes described as having "walked."

Wall Street Option refers to the power of shareholders in publicly held corporations to sell their holdings if they are dissatisfied with their investment.

Warranty Deed. *See* General Warranty Deed; Special Warranty Deed.

Whole Life Insurance provides a fixed benefit on the death of the insured with premiums that remain level from the date of the inception of the policy until the maturation of the policy. Whole life policies are also called Permanent Life Insurance or Ordinary Life Insurance policies.

Wilshire 5,000 index is an index of price movements covering 5,000 stocks traded on all the major securities markets.

Wire Transfer is a "paperless" transfer of funds by instant electronic communication between banks with funds being deposited directly into the account of the recipient. Wire transfers are wholesale transfers of funds, routinely used to settle very large transactions. The two wire transfer systems currently in use are "Fedwire" operated by the Federal Reserve System and the Clearinghouse Interbank Payment Systems ("CHIPS") operated by the New York Clearinghouse Association.

Wrap Accounts are arrangements offered by brokerage firms by which they agree to manage and invest a large sum of money for a fee fixed as a percentage of the amount in the account.

Wrap-Around Mortgage is an assumption-related device that was originally designed for use in connection with the financing of commercial real estate but is also used for assumptions of mortgages on residential real estate. A wrap-around mortgage is a second mortgage the payments from which are used in part to continue the payments on the first mortgage.

Writ of Execution is the basic device to collect upon a judgment in most states. A writ of execution directs the sheriff to seize nonexempt property of the judgment debtor and sell it at public sale. The proceeds of the public sale are used to satisfy the judgment in whole or in part.

Writer of an Annuity. *See* Seller of an Annuity.

Writer of an Option is the investor who commits to sell the optioned securities at the strike price in the case of a call or to buy the optioned securities at the strike price in the case of a put.

Yield. *See* Effective Rate of Interest.

Yield Curve shows the yield of equivalent-risk securities by date of maturity. Yield curves usually have a positive slope — the longer the maturity the higher the yield.

Yield-to-Maturity is the discount or interest rate that makes all future payments to be received on account of a debt security equal to the market value of that security. *See also* Current Yield.

Zero Coupon Bonds in securities trading parlance are bonds or debentures that pay no interest and are sold at significant discounts from face value. A zero coupon bond is often referred to as a zero.

Zero Uptick in securities trading parlance means that the current price quotation is above the price at which the last transaction that involved a change in price occurred. Under SEC regulations a short sale may be effectuated only on an uptick or zero uptick. *See* Uptick.

Zeroes are a nickname for zero coupon bonds.

Index

All references are to section numbers.

Index

Index

Index

Index

Index